Lecture Notes in Computer Science 3461

Paweł Urzyczyn (Ed.)

Typed Lambda Calculi and Applications

7th International Conference, TLCA 2005
Nara, Japan, April 21-23, 2005
Proceedings

Volume Editor

Paweł Urzyczyn
Warsaw University
Institute of Informatics
Banacha 2, 02-097 Warszawa, Poland
E-mail: urzy@mimuw.edu.pl

Library of Congress Control Number: Applied for

CR Subject Classification (1998): F.4.1, F.3, D.1.1, D.3

ISSN 0302-9743
ISBN-10 3-540-25593-1 Springer Berlin Heidelberg New York
ISBN-13 978-3-540-25593-2 Springer Berlin Heidelberg New York

Springer is a part of Springer Science+Business Media

springeronline.com

Printed in Germany

Typesetting: Camera-ready by author, data conversion by Scientific Publishing Services, Chennai, India
Printed on acid-free paper SPIN: 11417170 06/3142 5 4 3 2 1 0

Preface

The 7th International Conference on Typed Lambda Calculi and Applications (TLCA 2005) was held in Nara (Japan) from 21 to 23 April 2005, as part of the Joint Conference on Rewriting, Deduction and Programming (RDP 2005). This book contains the contributed papers, and extended abstracts of two invited talks, given by Thierry Coquand and Susumu Hayashi. A short abstract of the joint RDP invited lecture by Amy Felty is also included.

The 27 contributed papers were selected from 61 submissions of generally very high quality, and the Program Committee had a hard time making the selection. The editor would like to thank everyone who submitted a paper and to express his regret that many interesting works could not be included.

The editor also wishes to thank the invited speakers, the members of the Program and Organizing Committees, the Publicity Chair, and the referees for their joint effort towards the success of the conference. The support from the Nara Convention Bureau is gratefully acknowledged.

The typed lambda calculus continues to be an important tool in logic and theoretical computer science. Since 1993, the research progress in this area has been documented by the TLCA proceedings. The present volume contributes to this tradition.

February 2005 Paweł Urzyczyn

Organization

Steering Committee

Samson Abramsky, Oxford, chair
Henk Barendregt, Nijmegen
Mariangiola Dezani-Ciancaglini, Turin
Roger Hindley, Swansea
Martin Hofmann, Munich

Program Committee

Thorsten Altenkirch, Nottingham
Stefano Berardi, Turin
Adriana Compagnoni, Hoboken
Herman Geuvers, Nijmegen
Andy Gordon, Microsoft, Cambridge
Fritz Henglein, Copenhagen
Martin Hofmann, Munich
Assaf J. Kfoury, Boston
Atsushi Ohori, JAIST, Tatsunokuchi
Laurent Regnier, Marseille
Paweł Urzyczyn, Warsaw, chair
Marek Zaionc, Cracow

Organizing Committee

Masahito Hasegawa, Kyoto, chair
Ryu Hasegawa, Tokyo
Mitsu Okada, Keio, Tokyo
Masahiko Sato, Kyoto
Masako Takahashi, ICU, Mitaka

Publicity Chair

Masahito Hasegawa, Kyoto

Referees

Klaus Aehlig
Patrick Baillot
Adam Bakewell
Anindya Banerjee
Franco Barbanera
Henk Barendregt
Gilles Barthe
Denis Béchet
Marcin Benke
Chantal Berline
Marc Bezem
Frederic Blanqui
Eduardo Bonelli
Michele Bugliesi
Felice Cardone
Jesper Carlström
Juliusz Chroboczek
Jacek Chrząszcz
Paolo Coppola
Roy L. Crole
Luís Cruz-Filipe
Ugo Dal Lago
Vincent Danos
René David
Pietro Di Gianantonio
Thomas Ehrhard
Andrzej Filinski
Carsten Führmann
Ken-etsu Fujita
Pablo Garralda
Jacques Garrigue
Silvia Ghilezan
Andreas Goerdt
Healfdene Goguen
Philippe de Groote
Yves Guiraud

Christian Haack
Joe Hallett
Hugo Herbelin
Martin Hyland
Atsushi Igarashi
Patricia Johann
Jean-Baptiste Joinet
Delia Kesner
Siau-Cheng Khoo
Bartek Klin
Jan Willem Klop
Adam Kolany
Jean-Louis Krivine
Olivier Laurent
Pierre Lescanne
Paul Blain Levy
Ugo de'Liguoro
Henning Makholm
Simone Martini
Ralph Matthes
Conor McBride
Ricardo Medel
Marino Miculan
Dale Miller
Alexandre Miquel
Torben Mogensen
Peter Møller Neergaard
Larry Moss
César Muñoz
Andrzej Murawski
Tobias Nipkow
Luca Paolini
Zoran Petrić
Brigitte Pientka
Benjamin Pierce
Adolfo Piperno
Rinus Plasmeijer
Randy Pollack
François Pottier
Bernhard Reus
Eike Ritter
Mads Rosendahl
James Royer
Luca Roversi
Paul Ruet
Alejandro C. Russo
Takafumi Sakurai
Jeffrey Sarnat
Alexis Saurin
Aleksy Schubert
Carsten Schürmann
Philip Scott
Peter Selinger
Konrad Slind
Morten Heine Sørensen
Bas Spitters
Ian Stark
Jasper Stein
Charles Stewart
Lutz Straßburger
Eijiro Sumii
Makoto Takeyama
Makoto Tatsuta
Lorenzo Tortora de Falco
Silvio Valentini
René Vestergaard
Fer-Jan de Vries
Philip Wadler
David Walker
Daria Walukiewicz-Chrząszcz
Paweł Waszkiewicz
Joe Wells
Freek Wiedijk
Hongwei Xi
Yoriyuki Yamagata
Maddalena Zacchi

Table of Contents

Contributed Papers

Completeness Theorems and λ-Calculus

Thierry Coquand

Institutionen för Datavetenskap,
Chalmers Tekniska Högskola, Göteborg, Sweden
coquand@cs.chalmers.se

Abstract. The purpose of this note is to present a variation of Hindley's completeness theorem for simply typed λ-calculus based on Kripke model. This variation was obtained indirectly by simplifying an analysis of a fragment of polymorphic λ-calculus [2].

1 Introduction

One the most important problem in proof theory is the status of impredicative definitions. Since the sharp criticism of Poincaré [15] one of the goal of Hilbert's problem was precisely to show that such "circular" definitions cannot lead to contradictions. A typical example of impredicative definition is Leibnitz definition of equality, which defines "a is equal to b" by the formula

$$\forall X.X(a) \rightarrow X(b) \qquad (*)$$

Here $X(x)$ ranges over all possible properties. In particular it could be the property $P(x)$

$$P(x) \leftrightarrow_{def} x \text{ is equal to } b$$

and there is an apparent circularity. If we have a logic with a given equality $=$, it is clear that $(*)$ is equivalent to $a = b$: we have indeed that $a = b$ and $\phi(a)$ implies $\phi(b)$, and conversely, if $P(a)$ implies $P(b)$ for any propery $P(x)$ we can take $P(x) \leftrightarrow_{def} a = x$ and we get $a = b$ since $a = a$. In this case, an apparent impredicative definition is equivalent to a predicative one[1]. The intuitions of Poincaré have been confirmed by several works [3], which shows that impredicative definitions are proof theoretically very strong. According to Gödel [5], it is precisely the use of impredicative definitions that separates classical mathematics from intuitionistic mathematics, much more than the use of excluded middle (and a similar view is now taken by Martin-Löf).

One breakthrough was accomplished in the 60s by G. Takeuti [18], who showed that the first level of impredicative definitions, so called Π^1_1 comprehension, can be reduced to so a strong form of inductive definitions. G. Takeuti

[1] The purpose of the "reducibility axiom" [16] is precisely to postulate that one can always replace an impredicative definition by a predicative one. Theorems 2 and 5 are instances where a priori impredicative definitions can be replaced by predicative ones.

P. Urzyczyn (Ed.): TLCA 2005, LNCS 3461, pp. 1–9, 2005.

introduces a stratification of Π^1_1 comprehension, and the first level, which we shall call *strict* quantification, is obtained by limiting the quantification over predicate $\forall X.\phi(X)$ to formulae $\phi(X)$ which contain only first order quantification. In order to interpret this fragment we need only inductive definitions in a form already considered by Brouwer and thus Takeuti's result shows that strict Π^1_1-quantification can be understood intuitionistically[2]. It is quite remarkable that most use of impredicative definitions are done at this level. For instance, Leibnitz equality explained above uses only a strict quantification. Another example is provided by the greatest lower bound of a collection of reals. We represent a real as a Dedekind cut, i.e. a set of rational numbers which is downward closed. If the collection of real numbers is represented by a formula $\phi(X)$, the greatest lower bound, as a set of rationals, is the intersection of all properties satisfying $\phi(X)$. It can thus be represented by the formula $P(q)$ defined by

$$P(q) \leftrightarrow_{def} \forall X.\phi(X) \rightarrow X(q)$$

Takeuti's reduction was quite indirect: it was based first on ordinal analysis, and then an intuitionistic proof that the corresponding ordinal system is well-founded. It has been greatly simplified by W. Buchholz [4], by using the Ω-rule. One main intuition can be found in Lorenzen [8]: it is possible to explain the classical truth of a statement

$$\forall X.\phi(X)$$

where ϕ does not have any quantification on predicates, by saying that $\phi(X)$ is *provable*, where X is a variable. The key point is that we know how to express classical provability of such formulae using inductive definitions. Indeed the rules of ω-logic provides an intuitionistic way of explaining the truth of arithmetical formulae such as $\phi(X)$, which contains free variables ranging over predicates [13, 9, 10].

For instance, it can be seen in this way that $\forall X.X(5) \rightarrow X(5)$ is valid, without having to consider the notion of an arbitrary subset of $\mathbb{N}$, by checking instead that the formula $X(5) \rightarrow X(5)$ is provable. This idea of replacing a quantification over an arbitrary subset by a syntactical quantification over a free predicate variable will play an important rôle in this note.

In a previous work [2] we used the idea of the Ω-rule to analyse the system F_0, which is a natural restriction of system F, with only strict Π^1_1-quantification. This corresponds closely to the system analysed in [17]. We showed that, for this fragment, normalisation could be proved in Peano arithmetic. We learnt since then that a similar analysis had been done by I. Takeuti [18], following however the method of ordinal analysis of G. Takeuti, and showing that an upper-bound for the restricted system F is ϵ_0. The argument of [2] was simplified by Buchholz. In this version, we have to use a Kripke semantics where worlds are contexts of simply typed λ-calculus.

---

[2] The corresponding system of inductive definition is called ID_1. Stronger forms of inductive definitions are needed to interpret Π^1_1-comprehension in general, and the intuitionistic status of these stronger forms is not clear.

A natural question on this simplification was to understand if the use of Kripke model is necessary in this argument. It turned out that this question had been answered already by R. Hindley [6]. It is thus possible to use instead Hindley's completeness theorem and we obtain in this way an alternative simple way to analyse the system F_0.

This note is organised as follow. We first motivate the use of the Ω-rule to analyse impredicative quantifications on two examples. We then present a simplification of the argument presented in [2], which explains how to interpret the system F_0 in Peano arithmetic. We end by showing how Hindley's completeness theorem [6] can be used instead to give an alternative proof of this result.

2 Ω-Rule

In order to explain the use of the Ω-rule, we present two examples where one can interpret in a predicative way strict impredicative quantification. The first example is for minimal propositional calculus, and the second example explains how to give a predicative interpretation of second-order arithmetic with strict Π^1_1-quantification.

2.1 Minimal Propositional Calculus

We show in this way that the introduction to strict universal quantification over propositions is a conservative extension of the minimal logic, that is the logic with only $\rightarrow$ and $\wedge$. The axioms for these connectives are

$$[a \leq b \wedge c] \leftrightarrow [a \leq b \quad \wedge \quad a \leq c] \qquad\qquad [a \wedge b \leq c] \leftrightarrow [a \leq b \rightarrow c]$$

Let H be the free Heyting algebra over variables $x_1, x_2, \ldots$. We can think of the elements of H as finite expressions $a(x_1, \ldots, x_n)$ built from finitely variables with $\rightarrow$ and $\wedge$. We consider now the Heyting algebra D of downward closed subsets of H, with operations

$$X \wedge Y = X \cap Y, \qquad X \rightarrow Y = \{a \in H \mid \forall b. b \in X \rightarrow a \wedge b \in Y\}$$

Since H is free, any interpretation $\rho(x_i) \in D$ of the free variables $x_i \in H$ extends to a map $a \longmapsto \overline{\rho}(a)$, $H \rightarrow D$. The following lemma has a direct proof.

Lemma 1. *If $\rho(x_i) = \downarrow x_i$ then $\overline{\rho}(a) = \downarrow a$ for all $a \in H$*

Let $i : H \rightarrow D$ be the map $i(a) = \downarrow a$. We have clearly $i(a) \leq i(b)$ in D if and only if $a \leq b$ in H. Let now $p(x)$ be an arbitrary expression, containing only x as a free variable. If $u \in D$ we can consider $p(u) \in D$.

Lemma 2. *We have $i(a) \leq p(u)$ for all $u \in D$ if and only if $a \leq p(x)$ in H for x not free in a.*

Proof. If we take $u = i(x)$ we have $p(u) = i(p(x))$ and $i(a) \leq p(u)$ implies $a \leq p(x)$. Conversely, assume $a \leq p(x)$ in H with x not free in a and let u be an arbitrary element of D. Let ρ be defined by $\rho(x_i) = i(x_i)$ for x_i free in a and $\rho(x) = u$. We have then $\overline{\rho}(a) \leq \overline{\rho}(p(x))$ and hence $i(a) \leq p(u)$ in D.

Corollary 1. *For any expression $p(x)$ with only one free variable x there exists $v \in D$ such that $w \leq p(u)$ for all $u \in D$ if and only if $w \leq v$.*

Proof. We define v to be the subset of H of elements $a \in H$ such that $a \leq p(x)$ for x not free in a.

More generally, this shows how to interpret a proposition containing universal quantification, such that $\forall x.((z \to x) \to z) \to z$ as an element of D. In this case this would be the set of expressions a such that $a \leq ((z \to x) \to z) \to z$ for x not free in a. In the Heyting algebra D we can interpret proposition of the form $\forall x.p(x)$[3].

2.2 Interpretation of Strict Π^1_1-Quantification

We consider now σ-complete Heyting algebras, that is structures with $\to$ and finite and countable conjunctions. The axiom for countable conjunction is

$$[a \leq \wedge_n b_n] \quad \leftrightarrow \quad \forall n.[a \leq b_n]$$

Since the work of Lorenzen [9], it is known how to build constructively the free σ-complete Heyting algebra (see also [11]). We let $H(X_1, \dots, X_n)$ be the free σ-complete Heyting algebra on propositions $X_i(p)$, $i \leq n$, $p \in \mathbb{N}$ and H the union $\cup_n H(X_1, \dots, X_n)$. It is possible to interpret in H all arithmetical formulae built with predicates variables $X_1, X_2, \dots$ and $\to$, conjunction and universal quantification on natural numbers. For instance, $(\forall x.X_1(x)) \to X_1(5)$ is interpreted by $(\wedge_n X_1(n)) \to X_1(5)$. A normalisation theorem for a related proof system is proved in [11].

For interpreting strict quantification on predicates, we follow the same method as in the previous section. We consider the σ-complete Heyting algebra D of *downward closed* subsets of H. As before we have an embedding $i : H \to D$ such that $i(x) \leq i(y)$ if and only if $x \leq y$, by defining $i(x) = \downarrow x$. It is possible to give a semantics of strict universal quantification in D by interpreting $\forall X.\phi(X)$ as the subset of all $a \in H$ such that $a \leq \phi(X)$ for X not free in a.

One important point is that the construction of the σ-complete algebra D involves only inductive definitions provided by the system ID_1, since proofs in ω-logic are represented as well-founded trees with countable branching. We get in this way a quite simple proof of the following result.

Theorem 1. *The strength of second-order arithmetic with strict Π^1_1-comprehension is the same as the one of the system ID_1.*

---

[3] A. Pitts had shown [14] that, quite surprisingly, if we have also disjunction, one can already model in H these propositions, for instance $\forall x.(y \to x)$ is $y \to 0$.

3 A Finitary Analysis of a Fragment of System F

3.1 A Completeness Theorem

The completeness theorem we present was obtained by analysing Buchholz simplification of the argument of [2], following the method presented in the previous section.

We let Λ be the set of all untyped, maybe open, λ-terms, with β-conversion as equality.

We consider types of the form

$$T \ ::= \ \alpha \mid T \to T$$

We use the notation $T_1 \to T_2 \to T_3$ for $T_1 \to (T_2 \to T_3)$ and similarly $T_1 \to T_2 \to \ldots \to T_n$ for $T_1 \to (T_2 \to (\ldots \to T_n))$.

Let L, M range over *contexts*, that is finite sets of the form $x_1 : T_1, \ldots, x_k : T_k$ with $x_i \neq x_j$ if $i \neq j$. We let H be the set of downward closed subsets of the set of contexts, where the order is *reversed* inclusion. H is thought of as a set of generalised truth-values.

We define $C_T : \Lambda \to \mathsf{H}$ by

$$C_T(t) = \{L \in S \mid L \vdash t : T\}$$

If $A, B \in \mathsf{H}$ we define $A \Rightarrow B \in \mathsf{H}$ by

$$A \Rightarrow B = \{L \mid \forall M \supseteq L.M \in A \to M \in B\}$$

and for $X, Y : \Lambda \to \mathsf{H}$ we define $X \to Y : \Lambda \to \mathsf{H}$ by

$$(X \to Y)(t) = \cap_u X(u) \Rightarrow Y(t\ u)$$

We introduce the following typing rule for deriving $L \vdash t : T$, which defines the system TA_β, system analysed in the references [6, 7].

$$\frac{}{L \vdash x : T}\ x : T \in L$$

$$\frac{L, x : T \vdash t : U}{L \vdash \lambda x\ t : T \to U} \qquad \frac{L \vdash u : V \to T \quad L \vdash v : V}{L \vdash u\ v : T}$$

$$\frac{L \vdash t : T \quad t =_\beta u}{L \vdash u : T}$$

Simple properties are:

Lemma 3. *If $L \subseteq M$ and $L \vdash t : T$ then $M \vdash t : T$.*

Lemma 4. *If $L, x : T \vdash t : T_1$ and x is not free in t then $L \vdash t : T_1$.*

By these two lemmas, we derive

Lemma 5. *We have* $C_{T_1} \rightarrow C_{T_2} = C_{T_1 \rightarrow T_2}$.

Proof. It is indeed clear by Lemma 3 that if $L \vdash t : T_1 \rightarrow T_2$ and $M \vdash u : T_1$ and $M \supseteq L$ then $M \vdash t\ u : T_2$. Conversely if $L \in (C_{T_1} \rightarrow C_{T_2})(t)$ then for x not free in t we have $L, x : T_1 \in C_{T_1}(x)$ and hence $L, x : T_1 \in C_{T_2}(t\ x)$ and so $L, x : T_1 \vdash t\ x : T_2$. It follows from this that we have $L, x : T_1 \vdash t : T_1 \rightarrow T_2$ and hence by Lemma 4, $L \vdash t : T_1 \rightarrow T_2$.

If T is a first-order type and we have an assignment $\rho(\alpha) : \Lambda \rightarrow \mathsf{H}$ defined for at least all the free type variables α occuring in T, we define the interpretation $T\rho$ by induction as usual: $\alpha\rho = \rho(\alpha)$ and $(T_1 \rightarrow T_2)\rho = T_1\rho \rightarrow T_2\rho$.

Lemma 6. *If* $x_1 : T_1, \ldots, x_n : T_n \vdash t : T$ *then for any assigment* ρ*, we have in* H

$$T_1\rho(u_1) \cap \ldots \cap T_n\rho(u_n) \subseteq T\rho(t(x_1 = u_1, \ldots, x_n = u_n))$$

Corollary 2. *If* $M = x_1 : T_1, \ldots, x_n : T_n$ *and* $M \vdash t : T(\alpha)$ *and* $T(\alpha)$ *is a first-order type using only* α *as a free type variable, which does not appear in* $T_1, \ldots, T_n$ *then* $M \in T(\alpha = X)(t)$ *for any* $X : \Lambda \rightarrow \mathsf{H}$.

Proof. We take $\rho(\beta) = C_\beta$ for β free in $T_1, \ldots, T_n$ and $\rho(\alpha) = X$. By Lemma 5 we have $T_i\rho = C_{T_i}$ and since $M \in C_{T_i}(x_i)$ we get by Lemma 6 $M \in T\rho(t)$ that is, $M \in T(\alpha = X)(t)$.

Theorem 2. *If* $T(\alpha)$ *is a first-order type using only* α *as a free type variable, then*

$$\bigcap_{X:\Lambda \rightarrow \mathsf{H}} T(\alpha = X)(t)$$

is exactly $\{L \mid L \vdash T(\beta)\}$ *for* β *fresh w.r.t.* L.

This show that the a priori impredicative intersection $\bigcap_{X:\Lambda \rightarrow \mathsf{H}} T(\alpha = X)(t)$ has a predicative description.

3.2 A Fragment of System *F*

We apply Theorem 2 to give a finitary interpretation of the fragment F_0 of system F which involves only strict Π^1_1-quantification. We consider the following types

$$T \ ::= \ \alpha \mid T \rightarrow T \mid (\Pi\alpha)T$$

where in the quantification, T has to be built using only α and $\rightarrow$.

Let us give some examples to illustrate the restriction on quantification. We can have $T = (\Pi\alpha)[\alpha \rightarrow \alpha]$ or $(\Pi\alpha)[\alpha \rightarrow (\alpha \rightarrow \alpha) \rightarrow \alpha]$ or even $(\Pi\alpha)[((\alpha \rightarrow \alpha) \rightarrow \alpha) \rightarrow \alpha]$ but a type such as $(\Pi\alpha)[[(\Pi\beta)[\alpha \rightarrow \beta]] \rightarrow \alpha]$ is not allowed.

We have the following typing rules

$$\frac{}{\Gamma \vdash x : T} \quad x : T \in \Gamma$$

$$\frac{\Gamma \vdash t : T \qquad t =_\beta u}{\Gamma \vdash u : T}$$

$$\frac{\Gamma, x : T \vdash t : U}{\Gamma \vdash \lambda x\, t : T \to U} \qquad \frac{\Gamma \vdash u : V \to T \qquad \Gamma \vdash v : V}{\Gamma \vdash u\ v : T}$$

$$\frac{\Gamma \vdash t : (\Pi\alpha)T}{\Gamma \vdash t : T[U]} \qquad \frac{\Gamma \vdash t : T}{\Gamma \vdash t : (\Pi\alpha)T}$$

where Γ is a finite set of type declaration $x : T$, and in the last rule, α does not appear free in any type of Γ.

We let N be the type $(\Pi\alpha)[\alpha \to (\alpha \to \alpha) \to \alpha]$. and c_n be the lambda term $\lambda x \lambda f\ f^n\ x$. We have $\vdash c_n : N$ for each n. Our interpretation in H gives a *finitary proof* of the following result.

Theorem 3. *If* $\vdash t : N \to N$ *then for each* n *there exists* m *such that* $t\ c_n\ x\ f = f^m\ x$ *for* x, f *variables.*

Proof. Theorem 2 provides exactly a model of F_0, where types are interpreted as functions $\Lambda \to \mathsf{H}$. In particular since $\vdash t\ c_n : N$ we should have $L \vdash t\ c_n : \alpha \to (\alpha \to \alpha) \to \alpha$ for all L and, for $L = x : \alpha,\ f : \alpha \to \alpha$ we get $L \vdash t\ c_n\ x\ f : \alpha$ in TA_β, and hence $t\ c_n\ x\ f = f^m\ x$ for some n.

This gives a finitary interpretation of system F_0 since our use of the notion of subsets for building H is never done in an impredicative way. This implies that our argument could be formalised in second-order arithmetic with only arithmetical comprehension [3], and it is standard that second-order arithmetic with arithmetic comprehension is conservative over Peano arithmetic. An application of this is [2]:

Theorem 4. *A function in* $\mathbb{N} \to \mathbb{N}$ *is representable by a term* t *such that* $\vdash_{F_0} t : N \to N$ *if and only if it is provably total in Peano arithmetic.*

Had we consider instead the fragment F_N where the only quantified type that we can form is the type N, it would have been quite easy to give a finitary interpretation. This is because it is clear in this case that the subset $\bigcap_{X \subseteq \Lambda}(X \to (X \to X) \to X)$ which has a description *a priori* impredicative, can also be described in a finitary way as the set $\{c_n \mid n \in \mathbb{N}\}$. Indeed, all terms c_n are clearly in this intersection, and conversely if a term t is in this intersection we can take for X the subset $\{f^n\ x \mid n \in \mathbb{N}\}$ where x and f are free variables not in t. We should have $t\ x\ f \in X$ which implies that $t =_\beta c_n$ for some $n \in \mathbb{N}$. The next section shows that this idea actually extends to all types of the system F_0.

4 Hindley's Completeness Theorem

In all interpretations of strict impredicative quantifications we have seen so far, the use of some form of Kripke model has been essential. It is thus quite surprising that for the analysis of F_0, this use is not essential, and we can instead rely on a direct set-theoretical semantics. A first-order type $T(\alpha)$ is interpreted as a subset of Λ in the following intended way

$$[\![\alpha]\!]_{\alpha=X} = X, \quad [\![T_1 \to T_2]\!]_{\alpha=X} = \{t \in \Lambda \mid \forall u.u \in [\![T_1]\!]_{\alpha=X} \to t\ u \in [\![T_2]\!]_{\alpha=X}\}$$

Theorem 5. *(Hindley) We have $t \in [\![T]\!]_{\alpha=X}$ for* all *$X \subseteq \Lambda$ if and only if $\vdash t : T$.*

Proof. We refer to [6, 7]. The proof is similar to the proof of theorem 2 but it avoids the use of Kripke model by building first a suitable infinite context[4].

For instance, for $T = \alpha \to (\alpha \to \alpha) \to \alpha$ this gives another proof that

$$\bigcap_{X \subseteq \Lambda} (X \to (X \to X) \to X)$$

is the set of terms c_n, $n \in \mathbb{N}$, since it can be shown directly that $\vdash t : N$ if and only if $t = c_n$ for some $n \in \mathbb{N}$. The surprising fact is that it gives a finitary description of complicated sets such as

$$\bigcap_{X \subseteq \Lambda} ((X \to X) \to X) \to X$$

This is the set $\{t \in \Lambda \mid\ \vdash t : ((\alpha \to \alpha) \to \alpha) \to \alpha\}$. This is remarkable since it is difficult, contrary to the previous case, to have any clear intuition for the meaning of this intersection.

The work [1] extends the result of [2] by giving constructive interpretations of a hierarchy of stronger and stronger systems $F_0 \subset F_1 \subset \ldots$. For instance, we obtain F_1 by allowing types $(\Pi\alpha)T(\alpha)$ where in $T(\alpha)$ can appear also closed types of F_0. Typically the type of constructive ordinals [12]

$$(\Pi\alpha)[\alpha \to ((N \to \alpha) \to \alpha) \to \alpha]$$

is a type of the system F_1. It is shown in [1] that the functions $\mathbb{N} \to \mathbb{N}$ representable as terms of type $N \to N$ in the system F_1 are exactly the functions provably total in the system ID_1. This work is based on the use of the Ω-rule, and it might be interesting to analyse if one can give an alternative argument by a suitable generalisation of Theorem 5.

References

1. K. Aehlig. *On Fragments of Analysis with Strengths of Finitely Iterated Inductive Definitions.* PhD thesis, Munich, 2003.

---

[4] In this infinite context, each type T gets assigned countably many variables $x : T$. The construction of this infinite context relies on a non canonical enumeration of all types and all variables. The completeness Theorem 2 does not involve such non canonical enumeration, but relies instead on a non standard semantics.

2. Th. Altenkirch and Th. Coquand. A finitary subsystem of the polymorphic λ-calculus. Typed lambda calculi and applications (Krakw, 2001), 22–28, Lecture Notes in Comput. Sci., 2044, Springer, Berlin, 2001.
3. W. Buchholz, S. Feferman, W. Pohlers and W. Sieg. *Iterated inductive definitions and subsystems of analysis: recent proof-theoretical studies.* Lecture Notes in Mathematics, 897. Springer-Verlag, Berlin-New York, 1981.
4. W. Buchholz, and K. Schtte. *Proof theory of impredicative subsystems of analysis.* Studies in Proof Theory. Monographs, 2. Bibliopolis, Naples, 1988.
5. K. Gödel. Zur intuitionistischen Arithmetik und Zahlentheorie. Ergebnisse einers math. Koll., Heft 4 (1933), pp. 34-38.
6. R. Hindley. The completeness theorem for typing λ-terms. Theoret. Comput. Sci. 22 (1983), no. 1-2, 1–17.
7. R. Hindley. *Basic simple type theory.* Cambridge Tracts in Theoretical Computer Science, 42. Cambridge University Press, Cambridge, 1997.
8. P. Lorenzen. Logical reflection and formalism. J. Symb. Logic 23 1958 241–249.
9. P. Lorenzen. Algebraische und logistische Untersuchungen über freie Verbände. J. Symbolic Logic 16, (1951). 81–106.
10. P. Martin-Löf. *Notes on constructive mathematics.* Almquist and Wixsekk, Stockholm, 1968.
11. P. Martin-Löf. Infinite terms and a system of natural deduction. Compositio Math. 24 (1972), 93–103.
12. P. Martin-Löf. A construction of the provable wellorderings of the theory of species. Logic, meaning and computation, 343–351, Synthese Lib., 305, Kluwer Acad. Publ., Dordrecht, 2001.
13. P. Novikov. On the consistency of a certain logical calculus. Matematicesky sbovnik, 12(3):353-369, 1943.
14. A. Pitts. On an interpretation of second-order quantification in first-order intuitionistic propositional logic. J. Symbolic Logic 57 (1992), no. 1, 33–52.
15. H. Poincaré. La logique de l'infini. Revue de metaphysique et de morale, 1909.
16. B. Russell and A. Whitehead. *Principia Mathematica.* Cambridge, 1910-1913.
17. G. Takeuti. On the fundamental conjecture of GLC. I. J. Math. Soc. Japan 7 (1955), 249–275.
18. G. Takeuti. Consistency proofs of subsystems of classical analysis. Ann. of Math. (2) 86 1967 299–348.
19. I. Takeuti. Proof of calculability through cut elimination. Proof theory and reverse mathematics (Kyoto, 1993), pp. 78–93 .

A Tutorial Example of the Semantic Approach to Foundational Proof-Carrying Code: Abstract

Amy P. Felty

School of Information Science and Technology,
University of Ottawa, Canada
afelty@site.uottawa.ca

Proof-carrying code provides a mechanism for insuring that a host, or code consumer, can safely run code delivered by a code producer. The host specifies a safety policy as a set of axioms and inference rules. In addition to a compiled program, the code producer delivers a formal proof of safety expressed in terms of those rules that can be easily checked. Foundational proof-carrying code (FPCC) provides increased security and greater flexibility in the construction of proofs of safety. Proofs of safety are constructed from the smallest possible set of axioms and inference rules. For example, typing rules are not included. In our semantic approach to FPCC, we encode a semantics of types from first principles and the typing rules are proved as lemmas. In addition, we start from a semantic definition of machine instructions and safety is defined directly from this semantics.

Since FPCC starts from basic axioms and low-level definitions, it is necessary to build up a library of lemmas and definitions so that reasoning about particular programs can be carried out at a higher level, and ideally, also be automated. I describe a high-level organization that allows Hoare-style reasoning about machine code programs. This organization will be presented using a detailed example. The example, as well as illustrating the above mentioned approach to organizing proofs, is designed to provide a tutorial introduction to as many facets of our FPCC approach as possible. For example, it illustrates how to prove safety of programs that traverse input data structures as well as allocate new ones.

More information can be found in the full paper [1].

References

1. Felty, A.P.: A tutorial example of the semantic approach to foundational proof-carrying code. In: Sixteenth International Conference on Rewriting Techniques and Applications, Springer-Verlag Lecture Notes in Computer Science (2005)

P. Urzyczyn (Ed.): TLCA 2005, LNCS 3461, p. 10, 2005.

Can Proofs Be Animated By Games?

Susumu Hayashi*

Faculty of Engineering, Kobe University, Japan
susumu@shayashi.jp
http://www.shayashi.jp

Abstract. Proof animation is a way of executing proofs to find errors in the formalization of proofs. It is intended to be "testing in proof engineering". Although the realizability interpretation as well as the functional interpretation based on limit-computations were introduced as means for proof animation, they were unrealistic as an architectural basis for actual proof animation tools. We have found game theoretical semantics corresponding to these interpretations, which is likely to be the right architectural basis for proof animation.

1 Introduction -Proof Animation-

In this paper, we will discuss a possible application of game theoretic semantics to *proof animation*. Proof animation is an application of an extended Curry-Howard isomorphism. The notion of "proofs as programs" reads "if a program is extracted from a checked proof, then it does not have bugs." Proof animation is its contrapositive, "if a program extracted from a proof has a bug, then the proof is not correct." The objects of proof animation are not correct programs but formalized proofs.

By the late 80's, many people had still believed that formally verified programs would not have bugs. But, this has been proved wrong. Now, many software engineers have realized bugs in the formalization are far more serious than the bugs in the implementation. You cannot formally prove that your formal specifications correctly reflect your informal intentions or requirements in your mind. It was believed that building a system according to detailed specifications is more difficult than writing such a specification according to informal intentions or requirements. Probably, this was the right attitude at the time. However, the time has past and the environments for software engineering have changed. Thanks to excellent tools and software engineering technologies, such as design patterns, building systems correct to specifications has become much easier than before. In the changeable modern business environments, specifications tend to be changed even in the middle of a project. Requirement analysis, compliance test and validation are thus becoming more difficult and important in software development processes than verification.

* Partly supported by Monbushyo Kakenhi grant 1005-16650028. The address will change soon. Consult Web page for the new address.

P. Urzyczyn (Ed.): TLCA 2005, LNCS 3461, pp. 11–22, 2005.

The same will happen in formal proof developments. Although the proof checkers and methodologies to use them are not powerful enough for everyday usages in software developments, they are becoming ever more and more realistic. When formal verification technologies become a reality technology, the last problem left would be "how to show correctness of formalization."

Let us illustrate this problem by an example used in [9]. Assume that we are developing a formal theory of a metric $||x||$ on the interval $[m, n]$ of the set of integers by the distance from n. For example, $||n||$ is 0 and $||m||$ is $n - m$. A linear order is defined by means of the metric so that x is smaller than y iff $||x|| < ||y||$, i.e., x is closer to n than y. We wish to prove a minimum number principle for the ordering:

$$\exists x.\forall y.P_{m,n}(f(x), f(y)), \tag{1}$$

where f is any function from the natural numbers to the interval and $P_{m,n}(x, y)$ represent "x is less than or equals to y in the ordering". It maintains that there is some x such that $f(x)$ is the minimum among $f(0)$, $f(1), \ldots$, namely, a minimum number principle for the ordering $P_{m,n}$.

The metric of $x \in [m, n]$ is formally defined by $n - x$. Thus, the formal definition of $P_{m,n}(x, y)$ should be $\mathtt{n} - \mathtt{y} \geq \mathtt{n} - \mathtt{x}$. Suppose that our proof language has the built-in predicate for $\geq$ but not for $\leq$. Thus the $\geq$-sign was used instead of $\leq$-sign. However, it is a confusing usage of the inequality. It is plausible that we type $\mathtt{n} - \mathtt{x} \geq \mathtt{n} - \mathtt{y}$ by a slip of fingers in the definition of $P_{m,n}(x, y)$. Suppose this happened. Then, the order is defined by its reverse. Can we find this error by developing the fully formalized proof of the minimum number principle for the ordering $P_{m,n}$?

The answer is no. We can develop a formal proof of the principle with the wrong definition of $P_{m,n}(x, y)$ given above. This is because the ordering is isomorphic to its reverse. Formal proofs do not help us to find the error, since the wrong definition does not imply any contradictions. Only one thing is wrong with it, that is, the definition is not the one which we intended in our mind. Since the intention is in our mind, there is no formal way to compare it with the formal definition.

In the case of program developments, we can check our system against our intention by executing it. If the system is correct w.r.t. a specification, then we can check specifications against our intention through validating the system. This kind of activities are called *validation* [16]. Verification is to ask "Did we build the system right?". Validation is to ask "Did we build the right system?". We may build a wrong system which is *right* relative to wrong specifications.

Can we do validation in formal proof developments? In the example given above, if our proof checker is smart enough to evaluate truth values of simple formulas, we can check if a definition is correctly formulated. We expect $P_{2,7}(6, 3)$ holds, but the proof checker would return `false` by evaluating $\mathsf{7} - \mathsf{6} \geq \mathsf{7} - \mathsf{3}$.

When we can execute formalized notions, we can validate them. Quite often, specifications of realistic softwares are interactively executable by simulators, which are sometimes called animators. Thus, executing specifications by such tools are sometimes called *specification animation.* Using this terminology, the evaluation of $P_{2,7}(6,3)$ with the result `false` may be called "definition animation."

Although a large part of mathematics is non-executable, constructive mathematics is known to be executable by means of Curry-Howard isomorphism. This means that constructive mathematics can be animated. For example, the animation for $P_{2,7}(6,3)$ above, may be regarded as an execution of a constructive proposition $\forall x, y.(P_{2,7}(x,y) \vee \neg P_{2,7}(x,y))$. Then, the animation of definition turns to be an animation of the proof. The activity of animating proofs to validate them is called *proof animation.*

2 Limit Interpretations

Constructive mathematics can be animated and validated through their executions (see [8]). However, a large part of mathematics is non-constructive. Classical proofs have been known to be executable by some constructive interpretations, such as continuation. However, they are known *locally legible but not globally legible.* We can understand how each classical rule is executed. We call this property *local legibility.* However, when the interpretations are applied to actual mathematical proofs, even for the simplest proofs such as the proof of the minimum number principle, the resulting algorithms are too complicated to understand. We can understand their behaviors in only a few exceptional cases with non-trivial efforts. We call this difficulty *global ilegibility.*[1]. If proof animation is for finding useful information such as bounds for solutions and algorithms in classical proofs as proof mining in [14], global ilegibility is not a real obstacle. However, our aim is to test proofs to our intentions just as engineers test systems. Proof executions must be light and legible as test runs of programs. Thus, the global ilegibility is an essential defect for proof animations.

In [7, 15], we introduced a new realizability interpretation to overcome the global ilegibility. The definition of our new realizability interpretation of logical connectives is the same as the original one by Kleene. However, the recursive realizers are replaced with the Δ^0_2-partial functions. Since the Δ^0_2-partial functions satisfy an axiom system of abstract recursion theory, everything goes just as in the case of the original realizability interpretation [15].

According to such a realizability interpretation, some semi-classical principles are valid, e.g., the principles of excluded middle for Σ^0_1-formulas hold. The fragment of classical mathematics valid by this interpretation was named *LCM, Limit-Computable Mathematics.* It has been proved that there exists a fine hierarchy of classical principles in [1]. According to the results of [1], LCM corresponds to the lower part of the hierarchy. We cannot therefore derive all the classical theorems in LCM, but it is known that quite a large variety of non-constructive theorems belong to LCM: see, e.g. [18]. For example, the minimal number principle for the natural numbers (MNP)

[1] Local and global legibility are terminologies due to Stefano Berardi.

$$\exists x.\forall y.(f(x) \leq f(y)),$$

where x and y are natural numbers, holds in LCM if f is recursive.

LCM uses learning theoretic notions to make semi-classical proof execution legible. Let us explain it with the example of MNP. There is no recursive realizer for MNP. However, there is a Δ^0_2-function computing x. It is known that Δ^0_2-functions represent learning algorithms called *inductive inference* in Learning theory [17]. An inductive inference is a try-and-error algorithmic process to find a right solution in finite time.

Here is an inductive inference for MNP. At the beginning, we temporarily assume that $f(0)$ is the minimal value among $f(0)$, $f(1)$, ... Then, we start to compare the value of $f(0)$ with the values $f(1)$, $f(2)$, ... to confirm our hypothesis. If we find $f(n_1)$ smaller than $f(0)$, then we change mind and assume that $f(n_1)$ is the real minimal value instead. We repeat the process and continue to find $f(0) > f(n_1) > f(n_2) > \ldots$. Since the sequence is decreasing, we eventually reach the minimal value $f(n_m)$ in finite time. Then, we learned or discovered a right value for x.

Hilbert's main idea of the proof of the finite basis theorem in [10] was this argument on the learning process (see [7]). By applying the argument repeatedly to streams of algebraic forms, Hilbert gave a proof of his famous lemma, which opened the door to the modern abstract algebra. By the aid of limiting realizability interpretation, it is not so difficult to read the learning process of a basis of any ideal of algebraic forms recursively enumerated, from his proof in 1890 paper.

3 Animation via Games?

Execution of a proof in LCM is a kind of learning process as illustrated above. Using an analogy with learning processes, we can understand algorithmic contents of proofs of LCM rather intuitively. Nonetheless, it has not been known if such learning algorithms can be fully automatically extracted from formalized versions of such informal proofs.

According to our experiences with the PX system [6], algorithms which are automatically extracted from the proofs based on the mathematical soundness theorem or the original Curry-Howard isomorphism are much more complicated and illegible than the ones which human beings read from texts with realizability or Curry-Howard isomorphism in their minds. Human beings unconsciously refine and simplify extracted codes. In the PX system, we introduced some optimization procedures to mimic humans' natural refinements and simplifications. Natural codes could thus be extracted from proofs by the PX system.

We have to do similar things to build an LCM animator, and it is a non-trivial technological task. Furthermore, there is a rather serious theoretical obstacle. In the algorithmic learning theory, an inductive inference is defined by a limiting recursive function such as $f(x) = \lim_n .g(n, x)$, where g is a recursive function and n is a natural number. We compute $g(0, x)$, $g(1, x)$, ... and, if it stops changing at $g(n, x)$, then the value $g(n, x)$ is the value of the limit. Namely, the limit is "computed" through the discrete time line. Careful inspections of the soundness theorem in [15] shows that the learning processes extracted from proofs by the extraction method given there use a unique "global time" for the learning. However, Hilbert's proof in [10] apparently uses plural "local times". In a sense, a local time is generated by a occurrence of the principle of Σ^0_1-excluded middle. Since Σ^0_1-excluded middle is repeatedly used in Hilbert's proof, we have several limits, each of which has its own internal clock in the learning algorithm associated to Hilbert's proof.

It is not difficult to read these learning algorithms based on plural "local times", when you look at Hilbert's original proof texts.[2] However, we do not have any formal way to represent such intuition yet. This has been the main obstacle to build a real proof animation tool based on LCM. However, recently, a game theoretic equivalent of the interpretation has been found [3, 9], and we expect that it will give a right framework to solve this problem.

3.1 1-Backtracking Game

Game theoretical semantics of logical formulas are known to be a good substitute for Tarskian semantics of logic [13]. It is said that game semantics is easier to learn than Tarski semantics.

Coquand [5] introduced a game theoretical semantics of classical first order arithmetic. It allows Eloise, the player for existential quantifiers, to do backtracking as she likes. On the other hand, her opponent Abelard, the player for universal quantifiers, is not allowed to backtrack. Due to backtracks, existence of *recursive* winning strategy for Eloise was proven to be equivalent to the validity of the formula in Tarski's semantics. In standard games, e.g., Π^0_n-true sentences normally has a winning strategy at least of Δ^0_{n-1}. In this paper, Coquand's games will be referred to as *backtracking games* or *full backtracking games.* Since strategies are recursive, the backtracking game may be regarded as a way of executing classical logic.

It is known that this semantics still suffers global ilegibility, even though it is much more legible than the other constructivization of classical logic. However, when backtracks of the games are restricted to *simple backtracks*, the game semantics coincides with LCM semantics and become very legible. Such a game is called *1-game* or *1-backtracking game.* We now give its definition. To do so, we will define some game theoretic notions.

Definition 1. A *position* of a play is a finite sequence of moves, which are expressed as $[x = 0]$, $[x = 0; a = 3; b = 8; y = 11]$, $[x = 0; a = 3; b = 8]$. The empty position is $[]$. For example, a position $[x_1 = 7; y_1 = 11; x_2 = 18; y_2 = 4]$ for $\exists x_1.\forall y_1.\exists x_2.\forall y_2.x_1 + y_1 \leq x_2 + y_2$ leads to the true formula $7+11 \leq 18+4$, and represents a win by Eloise. Assignments such as $x_1 = 7$, $y_1 = 11, \ldots$ in

[2] His proof is the essentially the one of Dixon's lemma taught in the contemporary algebra courses. However, Hilbert's original proof is much more "learning theoretic" than the contemporary counterparts. Especially, the discussions in his course at Göttingen July 5th 1897 shows its learning theoretic nature[11].

a position are called *moves*. In the present paper, we assume that each player moves alternatively. This restriction is not essential, and makes things easier. If the last move of a position is played by a player A, we say that *A played the position*. **EndOfDef**

Let us note that the position of a play was called "occurrence" in [5]. In our [9], the notion of position was more restrictive so that the end of a position must be played by Abelard. In the present paper, we relax the condition. Notations are different, but these two notions are essentially the same.

Position S_1 is a *subposition* of position S_2 iff S_1 is an initial segment of S_2. Namely, S_1 is obtained from S_2 by "popping up" some rounds from the tail. Thus, we do not need to memorize stack contents, when we do backtracking. We now formulate 1-backtracking game.

Definition 2. A *play with 1-backtracking* consists of an infinite or finite sequence of positions $u_0, u_1, u_2, \ldots$ with the following conditions:

(i) It starts with empty position, $u_0 = []$.
(ii) For any position in the sequence, the last move of u_{n+1} is the opponent of the player who played the last move of u_n.
(iii) When Eloise plays a position u_{n+1}, u_{n+1} is an extension of a position u by Eloise's move, where u is a subposition of u_n and is played by Abelard.
(iv) When Abelard plays a position u_{n+1}, u_{n+1} is an extension of the position u_n, which is played by Eloise's move.

The game of plays with 1-backtracking is called *simple backtracking game* or *1-backtracking game*, *1-game* in short. **EndOfDef**

We introduce some more terminologies for the later discussions.

Definition 3. A move by Eloise (the move by the condition (iii) above) is called a *backtracking move*, when u is a proper subposition of u_n. All of the other moves are called *normal moves*. The normal moves are all of Abelard's moves by the rule (iv) and Eloise's move by (iii) of the case $u = u_n$.

Note that a backtracking move not only flush a tail of stack (position), but also adds a new move for an occurrence of existential quantifier, say $\exists x$. The move is said a *backtracking move to $\exists x$* or *backtracking to $\exists x$*. **EndOfDef**

We now give an example of 1-game session. Consider a Σ_1^0-EM (Σ_1^0-Excluded Middle):

$$\exists x.T(e,x) \vee \forall a.T^-(e,a). \tag{2}$$

It is transformed to the following prenex normal form:

$$\exists x.\forall a.((x > 0 \wedge T(e, x-1)) \vee (x = 0 \wedge T^-(e,a))). \tag{3}$$

Eloise has the following recursive 1-backtracking strategy for it as shown below. Observe that there is only 1-backtracking.

u_0: []. The initial empty position consisting of zero moves.
u_1: $[x = 0]$. The first move.
u_2: $[x = 0; a = A_1]$. The second move. A_1 is a number played by Abelard. After this, we have two cases. If $T^-(e, A_1)$ is true, then Eloise wins and she stops to play. If it's false, Eloise backtracks to $\exists x$, i.e., backtracks to u_0 and moves for $\exists x$ as follows:
u_3: $[x = A_1 + 1]$. Then Abelard plays, say $a = A_2$.
u_4: $[x = A_1 + 1; a = A_2]$. For any move $a = A_2$, Eloise wins, since $T^-(e, A_1)$ was false and so $T(e, (A_1 + 1) - 1)$ is true.

3.2 1-Game and LCM

It has been proved that 1-game for prenex normal forms are equivalent to LCM in the following sense:

Theorem 1. *For any prenex normal formula, there is a recursive winning strategy of 1-backtracking game for Eloise iff the formula is realizable by the LCM-realizability interpretation.*

We now prove the theorem.

"Only if" direction: We prove the theorem for $\exists x_1 \forall y_1 \exists x_2 \forall y_2.R$. The proof is easily extended to the general case.

Assume ϕ is Eloise's winning strategy for $\exists x_1 \forall y_1 \exists x_2 \forall y_2.R$. We have to define two Δ^0_2-functions $f()$ and $g(y_1)$ such that $\forall y_1.\forall y_2.R(f(), y_1, g(y_1), y_2)$ holds. Note that $f()$ is a function without arguments as in programming languages, or an expression for a constant.

First, we define $f()$ and $g(y_1)$ without considering if they are Δ^0_2. After we defined them, we will prove the defined functions are Δ^0_2.

Let $P(\phi)$ be the set of plays played after ϕ. Since all the plays of $P(\phi)$ are played after ϕ, they must be finite. (Infinite plays cannot be won in our game theoretical semantics.) Note that $P(\phi)$ is a recursive set.

There is a play p_0 in $P(\phi)$ satisfying the following conditions:

1. The last position of p_0 is of the form $[x_1 = a_1]$. Namely, it consists Eloise's move for the first existential quantifier $\exists x_1$.
2. Let p_0 be $u_0, \ldots, u_n$. If $u_0, \ldots, u_n, u_{n+1}, \ldots, u_m$ is an extension of p_0 in $P(\phi)$, then $u_{n+1}, \ldots, u_m$ never contains backtracking moves to $\exists x_1$.

Namely, p_0 is a play "stable" with respect to $\exists x_1$. Beyond the last move of the play, any move played after ϕ never backtracks to $\exists x_1$ anymore.

Then, we define $f() = a_1$, where $x_1 = a_1$ is the last move for a stable play p_0. There might be many stable plays. We may take the play smallest in some fixed ordering.

We must prove such p_0 exists. It is proved by reductio ad absurdum. Consider the set S_1 of the plays in $P(\phi)$ satisfying the first condition for p_0. Of course, it is not empty. Assume there is no plays satisfying the second condition in S_1. Then, we can build an infinite play played after the strategy ϕ. Let v_0 be any play in S_1. Since this does not satisfy the second condition for p_0, there is an extension

v_1 whose last move is a backtrack to $\exists x_1$. It again belongs to S_1. Repeatedly, we can define an infinite sequence v_1, $v_2, \ldots$ which is played after ϕ. Thus there is an infinite play played after ϕ. But, it is a contradiction, since ϕ is a winning strategy.

Now we verify that $f()$ is Δ^0_2-definable. The first condition for p_0 is a recursive statement and the second condition is Π^0_1-statement. Thus, p_0 is defined by an expression $\min_{p_0} P(p_0)$, where P is a Π^0_1-formula expressing the two conditions for p_0. Since any Π^0_1-predicates has Δ^0_2-characteristic functions, $f() = \min_{p_0} P(p_0)$ is Δ^0_2-definable.

After we defined $f()$, we consider the games $\exists x_2.\forall y_2.R(f(), b_1, x_2, y_2)$ for all b_1, which are fought with ϕ after p_0. More formally, we consider the set $P(\phi) \uparrow p_0$ that is the set of all the play of $P(\phi)$, for which p_0 is an initial segment.

By essentially the same argument, we can define a "stable play" $p_1^{b_1}$ for $\exists x_2$ for each b_1 in the new games, and define $g(b_1)$ from it. A play p_1 is *a stable play with respect to* $\exists x_2$ for b_1 is a play satisfying the following conditions:

1. $p_1 \in P(\phi) \uparrow p_0$
2. The last move of the last position of p_1 is Eloise's move for the second existential quantifier $\exists x_2$.
3. Let p_1 be $u_0, \ldots, u_n$. If $u_0, \ldots, u_n, u_{n+1}, \ldots, u_m$ is an extension of p_1 in $P(\phi) \uparrow p_0$, then $u_{n+1}, \ldots, u_m$ never contain backtracking moves to $\exists x_2$.

Note that all extensions of the stable play p_1 in $P(\phi) \uparrow p_0$ do not contain any backtracking moves at all. Backtracking to $\exists x_1$ is forbidden, since they are extensions of p_0 and backtracking to $\exists x_2$ is forbidden by the definition of p_1.

Let the last position of p_1 be $[x_1 = f(),\ y_1 = b_1,\ x_2 = a_2]$. Then, we set $g(b_1) = a_2$. Then $g(b_1)$ is again Δ^0_2-definable.

We must prove $R(f(), b_1, g(b_1), b_2)$ is true for any b_1 and b_2 to finish the proof. Assume $R(f(), b_1, g(b_1), b_2)$ were false. Then Eloise loses for the position $[x_1 = f(),\ y_1 = b_1,\ x_2 = g(b_1)]$. Since ϕ is a winning strategy, Eloise must be able to continue to play by backtracking and eventually win. Thus, $P(\phi) \uparrow p_0$ must contain a play with backtracking. But, we have shown that this cannot happen. Thus, $R(f(), b_1, g(b_1), b_2)$ is true for any b_1 and b_2. This ends the proof of only-if direction.

"If" direction: Assume that $\forall y_1.\forall y_2.R(f(), y_1, g(y_1), y_2)$ holds for two Δ^0_2-definable functions $f()$ and $g(y_1)$. There are recursive functions $h(t)$ and $k(t, y_1)$ (guessing functions in the terminology of learning theory) such that $f() = \lim_t h(t)$ and $g(y_1) = \lim_t k(t, y_1)$. Then, Eloise's winning strategy is as follows:

> She plays for $h(0)$ for $\exists x_1$, and, after Abelard's play b_1 for $\forall y_1$ she plays $k(0, b_1)$ for $\exists x_2$. If she wins for Abelard's play b_2 for $\forall y_2$, she stops. If she loses, she computes $h(1)$. When $h(1)$ changes from $h(0)$, she backtracks to $\exists x_1$, and restart the play using $h(1)$ and $k(1, -)$. When $h(1)$ does not changes from $h(0)$,i.e. $h(0) = h(1)$, she backtracks to $\exists x_2$ instead, and continue to play $k(1, -)$.

Note that Abelard's first play for $\forall y_1$ is kept in the latter case, incrementing t of $h(t)$ and $k(t, -)$. Eventually, $h(t)$ converges to $f()$. Assume $h(t)$ is stable after $t \geq t_0$. She never backtracks to $\exists x_1$ after t_0, for $h(t)$ does not change anymore after t_0. Then, Abelard's play b_1 for $\forall y_1$ is kept forever, since Eloise never backtracks beyond it. Eventually, $k(t_0, b_1)$ converges to $g(b_1)$ and then she can win for any move for $\forall y_2$. This ends the proof of if-direction.

3.3 General Formulation of Backtracking Games and Jump

The notion of 1-game has been further generalized and refined by Berardi [3]. We can associate a backtracking game bck(G) to each game G in the sense of set theory . In the setting of [3], both players are allowed to backtrack and winning conditions are defined even for infinite plays. This is natural from the standard game theoretic point of view, unlike the game presented in this paper.

Remarkably, Berardi has proved that having a winning strategy for bck(G) in a degree O is equivalent to having a strategy for G in the jump O'. Thus, the motto is "1-backtracking represents the first order quantifiers." We may say that, if we are allowed to change our hypotheses on a system (or on the nature), then we can cope with the "infinity" represented by arithmetical quantifiers.

Recall that Brouwer, Hilbert and their contemporaries in the research of the foundations of mathematics in the 1920's regarded arithmetical quantifiers as the gate to the infinite world from the finite world. We may say the jump, namely a single arithmetical quantifier, corresponds to the "smallest infinity." Although finitary human beings are bound to be recursive, human beings may virtually handle the smallest infinity (or the jump) with try-and-error investigations or experiments, i.e. 1-backtracking. It strongly suggests that the learning theoretic notion of inductive inference would be a right kind of theoretical foundations of researches on the notion of discovery.

3.4 1-Games and Proof Animation

Although there are some unsolved problems with the 1-game in applying it to proof animation, it seems to be the right framework for proof animation. In this subsection, we will discuss the problems of "approximation" and "semantics of implication."

In the limiting recursive realizability in [15], more the clock (the index n of $\lim_n$) ticks, the closer the guesses get to the correct answer. Thus we can regard that learning algorithms are *approximating* the right answer as time progresses. This simple notion of approximation is one of reasons why LCM-interpretation is legible than the other approaches.

In 1-games, there is no apparent notion of clocks. However, there is a kind of approximations. When Eloise picks, e.g. $x = 7$ for $\exists x.\forall y.A(x, y)$, Abelard starts to attack her hypothesis $x = 7$. He may be able to give a counterexample with a particular instance of y. Then, Eloise changes her hypothesis and continues to play. As shown in the proof of "only if"-part of the equivalence of the theorem above, Eloise eventually reaches a right solution for x. Namely, the more Abelard attacks Eloise's hypothesis, the close Eloise moves to the right answer guided by her recursive winning strategy.

In other words, Eloise is approximating the right solution, pushed by test cases given by Abelard. Namely, the set of test cases (or attacks) by Abelard advances the clock. As the set grows, Eloise gets closer to the right answer.[3]

To build a 1-game animator, we need a good notion of approximation formulated well. We have not found such a formulation on which a real software system can be built. We have just started to analyze the real proofs by means of 1-games, seeking such a notion. The initial results show that it remarkably fits our intuitive understanding of the proofs mentioned above. This suggests that the 1-game is likely to be the right framework for proof animation. However, more case studies are necessary.

We now discuss the problem of semantics of implication. Note that we considered only the prenex normal forms for the 1-game. We did not handle implications. Transformation of an implicational formula to the prenex normal form already includes classical reasonings. we have to give an game theoretical interpretation of implication which is equivalent to LCM-semantics of implication.

There are at least two ways to handle implication in game theoretical semantics (see [12]). The standard way is to regard $A \to B$ as $A^{\perp} \vee B$, where $A^{\perp}$ is the dual game. Another way is to use the notion of the *subgame*. Although some modifications are necessary, it is basically easy to extend our discussions to the full fragment of the first order arithmetic by the subgame approach in Chapter 3 of [12]. We regard $A \to B$ as the game to play B, provided we have a free access to a winning strategy for A. You can imagine that you are playing an online chess game. You are pondering on your next move for a configuration B. To do so, you wish to know a right move for another configuration A, which may turn up after B. You know how to win B, if you can win A. Instead of pondering on the next move for A, you may consult a chess program (it's an online game) how to win A. Then A is a subgame for $A \to B$. This scenario is natural, and easy to understand. However, it might obscure interactions between the strategies for A and B. To say "the strategy f for B can consult the strategy g for A", we mean that f is defined relative to g. Thus, the interaction is concealed in the computation of strategy f.

On the other hand, there is a way to use backtracks to represent communication between A and B in $A^{\perp} \vee B$. Since our backtrack is a kind of pops of stacks, we may simulate recursive function calls by 1-backtracking. It is expected that this approach and subgame approach are related.

However, from the system design point of view, these two are very different. If we take the latter approach, the interaction between A and B becomes part of plays of the game and it would give more legible animation of proofs. However, we have to allow Abelard to backtrack, since we must make the game symmetric to use the dual $A^{\perp}$ of A. If we identify Abelard's moves as test cases as explained above, test cases with backtracks must be introduced. After these differences, proof animation tools based on these two frameworks would be rather different.

[3] Berardi has introduced a series of limit-interpretations whose indexes are sets of conditions[2]. It is expected that these notions are closely related.

3.5 Why Is 1-Game Legible?

We will close this section by a remark on legibility of the 1-games. Since the full backtracking game needs only recursive strategies, there is no apparent reason to use the 1-game instead of the full backtracking game for proof animation. However, as already noted, the full backtracking game is not so legible as the 1-game. The ilegibility come from the lack of "stable play". If plays are stabilized, then the winning strategy is essentially that of 1-games. Thus, games won by stabilizing winning strategies must be 1-games. When, plays are not stabilized, we cannot "approximate" the truth. When, we say $A \vee B$ holds, we wish to know which of A and B holds. In constructive mathematics, we can effectively tell the answer. In LCM, we can approximate the truth. We may be wrong at the beginning, but we can move closer and closer to the right answer by try-and-error processes. The temporary guesses may oscillate between A and B, but eventually converge. In general, we cannot know when it converges, but, for many concrete cases, we can often find criteria by which we can see when guesses are stabilized.

We never have such stabilization for plays of the Σ^0_2-excluded middle for the universal Σ^0_2-formula $\exists x.\forall y.T(e,x,y) \vee \forall a.\exists b.T^-(e,a,b)$. A relatively simple winning strategy for this formula in the full backtracking game is given in [9]. However, the plays after it are never stabilized. Thus, we cannot have any useful information on which side of the disjunction operator holds, even though Abelard plays *all* possible moves. Contrary to this case, in the case of the Σ^0_1-excluded middle (2) above, when $\exists x.T(e,x)$ is correct, we will observe a backtracking and find this side is correct. When $\forall a.T^-(e,a)$ holds, we will observe the plays are stable and will have more and more confidence of the truth of $\forall a.T^-(e,a)$, as the game is repeatedly played.

The 1-game is expected to be a restricted backtracking game. Namely, we have found a subset of the full backtracking games, in which Eloise's winning strategies are guaranteed "legible" in the sense that the plays are eventually stabilized. Note that this does not exclude the possibility of some plays in Coquand's game beyond the 1-game may be legible in some particular cases. It is quite likely that there are some important classes of classical proofs beyond LCM, for which we can find legible computational contents through the full backtracking game or the like.

4 Conclusion

We have briefly surveyed proof animation, limit computable mathematics and backtracking games. We presented a version of 1-backtracking game and give a detailed proof of its equivalence to limiting recursive realizability. We also discussed how these notions and some results are expected to be useful for proof animation. We are now analyzing some simple LCM-proofs such as a proof of MNP from the Σ^0_1-excluded middle given in [9]. Doing so, we will eventually find the right way to handle implication semantics and approximation. After finding the solutions, we would design and build a prototype of proof animator. Then, we will see mathematical proofs, such as the ones of Hilbert's paper [10], animated by games.

The many materials of the present paper are outcomes of joint research with Stefano Berardi and Thierry Coquand. I thank them for many helpful suggestions and discussions.

References

1. Akama, Y., Berardi, S., Hayashi, S. and Kohlenbach, U.: An arithmetical hierarchy of the law of excluded middle and related principles,
2. Berardi, S.: Classical logic as Limit Completion, -a constructive model for non-recursive maps-, submitted, 2001, available at `http://www.di.unito.it/~stefano/`
3. Berardi, S., Coquand, T. and Hayashi, S.: Games with 1-Backtracking, submitted, 2005.
4. Coquand, T.: A Semantics of Evidence for Classical Arithmetic, in Géard Huet, Gordon Plotkin and Claire Jones, eds, Proceedings of the Second Workshop on Logical Frameworks, 1991, (a preliminary version of [5])
5. Coquand, T.: A Semantics of Evidence for Classical Arithmetic, Journal of Symbolic Logic, 60(1), 325-337, 1995.
6. Hayashi, S. and Nakano, H.: PX: A Computational Logic, 1988, The MIT Press, available free from the author's web page in PDF format.
7. Hayashi, S. and Nakata, M.: Towards Limit Computable Mathematics, in Types for Proofs and Programs, P. Challanghan, Z. Luo, J. McKinna, R. Pollack, eds., LNCS 2277 (2001) 125–144
8. Hayashi, S., Sumitomo, R. and Shii, K.: Towards Animation of Proofs - Testing Proofs by Examples -, Theoretical Computer Science, **272** (2002), 177–195
9. Hayashi, S.: Mathematics based on Incremental Learning, -Excluded middle and Inductive inference-, to appear in Theoretical Computer Science.
10. Hilbert, D.: *Über die Theorie der algebraische Formen*, Mathematische Annalen 36 (1890), 473–531.
11. Hilbert, D.: Theory of Algebraic Invariants, translated by Laubenbacher, R.L., Cambridge University Press, 1993.
12. Hintikka, J. and Kulas, J.: The Game of Language, Reidel, 1983.
13. Hintikka, J. and Sandu, G.: Game-Theoretical Semantics, in Handbook of Logic and Language, Part I, edited by van Benthem Jan F. A. K. et al., 1999.
14. Kohlenbach, U. and Oliva, P.: Proof mining: a systematic way of analysing proofs in Mathematics, in Proceedings of the Steklov Institute of Mathematics, Vol. 242 (2003), 136–164.
15. Nakata, M. and Hayashi, S.: Realizability Interpretation for Limit Computable Mathematics, Scientiae Mathematicae Japonicae, vol.5 (2001), 421–434.
16. Sommerville, I.: Software engineering, 6th edition, Addison Wesley, 2000.
17. Sanjay, J., Osherson, D., Royer, J.S., and Sharma, A.: Systems That Learn - 2nd Edition: An Introduction to Learning Theory (Learning, Development, and Conceptual Change), The MIT Press, 1999.
18. Toftdal, M.: *A Calibration of Ineffective Theorems of Analysis in a Hierarchy of Semi-Classical Logical Principles*, in Proceedings of ICALP '04, 1188–1200, 2004.

Untyped Algorithmic Equality for Martin-Löf's Logical Framework with Surjective Pairs

Andreas Abel* and Thierry Coquand

Department of Computer Science, Chalmers University of Technology
abel, coquand@cs.chalmers.se

Abstract. An untyped algorithm to test $\beta\eta$-equality for Martin-Löf's Logical Framework with strong Σ-types is presented and proven complete using a model of partial equivalence relations between untyped terms.

1 Introduction

Type checking in dependent type theories requires comparison of expressions for equality. In theories with β-equality, an apparent method is to normalize the objects and then compare their β-normal forms syntactically. In the theory we want to consider, an extension of Martin-Löf's logical framework with $\beta\eta$-equality by dependent surjective pairs (strong Σ types), which we call MLF_{Σ}, a naive *normalize and compare syntactically* approach fails since $\beta\eta$-reduction with surjective pairing is known to be non-confluent [Klo80].

We therefore advocate the incremental $\beta\eta$-convertibility test which has been given by the second author for dependently typed λ-terms [Coq91, Coq96], and extend it to pairs. The algorithm computes the weak head normal forms of the conversion candidates, and then analyzes the shape of the normal forms. In case the head symbols do not match, conversion fails early. Otherwise, the subterms are recursively weak head normalized and compared. There are two flavors of this algorithm.

Type-directed conversion. In this style, the type of the two candidates dictates the next step in the algorithm. If the candidates are of function type, both are applied to a fresh variable, if they are of pair type, their left and right projections are recursively compared, and if they are of base type, they are compared structurally, i. e., their head symbols and subterms are compared. Type-directed conversion has been investigated by Harper and Pfenning [HP05]. The advantage of this approach is that it can handle cases where the type provides extra information which is not already present in the shape of terms. An example is the unit type: any two terms of unit type, e. g., two variables, can be considered

* Research supported by the coordination action *TYPES* (510996) and thematic network *Applied Semantics II* (IST-2001-38957) of the European Union and the project *Cover* of the Swedish Foundation of Strategic Research (SSF).

P. Urzyczyn (Ed.): TLCA 2005, LNCS 3461, pp. 23–38, 2005.

equal. Harper and Pfenning report difficulties in showing transitivity of the conversion algorithm, in case of dependent types. To circumvent this problem, they erase the dependencies and obtain simple types to direct the equality algorithm. In the theory they consider, the Edinburgh Logical Framework [HHP93], erasure is sound, but in theories with types defined by cases (large eliminations), erasure is unsound and it is not clear how to make their method work. In this article, we investigate an alternative approach.

Shape-directed (untyped) conversion. As the name suggests, the shape of the candidates directs the next step. If one of the objects is a λ-abstraction, both objects are applied to a fresh variable, if one object is a pair, the algorithm continues with the left and right projections of the candidates, and otherwise, they are compared structurally. Since the algorithm does not depend on types, it is in principle applicable to many type theories with functions and pairs. In this article, we prove it complete for MLF_Σ, but since we are not using erasure, we expect the proof to extend to theories with large eliminations.

Main technical contributions of this article.

1. We extend the untyped conversion algorithm of the second author [Coq91] to a type system with Σ-types and surjective pairing. Recall that reduction in the untyped λ-calculus with surjective pairing is not Church-Rosser [Bar84] and, thus, one cannot use a presentation of this type system with conversion defined on raw terms.[1]
2. We take a modular approach for showing the completeness of the conversion algorithm. This result is obtained using a special instance of a general PER model construction. Furthermore this special instance can be described *a priori* without references to the typing rules.

Contents. We start with a syntactical description of MLF_Σ, in the style of equality-as-judgement (Section 2). Then, we give an untyped algorithm to check $\beta\eta$-equality of two expressions, which alternates weak head reduction and comparison phases (Section 3). The goal of this article is to show that the algorithmic equality of MLF_Σ is equivalent to the declarative one. Soundness is proven rather directly in Section 4, requiring inversion for the typing judgement in order to establish subject reduction for weak head evaluation. Completeness, which implies decidability of MLF_Σ, requires construction of a model. Before giving a specific model, we describe a class of PER models of MLF_Σ based on a generic model of the λ-calculus with pairs (Section 5). In Section 6 we turn to the specific model of expressions modulo β-equality, on which we define an inductive η-equality. Its transitive closure is regarded as the "universe" $\mathcal{S}$ of type interpretations, each interpretation is shown to be a subset of $\mathcal{S}$. As a consequence, two declaratively equal terms are related by $\mathcal{S}$. We complete the circle in Section 7 where we show that well-typed $\mathcal{S}$-related terms are algorithmically equal, using standardization

[1] In the absence of confluence, one cannot show injectivity of type constructors, hence subject reduction fails.

for λ-terms. Decidability of judgmental equality on well-typed terms in MLF_Σ ensues, which entails that type checking of normal forms is decidable as well.

The full version of the article, which contains additionally a bidirectional type-checking algorithm for MLF_Σ and more detailed proofs, is available on the homepage of the first author [AC05].

2 Declarative Presentation of MLF_Σ

This section presents the typing and equality rules for an extension of Martin-Löf's logical framework [NPS00] by dependent pairs. We show some standard properties like weakening and substitution, as well as injectivity of function and pair types and inversion of typing, which will be crucial for the further development.

Wellformed contexts $\Gamma \vdash \mathsf{ok}$.

$$\text{CXT-EMPTY}\ \frac{}{\diamond \vdash \mathsf{ok}} \qquad \text{CXT-EXT}\ \frac{\Gamma \vdash A : \mathsf{Type}}{\Gamma, x\!:\!A \vdash \mathsf{ok}}$$

Typing $\Gamma \vdash t : A$.

$$\text{HYP}\ \frac{\Gamma \vdash \mathsf{ok} \qquad (x\!:\!A) \in \Gamma}{\Gamma \vdash x : A} \qquad \text{CONV}\ \frac{\Gamma \vdash t : A \qquad \Gamma \vdash A = B : \mathsf{Type}}{\Gamma \vdash t : B}$$

$$\text{SET-F}\ \frac{\Gamma \vdash \mathsf{ok}}{\Gamma \vdash \mathsf{Set} : \mathsf{Type}} \qquad \text{SET-E}\ \frac{\Gamma \vdash t : \mathsf{Set}}{\Gamma \vdash \mathsf{El}\, t : \mathsf{Type}}$$

$$\text{FUN-F}\ \frac{\Gamma \vdash A : \mathsf{Type} \qquad \Gamma, x\!:\!A \vdash B : \mathsf{Type}}{\Gamma \vdash \mathsf{Fun}\, A\, (\lambda x B) : \mathsf{Type}}$$

$$\text{FUN-I}\ \frac{\Gamma, x\!:\!A \vdash t : B}{\Gamma \vdash \lambda x t : \mathsf{Fun}\, A\, (\lambda x B)} \qquad \text{FUN-E}\ \frac{\Gamma \vdash r : \mathsf{Fun}\, A\, (\lambda x B) \qquad \Gamma \vdash s : A}{\Gamma \vdash r\, s : B[s/x]}$$

$$\text{PAIR-F}\ \frac{\Gamma \vdash A : \mathsf{Type} \qquad \Gamma, x\!:\!A \vdash B : \mathsf{Type}}{\Gamma \vdash \mathsf{Pair}\, A\, (\lambda x B) : \mathsf{Type}} \qquad \text{PAIR-I}\ \frac{\Gamma \vdash s : A \qquad \Gamma \vdash t : B[s/x]}{\Gamma \vdash (s, t) : \mathsf{Pair}\, A\, (\lambda x B)}$$

$$\text{PAIR-E-L}\ \frac{\Gamma \vdash r : \mathsf{Pair}\, A\, (\lambda x B)}{\Gamma \vdash r\, \mathsf{L} : A} \qquad \text{PAIR-E-R}\ \frac{\Gamma \vdash r : \mathsf{Pair}\, A\, (\lambda x B)}{\Gamma \vdash r\, \mathsf{R} : B[r\, \mathsf{L}/x]}$$

Fig. 1. MLF_Σ rules for contexts and typing

Expressions (terms and types). We do not distinguish between terms and types syntactically. Dependent function types, usually written $\Pi x : A.\, B$, are written $\mathsf{Fun}\, A\, (\lambda x B)$; similarly, dependent pair types $\Sigma x : A.\, B$ are represented by

$\mathsf{Pair}\, A\, (\lambda x B)$. We write projections L and R postfix. The syntactic entities of MLF_Σ are given by the following grammar.

Var	$\ni x, y, z$		variables
Const	$\ni c$	$::= \mathsf{Fun} \mid \mathsf{Pair} \mid \mathsf{El} \mid \mathsf{Set}$	constants
Proj	$\ni p$	$::= \mathsf{L} \mid \mathsf{R}$	left and right projection
Exp	$\ni r, s, t, A, B, C$	$::= c \mid x \mid \lambda x t \mid r\, s \mid (t, t') \mid r\, p$	expressions
Cxt	$\ni \Gamma$	$::= \diamond \mid \Gamma, x\!:\!A$	typing contexts

We identify terms and types up to α-conversion and adopt the convention that in contexts Γ, all variables must be distinct; hence, the context extension $\Gamma, x\!:\!A$ presupposes $(x\!:\!B) \notin \Gamma$ for any B.

The inhabitants of Set are type codes; El maps type codes to types. E.g., $\mathsf{Fun}\ \mathsf{Set}\ (\lambda a.\ \mathsf{Fun}\ (\mathsf{El}\, a)\ (\lambda\_.\ \mathsf{El}\, a))$ is the type of the polymorphic identity $\lambda a \lambda x x$.

Judgements are inductively defined relations. If $\mathcal{D}$ is a derivation of judgement J, we write $\mathcal{D} :: J$. The type theory MLF_Σ is presented via five judgements:

$\Gamma \vdash \mathsf{ok}$	Γ is a well-formed context
$\Gamma \vdash A : \mathsf{Type}$	A is a well-formed type
$\Gamma \vdash t : A$	t has type A
$\Gamma \vdash A = A' : \mathsf{Type}$	A and A' are equal types
$\Gamma \vdash t = t' : A$	t and t' are equal terms of type A

Typing and well-formedness of types both have the form $\Gamma \vdash \_ : \_$. We will refer to them by the same judgement $\Gamma \vdash t : A$. If we mean typing only, we will require $A \not\equiv \mathsf{Type}$. The same applies to the equality judgements. Typing rules are given in Figure 1, together with the rules for well-formed contexts. The rules for the equality judgements are given in Figure 2. Observe that we have chosen a "parallel reduction" version for β- and η-rules, which has been inspired by Harper and Pfenning [HP05] and Sarnat [Sar04], in order to make the proof of functionality easier. In the following, we present properties of MLF_Σ which have easy syntactical proofs.

Admissible rules. MLF_Σ enjoys the usual properties of weakening, context conversion, substitution, functionality and inversion and injectivity for the type expressions $\mathsf{El}\, t$, $\mathsf{Fun}\, A\, (\lambda x B)$ and $\mathsf{Pair}\, A\, (\lambda x B)$. These rules can be found in the extended version of this article [AC05]. Note that in Martin-Löf's LF, injectivity is almost trivial since computation is restricted to the level of terms. This is also true for Harper and Pfenning's version of the Edinburgh LF which lacks type-level λ-abstraction [HP05]. In the Edinburgh LF with type-level λ it involves a normalization argument and is proven using logical relations [VC02].

Lemma 1 (Syntactic Validity).

1. *Typing: If* $\Gamma \vdash t : A$ *then* $\Gamma \vdash \mathsf{ok}$ *and either* $A \equiv \mathsf{Type}$ *or* $\Gamma \vdash A : \mathsf{Type}$.
2. *Equality: If* $\Gamma \vdash t = t' : A$ *then* $\Gamma \vdash t : A$ *and* $\Gamma \vdash t' : A$.

Equivalence, hypotheses, conversion.

$$\text{EQ-SYM}\ \frac{\Gamma \vdash t = t' : A}{\Gamma \vdash t' = t : A} \qquad \text{EQ-TRANS}\ \frac{\Gamma \vdash r = s : A \qquad \Gamma \vdash s = t : A}{\Gamma \vdash r = t : A}$$

$$\text{EQ-HYP}\ \frac{\Gamma \vdash \mathsf{ok} \qquad (x\!:\!A) \in \Gamma}{\Gamma \vdash x = x : A} \qquad \text{CONV}\ \frac{\Gamma \vdash t = t' : A \qquad \Gamma \vdash A = B : \mathsf{Type}}{\Gamma \vdash t = t' : B}$$

Sets.

$$\text{EQ-SET-F}\ \frac{\Gamma \vdash \mathsf{ok}}{\Gamma \vdash \mathsf{Set} = \mathsf{Set} : \mathsf{Type}} \qquad \text{EQ-SET-E}\ \frac{\Gamma \vdash t = t' : \mathsf{Set}}{\Gamma \vdash \mathsf{El}\,t = \mathsf{El}\,t' : \mathsf{Type}}$$

Dependent functions.

$$\text{EQ-FUN-F}\ \frac{\Gamma \vdash A = A' : \mathsf{Type} \qquad \Gamma, x\!:\!A \vdash B = B' : \mathsf{Type}}{\Gamma \vdash \mathsf{Fun}\,A\,(\lambda x B) = \mathsf{Fun}\,A'\,(\lambda x B') : \mathsf{Type}}$$

$$\text{EQ-FUN-I}\ \frac{\Gamma, x\!:\!A \vdash t = t' : B}{\Gamma \vdash \lambda x t = \lambda x t' : \mathsf{Fun}\,A\,(\lambda x B)}$$

$$\text{EQ-FUN-E}\ \frac{\Gamma \vdash r = r' : \mathsf{Fun}\,A\,(\lambda x B) \qquad \Gamma \vdash s = s' : A}{\Gamma \vdash r\,s = r'\,s' : B[s/x]}$$

$$\text{EQ-FUN-}\beta\ \frac{\Gamma, x\!:\!A \vdash t = t' : B \qquad \Gamma \vdash s = s' : A}{\Gamma \vdash (\lambda x t)\,s = t'[s'/x] : B[s/x]}$$

$$\text{EQ-FUN-}\eta\ \frac{\Gamma \vdash t = t' : \mathsf{Fun}\,A\,(\lambda x B)}{\Gamma \vdash (\lambda x.\,t\,x) = t' : \mathsf{Fun}\,A\,(\lambda x B)}\ x \notin \mathsf{FV}(t)$$

Dependent pairs.

$$\text{EQ-PAIR-F}\ \frac{\Gamma \vdash A = A' : \mathsf{Type} \qquad \Gamma, x\!:\!A \vdash B = B' : \mathsf{Type}}{\Gamma \vdash \mathsf{Pair}\,A\,(\lambda x B) = \mathsf{Pair}\,A'\,(\lambda x B') : \mathsf{Type}}$$

$$\text{EQ-PAIR-I}\ \frac{\Gamma \vdash s = s' : A \qquad \Gamma \vdash t = t' : B[s/x]}{\Gamma \vdash (s, t) = (s', t') : \mathsf{Pair}\,A\,(\lambda x B)}$$

$$\text{EQ-PAIR-E-L}\ \frac{\Gamma \vdash r = r' : \mathsf{Pair}\,A\,(\lambda x B)}{\Gamma \vdash r\,\mathsf{L} = r'\,\mathsf{L} : A} \qquad \text{EQ-PAIR-E-R}\ \frac{\Gamma \vdash r = r' : \mathsf{Pair}\,A\,(\lambda x B)}{\Gamma \vdash r\,\mathsf{R} = r'\,\mathsf{R} : B[r\,\mathsf{L}/x]}$$

$$\text{EQ-PAIR-}\beta\text{-L}\ \frac{\Gamma \vdash s = s' : A \quad \Gamma \vdash t : B}{\Gamma \vdash (s, t)\,\mathsf{L} = s' : A} \qquad \text{EQ-PAIR-}\beta\text{-R}\ \frac{\Gamma \vdash s : A \quad \Gamma \vdash t = t' : B}{\Gamma \vdash (s, t)\,\mathsf{R} = t' : B}$$

$$\text{EQ-PAIR-}\eta\ \frac{\Gamma \vdash r = r' : \mathsf{Pair}\,A\,(\lambda x B)}{\Gamma \vdash (r\,\mathsf{L},\ r\,\mathsf{R}) = r' : \mathsf{Pair}\,A\,(\lambda x B)}$$

Fig. 2. MLF_Σ equality rules

Lemma 2 (Inversion of Typing). *Let* $C \not\equiv \mathsf{Type}$.

1. *If* $\Gamma \vdash x : C$ *then* $\Gamma \vdash \Gamma(x) = C : \mathsf{Type}$.
2. *If* $\Gamma \vdash \lambda xt : C$ *then* $C \equiv \mathsf{Fun}\, A\, (\lambda x B)$ *and* $\Gamma, x{:}A \vdash t : B$.
3. *If* $\Gamma \vdash r\, s : C$ *then* $\Gamma \vdash r : \mathsf{Fun}\, A\, (\lambda x B)$ *with* $\Gamma \vdash s : A$ *and* $\Gamma \vdash B[s/x] = C : \mathsf{Type}$.
4. *If* $\Gamma \vdash (r, s) : C$ *then* $C \equiv \mathsf{Pair}\, A\, (\lambda x B)$ *with* $\Gamma \vdash r : A$ *and* $\Gamma \vdash s : B[r/x]$.
5. *If* $\Gamma \vdash r\mathsf{L} : A$ *then* $\Gamma \vdash r : \mathsf{Pair}\, A\, (\lambda x B)$.
6. *If* $\Gamma \vdash r\mathsf{R} : C$ *then* $\Gamma \vdash r : \mathsf{Pair}\, A\, (\lambda x B)$ *and* $\Gamma \vdash B[r\mathsf{L}/x] = C : \mathsf{Type}$.

3 Algorithmic Presentation

In this section, we present an algorithm for deciding equality. The goal of this article is to prove it sound and complete.

Syntactic classes. The algorithm works on weak head normal forms WVal. For convenience, we introduce separate categories for normal forms which can denote a function and for those which can denote a pair. In the intersection of these categories live the neutral expressions.

$$\begin{array}{lll}
\mathsf{WElim} \ni e & ::= s \mid p & \text{eliminations} \\
\mathsf{WNe} \ni n & ::= c \mid x \mid n\, e & \text{neutral expressions} \\
\mathsf{WFun} \ni w_f & ::= n \mid \lambda xt & \text{weak head function values} \\
\mathsf{WPair} \ni w_p & ::= n \mid (t, t') & \text{weak head pair values} \\
\mathsf{WVal} \ni w, W & ::= w_f \mid w_p & \text{weak head values}
\end{array}$$

Weak head evaluation $t \searrow w$ and active elimination $w@e \searrow w'$ are simultaneously given by the following rules:

$$\frac{r \searrow w_f \qquad w_f@s \searrow w}{r\, s \searrow w} \qquad \frac{r \searrow w_p \qquad w_p@p \searrow w}{r\, p \searrow w} \qquad \frac{}{t \searrow t}\; t \not\equiv r\, s \mid r\, p$$

$$\frac{}{n@e \searrow n\, e} \qquad \frac{t[w/x] \searrow w'}{(\lambda xt)@w \searrow w'} \qquad \frac{t \searrow w}{(t, t')@\mathsf{L} \searrow w} \qquad \frac{t' \searrow w}{(t, t')@\mathsf{R} \searrow w}$$

Weak head evaluation $t \searrow w$ is equivalent to multi-step weak head reduction to normal form. Since both judgements are deterministic, we can interpret them by two partial functions

$$\begin{array}{ll}
\downarrow\ \in \mathsf{Exp} \rightharpoonup \mathsf{WVal} & \text{weak head evaluation,} \\
@ \in \mathsf{WVal} \times \mathsf{WElim} \rightharpoonup \mathsf{WVal} & \text{active application.}
\end{array}$$

Conversion. Two terms t, t' are *algorithmically equal* if $t \searrow w$, $t' \searrow w'$, and $w \sim w'$. We combine these three propositions to $t\!\downarrow\ \sim t'\!\downarrow$. The algorithmic equality on weak head normal forms $w \sim w'$ is given inductively by these rules:

$$\text{AQ-C}\ \frac{}{c \sim c} \qquad \text{AQ-VAR}\ \frac{}{x \sim x}$$

$$\text{AQ-NE-FUN}\ \frac{n \sim n' \qquad s\!\downarrow\, \sim s'\!\downarrow}{n\, s \sim n'\, s'} \qquad \text{AQ-NE-PAIR}\ \frac{n \sim n'}{n\, p \sim n'\, p}$$

$$\text{AQ-EXT-FUN}\ \frac{w_f @ x \sim w'_f @ x}{w_f \sim w'_f}\ x \notin \mathsf{FV}(w_f, w'_f)$$

$$\text{AQ-EXT-PAIR}\ \frac{w_p @ \mathsf{L} \sim w'_p @ \mathsf{L} \qquad w_p @ \mathsf{R} \sim w'_p @ \mathsf{R}}{w_p \sim w'_p}$$

For two neutral values, the rules (AQ-NE-X) are preferred over AQ-EXT-FUN and AQ-EXT-PAIR. Thus, conversion is deterministic. It is easy to see that it is symmetric as well.

In our presentation, untyped conversion resembles type-directed conversion. In the terminology of Harper and Pfenning [HP05, Sar04], the first four rules AQ-C, AQ-VAR, AQ-NE-FUN and AQ-NE-PAIR compute *structural equality*, whereas the remaining two, the extensionality rules AQ-EXT-FUN and AQ-EXT-PAIR, compute type-directed equality. The difference is that in our formulation, the *shape* of a value—function or pair— triggers application of the extensionality rules.

Remark 1. In contrast to the corresponding equality for λ-terms without pairs [Coq91] (taking away AQ-NE-PAIR and AQ-EXT-PAIR), this relation is *not* transitive. For instance, $\lambda x.\, n\, x \sim n$ and $n \sim (n\mathsf{L},\, n\mathsf{R})$, but not $\lambda x.\, n\, x \sim (n\mathsf{L},\, n\mathsf{R})$.

4 Soundness

The soundness proof for conversion in this section is entirely syntactical and relies crucially on injectivity of El, Fun and Pair and inversion of typing. First, we show soundness of weak head evaluation, which subsumes subject reduction.

Lemma 3 (Soundness of Weak Head Evaluation).

1. *If* $\mathcal{D} :: t \searrow w$ *and* $\Gamma \vdash t : C$ *then* $\Gamma \vdash t = w : C$.
2. *If* $\mathcal{D} :: w @ e \searrow w'$ *and* $\Gamma \vdash w\, e : C$ *then* $\Gamma \vdash w\, e = w' : C$.

Proof. Simultaneously by induction on $\mathcal{D}$, making essential use of inversion laws.

Two algorithmically convertible well-typed expressions must also be equal in the declarative sense. In case of neutral terms, we also obtain that their types are equal. This is due to the fact that we can read off the type of the common head variable and break it down through the sequence of eliminations.

Lemma 4 (Soundness of Conversion).

1. *Neutral non-types: If* $\mathcal{D} :: n \sim n'$ *and* $\Gamma \vdash n : C \not\equiv \mathsf{Type}$ *and* $\Gamma \vdash n' : C' \not\equiv \mathsf{Type}$ *then* $\Gamma \vdash n = n' : C$ *and* $\Gamma \vdash C = C' : \mathsf{Type}$.
2. *Weak head values: If* $\mathcal{D} :: w \sim w'$ *and* $\Gamma \vdash w, w' : C$ *then* $\Gamma \vdash w = w' : C$.
3. *All expressions: If* $t{\downarrow} \sim t'{\downarrow}$ *and* $\Gamma \vdash t, t' : C$ *then* $\Gamma \vdash t = t' : C$.

Proof. The third proposition is a consequence of the second, using soundness of evaluation (Lemma 3) and transitivity. We prove the first two propositions simultaneously by induction on $\mathcal{D}$.

5 Models

To show completeness of algorithmic equality, we leave the syntactic discipline. Although a syntactical proof should be possible following Goguen [Gog99, Gog05], we prefer a model construction since it is more apt to extensions of the type theory.

The contribution of this section is that *any* PER model over a λ-model with full β-equality is a model of MLF_Σ. Only in the next section will we decide on a particular model which enables the completeness proof.

5.1 λ Models

We assume a set D with the four operations

$\_\cdot\_ \in \mathsf{D} \times \mathsf{D} \to \mathsf{D}$	application,
$\_\mathsf{L} \in \mathsf{D} \to \mathsf{D}$	left projection,
$\_\mathsf{R} \in \mathsf{D} \to \mathsf{D}$	right projection, and
$\_\_ \in \mathsf{Exp} \times \mathsf{Env} \to \mathsf{D}$	denotation.

Herein, we use the following entities:

c	$\in \mathsf{Const} := \{\mathsf{Set}, \mathsf{El}, \mathsf{Fun}, \mathsf{Pair}\}$	constants
$u, v, f, V, F \in \mathsf{D}$	$\supseteq \mathsf{Const}$	domain of the model
ρ, σ	$\in \mathsf{Env} := \mathsf{Var} \to \mathsf{D}$	environments

Let p range over the projection functions L and R. To simplify the notation, we write also $f\ v$ for $f \cdot v$. Update of environment ρ by the binding $x{=}v$ is written $\rho, x{=}v$. The operations $f \cdot v$, $v\,p$ and $t\rho$ must satisfy the following laws:

DEN-CONST	$c\rho = c$	if $c \in \mathsf{Const}$
DEN-VAR	$x\rho = \rho(x)$	
DEN-FUN-E	$(r\ s)\rho = r\rho\ (s\rho)$	
DEN-PAIR-E	$(r\ p)\rho = r\rho\ p$	
DEN-FUN-β	$(\lambda x t)\rho\ v = t(\rho, x{=}v)$	
DEN-PAIR-β-L	$(r, s)\rho\,\mathsf{L} = r\rho$	
DEN-PAIR-β-R	$(r, s)\rho\,\mathsf{R} = s\rho$	

DEN-FUN-ξ	$(\lambda xt)\rho = (\lambda xt')\rho'$	if $t(\rho, x{=}v) = t'(\rho', x{=}v)$ for all $v \in \mathsf{D}$
DEN-PAIR-ξ	$(r,s)\rho = (r',s')\rho'$	if $r\rho = r'\rho'$ and $s\rho = s'\rho'$
DEN-SET-F-INJ	$\mathsf{El}\, v = \mathsf{El}\, v'$	implies $v = v'$
DEN-FUN-F-INJ	$\mathsf{Fun}\, V\, F = \mathsf{Fun}\, V'\, F'$	implies $V = V'$ and $F = F'$
DEN-PAIR-F-INJ	$\mathsf{Pair}\, V\, F = \mathsf{Pair}\, V'\, F'$	implies $V = V'$ and $F = F'$

Lemma 5 (Irrelevance). *If $\rho(x) = \rho'(x)$ for all $x \in \mathsf{FV}(t)$, then $t\rho = t\rho'$.*

Proof. By induction on t. Makes crucial use of the ξ rules.

Lemma 6 (Soundness of Substitution). $(t[s/x])\rho = t(\rho, x{=}s\rho)$.

Proof. By induction on t, using the ξ rules and Lemma 5.

5.2 PER Models

In the definition of PER models, we follow a paper of the second author with Pollack and Takeyama [CPT03] and Vaux [Vau04]. The only difference is, since we have codes for types in D, we can define the semantical property of *being a type* directly on elements of D, whereas the cited works introduce an *intensional type equality* on closures $t\rho$.

Partial equivalence relation (PER). A PER is a symmetric and transitive relation. Let Per denote the set of PERs over D. If $\mathcal{A} \in \mathsf{Per}$, we write $v = v' \in \mathcal{A}$ if $(v, v') \in \mathcal{A}$. We say $v \in \mathcal{A}$ if v is in the carrier of $\mathcal{A}$, i. e., $v = v \in \mathcal{A}$. On the other hand, each set $\mathcal{A} \subseteq \mathsf{D}$ can be understood as the discrete PER where $v = v' \in \mathcal{A}$ holds iff $v = v'$ and $v \in \mathcal{A}$.

Equivalence classes and families. Let $\mathcal{A} \in \mathsf{Per}$. If $v \in \mathcal{A}$, then $\overline{v}_{\mathcal{A}} := \{v' \in \mathsf{D} \mid v = v' \in \mathcal{A}\}$ denotes the equivalence class of v in $\mathcal{A}$. We write $\mathsf{D}/\mathcal{A}$ for the set of all equivalence classes in $\mathcal{A}$. Let $\mathsf{Fam}(\mathcal{A}) = \mathsf{D}/\mathcal{A} \to \mathsf{Per}$. If $\mathcal{F} \in \mathsf{Fam}(\mathcal{A})$ and $v \in \mathcal{A}$, we use $\mathcal{F}(v)$ as a shorthand for $\mathcal{F}(\overline{v}_{\mathcal{A}})$.

Constructions on PERs. Let $\mathcal{A} \in \mathsf{Per}$ and $\mathcal{F} \in \mathsf{Fam}(\mathcal{A})$. We define two PERs $\mathcal{F}un(\mathcal{A}, \mathcal{F})$ and $\mathcal{P}air(\mathcal{A}, \mathcal{F})$ by

$$\begin{array}{ll} (f, f') \in \mathcal{F}un(\mathcal{A}, \mathcal{F}) & \text{iff } f\ v = f'\ v' \in \mathcal{F}(v) \text{ for all } v = v' \in \mathcal{A}, \\ (v, v') \in \mathcal{P}air(\mathcal{A}, \mathcal{F}) & \text{iff } v\, \mathsf{L} = v'\, \mathsf{L} \in \mathcal{A} \text{ and } v\, \mathsf{R} = v'\, \mathsf{R} \in \mathcal{F}(v\, \mathsf{L}). \end{array}$$

Semantical types. In the following, assume some $\mathcal{S}et \in \mathsf{Per}$ and some $\mathcal{E}\ell \in \mathsf{Fam}(\mathcal{S}et)$. We define inductively a new relation $\mathcal{T}ype \in \mathsf{Per}$ and a new function $[\_] \in \mathsf{Fam}(\mathcal{T}ype)$:

$\mathsf{Set} = \mathsf{Set} \in \mathcal{T}ype$ and $[\mathsf{Set}]$ is $\mathcal{S}et$.

$\mathsf{El}\ v = \mathsf{El}\ v' \in \mathcal{T}ype$ if $v = v' \in \mathcal{S}et$. Then $[\mathsf{El}\ v]$ is $\mathcal{E}\ell(v)$.

$\mathsf{Fun}\ V\ F = \mathsf{Fun}\ V'\ F' \in \mathcal{T}ype$ if $V = V' \in \mathcal{T}ype$ and $v = v' \in [V]$ implies $F\ v = F'\ v' \in \mathcal{T}ype$. We define then $[\mathsf{Fun}\ V\ F]$ to be $\mathcal{F}un([V], v \longmapsto [F\ v])$.

$\mathsf{Pair}\ V\ F = \mathsf{Pair}\ V'\ F' \in \mathcal{T}ype$ if $V = V' \in \mathcal{T}ype$ and $v = v' \in [V]$ implies $F\ v = F'\ v' \in \mathcal{T}ype$. We define then $[\mathsf{Pair}\ V\ F]$ to be $\mathcal{P}air([V], v \longmapsto [F\ v])$.

This definition is possible by the laws DEN-SET-F-INJ, DEN-FUN-F-INJ, and DEN-PAIR-F-INJ. Notice that in the last two clauses, we have

$$\mathcal{F}un([V], v \longmapsto [F\ v]) = \mathcal{F}un([V'], v \longmapsto [F'\ v]), \text{ and}$$
$$\mathcal{P}air([V], v \longmapsto [F\ v]) = \mathcal{P}air([V'], v \longmapsto [F'\ v]).$$

5.3 Validity

If Γ is a context, we define a corresponding PER on Env, written $[\Gamma]$. We define $\rho = \rho' \in [\Gamma]$ to mean that, for all $x{:}A$ in Γ, we have $A\rho = A\rho' \in \mathcal{T}ype$ and $\rho(x) = \rho'(x) \in [A\rho]$. Semantical contexts $\Gamma \in \mathcal{C}xt$ are defined inductively by the following rules:

$$\frac{}{\diamond \in \mathcal{C}xt} \qquad \frac{\Gamma \in \mathcal{C}xt \qquad A\rho = A\rho' \in \mathcal{T}ype \text{ for all } \rho = \rho' \in [\Gamma]}{(\Gamma, x\!:\!A) \in \mathcal{C}xt}$$

Theorem 1 (Soundness of the Rules of MLF_Σ).

1. *If $\mathcal{D} :: \Gamma \vdash \mathsf{ok}$ then $\Gamma \in \mathcal{C}xt$.*
2. *If $\mathcal{D} :: \Gamma \vdash A : \mathsf{Type}$ then $\Gamma \in \mathcal{C}xt$, and if $\rho = \rho' \in [\Gamma]$ then $A\rho = A\rho' \in \mathcal{T}ype$.*
3. *If $\mathcal{D} :: \Gamma \vdash t : A$ then $\Gamma \in \mathcal{C}xt$, and if $\rho = \rho' \in [\Gamma]$ then $A\rho = A\rho' \in \mathcal{T}ype$ and $t\rho = t\rho' \in [A\rho]$.*
4. *If $\mathcal{D} :: \Gamma \vdash A = A' : \mathsf{Type}$ then $\Gamma \in \mathcal{C}xt$, and if $\rho = \rho' \in [\Gamma]$ then $A\rho = A'\rho' \in \mathcal{T}ype$.*
5. *If $\mathcal{D} :: \Gamma \vdash t = t' : A$ then $\Gamma \in \mathcal{C}xt$, and if $\rho = \rho' \in [\Gamma]$ then $A\rho = A\rho' \in \mathcal{T}ype$ and $t\rho = t'\rho' \in [A\rho]$.*

Proof. Each by induction on $\mathcal{D}$, using lemmas 5 and 6.

5.4 Safe Types

We define an abstract notion of *safety*, similar to what Vaux calls "saturation" [Vau04]. A PER is safe if it lies between a PER $\mathcal{N}$ on *neutral* expressions and a PER $\mathcal{S}$ on *safe* expressions [Vou04]. In the following, we use set notation $\subseteq$ and $\cup$ also for PERs.

Safety. $\mathcal{N}, \mathcal{S}_{fun}, \mathcal{S}_{pair} \in \mathsf{Per}$ form a *safety range* if the following conditions are met:

SAFE-INT	$\mathcal{N} \subseteq \mathcal{S} = \mathcal{S}_{fun} \cup \mathcal{S}_{pair}$	
SAFE-NE-FUN	$u\,v = u'\,v' \in \mathcal{N}$	if $u = u' \in \mathcal{N}$ and $v = v' \in \mathcal{S}$
SAFE-NE-PAIR	$u\,p = u'\,p \in \mathcal{N}$	if $u = u' \in \mathcal{N}$
SAFE-EXT-FUN	$v = v' \in \mathcal{S}_{fun}$	if $v\,u = v'\,u' \in \mathcal{S}$ for all $u = u' \in \mathcal{N}$
SAFE-EXT-PAIR	$v = v' \in \mathcal{S}_{pair}$	if $v\,\mathsf{L} = v'\,\mathsf{L} \in \mathcal{S}$ and $v\,\mathsf{R} = v'\,\mathsf{R} \in \mathcal{S}$

A relation $\mathcal{A} \in \mathsf{Per}$ is called *safe* w.r.t. to a safety range $(\mathcal{N}, \mathcal{S}_{fun}, \mathcal{S}_{pair})$ if $\mathcal{N} \subseteq \mathcal{A} \subseteq \mathcal{S}$.

Lemma 7 (Fun and Pair Preserve Safety). *If* $\mathcal{A} \in \mathsf{Per}$ *is safe and* $\mathcal{F} \in \mathsf{Fam}(\mathcal{A})$ *is such that* $\mathcal{F}(v)$ *is safe for all* $v \in \mathcal{A}$ *then* $\mathcal{F}un(\mathcal{A}, \mathcal{F})$ *and* $\mathcal{P}air(\mathcal{A}, \mathcal{F})$ *are safe.*

Proof. By monotonicity of $\mathcal{F}un$ and $\mathcal{P}air$, if one considers the following reformulation of the conditions:

$$\begin{array}{ll} \text{SAFE-NE-FUN} & \mathcal{N} \subseteq \mathcal{F}un(\mathcal{S}, \_ \longmapsto \mathcal{N}) \\ \text{SAFE-NE-PAIR} & \mathcal{N} \subseteq \mathcal{P}air(\mathcal{N}, \_ \longmapsto \mathcal{N}) \\ \text{SAFE-EXT-FUN} & \mathcal{F}un(\mathcal{N}, \_ \longmapsto \mathcal{S}) \subseteq \mathcal{S}_{fun} \\ \text{SAFE-EXT-PAIR} & \mathcal{P}air(\mathcal{S}, \_ \longmapsto \mathcal{S}) \subseteq \mathcal{S}_{pair} \end{array}$$

Lemma 8 (Type Interpretations are Safe). *Let* $\mathcal{S}et$ *be safe and* $\mathcal{E}\ell(v)$ *be safe for all* $v \in \mathcal{S}et$. *If* $v \in \mathcal{T}ype$ *then* $[v]$ *is safe.*

Proof. By induction on the proof that $v \in \mathcal{T}ype$, using Lemma 7.

6 Term Model

In this section, we instantiate the model of the previous section to the set of expressions modulo β-equality. Application is interpreted as expression application and the projections of the model are mapped to projections for expressions.

Let $\overline{r}_\beta \in \mathcal{D}$ denote the equivalence class of $r \in \mathsf{Exp}$ with regard to $=_\beta$. We set $\mathsf{D} := \mathsf{Exp}/{=_\beta}$, $\overline{r}_\beta \cdot \overline{s}_\beta := \overline{r\,s}_\beta$, $\overline{r}_\beta\,\mathsf{L} := \overline{r\,\mathsf{L}}_\beta$, $\overline{r}_\beta\,\mathsf{R} := \overline{r\,\mathsf{R}}_\beta$, and $t\rho := \overline{t[\rho]}_\beta$. Herein, $t[\rho]$ denotes the substitution of $\rho(x)$ for x in t, carried out in parallel for all $x \in \mathsf{FV}(t)$. In the following, we abbreviate the equivalence class $\overline{r}_\beta$ by its representative r, if clear from the context.

Value classes. The β-normal forms $v \in \mathsf{Val}$, which can be described by the following grammar, completely represent the β-equivalence classes $\overline{t}_\beta \in \mathsf{Exp}/{=_\beta}$.

$$\begin{array}{llll} \mathsf{VNe} & \ni u & ::= c \mid x \mid u\,v \mid u\,p & \text{neutral values} \\ \mathsf{VFun} & \ni v_f & ::= u \mid \lambda x v & \text{function values} \\ \mathsf{VPair} & \ni v_p & ::= u \mid (v, v') & \text{pair values} \\ \mathsf{Val} & \ni v & ::= v_f \mid v_p & \text{values} \end{array}$$

An η-equality on β-equivalence classes. We define a relation $\simeq\ \subseteq \mathsf{Val} \times \mathsf{Val}$ inductively by the following rules.

$$\text{ETA-VAR}\ \frac{}{x \simeq x} \qquad \text{ETA-NE-FUN}\ \frac{u \simeq u' \qquad v \simeq v'}{u\,v \simeq u'\,v'} \qquad \text{ETA-NE-PAIR}\ \frac{u \simeq u'}{u\,p \simeq u'\,p}$$

$$\text{ETA-C}\ \frac{}{c \simeq c} \qquad \text{ETA-EXT-FUN}\ \frac{v_f\,x \simeq v'_f\,x}{v_f \simeq v'_f}\ x \notin \mathsf{FV}(v_f, v'_f)$$

$$\text{ETA-EXT-PAIR}\ \frac{v_p\,\mathsf{L} \simeq v'_p\,\mathsf{L} \qquad v_p\,\mathsf{R} \simeq v'_p\,\mathsf{R}}{v_p \simeq v'_p}$$

Note, since we are talking about equivalence classes, in the extensionality rules ETA-EXT-FUN and ETA-EXT-PAIR we actually mean the normal forms of the expressions appearing in the hypotheses. In the conclusion of an extensionality rule, we require one of the two values to be non-neutral.

As algorithmic equality, the relation $\simeq$ is symmetric, but not transitive. To turn it into a PER, we need to take the transitive closure $\simeq^+$ explicitly.

Lemma 9 (Admissible Rules for $\simeq^+$). *If we replace $\simeq$ by $\simeq^+$ consistently in the rules for $\simeq$, we get admissible rules for $\simeq^+$. We denote the admissible rule by appending a $^+$ to the rule name.*

Lemma 10 (Safety Range). *Let $\mathcal{S} := \simeq^+$, $\mathcal{N} := \mathcal{S} \cap (\mathsf{VNe} \times \mathsf{VNe})$, $\mathcal{S}_{fun} := \mathcal{S} \cap (\mathsf{VFun} \times \mathsf{VFun})$, and $\mathcal{S}_{pair} := \mathcal{S} \cap (\mathsf{VPair} \times \mathsf{VPair})$. Then $\mathcal{N}, \mathcal{S}_{fun}, \mathcal{S}_{pair}$ are PERs and form a safety range.*

Proof. SAFE-INT is shown by definition of $\mathcal{N}, \mathcal{S}_{fun}, \mathcal{S}_{pair}$. SAFE-EXT-FUN is satisfied by rule ETA-EXT-FUN$^+$ since $x = x \in \mathcal{N}$ for each variable. Each other requirement has its directly matching admissible rule.

Lemma 11 (Context Satisfiable). *Let $\rho_0(x) := x$ for all $x \in \mathsf{Var}$. If $\Gamma \vdash \mathsf{ok}$, then $\rho_0 \in [\Gamma]$.*

Corollary 1 (Equal Terms are Related). *If $\Gamma \vdash t = t' : C \not\equiv \mathsf{Type}$ then $\overline{t}_\beta \simeq^+ \overline{t}'_\beta$.*

Proof. By soundness of MLF_Σ (Thm. 1), $t\rho_0 = t'\rho_0 \in [C\rho_0]$. The claim follows since $[C\rho_0] \subseteq \mathcal{S}$ by Lemma 8.

It remains to show that $\overline{t}_\beta \simeq^+ \overline{t}'_\beta$ implies $t\!\downarrow\, \sim t'\!\downarrow$, which means that both t and t' weak head normalize and these normal forms are algorithmically equal.

7 Completeness

We establish completeness of the algorithmic equality in two steps. First we prove that η-equality of β-normal forms entails equality in the algorithmic sense. Then we show that for well-typed terms, transitivity is admissible for algorithmic equality. Combining this with the result of the last section, we are done.

Lemma 12 (Standardization).

1. *If $t =_\beta u\, v$ then $t \searrow n\, s$ with $n =_\beta u$ and $s =_\beta v$.*
2. *If $t =_\beta u\, p$ then $t \searrow n\, p$ with $n =_\beta u$.*
3. *If $t =_\beta v_f$ then $t \searrow w_f$ with $w_f =_\beta v_f$.*
4. *If $t =_\beta v_p$ then $t \searrow w_p$ with $w_p =_\beta v_p$.*

Proof. Fact about the λ-calculus [Bar84].

Lemma 13 (Completeness of $\sim$ w.r.t. $\simeq$). *If $\mathcal{D} :: \overline{n}_\beta \simeq \overline{n}'_\beta$ then $n \sim n'$ and if $\mathcal{D} :: \overline{t}_\beta \simeq \overline{t}'_\beta$ then $t\!\downarrow\, \sim t'\!\downarrow$.*

Proof. Simultaneously by induction on $\mathcal{D}$, using standardization.

While transitivity does not hold for the pure algorithmic equality (see Remark 1), it can be established for terms of the same type. The presence of types forbids comparison of function values with pair values, the stepping stone for transitivity of the untyped equality.

For a derivation $\mathcal{D}$ of algorithmic equality, we define the measure $|\mathcal{D}|$ which denotes the number of rule applications on the longest branch of $\mathcal{D}$, counting the rules AQ-EXT-FUN and AQ-EXT-PAIR *twice*.[2] We will use this measure for the proof of transitivity and termination of algorithmic equality.

Lemma 14 (Transitivity of Typed Algorithmic Equality).

1. *Let* $\Gamma \vdash n_1 : C_1$, $\Gamma \vdash n_2 : C_2$, *and* $\Gamma \vdash n_3 : C_3$. *If* $\mathcal{D} :: n_1 \sim n_2$ *and* $\mathcal{D}' :: n_2 \sim n_3$ *then* $n_1 \sim n_3$.
2. *Let* $\Gamma \vdash w_1, w_2, w_3 : C$. *If* $\mathcal{D} :: w_1 \sim w_2$ *and* $\mathcal{D}' :: w_2 \sim w_3$ *then* $w_1 \sim w_3$.
3. *Let* $\Gamma \vdash t_1, t_2, t_3 : C$. *If* $t_1{\downarrow} \sim t_2{\downarrow}$ *and* $t_2{\downarrow} \sim t_3{\downarrow}$ *then* $t_1{\downarrow} \sim t_3{\downarrow}$.

Proof. The third proposition is an immediate consequence of the second, using soundness of weak head evaluation. We prove 1. and 2. simultaneously by induction on $|\mathcal{D}| + |\mathcal{D}'|$, using inversion for typing and soundness of algorithmic equality.

Theorem 2 (Completeness of Algorithmic Equality).

1. *If* $\Gamma \vdash t = t' : C \not\equiv \mathsf{Type}$ *then* $t{\downarrow} \sim t'{\downarrow}$.
2. *If* $\mathcal{D} :: \Gamma \vdash A = A' : \mathsf{Type}$ *then* $A{\downarrow} \sim A'{\downarrow}$.

Proof. Completeness for terms (1): By Cor. 1 we have $\bar{t}_\beta \simeq^+ \bar{t}'_\beta$. Lemma 13 entails $t{\downarrow} \sim^+ t'{\downarrow}$, and since $\Gamma \vdash t, t' : C$, we infer $t{\downarrow} \sim t'{\downarrow}$ by transitivity. The completeness for types (2) is then shown by induction on $\mathcal{D}$, using completeness for terms in case EQ-SET-E.

We have shown that two judgmentally equal terms t, t' weak-head normalize to w, w' and a derivation of $w \sim w'$ exists, hence the equality algorithm, which searches deterministically for such a derivation, terminates with success. What remains to show is that the query $t{\downarrow} \sim t'{\downarrow}$ terminates for all well-typed t, t', either with success, if the derivation can be closed, or with failure, in case the search arrives at a point where there is no matching rule. For the following lemma, observe that $w \sim w$ iff w is weakly normalizing.

Lemma 15 (Termination of Equality). *If* $\mathcal{D}_1 :: w_1 \sim w_1$ *and* $\mathcal{D}_2 :: w_2 \sim w_2$ *then the query* $w_1 \sim w_2$ *terminates.*

Proof. By induction on $|\mathcal{D}_1| + |\mathcal{D}_2|$.

---

[2] A similar measure is used by Goguen [Gog05] to prove termination of algorithmic equality restricted to pure λ-terms [Coq91].

Theorem 3 (Decidability of Equality). *If* $\Gamma \vdash t, t' : C$ *then the query* $t\!\downarrow \sim t'\!\downarrow$ *succeeds or fails finitely and decides* $\Gamma \vdash t = t' : C$.

Proof. By Theorem 2, $t \searrow w$, $t' \searrow w'$, $w \sim w$, and $w' \sim w'$. By the previous lemma, the query $w \sim w'$ terminates. Since by soundness and completeness of the algorithmic equality, $w \sim w'$ if and only if $\Gamma \vdash t = t' : C$, the query decides judgmental equality.

8 Conclusion

We have presented a sound and complete conversion algorithm for MLF_Σ. The completeness proof builds on PERs over untyped expressions, hence, we need—in contrast to Harper and Pfenning's completeness proof for type-directed conversion [HP05]—no Kripke model and no notion of erasure, what we consider an arguably simpler procedure. We see in principle no obstacle to generalize our results to type theories with type definition by cases (large eliminations), whereas it is not clear how to treat them with a technique based on erasure.

The disadvantage of untyped conversion, compared to type-directed conversion, is that it cannot handle cases where the type of a term provides more information on equality than the shape of a terms, e. g., unit types, singleton types and signatures with manifest fields [CPT03].

A more general proof of completeness? Our proof uses a λ-model with full β-equality thanks to the ξ-rules. We had also considered a weaker model without ξ-rules which only equates weakly convertible objects. Combined with extensional PERs this would have been the model closest to our algorithm. But due to the use of substitution in the declarative formulation, we could not show MLF_Σ's rules to be valid in such a model. Whether it still can be done, remains an open question.

Related work. The second author, Pollack, and Takeyama [CPT03] present a model for $\beta\eta$-equality for an extension of the logical framework by singleton types and signatures with manifest fields. Equality is tested by η-expansion, followed by β-normalization and syntactic comparison. In contrast to this work, no syntactic specification of the framework and no incremental conversion algorithm are given.

Schürmann and Sarnat [Sar04] have been working on an extension of the Edinburgh Logical Framework (ELF) by Σ-types (LF_Σ), following Harper and Pfenning [HP05]. In comparison to MLF_Σ, syntactic validity (Lemma 1) and injectivity are non-trivial in their formulation of ELF. Robin Adams [Ada01] has extended Harper and Pfenning's algorithm to Luo's logical framework (i. e., MLF with typed λ-abstraction) with Σ-types and unit.

Goguen [Gog99] gives a typed operational semantics for Martin-Löf's logical framework. An extension to Σ-types has to our knowledge not yet been considered. Recently, Goguen [Gog05] has proven termination and completeness for both the type-directed [HP05] and the shape-directed equality [Coq91] from the standard meta-theoretical properties (strong normalization, confluence, subject reduction, etc.) of the logical framework.

Acknowledgments. We are grateful to Lionel Vaux whose clear presentation of models for this implicit calculus [Vau04] provided a guideline for our model construction. Thanks to Ulf Norell for proof-reading. The first author is indebted to Frank Pfenning who taught him type-directed equality at Carnegie Mellon University in 2000, and to Carsten Schürmann for communication on LF_{Σ}.

References

[AC05] A. Abel and T. Coquand. Untyped algorithmic equality for Martin-Löf's logical framework with surjective pairs (extended version). Tech. rep., Department of Computer Science, Chalmers, Göteborg, Sweden, 2005.

[Ada01] R. Adams. Decidable equality in a logical framework with sigma kinds, 2001. Unpublished note, see http://www.cs.man.ac.uk/~radams/.

[Bar84] H. Barendregt. *The Lambda Calculus: Its Syntax and Semantics*. North Holland, Amsterdam, 1984.

[Coq91] T. Coquand. An algorithm for testing conversion in type theory. In G. Huet and G. Plotkin, eds., *Logical Frameworks*, pp. 255–279. Cambridge University Press, 1991.

[Coq96] T. Coquand. An algorithm for type-checking dependent types. In *Mathematics of Program Construction (MPC 1995)*, vol. 26 of *Science of Computer Programming*, pp. 167–177. Elsevier Science, 1996.

[CPT03] T. Coquand, R. Pollack, and M. Takeyama. A logical framework with dependently typed records. In *Typed Lambda Calculus and Applications, TLCA'03*, vol. 2701 of *Lecture Notes in Computer Science*. Springer, 2003.

[Gog99] H. Goguen. Soundness of the logical framework for its typed operational semantics. In J.-Y. Girard, ed., *Typed Lambda Calculi and Applications, TLCA 1999*, vol. 1581 of *Lecture Notes in Computer Science*. Springer, 1999.

[Gog05] H. Goguen. Justifying algorithms for $\beta\eta$ conversion. In *FoSSaCS 2005*. To appear.

[HHP93] R. Harper, F. Honsell, and G. Plotkin. A Framework for Defining Logics. *Journal of the Association of Computing Machinery*, 40(1):143–184, 1993.

[HP05] R. Harper and F. Pfenning. On equivalence and canonical forms in the LF type theory. *ACM Transactions on Computational Logic*, 6(1):61–101, 2005.

[Klo80] J. W. Klop. Combinatory reducion systems. *Mathematical Center Tracts*, 27, 1980.

[NPS00] B. Nordström, K. Petersson, and J. Smith. Martin-löf's type theory. In *Handbook of Logic in Computer Science*, vol. 5. Oxford University Press, 2000.

[Sar04] J. Sarnat. LF_{Σ}: The metatheory of LF with Σ types, 2004. Unpublished technical report, kindly provided by Carsten Schürmann.

[Vau04] L. Vaux. A type system with implicit types, 2004. English version of his mémoire de maîtrise.

[VC02] J. C. Vanderwaart and K. Crary. A simplified account of the metatheory of Linear LF. Tech. rep., Dept. of Comp. Sci., Carnegie Mellon, 2002.

[Vou04] J. Vouillon. Subtyping union types. In J. Marcinkowski and A. Tarlecki, eds., *Computer Science Logic, CSL'04*, vol. 3210 of *Lecture Notes in Computer Science*, pp. 415–429. Springer, 2004.

The Monadic Second Order Theory of Trees Given by Arbitrary Level-Two Recursion Schemes Is Decidable

Klaus Aehlig*, Jolie G. de Miranda, and C.-H. Luke Ong

Oxford University Computing Laboratory,
Wolfson Building, Parks Road, Oxford OX1 3QD, UK
aehlig@math.lmu.de
{jgdm, lo}@comlab.ox.ac.uk

Abstract. A tree automaton can simulate the successful runs of a word or tree automaton working on the word or tree denoted by a level-2 lambda-tree. In particular the monadic second order theory of trees given by arbitrary, rather than only by safe, recursion schemes of level 2 is decidable. This solves the level-2 case of an open problem by Knapik, Niwiński and Urzyczyn.

1 Introduction and Related Work

Since Rabin [11] showed the decidability of the monadic second order theory of the binary tree this result has been applied and extended to various mathematical structures, including algebraic trees [4] and a hierarchy of graphs [3] obtained by iterated unfolding and inverse rational mappings from finite graphs. The interest in these kinds of structures arose in recent years in the context of verification of infinite state systems [9, 13].

Recently Knapik, Niwiński and Urzyczyn [6] showed that the monadic second order (MSO) theory of any infinite tree generated by a level-2 grammar satisfying a certain "safety" condition is decidable. Later they generalised [7] this result to grammars of arbitrary levels, but still requiring the "safety" condition. It remains open whether this condition is actually needed. In this article we give a partial answer: For grammars of level 2 the condition can be dropped.

Two observations are essential to obtain the result. The first, albeit trivial, is that if we go down to level 0, we will never actually perform a substitution, thus we need not worry that substitution is capture avoiding. *If you don't do a substitution, you'll never do a wrong substitution!*

The second observation is that even though first-order variables stand for words or trees of unbounded lengths, all the information we need to know in order to check for a *particular property* is the transition function of the automaton verifying this property. And this is a bounded amount of information!

* On leave from Ludwig-Maximilians-Universität München. Supported by a postdoctoral fellowship of the German Academic Exchange Service (DAAD).

P. Urzyczyn (Ed.): TLCA 2005, LNCS 3461, pp. 39–54, 2005.

Therefore the run of a Büchi automaton on an ω-word can be simulated by a Büchi tree automaton on a second order lambda tree denoting this word. Moreover, this idea extends to the simulation of an alternating parity-tree automaton by a two-way alternating parity tree automaton. It follows that the full MSO theory of the tree language generated by a level-2 recursion scheme is decidable.

It should be mentioned that in another article [1] the authors show a related result. For *word languages* general level-2 recursion schemes and safe recursion schemes indeed produce the same set of languages and the transformation is effective. It is yet unclear whether that result extends to tree languages. Moreover, the authors believe that the conceptual simplicity of the method presented here makes it worth being studied in its own right.

Only after finishing the work presented here the authors became aware of a manuscript by Knapik, Niwiński, Urzyczyn and Walukiewicz [8] who also solved the level-2 decidability problem. They used a new kind of automaton equipped with a limited "backtracking" facility.

The article is organised as follows. In Sections 2 and 3 we introduce lambda trees and recursion schemes. Section 4 shows the expected connection between the denotation of a recursion scheme and that of the associated lambda tree. Section 5 explains the main technical idea of the article: if we are interested in a particular property, all we need to know about a first-order object can be described by a bounded amount of information. Sections 6 and 7 show how the idea can be used to obtain the decidability of the MSO theory of words and trees given by level-2 recursion schemes.

2 Lambda Trees

Since the main technical idea for deciding properties of recursion schemes is to translate them to properties of infinitary lambda terms [5] we first have to consider these terms *qua* trees. In this section we will only handle abstractions that (morally) handle first-order abstractions (even though we give an untyped definition). The extension to function abstractions is explained in Section 5.

We presuppose a countably infinite set $\mathcal{V}$ of variables x.

Definition 1 (Lambda Trees). A *lambda tree* is a, not necessarily well-founded, tree built from the binary constructor *application* @, and for every variable x a unary *abstraction* constructor λ_x, and nullary *variable* constructor v_x. Moreover there is an unspecified but finite set Σ of constants, called "letters".

A lambda tree defines a, potentially partial, ω-word in a natural way made precise by the following definitions. They are motivated by ideas of geometry of interaction [2] and similar to the ones presented by Knapik *et al* [6].

Definition 2 (The Matching Lambda of a Variable). Let p be a node in a lambda tree that is a variable v_x. Its *matching path* is the shortest prefix (if it exists) of the path from p to the root of the tree that ends in a λ_x node. We call the last node of the matching path the *matching lambda* of the variable node p.

If no such path exists, we say the variable node p is a *free variable* v_x. Variable nodes that are not free are called *bound.*

In this definition, if we replace "root of the tree" by a node r we get the notion of a variable *free in the (located) subterm* r.

Definition 3 (Matching Argument of a Lambda or a Letter). For a lambda tree we define the k-th argument of a node, which is assumed to be a lambda or a letter, to be the right-hand child of the application node (if it exists) where, when walking from the given node to the root, for the first time the number of applications visited exceeds the number of abstractions visited (not including the starting node) by k. We presuppose that on this path, called the *matching path*, application nodes are only visited from the left child. We define the matching argument of a λ-node to be its first argument.

Definition 4 (Canonical Traversal of a Lambda-Tree). The *canonical traversal* of a lambda tree starts at the root of the tree. From an application we go to the left subtree, from an abstraction we go to the body. From a letter we go to its first argument. From a variable we first go to the matching lambda and then from there to the matching argument where we continue as above.

If we collect on the canonical traversal all the letters we pass downwards (that is, in direction from the root to the leaves) in order of traversal we get a, maybe partially defined, ω-word. This word is called *the word met on the canonical traversal.* If, instead of always going to the first argument when we meet a letter we branch and continue with the i'th argument, for $1 \leq i \leq k$ where k is the "arity" of the letter (assuming a fixed assignment), we obtain a tree, *the tree of the canonical traversal.*

Proposition 5. *In the canonical traversal (and in every path of the canonical tree traversal) every node is visited at most three times. More precisely, each node is visited at most once from each direction (top, left and right child).*

Remark 6. It should be noted that all the notions and results in this section are invariant under renaming of bound variables in a lambda tree in the usual way. This will be used tacitly in the sequel.

3 Recursion Schemes

Definition 7 (Simple Types and Their Level). Given a base type ι, the *simple types over* ι are inductively defined as the smallest set containing ι that is closed under forming arrow types $\sigma \to \tau$. We use the expression "simple type" if ι is understood from the context or irrelevant. We understand that $\to$ associates to the right, so $\sigma \to \tau \to \tau'$ is short for $\sigma \to (\tau \to \tau')$.

The level $\mathrm{lv}(\tau)$ of a simple type is inductively defined by $\mathrm{lv}(\iota) = 0$ and $\mathrm{lv}(\sigma \to \tau) = \max(\mathrm{lv}(\sigma) + 1, \mathrm{lv}(\tau))$. We use the expression "type of level i" to mean types τ with $\mathrm{lv}(\tau) = i$.

Definition 8 (Combinatory Terms). Given a set $\mathcal{C}$ of typed constants and a set $\mathcal{V}$ of typed variables, the sets $\mathcal{T}^\tau(\mathcal{C},\mathcal{V})$ of terms (over $\mathcal{C}$ and $\mathcal{V}$) of type τ is inductively defined as follows.

- $x \in \mathcal{T}^\tau(\mathcal{C},\mathcal{V})$ if $x \in \mathcal{V}$ is of type τ and $C \in \mathcal{T}^\tau(\mathcal{C},\mathcal{V})$ if $C \in \mathcal{C}$ is of type τ
- if $s \in \mathcal{T}^{\tau\to\sigma}(\mathcal{C},\mathcal{V})$ and $t \in \mathcal{T}^\tau(\mathcal{C},\mathcal{V})$ then $st \in \mathcal{T}^\sigma(\mathcal{C},\mathcal{V})$

Proposition 9. *Every term in $\mathcal{T}^\tau(\mathcal{C},\mathcal{V})$ is of one of the following forms.*

- $C\overrightarrow{t}$ *with* $C \in \mathcal{C}$ *of type* $\overrightarrow{\tau} \to \sigma$ *and* $t_i \in \mathcal{T}^{\tau_i}(\mathcal{C},\mathcal{V})$
- $x\overrightarrow{t}$ *with* $x \in \mathcal{V}$ *of type* $\overrightarrow{\tau} \to \sigma$ *and* $t_i \in \mathcal{T}^{\tau_i}(\mathcal{C},\mathcal{V})$

Definition 10 (Recursion Scheme). A level-2 *recursion scheme* is given by the following data.

- A finite set $\mathcal{N}$ of typed constants, called "non-terminals". Every non-terminal has a type of level at most 2. Moreover, there is a distinguished non-terminal S of level 0, called the start symbol.
- A finite set Σ of typed constants, called "terminal symbols". Every terminal symbol has a type of level at most 1.
- Maybe some binder symbol ℓ. If it is present, then for every variable x, a new constant ℓ_x of type $\iota \to \iota$ and a new constant v_x of type ι is present. We consider any occurrence of v_x in a term of the form $\ell_x t$ to be bound, and identify terms that are equal up to renaming of bound variables in the usual way. (However, we still formally consider the constants ℓ_x and v_x as additional terminal symbols.)
- A set of recursion equations of the form $N\overrightarrow{x} = e$, where N is a non-terminal, the $\overrightarrow{x}$ are pairwise distinct typed variables such that $N\overrightarrow{x}$ is a term of type ι and $e \in \mathcal{T}^\iota(\mathcal{N} \cup \Sigma, \{\overrightarrow{x}\})$.
  If a binder is present we require moreover, that every occurrence of a constant ℓ_x is in the context $\ell_x t$ and that every occurrence of v_x is bound in e.

Note that we do *not* insist that there is at most one equation for every non-terminal. In general a recursion scheme denotes a set of trees.

A level-1 or level-0 recursion scheme is a recursion scheme where all non-terminals have a type of level at most 1 or at most 0, respectively. A recursion scheme is said to be a "word recursion scheme", if all terminals have type $\iota \to \iota$; it is called "pure" if no binder is present.

Remark 11. Due to the native binding mechanism a non-pure recursion scheme currently is only a theoretical concept. However, in the only case where we need an effective construction on recursion schemes, that is for level-0 recursion schemes, we can always use the given names and needn't do any renaming.

Example 12. Let $\Sigma = \{a, b, f, e\}$ a set of terminal symbols, each of which has type $\iota \to \iota$. For $\mathcal{N} = \{F, A, B, S, E\}$ a set of non-terminals with F of type $(\iota \to \iota) \to \iota \to \iota \to \iota$ and E, A, B, S of type ι. The following equations define a pure level-2 recursion scheme.

$$F\varphi xy = F(F\varphi y)y(\varphi x) \qquad A = aE \qquad S = FfAB$$
$$F\varphi xy = y \qquad B = bE \qquad E = eE$$

Here x and y are variables of type ι and φ is a variable of type $\iota \to \iota$. It should be noted that this recursion scheme is neither safe nor deterministic.

Let $\tilde{\Sigma} = \Sigma \cup \{@\}$ with @ of type $\iota \to \iota \to \iota$ and λ a binder. Let $\tilde{F}$ be of type $\iota \to \iota$. Then a (non-pure) level-1 recursion scheme over $\tilde{\Sigma}$ with non-terminals $\tilde{\mathcal{N}} = \{\tilde{F}, \tilde{A}, \tilde{B}, \tilde{S}, \tilde{E}\}$ would be given by

$$\tilde{F}\varphi = \lambda_x(\lambda_y(@\ (@(\tilde{F}(@(\tilde{F}z)v_y))v_y)$$
$$(@\varphi v_x)))$$

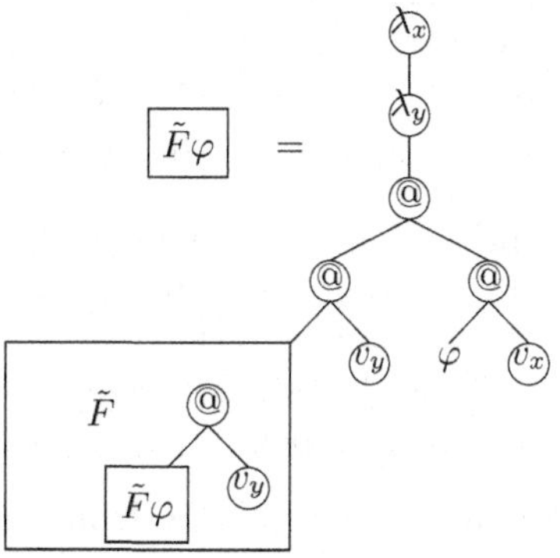

where φ is a variable of type ι. The other equations are

$$\tilde{F}\varphi = \lambda_x(\lambda_y y)$$
$$\tilde{A} = @a\tilde{E} \qquad \tilde{B} = @b\tilde{E}$$
$$\tilde{S} = @(@(\tilde{F}f)\tilde{A})\tilde{B} \qquad \tilde{E} = @e\tilde{E}$$

In fact, this is the reduced scheme (Definition 18) of the first scheme.

Proposition 13. *Let $t \in T^{\tau}(\mathcal{N}, \mathcal{X})$, with $\mathrm{lv}(\tau) \leq 1$ and all variables in $\mathcal{X}$ of level at most 1 and all symbols in $\mathcal{N}$ of level at most 2. Then every occurrence of an $N \in \mathcal{N}$ is in a context $N\overrightarrow{t}$ such that $N\overrightarrow{t}$ has type of level at most 1.*

Corollary 14. *In every term e at the right hand side of a recursion equation of a level-2 recursion scheme it is the case that every non-terminal has all its level-1 arguments present.*

Remark 15. Corollary 14 shows that we may assume without loss of generality that in every non-terminal symbol of a level-2 recursion scheme the higher order arguments come first. In other words, at level-2 we can assume types to be homogeneous [7]. From now on we will use this assumption tacitly.

Unwinding a recursion scheme yields a (potentially non well-founded) tree, labelled with terminal symbols. Following ideas of Knapik *et al* [6] we will now define the lambda tree associated with a level-2 pure recursion scheme. It will be generated by a level 1 grammar, the "reduced recursion scheme".

Definition 16 (Reduced Type of Level 2). For $\tau = \tau_1 \to \ldots \to \tau_n \to \iota \to \ldots \to \iota \to \iota$ with the τ_i types of level 1 we define inductively $\tau' = \tau_1' \to \ldots \to \tau_n' \to \iota$.

Definition 17 (Reduced Terms). For any term $e \in \mathcal{T}(\mathcal{N} \cup \Sigma, \{\overrightarrow{x}\})$ we define a reduced term e' inductively as follows.

$$\begin{array}{ll}(C\overrightarrow{t}\overrightarrow{s})' &= (C\overrightarrow{t'})@s'_1@\dots@s'_n\\(\varphi\overrightarrow{t})' &= \varphi@t'_1@\dots@t'_n\\x' &= v_x\end{array}$$

Here $C \in \mathcal{N} \cup \Sigma$ is a non-terminal or a letter with $\overrightarrow{t}$ terms of type of level 1 and $\overrightarrow{s}$ terms of level 0; $\varphi \in \{\overrightarrow{x}\}$ a variable of non-ground type with arguments $\overrightarrow{t}$ necessarily of type of level 0 and x a variable of ground type; @ is a terminal of type $\iota \to \iota \to \iota$, here written in infix.

Definition 18 (Reduced Recursion Scheme). For a level-2 recursion scheme, where we assume without loss of generality that all non-terminals have their first-order arguments first, we define a level-1 recursion scheme, the *reduced recursion scheme*, defining a lambda tree in the following way.

Terminals are those of the original recursion scheme, however with reduced type, and a new symbol $@\colon \iota \to \iota \to \iota$. The new recursion scheme has a binder λ. Non-terminals are the same as in the original, however with the type reduced.

For any rule of the original recursion scheme of the form $N\overrightarrow{\varphi}\overrightarrow{x} \to e$ where $\overrightarrow{\varphi}$ are the level-1 arguments and $\overrightarrow{x}$ the level-0 arguments we add a rule $N\overrightarrow{\varphi} \to \overrightarrow{\lambda_x}.e'$ with e' being the reduced term of e.

Definition 19 (Typed Lambda Trees). A *typed lambda tree* is a lambda tree with nodes labelled by simple types in such a way that

- Every variable is bound and if it is labelled with type σ, then the matching lambda has type $\sigma \to \tau$ for some τ; moreover, every abstraction node is labelled with a type of the form $\sigma \to \tau$ and its child is labelled with τ.
- If an application is labelled τ then, for some type σ the left child is labelled by $\sigma \to \tau$ and the right child by σ.
- Every terminal $f \in \Sigma$ is labelled by its type.

A lambda tree is *finitely typed* if it is a typed lambda tree and all types come from the same finite set.

Proposition 20. *The reduced recursion scheme of a pure level-2 word recursion scheme is finitely typed.*

Proposition 21. *If a lambda tree is finitely typed then the difference in the number of lambdas and applications seen on the matching path of an abstraction is bounded.*

Corollary 22. *In the reduced recursion scheme of a pure level-2 word recursion scheme the matching argument of an abstraction can be found by a finite state path walking automaton.*

4 Reductions and Denotations

In this section we make precise our intuitive notion of the tree denoted of recursion scheme, the (ω-word or) tree denoted by a lambda tree, and prove the needed properties. This essentially recasts results of Knapik *et al* [6].

Definition 23 (Reduction Relation). Let $\mathcal{S}$ be a recursion scheme. Its associated reduction relation $\to_{\mathcal{S}}$ on finite terms is inductively defined as follows.

- $N\overrightarrow{t} \to_{\mathcal{S}} e\left[\overrightarrow{t}/\overrightarrow{x}\right]$ if there is a recursion equation $N\overrightarrow{x} = e$ in $\mathcal{S}$.
- If $t \to_{\mathcal{S}} t'$ then $ts \to_{\mathcal{S}} t's$. If f is a terminal symbol and $t \to_{\mathcal{S}} t'$ then $f\overrightarrow{s}t \to_{\mathcal{S}} f\overrightarrow{s}t'$.
- In particular we have: If $t \to_{\mathcal{S}} t'$ then $\lambda_x t \to_{\mathcal{S}} \lambda_x t'$.

If in any reduction a variable is substituted in the scope of a binder then appropriate renaming is assumed to prevent the variable from getting bound at a new binder. In other words our reduction is capture avoiding in the usual sense. As we identify α-equal terms this is a well-defined notion.

Intuitively $t^{\perp}$ is t with all unfinished computations replaced by $\perp$. More precisely we have the following

Definition 24 (Constructed Part of a Term). For t a term we define $t^{\perp}$ inductively as follows.

- $f^{\perp} = f$ for $f \in \Sigma$ a terminal and $N^{\perp} = \perp$ for $N \in \mathcal{N}$ a non-terminal.
- If $s^{\perp} = \perp$ then $(st)^{\perp} = \perp$. Otherwise $(st)^{\perp}=s^{\perp}t^{\perp}$.
- In particular we have $(\lambda_x t)^{\perp} = \lambda_x t^{\perp}$.

Moreover, we define a partial order $\sqsubseteq$ on terms inductively as follows.

- $\perp \sqsubseteq t$ and $f \sqsubseteq f$ for every constant f.
- If $s \sqsubseteq s'$ and $t \sqsubseteq t'$ then $st \sqsubseteq s't'$.
- In particular: If $t \sqsubseteq t'$ then $\lambda_x t \sqsubseteq \lambda_x t'$.

This order is obviously reflexive, transitive and directed complete.

Lemma 25. *If $t \to_{\mathcal{S}} t'$ then $t^{\perp} \sqsubseteq t'^{\perp}$.*

Definition 26 (Terms Over a Signature). The set $\mathcal{T}^{\infty}(\Sigma)$ of not necessarily well founded terms over the signature Σ is coinductively defined by "If $t \in \mathcal{T}^{\infty}(\Sigma)$ then $t = f\overrightarrow{t}$ for some $t_1, \ldots, t_n \in \mathcal{T}^{\infty}(\Sigma)$ and $f \in \Sigma$ of type $\underbrace{\iota \to \ldots \to \iota}_{n} \to \iota$".

Definition 27 (Language of a Recursion Scheme). Let $\mathcal{S}$ be a recursion scheme with start symbol S. Then $t \in \mathcal{T}^{\infty}(\Sigma)$ *belongs to the language of* $\mathcal{S}$, in symbols $t \in L(\mathcal{S})$, if t is finite and there are terms $S = t_0 \to_{\mathcal{S}} t_1 \to_{\mathcal{S}} \ldots \to_{\mathcal{S}} t_n = t$; or t is infinite and there are terms $S = t_0 \to_{\mathcal{S}} t_1 \to_{\mathcal{S}} \ldots$ where t is the supremum of the $t_i^{\perp}$.

It should be noted that $\mathcal{T}^{\infty}(\Sigma)$, and hence the language of a recursion scheme, contains only total objects. This, however, is not a restriction, as introducing a new terminal $f_{\mathcal{R}} \colon \iota \to \iota$ and transforming every rule $N\overrightarrow{x} = e$ to $N\overrightarrow{x} = f_{\mathcal{R}}e$ guarantees the defined trees to be total. Note moreover, that "removing the repetition constructors $f_{\mathcal{R}}$" is MSO definable.

Remark 28 (Status of binder). If a binder is present in a recursion scheme, then Definition 27 is only defined up to renaming of bound variables, as α-equal terms are identified. However, as all our notions on lambda trees are invariant under α-equality we can safely assume that some canonical α-variants of the generated lambda trees are chosen.

We note moreover that in the only case where we actually need this construction to be effective, that is in the case of a level-0 recursion scheme, only closed terms are replaced by other closed terms, so we can (and will) always choose the variable named in the underlying equation.

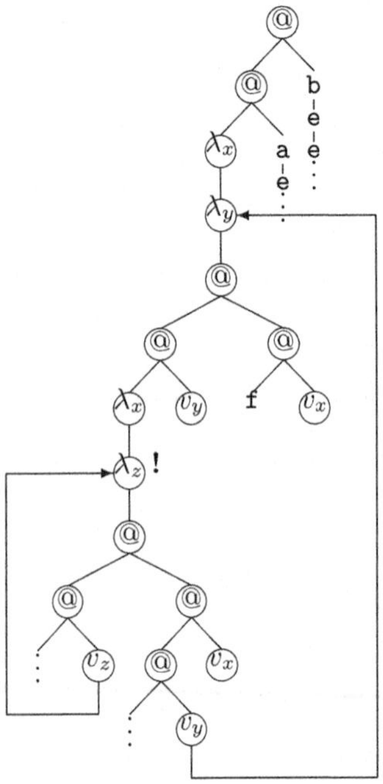

Example 29. The figure on the left shows a lambda tree of the language given by the second grammar in Example 12 with added arrows indicating some of the bindings; note in particular the renaming at the marked node. This example will be continued in Example 41.

Proposition 30 (Level-0 Trees). *Let $\mathcal{S}$ be a level-0 recursion scheme. Since in its reductions no capture can occur (since there are no substitutions), we may assume it to be pure (and consider λ_x and v_x as usual terminals). Then $L(\mathcal{S})$ is the language of a Büchi tree automaton.*

Definition 31 (Reduction Relation with Beta). Let $\mathcal{S}'$ be a recursion scheme with binder λ and distinguished binary terminal @. We define a relation $\to^{\beta}_{\mathcal{S}'}$ inductively as follows.

- $N\overrightarrow{t} \to^{\beta}_{\mathcal{S}'} e\left[\overrightarrow{t}/\overrightarrow{x}\right]$ if there is a recursion equation $N\overrightarrow{x} = e$ in $\mathcal{S}$.
- $(\lambda_x t)@s \to^{\beta}_{\mathcal{S}'} t\,[s/v_x]$. We recall that our notion of substitution is understood to be capture free.
- If $t \to^{\beta}_{\mathcal{S}'} t'$ then $t@s \to^{\beta}_{\mathcal{S}'} t'@s$. Moreover, if t is of the form $f@r_1@\ldots@r_n$ and $s \to s'$ then $t@s \to^{\beta}_{\mathcal{S}'} t@s'$.

We also define $t^{\perp\beta}$ as t with all unfinished computations replaced by $\perp$. This time, however, we consider @ as denoting application and the $f \in \Sigma$ as belonging to a reduced recursion scheme. That is we want $((\lambda_x \ldots)@a)^{\perp\beta} = \perp$ and $(f@a)^{\perp\beta} = fa$.

Definition 32 (Constructed Part of a Recursion Scheme with Beta). For t a term we define $t^{\perp\beta}$ inductively using the "vector notation" characterisation of terms, provided by Proposition 9.

- $f^{\perp\beta} = f$ for $f \in \Sigma$ and $\left(N\overrightarrow{t}\right)^{\perp\beta} = (\lambda_x t)^{\perp\beta} = \perp$.
- If $t^{\perp\beta} = f\overrightarrow{r}$ for some $f \in \Sigma$ then $(t@s)^{\perp\beta} = t^{\perp\beta} s^{\perp\beta}$; otherwise $(t@s)^{\perp\beta} = \perp$.

Lemma 33. *If* $t \to^{\beta}_{\mathcal{S}'} t'$ *then* $t^{\perp\beta} \sqsubseteq t'^{\perp\beta}$.

Definition 34 (The Beta-Language of a Recursion Scheme). Let $\mathcal{S}'$ be a recursion scheme with start symbol S, binder λ and distinguished non-terminal @. Then $t \in \mathcal{T}^{\infty}(\Sigma)$ *belongs to the* β*-language of* $\mathcal{S}'$, in symbols $t \in L^{\beta}(\mathcal{S}')$, if t is finite and there are terms $S = t_0 \to^{\beta}_{\mathcal{S}'} t_1 \to^{\beta}_{\mathcal{S}'} \dots \to^{\beta}_{\mathcal{S}'} t_n$ with $t_n^{\perp\beta} = t$, or t is infinite and there are terms $S = t_0 \to^{\beta}_{\mathcal{S}'} t_1 \to^{\beta}_{\mathcal{S}'} \dots$ and t is the supremum of the $t_i^{\perp\beta}$.

Lemma 35. *Let* $\mathcal{S}$ *be a recursion scheme and* $\mathcal{S}'$ *the reduced scheme. Then* $w \in L(\mathcal{S}) \Leftrightarrow w \in L^{\beta}(\mathcal{S}')$.

Proof. First we note that $N\overrightarrow{s}\overrightarrow{t} \to^{\beta}_{\mathcal{S}'} (\overrightarrow{\lambda_x}.e[\overrightarrow{s}/\overrightarrow{\varphi}])@t_0@\dots@t_n \to^{\beta}_{\mathcal{S}'} \dots \to^{\beta}_{\mathcal{S}'} e[\overrightarrow{s}\overrightarrow{t}/\overrightarrow{\varphi}\overrightarrow{x}]$. So a reduction sequence for $\mathcal{S}$ approximating some term $w \in L(\mathcal{S})$ can be transformed into a reduction sequence for $\mathcal{S}'$ approximating the same $w \in L(\mathcal{S}')$.

Moreover, we note that if in $\mathcal{S}'$ we have that $t \to^{\beta}_{\mathcal{S}'} t'$ by unfolding of a non-terminal, that is, by replacing somewhere in t the expression $N\overrightarrow{s}$ by $\overrightarrow{\lambda_x}.e[\overrightarrow{s}/\overrightarrow{\varphi}]$ then this happens in a context to produce $r = (\overrightarrow{\lambda_x}.e[\overrightarrow{s}/\overrightarrow{\varphi}])@t_1@\dots@t_n$. Moreover $r^{\perp\beta} = \perp$ and every $\to^{\beta}_{\mathcal{S}'}$-reduction sequence starting with r has to first reduce the obvious beta redexes yielding $e[\overrightarrow{s},\overrightarrow{t}/\overrightarrow{\varphi},\overrightarrow{x}]$ with all reducts r' before obtaining $r'^{\perp\beta} \neq \perp$.

Lemma 36. *Let* $\mathcal{S}'$ *be the reduced recursion scheme of a pure level-2 recursion scheme* $\mathcal{S}$*. Then the word or tree met on the canonical traversal of the lambda-tree denoted by* $\mathcal{S}'$ *and the word denoted by* $\mathcal{S}'$ *coincide.*

Corollary 37. *For a pure recursion scheme, its language can also be described as the words met on the canonical traversals of the trees obtained by the reduced recursion scheme.*

5 First Order Functions

Recall that our main idea is to simulate an automaton walking along the word or tree met on the canonical traversal. By Corollary 37 this suffices to test for a given ω-regular property. However, we currently have two unsolved problems.

- The definition of the tree denoted by a first-order recursion scheme involves binders and substitution is assumed to be performed in a capture avoiding manner. This no longer results in local conditions on testing whether a tree is generated by a given recursion scheme.
- There is no obvious way to characterise level-1 trees by automata. So the idea of intersecting an automaton testing whether the tree belongs to the language of the recursion scheme and an automaton simulating the Büchi-automaton does not work.

Fortunately, both problems simultaneously disappear if we perform the same trick again, and denote parts of the lambda tree by second-order abstractions.

Definition 38 (Second Order Lambda Trees). A *second-order lambda tree* is a tree built from the following constructors.

- Letters f, g, h, … , "application" $\underline{@}$, "abstraction" λ_x and "variables" v_x
- "function abstraction $\underline{\lambda}\varphi$" and "function variables φ" and "function application $\underline{@}$".

Definition 39 (Typed Second Order Lambda Trees). A second-order lambda tree is called *typed* if it arises from a level-2 recursion scheme by replacing every rule $N\overrightarrow{\varphi}\overrightarrow{x} \to e$ by

$$N \to \overrightarrow{\underline{\lambda}\varphi}\,\overrightarrow{\lambda_x}\, e''$$

where the $\overrightarrow{\varphi}$ are the first-order arguments of N and the $\overrightarrow{x}$ are the ground type arguments of N. Here e'' is the term e reduced twice in the sense of Definition 17; the first time with respect to λ and @ and the second time with respect to $\underline{\lambda}$ and $\underline{@}$.

Remark 40. Note that in a level-0 recursion scheme no substitution is performed and hence no variable renaming is necessary. Therefore, in accordance with Remark 28, we assume that always the variable name of the underlying equation is chosen. In particular we only need a fixed amount of variables.

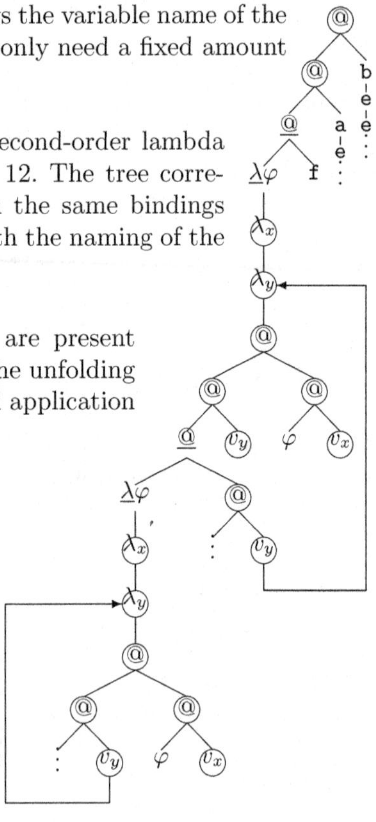

Example 41. The figure on the right shows a second-order lambda tree associated with the grammar in Example 12. The tree corresponds to the one shown in Example 29, with the same bindings indicated. Note that no care had to be taken with the naming of the variables.

Remark 42. Since all higher order arguments are present and the function abstractions $\underline{\lambda}\varphi$ come first in the unfolding of every nonterminal, first-order abstraction and application come always in the pattern

$$(\underline{\lambda}\overrightarrow{\varphi}.t)\underline{@}t_1\underline{@}\dots\underline{@}t_n$$

which we will in the following abbreviate by

$$\underline{\text{subst}}(t, \overrightarrow{\varphi}, \overrightarrow{t})$$

It should be noted that –as only finitely many arities are possible– this introduction of new $\underline{\text{subst}}(\cdot, \overrightarrow{\varphi}, \cdot)$ constructor symbols does not destroy the automata-theoretic description of the tree language.

Proposition 43. *Consider a typed lambda tree for words, that is, with every letter $f \in \Sigma$ of type $\iota \to \iota$. The canonical traversal continues in one of the following ways when entering a subterm of type* $\underbrace{\iota \to \ldots \to \iota}_{k} \to \iota$.

- *continues forever within this subterm*
- *passes finitely many letters and eventually hits a variable denoting one of the k function arguments*
- *it passes finitely letters and eventually hits a free variable of the subterm*

The crucial point about Proposition 43 is that it shows that only a *fixed amount of information* is needed to describe a first-order variable φ. This will allow us to split the traversal into two parts in the style of a logical "cut", and non-deterministically guess the splittings, carrying our guesses in the state of the automaton.

6 Word Languages

Theorem 44. *For any ω-regular property of words, fixed set of types and variables, there is a Büchi tree automaton that accepts precisely those second order lambda trees over the given set of variables and typed by the given types, where the denoted word satisfies the regular property. (We do not care what the automaton does on input trees that are not appropriately typed second-order lambda-trees.)*

Proof. Let the ω-regular property be given as a nondeterministic Büchi word automaton. First assume that there are no first-order variables. Then what we have to do is to assign each of the visited letters the state it has in a successful run (which we guess) and check local correctness and acceptance condition.

To make the transitions completely local, we use the fact that every node is visited at most three times so that we can guess for each node up to three annotations of the form "a automaton coming from direction ... in state ... is continuing its path here", " ... is searching upwards for variable x" or " ... is looking for the k'th argument". Since the number of arguments is bounded by the type for every such statement only a fixed amount of information is needed and the correctness of the guessed traversal can be checked locally.

Concerning the acceptance condition: given that each node of the lambda tree is visited only finitely many times, it must be the case that we visit infinitely many nodes in order to traverse an infinite word. As the automaton moves locally, at every node where an automaton enters, but doesn't come back there must be a child where an automaton enters but doesn't come back. Following these nodes traces a path that is visited infinitely often by the simulated automaton. Acceptance checking results in only signalling acceptance on the distinguished path (which we can guess) only if the automaton visits it having visited an accepting state since the last visit of the distinguished path.

Now assume that first-order variables are present. If we then consider walking just down the $\underline{\text{subst}}(t, \overrightarrow{\varphi}, \overrightarrow{t})$ nodes as if they were not present, we might at some point hit a first-order variable φ, that stands for a tree. The path might either continue forever in the tree denoted by φ or come back after finitely many steps asking to continue in one of its k arguments.

We note that there is still a path that is visited infinitely often: either the main branch of a $\underline{\text{subst}}(\cdot, \overrightarrow{\varphi}, \cdot)$ node or the subtree the variable stands for where the automaton enters, but never returns.

What remains to be shown is that local correctness can be tested. To do so, we keep for every of the (finitely many!) first-order variables a table with our guess of the behaviour of the variable in the current context. Such an entry is one of the following.

- "The variable will not be needed."
- "The successful run will enter in state q and will remain there forever."
- "When entering this variable the path will come back asking for argument k and the transition table for the word read in between is δ."

Here a "transition table" is understood as a table saying for every pair (p, q) of states of the simulated automaton, whether, when entering with state p we can leave with state q and whether we can do so with a visit of an accepting state in between.

Obviously only a fixed amount of information is needed to store this table. At every $\underline{\text{subst}}(t, \overrightarrow{\varphi}, \overrightarrow{t})$-"node" we update the table for the variables $\overrightarrow{\varphi}$ and our offspring to subtree t_i verifies our guess for φ_i.

- For the guess "The variable will not be needed" we need to verify nothing. So we just accept this subtree.
- For the guess "The successful run will enter here with state q" we have to simulate a successful run starting in state q.

  Note that we will continue producing the successful run even if this involves going upwards beyond the $\underline{\text{subst}}(\cdot, \overrightarrow{\varphi}, \cdot)$ where we entered the side branch. *This is precisely the device that allows us to work without a safety condition.*

  The picture on the right shows an example of such a run in a situation where blind substitution would produce variable capture. It should be noted that above the $\underline{\text{subst}}(\cdot, \varphi, \cdot)$ node all the annotations are the same, as if the automaton looking for variable x came directly from the main branch, correctly jumping over the λ_x there.

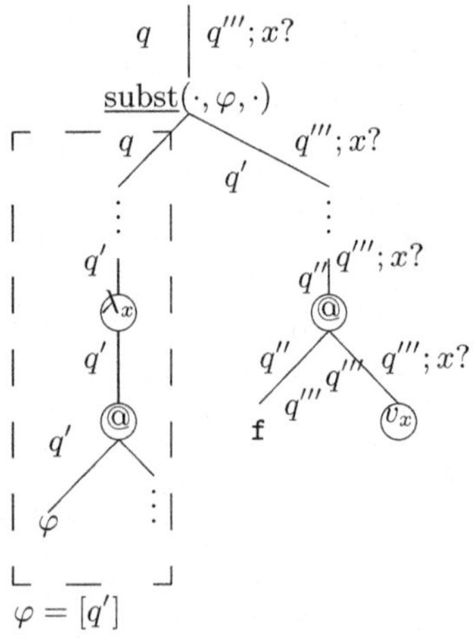

- For the guess "will come back to argument k with transition table δ", we have to produce a symbolic run, i.e., a run with transition tables rather than just states. But as transition tables can be updated locally when reading a letter we can produce such a symbolic run in the same way, as we would produce a usual run.

All this can be checked locally. Here we note that the guessing and verifying mechanism can be used for first-order variables, even if we are in a branch that currently verifies a guess. The reason is that our guesses are absolute ones and we needn't care what we use them for. The figure after this proof shows an example of such a guessed and verified run.

When our path now hits a second order variable φ, we do the following, depending on our guess of how φ behaves. If we have guessed that φ will not be needed, we fail. If we have guessed that φ will be entered in state q then we accept if and only if the current state is q. If we have guessed that the path will come back asking for argument k, we choose a state q' in accordance with the guessed transition table and make sure the node above has annotation "an automaton in state q' coming from left below searching for argument k".

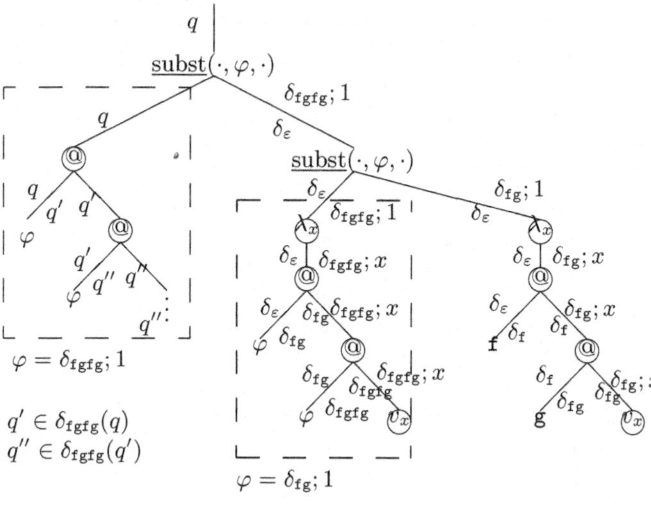

Corollary 45. *Given a level-2 word recursion scheme and an MSO property, it is decidable whether some word can be generated with the given recursion scheme that has the given property.*

7 Tree Languages

In this section we show how the proof of Theorem **??** can be extended to tree languages. To do so, we will use a result of Vardi [12] showing that the emptiness problem for *two way alternating parity tree automata* is decidable.

This has the advantage that we can follow the canonical paths directly (even upwards) and we can use our own alternating power to follow the alternations of the simulated automata and we use our own parity conditions to check the parity conditions of the simulated automaton. The only non-trivial point is still the case when we meet a first-order variable. Here we branch and do the same "guess and verify" as in the word case; this time with guesses of the form

"There is a successful run in the tree denoted by φ, starting from state q with automata entering the arguments of this function with at most the given states and the given parities visited in between."

Theorem 46. *For any alternating parity tree automaton there is a two-way alternating parity tree automaton that accepts precisely those typed second order lambda-trees denoting trees that have an accepting run of the given automaton.*

Proof. Our aim is to simulate an accepting run of an alternating *one-way* parity tree automaton on a tree denoted by the recursion scheme.

Since we now can also walk backwards we follow the path directly and we use our own alternating power to do the alternating of the simulated automaton. The only thing that remains to show is what we do, if we hit a first-order variable.

In short, we guess what the run through that variable would look like and then, on the one hand, send an automaton upwards to verify the guess and on the other hand simulate those paths of the tree that come up from the variable again. Of course we must make sure that the guess can be stored in the state of the automaton walking upwards and that there is only a bounded number of possible automata coming out of the variable and continue their run here (so that we can use our alternating power to branch off in such a strong way). This is achieved by the following observations.

- Automata coming out in the same state, with the same set of parities visited, and asking for the same argument can be merged into a single automaton, as automata entering the same tree with the same condition either all have an accepting run, or none.
- The question whether the automata on the paths that never leave the (tree denoted by) the first-order variable have an accepting run can be checked by the automaton walking upwards towards the variable.

Hence our guess "There is a successful run with automata entering the arguments of this function with at most the given states" can be described by a subset of $Q \times \{1, \ldots, k\} \times \mathfrak{P}(\Omega)$ where Q is the set of states of the simulated automaton, k the arity of the variable (which is bounded by the maximal number of arrows in any non-terminal of the original grammar) and $\mathfrak{P}(\Omega)$ the power set of the set of parities of the original automaton. So our guess comes from a fixed finite set.

The automaton walking upwards verifies its guess in the following way. It enters in the designated start state and simulates a run in the usual way, except that it remembers in its states the following information.

- The fact that we are in verifying a guess and its minimal parity visited since entering here.
- The set of allowed state/argument/acceptance triples for leaving the subtree "upwards"

This information is only used when walking upwards and hitting the $\underline{\text{subst}}(\cdot, \overrightarrow{\varphi}, \cdot)$-node from somewhere different than the main-branch, i.e., when leaving the subtree denoted by the variable. Then we check, whether we leave in one of the allowed states. Of course when hitting the subst$(\cdot, \overrightarrow{\varphi}, \cdot)$ node while searching for a variable, we continue our simulation (just forgetting that we were in verifying mode); we can do this, as this path will never ask for an argument of φ_i. *Again, this is the device, that allows us to work without a safety condition.*

Corollary 47. *The MSO theory of tree languages given by level-2 recursion schemes (that need not be safe or deterministic) is decidable.*

Proof. For every MSO formula there is an alternating parity tree automaton accepting those trees that satisfy it [11, 10]. Since level-0 recursion schemes are given by tree automata, we can intersect the language of the automaton obtained by Theorem 46 with the language of the corresponding level-0 recursion scheme. The decidability of the non-emptiness of two-way alternating parity tree automata was shown by Vardi [12].

References

1. Klaus Aehlig, Jolie G de Miranda, and C H Luke Ong. Safety is not a restriction at level two for string languages. In *Foundations of Software Science and Computation Structures (FOSSACS '05)*, April 2005. To appear.
2. A. Asperti, V. Danos, C. Laneve, and L. Regnier. Paths in the lambda-calculus. In *Proceedings of the Ninth Annual IEEE Symposium an Logic in Computer Science (LICS '94)*, pages 426–436, July 1994.
3. D. Caucal. On infinite transition graphs having a decidable monadic theory. In F. M. auf der Heide and B. Monien, editors, *Proceedings of the 23th International Colloquium on Automata, Languages and Programming (ICALP '96)*, volume 1099 of *Lecture Notes in Computer Science*, pages 194–205. Springer Verlag, 1996.
4. B. Courcelle. The monadic second-order logic of graphs IX: Machines and their behaviours. *Theoretical Comput. Sci.*, 151(1):125–162, 1995.
5. J. R. Kennaway, J. W. Klop, and F. J. d. Vries. Infinitary lambda calculus. *Theoretical Comput. Sci.*, 175(1):93–125, Mar. 1997.
6. T. Knapik, D. Niwiński, and P. Urzyczyn. Deciding monadic theories of hyperalgebraic trees. In S. Abramsky, editor, *Proceedings of the 5th International Conference on Typed Lambda Caculi and Applications (TLCA '01)*, volume 2044 of *Lecture Notes in Computer Science*, pages 253–267. Springer Verlag, 2001.
7. T. Knapik, D. Niwiński, and P. Urzyczyn. Higher-order pushdown trees are easy. In M. Nielson, editor, *Proceedings of the 5th International Conference Foundations of Software Science and Computation Structures (FOSSACS '02)*, volume 2303 of *Lecture Notes in Computer Science*, pages 205–222, Apr. 2002.
8. T. Knapik, D. Niwiński, P. Urzyczyn, and I. Walukiewicz. Unsafe grammars, panic automata, and decidability. Manuscript, Oct. 2004.
9. O. Kupferman and M. Y. Vardi. An automata-theoretic approach to reasoning about infinite-state systems. In E. A. Emerson and A. P. Sistla, editors, *12th International Conference on Computer Aided Verification (CAV '00)*, volume 1855 of *Lecture Notes in Computer Science*, pages 36–52. Springer Verlag, 2000.
10. D. E. Muller and P. E. Schupp. Alternating automata on infinite trees. *Theoretical Comput. Sci.*, 54:267–276, 1987.
11. M. O. Rabin. Decidability of second-order theories and automata on infinite trees. *Transactions of the American Mathematical Society*, 141:1–35, July 1969.

12. M. Y. Vardi. Reasoning about the past with two-way automata. In K. G. Larsen, S. Skyum, and G. Winskel, editors, *Proceedings of the 25th International Colloquium on Automata, Languages and Programming (ICALP 98)*, volume 1443 of *Lecture Notes in Computer Science*, pages 628–641. Springer Verlag, 1998.
13. I. Walukiewicz. Pushdown processes: Games and model-checking. *Information and Computation*, 164(2):234–263, Jan. 2001.

A Feasible Algorithm for Typing in Elementary Affine Logic

Patrick Baillot[1,*] and Kazushige Terui[2,**]

[1] Laboratoire d'Informatique de Paris-Nord / CNRS, Université Paris-Nord, France
pb@lipn.univ-paris13.fr
[2] National Institute of Informatics, Tokyo, Japan
terui@nii.ac.jp

Abstract. We give a new type inference algorithm for typing lambda-terms in Elementary Affine Logic (EAL), which is motivated by applications to complexity and optimal reduction. Following previous references on this topic, the variant of EAL type system we consider (denoted $\mathrm{EAL}^{\star}$) is a variant where sharing is restricted to variables and without polymorphism. Our algorithm improves over the ones already known in that it offers a better complexity bound: if a simple type derivation for the term t is given our algorithm performs $\mathrm{EAL}^{\star}$ type inference in polynomial time in the size of the derivation.

1 Introduction

Linear logic (LL) has proved a fruitful logical setting in which computational complexity can be brought into the picture of the proofs-as-programs correspondence, since the early work [GSS92]. In particular Light linear logic ([Gir98]) and Soft linear logic ([Laf04]) are variants of LL in which all numerical functions programmed are polynomial time. Another system, Elementary linear logic (ELL, see [Gir98, DJ03]) corresponds to Kalmar elementary complexity.

Hence one can consider specific term calculi designed through the Curry-Howard correspondence and program directly in these languages with the guaranteed complexity bound ([Rov98, Ter01]). However this turns out in practice to be a difficult task, in particular because these languages require managing specific constructs corresponding to the logical modalities. Considering the *affine* variant (i.e. with unrestricted weakening) of these systems is an advantage ([Asp98]) but does not suppress the difficulty.

An alternative point of view is to keep ordinary lambda-calculus and use the logic as a type system: then if a program is well-typed the logic provides a way to execute it with the guaranteed complexity bound. The difficulty is then moved to the problem of type inference. This approach and the corresponding type inference problems have been studied in [CM01, CRdR03] for Elementary affine logic (EAL) and [Bai02, Bai04] for

* Work partially supported by project CRISS ACI *Sécurité informatique* and project GEOCAL ACI *Nouvelles interfaces des mathématiques*.

** Work partially supported by Grant-in-Aid for Scientific Research, MEXT, Japan. This work was started during a visit of this author at Université Paris-Nord, in september 2004.

P. Urzyczyn (Ed.): TLCA 2005, LNCS 3461, pp. 55–70, 2005.

Light affine logic (LAL). It was shown that type inference in the propositional fragments of these systems is decidable.

Typing in EAL is actually also motivated by another goal (see [CM01, ACM00]): EAL-typed terms can be evaluated with the optimal reduction discipline much more easily than general terms, by using only the abstract part of Lamping's algorithm. Thus EAL has been advocated as a promising type system for performing efficient optimal reduction, using the following strategy: given a term, first try to infer an EAL type and if there is one then evaluate the term using Lamping's abstract algorithm. To succeed, this approach would require: an efficient type inference algorithm, evidence that the class of EAL-typable terms is large enough and includes interesting programs, and finally a proof that those terms are indeed evaluated in a faster way with Lamping's algorithm. Maybe intersection types could also be a useful tool in this direction ([Car04]).

However though the type inference problems for EAL and LAL have been shown decidable the algorithms provided, either for EAL or LAL, are not really efficient. They all run at least in exponential time, even if one considers as input a simply typed lambda-term. Our goal is to improve this state-of-the-art by providing more efficient and possibly simpler algorithms.

In this paper we propose a new algorithm for EAL typing, which is therefore a contribution to the perspective of EAL-driven optimal reduction discussed above. This is also a first step for designing an efficient inference procedure for Dual light affine logic (DLAL, [BT04a]) which is a simplification of LAL and corresponds to Ptime computation.

Contribution. Technically speaking the main difficulty with EAL typing is to find out *where* in the derivation to place !-rules and to determine *how many* of them to put. This corresponds in proof-nets terminology to placing *boxes*. The algorithms in [CM01] and [CRdR03] are based on two tactics for *first* placing abstract boxes and *then* working out their number using linear constraints. Our approach also uses linear constraints but departs from this point of view by determining the place of boxes *dynamically*, at the time of constraints solving. This method was actually already proposed in [Bai02] for LAL typing but with several conditions; in particular the term had to be in normal form. In the present work we show that in a system without sharing of subterms other than variables (like DLAL, but unlike LAL), this approach is considerably simplified. In particular it results that:

- one can use as intermediary syntax a very simple term calculus (introduced in [AR02]) instead of proof-nets like in [Bai02];
- the procedure can be run in polynomial time, if one considers as input a simply typed lambda-term (instead of an untyped lambda-term).

Outline. The paper will proceed as follows: in section 2 we introduce Elementary affine logic and the type system $\mathrm{EAL}^\star$ we consider for lambda-calculus; in section 3 we describe the term calculus (*pseudo-terms*, or *concrete syntax*) we will use to denote $\mathrm{EAL}^\star$ derivations and we prove a theorem (Theorem 8) on $\mathrm{EAL}^\star$ typability; finally in section 4 we give an $\mathrm{EAL}^\star$ decoration algorithm (based on Theorem 8), prove it can be run in polynomial time (4.2) and derive from it an $\mathrm{EAL}^\star$ type inference algorithm (4.3).

Acknowledgements. We are grateful to an anonymous referee who suggested important remarks about optimal reduction and possible improvement of the present work.

Notations. Given a lambda-term M we denote by $FV(M)$ the set of its free variables. Given a variable x we denote by $no(x, M)$ the number of occurrences of x in M. We denote by $|M|$ the structural size of a term M. We denote substitution (without capture of variable) by $M[N/x]$. When there is no ambiguity we will write $M[M_i/x_i]$ for $M[M_1/x_1, \dots, M_n/x_n]$.

Notations for lists: ϵ will denote the empty list and pushing element a on list l will be denoted by $a :: l$. The prefix relation on lists will be denoted by $\leq$.

2 Typing in Elementary Affine Logic

The formulas of Intuitionistic multiplicative Elementary affine logic (Elementary affine logic for short, EAL) are given by the following grammar:

$$A, B ::= \alpha \mid A \multimap B \mid !A \mid \forall \alpha.A$$

We restrict here to propositional EAL (without quantification). A natural deduction presentation for this system is given on Figure 1.

$$\frac{}{A \vdash A}\ \text{(var)} \qquad \frac{\Gamma \vdash B}{\Gamma, A \vdash B}\ \text{(weak)}$$

$$\frac{\Gamma_1 \vdash A \multimap B \quad \Gamma_2 \vdash A}{\Gamma_1, \Gamma_2 \vdash B}\ \text{(appl)} \qquad \frac{\Gamma, A \vdash B}{\Gamma \vdash A \multimap B}\ \text{(abst)}$$

$$\frac{\Gamma \vdash !A \quad !A, \dots, !A, \Delta \vdash B}{\Gamma, \Delta \vdash B}\ \text{(contr)}$$

$$\frac{\Gamma_1 \vdash !A_1 \quad \cdots \quad \Gamma_n \vdash !A_n \quad A_1, \dots, A_n \vdash B}{\Gamma_1, \dots, \Gamma_n \vdash !B}\ \text{(prom)}$$

Fig. 1. Natural deduction for EAL

We call *erasure* A^- of an EAL formula A the simple type defined inductively by:

$$\alpha^- = \alpha,\ (!A)^- = A^-,\ (A \multimap B)^- = A^- \to B^-.$$

Conversely, given a simple type T we say that an EAL formula A is a *decoration* of T if we have $A^- = T$.

We will use EAL as a type system for lambda-terms, but in a way more constrained than that allowed by this natural deduction presentation:

Definition 1. Let M be a lambda-term; we say M is typable in EAL* with type $\Gamma \vdash M : A$ if there is a derivation of this judgment in the system from Figure 2.

Notice that the rule (contr) is restricted and an affinity condition is imposed on the rule (prom). The effect is that it does not allow *sharing* of subterms other than variables. This comes in contrast with the computational study of ELL carried out for instance in [DJ03] but is motivated by several points:

- With our restrictions, terms and derivations correspond more closely to each other. For instance, the size of a typed term M is always linear in the length (i.e. the number of typing rules) of its type derivation.
- This approach where sharing is restricted to variables (and not arbitrary subterms) is enough to define Dual Light Affine Logic (DLAL) typing ([BT04a]) which is sufficient to capture polynomial time computation.
- It is not hard to see that our notion of EAL*-typability precisely coincides with the EAL-typability for lambda-terms considered by Coppola and Martini in [CM01] (see [BT04b]). As argued in their paper [CM01], sharing-free derivations are necessary to be able to use EAL for optimal reduction with the abstract part of Lamping's algorithm.
- Finally: using sharing of arbitrary subterms would make type inference more difficult …

$$\frac{}{x : A \vdash x : A}\ (\text{var}) \qquad \frac{\Gamma \vdash M : B}{\Gamma, x : A \vdash M : B}\ (\text{weak})$$

$$\frac{\Gamma_1 \vdash M_1 : A \multimap B \quad \Gamma_2 \vdash M_2 : A}{\Gamma_1, \Gamma_2 \vdash (M_1)M_2 : B}\ (\text{appl}) \qquad \frac{\Gamma, x : A \vdash M : B}{\Gamma \vdash \lambda x.M : A \multimap B}\ (\text{abst})$$

$$\frac{x_1 : !A, \ldots, x_n : !A, \Delta \vdash M : B}{x : !A, \Delta \vdash M[x/x_1, \ldots, x_n] : B}\ (\text{contr})$$

$$\frac{\Gamma_1 \vdash M_1 : !A_1 \quad \cdots \quad \Gamma_n \vdash M_n : !A_n \quad x_1 : A_1, \ldots, x_n : A_n \vdash M : B}{\Gamma_1, \ldots, \Gamma_n \vdash M[M_i/x_i] : !B}\ (\text{prom})$$

In the rule (prom), each x_i occurs at most once in M.

Fig. 2. Typing rules for EAL*

3 Concrete Syntax and Box Reconstruction

3.1 Pseudo-Terms

In order to describe the structure of type derivations we need a term calculus more informative than lambda-calculus. We will use the language introduced in [AR02] (called *concrete syntax* in this paper), which is convenient because it has no explicit construct neither for boxes, nor for contractions. It was stressed in this reference that this syntax is not faithful for LAL: several type derivations (LAL proofs) correspond to the same term. However it is faithful for EAL*, precisely because sharing is restricted to variables and there is no ambiguity on the placement of contractions.

Let us introduce *pseudo-terms*:

$$t, u ::= x \mid \lambda x.t \mid (t)u \mid !t \mid \bar{!}t$$

The basic idea is that ! constructs correspond to main doors of boxes in *proof-nets* ([Gir87, AR02]) while $\bar{!}$ constructs correspond to auxiliary doors of boxes. But note that there is no information in the pseudo-terms to link occurrences of ! and $\bar{!}$ corresponding to the same box.

There is a natural erasure map $(.)^-$ from pseudo-terms to lambda-terms consisting in removing all occurrences of ! and $\bar{!}$. When $t^- = M$, t is called a *decoration* of M.

For typing pseudo-terms the rules are the same as in Definition 1 and Figure 2, but for (prom):

$$\frac{\Gamma_1 \vdash t_1 : !A_1 \quad \cdots \quad \Gamma_n \vdash t_n : !A_n \quad x_1 : A_1, \ldots, x_n : A_n \vdash t : B}{\Gamma_1, \ldots, \Gamma_n \vdash !t\ [\bar{!}t_i / x_i] : !B} \text{(prom)}$$

We want to give an algorithm to determine if a pseudo-term can be typed in EAL*: this can be seen as a kind of correctness criterion allowing to establish if boxes can be reconstructed in a suitable way; this issue will be examined in 3.2.

Actually, when searching for EAL* type derivations for (ordinary) lambda-terms it will be interesting to consider a certain subclass of derivations. A type derivation in EAL* is *restricted* if in all applications of the rule (prom),

(i) the subject M of the main premise $x_1 : A_1, \ldots, x_n : A_n \vdash M : B$ is not a variable, and
(ii) the last rules to derive auxiliary premises $\Gamma_i \vdash M_i :!A_i$ $(1 \leq i \leq n)$ are either (var) or (appl).

A pseudo-term is *restricted* if it is obtained by the following grammar:

$$a ::= x \mid \lambda x.t \mid (t)t$$
$$t ::= !^m a,$$

where m is an arbitrary value in $\mathbb{Z}$ and $!^m a$ is defined by:

$$!^m a = \underbrace{! \cdots !}_{m\ times}\ a \quad \text{if } m \geq 0; \quad !^m a = \underbrace{\bar{!} \cdots \bar{!}}_{-m\ times}\ a \quad \text{if } m < 0.$$

We then have the following proposition (see [BT04b] for the proof):

Proposition 2.

1. *(For lambda-terms) if $\Gamma \vdash M : A$ has a type derivation, then it also has a restricted type derivation.*
2. *(For pseudo-terms) Every restricted derivation yields a restricted pseudo-term.*

As a consequence, when a lambda-term M is typable in EAL* one can always find a decoration of M (of the same type) in the set of restricted pseudo-terms.

3.2 Box Reconstruction

We will consider words over the language $\mathcal{L} = \{!, \bar{!}\}^\star$.

If t is a pseudo-term and x is an occurrence of variable (either free or bound) in t, we define $t\langle x\rangle$ as the word of $\mathcal{L}$ obtained by listing the occurrences of $!$, $\bar{!}$ holding x in their scope. More formally:

$$
\begin{array}{lll}
x\langle x\rangle & = \epsilon, & (!t)\langle x\rangle = \,! :: (t\langle x\rangle), \\
(\lambda y.t)\langle x\rangle & = t\langle x\rangle, \ (y \text{ might be equal to } x) & (\bar{!}t)\langle x\rangle = \bar{!} :: (t\langle x\rangle), \\
((t_1)t_2)\langle x\rangle & = t_i\langle x\rangle \ \text{ where } t_i \text{ is the subterm containing } x. &
\end{array}
$$

We define a map: $s : \mathcal{L} \to \mathbb{Z}$ by:

$$s(\epsilon) = 0, \quad s(! :: l) = 1 + s(l), \quad s(\bar{!} :: l) = -1 + s(l).$$

We call $s(l)$ the *sum* associated to l.

Let t be a pseudo-term. We say that t satisfies the *bracketing condition* if

– for any occurrence of variable x in t:

$$\forall l \leq t\langle x\rangle, \ s(l) \geq 0,$$

– moreover if x is an occurrence of free variable:

$$s(t\langle x\rangle) = 0.$$

That is to say: if $!$ is seen as an opening bracket and $\bar{!}$ as a closing bracket, in $t\langle x\rangle$ any $\bar{!}$ matches a $!$ (we will say that $t\langle x\rangle$ is *weakly well-bracketed*) and if x is free $t\langle x\rangle$ is well-bracketed.

We say t satisfies the *scope condition* if: for any subterm $\lambda x.v$ of t, for any occurrence x_i of x in v, $v\langle x_i\rangle$ is well-bracketed:

– $\forall l \leq v\langle x_i\rangle, \ s(l) \geq 0,$
– and $s(v\langle x_i\rangle) = 0$.

It is obvious that:

Lemma 3. *If t is a pseudo-term which satisfies the scope condition, then any subterm of t also satisfies this condition.*

Proposition 4. *If t is an EAL* typed pseudo term, then t satisfies the bracketing and scope conditions.*

Proof. By induction on the EAL* type derivations.

For instance the two following pseudo-terms are *not* EAL* typable:

$$!\lambda f.!((\bar{!}f)(\bar{!}f)\bar{!}^3 x), \qquad !\lambda f.!((\bar{!}^2 f)(\bar{!}f)\bar{!}^2 x),$$

the first one because it does not satisfy bracketing, and the second one because it does not satisfy the scope condition (because of the first occurrence of f).

Now, we can observe the following property:

Lemma 5 (Boxing). *If $!u$ is a pseudo-term which satisfies the bracketing and scope conditions then there exist v, u_1, ..., u_n unique (up to renaming of v's free variables) such that:*

- *$FV(v) = \{x_1, \dots, x_n\}$ and for $1 \leq i \leq n$, $no(x_i, v) = 1$,*
- *$!u = !v[\bar{!}u_1/x_1, \dots, \bar{!}u_n/x_n]$,*
- *v and u_i, for $1 \leq i \leq n$, satisfy the bracketing condition.*

Proof. We denote by $!_0$ the first occurrence of ! in the term considered: $!_0u$. Denote by $\bar{!}_1, \dots, \bar{!}_n$ the occurrences of $\bar{!}$ matching $!_0$ in the words $!u\langle x\rangle$, where x ranges over the occurrences of variables in $!u$. Let u_i, with $1 \leq i \leq n$, be the subterms of $!u$ such that $\bar{!}_iu_i$ is a subterm of $!u$, for $1 \leq i \leq n$. Then it is clear that no u_i is a subterm of a u_j, for $i \neq j$.

Let now v be the pseudo-term obtained from u by replacing each $\bar{!}_iu_i$ by a distinct variable x_i. Let us show that inside t, no occurrence of variable in u_i can be bound by a λ in v. Indeed assume it was the case for an occurrence y in u_i and let $\lambda y.w$ denote the subterm of t starting with λy. Then $\lambda y.w$ would be of the form $\lambda y.w'\{\bar{!}u_i/x_i\}$, where $v_1\{v_2/x\}$ denotes the syntactic substitution of x by v_2 in v_1 (i.e. possibly with variable capture). One can check that the scope condition for t would then be violated, hence a contradiction.

Therefore we have $!u = !v[\bar{!}u_1/x_1, \dots, \bar{!}u_n/x_n]$ (without variable capture), and by definition of $\bar{!}_i$ we know that for $1 \leq i \leq n$, $v\langle x_i\rangle$ is well-bracketed.

Finally let us assume x is an occurrence of free variable in v distinct from x_i, for $1 \leq i \leq n$. Then x is an occurrence of free variable in $!u$, and as $!u$ is well-bracketed we have that $s(!u\langle x\rangle) = 0$, hence x is in the scope of a $\bar{!}_0$ matching $!_0$. Then $\bar{!}_0$ must be one of the $\bar{!}_i$, for $1 \leq i \leq n$, hence x is in u_i and thus does not occur in v, which gives a contradiction. Therefore we have $FV(v) = \{x_1, \dots, x_n\}$.

Let us show that v satisfies bracketing. Let y be an occurrence of variable in v. If y is free we already know that $v\langle y\rangle$ is well-bracketed. If y is bound then $!v\langle y\rangle = !u\langle y\rangle$. So if $l \leq !v\langle y\rangle$ and $l \neq \epsilon$, then $s(l) \geq 1$, therefore $\forall l \leq v\langle y\rangle,\ s(l) \geq 0$. So v satisfies the bracketing condition. It is easy to check that the u_is also satisfy the bracketing condition.

Given a pseudo-term t we call *EAL type assignment* for t a map Γ from the variables of t (free or bound) to EAL formulas. EAL type assignments are simply called *assignments* when there is no danger of confusion. This map Γ is extended to a partial map from subterms of t to EAL formulas by the following inductive definition:

$$
\begin{array}{lll}
\Gamma(!u) & = !A, & \text{if } \Gamma(u) = A, \\
\Gamma(\bar{!}u) & = A, & \text{if } \Gamma(u) = !A, \text{ undefined otherwise}, \\
\Gamma(\lambda x.u) & = A \multimap B, & \text{if } \Gamma(x) = A, \Gamma(u) = B, \\
\Gamma((u_1)u_2) & = B, & \text{if } \Gamma(u_2) = A \text{ and } \Gamma(u_1) = A \multimap B, \text{ undefined otherwise.}
\end{array}
$$

Given a pair (t, Γ) of a pseudo-term t and an assignment Γ (we omit Γ if it is natural from the context) we say that (t, Γ) satisfies the *typing condition* if:

- $\Gamma(t)$ is defined (so in particular each subterm of t of the form $(u_1)u_2$ satisfies the condition above),

– for any variable x of t which has at least 2 occurrences we have: $\Gamma(x)$ is of the form $!B$ for some formula B.

Given an EAL* type derivation for a pseudo-term t there is a natural assignment Γ obtained from this derivation: the value of Γ on free variables is obtained from the environment of the final judgment and its value on bound variables from the type of the variable in the premise of the abstraction rule in the derivation.

Proposition 6. *If t is an EAL* typed pseudo-term and Γ is an associated assignment then (t, Γ) satisfies the typing condition.*

Moreover it is easy to observe that:

Lemma 7. *If (t, Γ) satisfies the typing condition and u is a subterm of t, then (u, Γ) also satisfies the typing condition.*

Now, the conditions on pseudo-terms we have listed up to now are sufficient to ensure that t is an EAL* typed pseudo-term:

Theorem 8. *If t is a pseudo-term and Γ an assignment such that:*

- *t satisfies the bracketing and scope conditions,*
- *(t, Γ) satisfies the typing condition,*

then t is typable in EAL* with a judgment $\Delta \vdash t : A$ such that: $\Gamma(t) = A$ and Δ is the restriction of Γ to the free variables of t.

Proof. Let us use the following enumeration for the conditions:
(i) bracketing, (ii) scope, (iii) typing.

The proof proceeds by structural induction on the pseudo-term t. Let us just deal here with the case $t = !u$. The complete proof can be found in [BT04b].

By the Boxing Lemma 5, t can be written as $t = !v[\bar{!}u_1/x_1, \ldots, \bar{!}u_n/x_n]$ where $FV(v) = \{x_1, \ldots, x_n\}$ and each $v\langle x_i \rangle$ is well-bracketed. By Lemma 5 again, each u_i satisfies (i).

By Lemmas 3 and 7 as t satisfies (ii) and (iii), u_i also satisfies (ii) and (iii). Therefore by induction hypothesis we get that there exists an EAL* derivation of conclusion:

$$\Delta_i \vdash u_i : A_i,$$

where $A_i = \Gamma(u_i)$, for $1 \leq i \leq n$.

Let us now examine the conditions for v. As t satisfies the bracketing condition and by the Boxing Lemma 5, we get that v satisfies (i). By the Boxing Lemma again we know that all free variables of v have exactly one occurrence. It is easy to check that as t satisfies the scope condition (ii), so does v.

Consider now the typing condition. Let $\tilde{\Gamma}$ be defined as Γ but $\tilde{\Gamma}(x_i) = \Gamma(\bar{!}u_i)$ for $1 \leq i \leq n$. If y has several occurrences in v then it has several occurrences in t, hence $\Gamma(y) = !B$, so $\tilde{\Gamma}(y) = !B$. If $(v_1)v_2$ is a subterm of v then $(v_1')v_2'$, where $v_i' = v_i[\bar{!}u_1/x_1, \ldots, \bar{!}u_n/x_n]$, is a subterm of t and $\tilde{\Gamma}(v_i') = \Gamma(v_i)$. Therefore as (t, Γ) satisfies the typing condition, then so does $(v, \tilde{\Gamma})$.

As $\Gamma(u_i) = A_i$ and $\Gamma(\bar{!}u_i)$ is defined we have $A_i = !B_i$ and $\tilde{\Gamma}(x_i) = B_i$. Finally as v satisfies conditions (i)–(iii), by i.h. there exists an EAL* derivation of conclusion:

$$x_1 : B_1, \ldots, x_n : B_n \vdash v : C,$$

where $C = \tilde{\Gamma}(v)$.

If u_i and u_j for $i \neq j$ have a free variable y in common then as t satisfies the typing condition we have $\Gamma(y) = !B$. We rename the free variables common to several of the u_is, apply a (prom) rule to the judgments on u_i and the judgment on v, then some (contr) rules and get a judgment: $\Delta' \vdash t : !C$. Hence the i.h. is valid for t.

4 A Decoration Algorithm

4.1 Decorations and Instantiations

We consider the following *decoration problem*:

Problem 9 (decoration). Let $x_1 : A_1, \ldots, x_n : A_n \vdash M : B$ be a simply typed term; does there exist EAL decorations A'_i of the A_i for $1 \leq i \leq n$ and B' of B such that $x_1 : A'_1, \ldots, x_n : A'_n \vdash M : B'$ is a valid EAL* judgment for M?

For that we will need to find out the possible concrete terms corresponding to M. Actually following section 3.1 and Prop. 2 it is sufficient to search for a suitable term in the set of restricted pseudo-terms, instead of considering the whole set of pseudo-terms. To perform this search we will use *parameters*: $\mathbf{n}, \mathbf{m}, \mathbf{k}, \ldots$. The *parameterized pseudo-terms* are defined by the following grammar:

$$a ::= x \mid \lambda x.t \mid (t)t, \qquad t ::= !^{\mathbf{n}}a,$$

where $\mathbf{n}$ is a parameter (and not an integer).

To parameterize types, we will also use *linear combinations of parameters* $\mathbf{c}, \mathbf{d}, \ldots$ defined by:

$$\mathbf{c} ::= 0 \mid \mathbf{n} \mid \mathbf{n} + \mathbf{c}.$$

The *parameterized types* are defined by:

$$A ::= !^{\mathbf{c}}\alpha \mid !^{\mathbf{c}}(A \multimap A).$$

Given a parameterized pseudo-term t, a *parameterized type assignment* Σ for t is a map from the variables of t (free or bound) to the parameterized types.

We denote by $par(t)$ ($par(A)$, resp.) the set of parameters occurring in t (A, resp.), and by $par(\Sigma)$ the union of $par(\Sigma(x))$ with x ranging over all the variables of t.

An *instantiation* ϕ for t is a map $\phi : par(t) \rightarrow \mathbb{Z}$. It allows to define a restricted pseudo-term $\phi(t)$ obtained by substituting the integer $\phi(\mathbf{n})$ for each parameter $\mathbf{n}$. Similarly, an *instantiation* ϕ for (t, Σ) is a map $\phi : par(t) \cup par(\Sigma) \rightarrow \mathbb{Z}$. The map ϕ is naturally extended to the linear combinations of parameters. If A is a parameterized type such that $par(A) \subseteq par(\Sigma)$ and moreover $\phi(\mathbf{c})$ is *non-negative* whenever $!^{\mathbf{c}}B$ occurs in A, one can obtain an EAL type $\phi(A)$ by substituting $\phi(\mathbf{n})$ for each parameter $\mathbf{n}$ as above. For instance, $\phi(!^{\mathbf{n}}(!^{0}\alpha \multimap !^{\mathbf{n}+\mathbf{n}}\alpha)) = !^{3}(\alpha \multimap !^{6}\alpha)$ when $\phi(\mathbf{n}) = 3$. An EAL type assignment $\phi\Sigma$ for $\phi(t)$ is then obtained by $\phi\Sigma(x) = \phi(\Sigma(x))$ when $\phi(\Sigma(x))$ is defined for all variables x of t.

We define the *size* $|A|$ of a parameterized formula A as the structural size of its underlying simple type (so the sum of the number of $\multimap$ connectives and atomic subtypes), and $|\Sigma|$ as the maximum of $|\Sigma(x)|$ for all variables x. The *erasure map* $(.)^{-}$ is defined for parameterized pseudo-terms and parameterized types analogously to those for pseudo-terms and EAL types.

It is clear that given a lambda-term M there exists a parameterized pseudo-term t such that $t^{-} = M$ and all occurrences of parameter in t are distinct. We denote t, which is unique up to renaming of its parameters, by $\overline{M}$ and call it the *free decoration* of M. Note that the size of $\overline{M}$ is linear in the size of M. Given a simple type T, its *free decoration* $\overline{T}$ is defined by:

$$\overline{\alpha} = !^{\mathbf{n}}\alpha, \qquad \overline{A \multimap B} = !^{\mathbf{n}}(\overline{A} \multimap \overline{B}),$$

where in the second case we have taken $\overline{A}$ and $\overline{B}$ with disjoint sets of parameters and $\mathbf{n}$ a fresh parameter. Finally, a *simple type assignment* Θ for M is a map from the variables of M to the simple types. Its *free decoration* $\overline{\Theta}$ is defined pointwise, by taking $\overline{\Theta}(x) = \overline{\Theta(x)}$, where all these decorations are taken with disjoint parameters.

The following picture illustrates the relationship among various notions introduced so far:

pseudo-terms EAL types EAL typ. assign.	instantiation $\longleftarrow$	param. pseudo-terms param. types param. typ. assign.	erasure $\longrightarrow$ $\longleftarrow$ free decoration	lambda-terms simple types simple typ. assign.

Given a simple type derivation of $x_1 : T_1, \dots, x_n : T_n \vdash M : T$, one can naturally obtain a simple type assignment Θ for M. Furthermore, it is automatic to build a parameterized pseudo-term $\overline{M}$ and a parameterized type assignment $\overline{\Theta}$ for $\overline{M}$. If ϕ is an instantiation for $(\overline{M}, \overline{\Theta})$ such that $\phi(\overline{T_i})$ and $\phi(\overline{T})$ are defined (i.e. $\phi(\mathbf{n}) \geq 0$ for all $\mathbf{n} \in par(\overline{T_1}) \cup \cdots par(\overline{T_n}) \cup par(\overline{T})$), then $\phi(\overline{T_i})$ is a decoration of T_i for $1 \leq i \leq n$ and $\phi(\overline{T})$ is a decoration of T. Conversely, any decorations of T_i's and T are obtained through some instantiations for $(\overline{M}, \overline{\Theta})$. Therefore, the decoration problem boils down to the following *instantiation problem*:

Problem 10 (instantiation). Given a parameterized pseudo-term t and a parameterized type assignment Σ for it: does there exist an instantiation ϕ for (t, Σ) such that $\phi(t)$ has an EAL* type derivation associated to $\phi\Sigma$?

To solve this problem we will use Theorem 8 to find suitable instantiations ϕ if there exists any. For that we will need to be able to state the conditions of this theorem on parameterized pseudo-terms; they will yield linear constraints. We will speak of *linear inequations*, meaning in fact both linear equations and linear inequations.

We will consider lists over parameters $\mathbf{n}$. Let us denote by $\mathcal{L}'$ the set of such lists.

As for pseudo-terms we define for t a parameterized pseudo-term and x an occurrence of variable in t, a list $t\langle x\rangle$ in $\mathcal{L}'$ by:

$$x\langle x\rangle \;=\; \epsilon, \qquad ((t_1)t_2)\langle x\rangle = t_i\langle x\rangle \text{ where } t_i \text{ is the subterm containing } x,$$
$$(!^{\mathbf{n}}a)\langle x\rangle = \mathbf{n} :: (a\langle x\rangle), \qquad (\lambda y.t)\langle x\rangle \;=\; t\langle x\rangle \;\; (y \text{ might be equal to } x).$$

The sum $s(l)$ of an element l of $\mathcal{L}'$ is a linear combination defined by:

$$s(\epsilon) = 0, \quad s(\mathbf{n} :: l) = \mathbf{n} + s(l).$$

Let t be a parameterized pseudo-term. We define the *boxing constraints* for t as the set of linear inequations $\mathcal{C}^b(t)$ obtained from t in the following way:

- bracketing: for any occurrence of variable x in t and any prefix l of $t\langle x\rangle$, add the inequation: $s(l) \geq 0$; moreover if x is an occurrence of free variable add the equation $s(t\langle x\rangle) = 0$.
- scope: for any subterm $\lambda x.v$ of t, for any occurrence x_i of x in v, add similarly the inequations expressing the fact that $v\langle x_i\rangle$ is well-bracketed.

It is then straightforward that:

Proposition 11. *Given an instantiation ϕ for t, we have: $\phi(t)$ satisfies the bracketing and scope conditions iff ϕ is a solution of $\mathcal{C}^b(t)$.*

Note that the number of inequations in $\mathcal{C}^b(t)$ is polynomial in the size of t (hence also in the size of t^-).

In the sequel, we will need to unify parameterized types. For that, given 2 parameterized types A and B we define their unification constraints $U(A, B)$ by:

$$U(!^{\mathbf{c}}\alpha, !^{\mathbf{d}}\alpha) = \{\mathbf{c} = \mathbf{d}\}$$
$$U(!^{\mathbf{c}}(A_1 \multimap A_2), !^{\mathbf{d}}(B_1 \multimap B_2)) = \{\mathbf{c} = \mathbf{d}\} \cup U(A_1, B_1) \cup U(A_2, B_2)$$

and $U(A, B) = \{\text{FALSE}\}$ (unsolvable constraint) in the other cases.

Let Σ be a parameterized type assignment for t. Then we extend Σ to a partial map from the subterms of t to parameterized types in the following way:

$$\begin{array}{lll} \Sigma(!^{\mathbf{n}}a) & = !^{\mathbf{n}+\mathbf{c}}A & \text{if } \Sigma(a) = !^{\mathbf{c}}A, \\ \Sigma(\lambda x.u) & = !^0(A \multimap B) & \text{if } \Sigma(x) = A, \Sigma(u) = B, \\ \Sigma((u_1)u_2) & = B, & \text{if } \Sigma(u_1) = !^{\mathbf{c}}(A \multimap B), \text{ undefined otherwise.} \end{array}$$

We define the *typing constraints* for (t, Σ) as the set of linear inequations $\mathcal{C}^{typ}(t, \Sigma)$ obtained from t, Σ as follows. When $\Sigma(t)$ is not defined, then $\mathcal{C}^{typ}(t, \Sigma) = \{\text{FALSE}\}$. Otherwise:

(***applications***) for any subterm of t of the form $(u_1)u_2$ with $\Sigma(u_1) = !^{\mathbf{c}}(A_1 \multimap B_1)$ and $\Sigma(u_2) = A_2$ add the constraints $U(A_1, A_2) \cup \{\mathbf{c} = 0\}$.

(***bangs***) for any subterm of t of the form $!^{\mathbf{n}}u$ with $\Sigma(u) = !^{\mathbf{c}}A$, add the constraint $\mathbf{n} + \mathbf{c} \geq 0$.

(***contractions***) for any variable x of t which has at least 2 occurrences and $\Sigma(x) = !^{\mathbf{c}}A$, add the constraint $\mathbf{c} \geq 1$.
(***variables***) for any $\mathbf{c}$ such that $!^{\mathbf{c}}B$ is a subtype of $\Sigma(x)$ for some variable x of t, add the constraint $\mathbf{c} \geq 0$.

We then have:

Proposition 12. *Let t be a parameterized pseudo-term and Σ be a parameterized type assignment for t. Given an instantiation ϕ for (t, Σ), we have: $\phi\Sigma$ is defined and $(\phi(t), \phi\Sigma)$ satisfies the typing condition iff ϕ is a solution of $\mathcal{C}^{typ}(t, \Sigma)$.*

Note that the number of inequations in $\mathcal{C}^{typ}(t, \Sigma)$ is polynomial in $(|t| + |\Sigma|)$.

We define $\mathcal{C}(t, \Sigma) = \mathcal{C}^b(t) \cup \mathcal{C}^{typ}(t, \Sigma)$. Using the two previous Propositions and Theorem 8 we get the following result, which solves the instantiation problem:

Theorem 13. *Let t be a parameterized pseudo-term, Σ be a parameterized type assignment for t, and ϕ be an instantiation for (t, Σ). The two following conditions are equivalent:*

- *$\phi\Sigma$ is defined and $\phi(t)$ is typable in EAL* with a judgment $\Delta \vdash \phi(t) : A$ such that $\phi\Sigma(\phi(t)) = A$ and Δ is the restriction of $\phi\Sigma$ to the free variables of $\phi(t)$,*
- *ϕ is a solution of $\mathcal{C}(t, \Sigma)$.*

Moreover the number of inequations in $\mathcal{C}(t, \Sigma)$ is polynomial in $(|t| + |\Sigma|)$.

Finally, we obtain the following result, which solves the decoration problem:

Theorem 14. *Let $x_1 : A_1, \ldots, x_n : A_n \vdash M : B$ be a simply typed term and let Θ be the associated simple type assignment. There exist decorations A'_i of the A_i for $1 \leq i \leq n$ and B' of B such that $x_1 : A'_1, \ldots, x_n : A'_n \vdash M : B'$ is a valid EAL* judgment iff there is a solution ϕ of $\mathcal{C}(\overline{M}, \overline{\Theta})$.*

In this case each solution ϕ gives a suitable EAL* judgment $x_1 : A'_1, \ldots, x_n : A'_n \vdash M : B'$. Moreover the number of inequations and the number of parameters in $\mathcal{C}(\overline{M}, \overline{\Theta})$ are polynomial in $(|M| + |\Theta|)$.

4.2 Solving the Constraints

Now we turn our attention to the constraints and their solutions. Let t be a parameterized pseudo-term and Σ be an assignment. We consider instead of the previous instantiation maps with values in $\mathbb{Z}$, maps with rational numbers as values: $\psi : par(t) \cup par(\Sigma) \rightarrow \mathbb{Q}$. If ψ is such a map and k is a non-negative integer we defined the map $k\psi$ by: $(k\psi)(\mathbf{n}) = k.\psi(\mathbf{n})$, for any parameter $\mathbf{n}$.

Lemma 15. *If ψ is a solution of $\mathcal{C}(t, \Sigma)$ and k is a strictly positive integer then $k\psi$ is also a solution of $\mathcal{C}(t, \Sigma)$.*

Proof. It is enough to observe that for any inequation of $\mathcal{C}^b(t)$ and $\mathcal{C}^{typ}(t, \Sigma)$ if ψ is a solution then so is $k\psi$:

- all inequations from $\mathcal{C}^b(t)$ and all those from $\mathcal{C}^{typ}(t, \Sigma)$ except the contraction cases are homogeneous (no constant element in combinations) and as $k \geq 0$ the inequalities are preserved when multiplying both members by k;

- the inequations coming from the contraction cases in $\mathcal{C}^{typ}(t, \Sigma)$ are of the form $\mathbf{m} \geq 1$, so as $k \geq 1$ we have: if $\psi(\mathbf{m}) \geq 1$ holds then so does $k\psi(\mathbf{m}) \geq 1$.

Recall that the problem of finding if a linear system of inequations $\mathcal{C}$ admits a solution in $\mathbb{Q}$ can be solved in polynomial time in the size of $\mathcal{C}$ and its number of variables. Hence we have:

Proposition 16. *The problem of whether the system $\mathcal{C}(t, \Sigma)$ admits a solution with values in $\mathbb{Z}$ can be solved in time polynomial in* $(|t| + |\Sigma|)$.

Proof. As the number of inequations and the number of parameters in $\mathcal{C}^{typ}(t, \Sigma)$ are polynomial in $(|t| + |\Sigma|)$ and by the result we recalled above we have: one can decide if $\mathcal{C}^{typ}(t, \Sigma)$ admits a solution with values in $\mathbb{Q}$ in time polynomial in $(|t| + |\Sigma|)$.

Then, if there is no solution in $\mathbb{Q}$ there is no solution in $\mathbb{Z}$. Otherwise if ψ is a solution in $\mathbb{Q}$ take for k the least multiple of the denominators of $\psi(\mathbf{n})$, for all parameters $\mathbf{n}$. Then by Lemma 15, $k\psi$ is a solution in $\mathbb{Z}$.

It then follows that:

Theorem 17. *The decoration problem of Theorem 14 can be solved in time polynomial in* $(|M| + |\Theta|)$.

4.3 Type Inference

The procedure for EAL* decoration we have given can be extended to a type inference procedure for EAL* in the way used in [CM01]: given an ordinary term M,

- compute the principal assignment Θ for M (giving the principal simple type),
- use the procedure of Theorem 14 to find if M, Θ admits a suitable EAL* decoration.

It follows from a result of [CRdR03] that:

Proposition 18. *if M is EAL* typable and admits as principal simple type judgment $\Delta \vdash M : A$, then M admits an EAL* type judgment which is a decoration of this judgment.*

See [BT04b] for a self-contained proof of this proposition.

As a consequence, searching for an EAL* decoration of the principal type judgment of M is sufficient to decide if M is EAL* typable. It then follows from Theorem 17 that our EAL* type inference algorithm applied to a term M can be executed in time bounded by a polynomial in $(|M| + |\Theta|)$ where Θ is the principal (simple type) assignment of M.

Note, however, that this does not mean that the overall algorithm is polynomial time in $|M|$, as the principal simple type assignment for M can have a size exponential in $|M|$. Still, type inference in simples types can be performed in polynomial time if one uses a representation with sharing for the types. Further work is needed to examine if using a shared representation for types one can design an algorithm for EAL typing polynomial w.r.t. the size of the untyped term.

4.4 Example

Let us consider a small example to illustrate our method: take $M = \lambda y.\lambda z.(y)(y)z$ (the Church integer 2). The decoration $\overline{M}$ is given by:

$$\overline{M} = !^{\mathbf{m_1}}\lambda y.!^{\mathbf{m_2}}\lambda z.!^{\mathbf{m_3}}[\,(!^{\mathbf{m_4}}y_1)\ !^{\mathbf{m_5}}[\,(!^{\mathbf{m_6}}y_2)!^{\mathbf{m_7}}z\,]\,]$$

(we have distinguished the 2 occurrences of y in y_1 and y_2). We get for the boxing constraints:

$$\mathcal{C}^b(\overline{M}) = \left\{ \begin{array}{rlrl} \mathbf{m_1} & \geq 0\ (1) & \mathbf{m_2} & \geq 0\ (8) \\ \mathbf{m_1}+\mathbf{m_2} & \geq 0\ (2) & \mathbf{m_2}+\mathbf{m_3} & \geq 0\ (9) \\ \mathbf{m_1}+\mathbf{m_2}+\mathbf{m_3} & \geq 0\ (3) & \mathbf{m_2}+\mathbf{m_3}+\mathbf{m_4} & = 0\ (10) \\ \mathbf{m_1}+\mathbf{m_2}+\mathbf{m_3}+\mathbf{m_4} & \geq 0\ (4) & \mathbf{m_2}+\mathbf{m_3}+\mathbf{m_5} & \geq 0\ (11) \\ \mathbf{m_1}+\mathbf{m_2}+\mathbf{m_3}+\mathbf{m_5} & \geq 0\ (5) & \mathbf{m_2}+\mathbf{m_3}+\mathbf{m_5}+\mathbf{m_6} & = 0\ (12) \\ \mathbf{m_1}+\mathbf{m_2}+\mathbf{m_3}+\mathbf{m_5}+\mathbf{m_6} & \geq 0\ (6) & \mathbf{m_3} & \geq 0\ (13) \\ \mathbf{m_1}+\mathbf{m_2}+\mathbf{m_3}+\mathbf{m_5}+\mathbf{m_7} & \geq 0\ (7) & \mathbf{m_3}+\mathbf{m_5} & \geq 0\ (14) \\ & & \mathbf{m_3}+\mathbf{m_5}+\mathbf{m_7} & = 0\ (15) \end{array} \right.$$

where (1)–(7) express bracketing, (8)–(12) scope for λy and (13)–(15) scope for λz.

Now let us examine the typing constraints. We consider the principal typing assignment: $\Theta(y) = \alpha \to \alpha$, $\Theta(z) = \alpha$, which yields $\Theta(M) = (\alpha \to \alpha) \to (\alpha \to \alpha)$. Thus we have: $\overline{\Theta}(y) = !^{\mathbf{p_1}}(!^{\mathbf{p_2}}\alpha \multimap !^{\mathbf{p_3}}\alpha)$, $\overline{\Theta}(z) = !^{\mathbf{p_4}}\alpha$. We get for instance:

$$\begin{array}{ll} \overline{\Theta}(!^{\mathbf{m_7}}z) & = !^{\mathbf{m_7}+\mathbf{p_4}}\alpha \\ \overline{\Theta}(!^{\mathbf{m_6}}y_2) & = !^{\mathbf{m_6}+\mathbf{p_1}}(!^{\mathbf{p_2}}\alpha \multimap !^{\mathbf{p_3}}\alpha) \\ \overline{\Theta}((!^{\mathbf{m_6}}y_2)!^{\mathbf{m_7}}z) & = !^{\mathbf{p_3}}\alpha \\ \overline{\Theta}(!^{\mathbf{m_5}}((!^{\mathbf{m_6}}y_2)!^{\mathbf{m_7}}z)) & = !^{\mathbf{m_5}+\mathbf{p_3}}\alpha \\ \overline{\Theta}(!^{\mathbf{m_4}}y_1) & = !^{\mathbf{m_4}+\mathbf{p_1}}(!^{\mathbf{p_2}}\alpha \multimap !^{\mathbf{p_3}}\alpha) \\ \overline{\Theta}((!^{\mathbf{m_4}}y_1)\ !^{\mathbf{m_5}}[\,(!^{\mathbf{m_6}}y_2)!^{\mathbf{m_7}}z\,]) & = !^{\mathbf{p_3}}\alpha \\ \overline{\Theta}(\overline{M}) & = !^{\mathbf{m_1}}(!^{\mathbf{p_1}}(!^{\mathbf{p_2}}\alpha \multimap !^{\mathbf{p_3}}\alpha) \multimap !^{\mathbf{m_2}}(!^{\mathbf{p_4}}\alpha \multimap !^{\mathbf{m_3}+\mathbf{p_3}}\alpha)) \end{array}$$

We obtain the following typing constraints (omitting some obvious constraints):

$$\mathcal{C}^{typ}(\overline{M}) = \left\{ \begin{array}{rcll} \mathbf{m_7}+\mathbf{p_4} & \geq & 0 & (16) \\ \mathbf{m_6}+\mathbf{p_1} & \geq & 0 & (17) \\ \mathbf{m_6}+\mathbf{p_1} & = & 0 & (18) \\ \mathbf{p_2} & = & \mathbf{m_7}+\mathbf{p_4} & (19) \\ \mathbf{m_5}+\mathbf{p_3} & \geq & 0 & (20) \end{array} \quad \begin{array}{rcll} \mathbf{m_4}+\mathbf{p_1} & \geq & 0 & (21) \\ \mathbf{m_4}+\mathbf{p_1} & = & 0 & (22) \\ \mathbf{p_2} & = & \mathbf{m_5}+\mathbf{p_3} & (23) \\ \mathbf{p_1},\dots,\mathbf{p_4} & \geq & 0 & (24) \\ \mathbf{p_1} & \geq & 1 & (25) \end{array} \right.$$

Putting $\mathcal{C}^b(\overline{M})$ and $\mathcal{C}^{typ}(\overline{M})$ together we get that $\mathcal{C}(\overline{M})$ is equivalent to:

$$\begin{array}{l} \{\mathbf{m_1},\mathbf{m_2},\mathbf{m_3} \geq 0;\ \mathbf{m_2}+\mathbf{m_3} = -\mathbf{m_4} = -\mathbf{m_6} = \mathbf{p_1} \geq 1; \\ \mathbf{m_5} = 0;\ \mathbf{m_3}+\mathbf{m_7} = 0;\ \mathbf{p_2} = \mathbf{p_3} \geq 0;\ \mathbf{p_4} = \mathbf{p_2}+\mathbf{m_3}\}. \end{array}$$

This finally gives the following (informally written) parameterized term and type with constraints, which describe all solutions to this decoration problem:

$$\begin{cases} \overline{M} = !^{\mathbf{m_1}} \lambda y. !^{\mathbf{m_2}} \lambda z. !^{\mathbf{m_3}} [\, (\bar{!}^{\mathbf{m_2}+\mathbf{m_3}} y_1)\, [\, (\bar{!}^{\mathbf{m_2}+\mathbf{m_3}} y_2) \bar{!}^{\mathbf{m_3}} z \,]\,] \\ !^{\mathbf{m_1}} (!^{\mathbf{m_2}+\mathbf{m_3}} (!^{\mathbf{p_2}} \alpha \multimap !^{\mathbf{p_2}} \alpha) \multimap !^{\mathbf{m_2}} (!^{\mathbf{p_2}+\mathbf{m_3}} \alpha \multimap !^{\mathbf{p_2}+\mathbf{m_3}} \alpha)) \\ \text{constraints: } \{\mathbf{m_1}, \mathbf{m_2}, \mathbf{m_3}, \mathbf{p_2} \geq 0, \mathbf{m_2} + \mathbf{m_3} \geq 1\}. \end{cases}$$

Observe that this representation corresponds to several canonical forms (6 in this particular example) in the approach of Coppola and Ronchi della Rocca (see [CRdR03]).

5 Conclusion

We have given a new type inference algorithm for EAL* which is more efficient and we think simpler than the previous ones. It generates a set of constraints which consists of two parts: one which deals with placing suitable (potential) boxes and the other one with typing the boxed term obtained. We believe the first part is not specific to EAL* typing and could be used for typing with other Linear logic systems which require determining boxes; what would need to be adapted to each case is the second (typing) part. This was already stressed by Coppola and Martini for their EAL type inference procedure ([CM04]). In particular we plan to study in this way second-order EAL typing (assuming a system F type given) and DLAL typing ([BT04a]).

We have shown that the set of constraints needed in our algorithm is polynomial in the size of the term and its simple type assignment. Finally we have also shown that by using resolution of linear inequations over rationals our algorithm can be executed in polynomial time with respect to the size of the initial term and its principal simple type assignment.

References

[ACM00] A. Asperti, P. Coppola, and S. Martini. (Optimal) duplication is not elementary recursive. In *Proceedings of POPL'00*, pages 96–107, 2000.

[AR02] A. Asperti and L. Roversi. Intuitionistic light affine logic. *ACM Transactions on Computational Logic*, 3(1):1–39, 2002.

[Asp98] A. Asperti. Light affine logic. In *Proceedings of LICS'98*, pages 300–308, 1998.

[Bai02] P. Baillot. Checking polynomial time complexity with types. In *Proceedings of IFIP TCS'02*, pages 370–382, Montreal, 2002.

[Bai04] P. Baillot. Type inference for light affine logic via constraints on words. *Theoretical Computer Science*, 328(3):289–323, 2004.

[BT04a] P. Baillot and K. Terui. Light types for polynomial time computation in lambda-calculus. In *Proceedings of LICS'04*, pages 266–275, 2004. Long version available at http://arxiv.org/abs/cs.LO/0402059.

[BT04b] P. Baillot and K. Terui. A feasible algorithm for typing in elementary affine logic (long version). Technical Report cs.LO/0412028, arXiv, 2004. Available from http://arxiv.org/abs/cs.LO/0412028.

[Car04] D. de Carvalho. Intersection types for light affine lambda calculus. In *Proceedings of 3rd Workshop on Intersection Types and Related Systems (ITRS'04)*, 2004. To appear in ENTCS.

[CM01] P. Coppola and S. Martini. Typing lambda-terms in elementary logic with linear constraints. In *Proceedings of TLCA'01*, volume 2044 of *LNCS*, pages 76–90, 2001.

[CM04] P. Coppola and S. Martini. Optimizing optimal reduction. A type inference algorithm for elementary affine logic. *ACM Transactions on Computational Logic*, 2004. To appear.

[CRdR03] P. Coppola and S. Ronchi della Rocca. Principal typing in Elementary Affine Logic. In *Proceedings of TLCA'03*, volume 2701 of *LNCS*, pages 90–104, 2003.

[DJ03] V. Danos and J.-B. Joinet. Linear logic & elementary time. *Information and Computation*, 183(1):123–137, 2003.

[DJS95] V. Danos, J.-B. Joinet, and H. Schellinx. On the linear decoration of intuitionistic derivations. *Archive for Mathematical Logic*, 33(6):387–412, 1995.

[Gir87] J.-Y. Girard. Linear logic. *Theoretical Computer Science*, 50:1–102, 1987.

[Gir98] J.-Y. Girard. Light linear logic. *Information and Computation*, 143:175–204, 1998.

[GSS92] J.-Y. Girard, A. Scedrov, and P. Scott. Bounded linear logic: A modular approach to polynomial time computability. *Theoretical Computer Science*, 97:1–66, 1992.

[Laf04] Y. Lafont. Soft linear logic and polynomial time. *Theoretical Computer Science*, 318(1–2):163–180, 2004.

[Rov98] L. Roversi. A polymorphic language which is typable and poly-step. In *Proceedings of the Asian Computing Science Conference (ASIAN'98)*, volume 1538 of *LNCS*, pages 43–60, 1998.

[Ter01] K. Terui. Light affine lambda-calculus and polytime strong normalization. In *Proceedings of LICS'01*, pages 209–220, 2001. Full version to appear in *Archive for Mathematical Logic*.

Practical Inference for Type-Based Termination in a Polymorphic Setting

Gilles Barthe[1], Benjamin Grégoire[1], and Fernando Pastawski[2,*]

[1] INRIA Sophia-Antipolis, France
{Gilles.Barthe, Benjamin.Gregoire}@sophia.inria.fr
[2] FaMAF, Univ. Nacional de Córdoba, Argentina
fernandopastawski@arnet.com.ar

Abstract. We introduce a polymorphic λ-calculus that features inductive types and that enforces termination of recursive definitions through typing. Then, we define a sound and complete type inference algorithm that computes a set of constraints to be satisfied for terms to be typable. In addition, we show that Subject Reduction fails in a naive use of typed-based termination for a λ-calculus *à la* Church, and we propose a general solution to this problem.

1 Introduction

Type-based termination is a method to enforce termination of recursive functions through typing, using an enriched type system that conveys size information about the inhabitants of inductive types. Tracing back to N. P. Mendler's work on inductive types [13], type-based termination offers several distinctive advantages over termination checking through syntactic criteria, e.g. the possibility for separate compilation. However, there is no widely used implementation of a type system that relies on type-based termination. There are two main reasons for the lack of such an implementation:

- termination of recursive definitions is mostly relevant for proof assistants, but less so for programming languages. However, proof assistants that enforce termination through syntactic means often rely on dependent type theories *à la* Church, for which type-based termination is not completely understood, despite preliminary work in this direction [4, 6, 11];
- the problem of size inference is seldom considered, and existing algorithms [7, 16] for inferring size annotations are complex, and typically return for every program an annotated type and a formula (in a decidable fragment of arithmetic) to be satisfied by the size variables.

The principal contribution of this article is to provide a practical inference algorithm for a polymorphic λ-calculus featuring type-based termination. The inference algorithm is scalable, in the sense that it computes size annotations

* Most of the work was done while supported by an INRIA International Internship.

P. Urzyczyn (Ed.): TLCA 2005, LNCS 3461, pp. 71–85, 2005.

efficiently, and returns types that are easily understood. We achieve practicality by two means: first of all, we require recursive definitions to carry annotations about the dependency between the arguments and results of a recursive function definition. Due to the limited overhead they introduce (they should be compared to the {`struct` *id*} declarations in recursive definitions of Coq V8 [8]), we consider it perfectly acceptable to require users to provide such annotations when writing programs. Second of all, we consider a simple grammar for stage expressions: stage expressions are either stage variables, or ∞ (which denotes the maximal, closing stage of a datatype), or the successor of a stage expression. Thus our approach departs from the philosophy of many works on type-based termination which aim at typing as many terminating recursive definitions as possible. Nevertheless, our approach is more powerful than syntactic criteria for termination checking, see e.g. [5].

The combination of minimal annotations and a restricted language for stages enables us to guarantee that inferred types are of the form $C \Rightarrow \tau$, where τ is a type, and C is a finite conjunction of stage inequalities (our system features an obvious partial order on stages; hence the inference algorithm generates inequality constraints). The inference algorithm takes as input a pair (Γ, e) where Γ is a context and e is an expression, and returns an error if e is not typable in Γ, or a type τ *and* a set C of inequality between size expressions such that:

Soundness: for every stage substitution ρ satisfying C, we have $\rho\Gamma \vdash e : \rho\tau$.
Completeness: for every stage substitution ρ' such that $\rho'\Gamma \vdash e : \tau'$, there exists a stage substitution such that ρ satisfies C and $\rho\Gamma = \rho'\Gamma$ and $\rho\tau \preceq \tau'$, where the subtyping relation $\preceq$ is inherited from the partial order on stages.

Contents of the paper. Section 2 introduces $F^{\frown}$, which gives the setting of our work. Section 3 introduces the inference algorithm and establishes its soundness and completeness. Section 3.5 briefly describes an implementation of the size inference algorithm for $F^{\frown}$. Section 4 provides an overview of related work. We conclude in Section 5.

2 System $F^{\frown}$

The system $F^{\frown}$ is an extension of System F with inductive types and type-based termination. As such, $F^{\frown}$ shares many features of $\lambda^{\frown}$ [5], from which it is inspired: simple stage arithmetic, implicit stage polymorphism, and a subtyping relation inherited from the partial order between stages. Unlike $\lambda^{\frown}$, the system $F^{\frown}$ features abstractions *à la* Church, i.e. of the form $\lambda x : \tau.e$, and $\mathsf{letrec}\ f : \sigma = e$.

2.1 Types and Datatypes Declarations

In order to achieve subject reduction and efficient type inference, we are led to consider three different families of types: size types, which record size information, bare types, which do not contain any size information and are used to tag variables in λ-abstractions, position types which are used to tag fixpoint variables in recursive definitions and indicate which positions in the type of a recursive function have the same stage variable as the recursive argument (we use a $\star$ to indicate those positions). The need for bare types and position types is further justified in Sections 2.4 and 3.1 below.

Types are built from type variables and datatypes using type constructors for universal quantification and function space. Formally, we assume given a set $\mathcal{X}$ of type variables, and a set $\mathcal{D}$ of datatype identifiers. Each datatype identifier comes equipped with an arity $\mathsf{ar}(d)$.

Definition 1 (Stages and Types).

1. *The set* $\mathcal{S}$ *of* stage expressions *is given by the abstract syntax:*

$$s, r ::= \imath \mid \infty \mid \widehat{s}$$

where $\imath$ ranges over stage variables. Stage substitution is defined in the obvious way, and we write $s[\imath := s']$ to denote the stage obtained by replacing $\imath$ by s' in s. Furthermore, the base stage of a stage expression is defined by the clauses $\lfloor \imath \rfloor = \imath$ and $\lfloor \widehat{s} \rfloor = \lfloor s \rfloor$ (the function is not defined on stages that contain ∞).

2. *The sets $\mathcal{T}$, $\overline{\mathcal{T}}$ and $\mathcal{T}^\star$ of* bare types, (size) types, *and* position types *are given by the abstract syntaxes:*

$$\begin{aligned}
\mathcal{T} &::= \mathcal{X} \mid \mathcal{T} \to \mathcal{T} \mid \forall \mathcal{X}.\mathcal{T} \mid \mathcal{D}\ \boldsymbol{\mathcal{T}} \\
\overline{\mathcal{T}} &::= \mathcal{X} \mid \overline{\mathcal{T}} \to \overline{\mathcal{T}} \mid \forall \mathcal{X}.\overline{\mathcal{T}} \mid \mathcal{D}^{\mathcal{S}}\ \overline{\boldsymbol{\mathcal{T}}} \\
\mathcal{T}^\star &::= \mathcal{X} \mid \mathcal{T}^\star \to \mathcal{T}^\star \mid \forall \mathcal{X}.\mathcal{T}^\star \mid \mathcal{D}^\star\ \boldsymbol{\mathcal{T}}^\star \mid \mathcal{D}\ \boldsymbol{\mathcal{T}}^\star
\end{aligned}$$

where in the clauses for datatypes, it is assumed that the length of the vectors $\boldsymbol{\mathcal{T}}$, $\overline{\boldsymbol{\mathcal{T}}}$, and $\boldsymbol{\mathcal{T}}^\star$ is exactly the arity of the datatype.

Types are related by a subtyping relation inherited from stages.

Definition 2 (Subtyping). *The relations* s is a substage of s', *written* $s \sqsubseteq s'$, *and* τ is a subtype of σ, *written* $\tau \preceq \sigma$, *are defined by the rules:*

$$(\mathit{refl})\frac{}{s \sqsubseteq s} \qquad (\mathit{trans})\frac{s \sqsubseteq r \quad r \sqsubseteq p}{s \sqsubseteq p} \qquad (\mathit{hat})\frac{}{s \sqsubseteq \widehat{s}} \qquad (\mathit{infty})\frac{}{s \sqsubseteq \infty}$$

$$(\mathit{refl})\frac{}{\sigma \preceq \sigma} \qquad (\mathit{data})\frac{s \sqsubseteq r \quad \overline{\boldsymbol{\tau}} \preceq \overline{\boldsymbol{\tau}'}}{d^s \overline{\boldsymbol{\tau}} \preceq d^r \overline{\boldsymbol{\tau}'}} \qquad (\mathit{func})\frac{\tau' \preceq \tau \quad \sigma \preceq \sigma'}{\tau \to \sigma \preceq \tau' \to \sigma'} \qquad (\mathit{prod})\frac{\sigma \preceq \sigma'}{\forall A.\sigma \preceq \forall A.\sigma'}$$

Remark that the rule *(infty)* imply that $\widehat{\infty} \sqsubseteq \infty$. We now turn to datatype declarations. We assume given a fixed set $\mathcal{C}$ of *constructors*, and a function $\mathsf{C} : \mathcal{D} \to \wp(\mathcal{C})$ such that $\mathsf{C}(d) \cap \mathsf{C}(d') = \emptyset$ for every distinct $d, d' \in \mathcal{D}$.

Definition 3.

1. *A size type $\overline{\sigma} \in \overline{\mathcal{T}}$ is a $(d, \imath, \boldsymbol{A})$-*constructor type *if it is of the form*

$$\forall \boldsymbol{B}.\overline{\theta}_1 \to \ldots \to \overline{\theta}_k \to \widehat{d^\imath}\ \boldsymbol{A}$$

and every $\overline{\theta}_i$ belongs to the set $\overline{\mathcal{T}}_{(d,\imath,\boldsymbol{A})} \subseteq \overline{\mathcal{T}}$ defined by the syntax:

$$\mathcal{X} \mid \overline{\mathcal{T}}_{(d,\imath,\boldsymbol{A})} \to \overline{\mathcal{T}}_{(d,\imath,\boldsymbol{A})} \mid \forall \mathcal{X}.\overline{\mathcal{T}}_{(d,\imath,\boldsymbol{A})} \mid d^\imath\ \boldsymbol{A} \mid d'^\infty\ \overline{\boldsymbol{\mathcal{T}}}_{(d,\imath,\boldsymbol{A})}$$

(Note that $\imath$ is the sole stage variable in $(d, \imath, \boldsymbol{A})$-constructor type.) In the sequel, we let $\mathsf{Inst}(\overline{\sigma}, s, \overline{\boldsymbol{\tau}}, \overline{\sigma}') = \overline{\theta}_1[\boldsymbol{A} := \overline{\boldsymbol{\tau}}, \imath := s] \to \ldots \to \overline{\theta}_k[\boldsymbol{A} := \overline{\boldsymbol{\tau}}, \imath := s] \to \sigma'$.

2. A datatype definition *is a declaration of the form:*

$$\textbf{Inductive } d\ \boldsymbol{A} := c_1 : \overline{\sigma}_1 \mid \ \ldots \ \mid c_n : \overline{\sigma}_n$$

where $\mathsf{C}(d) = \{c_1, \ \ldots \ , c_n\}$ *and* $\overline{\sigma}_1 \ \ldots \ \overline{\sigma}_n$ *are* $(d, \imath, \boldsymbol{A})$*-constructor types in which* $\boldsymbol{A}, d^{\imath}\ \boldsymbol{A}$ *occur positively. We let* $\mathsf{Type}(c_i, s) = \forall \boldsymbol{A}.\overline{\sigma}_i[\imath := s]$ *and*

$$\mathsf{Inst}(c_i, s, \boldsymbol{\tau}, \sigma) = \mathsf{Inst}(\overline{\sigma}_i, s, \boldsymbol{\tau}, \sigma)$$

3. An environment is a set of datatype definitions $I_1 \ldots I_n$ in which constructors of the datatype definition I_k only use datatypes introduced by $I_1 \ldots I_k$.

Note that the definition of constructor types and environments rules out heterogeneous and mutually recursive datatypes. Besides, the positivity requirement for $d^{\imath}\ \boldsymbol{A}$ is a standard assumption to guarantee strong normalization. Also, the positivity requirement for $\boldsymbol{A}$ is added to guarantee the soundness of the subtyping rule for datatypes, and to avoid considering polarity, as in e.g. [14]. See e.g. [5] for a definition of positivity.

In the remaining of the paper, we implicitly assume given an environment in which every $d \in \mathcal{D}$ has a corresponding datatype definition.

2.2 Terms and Reduction

Terms are built from variables, abstractions, applications, constructors, case-expressions and recursive definitions. Formally we assume given a set $\mathcal{V}$ of *(object) variables.*

Definition 4 (Terms). *The set $\mathcal{E}$ of* terms *is given by the abstract syntax:*

$$e, e' ::= x \mid \lambda x : \tau.e \mid \Lambda A.e \mid e\ e' \mid e\ \tau \mid c \mid \mathsf{case}_{\tau}\ e' \ \mathsf{of}\ \{\mathbf{c} \Rightarrow \mathbf{e}\} \mid \mathsf{letrec}\ f : \tau^{\star} = e$$

Free and bound variables, substitution, etc. are defined as usual. We let $e[x := e']$ be the result of replacing all free occurrences of x in e with e'.

The reduction calculus is given by β-reduction for function application, $\imath$-reduction for case analysis and μ-reduction for unfolding recursive definitions, which is only allowed in the context of application to a constructor application.

Definition 5 (Reduction Calculus). *The notion of $\beta\imath\mu$-reduction $\to_{\beta\imath\mu}$ is defined as $\to_\beta \cup \to_\imath \cup \to_\mu$, where $\to_\beta$, $\to_\imath$, and μ-reduction are defined as the compatible closure of the rules*

$$\begin{array}{c}
(\lambda x : \tau.e)\ e' \ \to_\beta \ e[x := e'] \\
(\Lambda \alpha.e)\ \tau \ \to_\beta \ e[\alpha := \tau] \\
\mathsf{case}_{\tau}\ (c_i\ \boldsymbol{a})\ \mathsf{of}\ \{c_1 \Rightarrow e_1 \mid \ldots \mid c_n \Rightarrow e_n\} \ \to_\imath \ e_i\ \boldsymbol{a} \\
(\mathsf{letrec}\ f : \tau^{\star} = e)\ (c\ \boldsymbol{a}) \ \to_\mu \ e[f := (\mathsf{letrec}\ f : \tau^{\star} = e)]\ (c\ \boldsymbol{a})
\end{array}$$

The rewrite system $\beta\imath\mu$ is orthogonal and confluent.

(var) $\dfrac{}{\overline{\Gamma} \vdash x : \overline{\sigma}}$ if $(x : \overline{\sigma}) \in \overline{\Gamma}$

(abs) $\dfrac{\overline{\Gamma}; x : \overline{\tau} \vdash e : \overline{\sigma}}{\overline{\Gamma} \vdash \lambda x : |\overline{\tau}|.e : \overline{\tau} \to \overline{\sigma}}$

(app) $\dfrac{\overline{\Gamma} \vdash e : \overline{\tau} \to \overline{\sigma} \qquad \overline{\Gamma} \vdash e' : \overline{\tau}}{\overline{\Gamma} \vdash e\ e' : \overline{\sigma}}$

(T-abs) $\dfrac{\overline{\Gamma} \vdash e : \overline{\sigma}}{\overline{\Gamma} \vdash \Lambda A.e : \forall A.\overline{\sigma}}$ if $A \notin \overline{\Gamma}$

(T-app) $\dfrac{\overline{\Gamma} \vdash e : \forall A.\overline{\sigma}}{\overline{\Gamma} \vdash e\ |\overline{\tau}| : \overline{\sigma}[A := \overline{\tau}]}$

(cons) $\dfrac{}{\overline{\Gamma} \vdash c : \mathsf{Type}(c, s)}$ if $c \in \mathsf{C}(d)$ for some d

(case) $\dfrac{\overline{\Gamma} \vdash e' : d^{\widehat{s}}\overline{\boldsymbol{\tau}} \qquad \overline{\Gamma} \vdash e_i : \mathsf{Inst}(c_i, s, \overline{\boldsymbol{\tau}}, \overline{\theta}) \quad (1 \le i \le n)}{\overline{\Gamma} \vdash \mathsf{case}_{|\overline{\theta}|}\ e'\ \mathsf{of}\ \{c_1 \Rightarrow e_1 \mid \ldots \mid c_n \Rightarrow e_n\} : \overline{\theta}}$ if $\mathsf{C}(d) = \{c_1, \ldots, c_n\}$

(rec) $\dfrac{\overline{\Gamma}; f : d^{\imath}\overline{\boldsymbol{\tau}} \to \overline{\theta} \vdash e : d^{\widehat{\imath}}\overline{\boldsymbol{\tau}} \to \overline{\theta}[\imath := \widehat{\imath}]}{\overline{\Gamma} \vdash \mathsf{letrec}\ f : \tau^\star = e : d^s\boldsymbol{\tau} \to \theta[\imath := s]}$ if $\begin{cases} \imath \text{ not in } \overline{\Gamma}, \overline{\boldsymbol{\tau}} \text{ and } \imath \ \mathsf{pos}\ \overline{\theta} \\ \tau^\star \text{ is } \imath-\text{compatible with } d^{\imath}\boldsymbol{\tau} \to \theta \end{cases}$

(sub) $\dfrac{\overline{\Gamma} \vdash e : \overline{\sigma} \qquad \overline{\sigma} \preceq \overline{\sigma}'}{\overline{\Gamma} \vdash e : \overline{\sigma}'}$

Fig. 1. Typing rules for $F^{\frown}$

2.3 Typing Rules

The type system is adapted from [5], and uses an erasure function $|.|$ that maps types to bare types by removing all size information.

Definition 6 (Contexts and Judgments).

1. *A* context *is a finite sequence* $x_1 : \overline{\sigma}_1, \ldots, x_n : \overline{\sigma}_n$ *where* $x_1, \ldots, x_n$ *are pairwise disjoint (object) variables and* $\overline{\sigma}_1, \ldots, \overline{\sigma}_n$ *are (size) types.*
2. *A* typing judgment *is a triple of the form* $\overline{\Gamma} \vdash e : \overline{\sigma}$*, where* $\overline{\Gamma}$ *is a context, e is a term and* $\overline{\sigma}$ *is a (size) type.*
3. *A typing judgment is* derivable *if it can be inferred from the rules of Figure 1 where the positivity condition* $\imath\ \mathsf{pos}\ \overline{\sigma}$ *in the (rec) rule is defined in the usual way [5], and an annotated type* $\sigma^\star$ *is* $\imath$-compatible *with a size type* $\overline{\sigma}$ *if* $\sigma^\star$ *can be obtained from* $\overline{\sigma}$ *by replacing all stage annotations containing* $\imath$ *by* $\star$ *and by erasing all other size annotations.*
4. *A term* $e \in \mathcal{E}$ *is typable if* $\overline{\Gamma} \vdash e : \overline{\sigma}$ *is derivable for some context* $\overline{\Gamma}$ *and (size) type* $\overline{\sigma}$.

In the (rec) rule the side condition on $\imath$-compatibility is only relevant for the inference algorithm. Note also that the expression $\lambda x : \mathrm{Nat}.x$ has type $\mathrm{Nat}^s \to \mathrm{Nat}^s$ for all stages s. We refer to [5] for further explanations on the typing rules.

2.4 Subject Reduction

The system $F^{\frown}$ enjoys subject reduction. The proof is routine.

Lemma 1. *If* $\overline{\Gamma} \vdash e : \overline{\tau}$ *and* $e \rightarrow_{\beta\iota\mu} e'$, *then* $\overline{\Gamma} \vdash e' : \overline{\tau}$.

On the contrary, subject reduction would fail if annotated terms were used to tag expressions. Indeed, consider for a moment that terms carry annotated types. With the obvious adaptation of the typing rules, we would be able to derive $y : \mathrm{Nat}^{\jmath} \vdash M\ (\mathsf{s}\ y) : \mathrm{Nat}^{\jmath}$, where M is

$$\mathsf{letrec}\ f : \mathrm{Nat}^{\imath} \rightarrow \mathrm{Nat}^{\imath} = \lambda x : \mathrm{Nat}^{\widehat{\imath}}.\ \mathsf{case}_{\mathrm{Nat}^{\imath}}\ x\ \mathsf{of}\ \{\mathsf{o} \Rightarrow \mathsf{o} \mid \mathsf{s}\ x' \Rightarrow (\lambda z : \mathrm{Nat}^{\imath}.z)\ x'\}$$

With the obvious adaptation of the reduction rules, one would also derive that $M\ (\mathsf{s}\ y)$ reduces to $(\lambda z : \mathrm{Nat}^{\imath}.z)y$. However, the latter is obviously ill-typed. Intuitively, the failure of subject reduction is caused by the combination of implicit stage polymorphism with explicit stage annotations in the tags of λ-expressions.

2.5 Strong Normalization

Type-based termination is meant to enforce strong normalization of recursive definitions, therefore it is important to show that every typable expression in $F^{\frown}$ is strongly normalizing. The latter can be established by adapting standard model constructions based on saturated sets, see [5].

3 Inference Algorithm

The purpose of this section is to define a sound and complete inference algorithm which computes for every context and expression a most general typing of the form $C \Rightarrow \overline{\sigma}$ where C is a set (i.e. conjunction) of constraints, and $\overline{\sigma}$ is an annotated type.

Definition 7 (Constraint and Constraint Systems).

1. *A* stage constraint *is a pair of stages, written* $s_1 \sqsubseteq s_2$.
2. *A* constraint system *is a finite set of stage constraints.*
3. *A stage substitution* ρ *satisfies a constraint system* C, *written* $\rho \models C$, *if for every constraint* $s_1 \sqsubseteq s_2$ *in* C, *we have* $\rho s_1 \sqsubseteq \rho s_2$.

Every constraint system has an obvious solution which maps all stage variables for ∞. Furthermore, each subtyping constraint $\overline{\sigma} \preceq \overline{\tau}$ which has a solution yields a constraint system C. In the sequel, we often write $\overline{\sigma} \preceq \overline{\tau}$ instead of C. Finally, we equate ∞ with $\widehat{\infty}$.

3.1 Discussion

Before describing the algorithm, we would like to illustrate two issues with efficient size annotation: the lack of unconstrained principal types, and the need for position types.

Lack of unconstrained principal types. This issue is pervasive in type systems with subtyping, but we sketch how it can be cast it to our setting. Consider the expression twice, defined as $\lambda f : \mathrm{Nat} \rightarrow \mathrm{Nat}.\lambda x : \mathrm{Nat}.f\ (f\ x)$, and which can be

given the typings $\tau_1 \equiv (\mathrm{Nat}^{\imath} \to \mathrm{Nat}^{\imath}) \to \mathrm{Nat}^{\imath} \to \mathrm{Nat}^{\imath}$ and also $\tau_2 \equiv (\mathrm{Nat}^{\imath} \to \mathrm{Nat}^{\infty}) \to \mathrm{Nat}^{\imath} \to \mathrm{Nat}^{\infty}$. If there would exist an unconstrained principal type $\tau_0 \equiv (\mathrm{Nat}^{s_1} \to \mathrm{Nat}^{s_2}) \to \mathrm{Nat}^{s_3} \to \mathrm{Nat}^{s_4}$, such that $\mathsf{twice} : \tau_0$ then we would have two stage substitutions ρ and ρ' such that $\rho\tau_0 \preceq \tau_1$ and $\rho'\tau_0 \preceq \tau_2$. Using the soundness of the inference algorithm (Proposition 5) and some elementary reasoning one can show that no such substitutions exist.
The same example can be used to show that the completeness statement of the inference algorithm must involve both subtyping and stage substitution.

Need for annotated types. Consider the most general typings

$$\begin{array}{c} \mathsf{letrec}\ f : \mathrm{Nat}^{\star} \to \mathrm{Nat}^{\star} = \lambda x : \mathrm{Nat}.\mathsf{o} : \mathrm{Nat}^{\imath} \to \mathrm{Nat}^{\imath} \\ \mathsf{letrec}\ f : \mathrm{Nat}^{\star} \to \mathrm{Nat} = \lambda x : \mathrm{Nat}.\mathsf{o} : \mathrm{Nat}^{\imath} \to \mathrm{Nat}^{\widehat{\jmath}} \end{array}$$

Would we omit $\star$ in the tags of the recursive definitions, then $\mathsf{letrec}\ f : \mathrm{Nat} \to \mathrm{Nat} = \lambda x : \mathrm{Nat}.\mathsf{o}$ would not have a most general typing. Indeed, such a most general typing would be of the form $C \Rightarrow \mathrm{Nat}^{\imath_1} \to \mathrm{Nat}^{\imath_2}$ with the substitutions $[\imath_1 := \imath, \imath_2 := \imath] \models C$ and $[\imath_1 := \imath, \imath_2 := \widehat{\jmath}] \models C$. By elementary reasoning, we can show that it is impossible. In order to recover a most general typing, it will be required to allow both disjunctions and conjunctions of constraints in C. Unfortunately, disjunction makes types more complex to compute and to grasp.

3.2 Algorithm

The inference algorithm $\mathrm{Infer}(V, \overline{\Gamma}, t)$ take as input a context $\overline{\Gamma}$, an expression e and an auxiliary parameter V that represents the stage variables that have been previously used during inference (we need the latter to guarantee that we only introduce fresh variables). It returns a tuple $(V', C, \overline{\tau})$ where $\overline{\tau}$ is an annotated type, C is a constraint system, and V' is an extended set of stage variables that has been used by the algorithm. The invariants are $\mathsf{FV}(\overline{\Gamma}) \subseteq V$ and $V \subseteq V'$ and $\mathsf{FV}(C, \overline{\tau}) \subseteq V'$. For practical reasons, we also use a second algorithm $\mathrm{Check}(V, \overline{\Gamma}, t, \overline{\tau})$ which return a pair (V', C) ensuring that t has type $\overline{\tau}$ in environment $\overline{\Gamma}$. The invariants are $\mathsf{FV}(\overline{\Gamma}, \overline{\tau}) \subseteq V$ and $V \subseteq V'$ and $\mathsf{FV}(C) \subseteq V'$.

Definition 8. *The algorithms* Infer *and* Check *are defined in Figure 2.*

Note that the algorithms rely on auxiliary functions Annot, AnnotRec and RecCheck. $\mathrm{Annot}(\sigma, V) = (\overline{\sigma}, V')$ where V is a set of stage variables, σ a bare type. $\overline{\sigma}$ is an annotated version of σ with fresh stage variables (that do not belong to V) and $V' = V \bigcup \mathsf{FV}(\overline{\sigma})$. The only stage expressions that appear in $\overline{\sigma}$ are distinct and fresh stage variables. The second function AnnotRec is similar, but takes as input a position type instead of a bare type and returns $(\overline{\sigma}, V', V^{\star})$ where $V^{\star}$ is the set of fresh stage variables that appear in $\overline{\sigma}$ where there was a $\star$ in the original position type.

The function RecCheck is at the core of guaranteeing termination: it takes as input the set of constraints that has been inferred for the body of the recursive definition, and either returns an error if the definition is unsound w.r.t. the type

$$
\begin{array}{lll}
\text{Check}(V,\overline{\Gamma},e,\overline{\tau}) & = & V_e, C_e \cup \overline{\tau}_e \preceq \overline{\tau} \\
& & \text{where } (V_e, C_e, \overline{\tau}_e) := \text{Infer}(\overline{\Gamma}, e) \\
\text{Infer}(V,\overline{\Gamma},x) & = & V, \emptyset, \overline{\Gamma}(x) \\
\text{Infer}(V,\overline{\Gamma},\lambda x:\tau_1.e) & = & V_e, C_e, \overline{\tau}_1 \to \overline{\tau}_2 \\
& & \text{where } V_1, \overline{\tau}_1 := \text{annot}(V,\tau_1) \\
& & \quad (V_e, C_e, \overline{\tau}_2) := \text{Infer}(V_1, \overline{\Gamma}; x{:}\overline{\tau}_1, e) \\
\text{Infer}(V,\overline{\Gamma},\Lambda A.e) & = & V_e, C_e, \forall A.\overline{\tau} \\
& & \text{where } (V_e, C_e, \overline{\tau}) := \text{Infer}(V, \overline{\Gamma}, e) \\
& & \text{if } A \text{ does not occur in } \overline{\Gamma} \\
\text{Infer}(V,\overline{\Gamma},e_1\, e_2) & = & V_2, C_1 \cup C_2, \overline{\tau} \\
& & \text{where } (V_1, C_1, \overline{\tau}_2 \to \overline{\tau}) := \text{Infer}(V, \overline{\Gamma}, e_1) \\
& & \quad (V_2, C_2) := \text{Check}(V_1, \overline{\Gamma}, e_2, \overline{\tau}_2) \\
\text{Infer}(V,\overline{\Gamma},e\, \tau) & = & V_e, C_e, \overline{\tau}_e[A := \overline{\tau}] \\
& & \text{where } V_1, \overline{\tau} := \text{annot}(V,\tau) \\
& & \quad (V_e, C_e, \forall A.\overline{\tau}_e) := \text{Infer}(V_1, \overline{\Gamma}, e) \\
\text{Infer}(V,\overline{\Gamma},c) & = & V \cup \{\alpha\},, \mathsf{Type}(c,\alpha) \\
& & \text{with } \alpha \notin V \\
\text{Infer}(V,\overline{\Gamma},\mathsf{case}_\theta\; e' \;\mathsf{of}\; \{c_i \Rightarrow e_i\}) & = & V_n, s \sqsubseteq \widehat{\alpha} \cup C_{e'} \cup \bigcup_{i=1}^n C_i, \overline{\theta} \\
& & \text{where } \alpha \notin V \\
& & \quad V_\theta, \overline{\theta} := \text{annot}(V \cup \{\alpha\}, \theta) \\
& & \quad (V_0, C_{e'}, d^s\overline{\boldsymbol{\tau}}) := \text{Infer}(V_\theta, \overline{\Gamma}, e') \\
& & \quad (V_i, C_i) := \text{Check}(V_{i-1}, \overline{\Gamma}, e_i, \mathsf{Inst}(c_i, \alpha, \overline{\boldsymbol{\tau}}, \overline{\theta})) \\
& & \text{if } \mathsf{C}(d) = \{c_1, \ldots, c_n\} \\
\text{Infer}(V,\overline{\Gamma},\mathsf{letrec}\; f : d^\star\boldsymbol{\tau} \to \theta = e') & = & V_{e'}, C_f, d^\alpha\overline{\boldsymbol{\tau}} \to \overline{\theta} \\
& & \text{where } (V_1, V^\star, d^\alpha\overline{\boldsymbol{\tau}} \to \overline{\theta}) := \text{annotrec}(V, d^\star\boldsymbol{\tau} \to \theta) \\
& & \quad \widehat{\theta} := \overline{\theta}[\alpha_i := \widehat{\alpha_i}]_{\alpha_i \in V^\star} \\
& & (V_{e'}, C_{e'}) := \text{Check}(V_1, \overline{\Gamma}; f{:}d^\alpha\overline{\boldsymbol{\tau}} \to \overline{\theta}, e', d^{\widehat{\alpha}}\overline{\boldsymbol{\tau}} \to \widehat{\theta}) \\
& & \quad C_f := \text{RecCheck}(\alpha, V^\star, V_1 \backslash V^\star, C_{e'} \cup \overline{\theta} \preceq \widehat{\theta})
\end{array}
$$

Fig. 2. Inference Algorithm

system, or the set of constraints for the recursive definition, if the definition is sound w.r.t. the type system. Formally, the function RecCheck takes as input:

- the stage variable α which corresponds to the recursive argument, and which must be mapped to a fresh base stage $\imath$;
- a set of stage variables $V^\star$ that must be mapped to a stage expression with the same base stage as α. The set $V^\star$ is determined by the position types in the tag of the recursive definition. In particular, we have $\alpha \in V^\star$;
- a set of stage variables $V^{\neq}$ that must be mapped to a stage expression with a base stage different from $\imath$;
- a set of constraints C';

and returns an error or a set of constraints subject to the conditions below. To express these conditions concisely, we use $\rho \leq_{V_1}^{V_2} \rho'$ as a shorthand for $\rho(\alpha) \sqsubseteq \rho'(\alpha)$

for all $\alpha \in V_1$ and $\rho(\alpha) = \rho'(\alpha)$ for all $\alpha \in V_2$ and $\circ$ to denote the usual composition of substitutions. Furthermore, we freely use set notation.

Soundness (SRC): if $\text{RecCheck}(\alpha, V^\star, V^{\neq}, C') = C$ then for all stage substitutions ρ such that $\rho \models C$ there exists a fresh stage variable $\imath$ and a stage substitution ρ' such that $\rho' \models C'$, and $\rho'(\alpha) = \imath$, and $[\imath := \rho(\alpha)] \circ \rho' \leq_{V^\star}^{V^{\neq}} \rho$, and $\lfloor \rho'(V^\star) \rfloor = \imath$, and $\lfloor \rho'(V^{\neq}) \rfloor \neq \imath$ (the last two formulas state respectively that for all $\alpha_i \in V^\star$, $\lfloor \rho'(\alpha_i) \rfloor = \imath$, and for all $\beta \in V^{\neq}$, $\lfloor \rho'(\beta) \rfloor \neq \imath$).

Completeness (CRC): if $\rho(\alpha) = \imath$ and $\lfloor \rho(V^\star) \rfloor = \imath$ and $\lfloor \rho(V^{\neq}) \rfloor \neq \imath$ and also $\rho \models C'$ then $\text{RecCheck}(\alpha, V^\star, V^{\neq}, C')$ is defined and

$$\rho \models \text{RecCheck}(\alpha, V^\star, V^{\neq}, C')$$

The algorithm for computing RecCheck, and the proofs of correctness, are given in Section 3.4.

3.3 Soundness and Completeness

In order to establish soundness and completeness of the inference and checking algorithms, we must prove some preliminary lemmas. The first lemma provides a characterization of positivity which we use for dealing with the positivity constraints of the (rec) rule.

Lemma 2. $\imath \ \mathsf{pos}\ \overline{\tau} \Leftrightarrow \overline{\tau} \preceq \overline{\tau}[\imath := \widehat{\imath}]$

In the sequel, we use the notation $V \ \mathsf{pos}\ \overline{\tau}$ as a shorthand for $\overline{\tau} \preceq \overline{\tau}[\alpha := \widehat{\alpha}]_{\alpha \in V}$. The second and third lemmas are concerned with stage substitutions.

Lemma 3. *If* $\rho \leq_{V_1}^{V_2} \rho' \wedge \mathsf{FV}(\overline{\tau}) \subseteq V_1 \cup V_2 \wedge V_1 \ \mathsf{pos}\ \overline{\tau}$ *then* $\rho(\overline{\tau}) \preceq \rho'(\overline{\tau})$

Lemma 4. *If* $\lfloor \rho(V) \rfloor = \imath$ *then* $\rho(\overline{\tau})[\imath := \widehat{\imath}] = \rho(\overline{\tau}[\alpha_i := \widehat{\alpha_i}]_{\alpha_i \in V})$.

We now turn to soundness.

Lemma 5 (Soundness). *Check and Infer are sound:*

$$\begin{array}{rcl} \mathit{Check}(V, \overline{\Gamma}, e, \overline{\tau}) = (V', C) & \Rightarrow & \forall \rho \models C.\ \rho(\overline{\Gamma}) \vdash e : \rho(\overline{\tau}) \\ \mathit{Infer}(V, \overline{\Gamma}, e) = (V', C, \overline{\tau}) & \Rightarrow & \forall \rho \models C.\ \rho(\overline{\Gamma}) \vdash e : \rho(\overline{\tau}) \end{array}$$

Proof. We prove the two statements simultaneously. Note that the first statement can be deduced easily from the second one.

Indeed, assume that $\text{Check}(V, \overline{\Gamma}, e, \overline{\tau}) = (V', C)$ and that $\rho \models C$. By definition of Check, we have $\text{Infer}(V, \overline{\Gamma}, e) = (V', C_e, \overline{\tau}_e)$ and $\rho \models C_e \cup \overline{\tau}_e \preceq \overline{\tau}$, so $\rho \models C_e$ and $\rho(\overline{\tau}_e) \preceq \rho(\overline{\tau})$. Assuming the first statement, it follows that $\rho(\overline{\Gamma}) \vdash e : \rho(\overline{\tau}_e)$ and we conclude using the (sub) rule.

Therefore we focus on the proof of the second statement, by induction on the structure of e:

Cases $e \equiv x$ and $e \equiv \Lambda A.e_1$ $e \equiv c$. Trivial.

Cases $e \equiv \lambda x : \tau_1.e_1$ and $e \equiv t\ \tau_1$. The result follows from the induction hypothesis and the facts that both $|\mathrm{annot}(\tau_1, V)| = \tau_1$ and $\rho(\overline{\tau}_e[A := \overline{\tau}_1]) = \rho(\overline{\tau}_e)[A := \rho(\overline{\tau}_1)]$.

Case $e \equiv e_1\ e_2$. By hypothesis, $\rho \models C_1 \cup C_2$ so $\rho \models C_1$ and $\rho \models C_2$. By the induction hypotheses, $\rho(\overline{\Gamma}) \vdash e_1 : \rho(\overline{\tau}_2) \to \rho(\overline{\tau})$ and $\rho(\overline{\Gamma}) \vdash e_2 : \rho(\overline{\tau}_2)$. We conclude using the (app) rule.

Case $e \equiv \mathsf{case}_\theta\ e'$ of $\{c_i \Rightarrow e_i\}$. By hypothesis, $\rho \models s \sqsubseteq \widehat{\alpha} \cup C_{e'} \cup \bigcup_{i=1}^{n} C_i$. By induction hypotheses, $\rho(\overline{\Gamma}) \vdash e' : \rho(d^s \boldsymbol{\tau})$ and for every $c_i \in \mathsf{C}(d)$

$$\rho(\overline{\Gamma}) \vdash e_i : \rho(\mathsf{Inst}(c_i, \alpha, \overline{\boldsymbol{\tau}}, \overline{\theta})) = \mathsf{Inst}(c_i, \rho(\alpha), \rho(\overline{\boldsymbol{\tau}}), \rho(\overline{\theta}))$$

Using the (sub) rule and the fact that $\rho(s) \sqsubseteq \rho(\widehat{\alpha})$, we derive

$$\rho(\overline{\Gamma}) \vdash e' : \rho(d^{\widehat{\alpha}} \boldsymbol{\tau})$$

and conclude using the (case) rule.

Case $e \equiv \mathsf{letrec}\ f : d^\star \boldsymbol{\tau} \to \theta = e'$. By hypothesis,

$$\rho \models \mathrm{RecCheck}(\alpha, V^\star, V_1^{\neq}, C_{e'} \cup \overline{\theta} \preceq \widehat{\theta})$$

By (SRC), there exists $\imath$ and ρ' such that $\rho' \models C_{e'}$. Using the induction hypothesis with ρ', we get $\rho'(\overline{\Gamma}); f : d^{\imath} \rho'(\overline{\boldsymbol{\tau}}) \to \rho'(\overline{\theta}) \vdash e' : d^{\widehat{\imath}} \rho'(\overline{\boldsymbol{\tau}}) \to \rho'(\widehat{\theta})$. So by Lemma 4 : $\rho'(\overline{\Gamma}); f : d^{\imath} \rho'(\overline{\boldsymbol{\tau}}) \to \rho'(\overline{\theta}) \vdash e' : d^{\imath} \rho'(\overline{\boldsymbol{\tau}}) \to \rho'(\overline{\theta})[\imath := \widehat{\imath}]$.
Because $\rho' \models \overline{\theta} \preceq \widehat{\theta}$, we know that $\imath$ pos $\rho'(\overline{\theta})$ by lemma 2. We also know from (SRC) that $\imath \notin \rho'(\overline{\Gamma}), \rho'(\overline{\boldsymbol{\tau}})$. Let s be $\rho(\alpha)$, by application of the (rec) typing rule we obtain $\rho'(\overline{\Gamma}) \vdash e : d^s \rho'(\overline{\boldsymbol{\tau}}) \to \rho'(\overline{\theta})[\imath := s]$. Finally we use the facts that $[\imath := s] \circ \rho' \leq_{V^\star}^{V_1^{\neq}} \rho$, $V^\star$ pos $\overline{\theta}$ and Lemma 3 to conclude that e has the expected type.

We now turn to completeness. Note that, for the proofs to go through, the statement of completeness is slightly stronger than the one of the introduction: we require $\rho =_V \rho'$ instead of $\rho(\overline{\Gamma}) = \rho'(\overline{\Gamma})$, where $\rho =_V \rho'$ iff $\rho(\alpha) = \rho'(\alpha)$ for all $\alpha \in V$.

Lemma 6 (Completeness). *Check and Infer are complete:*

1. *If* $\rho(\overline{\Gamma}) \vdash e : \rho\overline{\tau}$ *and* $\mathsf{FV}(\overline{\Gamma}, \overline{\tau}) \subseteq V$ *then there exist* V', C, ρ' *such that* *Check*$(V, \overline{\Gamma}, e, \overline{\tau}) = (V', C)$ *and* $\rho' \models C \wedge \rho =_V \rho'$.
2. *If* $\rho(\overline{\Gamma}) \vdash e : \overline{\theta}$ *and* $\mathsf{FV}(\overline{\Gamma}) \subseteq V$ *there exist* $V', C, \overline{\tau}, \rho'$ *such that* *Infer*$(V, \overline{\Gamma}, e) = (V', C, \overline{\tau})$ *and* $\rho' \models C$ *and* $\rho'(\overline{\tau}) \preceq \overline{\theta}$ *and* $\rho' =_V \rho$

Proof. We prove the two statements simultaneously. Note that the first statement can be deduced easily from the second one. Indeed, assume that $\rho(\overline{\Gamma}) \vdash e : \rho\overline{\tau}$ with $\mathsf{FV}(\overline{\Gamma}, \overline{\tau}) \subseteq V$. Using the completeness of inference, there exists V', C, $\overline{\tau}_1$, ρ' such that $\mathrm{Infer}(V, \overline{\Gamma}, e) = (V', C, \overline{\tau}_1)$, $\rho' \models C$, $\rho'(\overline{\tau}_1) \preceq \rho(\overline{\tau})$ and $\rho' =_V \rho$. Because $\mathsf{FV}(\overline{\tau}) \subseteq V$, we have $\rho(\overline{\tau}) = \rho'(\overline{\tau})$, so we conclude easily.

Therefore, we focus on the proof of the second statement, by induction on the typing derivation:

Cases (var) and (sub). Trivial.

Case (abs). Let $e = \lambda x : \overline{\tau}_1.e'$ and $(V_1, \overline{\tau}_1) = \text{annot}(V, |\overline{\sigma}_1|)$, by definition of annot, variables in $\overline{\tau}_1$ do not appear in V, so we can choose ρ_1 such that $\rho_1 =_V \rho$ and $\rho_1(\overline{\tau}_1) = \overline{\sigma}$. By induction hypotheses we have that $\text{Infer}(V_1, \overline{\Gamma}; x : \overline{\tau}_1, e') = (V', C, \overline{\tau}_2)$ and $\rho' \models C$, $\rho'(\overline{\tau}_2) \preceq \overline{\sigma}_2$ $\rho' =_{V_1} \rho_1$. It is easy to conclude.

Case (app), (T-abs), (T-app). Similar to (abs), just remark for the last one that $\overline{\tau} \preceq \overline{\sigma}$ implies $\overline{\tau}[A := \overline{\tau}'] \preceq \overline{\sigma}[A := \overline{\tau}']$.

Case (cons). Choose $\rho' = \rho[\alpha := s]$ and conclude.

Case (case). Let $e = \mathsf{case}_{|\overline{\sigma}|}\ e'\ \mathsf{of}\ \{\boldsymbol{c_i} \Rightarrow \boldsymbol{e_i}\}$ and $(V_\sigma, \overline{\sigma}') = \text{annot}(V \cup \{\alpha\}, |\overline{\sigma}|)$. Choose ρ_σ such that $\rho_\sigma =_V \rho$, $\rho_\sigma(\alpha) = s$ and $\rho_\sigma(\overline{\sigma}') = \overline{\sigma}$. By induction hypotheses, the type checking of branches succeeds. So we can easily conclude.

Case (rec). Let $e = \mathsf{fix}\ f : \tau^\star.e'$, with $\tau^\star$ is $\imath$-compatible with $d^\imath\overline{\boldsymbol{\tau}} \to \overline{\theta}$. Let $(V_1, V^\star, d^\alpha\overline{\boldsymbol{\tau}}' \to \overline{\theta}') = \text{annotrec}(V, \tau^\star)$ and choose ρ_1 such that $\rho_1 =_V \rho$, $\rho_1(d^\alpha\overline{\boldsymbol{\tau}}' \to \overline{\theta}') = d^\imath\overline{\boldsymbol{\tau}} \to \overline{\theta}$, in particular we have $\rho_1(\alpha) = \imath$. By induction hypothesis $\text{Check}(V_1, \overline{\Gamma}; f : d^\alpha\overline{\boldsymbol{\tau}}' \to \overline{\theta}', e', d^{\widehat{\alpha}}\overline{\boldsymbol{\tau}}' \to \widehat{\theta}') = (V_{e'}, C_{e'})$ and there exists $\rho_{e'} =_{V_1} \rho_1$ such that $\rho_{e'} \models C_{e'}$. By soundness,

$$\rho_{e'}(\overline{\Gamma}; f : d^\alpha\overline{\boldsymbol{\tau}}' \to \overline{\theta}') \vdash e' : \rho_{e'}(d^{\widehat{\alpha}}\overline{\boldsymbol{\tau}}' \to \widehat{\theta}')$$

By CRC, $\rho_{e'}$ is a solution for C_f. Choose $\rho' = [i := s] \circ \rho_{e'}$ to conclude.

3.4 Implementation of the RecCheck Algorithm

Constraint systems can be represented by a graph where the nodes are stage variables and ∞, and the edges are integers. Concretely, each constraint in C is of the form $\infty \sqsubseteq \widehat{\alpha}^n$, or $\widehat{\alpha}_1^{n_1} \sqsubseteq \widehat{\alpha}_2^{n_2}$. In the first case, one adds an edge from α to ∞ labeled with 0, in the second case one adds an edge from α_2 to α_1 labeled with $n_2 - n_1$. Using Bellman's algorithm, one can then detect negative cycles in the graph, i.e. cycles where the sums of the edges are strictly negative. Such cycles imply $\widehat{\alpha}^{k+1} \sqsubseteq \alpha$, or equivalently $\infty \sqsubseteq \alpha$, for the stage variable α at the beginning of the cycle.

We now turn to the computation of $RecCheck(\alpha, V^\star, V^{\neq}, C)$. Assuming that we intend to map α to a fresh stage variable $\imath$, the computation proceeds as follows:

1. it computes the downwards closed set $S_\imath$ of stage variables that must be mapped to a stage expression with base stage $\imath$. The rules are $V^\star \subseteq S_\imath$, and if $\alpha_1 \in S_\imath$ and $\widehat{\alpha}_2^{n_2} \sqsubseteq \widehat{\alpha}_1^{n_1} \in C$ then $\alpha_2 \in S_\imath$;
2. the algorithm must enforce that α is the smallest variable in $S_\imath$. It does so by adding to C the constraints $\alpha \sqsubseteq S_\imath$. Let $C_1 = C \cup \alpha \sqsubseteq S_\imath$;
3. the algorithm checks for negative cycles in the graph representation of C_1. Each time it finds such a cycle starting from β, the algorithm computes the set $V_{\sqsupseteq\beta}$ of variables greater or equal to β, removes all inequalities about variables in $V_{\sqsupseteq\beta}$ and adds the constraints $\infty \sqsubseteq V_{\sqsupseteq\beta}$. At the end of this step there are no more negative cycles in the graph, and we get a new set of constraints C_2;

4. the algorithm computes the upwards closed set $S_{\imath\sqsubseteq}$ of stage variables that must be mapped to ∞ or to a stage expression with base stage $\imath$. The rules are $S_\imath \subseteq S_{\imath\sqsubseteq}$ and if $\alpha_1 \in S_{\imath\sqsubseteq}$ and $\widehat{\alpha}_1^{n_1} \sqsubseteq \widehat{\alpha}_2^{n_2} \in C_2$ then $\alpha_2 \in S_{\imath\sqsubseteq}$;
5. the algorithm computes the upwards closed set $S_{\neg\imath}$ of stage variables that cannot be mapped to a stage expression with base stage $\imath$. The rules are $V^{\neq} \subseteq S_{\neg\imath}$ and if $\alpha_1 \in S_{\neg\imath}$ and $\widehat{\alpha}_1^{n_1} \sqsubseteq \widehat{\alpha}_2^{n_2} \in C_2$ then α_2 is in $S_{\neg\imath}$;
6. the algorithm sets all variables $\beta \in S_{\neg\imath} \cap S_{\imath\sqsubseteq}$ to ∞ (as in Step 3). At the end of this step we get a new set of constraints C_3;
7. the algorithm computes the upwards closed set S_∞ of stage variables that must be mapped to ∞. If $\infty \sqsubseteq \widehat{\beta}^k \in C_3$ then β is in S_∞, and if $\alpha_1 \in S_\infty$ and $\widehat{\alpha}_1^{n_1} \sqsubseteq \widehat{\alpha}_2^{n_2} \in C_3$ then α_2 is in S_∞.
8. if $S_\infty \cap S_\imath = \emptyset$ the algorithm returns the new set of constraints, else it fails.

Lemma 7 (Soundness of RecCheck). *The algorithm guarantees (SRC).*

Proof. Assume RecCheck$(\alpha, V^\star, V^{\neq}, C') = C$ and let ρ be a stage substitution such that $\rho \models C$. Let $\imath$ be a fresh base stage that does not appear in the codomain of ρ, and let $C_\imath$ be the subset of C that only contains inequalities of the form $\widehat{\alpha}_1^{n_1} \sqsubseteq \widehat{\alpha}_2^{n_2}$ with both $\alpha_i \in S_{\imath\sqsubseteq}$ and $\rho(\alpha_i) \neq \infty$. By definition of the algorithm, there is no negative cycle in the graph representation of $C_\imath$. So we can use the Floyd-Warshall algorithm to compute the shortest path (SP) from α to each variable of $S_{\imath\sqsubseteq}$. Then we set

$$\rho'(\beta) = \begin{cases} \widehat{\imath}^{\mathrm{SP}(\beta)} \text{if } \beta \in S_\imath \vee (\beta \in S_{\imath\sqsubseteq} \wedge \rho(\beta) \neq \infty) \\ \rho(\beta) \text{ otherwise} \end{cases}$$

Let us show that ρ' has the expected properties. By construction, $\imath$ does not appear in $\rho(\beta)$ for $\beta \in V^{\neq}$ and ρ' verifies the first and last two properties required from it in (SRC); hence are left to verify that $\rho' \models C'$ and $[\imath := \rho(\alpha)] \circ \rho' \leq_{V^\star}^{V^{\neq}} \rho$.

We first prove $\rho' \models C'$. Note that constraints of the form $s \sqsubseteq \infty$ are trivially satisfied by ρ', and that $\rho'(s) = \rho(s)$ whenever there is a constraint of the form $\infty \sqsubseteq s$ in C' (in which case the constraint is derivable from C, and hence satisfied by ρ and ρ'). Hence we only need to focus on constraints of the form $\widehat{\beta}_1^{n_1} \sqsubseteq \widehat{\beta}_2^{n_2} \in C'$. We write $\beta \in S_{\mathrm{LP}}$ if $\beta \in S_\imath \vee (\beta \in S_{\imath\sqsubseteq} \wedge \rho(\beta) \neq \infty)$. We proceed by case analysis. There are three cases to treat:

- $\beta_1, \beta_2 \in S_{\mathrm{LP}}$. By definition of SP, the constraint is satisfied by ρ'.
- $\beta_1 \in S_{\mathrm{LP}}$ and $\beta_2 \notin S_{\mathrm{LP}}$. Since $\beta_2 \in S_{\imath\sqsubseteq}$, we must have $\rho(\beta_2) = \infty$. Therefore $\rho'(\beta_2) = \infty$ and the constraint is satisfied by ρ'.
- $\beta_1 \notin S_{\imath\sqsubseteq}$. Necessarily $\beta_2 \notin S_{\imath\sqsubseteq}$ and we conclude as for constraints of the form $\infty \sqsubseteq s$.

Now we prove that $[\imath := \rho(\alpha)] \circ \rho' \leq_{V^\star}^{V^{\neq}} \rho$:

- if $\beta \in V^{\neq}$, we must prove $\rho'(\beta) = \rho(\beta)$. By definition of ρ' it is sufficient to show for all $\beta \in V^{\neq}$ that $\beta \notin S_\imath$, and that if $\beta \in S_{\imath\sqsubseteq}$ then $\rho(\beta) = \infty$.
  For the first statement, we have $S_\imath \cap V^{\neq} = \emptyset$, and for the second statement, we have that if $\beta \in V^{\neq} \cap S_{\imath\sqsubseteq}$ then the algorithm has added a constraint $\infty \sqsubseteq \beta$ so that $\rho(\beta) = \infty$;

– if $\beta \in V^\star$, we must prove $\rho'(\beta)[\imath := \rho(\alpha)] \sqsubseteq \rho(\beta)$. As $\rho \models C$ we have

$$\rho'(\beta)[\imath := \rho(\alpha)] = \widehat{\rho(\alpha)}^{\mathrm{SP}(\beta)} \sqsubseteq \rho(\beta)$$

which concludes the proof.

Note that in the above SP is only used to establish the soundness of RecCheck.

Lemma 8 (Completeness of RecCheck). *The algorithm guarantees (CRC).*

Proof. Assume RecCheck$(\alpha, V^\star, V^{\neq}, C') = C$ and let ρ be a stage substitution s.t. $\rho(\alpha) = \imath$ and $\lfloor \rho(V^\star) \rfloor = \imath$ and $\lfloor \rho(V^{\neq}) \rfloor \neq \imath$ and $\rho \models C'$. To show $\rho \models$ RecCheck$(\alpha, V^\star, V^{\neq}, C')$. We proceed by showing that the constraints introduced by each step of the algorithm are satisfied.

During Step (2), the algorithm adds the constraints $\alpha \sqsubseteq S_\imath$; because $\lfloor \rho(S_\imath) \rfloor = \imath$, and by construction of $S_\imath$, it follows that these constraints are satisfied by ρ.

During Step (3) the algorithm adds the constraints $\infty \sqsubseteq V_{\sqsupseteq \beta}$ each time it finds a negative cycle starting from β. By construction, negative cycles entail that $\widehat{\beta}^{k+1} \sqsubseteq \beta$ is derivable from C. Since ρ satisfies C, it must satisfy all inequalities derivable from C, so necessarily $\infty \sqsubseteq \rho(\beta)$, as expected.

During Step (6) the algorithm adds constraints $\infty \sqsubseteq S_{\neg\imath} \cap S_{\imath\sqsubseteq}$. However, a constraint $\infty \sqsubseteq \alpha$ is only added if one can derive from C that $\widehat{\beta}^k \sqsubseteq \widehat{\alpha}^{k'}$ with $\beta \in V^{\neq}$ and $\imath \sqsubseteq \alpha$. Since ρ satisfies C, it must satisfy all inequalities derivable from C, which forces $\infty \sqsubseteq \rho(\alpha)$, as expected.

3.5 Implementation Issues and Complexity

We have implemented the inference algorithm in OCaml. The implementation also supports global declarations, and performs some additional heuristics to increase readability and compactness of constraints. Roughly speaking, heuristics either try to remove constraints that involve stage variables not occurring in the inferred type (these stage variables are implicitly quantified existentially), or try to exploit positivity or negativity information about the positions in which stage variables occur (we do not loose any solutions by maximizing stage variables that occur negatively, or by minimizing stage variables that occur positively; in the first case it amounts replacing the variable by ∞).

The complexity of the RecCheck algorithm is in n^2 where n is the number of distinct stage variables used in the set of constraints, since it is equivalent to the complexity of Bellman algorithm.

4 Related Work

The origins of type-based termination can be traced back to N. Mendler [13], who considered recursors and corecursors in a fixpoint-like style. The study of type-based termination was further pursued by H. Geuvers [9] who established a comparison between Mendler's formulation and the traditional formulation of recursors, and by E. Giménez [10, 11], who developed a variant of the Calculus of Inductive Definitions based on type-based termination, and established its relationship with the variant that uses a syntactic criterion for termination. Independently, J. Hughes, L. Pareto and A. Sabry [12] studied the use of size types to ensure productivity of reactive programs, and provided a type-checking algorithm for size types.

In an attempt to gain a better understanding of [11] and [12], several authors have studied the meta-theoretical properties of these systems or their variants. In particular, R. Amadio and S. Coupet-Grimal [2] considered type-based termination for coinductive types. Decidability of type-checking for this system is further established in [3]. More recently, G. Barthe, M.J. Frade, E. Giménez, L. Pinto and T. Uustalu [5] introduced $\lambda\widehat{}$ and showed its strong normalization, but did not consider the issue of type checking. Furthermore, A. Abel [1] has studied type-based termination in a non-dependent setting and established decidability of type-checking for his type system (strictly speaking, his result only applies to terms in normal form, as a result of considering a calculus with domain-free abstractions). In a dependent setting, B. Barras [4] pursued the work of [11] by formalizing a variant of Giménez's system, and showed decidability of type-checking. Finally, F. Blanqui [6] considered a variant of the Calculus of Algebraic Constructions where termination of rewrite systems is enforced through typing.

However, these works do not consider the problem of inferring size annotations. To our best knowledge, the first inference algorithm for size types has been developed by W.-N. Chin and S.-C. Khoo [7], who provide an algorithm that infers for every program an annotated type and a formula in Presburger arithmetic to be satisfied by the size variables. Their type system is more powerful than ours, but has a greater complexity. In a similar line of work, H. Xi [16] proposes a system of restricted dependent types, built upon DML [17], to ensure program termination. As in [7], his system features a very rich system with stage arithmetic, and a notion of metric that is very useful to handle functions in several arguments. Expressiveness is achieved at the cost of practicality (some difficulties with scalability are discussed in [7]).

5 Conclusion

The main contribution of this paper is the definition and justification of a practical size inference algorithm for a polymorphic typed λ-calculus combining type-based termination and λ-abstractions *à la Church*. We have tried to motivate our choices in the design of the inference algorithm, and shown its soundness and completeness. Experimentations with an implementation of the algorithm suggests that the algorithm is practical.

In a companion article, we define a sound, complete and terminating size inference algorithm for a type-based variant of the Calculus of Inductive Constructions [15]. We also discuss some experiments with an implementation of the system, notably a formal proof of the correctness of sorting algorithms. Taken together, the results of the two articles demonstrate that it is feasible and indeed desirable that proof assistants such as Coq use type-based termination instead of syntactic termination criteria.

Future work includes implementing type-based termination for Coq, and experimenting with extensions that increase the expressiveness of the type system without compromising the practicality of the inference algorithm.

Acknowledgments. Thanks to the anonymous referees and F. Blanqui for their comments on the paper.

References

1. A. Abel. Termination checking with types. *RAIRO– Theoretical Informatics and Applications*, 38:277–320, October 2004.
2. R. Amadio and S. Coupet-Grimal. Analysis of a guard condition in type theory. In M. Nivat, editor, *Proceedings of FOSSACS'98*, volume 1378 of *Lecture Notes in Computer Science*, pages 48–62. Springer-Verlag, 1998.
3. A. Bac. Un algorithme d'inférence de types pour les types coinductifs. Master's thesis, École Normale Supérieure de Lyon, 1998.
4. B. Barras. *Auto-validation d'un système de preuves avec familles inductives.* PhD thesis, Université Paris 7, 1999.
5. G. Barthe, M. J. Frade, E. Giménez, L. Pinto, and T. Uustalu. Type-based termination of recursive definitions. *Mathematical Structures in Computer Science*, 14:97–141, February 2004.
6. F. Blanqui. A type-based termination criterion for dependently-typed higher-order rewrite systems. In V. van Oostrom, editor, *Proceedings of RTA'04*, volume 3091 of *Lecture Notes in Computer Science*, pages 24–39, 2004.
7. W.-N. Chin and S.-C. Khoo. Calculating sized types. *Higher-Order and Symbolic Computation*, 14(2–3):261–300, September 2001.
8. Coq Development Team. *The Coq Proof Assistant User's Guide. Version 8.0*, January 2004.
9. H. Geuvers. Inductive and coinductive types with iteration and recursion. In B. Nordström, K. Pettersson, and G. Plotkin, editors, *Informal proceedings of Logical Frameworks'92*, pages 193–217, 1992.
10. E. Giménez. *Un calcul de constructions infinies et son application à la vérification de systèmes communicants.* PhD thesis, Ecole Normale Superieure de Lyon, 1996.
11. E. Giménez. Structural recursive definitions in Type Theory. In K.G. Larsen, S. Skyum, and G. Winskel, editors, *Proceedings of ICALP'98*, volume 1443 of *Lecture Notes in Computer Science*, pages 397–408. Springer-Verlag, 1998.
12. J. Hughes, L. Pareto, and A. Sabry. Proving the correctness of reactive systems using sized types. In *Proceedings of POPL'96*, pages 410–423. ACM Press, 1996.
13. N. P. Mendler. Inductive types and type constraints in the second-order lambda calculus. *Annals of Pure and Applied Logic*, 51(1-2):159–172, March 1991.
14. M. Steffen. *Polarized Higher-order Subtyping.* PhD thesis, Department of Computer Science, University of Erlangen, 1997.
15. B. Werner. *Méta-théorie du Calcul des Constructions Inductives.* PhD thesis, Université Paris 7, 1994.
16. H. Xi. Dependent Types for Program Termination Verification. In *Proceedings of LICS'01*, pages 231–242. IEEE Computer Society Press, 2001.
17. H. Xi and F. Pfenning. Dependent types in practical programming. In *Proceedings of POPL'99*, pages 214–227. ACM Press, 1999.

Relational Reasoning in a Nominal Semantics for Storage

Nick Benton[1] and Benjamin Leperchey[2]

[1] Microsoft Research, Cambridge
[2] PPS, Université Denis Diderot, Paris

Abstract. We give a monadic semantics in the category of FM-cpos to a higher-order CBV language with recursion and dynamically allocated mutable references that may store both ground data and the addresses of other references, but not functions. This model is adequate, though far from fully abstract. We then develop a relational reasoning principle over the denotational model, and show how it may be used to establish various contextual equivalences involving allocation and encapsulation of store.

1 Introduction

The search for good models and reasoning principles for programming languages with mutable storage has a long history [21], and we are still some way from a fully satisfactory account of general dynamically-allocated storage in higher-order languages. Here we take a small step forward, building on the work of Pitts and Stark on an operational logical relation for an ML-like language with integer references [12], that of Reddy and Yang on a parametric model for a divergence-free, Pascal-like language with heap-allocated references [14] and that of Shinwell and Pitts on an FM-cpo model of FreshML [17].

Section 2 introduces MILler, a monadic, monomorphic, ML-like language with references storing integers or the addresses of other references. Section 3 defines a computationally adequate denotational semantics for MILler by using a continuation monad over FM-cpos (cpos with an action by permutations on location names). Working with FM-cpos is much like doing ordinary domain theory; although it is technically equivalent to using pullback preserving functors from the category of finite sets and injections into Cpo, it is significantly more concrete and convenient in practice. The basic model in FM-cpo gives us an elegant interpretation of dynamic allocation, but fails to validate most interesting equivalences involving the use of encapsulated state.

Section 4 defines a logical relation over our model, parameterized by relations on stores that specify explicitly both a part of the store accessible to an expression and a separated (non-interfering) invariant that is preserved by the context. Section 5 uses the relation to establish a number of equivalences involving the encapsulation of dynamically allocated references, and shows the incompleteness of our reasoning principle. A fuller account of this work, including proofs, more discussion and examples may be found in the companion technical report [2].

P. Urzyczyn (Ed.): TLCA 2005, LNCS 3461, pp. 86–101, 2005.

2 The Language

MILler (MIL-lite with extended references), is a CBV, monadically-typed λ-calculus with recursion and dynamically allocated references. It is a close relative of the MIL-lite fragment [1] of the intermediate language of MLj and SML.NET, and of ReFS [12]. MILler distinguishes *value types*, τ, from *computation types*, of the form $\mathbf{T}\tau$. The *storable types*, σ, are a subset of the value types:

$$\begin{aligned}\tau &::= \text{unit} \mid \text{int} \mid \sigma\ \text{ref} \mid \tau \times \tau \mid \tau + \tau \mid \tau \to \mathbf{T}\tau\\ \sigma &::= \text{int} \mid \sigma\ \text{ref}\\ \gamma &::= \tau \mid \mathbf{T}\tau\end{aligned}$$

Typing contexts, Γ, are finite maps from variable names to value types. We assume an infinite set of locations $\mathbb{L}$, ranged over by ℓ. Store types Δ are finite maps from locations to storable types. Terms, G, are subdivided into values, V, and computations, M:

$$\begin{aligned}V &::= x \mid \underline{n} \mid \underline{\ell} \mid () \mid (V, V') \mid \text{in}_i^{\tau} V \mid \text{rec}\ f(x{:}\tau){:}\tau' = M\\ M &::= V\ V' \mid \text{let}\ x \Leftarrow M\ \text{in}\ M' \mid \text{val}\ V \mid \pi_i V \mid \text{ref}\ V \mid !V \mid V := V'\\ &\mid \text{case}\ V\ \text{of}\ \text{in}_1 x \Rightarrow M\ ;\ \text{in}_2 x \Rightarrow M'\\ &\mid V = V' \mid V + V' \mid \text{iszero}\ V\end{aligned}$$

Some of the typing rules for MILler are shown in Figure 1. One can define syntactic sugar for booleans, conditionals, non-recursive λ-abstractions, sequencing of commands, etc. in the obvious way.

States, Σ, are finite maps from locations to $\mathbb{Z} + \mathbb{L}$. We write $\text{in}_{\mathbb{Z}}$,$\text{in}_{\mathbb{L}}$ for the injections and $\Sigma[\ell \mapsto \text{in}_{\mathbb{Z}} n]$ (resp.$\text{in}_{\mathbb{L}}$) for updating.

Definition 1 (Typed States and Equivalence). If Σ,Σ' are states, and Δ is a store type, we write $\Sigma \sim \Sigma' : \Delta$ to mean $\forall \ell \in \text{dom}\,\Delta, \Sigma \sim \Sigma' : (\ell : \Delta(\ell))$,

$$(rec)\frac{\Delta; \Gamma, x : \tau, f : \tau \to \mathbf{T}(\tau') \vdash M : \mathbf{T}(\tau')}{\Delta; \Gamma \vdash (\text{rec}\ f(x{:}\tau){:}\tau' = M) : \tau \to \mathbf{T}(\tau')} \qquad (loc)\frac{\ell : \sigma \in \Delta}{\Delta; \Gamma \vdash \underline{\ell} : \sigma\ \text{ref}}$$

$$(app)\frac{\Delta; \Gamma \vdash V_1 : \tau \to \mathbf{T}\tau' \quad \Delta; \Gamma \vdash V_2 : \tau}{\Delta; \Gamma \vdash V_1\ V_2 : \mathbf{T}\tau'}$$

$$(let)\frac{\Delta; \Gamma \vdash M_1 : \mathbf{T}(\tau_1) \quad \Delta; \Gamma, x : \tau_1 \vdash M_2 : \mathbf{T}(\tau_2)}{\Delta; \Gamma \vdash \text{let}\ x \Leftarrow M_1\ \text{in}\ M_2 : \mathbf{T}(\tau_2)} \qquad (val)\frac{\Delta; \Gamma \vdash V : \tau}{\Delta; \Gamma \vdash \text{val}\ V : \mathbf{T}(\tau)}$$

$$(eq)\frac{\Delta; \Gamma \vdash V_1 : \sigma\ \text{ref} \quad \Delta; \Gamma \vdash V_2 : \sigma\ \text{ref}}{\Delta; \Gamma \vdash V_1 = V_2 : \mathbf{T}(\text{unit} + \text{unit})} \qquad (deref)\frac{\Delta; \Gamma \vdash V : \sigma\ \text{ref}}{\Delta; \Gamma \vdash !V : \mathbf{T}\sigma}$$

$$(alloc)\frac{\Delta; \Gamma \vdash V : \sigma}{\Delta; \Gamma \vdash \text{ref}\ V : \mathbf{T}(\sigma\ \text{ref})} \qquad (assign)\frac{\Delta; \Gamma \vdash V_1 : \sigma\ \text{ref} \quad \Delta; \Gamma \vdash V_2 : \sigma}{\Delta; \Gamma \vdash V_1 := V_2 : \mathbf{T}(\text{unit})}$$

Fig. 1. Type Rules for MILler (extract)

$$\frac{}{\Sigma, \text{let } x \Leftarrow \text{val } V \text{ in val } x \downarrow} \qquad \frac{\Sigma, \text{let } y \Leftarrow M[V/x] \text{ in } K \downarrow}{\Sigma, \text{let } x \Leftarrow \text{val } V \text{ in } (\text{let } y \Leftarrow M \text{ in } K) \downarrow}$$

$$\frac{\Sigma, \text{let } x_2 \Leftarrow M_1 \text{ in } (\text{let } x_1 \Leftarrow M_2 \text{ in } K) \downarrow}{\Sigma, \text{let } x_1 \Leftarrow (\text{let } x_2 \Leftarrow M_1 \text{ in } M_2) \text{ in } K \downarrow}$$

$$\frac{\Sigma, \text{let } x_1 \Leftarrow M[V/x_2, (\text{rec } f(x_2 : \tau_1) : \tau_2 = M)/f] \text{ in } K \downarrow}{\Sigma, \text{let } x_1 \Leftarrow (\text{rec } f(x_2 : \tau_1) : \tau_2 = M)\ V \text{ in } K \downarrow}$$

$$\frac{\Sigma, \text{let } x \Leftarrow \text{val } \mathit{false} \text{ in } K \downarrow}{\Sigma, \text{let } x \Leftarrow \underline{\ell} = \underline{\ell'} \text{ in } K \downarrow}\ \ell \neq \ell' \qquad \frac{\Sigma[\ell \mapsto \mathit{in}_{\mathbb{L}}\ell'], \text{let } x \Leftarrow \text{val } () \text{ in } K \downarrow}{\Sigma, \text{let } x \Leftarrow \underline{\ell} := \underline{\ell'} \text{ in } K \downarrow}$$

$$\frac{\Sigma(\ell) = \mathit{in}_{\mathbb{L}}\ell' \quad \Sigma, \text{let } x \Leftarrow \text{val } \underline{\ell'} \text{ in } K \downarrow}{\Sigma, \text{let } x \Leftarrow !\underline{\ell} \text{ in } K \downarrow}$$

$$\frac{\Sigma[\ell \mapsto \mathit{in}_{\mathbb{L}}\ell'], \text{let } x \Leftarrow \text{val } \underline{\ell} \text{ in } K \downarrow}{\Sigma, \text{let } x \Leftarrow \text{ref } \underline{\ell'} \text{ in } K \downarrow}\ \ell \notin \mathit{locs}(\Sigma) \cup \mathit{locs}(K) \cup \{\ell'\}$$

Fig. 2. Operational Semantics of MILler (extract)

where $\Sigma \sim \Sigma' : (\ell : \text{int})$ means $\exists n \in \mathbb{Z}. \Sigma\ell = \text{in}_{\mathbb{Z}} n = \Sigma'\ell$ and $\Sigma \sim \Sigma' : (\ell : \sigma' \text{ ref})$ means $\exists \ell' \in \mathbb{L}. \Sigma\ell = \text{in}_{\mathbb{L}}\ell' = \Sigma'\ell \wedge \Sigma \sim \Sigma' : (\ell' : \sigma')$. We say that a state Σ has type Δ, and we write $\Sigma : \Delta$, when $\Sigma \sim \Sigma : \Delta$.

The restricted grammar of storable types means that if $\Sigma : \Delta$ then the part of Σ accessible from $\mathit{dom}(\Delta)$ will be acyclic.

The operational semantics is defined using a termination judgement [12] $\Sigma, \text{let } x \Leftarrow M \text{ in } K \downarrow$ where M is closed and K is a *continuation term in* x. Typed continuation terms are defined by

$$\frac{}{\Delta; \vdash \text{val } x : (x : \tau)^{\top}} \qquad \frac{\Delta; x : \tau \vdash M : \mathbf{T}\tau' \quad \Delta; \vdash K : (y : \tau')^{\top}}{\Delta; \vdash \text{let } y \Leftarrow M \text{ in } K : (x : \tau)^{\top}}$$

and the rules for defining untyped ones are the same with types (though not variables) erased. Some of the rules defining the termination predicate are shown in Figure 2.

Definition 2 (Contextual Equivalence). Contexts, $C[\cdot]$, are 'computation terms with holes in' and we write $C[\cdot] : (\Delta; \Gamma \vdash \gamma) \Rightarrow (\Delta; - \vdash \mathbf{T}\tau)$ to mean that whenever $\Delta; \Gamma \vdash G : \gamma$ then $\Delta; \vdash C[G] : \mathbf{T}\tau$. If $\Delta; \Gamma \vdash G_i : \gamma$ for $i = 1, 2$ then we write $\Delta; \Gamma \vdash G_1 =_{\text{ctx}} G_2 : \gamma$ to mean

$$\begin{array}{l}\forall \tau. \forall C[\cdot] : (\Delta; \Gamma \vdash \gamma) \Rightarrow (\Delta; - \vdash \mathbf{T}\tau). \forall \Sigma : \Delta. \\ \quad \Sigma, \text{let } x \Leftarrow C[G_1] \text{ in val } x \downarrow \iff \Sigma, \text{let } x \Leftarrow C[G_2] \text{ in val } x \downarrow\end{array}$$

3 Denotational Semantics

We first summarize basic facts about FM-cpos. A more comprehensive account appears in Shinwell's thesis [16].

Fix a countable set of *atoms*, which in our case will be the locations, $\mathbb{L}$. Then an *FM-set* X is a set equipped with a *permutation action*: an operation $\pi \bullet - : perms(\mathbb{L}) \times X \to X$ that preserves composition and identity, and such that each element $x \in X$ is *finitely supported*: there is a finite set $L \subseteq \mathbb{L}$ such that whenever π fixes each element of L, the action of π fixes x: $\pi \bullet x = x$. There is a smallest such set, which we write $supp(x)$. A morphism of FM-sets is a function $f : X \to Y$ between the underlying sets that is *equivariant*: $\forall x.\forall \pi.\, \pi \bullet (f\, x) = f\,(\pi \bullet x)$.

An *FM-cpo* is an FM-set with an equivariant partial order relation $\sqsubseteq$ and least upper bounds of all finitely-supported ω-chains. A morphism of FM-cpos is a morphism of their underlying FM-sets that is monotone and preserves lubs of finitely-supported chains. We only require the existence and preservation of finitely-supported chains, so an FM-cpo may not be a cpo in the usual sense. The sets $\mathbb{Z}$, $\mathbb{N}$, etc. are discrete FM-cpos with the trivial action. The set of locations, $\mathbb{L}$, is a discrete FM-cpo with the action $\pi \bullet \ell = \pi(\ell)$.

The category of FM-cpos is bicartesian closed: we write 1 and $\times$ for the finite products, $\Rightarrow$ for the internal hom and $0,+$ for the coproducts. The action on products is pointwise, and on functions is given by conjugation: $\pi \bullet f \stackrel{def}{=} \lambda x.\pi \bullet (f\,(\pi^{-1} \bullet x))$. The category is not well-pointed: morphisms $1 \to D$ correspond to elements of $1 \Rightarrow D$ with empty support.

The lift monad, $(\cdot)_\perp$, is defined as usual with the obvious action. The Kleisli category is the category of pointed FM-cpos (FM-cppos) and strict continuous maps, which is symmetric monoidal closed, with smash product $\otimes$ and strict function space $\multimap$. We use the same notation for partial constructions on the category of FM-cpos, defined on the range of the forgetful functor from FM-cppo. If D is a pointed FM-cpo then $fix : (D \Rightarrow D) \multimap D$ is defined by the lub of an ascending chain in the usual way.

We now turn to the denotational semantics of MILler. Define the FM-cpo of states, $\mathbb{S}$, to be $\mathbb{L} \Rightarrow (\mathbb{Z}+\mathbb{L})$, the finitely-supported functions mapping locations to either locations or integers, and write $[\![\Sigma]\!]$ for $\{S \in \mathbb{S} \mid \forall \ell \in dom\Sigma.S(\ell) = \Sigma(\ell)\}$. The update operation $\cdot[\cdot \mapsto \cdot]$ of type $\mathbb{S} \times \mathbb{L} \times (\mathbb{Z}+\mathbb{L}) \to \mathbb{S}$ is equivariant and continuous. The equivalence of operational states at a type of Definition 1 extends naturally to denotational states.

We write $\mathbb{O}$ for the flat two-element FM-cpo $\{\perp \sqsubseteq \top\}$, with the trivial action and then define the FM-cpo $[\![\gamma]\!]$, interpreting the type γ, inductively:

$$\begin{array}{rlrl} [\![\text{unit}]\!] &= 1 & [\![\tau_1 \times \tau_2]\!] &= [\![\tau_1]\!] \times [\![\tau_2]\!] \\ [\![\text{int}]\!] &= \mathbb{Z} & [\![\tau_1 + \tau_2]\!] &= [\![\tau_1]\!] + [\![\tau_2]\!] \\ [\![\sigma\ \text{ref}]\!] &= \mathbb{L} & [\![\tau_1 \to \mathbf{T}\tau_2]\!] &= [\![\tau_1]\!] \Rightarrow \mathbf{T}[\![\tau_2]\!] \\ \mathbf{T}D &= (\mathbb{S} \Rightarrow D \Rightarrow \mathbb{O}) \multimap (\mathbb{S} \Rightarrow \mathbb{O}) & & \end{array}$$

$$[\![\Delta;\Gamma \vdash \underline{\ell} : \sigma\,\mathrm{ref}]\!]\ \rho \ = \ \ell$$

$$[\![\Delta;\Gamma \vdash \mathrm{let}\, x \Leftarrow M_1 \,\mathrm{in}\, M_2 : \mathbf{T}\tau_2]\!]\ \rho\, k\, S \ = \\ [\![\Delta;\Gamma \vdash M_1 : \mathbf{T}\tau_1]\!]\ \rho\ (\lambda S' : \mathbb{S}.\lambda d : [\![\tau_1]\!].[\![\Delta;\Gamma, x:\tau_1 \vdash M_2 : \mathbf{T}\tau_2]\!]\ \rho[x \mapsto d]\ k\ S')\ S$$

$$[\![\Delta;\Gamma \vdash \mathrm{val}\, V : \mathbf{T}\tau]\!]\ \rho\, k\, S \ = \ k\, S\, ([\![\Delta;\Gamma \vdash V : \tau]\!]\ \rho)$$

$$[\![\Delta;\Gamma \vdash !V : \mathbf{T}\sigma]\!]\ \rho\, k\, S \ = \begin{cases} k\ S\ v \ \text{if}\ S([\![\Delta;\Gamma \vdash V : \sigma\,\mathrm{ref}]\!]\ \rho) = in_{[\![\sigma]\!]}v \\ \bot \quad\ \text{otherwise} \end{cases}$$

$$[\![\Delta;\Gamma \vdash V_1 := V_2 : \mathbf{T}\mathrm{unit}]\!]\ \rho\, k\, S \ = \\ k\ S[([\![\Delta;\Gamma \vdash V_1 : \sigma\,\mathrm{ref}]\!]\ \rho) \ \mapsto\ in_{[\![\sigma]\!]}([\![\Delta;\Gamma \vdash V_2 : \sigma]\!]\ \rho)]\ *$$

$$[\![\Delta;\Gamma \vdash \mathrm{ref}\, V : \mathbf{T}\sigma\,\mathrm{ref}]\!]\ \rho\, k\, S \ = \ k\, S[\ell \mapsto in_{[\![\sigma]\!]}([\![\Delta;\Gamma \vdash V : \sigma]\!]\rho)]\ \ell \\ \text{for some/any}\ \ell \notin supp(\lambda \ell'.k\, S[\ell' \mapsto in_\sigma([\![\Delta;\Gamma \vdash V : \sigma]\!]\rho)]\ \ell').$$

$$[\![\Delta;\Gamma \vdash (\mathrm{rec}\, f\, x = M) : \tau \to \mathbf{T}\tau']\!]\ \rho \ = \\ fix(\lambda f' : [\![\tau \to \mathbf{T}\tau']\!].\lambda x' : [\![\tau]\!].[\![\Delta;\Gamma, f:\tau \to \mathbf{T}\tau', x:\tau \vdash M : \mathbf{T}\tau']\!]\ \rho[f \mapsto f', x \mapsto x'])$$

Fig. 3. Denotational Semantics of MILler (extract)

For terms in context, we define $[\![\Delta;\Gamma \vdash G : \gamma]\!] \in [\![\Gamma]\!] \Rightarrow [\![\gamma]\!]$, where $[\![x_1 : \tau_1, \dots, x_n : \tau_n]\!]$ is the record $\{x_1 : [\![\tau_1]\!], \cdots, x_n : [\![\tau_n]\!]\}$, inductively. Some of the cases are shown in Figure 3. The most interesting case is the definition of the semantics of allocation. Note that the monad T combines state with continuations, even though there are no control operators in MILler. However, explicit continuations give us a handle on just what the new location has to be fresh *for*, whilst the ambient use of FM-cpos is exactly what we need to ensure that this really is a good definition, i.e. that one *can* pick a sufficiently fresh ℓ and, moreover, one gets the *same* result in $\mathbb{O}$ for any such choice. An equivalent, perhaps simpler, definition uses the quantification

$$\text{`}\dots\ \text{for some/any}\ \ell \notin supp(k) \cup supp(S) \cup supp([\![\Delta;\Gamma \vdash V : \sigma]\!]\rho)\text{'}$$

Our formulation emphasizes that the notion of support is semantic, not syntactic. The quantification can be seen as ranging not merely over locations that have not previously been allocated (as in the operational semantics), but over all locations that the specific continuation does not distinguish from any of the unallocated ones, i.e. including those which are 'extensionally garbage'.

Writing $[\![\Delta;\vdash K : (x:\tau)^\top]\!]^{\mathcal{K}}$ for $\lambda Sd.[\![\Delta; x:\tau \vdash K : \mathbf{T}\tau']\!]\{x \mapsto d\}(\lambda Sd.\top)\,S$, the following is proved via a logical 'formal approximation' relation:

Theorem 3 (Soundness and Adequacy). *If* $\Delta;\vdash M : \mathbf{T}\tau$, $\Delta;\vdash K : (x:\tau)^\top$, $\Sigma : \Delta$ *and* $S \in [\![\Sigma]\!]$ *then*

$$\Sigma, let\, x \Leftarrow M\ in\, K \downarrow \iff [\![\Delta;\vdash M : \mathbf{T}\tau]\!]\{\}[\![\Delta;\vdash K : (x:\tau)^\top]\!]^{\mathcal{K}}\,S = \top.$$

Corollary 4. $[\![\Delta;\Gamma \vdash G_1 : \gamma]\!] = [\![\Delta;\Gamma \vdash G_2 : \gamma]\!]$ *implies* $\Delta;\Gamma \vdash G_1 =_{ctx} G_2 : \gamma$.

The denotational semantics validates as contextual equivalences the basic equalities of the computational metalanguage and simple properties of assignment and dereferencing. It also proves the 'swap' equivalence:

$$\frac{\Delta;\Gamma \vdash V_1 : \sigma_1 \quad \Delta;\Gamma \vdash V_2 : \sigma_2 \quad \Delta;\Gamma, x : \sigma_1\,\mathrm{ref}, y : \sigma_2\,\mathrm{ref} \vdash N : \mathbf{T}\tau}{\Delta;\Gamma \vdash \begin{array}{l} \mathrm{let}\; x \Leftarrow \mathrm{ref}\, V_1\; \mathrm{in}\; (\mathrm{let}\; y \Leftarrow \mathrm{ref}\, V_2\; \mathrm{in}\; N) \\ =_{\mathrm{ctx}} \mathrm{let}\; y \Leftarrow \mathrm{ref}\, V_2\; \mathrm{in}\; (\mathrm{let}\; x \Leftarrow \mathrm{ref}\, V_1\; \mathrm{in}\; N) : \mathbf{T}\tau \end{array}}$$

But many interesting valid equivalences, including the garbage collection rule

$$\frac{\Delta;\Gamma \vdash V : \sigma \quad \Delta;\Gamma \vdash N : \mathbf{T}\tau}{\Delta;\Gamma \vdash \mathrm{let}\; x \Leftarrow \mathrm{ref}\, V\; \mathrm{in}\; N \;=_{\mathrm{ctx}}\; N : \mathbf{T}\tau}\; x \notin fvN$$

are, unfortunately, not equalities in the model. The above fails because the model contains undefinable elements that test for properties like $\exists \ell \in \mathbb{L}.S(\ell) = in_{\mathbb{Z}}(3)$ (note that this has empty support) and so make the effect of the initialization visible. The garbage collection and swap equations correspond to two of the structural congruences for restriction in the π-calculus. One might regard them as rather minimal requirements for a useful model, but they also fail in other models in the literature: Levy's possible worlds model [3] fails to validate either and, like ours, a model due to Stark [19–Chapter 5] fails to validate the garbage collection rule.

4 A Parametric Logical Relation

We now embark on refining our model using parameterized logical relations. Many authors have used forms of parametricity to reason about storage; our approach is particularly influenced by the work of Pitts and Stark [12] and of Reddy and Yang [14]. We will define a partially ordered set of *parameters*, p, and a parameter-indexed collection of binary relations on the FM-cpos interpreting states and types: $\forall p.\, \mathcal{R}_{\mathbb{S}}(p) \subseteq \mathbb{S} \times \mathbb{S}$ and $\forall p.\, \forall \gamma.\, \mathcal{R}_{\gamma}(p) \subseteq [\![\gamma]\!] \times [\![\gamma]\!]$. We then show that the denotation of each term is related to itself and, as a corollary, that typed terms with related denotations are contextually equivalent.

An important feature of the state relations we choose will be that they depend on only part of the state: this will allow us to reason that related states are still related if we update them in parts on which the relation does not depend.

One might expect that the notion of support, which is already built into our denotational model, would help here; for example by taking relations to be finitely-supported functions in $\mathbb{S} \times \mathbb{S} \Rightarrow 1 + 1$. Unfortunately, the support is not the right notion for defining separation of relations. For example, the relation

$$\{S_1, S_2 \mid \exists \ell_1, \ell_2. S_1(\ell_1) = S_2(\ell_2) = in_{\mathbb{Z}}0 \wedge S_1(\ell) = in_{\mathbb{L}}\ell_1 \wedge S_2(\ell) = in_{\mathbb{L}}\ell_2\}$$

has only ℓ in its support, but writing to the existentially quantified locations 'in the middle' can make related states unrelated. Even with only integers in the store, a relation like $\{(S_1, S_2) \mid \exists \ell, S_1\ell = 0 = S_2\ell\}$ can be perturbed by writes outside of its (empty) support.

Separation logic [6] leaves the part of the store which is 'relevant' to a predicate implicit and enforces separation by existential quantification over partial stores in the definition of the (partial) separating conjunction $*$. We instead make the finite part of the state on which our relations depend explicit, using what we call *accessibility maps*. Because, as above, relations can 'follow pointers', the set of locations on which a relation depends can itself be a function of the states. We make no explicit use of support in this section, though working with FM-cpos allows the use of equality of locations, rather than partial bijections, in our definitions.

Definition 5 (Accessibility Map). An accessibility map A is a function from $\mathbb{S}$ to finite subsets of $\mathbb{L}$, such that:

$$\forall S, S' \in \mathbb{S}, (\forall \ell \in AS, S\ell = S'\ell) \Longrightarrow A(S) = A(S')$$

The subtyping ordering $<:$ is defined as:

$$A <: A' \iff \forall S, A(S) \supseteq A'(S)$$

The subtype relation is a partial order, and the function $\lambda S.\emptyset$, abbreviated $\emptyset$, is the greatest accessibility map with respect to $<:$. One source of concrete accessibility maps is our existing notion of state type:

Definition 6 (Accessible Part of a State at a Type). If Δ is a state type, then $\mathrm{Acc}_\Delta : \mathbb{S} \to \mathbb{P}_{fin}(\mathbb{L})$ is defined by $\mathrm{Acc}_\Delta(S) = \bigcup_{(\ell:\sigma)\in\Delta} \mathrm{Acc}(\ell, \sigma, S)$ where $\mathrm{Acc}(\ell, \mathrm{int}, S) \stackrel{def}{=} \{\ell\}$ and

$$\mathrm{Acc}(\ell, \sigma\ \mathrm{ref}, S) \stackrel{def}{=} \{\ell\} \cup \begin{cases} \mathrm{Acc}(\ell', \sigma, S) & \text{if } S\,\ell = \mathrm{in}_{\mathbb{L}}\ell' \\ \emptyset & \text{otherwise} \end{cases}$$

Lemma 7. *Acc_Δ is an accessibility map, and if $\Delta \subseteq \Delta'$ then $Acc_{\Delta'} <: Acc_\Delta$.*

Definition 8 (Accessible Equality of States). If A is an accessibility map, we define $S \sim S' : A$ to mean $\forall \ell \in A(S), S\ell = S'\ell$.

Definition 9 (Finitary State Relation). A finitary state relation r is a pair $\langle |r|, A_r \rangle$ where $|r| \subseteq \mathbb{S} \times \mathbb{S}$ and A_r is an accessibility map, subject to the following saturation condition: if $S_1 \sim S_1' : A_r$ and $S_2 \sim S_2' : A_r$ then $(S_1, S_2) \in |r| \iff (S_1', S_2') \in |r|$.

Lemma 10.

1. *If A and A' are accessibility maps then so is $A \wedge A'$, where $\forall S. (A \wedge A')(S) = (A(S)) \cup (A'(S))$.*
2. *$\top \stackrel{def}{=} \langle \mathbb{S} \times \mathbb{S}, \emptyset \rangle$ is a finitary state relation.*

3. *If* $\langle|r|, A\rangle$ *is a finitary state relation and* $A' <: A$ *then* $\langle|r|, A'\rangle$ *is a finitary state relation.*
4. $id_\Delta \stackrel{def}{=} \langle\sim_\Delta, Acc_\Delta\rangle$ *is a finitary state relation.*

Definition 11 (Separating Conjunction). Given two finitary state relations, $r_1 = \langle|r^1|, A^1\rangle$ and $r_2 = \langle|r^2|, A^2\rangle$, define $r^1 \otimes r^2 \stackrel{def}{=} \langle|r^1 \otimes r^2|, A^1 \wedge A^2\rangle$ where

$$(S_1, S_2) \in |r^1 \otimes r^2| \iff \begin{cases} (S_1, S_2) \in |r^1| \cap |r^2| \\ \forall i \in \{1, 2\}, A^1(S_i) \cap A^2(S_i) = \emptyset \end{cases}$$

Lemma 12. *If* r^1 *and* r^2 *are finitary state relations, so is* $r^1 \otimes r^2$*. The conjunction is associative and commutative, with* $\top$ *as a unit.*

We now have all the ingredients needed to define the parameters of our relations. The intuition is that the parameters express that one part of the store is directly accessible, or *visible*, and that functions in the context also give access to other locations. Since we can do anything with visible locations, related states must be equal on that part. Moreover, we will preserve any invariant on hidden locations that is preserved by all the functions we can use, provided that invariant does not also depend on the contents of visible locations. Our parameters comprise these two components: the set of visible locations and a hidden invariant.[1]

Definition 13 (Parameters). A parameter is a pair (Δ, r), where Δ is a state type and r is a finitary relation; we will abbreviate this to Δr. If Δr is a parameter, we define the binary relation on states $\mathcal{R}_{\mathbb{S}}(\Delta r) \stackrel{def}{=} |id_\Delta \otimes r|$ and define the partial order $\rhd$ on parameters by

$$\Delta r \rhd \Delta' r' \iff (\Delta \supseteq \Delta') \wedge (\exists r'', r = r' \otimes r'')$$

Definition 14 (Logical Relation). We define the parameter- and typed- indexed family of relations $\mathcal{R}_\gamma(\Delta r)$ by induction over the types:

$$\begin{aligned}
\mathcal{R}_{\text{unit}}(\Delta r) &= \{(*, *)\} \\
\mathcal{R}_{\text{int}}(\Delta r) &= \{(n, n) \mid n \in N\} \\
\mathcal{R}_{\tau\times\tau'}(\Delta r) &= \{((d_1, d_1'), (d_2, d_2')) \mid (d_1, d_2) \in \mathcal{R}_\tau(\Delta r) \wedge (d_1', d_2') \in \mathcal{R}_{\tau'}(\Delta r)\} \\
\mathcal{R}_{\tau_1+\tau_2}(\Delta r) &= \{(\text{in}_1 d_1, \text{in}_1 d_2) \mid (d_1, d_2) \in \mathcal{R}_{\tau_1}(\Delta r)\} \\
&\quad \cup \{(\text{in}_2 d_1, \text{in}_2 d_2) \mid (d_1, d_2) \in \mathcal{R}_{\tau_2}(\Delta r)\} \\
\mathcal{R}_{\sigma\ \text{ref}}(\Delta r) &= \{(\ell, \ell) \mid (\ell : \sigma) \in \Delta\} \\
\mathcal{R}_{\tau\to\mathbf{T}\tau'}(\Delta r) &= \\
&\{(f_1, f_2) \mid \forall \Delta' r' \rhd \Delta r, (v_1, v_2) \in \mathcal{R}_\tau(\Delta' r'), (f_1 v_1, f_2, v_2) \in \mathcal{R}_{\mathbf{T}\tau'}(\Delta' r')\}
\end{aligned}$$

---

[1] This is in the style of Reddy and Yang [14]. Pitts and Stark [12] got away with simpler parameters, adding a new visible location ℓ to a parameter r by $r \otimes id_{\{\ell\}}$. In the presence of references to references, this doesn't work, as it prevents one visible location pointing to another.

For continuations, we define $\mathcal{R}_{\tau^\top}(\Delta r)$ to be

$$\{(k_1, k_2) \mid \forall \Delta' r' \rhd \Delta r, (v_1, v_2) \in \mathcal{R}_\tau(\Delta' r'), (S_1, S_2) \in \mathcal{R}_{\mathbb{S}}(\Delta' r'), k_1 S_1 v_1 = k_2 S_2 v_2\}$$

and for computations, $\mathcal{R}_{\mathbf{T}\tau}(\Delta r)$ is defined as $\{(f_1, f_2) \mid \forall \Delta' r' \rhd \Delta r, (k_1, k_2) \in \mathcal{R}_{\tau^\top}(\Delta' r'), (S_1, S_2) \in \mathcal{R}_{\mathbb{S}}(\Delta' r'), f_1 k_1 S_1 = f_2 k_2 S_2\}$.

Definition 15 (Relations in Context). We define $\mathcal{R}_\Gamma(\Delta r)$ to be $\{(\rho_1, \rho_2) \mid \forall (x_i : \tau_i) \in \Gamma, (\rho_1 x_i, \rho_2 x_i) \in \mathcal{R}_{\tau_i}(\Delta r)\}$ and $\mathcal{R}_{\Gamma \vdash \gamma}(\Delta r)$ to be $\{(v_1, v_2) \mid \forall \Delta' r' \rhd \Delta r, \forall (\rho_1, \rho_2) \in \mathcal{R}_\Gamma(\Delta' r'), (v_1 \rho_1, v_2 \rho_2) \in \mathcal{R}_\gamma(\Delta' r')\}$.

We now have to prove a number of non-trivial technical lemmas, which we omit here. These allow us to show that the interpretations of all the MILler typing rules preserve the logical relation, and hence deduce:

Theorem 16 (Fundamental Lemma). *If $\Delta; \Gamma \vdash G : \gamma$, then*

$$\forall r. ([\![\Delta; \Gamma \vdash G : \gamma]\!], [\![\Delta; \Gamma \vdash G : \gamma]\!]) \in \mathcal{R}_{\Gamma \vdash \gamma}(\Delta r).$$

Theorem 17 (Soundness of Relational Reasoning). *If $\Delta; \Gamma \vdash G_i : \gamma$ for $i = 1, 2$ and*

$$([\![\Delta; \Gamma \vdash G_1 : \gamma]\!], [\![\Delta; \Gamma \vdash G_2 : \gamma]\!]) \in \mathcal{R}_{\Gamma \vdash \mathbf{T}\tau}(\Delta \top)$$

then $\Delta; \Gamma \vdash G_1 =_{ctx} G_2 : \gamma$.

Accessibility maps are convenient to prove generic results, but working with specific ones can be a little awkward. In most examples we do not need their full generality (for example, allowing the accessible locations to depend on the integer contents of a particular location). We find it useful to generalize the notion of state type a little, introducing a top type and a simple form of subtyping. This allows a corresponding generalization of the accessibility map associated with a state type that suffices to specify the accessiblity maps we need even in tricky cases in which there are pointers between the visible and hidden parts of the state, but the invariant does not follow them far enough to be affected.

Definition 18 (Extended Storable Types). Extended storable types are given by the grammar $\alpha ::= \mathbb{T} \mid \text{int} \mid \alpha\ \text{ref}$. We define an order $<:$ between extended storable types by: int $<: \mathbb{T}$, αref $<: \mathbb{T}$, and if $\alpha <: \alpha'$ then αref $<: \alpha'$ref.

Definition 19 (Extended State Type). An extended state type θ is a map from $\mathbb{L}$ to location types which is $\mathbb{T}$ for all but a finite number of locations. Subtyping is defined pointwise.

The types α say how much of the value stored in a location is relevant: $\mathbb{T}$ means that we do not care about the value of the location. For instance, a location has type $\mathbb{T}$ ref if the value it carries is always a location, but we do not specify the type of this location: it might be an integer or a location.

Definition 20 (Accessibility Map for Extended State Type). The map Acc_θ is defined as in Definition 6, with the extra clause $\text{Acc}(\ell, \mathbb{T}, S) \stackrel{def}{=} \emptyset$.

Lemma 21. *Acc_θ is an accessibility map. If $\theta <: \theta'$, $Acc_{\theta'} <: Acc_\theta$.*

5 Examples

Garbage Collection. If x is not free in M, and $\Delta; \Gamma \vdash M : \mathbf{T}\tau$, then

$$\Gamma \vdash \text{let } x \Leftarrow \text{ref } V \text{ in } M =_{\text{ctx}} M : \mathbf{T}\tau$$

We prove that $[\![\text{let } x \Leftarrow \text{ref } V \text{ in } M]\!]$ and $[\![M]\!]$ are related by $\mathcal{R}_{\Gamma \vdash \mathbf{T}\tau}(\Delta\top)$, and we conclude using Theorem 17. Let $\Delta' r' \rhd \Delta\top$ be a parameter and $(\rho_1, \rho_2) \in \mathcal{R}_\Gamma(\Delta' r')$. We need to prove that $([\![\text{let } x \Leftarrow \text{ref } V \text{ in } M]\!]\rho_1, [\![M]\!]\rho_2) \in \mathcal{R}_{\mathbf{T}\tau}(\Delta' r')$. Let $\Delta'' r'' \rhd \Delta' r'$, $(k_1, k_2) \in \mathcal{R}_{\tau\top}(\Delta'' r'')$ and $(S_1, S_2) \in \mathcal{R}_{\mathbb{S}}(\Delta'' r'')$. We have to prove that

$$[\![\text{let } x \Leftarrow \text{ref } V \text{ in } M]\!]\rho_1 k_1 S_1 = [\![M]\!]\rho_2 k_2 S_2$$

For $\ell \notin supp(\lambda\ell'.k_1 S_1[\ell' \to [\![V]\!]\rho]\ell')$

$$[\![\text{let } x \Leftarrow \text{ref } V \text{ in } M]\!]\rho_1 k_1 S_1 = [\![M]\!]\rho_1 k_1 S_1[\ell \to [\![V]\!]\rho_1]$$

because x is not free in M. Since we can pick *any* such ℓ, we actually choose one also out of $\text{Acc}_{\Delta''}(S_i) \cup A_{r''}(S_i)$ for $i = 1, 2$. By the fundamental lemma, $[\![M]\!]$ is related to itself by $\mathcal{R}_{\Gamma \vdash \mathbf{T}\tau}(\Delta\top)$, so if we prove that $(S_1[\ell \to [\![V]\!]\rho_1], S_2) \in \mathcal{R}_{\mathbb{S}}(\Delta'' r'')$ we are done.

First, since $\ell \notin \text{Acc}_{\Delta''}(S_i)$, $(S_1[\ell \to [\![V]\!]\rho_1], S_2) \in id_{\Delta''}$, and since $\ell \notin A_{r''}(S_i)$, $(S_1[\ell \to [\![V]\!]\rho_1], S_2) \in r''$. By definition of accessibility maps, $\text{Acc}_{\Delta''}$ and $A_{r''}$ are unchanged, so they still do not overlap, which concludes the proof.

Meyer-Sieber 6. We can validate all the Meyer-Sieber examples [4]. We explain here example 6, which can be translated in MILler as the program M:

$$
\begin{array}{l}
\text{let } x \Leftarrow \text{ref } \underline{0} \text{ in} \\
\quad \text{let } almost\_add2 \Leftarrow \lambda z.\text{if } z = x \\
\qquad\qquad\qquad\qquad\qquad \text{then } x := 1 \\
\qquad\qquad\qquad\qquad\qquad \text{else let } y \Leftarrow !x \text{ in let } y' \Leftarrow y + 2 \text{ in } x := y' \text{in} \\
\qquad p(almost\_add2); \\
\qquad \text{let } y \Leftarrow !x \text{ in} \\
\qquad\quad \text{if } !x \bmod 2 = 0 \text{ then diverge}_{\text{unit}} \text{ else val } ()
\end{array}
$$

This program always diverges: we prove that $([\![; \Gamma \vdash M : \mathbf{T}\text{unit}]\!], \lambda\rho ks.\bot) \in \mathcal{R}_{\Gamma \vdash \mathbf{T}\text{unit}}(\emptyset\top)$. We have, for some fresh ℓ:

$$[\![M]\!]\rho k S = \rho(p) f \left(\lambda S' v. \begin{cases} kS' * & \text{if } S\ell = \text{in}_{\mathbb{Z}} n \text{ for some odd } n \\ \bot & \text{otherwise} \end{cases} \right) S[\ell \to 0]$$

where

$$fzks = \begin{cases} ks[\ell \to 1]* & \text{if } z = \ell \\ ks[\ell \to n+2]* & \text{if } z \neq \ell \text{ and } s\ell = \text{in}_{\mathbb{Z}} n \\ \bot & \text{otherwise} \end{cases}$$

Let $\Delta' r' \triangleright \Delta r$ be two parameters, $(\rho_1, \rho_2) \in \mathcal{R}_\Gamma(\Delta r)$, $(k_1, k_2) \in \mathcal{R}_{\text{unit}^\top}(\Delta' r')$ and $(S_1, S_2) \in \mathcal{R}_{\mathbb{S}}(\Delta' r')$. We let $r'' = r' \otimes \langle \{(S_1, S_2) \mid S_1\ell \text{ and } S_2\ell \text{ hold even integers}\}, \text{Acc}_{\{\ell:\text{int}\}}\rangle$ and prove that

$$(f, f) \in \mathcal{R}_{\text{int ref} \to \mathbf{T}\text{unit}}(\Delta' r'')$$

the proof is then straightforward.

Suppose $\Delta^4 r^4 \triangleright \Delta^3 r^3 \triangleright \Delta' r''$, $(v_1^3, v_2^3) \in \mathcal{R}_{\text{int ref}}(\Delta^3 r^3)$, $(k_1^4, k_2^4) \in \mathcal{R}_{\text{unit}}(\Delta^4 r^4)$, $(S_1^4, S_2^4) \in \mathcal{R}_{\mathbb{S}}(\Delta^4 r^4)$. As $\Delta^4 r^4 \triangleright \Delta' r''$, $(S_1, S_2) \in r^4 \subseteq r''$, so S_1 and S_2 hold even integers n_1 and n_2. $v_1^3 = v_2^3$ is a visible location. As $A_{r^4} <: A_{r''}$, $\ell \in A_{r^4}(S_i)$, which entails that $v_i^3 \neq \ell$. We get

$$f v_i^3 k_i^4 S_i^4 = k_i^4 S_i^4 [\ell \to n_i + 2]$$

$(S_1[\ell \to n_i + 2], S_2[\ell \to n_i + 2]) \in \mathcal{R}_{\mathbb{S}}(\Delta^4 r^4)$, because our invariant is preserved, and, by non interference, the other parts of the invariant are preserved too, so

$$f v_1 k_1 S_1 = k_1 S_1[\ell \to n_1 + 2] = k_2 S_2[\ell \to n_2 + 2] = f v_2 k_2 S_1$$

Extended Types. To illustrate the extended types, we give an example involving a pointer from the invariant to the visible locations. We show that the following program M diverges:

let $x \Leftarrow$ ref 0 in
let $y \Leftarrow$ ref x in
$p\ x$;
let $z \Leftarrow !y$ in
if $z = x$ then diverge$_{\text{unit}}$ else val ()

As before, we prove that $([\![M]\!], \bot) \in \mathcal{R}_{\Gamma \vdash \mathbf{T}\text{unit}}(\emptyset \top)$. For any fresh ℓ_x, ℓ_y:

$$[\![M]\!]\rho k S = \rho(p)\ell \left(\lambda S'' v. \begin{cases} \bot & \text{if } S''\ell_y = \text{in}_{\mathbb{L}} \ell_x \\ k_1 S'' * & \text{otherwise} \end{cases} \right) S_1'$$

where $S_1' = S_1[\ell_y \to \ell_x, \ell_x \to 0]$. We want to prove that when we reach the continuation, the value held in ℓ_y is ℓ_x. ℓ_x is given to p, so it must be visible, but the invariant "ℓ_y holds ℓ_x" is about the location held by ℓ_y, but not about what this location holds. We have to define an accessibility map that does not contain ℓ_x: the invariant is

$$dr = \langle \{(S_1, S_2) \mid S_1 \ell_y = \text{in}_{\mathbb{L}} \ell_x\}, \text{Acc}_{\{\ell_y : \mathbb{T}\ \text{ref}\}} \rangle$$

Secrecy. We can prove some examples (very) loosely inspired by the work of Sumii and Pierce [20] on logical relations and encryption. The idea, though we certainly do not claim this is a particularly good model of cryptography, is that encrypted messages are sent through hidden locations. Encrytion is encoded as writing in a hidden location, and decryption as reading the same hidden location. The visible locations are the keys the context knows, and the locations in the invariant the private keys. We can represent public keys by providing a function that wraps the assignment.

For instance, in the following dummy protocol, A (the first function) sends a message to B (the second function) containing a fresh key, and B reads this key and sends a message i using this key. The program M_i is

$$\begin{array}{l} \text{let } x \Leftarrow \text{ref } 0 \text{ in} \\ \text{let } k_b \Leftarrow \text{ref } x \text{ in} \\ \text{let cipher} \Leftarrow \text{val } \lambda\langle k, n\rangle.k := n \text{ in} \\ \text{let decipher} \Leftarrow \text{val } \lambda k.!k \text{ in} \\ \text{val } \langle \lambda().\text{let } k_a \Leftarrow \text{ref } 0 \text{ in cipher } \langle k_b, k_a\rangle, \\ \qquad \lambda().\text{let } k \Leftarrow \text{decipher } k_b \text{ in cipher } \langle k, i\rangle\rangle \end{array}$$

We prove that M_1 is equivalent to M_2, which shows that the information written in k is not accessible from the context, thus kept secret.[2] An easy calculation gives, for fresh ℓ_x and ℓ_b:

$$[\![M_i]\!]kS = kS[\ell_b \to \ell_x \to 0]\langle \phi^A, \phi_i^B\rangle$$

where

$$\begin{array}{l} \phi^A = \lambda * kS.kS[\ell_b \to \ell_a \to 0] * \quad \text{for a fresh } \ell_a \\ \phi_i^B = \lambda * kS. \begin{cases} kS[\ell \to i]* \text{ if } S\ell_b = \text{in}_{\mathbb{L}}\ell \\ \bot \qquad\qquad \text{otherwise} \end{cases} \end{array}$$

Let Δr be a parameter $(k_1, k_2) \in \mathcal{R}_{(\tau\times\tau)^\top}(\Delta r)$ and $(S_1, S_2) \in \mathcal{R}_{\mathbb{S}}(\Delta r)$, where $\tau = \text{unit} \to \mathbf{T}\text{unit}$ is the type of the processes A and B. The invariant dr says that ℓ_b holds a reference to an integer, which makes ℓ_b and, later, ℓ_a secret. Let $r' = r \otimes dr$, and $S_i' = S_i[\ell_b \to \ell_x \to 0]$. Of course $(S_1', S_2') \in \mathcal{R}_{\mathbb{S}}(\Delta r')$. If we show that (ϕ^A, ϕ^A) and (ϕ_1^B, ϕ_2^B) are in $\mathcal{R}_\tau(\Delta r')$, then we are done.

Let $\Delta'' r'' \rhd \Delta r'$, $(k_1'', k_2'') \in \mathcal{R}_{\text{unit}^\top}(\Delta'' r'')$ and $(S_1'', S_2'') \in \mathcal{R}_{\mathbb{S}}(\Delta'' r'')$. We write $r'' = r \otimes dr \otimes dr'$. We can pick a fresh ℓ_a such that, for both $i = 1, 2$:

$$\phi^A * k_i'' S_i'' = k_i'' S_i''[\ell_b \to \ell_a \to 0]*$$

It is easy to check that the new states are still related by $\mathcal{R}_{\mathbb{S}}(\Delta'' r'')$: they are in dr, they also are in the other parts of the relation $id_{\Delta''}$, r and dr' thanks to the separating condition, because the only locations that were changed are ℓ_b (which is in $A_{dr} S_i$) and ℓ_a (which was fresh), and there is no new cross pointer between these parts. This gives $(\phi^A, \phi^A) \in \mathcal{R}_\tau(\Delta r')$.

The same holds for ϕ_1^B and ϕ_2^B because the relation dr only states that ℓ_x holds an integer, not which integer. We get the expected contextual equivalence of M_1 and M_2.

---

[2] The equivalence of two pairs of functions of type unit $\to$ **T**unit with no free locations is not *completely* trivial: each pair might have differing intertwined termination behaviour, depending on hidden state.

On the other hand, if the key is public, *i.e.* we give an encryption function to the context, then the secrecy is broken: the opponent can write a message to B, giving it a channel it can read, so that the value i written by B can be deciphered afterwards. We give to the context (as a third element in the tuple) the function

$$\text{public\_cipher} = \lambda n.\text{cipher}\ \langle k_b, n\rangle$$

public_cipher does not respect the relation $\mathcal{R}_{\mathbb{S}}(\Delta r')$:

$$\text{public\_cipher}\ \ell k S = kS[\ell_b \to \ell]*$$

ℓ_b certainly points to a reference to an integer after it is called, so it is in dr as before, but now this reference is ℓ, which is visible (since it is given by the context), so the separating condition between id_Δ and dr no longer holds.

Snapback. Our logical relation fails to capture the irreversibility of state changes, which is a source of incompleteness relative to contextual equivalence. Consider the element 'snapback' of $[\![(\text{unit} \to \mathbf{T}\text{int}) \to \mathbf{T}\text{unit}]\!]$ defined by

$$\text{snapback}\ f\ k\ S \ = \ f\ *\ (\lambda S'.\lambda n.k\ S\ n)\ S$$

Snapback calls its argument f, passing it the state S and a continuation that will set the state *back* to S, discarding any updates made by f. Snapback is not definable, but it *is* parametric: assume $\Delta' r' \rhd \Delta r$ are parameters, $(f_1, f_2) \in \mathcal{R}_{\text{unit}\to\mathbf{T}\text{int}}(\Delta r)$, $(k_1, k_2) \in \mathcal{R}_{\text{int}^\top}(\Delta' r')$ and $(S_1, S_2) \in \mathcal{R}_{\mathbb{S}}(\Delta' r')$. We only have to show that the continuations $\lambda S' n.k_i S_i n$ are related by $\mathcal{R}_{\text{int}^\top}(\Delta' r')$. Let $\Delta'' r'' \rhd \Delta' r'$ and $(S_1'', S_2'') \in \mathcal{R}_{\mathbb{S}}(\Delta'' r'')$. The only values related by $\mathcal{R}_{\text{int}}(\Delta'' r'')$ are (m, m) for some $m \in \mathbb{N}$. We have $(\lambda S' n.k_i S_i n) S_i'' m = k_i S_i m$, and, since $(k_1, k_2) \in \mathcal{R}_{\text{int}^\top}(\Delta' r')$ and $(S_1, S_2) \in \mathcal{R}_{\mathbb{S}}(\Delta' r')$, $k_1 S_1 m = k_2 S_2 m$, so we're done.

The fact that our relation does not eliminate snapback prevents us from proving some useful and valid contextual equivalences. For example, $; p : (\text{unit} \to \mathbf{T}\text{int}) \to \mathbf{T}\text{unit}) \vdash M =_{\text{ctx}} N : \mathbf{T}\text{unit}$ where

$$\begin{aligned} M = {} & \text{let}\ x \Leftarrow \text{ref}\ 0\ \text{in} \\ & \quad p(\lambda\_.\, x := 1;\ 0); \\ & \quad \text{let}\ y \Leftarrow !x\ \text{in} \\ & \quad \text{if iszero}\ y\ \text{then val}\ ()\ \text{else diverge}_{\text{unit}} \end{aligned} \qquad N = p\ (\lambda\_.\, \text{diverge}_{\text{int}})$$

but this is not provable with our relation, as if p is snapback, then M converges and N diverges. Intuitively, the problem here is one of linearity: note that snapback duplicates S and discards S'.

6 Discussion and Further Work

There is much related work on the semantics of Algol-like languages; we can only pick out a few relevant highlights. Meyer and Sieber [4] gave a model for an Algol-like language with local integer variables which was based on a notion of 'support' and a refined model based on the preservation of (unary) predicates on stores that depend only on a finite number of locations. Reynolds [15] and Oles [9] pioneered the functor-category, or *possible-worlds* approach to modelling storage, further developed by O'Hearn and Tennent [7] and Sieber [18] to incorporate relational parametricity. This gives a good semantics for the locality of local variables but, like our relation, still does not account for the irreversibility of state changes: essentially the same snapback example as we have given above causes incompleteness. Reynolds and O'Hearn [5] gave models via translations from Algol-like languages into a predicatively polymorphic *linear* lambda calculus, ruling out snapback. Pitts [10] used that idea to give an operationally-based logical relation for an Algol-like language that is complete for contextual equivalence. Following [5, 10], we believe a relatively small modification to the logical relation (involving lifting of states) may rule out snapback in our model too (strict relations over pointed cpos give a rather weak model of the polymorphic linear lambda calculus, but as snapback relies on both contraction and weakening, this seems to suffice), but we have not yet worked through all the details.

General dynamic allocation is more complex than the stack-structured local variables of Algol. Pitts and Stark [11, 19] introduced the *ν-calculus*, a simply-typed (and recursion-free) CBV lambda calculus with dynamic generation of pure names. They present both operational logical relations and monadically-structured denotational models, based on parametric functor categories, for the ν-calculus. We have already mentioned their later work [12] and that of Reddy and Yang [14], from which we drew much inspiration. Levy [3] has given an adequate, but non-parametric, possible-worlds semantics for an ML-like language with storage of arbitrary values, including functions. Our FM-cpo semantics for MILler derives from a model for FreshML due to Shinwell and Pitts [17, 16].

Although most of the pieces of our model and logical relation are closely related to ones in the literature, the way they are combined here is novel (possibly the first domain-theoretic, parametric treatment of dynamic allocation), elegant and, above all, elementary. Our basic model is considerably easier to work with than a functor category, and the relational reasoning principle is easy to apply. We believe our formulation of separation is more powerful than that of [14].

We would like to be able to reason relationally about references to values of functional (and recursive) types. Appropriate technology seems to exist [13], but it remains to be seen whether we can apply it successfully in our setting.

We have experimented with a simple inference system for proving expressions are related. Developing this, perhaps using ideas from nominal logic, may open the way to automated support. We have also looked at methods to prove the soundness of the effect-based transformations we previously studied operationally (and rather unsatisfactorily) in [1]. Something can certainly be pushed through using our current definitions, but making it work smoothly seems to call for some interesting modifications to our logical relation. We also plan to investigate more seriously the applications to secure information flow and the correctness of cryptographic protocols.

References

1. N. Benton and A. Kennedy. Monads, effects and transformations. In *3rd International Workshop on Higher Order Operational Techniques in Semantics (HOOTS), Paris*, volume 26 of *Electronic Notes in Theoretical Computer Science*. Elsevier, September 1999.
2. N. Benton and B. Leperchey. Relational reasoning in a nominal semantics for storage. Technical report, Microsoft Research, February 2005.
3. P. B. Levy. Possible world semantics for general storage in call-by-value. In *Proceedings of the Annual Conference of the European Association for Computer Science Logic (CSL)*, volume 2471 of *Lecture Notes in Computer Science*. Springer-Verlag, September 2002.
4. A. R. Meyer and K. Sieber. Towards a fully abstract semantics for local variables: Preliminary report. In *Proceedings of the 15th Annual ACM SIGACT-SIGPLAN Symposium on Principles of Programming Languages (POPL)*, January 1988.
5. P. W. O'Hearn and J. C. Reynolds. From Algol to polymorphic linear lambda-calculus. *Journal of the ACM*, 47(1):167–223, January 2000.
6. P. W. O'Hearn, J. C. Reynolds, and H. Yang. Local reasoning about programs that alter data structures. In *Proceedings of the Annual Conference of the European Association for Computer Science Logic (CSL)*, 2001.
7. P. W. O'Hearn and R. D. Tennent. Parametricity and local variables. *Journal of the ACM*, 42(3):658–709, May 1995.
8. P. W. O'Hearn and R. D. Tennent, editors. *Algol-like Languages*. Progress in Theoretical Computer Science. Birkhäuser, 1997. Two volumes.
9. F. J. Oles. *A Category-Theoretic Approach to the Semantics of Programming Languages*. PhD thesis, Syracuse University, 1982.
10. A. M. Pitts. Reasoning about local variables with operationally-based logical relations. In [8], 1997.
11. A. M. Pitts and I. D. B. Stark. Observable properties of higher order functions that dynamically create local names, or: What's new? In *Proceedings of the 18th International Symposium on Mathematical Foundations of Computer Science*, volume 711 of *Lecture Notes in Computer Science*, pages 122–141. Springer-Verlag, 1993.
12. A. M. Pitts and I. D. B. Stark. Operational reasoning for functions with local state. In A. D. Gordon and A. M. Pitts, editors, *Higher Order Operational Techniques in Semantics*, Publications of the Newton Institute, pages 227–273. Cambridge University Press, 1998.
13. A.M. Pitts. Relational properties of domains. *Information and Computation*, 127(2), 1996.
14. U. S. Reddy and H. Yang. Correctness of data representations involving heap data structures. *Science of Computer Programming*, 50(1–3):129–160, March 2004.
15. J. C. Reynolds. The essence of Algol. In *Proceedings of the International Symposium on Algorithmic Languages*, 1981. Reprinted in [8].
16. M. R. Shinwell. *The Fresh Approach: Functional Programming with Names and Binders*. PhD thesis, Computer Laboratory, University of Cambridge, December 2004.
17. M. R. Shinwell and A. M. Pitts. On a monadic semantics for freshness. *Theoretical Computer Science*, 2005. To appear.
18. K. Sieber. New steps towards full abstraction for local variables. In *Proceedings of the ACM SIGPLAN Workshop on State in Programming Languages*, 1993.

19. I. D. B. Stark. *Names and Higher-Order Functions.* PhD thesis, Computer Laboratory, University of Cambridge, December 1994. Available as Technical Report 363.
20. E. Sumii and B. C. Pierce. Logical relations for encryption. *Journal of Computer Security*, 11(4), 2003.
21. R. D. Tennent and D. R. Ghica. Abstract models of storage. *Higher-Order and Symbolic Computation*, 13(1/2):119–129, 2000.

Filters on CoInductive Streams, an Application to Eratosthenes' Sieve

Yves Bertot

INRIA Sophia Antipolis
Yves.Bertot@sophia.inria.fr

Abstract. We present the formal description of an algorithm to filter values from an infinite steam using a type theory based prover. The key aspect is that filters are partial co-recursive functions and we solve the problem of expressing partiality. We then show how to prove properties of this filter algorithm and we study an application computing the stream of all prime numbers.

Our objective is to describe a formal proof of correctness for the following Haskell [14] program in a type theory-based proof verification system, like the Coq system [10, 1].

```
sieve (p:rest) = p:sieve [r | r <- rest, r `rem` p /= 0]
primes = sieve [2..]
```

This program is a functional implementation of Eratosthenes' sieve that consists in removing all multiples of previously found primes from the sequence of natural numbers. We want to prove that the expression `primes` is the stream containing all the prime numbers in increasing order.

This work relies on co-inductive types [5, 12, 13] because the program manipulates infinite lists, also known as streams. This example was used as an illustration of a program and its proof of correctness in a language for co-routines in [15]. The exact formulation of the program given here was found in [7], who describes it as a re-phrasing of an program SASL [21]. A proof of Eratosthenes' sieve in type theory was already studied in 1993 [16], but their program has a different structure and does not exhibit the filter problem that is central here. Another program computing the stream of prime numbers is given as example in [8], which relies on a more general notion of ultra-metric spaces to combine inductive and co-inductive aspects in recursive definitions. It is later extended to sheaves [9].

Before performing the verification proof of such a program in type theory, we need to be able to formulate it. This is difficult, because type theory based frameworks only provide restricted capabilities for the definition of recursive functions, which basically ensure that all functions are total. The Haskell program uses a filter function. This function receives a boolean predicate and a stream as argument and it is supposed to take from the stream all the elements of the stream that satisfy the predicate and place them in the resulting stream. Because the result is an infinite stream, it means that an infinity of values should be found in the input, but this is not always possible and actually depends on the input: filter functions are partial. Our principal contribution is actually to find a solution to the problem a large class of partial co-recursive functions.

P. Urzyczyn (Ed.): TLCA 2005, LNCS 3461, pp. 102–115, 2005.

When computing on usual inductive structures, the termination of computation is usually ensured by a syntactic restriction on the way functions may be defined: they have to be "guarded-by-destructors". Intuitively, this contraint imposes a bound on the number of possible recursive calls using the size of the algebraic term given as input. In spite of its apparent simplicity, this criterion is quite powerful, because inductive types are more general than simple algebraic types: infinitely branching nodes are allowed and it is only the absence of infinite branches that is used to restrict computation.

For functions that produce terms in co-inductive types, recursive functions are also allowed, but this time restrictions are not placed on the way the input is used, but on the way the output data is produced. A common syntactic criterion is to accept a recursive call to a co-recursive function only if some information has been produced in the result, in the form of a constructor . The terminology is that calls must be "guarded-by-constructors" [12]. In their usual form, filters do not respect this syntactic criterion.

We propose to combine insights coming from reasoning techniques on linear temporal logic [4, 6] and on general recursion with partial functions, essentially the techique advocated in [11, 2]. We transpose this technique to the Calculus of Inductive Constructions, the underlying theory for the Coq system, with some added difficulties coming from the use of two sorts. Coping with these two sorts also has advantages; we obtain the possibility to extract our model back to conventional programming languages and to execute the programs that were proved correct.

In a first part we give an overview of co-recursive programming techniques in the Calculus of Constructions. In a second part we show that filters cannot be programmed directly, mainly because not all streams are valid inputs for filters, and we describe a few notions of linear temporal logic to characterize the valid inputs. We show that this can be used as a basis to program a filter function. In a third part, we describe how this adapts to the context of Eratosthene's sieve. The fourth part concludes and underlines the opportunities for future improvement.

1 Co-induction and Co-recursion

Co-inductive types are defined by giving together a type and a collection of constructors. A pattern-matching construct expresses that all elements of a co-inductive type are obtained through one of the constructors. However, there is no obligation that the process of constructing a term in a co-inductive type should be finite as is the case for inductive types [19, 12].

For instance, we can work in a context where some type `A` is declared and use the type of streams of elements of `A`. We later instantiate `A` with the type `Z` of integers.

```
CoInductive str : Set := SCons: A → str → str.
```

A stream of type `str` is like a list of elements of A: it has a first element and a tail, grouped together using the constructor `SCons`. Inductive definitions of lists usually contain a constructor for the empty list, but here there is none: all our streams are infinite.

Writing programs with streams as inputs, we have to avoid traversing the whole data structure, because this operation never terminates. In the calculus of constructions, there are a few safeguard that prevent this. The first safeguard is that computation of values in co-inductive types is not performed unless explicitely requested by a pattern-matching operation.

The second safeguard is that the definitions of recursive functions returning co-inductive types must respect a few constraints, like for recursive functions over inductive types, except that the constraints are not expressed in terms of using the input but in terms of producing the output. The intuitive motto is "every recursive call must produce some information". In practice, every recursive call must be embedded in a constructor of the co-inductive type, the whole expression being allowed to appear only inside a pattern-matching construct, an abstraction, or another constructor of this co-inductive type. We say that such a recursive function is *guarded by constructors*.

The criterion is theoretically justified by the fact that a co-inductive type is a final co-algebra in the category of co-algebras associated to the collection of constructors given in the co-inductive definition and a guarded function actually defines another co-algebra in this category. The existence of value in the final co-algebra is a consequence of the finality property.

Here is an example of a well-formed function, that will be used in our work (in this example, the type `A` is not used implicitely anymore and we use the type of streams of integers, `str Z`).

```
CoFixpoint nums (n : Z) : str Z := SCons n (nums (n+1))
```

Every recursive call produces a new element of the stream. The value "`nums 2`" is exactly the model for the Haskell value `[2 ..]`.

Proofs by co-induction are co-recursive functions whose type concludes on a co-inductive predicate, a type with logical content (a co-inductive type in sort `Prop`). When performing a proof by co-induction, we have the same constraints as when defining a co-recursive function: the co-inductive hypothesis expresses the same logical content as the whole theorem, but it can only be used to prove a statement appearing as a premise of one of the constructors in the co-inductive predicate.

2 The Filter Problem

A filter function is a function that takes a predicate and a stream as arguments and returns the stream that contains all the elements of the argument that satisfy the predicate. It can be programmed in Haskell using the following text:

```
filter f (x:tl) | f x = x:(filter f tl)
filter f (x:tl)       = (filter f tl)
```

The notation `[x | x <- rest, x 'rem' p /= 0]` actually stands for the following more traditional functional expression:

```
 filter (\x -> x 'rem' p /= 0) rest
```

When translated into Coq, this gives the following (invalid) code:

```
CoFixpoint filter (f:A→Prop)(s:str) : str :=
 match s with
```

```
  SCons x tl =>
  match f x with
    true => SCons x (filter f tl)
  | false => filter f tl
  end.
```

There are more palatable notations, this formulation emphasizes the fact that the second recursive call appearing in this program is not valid: it is a recursive call not embedded inside a constructor. The function needs to perform several recursive calls before returning the next data and this is rejected. This is consistent with the constraint that there should be no infinite computation: if we take a predicate and a stream where no element satisfies the predicate, the program will loop forever without producing any result. Understanding this counter-example gives us a key to a technique to model filter functions.

2.1 Characterizing Valid Filter Inputs

If we want to use a filter function, we need to give it arguments that won't make it loop. We use the same technique as in in [11, 2]: an extra argument expresses that the input satisfies the right conditions to ensure data production.

For a given predicate `P`, a stream is correct if we can find an element of the stream that satisfies the predicate and if the sub-stream starting after that element is also correct. We can simplify this analysis by saying that a stream is correct if we can find an element satisfying the predicate and if its tail is also correct.

That there is one element satisfying the predicate actually is an inductive property, not a co-inductive one, so we will characterize the correct streams for a given predicate using both an inductive predicate and a co-inductive predicate.

This is reminiscent of linear temporal logic, viewing the different elements of the stream as a succession of states in time. The property that the predicate is eventually satisfied means that the property `eventually P` is satisfied. The property that must be repeated for all streams is an `always (eventually P)`. The encoding of these linear logic predicates as inductive predicates has already been studied in [4, 6] have already studied how these linear logic predicates can be encoded as inductive predicates. In our case, we assume that we are working in a context where the predicate `P` is given, and we encode directly the combination of `always` and `eventually` as a predicate on streams, which we call `F_infinite` (the predicates `always`, `eventually` and `F_infinite` are similar to the ones with the same name in [1]).

```
Inductive eventually : str → Prop :=
   ev_b: ∀x s, P x → eventually (SCons x s)
 | ev_r: ∀x s, eventually s → eventually (SCons x s).

CoInductive always : str →  Prop :=
  as_cons: ∀x s, P x → always s → always (SCons x s).

CoInductive F_infinite : str → Prop :=
   al_cons:
```

```
∀x s, eventually (SCons x s) → F_infinite s →
  F_infinite (SCons x s).
```

Now, a filter function should have the following type :

```
∀s, F_infinite s → s
```

We have shown that characterizing the correct inputs for the filter function relies on both a co-inductive and an inductive part; this suggests that the filter function should have both a recursive part and a co-recursive part. The recursive part is responsible for finding the first element, making as many recursive calls as necessary without producing any data, but being guarded by an `eventually` property on the input, when the first element is found, we can produce it and have a co-recursive call, which is now valid.

Programming the Recursive Part. The recursive part of the filter function is defined by recursion on the ad-hoc predicate `eventually`. It also uses a function `P_dec` that is supposed to compute whether the property `P` is satisfied or not.

Here is a first attempt where we only produce the first value that satisfies the predicate.

```
Fixpoint
 pre_filter_i (s:str)(h:eventually s){struct h}:A :=
 match s as b return s = b →  A with
    SCons x s' =>
      fun heq =>
         match P_dec x with
           left _ => x
         | right hn => pre_filter_i s'
                (eventually_inv s h x s' heq hn)
         end
 end (refl_equal s).
```

The theorem `eventually_inv` has the following statement:

```
∀s, eventually s →
  ∀x s', s = SCons x s'→ not(P x) → eventually s'
```

For this definition to be accepted, the expression `eventually_inv s h x s' heq hn` must be recognized as a sub-term of `h`. This is achieved because this proof is actually obtained through a pattern-matching construct on the proof `h`. In this pattern-matching construct, we must ensure that the sub-expression that is returned in each possible case is a sub-term of `h`. There are two cases.

1. Either the proof `h` was obtained with the constructor `ev_r` applied to three arguments arguments `x1`, `s1`, and `h1`. In this case, `s1` $=$ `s'` and `h1` is a sub-term of `h` that is also a proof of `eventually s1`. We can return `h1`.
2. Either the proof `h` was obtained with the constructor `ev_b` applied to `x1`, `s1`, and `hp`. In this case, `x1` $=$ `x` and `hp` is a proof that `P x1` holds. The fact `hp` is inconsistent with the fact `hn` which must be a proof of `not(P x)`. Because of this inconsistency, we are relieved from the need to produce a sub-term proof.

In other words, we only need to produce a sub-term proof for the consistent cases. When the constructor that is used does not contain a sub-term proof for the recursive call, the fact that this constructor may have been used is inconsistent.

The function pre_filter_i is not satisfactory, because we also need the recursive function to produce the stream, on which filtering carries on, together with a proof that this stream contains an infinity of satisfactory elements. Thus we want to program a function filter_i with the following type:

```
∀s, eventually s → F_infinite s →
   {x:A, P x}*{s':str, F_infinite s'}
```

This function takes one extra argument that is a proof that all the sub-streams eventually satisfy the predicate, it returns two pieces of data annotated with logical information. The first piece of data is a number x and the annotation is a proof that x satisfies the predicate P, the second piece of data is a stream s' and the annotation is a proof that an infinity of elements of s' satisfy P. We do not describe the code of filter_i here, it has the same structure as the function pre_filter_i, but it contains more code to handle the logical information.

Programming the Co-recursive Part. Assuming the filter_i function and a theorem always_eventually, which indicates that any stream that satisfies the predicate F_infinite also satisfies eventually, we can produce the filter function, which contains a single co-recursive call using the data returned by filter_i.

```
CoFixpoint filter (s : str) (hs : F_infinite s): str :=
 let (a, b) := filter_i s (always_eventually s hs) hs in
 let (n, hn) := a in let (s', hs') := b in
 SCons n (filter s' hs').
```

Proving Properties of the Result Stream. Because the filter function has a recursive and a co-recursive part, all proofs about the resulting stream will have an inductive and a co-inductive part. For instance, we can prove that every property that is satisfied by all the elements of the initial stream is also satisfied by all the elements of the resulting stream. To state this theorem we have to change our implicit notations: the predicates always and F_infinite and the function filter are not implicitely applied to P anymore. This results in extra arguments for the various predicates and functions.

```
Theorem filter_keep:
 ∀(P Q:A → Prop)(P_dec:∀x,{P x}+{not(P x)})(s:str)
  (h:F_infinite P s),
 always Q s → always Q (filter P P_dec s h).
```

To establish this theorem, we first have to prove that the element and the stream returned by filter_i satisfy the properties Q and always Q, respectively. This proof uses an induction over a proof of eventually P s. The theorem has the following statement:

```
Theorem filter_i_keep:
 ∀(P Q:A → Prop)(P_dec:∀x,{P x}+{not(P x)})(s:str)
   (h:eventually P s)(ha : F_infinite P s),
 always Q s →
 ∀x hx s' hs',
 filter_i P P_dec s h ha =
 (exist (fun n => P n) x hx,
  exist (fun s => F_infinite P s) s' hs') →
  Q x /\ always Q s'.
```

This proof is tricky and we have to use a maximal induction principle as described in [1] (sect. 14.1.5).

We can also prove that all elements of the resulting stream satisfy the predicate P.

```
Theorem filter_always:
 ∀(s:str)(h:F_infinite s), always (filter s h).
Proof.
 cofix.
 intros s h; rewrite (st_dec_eq (filter s h)); simpl.
 case (filter_i s (always_eventually s h) h).
 intros [n hn][s' hs']; apply as_cons.
 assumption.
 apply filter_always.
Qed.
```

We give the script to perform the proof using the tactic language provided in Coq. The `cofix` tactic provides an assumption that expresses exactly the same statement as the theorem we want to prove, but this assumption can only be used after a use of `as_cons` (the constructor of `always`). Here we need to prove that the first element satisfies `P`, but this is already given in the result of `filter_i`, so that we do not need an extra inductive proof.

This proof contains a rewriting step with a theorem `st_dec_eq`. This theorem is used to force the evaluation of the co-inductive value `(filter s h)` because otherwise, co-inductive values remain unevaluated. This method to force evaluation for at least one step is described in [1], along with other techniques for proofs about co-inductive data.

Non-local Properties. With only `filter_always` and `filter_keep`, there are two important characteristics that we are still unable to express. The first characteristic is that no value present in the input and satisfying `P` is forgotten, the second is that the elements in the result are in the same order, with no repetition as long as there were no repetitions in the input. These characteristics seem more complex to express because they are not local properties of each stream element taken separately, but they are global properties of the streams. We propose a solution to express them as properties between consecutive elements, using a new co-inductive predicate named `connected`. Intuitively, a stream is *connected* by some binary relation `R` with respect to some value `x` if any two consecutive elements of the stream are connected by `R` and the stream's first element is connected with `x`. Here is the co-inductive definition:

```
CoInductive connected(R:A→A→Prop):A→str→Prop:=
 connected_cons:
 ∀k x s, R k x → connected R x s →
  connected R k (SCons x s).
```

For instance, to express that some stream contains all the natural numbers above a given k that satisfy the property P in increasing order, we can use the following binary relation:

```
Definition step_all P x y :=
  x < y /\ (∀z, x < z < y → not(P z)) /\ P y
```

and we say that the stream satisfies the property `connected (step_all P) k`. We proved the following two theorems:

```
Theorem step_all_always :
 ∀P k s, connected (step_all P) k s → always P s.

Theorem step_all_present :
 ∀P k s,
  connected (step_all P) k s →
  ∀x, k < x → P x → eventually (fun y => y=x) s.
```

The first theorem expresses that all numbers in the stream satisfy P, and the second one expresses that all numbers larger than k and satisfying P are in the stream.

Our main theorem for `filter` will simply express that it maps any connected stream for a relation R1 to a connected stream for a relation R2, provided the relations R1 and R2 satisfy proper conditions with respect to P.

```
Theorem filter_connected:
 ∀(R1 R2:A → A → Prop),
 (∀x y z, R1 x y → not(P y) → R2 y z → R2 x z) →
 (∀x y, P y → R1 x y → R2 x y) →
 ∀s (h:F_infinite s) x,
  connected R1 x s → connected R2 x (filter s h).
```

The two conditions that R1 and R2 must satisfy express that if $x_1, \ldots x_k$ is a sequence of values such that P x_1 and P x_k hold, not(P x_i) holds for all the other indices i from 1 and k, and R1 x_i x_{i+1} holds, then R2 x_1 x_k holds.

The theorem `filter_connected` sepersedes the other two theorems. The theorem `filter_always` is a obtained with `filter_connected` for R1 the relation that is always satisfied and R2 the relation of x and y that holds if and only if `P y` holds. The theorem `filter_keep Q` is a corollary for R1 and R2 that are both the relation of x and y that holds if and only if `Q y` holds.

We thus have a generic implementation of a filter function, together with a powerful generic theorem to prove most of its properties. This package can be re-used for any development using filters on arbitrary streams, as long as users provide the predicate, the decision function, and proofs that the streams taken as arguments satisfy the predicate infinitely many times. To perform proofs about the filtered streams, users simply need to exhibit the relations `R1` and `R2` and proofs of the properties they have to satisfy. Even though we used a clever technique to implement the filter function, it can be used and reasoned about with much simpler proof techniques.

Some properties are not captured by the theorem `filter_connected`. For instance, if the input stream contains several instances of the same element satisfying `P` then the same number of instances will occur in the result, but this cannot be expressed using the `connected` predicate only.

3 Application to Eratosthenes' Sieve

We can now come back to our initial objective and use our filter function to model Eratosthenes' sieve.

3.1 The Sieve's Specification

Defining Primality. Our model does not follow strictly the initial Haskell program in the sense that we change our filtering predicate for a predicate `not_mult m`, which accepts all numbers that are not multiples of `m` and we use a function `mult_dec` with the following type:

```
∀m, m > 0 → ∀n, {not_mult m n}+{not(not_mult m n)}
```

We use an auxiliary notion of *partial primes*. We say that a number `n` is partially prime up to another number `m` if it is not a multiple of any number larger than 1 and smaller than `m` (the bounds are excluded). This notion is useful to characterize the streams that are given as arguments to the `filter` function, as we see later. We then define the notion of *pre-prime* numbers, which are partially prime up to themselves. The pre-prime numbers actually are 0, 1, and the prime numbers. We prove a few theorems around these notions:

`partial_prime_le`. If a number is partially prime up to m, it is partial prime up to any positive n less than or equal to m.

`partial_prime_step`. If a number is partially prime up to m and not a multiple of m, then it is partially prime up to $1 + m$.

`pre_prime_decompose`. For every positive number n that is not pre-prime, there exists a pre-prime divisor of n between 1 and n (bounds excluded).

`infinite_primes`. For every number, there exists a larger pre-prime number.

`partial_prime_next`. If a number is partially prime up to m and there are no pre-prime numbers between m and n (m included, n excluded), then it is partially prime up to n. The proof of this theorem uses the previous one.

Specifications for Input and Output Streams. Obviously the `connected` predicate is well-suited to express that some stream contains all the prime numbers above a given bound, using the following binary relation:

```
Definition step_prime := step_all pre_prime.
```

The input must be a stream containing partial primes, so we use `connected` with the following relation to describe this specification:

```
Definition step_partial_prime m := step_all (partial_prime m).
```

This gives us different binary relations for different values of `m`.

Main Theorems. We have two main theorems concerning the filter function. The first theorem expresses that the filter function can be used. We need to express that the right `F_infinite` property holds to use the `filter` function. This is expressed with the following theorem.

```
Theorem partial_primes_to_F_infinite:
 ∀m, 1 < m →
 ∀k s, 1 < k → connected (step_partial_prime m) k s →
 F_infinite (not_mult m) s.
```

The proof of this theorem relies on the basic theorem that there are infinitely many primes. It contains both a co-inductive step to prove that the stream tail also satisfies the `F_infinite` property and an inductive step to prove that we can find a number that is not a multiple of `m` in the stream. The inductive part of the proof is done by general induction over the distance to an arbitrary prime number above the first element of the stream, this distance is bound to decrease and stay positive as we traverse the stream while finding only multiples of `m`, because this arbitrary prime number is necessary in the stream and not a multiple of `m`.

The second theorem about the `filter` function shows that when `h` is a proof that `m` is positive the function, `filter (not_mult m) (mult_dec m h)` maps any stream satisfying

```
connected (step_partial_prime m) k
```

to a stream satisfying

```
connected (step_partial_prime (m + 1)) k.
```

This theorem is not proved using any form of induction, we only need to check that the `step_partial_prime` relations satisfy the right conditions for the theorem `filter_connected`.

The other theorems concentrate on streams that are connected for the relations `step_partial_prime`. First, the theorem `partial_prime_next`, which we described in section 3.1, can be lifted to connected streams. Second, the first element of some connected streams are prime numbers:

```
Theorem pre_prime_connect_partial_prime:
 ∀m s, 0 ≤ m →
 connected (step_partial_prime(m + 1)) m s → pre_prime (hd s).
```

3.2 Obtaining the Main Function

The streams that are manipulated in the main function are the streams of all partial primes up to m, starting at m. For this reason, we have defined another property that characterizes the main streams.

```
Definition start_partial_primes s :=
 1 < hd s /\ connected (step_partial_prime (hd s)) (hd s) (tl s).
```

After filtering out the multiples of the stream's first element, we obtain a new stream where the first element p is itself prime and the rest is another stream that satisfies the property `start_partial_primes`. This property is the invariant that is respected by arguments to `sieve` throughout the recursion, this invariant is expressed in a theorem named `start_partial_primes_invariant`. With this invariant we can now define a Coq model for the `sieve` function.

```
CoFixpoint sieve s: start_partial_primes s → str Z :=
 match s return start_partial_primes s → str Z with
  SCons p rest =>
   fun H : start_partial_primes (SCons p rest) =>
   let (Hm, Hpprs) := H in
   let Ha := partial_primes_to_F_infinite p Hm p rest Hm Hpprs
   in SCons p
    (sieve
     (filter (not_mult p) (mult_dec p (lt1_gt0 _ Hm)) rest Ha)
     (start_partial_primes_invariant p rest Ha Hm Hpprs))
 end.
```

Although this definition is cluttered with logical information, the reader should be convinced that this function really follows the same structure as the initial Haskell function we used as a guideline: construct a stream with the first element of the input and then call the `sieve` function on the result of filtering out the multiples of this first element. We can show that the result is connected for the property `step_prime`, this is a simple proof by co-induction.

The last step is to verify that the stream of natural numbers starting from k is also the streams of partial primes up to 2 starting from k (this theorem is called `pprs2`) and can construct the stream of all prime numbers (`lt12` is a proof of $1 < 2$ and `le22` is a proof of $2 \leq 3$):

```
Definition primes := sieve (nums 2)(conj lt12 (pprs2 2 le22)).
```

We finally obtain the following theorem.

```
Theorem pre_primes: connected step_prime 1 primes.
```

Using the theorems `step_all_always` and `step_all_present`, we show that all the prime numbers and only prime numbers are in the result. The proof has been verified using the Coq system. The files are available at the following address:
`ftp://ftp-sop.inria.fr/lemme/Yves.Bertot/filters.tar.gz`

3.3 Code Extraction

We can map the `sieve` function back to Haskell code using the extraction facility [17, 20]. The code we obtain for the `sieve` function is close to the one we initially intended to certify, except that it uses a re-defined type of streams, instead of using the built-in type of lists.

```
sieve s =
  case s of
    SCons p rest →
    SCons p (sieve (filter (\x → mult_dec p x) rest))
```

The code we obtain for the `filter` function is less easy to recognize. A simple difference with the original code is that the extracted code uses its own datatype for boolean values, where `Left` is used to represent `True` and `Right` is used to represent `False`. The main difference is that the function is decomposed into two recursive functions. However, we maintain that this code is equivalent, up to the *unfolding/folding* technique of [3] to the initial `filter`.

```
filter_i p_dec s =
  case s of
    SCons x s' →
      (case p_dec x of
         Left → Pair x s'
         Right → filter_i p_dec s')

filter p_dec s =
  case filter_i p_dec s of
    Pair a b → SCons a (filter p_dec b)
```

4 Conclusion

Our first experiments was actually carried out on a more complex but very similar program, stated as follows:

```
fm a n (x:l) | n < x = fm a (n+a) (x:l)
fm a n (x:l) | n = x = fm a (n+a) l
fm a n (x:l) | x < n = x:(fm a n l)

sieve (x:l) = x:(sieve (fm x (x+x) l))

primes = sieve [2 ..]
```

The function `fm` actually performs the filter step of removing all the multiples of a number in a stream, but it avoids the computation of remainders by keeping the next expected multiple in an auxiliary variable. This is probably closer to the initial description of the sieve by Eratosthenes. This function has an internal state and it does not behave in the same manner as `filter`. Actually, there are streams for which `filter (not_mult m) ...` behaves properly and `fm` does not, since this function relies more crucially on the property that all the values found in the streams are in increasing order. Another significant difference is that this paper presents a separation between algorithm description and proof development, mostly because we believe this makes the method easier to understand. In our previous work, we practiced a more "integrated" development, where the algorithm and the proof that it satisfies its specifications were described at the same time. In spite of these differences, defining this function and reasoning about it still relies on the same technique of mixing inductive and co-inductive predicates and developing an auxiliary function that is recursive on the inductive predicate. This previous work was done together with Damien Galliot as part of a student project in 2003.

The first result of this paper is to show that we can model more general recursive programming than what seems imposed by the basic "guarded-by-constructors" constraint. We believe this work describes an improvement on the domain of co-inductive reasoning that is similar to the improvement brought by well-founded recursion when compared to plain structural recursion. The key point was to adapt the technique of ad-hoc predicates for partial functions to co-inductive structures while respecting the sort constraints of the calculus of constructions. This was made possible thanks to a remark by C. Paulin-Mohring that sub-terms were not restricted to variables. This approach can be re-used to other more practical applications of co-inductive data. In particular, we think it can be adapted to the co-inductive data used to implement real number arithmetic as proposed in [18].

The second important contribution is to describe a filter function in a general form, together with a general theorem that makes it possible to prove properties of this function's result. While the function relies on a lot of expertise in the description of inductive and co-inductive programs, the general theorem makes it possible to relieve users from the task of performing inductive or co-inductive proofs, by simply coming back to relations between successive elements of the input and the output. We have shown the usability of our general theorem on the example of Eratosthenes' sieve. It is interesting to compare our proof to the one proposed in [15]. Our proof only uses local notions: the properties of two consecutive elements in a stream, while their proof uses more general notions concerning whole streams.

Acknowledgements

The author wishes to thank Pierre Castéran for teaching him the techniques of co-induction in the Calculus of Inductive Constructions and for his remarks on early drafts of this paper, Gilles Kahn for discussions on the sieve example, Venanzio Capretta for sharing his knowledge on the technique of recursion on an ad-hoc predicate, Christine Paulin-Mohring for describing the extensions to the guard systems, and Laurence Rideau and Laurent Théry for their comments on early drafts of the paper.

References

1. Yves Bertot and Pierre Castéran. *Interactive Theorem Proving and Program Development, Coq'Art:the Calculus of Inductive Constructions*. Springer-Verlag, 2004.
2. Ana Bove. Simple general recursion in type theory. *Nordic Journal of Computing*, 8(1):22–42, 2001.
3. Rod M. Burstall and John Darlington. A transformation system for developing recursive programs. *Journal of the ACM*, 24(1):44–67, 1977.

4. Pierre Castéran and Davy Rouillard. Reasoning about parametrized automata. In *Proceedings, 8-th International Conference on Real-Time System*, volume 8, pages 107–119, 2000.
5. Thierry Coquand. Infinite objects in Type Theory. In Henk Barendregt and Tobias Nipkow, editors, *Types for Proofs and Programs*, volume 806 of *LNCS*, pages 62–78. Springer Verlag, 1993.
6. Solange Coupet-Grimal. An axiomatization of linear temporal logic in the calculus of inductive constructions. *Journal of Logic and Computation*, 13(6):801–813, 2003.
7. Antony J. T. Davie. *An introduction to functional programming systems using Haskell*. Cambridge Computer Science texts. Cambridge University Press, 1992.
8. Pietro di Gianantonio and Marino Miculan. A unifying approach to recursive and corecursive definitions. In Herman Geuvers and Freek Wiedijk, editors, *Types for Proofs and Programs*, volume 2646 of *LNCS*, pages 148–161. Springer Verlag, 2003.
9. Pietro di Gianantonio and Marino Miculan. Unifying recursive and co-recursive definitions in sheaf categories. In Igora Walukiewicz, editor, *Foundations of Software Science and Computation Structures (FOSSACS'04)*, volume 2987 of *LNCS*. Springer Verlag, 2004.
10. Gilles Dowek, Amy Felty, Hugo Herbelin, Gérard Huet, Chet Murthy, Catherine Parent, Christine Paulin-Mohring, and Benjamin Werner. *The Coq Proof Assistant User's Guide*. INRIA, May 1993. Version 5.8.
11. Catherine Dubois and Véronique Viguié Donzeau-Gouge. A step towards the mechanization of partial functions: domains as inductive predicates, July 1998. `www.cs.bham.ac.uk/~mmk/cade98-partiality`.
12. Eduardo Giménez. Codifying guarded definitions with recursive schemes. In Peter Dybjer, Bengt Nordström, and Jan Smith, editors, *Types for proofs and Programs*, volume 996 of *LNCS*, pages 39–59. Springer Verlag, 1994.
13. Eduardo Giménez. An application of co-inductive types in Coq: Verification of the alternating bit protocol. In *Proceedings of the 1995 Workshop on Types for Proofs and Programs*, volume 1158 of *Lecture Notes in Computer Science*, pages 135–152. Springer-Verlag, 1995.
14. P. Hudak, S. Peyton Jones, P. Wadler, et al. *Report on the Programming Language Haskell*. Yale University, New Haven, Connecticut, USA, 1992. Version 1.2.
15. Gilles Kahn and David B. MacQueen. Coroutines and networks of parallel processes. In *IFIP Congress 77*, pages 993–998. North-Holland, 1977.
16. François Leclerc and Christine Paulin-Mohring. Programming with streams in coq. A case study: the sieve of Eratosthenes. In Henk Barendregt and Tobias Nipkow, editors, *Types for Proofs and Progams*, volume 806 of *LNCS*, pages 191–212. Springer Verlag, 1993.
17. Pierre Letouzey. A new extraction for Coq. In Herman Geuvers and Freek Wiedijk, editors, *TYPES 2002*, volume 2646 of *Lecture Notes in Computer Science*. Springer-Verlag, 2003.
18. Milad Niqui. *Formalising Exact Arithmetic, Representations, Algorithms, and Proofs*. PhD thesis, University of Nijmegen, September 2004. ISBN 90-9018333-7.
19. Christine Paulin-Mohring. Inductive Definitions in the System Coq - Rules and Properties. In M. Bezem and J.-F. Groote, editors, *Proceedings of the conference Typed Lambda Calculi and Applications*, number 664 in Lecture Notes in Computer Science, 1993. LIP research report 92-49.
20. Christine Paulin-Mohring and Benjamin Werner. Synthesis of ML programs in the system Coq. *Journal of Symbolic Computation*, 15:607–640, 1993.
21. David A. Turner. *SASL Language Manual*. St. Andrews University Department of Computer Science, 1976.

Recursive Functions with Higher Order Domains

Ana Bove[1] and Venanzio Capretta[2]

[1] Department of Computing Science, Chalmers University of Technology,
412 96 Göteborg, Sweden
telephone: +46-31-7721020, fax: +46-31-165655
bove@cs.chalmers.se

[2] Department of Mathematics and Statistics, University of Ottawa,
585 King Edward, Ottawa, Canada
telephone: +1-613-562-5800 extension 2103, fax: +1-613-562-5776
venanzio.capretta@mathstat.uottawa.ca

Abstract. In a series of articles, we developed a method to translate general recursive functions written in a functional programming style into constructive type theory. Three problems remained: the method could not properly deal with functions taking functional arguments, the translation of terms containing λ-abstractions was too strict, and partial application of general recursive functions was not allowed. Here, we show how the three problems can be solved by defining a type of partial functions between given types. Every function, including arguments to higher order functions, λ-abstractions and partially applied functions, is then translated as a pair consisting of a domain predicate and a function dependent on the predicate. Higher order functions are assigned domain predicates that inherit termination conditions from their functional arguments. The translation of a λ-abstraction does not need to be total anymore, but generates a local termination condition. The domain predicate of a partially applied function is defined by fixing the given arguments in the domain of the original function. As in our previous articles, simultaneous induction-recursion is required to deal with nested recursive functions. Since by using our method the inductive definition of the domain predicate can refer globally to the domain predicate itself, here we need to work on an impredicative type theory for the method to apply to all functions. However, in most practical cases the method can be adapted to work on a predicative type theory with type universes.

1 Introduction

In functional programming, functions can be defined by recursive equations where the arguments of the recursive calls are not required to be smaller than the input, hence allowing the definition of general recursive functions. Thus, the termination of a program is not guaranteed by its structure. On the other hand, in type theory, only structurally recursive functions are allowed, that is, functions where the recursive calls are performed only on arguments structurally smaller than the input. Thus, some functional programs have no direct translation into type theory.

P. Urzyczyn (Ed.): TLCA 2005, LNCS 3461, pp. 116–130, 2005.

In a series of articles, we have developed a method to translate functional programs into constructive type theory. Given a general recursive function, the method consists in defining an inductive predicate that characterises the inputs on which the function terminates. We can think of this predicate as the domain of the function. The type-theoretic version of the function can then be defined by structural recursion on the proof that the input values satisfy this predicate. A similar method was independently developed by Dubois and Viguié Donzeau-Gouge [DDG98], however they treat nested recursion in a different way and they do not consider the issues we tackle in the present article.

Given a general recursive function $\mathtt{f}$ from σ to τ, its formalisation in type theory following our method consists of an inductive predicate fAcc and a function f with types

$$\mathsf{fAcc}\colon \widehat{\sigma} \to \mathsf{Prop}$$
$$\mathsf{f}\colon (x\colon \widehat{\sigma}; \mathsf{fAcc}\ x) \to \widehat{\tau}$$

where $\widehat{\sigma}$ and $\widehat{\tau}$ are the type-theoretic translations of σ and τ, respectively, and f is defined by structural recursion on its second argument.

Intuitively, if the ith recursive equation of the original program is

$$\mathtt{f}(p) = \cdots \mathtt{f}(a_1) \cdots \mathtt{f}(a_n) \cdots$$

calling itself recursively on the arguments $a_1, \ldots, a_n$, then the ith constructor of fAcc has type

$$\mathsf{facc}_i\colon (\ldots ; \mathsf{fAcc}\ a_1; \ldots ; \mathsf{fAcc}\ a_n)(\mathsf{fAcc}\ p)$$

and the ith structural recursive equation of f is

$$\mathsf{f}\ p\ (\mathsf{facc}_i\ \cdots\ h_1\ \cdots\ h_n) = \cdots (\mathsf{f}\ a_1\ h_1) \cdots (\mathsf{f}\ a_n\ h_n) \cdots .$$

In practise, the types of the constructors of fAcc and the structure of the equations of f may be more complex, but the idea remains the same: fAcc is inductively defined so that proving fAcc on an input p requires proofs of fAcc for the arguments of all the recursive calls that $\mathtt{f}$ performs when applied to p.

The method was introduced by Bove [Bov01] to formalise simple general recursive algorithms in constructive type theory (by simple we mean non-nested and non-mutually recursive). It was extended by Bove and Capretta [BC01] to treat nested recursion by using Dybjer's simultaneous induction-recursion, and by Bove [Bov02a] to treat mutually recursive algorithms, nested or not. A formal description of the method is given in [BC04] where we also prove a soundness and a weak completeness theorem. The first three papers mentioned above and a previous version of [BC04] have been put together into the first author's Ph.D. thesis [Bov02b]. A tutorial on the method can be found in [Bov03].

The method of [BC04] separates the computational and logical parts of the type-theoretic versions of the functional programs. An immediate consequence is that it allows the formalisation of partial functions: proving that a certain function is total amounts to proving that the corresponding domain predicate is satisfied by every input. Another consequence is that the resulting type-theoretic algorithms are clear, compact and easy to understand. They are as simple as their counterparts in a functional programming language. However, our method has some problems and limitations which we have already mentioned in [BC04].

The first problem concerns higher order functions, that is, functions that take other functions as arguments. For example, let us consider the function `map`: $(\sigma \to \tau) \to [\sigma] \to [\tau]$, as defined in the Haskell [Jon03] prelude, which has a first argument in a functional type. Since `map` is structurally recursive on its list argument, in [BC04] we translate it into a structurally recursive function map in type theory with type $(\widehat{\sigma} \to \widehat{\tau}) \to [\widehat{\sigma}] \to [\widehat{\tau}]$. This means that the first argument of map can only be instantiated to a total function of type $\widehat{\sigma} \to \widehat{\tau}$. But in functional programming `map` could be applied to potentially non-terminating functions. Therefore, even if `map` is structurally recursive, it is still liable to non-termination since its functional argument f might be undefined on some (or all) of the elements to which it will be applied. In other words, `map` inherits the termination conditions from its functional argument. In [BC04] we had no way to express this fact. Therefore, our translation was too restrictive with respect to the original functional program.

Another problem is that whenever there is a λ-abstraction in the right-hand side of an equation, the method of [BC04] translates it as a total function in type theory. This interpretation is too strict, since the corresponding function could diverge on arguments to which it is not actually applied during execution, without jeopardising the termination behaviour of the program. More specifically, if under the scope of the λ-abstraction there is a call to one of the general recursive functions we are defining in our program, let us say `f`, the method inductively requires every instantiation of the argument of the λ-abstraction to be in the domain of f. However, this constraint might be stronger than actually needed since the λ-abstraction may just be applied to a proper subset of all the instantiations. This problem is already present in a classical setting in the work of Finn, Fourman, and Longley [FFL97].

The third problem is that partial applications of general recursive functions are not allowed in [BC04]. When applying a recursive function f taking m arguments $a_1, \ldots, a_m$, we must also provide a proof h of the accessibility of $a_1, \ldots, a_m$. If f is applied to an insufficient number of arguments $a_1, \ldots, a_k$ with $k < m$, then the accessibility condition cannot even be formulated and it is not possible to prove that the result of the application converges. Therefore, we barred partial applications of general recursive functions.

Here, we introduce a type of partial functions in type theory and we present a new method to translate functional programs into their type-theoretic equivalents. The method is based on the one presented in [BC04] but, now, it translates every function in the functional side into an element of the new type of partial functions. With this new approach, the problems we mention above disappear.

For our new method to be applicable to any function, we need to work in a type theory with an impredicative universe Set with inductive-recursive definitions à la Dybjer [Dyb00]. Both datatypes and propositions are represented as elements of Set. Therefore, we use the Calculus of Construction [CH88] extended with a schema for simultaneous inductive-recursive definitions. A justification of the soundness of inductive-recursive definitions in the Calculus of Constructions is given by [Bla03] and [Cap04]. The method works also in the slightly different type architecture used in the proof assistant Coq [Coq02]. There are in Coq two impredicative universes, Set and Prop, both being elements of the predicative universe Type. For the purpose of this work, it is possible to use Prop for the domain predicate and Set for the functions. Usually, elimination of a proposition over a set (essential in our method) is not allowed in Coq, a feature intended to prevent mixing logical information with pure computational content. However, Christine Paulin [Pau] devised a way around this difficulty, consisting in defining structural deconstruction functions on propositions that have the property of uniqueness of proofs, as is the case of our domain predicates. Therefore, we use the notation Set for datatypes and Prop for propositions, to be interpreted as either the same impredicative universe or two distinct impredicative universes, in which case Paulin's method is to be used in place of structural recursion on the proofs of accessibility. As we point out later, it would be possible to adapt the method to work on a predicative type theory. However, we would loose generality since then the method could not be used to translate all functions (see function `itz` in section 4).

An extension of type theory with a constructor $A \rightsquigarrow B$ for partial functions from A to B was already proposed by Constable and Mendler in [CM85]. Together with the type $A \rightsquigarrow B$ they introduce a new form of canonical elements, which is not the case in our partial functions type. They are of the form $fix(f, x.F)$, to be intended as the functions with definition $f(x) = F$. From the definition of f one can construct its domain $dom(f)(x)$, essentially as in our method, as a recursive predicate generated structurally by the recursive calls to f in F. The roles of both domain predicates are however quite different. While our functions are defined by structural recursion on their domain predicates, the predicates in [CM85] serve only as a way to characterise the valid inputs and the functions in [CM85] are defined independently of their domain predicates.

This paper is mainly intended for readers with some knowledge in type theory. This said, what follows is just intended to fix the notation.

A *context* Γ is a sequence of assumptions $\Gamma \equiv x_1 : \alpha_1; \ldots ; x_n : \alpha_n$ where $x_1, \ldots , x_n$ are distinct variables and each α_i is a type that can contain occurrences of the variables that precede it. We call a sequence of variable assumptions Δ a *context extension* of the context Γ if $\Gamma; \Delta$ is a context.

If α is a type and β is a family of types over α, we write $(x : \alpha)\beta(x)$ for the type of dependent functions from α to β. If β does not depend on values of type α we might simply write $\alpha \to \beta$ for the type of functions from α to β. Functions have abstractions as canonical values, which we write $[x : \alpha]e$. Consecutive dependent function types and abstractions are written $(x_1 : \alpha_1; \ldots ; x_n : \alpha_n)\beta(x_1, \ldots , x_n)$ and $[x_1 : \alpha_1, \ldots , x_n : \alpha_n]e$, respectively. In either case, each α_i can contain occurrences of the variables that precede it. If β doest not depend on the last assumption x_n, then we can write $(x_1 : \alpha_1; \ldots ; x_{n-1} : \alpha_{n-1}; \alpha_n) \to \beta(x_1, \ldots , x_{n-1})$.

For the sake of simplicity, we will use the same notation as much as possible both in the functional programming side and in the type-theoretic side. In addition, names in the functional programming side will be written with `typewriter` font while names in the type-theoretic side will be written with Sans Serif font.

The article has the following organisation. Section 2 briefly presents the method of [BC04]. Section 3 defines the type of partial functions and gives a formal definition of the new translation. Section 4 illustrates the translation on some examples. Finally, Section 5 discusses advantages and disadvantages of the new method.

2 Brief Summary of the Original Translation

We start from a Haskell-like functional programming language $\mathcal{FP}$. The types allowed in $\mathcal{FP}$ are: variable types, inductive data types, and function types.

Elements of inductive types are generated by constructors which must always be used fully applied.

There are two kinds of functions, that is, of elements in the functional type: those defined by structural recursion and those defined by general recursion. Since the two kinds need to be translated differently, we distinguish them in the functional programming notation. Structurally recursive functions acquire the usual Haskell-like functional types, $\sigma \to \tau$. On the other hand, general recursive functions must always be used fully applied. We reflect this requirement in the syntax by assigning them a *specification* $\sigma_1, \ldots, \sigma_m \Rightarrow \tau$ rather than a proper functional type.

The two kinds of functions give rise to two kinds of applications: those dealing with proper functional types and those dealing with specifications.

The form of the definition of a general recursive function is:

$$\begin{array}{l} \texttt{fix f} : \sigma_1, \ldots, \sigma_m \Rightarrow \tau \\ \quad \texttt{f}(p_{11}, \ldots, p_{1m}) = e_1 \\ \quad \vdots \\ \quad \texttt{f}(p_{l1}, \ldots, p_{lm}) = e_l \end{array}$$

where the p_{ij}'s are exclusive linear patterns of the corresponding types and the e_i's are valid terms of type τ (see Definition 1 below). We also allow guarded equations in the definition of a function, where the condition in the equation must be a valid term of type `Bool`. In any case, the equations must satisfy the exclusivity condition: for every particular argument, at most one equation can apply. It is possible that, for some argument, no equation applies, in which case the function is undefined on the given input.

Since the definition of the set of valid terms of a certain type (definition 4 in [BC04]) is important for the understanding of this work, we transcribe it below.

Let us call $\mathcal{F}$ the set of all structurally recursive functions together with their types. Then, the valid terms that we allow in the definition of a recursive function depend on two components: (a) the set $\mathcal{X}$ of variables that can occur free in the terms, and (*b*) the set $\mathcal{SF}$ of functions that are being defined (we might define several mutually recursive functions simultaneously), which can be used in the recursive calls.

Definition 1. *Let $\mathcal{X}$ be a set of variables together with their types. Let $\mathcal{SF}$ be a set of function names together with their specifications. Let the set of names of the variables in $\mathcal{X}$, the set of names of the functions in $\mathcal{SF}$, and the set of names of the functions in $\mathcal{F}$ be disjoint. We say that t* is a valid term of type τ *with respect to $\mathcal{X}$ and $\mathcal{SF}$, if the judgement $\mathcal{X};\mathcal{SF} \vdash t\colon \tau$ can be derived from the rules in Figure 1.* □

$$\frac{x\colon \sigma \in \mathcal{X}}{\mathcal{X};\mathcal{SF} \vdash x\colon \sigma} \qquad \frac{f\colon \sigma \to \tau \in \mathcal{F}}{\mathcal{X};\mathcal{SF} \vdash f\colon \sigma \to \tau}$$

$$\frac{\mathtt{f}\colon \sigma_1, \ldots, \sigma_m \Rightarrow \tau \in \mathcal{SF} \quad \mathcal{X};\mathcal{SF} \vdash a_i\colon \sigma_i \text{ for } 1 \leqslant i \leqslant m}{\mathcal{X};\mathcal{SF} \vdash f(a_1, \ldots, a_m)\colon \tau}$$

$$\frac{\mathsf{c}\colon \tau_1, \ldots, \tau_k \Rightarrow \mathtt{T} \qquad \mathsf{c} \text{ constructor of } \mathtt{T} \qquad \mathcal{X};\mathcal{SF} \vdash a_i\colon \tau_i \text{ for } 1 \leqslant i \leqslant k}{\mathcal{X};\mathcal{SF} \vdash \mathsf{c}(a_1, \ldots, a_k)\colon \mathtt{T}}$$

$$\frac{(\mathcal{X}\backslash x) \bigcup \{x\colon \sigma\};\mathcal{SF} \vdash b\colon \tau}{\mathcal{X};\mathcal{SF} \vdash [x]b\colon \sigma \to \tau} \qquad \frac{\mathcal{X};\mathcal{SF} \vdash f\colon \sigma \to \tau \quad \mathcal{X};\mathcal{SF} \vdash a\colon \sigma}{\mathcal{X};\mathcal{SF} \vdash (f\ a)\colon \tau}$$

Fig. 1. Rules for deriving valid terms judgements

Next, we briefly explain the translation of programs into type theory presented in [BC04]. Below, we call $\widehat{\sigma}$ the translation of the type σ.

Variable types and variables, and inductive data types and their constructors are translated straightforwardly. A function type $\sigma \to \tau$ is translated as the total function type $\widehat{\sigma} \to \widehat{\tau}$ in type theory. Structurally recursive functions are directly translated as structurally recursive functions in type theory with the same functional type (except for some possible changes in the notation).

As we have already mentioned in Section 1, a function $\mathtt{f}\colon \sigma_1, \ldots, \sigma_m \Rightarrow \tau$ is translated as a pair

$$\begin{aligned} &\mathsf{fAcc}\colon \widehat{\sigma_1} \to \ldots \to \widehat{\sigma_m} \to \mathsf{Prop} \\ &\mathsf{f}\colon (x_1\colon \widehat{\sigma_1}; \ldots; x_m\colon \widehat{\sigma_m}; \mathsf{fAcc}\ x_1 \cdots x_m) \to \widehat{\tau} \end{aligned}$$

In order to complete the translation of $\mathtt{f}$ we need to give the types of the constructors of fAcc and the equations defining f.

For each equation in $\mathtt{f}$ (i.e., in the functional side) we define a constructor for fAcc and an equation for f (i.e., in the type-theoretic side) as follows. Let

$$\mathtt{f}(p_1, \ldots, p_m) = e \quad \mathtt{if}\ c$$

be a guarded equation of $\mathtt{f}$, let Γ be the context of variables occurring in the patterns $p_1, \ldots, p_m$ and let $\widehat{\Gamma}$ be its type-theoretic translation. Given the term

e, we define a type-theoretic context Φ_e which extends $\widehat{\Gamma}$, and a type-theoretic translation $\widehat{e}$ of e whose free variables are included in $\widehat{\Gamma}; \Phi_e$. Similarly, we define Φ_c and $\widehat{c}$.

The type of the constructor of fAcc corresponding to the above equation is

$$\mathsf{facc}\colon (\widehat{\Gamma}; \Phi_c; q\colon \widehat{c} = \mathsf{true}; \Phi_e)(\mathsf{fAcc}\ \widehat{p_1} \cdots \widehat{p_m})$$

and the corresponding equation of f is

$$\mathsf{f}\ \widehat{p_1} \cdots \widehat{p_m}\ (\mathsf{facc}\ \overline{x}\ \overline{y}\ q\ \overline{z}) = \widehat{e}$$

where $\overline{x}$, $\overline{y}$ and $\overline{z}$ are the variables defined in $\widehat{\Gamma}$, Φ_c and Φ_e, respectively, and $\widehat{p_i}$ is the type-theoretic version of p_i. For non-conditional equations, we simply omit all the parts related with the condition c.

The translation of the application of a function to an argument must consider two cases. If the function has a regular function type $\sigma \to \tau$, that is, it is defined without using general recursion, then the application is translated straightforwardly. When we translate the application of a general recursive function to *all* its arguments, we have to make sure that the arguments are in the domain of the function. Hence, we must add a constraint expressing this fact in the translation context of the application. Concretely, when translating a term of the form $\mathtt{f}(a_1, \ldots, a_m)$, we must add an assumption $(h\colon \mathsf{fAcc}\ \widehat{a_1} \cdots \widehat{a_m})$ to the translation context of the application, where $\widehat{a_i}$ is the type-theoretic translation of a_i. The application itself is translated as $(\mathsf{f}\ \widehat{a_1} \cdots \widehat{a_m}\ h)$. The argument h is needed to make sure that f is only applied to arguments in its domain.

The crucial part of the method in [BC04] is the definition of the context Φ_a and the type-theoretic term $\widehat{a}$ associated with a term a. Both Φ_a and $\widehat{a}$ are defined simultaneously by recursion over the structure of a.

For a formal description of the language $\mathcal{FP}$ and the translation of its programs into type theory, the reader can refer to [BC04].

We finish this section with the definition of the partial function my_mod and its translation into type theory following the method we have just described. This function is such that $\mathtt{my\_mod}(m, n) = n \ \mathtt{mod}\ m$ whenever $m \neq 0$, where mod is the standard modulo function defined as in the Haskell prelude.

We define the functional version of my_mod as:

$$\begin{array}{ll}
\mathtt{fix\ my_mod}\colon \mathtt{N}, \mathtt{N} \Rightarrow \mathtt{N} & \\
\quad \mathtt{my_mod}(m, n) = n & \mathtt{if}\ m \neq \mathsf{0} \wedge n < m \\
\quad \mathtt{my_mod}(m, n) = \mathtt{my_mod}(m, n - m) & \mathtt{if}\ m \neq \mathsf{0} \wedge n \geqslant m
\end{array}$$

where $-$, $<$, $\geqslant$, $\neq$ and $\wedge$ are defined as expected.

This function is translated into type theory as follows:

$$\begin{array}{l}
\mathsf{my_modAcc}\colon \mathsf{N} \to \mathsf{N} \to \mathsf{Prop} \\
\quad \mathsf{my_mod_acc}_{<}\colon (m\colon \mathsf{N}; n\colon \mathsf{N}; q\colon (m \neq \mathsf{0} \wedge n < m) = \mathsf{true})(\mathsf{my_modAcc}\ m\ n) \\
\quad \mathsf{my_mod_acc}_{\geqslant}\colon (m\colon \mathsf{N}; n\colon \mathsf{N}; q\colon (m \neq \mathsf{0} \wedge n \geqslant m) = \mathsf{true}; \\
\qquad\qquad\qquad\quad h\colon \mathsf{my_modAcc}\ m\ (n - m))(\mathsf{my_modAcc}\ m\ n)
\end{array}$$

$$\begin{array}{l}
\mathsf{my_mod}\colon (m\colon \mathsf{N}; n\colon \mathsf{N}; \mathsf{my_modAcc}\ m\ n) \to \mathsf{N} \\
\quad \mathsf{my_mod}\ m\ n\ (\mathsf{my_mod_acc}_{<}\ m\ n\ q) = n \\
\quad \mathsf{my_mod}\ m\ n\ (\mathsf{my_mod_acc}_{\geqslant}\ m\ n\ q\ h) = \mathsf{my_mod}\ m\ (n - m)\ h
\end{array}$$

Observe that we will never be able to apply the function $\mathsf{my\_mod}$ to the arguments 0 and $i\colon \mathsf{N}$ since we cannot construct a proof of $(\mathsf{my\_modAcc}\ 0\ i)$.

3 New Translation of Functional Programs

We now introduce the type of *partial functions* in our impredicative type theory. If $\alpha\colon \mathsf{Set}$ and $\beta\colon \mathsf{Set}$, then we define the type of partial functions as

$$\alpha \rightharpoonup \beta \equiv \Sigma D\colon \alpha \to \mathsf{Prop}.(x\colon \alpha; D\ x) \to \beta\colon \mathsf{Set}.$$

Thus, a partial function $f\colon \alpha \rightharpoonup \beta$ is actually a pair consisting of the domain of the function and the function itself, which depends on a proof that the input value is in the domain of the function. The definition can be extended to consider partial functions of several arguments. If $\alpha_1, \ldots, \alpha_m\colon \mathsf{Set}$ and $\beta\colon \mathsf{Set}$, we define

$$\begin{aligned}\alpha_1, \ldots, \alpha_m \rightharpoonup \beta \equiv\ & \Sigma D\colon \alpha_1 \to \cdots \to \alpha_m \to \mathsf{Prop}.\\ & (x_1\colon \alpha_1; \ldots; x_m\colon \alpha_m; D\ x_1\ \cdots\ x_m) \to \beta.\end{aligned}$$

If $f\colon \alpha_1, \ldots, \alpha_m \rightharpoonup \beta$, we write dom_f for $(\pi_1\ f)$ and, if $a_i\colon \alpha_i$ for $1 \leqslant i \leqslant m$ and $(h\colon \mathsf{dom}_f\ a_1\ \cdots\ a_m)$, we use the notation $f_{[h]}(a_1, \ldots, a_m)$ for $(\pi_2\ f\ a_1\ \cdots\ a_m\ h)$.

In the case of functions of many arguments, we may partially apply the function to only $k < m$ arguments. Then we write:

$$\begin{aligned}& f(a_1, \ldots, a_k) = \langle D', f'\rangle\colon \alpha_{k+1}, \ldots, \alpha_m \rightharpoonup \beta\\ & \text{where } D'\ x_{k+1}\ \cdots\ x_m = \mathsf{dom}_f\ a_1\ \cdots\ a_k\ x_{k+1}\ \cdots\ x_m\\ & \qquad f'\ x_{k+1}\ \cdots\ x_m\ h = f_{[h]}(a_1, \ldots, a_k, x_{k+1}, \ldots, x_m)\end{aligned} \qquad (*)$$

This definition amounts to an outline of a proof of the left-to-right direction of the following equivalence:

$$\alpha_1, \ldots, \alpha_m \rightharpoonup \beta \cong \alpha_1 \to \cdots \to \alpha_k \to (\alpha_{k+1}, \ldots, \alpha_m \rightharpoonup \beta).$$

The right-to-left direction is straightforward.

In what follows, we give a modification of the method of [BC04] that uses the type of partial functions in place of the standard type of total functions.

First, we apply the translation method also to structurally recursive functions since we want all the functions to have a partial function type. Hence, structurally and general recursive functions are now all assigned specifications, so now the set $\mathcal{SF}$ contains also the functions previously in $\mathcal{F}$. As a consequence, the second rule in Definition 1 of valid terms simply disappears.

In addition, the definition of valid terms required every occurrence of a general recursive function to be fully applied. Now we lift this restriction and we replace the third rule in Definition 1 by the following rule:

$$\frac{\mathtt{f}\colon \sigma_1, \ldots, \sigma_m \Rightarrow \tau \in \mathcal{SF} \quad \mathcal{X}; \mathcal{SF} \vdash a_i\colon \sigma_i \text{ for } 1 \leqslant i \leqslant k \text{ and } k \leqslant m}{\mathcal{X}; \mathcal{SF} \vdash f(a_1, \ldots, a_k)\colon \sigma_{k+1}, \ldots, \sigma_m \Rightarrow \tau}$$

where if $k = m$, $\sigma_{k+1}, \ldots, \sigma_m \Rightarrow \tau$ is understood simply as τ.

A similar modification has to be made to the fourth rule of the same definition, which deals with constructors, since they must also be used fully applied in [BC04].

Next, we modify the definition of the translation into type theory.

Variable types and inductive datatypes are translated as before. The function type $\sigma \rightarrow \tau$ is now translated into the partial function type $\widehat{\sigma} \rightharpoonup \widehat{\tau}$. In our previous work, specifications were not translated into a type. Now, given the specification $\sigma_1, \ldots, \sigma_m \Rightarrow \tau$ we define its translation as the type of partial functions $\widehat{\sigma_1}, \ldots, \widehat{\sigma_m} \rightharpoonup \widehat{\tau}$.

Constructors are assigned specifications in [BC04] rather than types. With the translation we give of specifications, a constructor is now expected to have a domain predicate. However, the application of a constructor to arguments of the corresponding types should always be defined. Let $\mathsf{c}\colon \sigma_1, \ldots, \sigma_m \Rightarrow \mathtt{T}$ be one of the constructors of the inductive type $\mathtt{T}$. In type theory, the corresponding constructor would have type $\mathsf{c}\colon \widehat{\sigma_1} \rightarrow \cdots \rightarrow \widehat{\sigma_m} \rightarrow \mathsf{T}$. The translation of c is then defined as $\mathsf{C} = \langle \mathsf{cAcc}, \mathsf{c}' \rangle \colon \widehat{\sigma_1}, \ldots, \widehat{\sigma_m} \rightharpoonup \mathsf{T}$ with

$$\begin{aligned}
&\mathsf{cAcc} = [x_1\colon \widehat{\sigma_1}; \ldots; x_m\colon \widehat{\sigma_m}]\mathbb{T}\colon \widehat{\sigma_1} \rightarrow \cdots \rightarrow \widehat{\sigma_m} \rightarrow \mathsf{Prop} \\
&\mathsf{c}'_{[h]}(a_1, \ldots, a_m) = \mathsf{c}(a_1, \ldots, a_m)
\end{aligned}$$

where $\mathbb{T}$ is a set containing only the element $\mathtt{tt}$.

Below we present the definition of the context Φ_a and the type-theoretic expression $\widehat{a}$ associated with a term a. The cases of function calls and constructors are now split into two cases, according to whether the function or the constructor is fully or partially applied; this distinction was not relevant in [BC04].

Definition 2. *Given a term a and a context Γ containing type assumptions for the free variables in a, we define the context extension Φ_a and the type-theoretic term $\widehat{a}$ by recursion on the structure of a. Note that, since Φ_a extends Γ, we should only introduce fresh variables in Φ_a.*

$a \equiv z$**:** *If the term a is the variable z, then $\Phi_a \equiv ()$ and $\widehat{a} \equiv z$.*

$a \equiv \mathtt{f}(a_1, \ldots, a_m)$**:** *Here, $\mathtt{f}\colon \sigma_1, \ldots, \sigma_m \Rightarrow \tau$, and $a_1, \ldots, a_m$ are arguments of the appropriate types. Hence, the function is fully applied. First, we determine $\Phi_{a_1}, \ldots, \Phi_{a_m}$ and $\widehat{a_1} \ldots, \widehat{a_m}$ by structural recursion. We then define*

$$\Phi_a \equiv \Phi_{a_1}; \ldots; \Phi_{a_m}; (h\colon \mathsf{fAcc}\ \widehat{a_1}\ \cdots\ \widehat{a_m}) \quad \text{and} \quad \widehat{a} \equiv \mathsf{f}_{[h]}(\widehat{a_1}, \ldots, \widehat{a_m})$$

$a \equiv \mathtt{f}(a_1, \ldots, a_k)$**:** *Let $\mathtt{f}$ be as above and $k < m$. In this case the function is not fully applied. Under similar assumptions as in the previous case, we define $\Phi_a \equiv \Phi_{a_1}; \ldots; \Phi_{a_k}$ and $\widehat{a} \equiv \mathsf{f}(\widehat{a_1}, \ldots, \widehat{a_k})$. See $(*)$ for the meaning of the partial application of f to only k of its m arguments.*

$a \equiv \mathsf{c}(a_1, \ldots, a_m)$**:** *Let c be a constructor fully applied to arguments of the appropriate types. Under similar assumptions as in the case of fully applied functions, we define $\Phi_a \equiv \Phi_{a_1}; \ldots; \Phi_{a_m}$ and $\widehat{a} \equiv \mathsf{c}(\widehat{a_1}, \ldots, \widehat{a_m})$. Notice that this is equal to $\mathsf{c}'_{[\mathtt{tt}]}(\widehat{a_1}, \ldots, \widehat{a_m})$, so the translation is consistent with that of recursive functions.*

$a \equiv \mathsf{c}(a_1, \ldots, a_k)$: *Let* c *be a constructor applied to only* k *of its* m *arguments. This case is similar to the case of partially applied functions.*

$a \equiv [z]b$: *Let* σ *be the type of* z. *We start by calculating* Φ_b *and* $\widehat{b}$ *recursively. Notice that now, the context with the assumptions for the free variables in* b *is* $\widehat{(\Gamma; z\colon \sigma)}$. *We define* $\Phi_{[z]b} \equiv ()$ *and* $\widehat{[z]b} \equiv \langle \mathsf{gAcc}, \mathsf{g} \rangle$ *with*

$$\mathsf{gAcc} = [z\colon \widehat{\sigma}]\Sigma\Phi_b$$
$$\mathsf{g} = [z\colon \widehat{\sigma}; h\colon \mathsf{gAcc}\ z]\mathsf{Cases}\ h\ \mathsf{of}\ \left\{ \langle \overline{y_{\Phi_b}} \rangle \mapsto \widehat{b} \right.$$

where $\Sigma\Phi_b$ *is a big* Σ*-type defining the conjunction of all the preconditions contained in* Φ_b *and* $\overline{y_{\Phi_b}}$ *is the sequence of variables in* Φ_b. *If* Φ_b *is empty then* $\Sigma\Phi_b$ *is simply understood as* $\mathbb{T}$ *and the whole case-expression can just be replaced by* $\widehat{b}$. *On the other hand, if* Φ_b *contains only one assumption then* $\Sigma\Phi_b$ *is simply* Φ_b. *Moreover, the case-expression can just be replaced by* $\widehat{b}[y_b := h]$, *where* y_b *is the variable assumed in* Φ_b.

$a \equiv (g\ b)$: *Here* g *stands for any function with a functional type (not a specification). As usual, we define* Φ_a *and* $\widehat{a}$ *in terms of* $\Phi_g, \widehat{g}, \Phi_b$ *and* $\widehat{b}$. *Since* g *is (potentially) a partial function, it has a partial function type in type theory, so we have to make sure that it is only applied to elements in its domain. Hence, we have* $\Phi_a = \Phi_g; \Phi_b; (h\colon \mathsf{dom}_{\widehat{g}}\ \widehat{b})$ *and* $\widehat{a} = \widehat{g}_{[h]}(\widehat{b})$. □

Theorem 1 of [BC04] can be strengthened: now, it states that the functional program `f` and its type-theoretic translation f denote the same partial recursive function. The proof is similar to those of Theorems 1 and 2 in [BC04] and it relies on a correspondence between computation of terms in functional programming and reduction of their translations in type theory. Given the application of a general recursive function, this correspondence depends, in turn, on the correspondence between the trace of the computation of the application in functional programming and a normal form of the proof that the type-theoretic versions of the arguments satisfy the corresponding domain predicate.

Lemma 1. *Let* $e\colon \tau$ *be a valid term in* $\mathcal{FP}$ *with respect to* Γ *and* $\mathcal{SF}$, *and let* $\widehat{\Gamma}$ *be the type-theoretic translation of* Γ. *Let* Φ_e *be the translation context generated by the method,* $\overline{z}$ *the sequence of variables in* Φ_e, *and* $\overline{d}$ *an instantiation of* Φ_e *depending only on variables in* $\widehat{\Gamma}$. *Then the computation of* e *in* $\mathcal{FP}$ *terminates with a term* r *whose type-theoretic translation* $\widehat{r}$ *is convertible with* $\widehat{e}[\overline{z := d}]$.

Proof. We do induction on the pair (l, e) where l is the maximum length of a normalisation path of $\widehat{e}[\overline{z := d}]$ (notice that the path is finite because type theory enjoys strong normalisation) and the order $<$ is the lexicographic order on pairs, that is: $(l', e') < (l, e)$ iff either $l' < l$ or $l' \leqslant l$ and e' is structurally smaller than e. This part of the proof does not present any substantial change with respect to our previous work. □

Lemma 2. *Let* e *and* Φ_e *be as in the previous lemma. If the computation of* e *terminates in* $\mathcal{FP}$ *then there is an instantiation* $\overline{d}$ *of* Φ_e.

Proof. We do induction on the pair (l, e) where l is the length of the trace of the computation of e and the order is the lexicographic order on pairs as in lemma 1.

The fact that we assign domain predicates also to local functions generated by λ-abstraction entails that, when computing a local function on a specific argument, we can generate a proof of the local termination predicate whenever the application terminates in the functional side. This is an improvement on [BC04], where we needed to generate a proof of totality for the local function. □

Theorem 1. *Let* $\mathtt{f}\colon \sigma_1, \ldots, \sigma_m \Rightarrow \tau$ *be a function in* $\mathcal{FP}$. *Let* fAcc *and* f *be the domain predicate for* $\mathtt{f}$ *and the type-theoretic version of* $\mathtt{f}$, *respectively. Then, for every sequence of values* $v_1\colon \sigma_1, \ldots, v_m\colon \sigma_m$ *we have that*

$$(\mathsf{fAcc}\ \widehat{v_1}\ \cdots\ \widehat{v_m})\ \textit{is provable} \quad\Longleftrightarrow\quad \mathtt{f}\ \textit{is defined on}\ v_1, \ldots, v_m$$

and if $(h\colon \mathsf{fAcc}\ \widehat{v_1}\ \cdots\ \widehat{v_m})$ *is a closed proof, then*

$$\mathsf{f}_{[h]}(\widehat{v_1}, \ldots, \widehat{v_m}) = \widehat{\mathtt{f}(v_1, \ldots, v_m)}.$$

Proof. Immediate by applying the previous lemmas to $e \equiv \mathtt{f}(v_1, \ldots, v_m)$. □

4 Illustration of the Method

We illustrate the advantages of the new method on some examples containing the features that were problematic in our previous work. The function `map` shows how to deal with functional arguments, the function `sumdel` illustrates how λ-abstractions are treated, and the function `is_div2` shows how to deal with partial applications.

In addition, we demonstrate that the impredicativity of the sort Prop is necessary for the generality of the method, by giving an example `itz` that gives rise to a polymorphic domain predicate. The example `itz` is also the only one with nested recursion, so it is the only one that needs induction-recursion.

Functional Arguments: `map`. Functional version:

$$\begin{aligned}&\mathtt{fix\ map}\colon \gamma \to \delta, \mathtt{List}\ \gamma \Rightarrow \mathtt{List}\ \delta\\ &\qquad \mathtt{map}(f, \mathtt{nil}) = \mathtt{nil}\\ &\qquad \mathtt{map}(f, \mathtt{cons}(x, xs)) = \mathtt{cons}(f\ x, \mathtt{map}(f, xs))\end{aligned}$$

Type-theoretic version: $\mathsf{Map} = \langle \mathsf{mapAcc}, \mathsf{map}\rangle\colon (\gamma \rightharpoonup \delta), \mathsf{List}\ \gamma \rightharpoonup \mathsf{List}\ \delta$ with:

$$\begin{aligned}&\mathsf{mapAcc}\colon (\gamma \rightharpoonup \delta) \to \mathsf{List}\ \gamma \to \mathsf{Prop}\\ &\quad \mathsf{mapacc}_{\mathsf{nil}}\colon (f\colon \gamma \rightharpoonup \delta)(\mathsf{mapAcc}\ f\ \mathsf{nil})\\ &\quad \mathsf{mapacc}_{\mathsf{cons}}\colon (f\colon \gamma \rightharpoonup \delta; x\colon \gamma; xs\colon \mathsf{List}\ \gamma; h\colon \mathsf{dom}_f\ x; h_1\colon \mathsf{dom}_{\mathsf{Map}}\ f\ xs)\\ &\qquad\qquad\quad (\mathsf{mapAcc}\ f\ \mathsf{cons}(x, xs))\end{aligned}$$

$$\begin{aligned}&\mathsf{map}\colon (f\colon \gamma \rightharpoonup \delta; ys\colon \mathsf{List}\ \gamma; \mathsf{mapAcc}\ f\ ys) \to \mathsf{List}\ \delta\\ &\quad \mathsf{map}\ f\ \mathsf{nil}\ (\mathsf{mapacc}_{\mathsf{nil}}\ f) = \mathsf{nil}\\ &\quad \mathsf{map}\ f\ \mathsf{cons}(x, xs)\ (\mathsf{mapacc}_{\mathsf{cons}}\ f\ x\ xs\ h\ h_1) = \mathsf{cons}(f_{[h]}(x), \mathsf{Map}_{[h_1]}(f, xs))\end{aligned}$$

Recall that ($\mathsf{dom_{Map}}\ f\ xs$) and $\mathsf{Map}_{[h_1]}(f, xs)$ reduce to ($\mathsf{mapAcc}\ f\ xs$) and ($\mathsf{map}\ f\ xs\ h_1$), respectively. In addition, when map is applied to a concrete partial function $\langle \mathsf{fAcc}, \mathsf{f}\rangle$, ($\mathsf{dom}_f\ x$) and $f_{[h]}(x)$ reduce to ($\mathsf{fAcc}\ x$) and ($\mathsf{f}\ x\ h$), respectively. When checking the validity of the inductive-recursive definitions, we have to expand such terms.

Abstractions: sumdel. Here, the functions $+$, `sum` and `delete` are all structurally recursive. The function $+$ is defined as expected, and `sum` and `delete` are as in the Haskell prelude. Below, we assume that the mentioned functions have already been translated into type theory. Moreover, for simplicity reasons, we use the structurally recursive versions of these functions rather than the formal translations we would obtain with our new method.

Functional version:

$$\begin{array}{l} \mathtt{fix\ sumdel} \colon \mathtt{List\ N} \Rightarrow \mathtt{N} \\ \quad \mathtt{sumdel}(\mathtt{nil}) = 0 \\ \quad \mathtt{sumdel}(\mathtt{cons}(n, l)) = n + \mathtt{sum}(\mathtt{map}([x]\mathtt{sumdel}(\mathtt{cons}(n, \mathtt{delete}(x, l))), l)) \end{array}$$

The actual value computed by the function is $\mathtt{sumdel}(n_1, \ldots, n_k) = n_1 \mathtt{sd}(k)$ where $\mathtt{sd}(0) = 0$ and $\mathtt{sd}(k+1) = k\mathtt{sd}(k) + 1$.

Type-theoretic version: $\mathsf{Sumdel} = \langle \mathsf{sumdelAcc}, \mathsf{sumdel}\rangle \colon \mathsf{List\ N} \rightharpoonup \mathsf{N}$ with:

$$\begin{array}{l} \mathsf{sumdelAcc} \colon \mathsf{List\ N} \to \mathsf{Prop} \\ \quad \mathsf{sumdelacc_{nil}} \colon (\mathsf{sumdelAcc\ nil}) \\ \quad \mathsf{sumdelacc_{cons}} \colon (n \colon \mathsf{N}; l \colon \mathsf{List\ N}; h \colon \mathsf{mapAcc\ G}\ l)(\mathsf{sumdelAcc\ cons}(n, l)) \end{array}$$

$$\begin{array}{l} \mathsf{sumdel} \colon (l \colon \mathsf{List\ N}; \mathsf{sumdelAcc}\ l) \to \mathsf{N} \\ \quad \mathsf{sumdel\ nil\ sumdelacc_{nil}} = 0 \\ \quad \mathsf{sumdel\ cons}(n, l)\ (\mathsf{sumdelacc_{cons}}\ n\ l\ h) = n + \mathsf{sum}\ \ \mathsf{Map}_{[h]}(\mathsf{G}, l) \end{array}$$

with $\mathsf{G} \equiv \langle \mathsf{gAcc}, \mathsf{g}\rangle \colon \mathtt{N} \rightharpoonup \mathtt{N}$ where

$$\begin{array}{l} \mathsf{gAcc} = [x \colon \mathtt{N}](\mathsf{sumdelAcc\ cons}(n, (\mathsf{delete}\ x\ l))) \colon \mathsf{N} \to \mathsf{Prop} \\ \mathsf{g} = [x \colon \mathtt{N}; h \colon \mathsf{gAcc}\ x]\mathsf{Sumdel}_{[h]}(\mathsf{cons}(n, (\mathsf{delete}\ x\ l))) \colon (x \colon \mathsf{N}; \mathsf{gAcc}\ x) \to \mathsf{N} \end{array}$$

Notice that G is local to Sumdel and hence, n and l are known while defining G.

The important feature of this translation, not possible in the old one, is that we can assign a precise domain predicate gAcc to the local function generated by the λ-abstraction. Notice that in the body of the main function, the local function is applied only to arguments that satisfy gAcc, so termination is ensured.

Partial Application: is_div2. Functional version:

$$\begin{array}{l} \mathtt{fix\ is\_div2} \colon \mathtt{List\ N} \Rightarrow \mathtt{List\ N} \\ \qquad \mathtt{is\_div2}(xs) = \mathtt{map}(\mathtt{my\_mod}(2), xs) \end{array}$$

where the function `my_mod` is the one defined at the end of Section 2. Given a list of numbers, this function returns a list of 0's and 1's depending on whether the numbers in the list are divisible by 2 or not, respectively.

Observe that the type-theoretic version of my_mod is the same as before since this function does not present any of the problematic aspects on which the method has been changed. Let $\mathsf{My\_Mod} = \langle \mathsf{my\_modAcc}, \mathsf{my\_mod}\rangle \colon \mathsf{N}, \mathsf{N} \rightharpoonup \mathsf{N}$ with my_modAcc and my_mod as defined on page 122.

Type-theoretic version: $\mathsf{Is\_Div2} = \langle \mathsf{is\_div2Acc}, \mathsf{is\_div2}\rangle \colon \mathsf{List}\ \mathsf{N} \rightharpoonup \mathsf{List}\ \mathsf{N}$ with:

$$\begin{array}{l} \mathsf{is\_div2Acc} \colon \mathsf{List}\ \mathsf{N} \to \mathsf{Prop} \\ \quad \mathsf{is\_div2acc} \colon (xs \colon \mathsf{List}\ \mathsf{N}; h \colon \mathsf{mapAcc}\ \mathsf{My\_Mod}(2)\ xs)(\mathsf{is\_div2Acc}\ xs) \end{array}$$

$$\begin{array}{l} \mathsf{is\_div2} \colon (xs \colon \mathsf{List}\ \mathsf{N}; \mathsf{is\_div2Acc}\ xs) \to \mathsf{List}\ \mathsf{N} \\ \quad \mathsf{is\_div2}\ xs\ (\mathsf{is\_div2acc}\ xs\ h) = \mathsf{Map}_{[h]}(\mathsf{My\_Mod}(2), xs) \end{array}$$

Notice that the translation of the partial application my_mod(2) does not introduce any domain constrains in the type of the constructor is_div2acc. Given an element x in the list xs, the application of the function My_Mod(2) to the argument x will only be possible if we can find a proof of (my_modAcc 2 x). This is taken care of in the definition of mapAcc.

Necessity of Impredicativity: itz. The following example shows that it is necessary to have an impredicative type theory if we want our method to apply to every functional program. Functional version:

$$\begin{array}{l} \mathtt{fix}\ \mathtt{itz} \colon \mathtt{N} \to \mathtt{N}, \mathtt{N} \Rightarrow \mathtt{N} \\ \qquad \mathtt{itz}(f, 0) = f\ 0 \\ \qquad \mathtt{itz}(f, \mathtt{succ}(n)) = f\ \ \mathtt{itz}(\mathtt{itz}(f), n) \end{array}$$

Type-theoretic version: $\mathsf{Itz} = \langle \mathsf{itzAcc}, \mathsf{itz}\rangle \colon (\mathsf{N} \rightharpoonup \mathsf{N}), \mathsf{N} \rightharpoonup \mathsf{N}$ with:

$$\begin{array}{l} \mathsf{itzAcc} \colon (\mathsf{N} \rightharpoonup \mathsf{N}) \to \mathsf{N} \to \mathsf{Prop} \\ \quad \mathsf{itzacc}_0 \colon (f \colon \mathsf{N} \rightharpoonup \mathsf{N}; h \colon \mathsf{dom}_f\ 0)(\mathsf{itzAcc}\ f\ 0) \\ \quad \mathsf{itzacc}_{\mathsf{succ}} \colon (f \colon \mathsf{N} \rightharpoonup \mathsf{N}; n \colon \mathsf{N}; h_1 \colon \mathsf{itzAcc}\ \mathsf{Itz}(f)\ n; \\ \qquad\qquad h_2 \colon \mathsf{dom}_f\ \mathsf{Itz}_{[h_1]}(\mathsf{Itz}(f), n))(\mathsf{itzAcc}\ f\ \mathsf{succ}(n)) \end{array}$$

$$\begin{array}{l} \mathsf{itz} \colon (f \colon \mathsf{N} \rightharpoonup \mathsf{N}; n \colon \mathsf{N}; \mathsf{itzAcc}\ f\ n) \to \mathsf{N} \\ \quad \mathsf{itz}\ f\ 0\ (\mathsf{itzacc}_0\ f\ h) = f_{[h]}(0) \\ \quad \mathsf{itz}\ f\ \mathsf{succ}(n)\ (\mathsf{itzacc}_{\mathsf{succ}}\ f\ n\ h_1\ h_2) = f_{[h_2]}(\mathsf{Itz}_{[h1]}(\mathsf{Itz}(f), n)) \end{array}$$

We see that impredicativity is essential when we follow our method to formalise this example. When defining itzAcc, the constructor $\mathsf{itzacc}_{\mathsf{succ}}$ quantifies over all partial functions $f \colon \mathsf{N} \rightharpoonup \mathsf{N}$ (and, therefore, over the domain predicates of all those functions) and in the body of the constructor $\mathsf{itzacc}_{\mathsf{succ}}$ the function $\mathsf{Itz}(f)$ is itself an argument of itzAcc.

The alternative to use a predicative hierarchy of type universes $\mathsf{U}_0, \mathsf{U}_1, \mathsf{U}_2, \ldots$ does not work in this example. Function spaces would need to be stratified too, according to the universe in which the domain predicate lives, so we would have

$$A \rightharpoonup_i B = \Sigma P \colon A \to \mathsf{U}_i.(x \colon A; P\ x) \to B$$

Since we are quantifying over $A \to \mathsf{U}_i$, predicatively it must be $A \rightharpoonup_i B \colon \mathsf{U}_j$ with $j > i$. That is, we have at least $A \rightharpoonup_i B \colon \mathsf{U}_{i+1}$.

In the case of Itz, if we try to assign universe levels, that is, if we try to give it the type $\mathsf{Itz}\colon (\mathsf{N} \rightharpoonup_i \mathsf{N}), \mathsf{N} \rightharpoonup_j \mathsf{N}$ for some i and j, we reach a contradiction regardless of what i and j are. To start with, we have $\mathsf{itzAcc}\colon (\mathsf{N} \rightharpoonup_i \mathsf{N}) \to \mathsf{N} \to \mathsf{U}_j$. The first constructor itzacc_0 contains a quantification on $\mathsf{N} \rightharpoonup_i \mathsf{N}$, so its type must be at least in U_{i+1}. Thus, also the universe of itzAcc must be at least U_{i+1}, that is, $j \geqslant i+1$. Now, in the constructor $\mathsf{itzacc}_{\mathsf{succ}}$ we have the subterm $\mathsf{Itz}(\mathsf{Itz}(f), n)$, but this term does not type-check because $\mathsf{Itz}\colon (\mathsf{N} \rightharpoonup_i \mathsf{N}), \mathsf{N} \rightharpoonup_j \mathsf{N}$ and $\mathsf{Itz}(f)\colon \mathsf{N} \rightharpoonup_j \mathsf{N}$ with $j \geqslant i+1$. Hence, Itz cannot be applied to $\mathsf{Itz}(f)$ because the type is not correct: it expects an argument of type $\mathsf{N} \rightharpoonup_i \mathsf{N}$ and it gets one of type $\mathsf{N} \rightharpoonup_j \mathsf{N}$ with $j \geqslant i+1$.

5 Conclusions

This article presents a method to translate functional programs into type theory based on the one previously presented in [BC04]. The new approach relies on a type of partial functions whose elements are pairs consisting of a domain predicate and a function depending on a proof of the predicate. The problems that were left open in [BC04] are now solved: functional arguments are dealt with by lifting their domain conditions to the main call; λ-abstractions denote partial functions with domain condition generated locally; partial application is interpreted by just fixing the given parameters both in the domain predicate and the function.

These results are obtained at the cost of two disadvantages. First of all, we need an impredicative type theory for the method to be applicable to all functional programs (see example `itz`). This is indispensable to obtain a general result, but in most practical cases the method could be adapted to work on a predicative type theory with type universes.

As we have already mentioned, this paper is the last in a series of articles [Bov01, BC01, Bov02a, Bov02b, Bov03, BC04] aimed at representing general recursive functions in type theory. See the section on related work in [BC04] for a thorough discussion of the literature regarding representations of recursive functions in logical frameworks.

Acknowledgements. We would like to thank Thierry Coquand for his constructive criticism on earlier versions of this article and for useful comments on the type of partial functions and on the use of impredicativity. We are also grateful to Christine Paulin-Mohring for giving us a clarifying explanation of her method to extract computational content from the accessibility predicates.

References

[BC01] A. Bove and V. Capretta. Nested general recursion and partiality in type theory. In R. J. Boulton and P. B. Jackson, editors, *Theorem Proving in Higher Order Logics: 14th International Conference, TPHOLs 2001*, volume 2152 of *Lecture Notes in Computer Science, Springer-Verlag*, pages 121–135, September 2001.

[BC04] A. Bove and V. Capretta. Modelling general recursion in type theory. To appear in *Mathematical Structures in Computer Science*. Available on the WWW: `http://www.cs.chalmers.se/~bove/Papers/general_presentation.ps.gz`, May 2004.

[Bla03] Frédéric Blanqui. Inductive types in the calculus of algebraic constructions. In M. Hofmann, editor, *Typed Lambda Calculi and Applications: 6th International Conference, TLCA 2003*, volume 2701 of *LNCS*, pages 46–59. Springer-Verlag, 2003.

[Bov01] A. Bove. Simple general recursion in type theory. *Nordic Journal of Computing*, 8(1):22–42, Spring 2001.

[Bov02a] A. Bove. Mutual general recursion in type theory. Technical Report, Chalmers University of Technology. Available on the WWW: `http://www.cs.chalmers.se/~bove/Papers/mutual_rec.ps.gz`, May 2002.

[Bov02b] Ana Bove. *General Recursion in Type Theory*. PhD thesis, Chalmers University of Technology, Department of Computing Science, November 2002. Available on the WWW: `http://cs.chalmers.se/~bove/Papers/phd_thesis.ps.gz`.

[Bov03] A. Bove. General recursion in type theory. In H. Geuvers and F. Wiedijk, editors, *Types for Proofs and Programs, International Workshop TYPES 2002, The Netherlands*, number 2646 in Lecture Notes in Computer Science, pages 39–58, March 2003.

[Cap04] Venanzio Capretta. A polymorphic representation of induction-recursion. Draft paper. Available from `http://www.science.uottawa.ca/~vcapr396/`, 2004.

[CH88] T. Coquand and G. Huet. The Calculus of Constructions. *Information and Computation*, 76:95–120, 1988.

[CM85] R. L. Constable and N. P. Mendler. Recursive definitions in type theory. In Rohit Parikh, editor, *Logic of Programs*, volume 193 of *Lecture Notes in Computer Science*, pages 61–78. Springer, 1985.

[Coq02] Coq Development Team. LogiCal Project. *The Coq Proof Assistant. Reference Manual. Version 7.4*. INRIA, 2002.

[DDG98] C. Dubois and V. Viguié Donzeau-Gouge. A step towards the mechanization of partial functions: Domains as inductive predicates. In M. Kerber, editor, *CADE-15, The 15th International Conference on Automated Deduction*, pages 53–62, July 1998. WORKSHOP Mechanization of Partial Functions.

[Dyb00] P. Dybjer. A general formulation of simultaneous inductive-recursive definitions in type theory. *Journal of Symbolic Logic*, 65(2), June 2000.

[FFL97] S. Finn, M.P. Fourman, and J. Longley. Partial functions in a total setting. *Journal of Automated Reasoning*, 18(1):85–104, 1997.

[Jon03] S. Peyton Jones, editor. *Haskell 98 Language and Libraries. The Revised Report*. Cambridge University Press, April 2003.

[Pau] Christine Paulin. How widely applicable is Coq? Contribution to the Coq mailing list, 19 Aug 2002, `http://pauillac.inria.fr/bin/wilma_hiliter/coq-club/200208/msg00003.html`.

Elementary Affine Logic and the Call-by-Value Lambda Calculus*

Paolo Coppola[1], Ugo Dal Lago[2], and Simona Ronchi Della Rocca[3]

[1] Dipartimento di Matematica e Informatica, Università di Udine,
via delle Scienze 206, 33100 Udine, Italy
coppola@dimi.uniud.it

[2] Dipartimento di Scienze dell'Informazione, Università di Bologna,
via Mura Anteo Zamboni 7, 40127 Bologna, Italy
dallago@cs.unibo.it

[3] Dipartimento di Informatica, Università di Torino,
corso Svizzera 185, 10129 Torino, Italy
ronchi@di.unito.it

Abstract. The so-called light logics [1, 2, 3] have been introduced as logical systems enjoying quite remarkable normalization properties. Designing a type assignment system for pure lambda calculus from these logics, however, is problematic, as discussed in [4]. In this paper we show that shifting from usual call-by-name to call-by-value lambda calculus allows regaining strong connections with the underlying logic. This will be done in the context of Elementary Affine Logic (EAL), designing a type system in natural deduction style assigning EAL formulae to lambda terms.

1 Introduction

The so-called light logics [1, 2, 3] were all introduced as logical counterparts of complexity classes, namely polynomial and elementary time functions. After their introduction, they have been shown to be relevant for optimal reduction [5, 6], programming language design [3, 7] and set theory [8]. However, proof languages for these logics, designed through the Curry-Howard correspondence, are syntactically quite complex and can hardly be proposed as programming languages. An interesting research challenge is the design of type systems assigning light logics formulae to pure lambda-terms, forcing the class of typable terms to enjoy the same remarkable normalization properties which can be proved on logical systems. The difference between β-reduction and the normalization step in the logics, however, makes it difficult both getting the subject reduction property and inheriting the complexity properties from the logic, as discussed in [4]. Indeed, β-reduction is more permissive than the restrictive copying discipline governing calculi directly derived from light logics. Consider, for example, the following expression in Λ_{LA} (see [7]):

* The three authors are partially supported by PRIN projects PROTOCOLLO (2002) and FOLLIA (2004).

P. Urzyczyn (Ed.): TLCA 2005, LNCS 3461, pp. 131–145, 2005.

$$let\ \ M\ \ be\ \ !x\ \ in\ \ N$$

This rewrites to $N\{x/P\}$ if M is $!P$, but is not a redex if M is, say, an application. It is not possible to map this mechanism into pure lambda calculus. The solution proposed by Baillot and Terui [4] in the context of Light Affine Logic (LAL, see [2, 3]) consists in defining a type-system which is strictly more restrictive than the one induced by the logic. In this way, they both achieve subject reduction and a strong notion of polynomial time soundness. The system, however, is not complete with respect to LAL, i.e. there are proofs that cannot be mapped into typable terms.

Now, notice that mapping the above let expression to the application

$$(\lambda x.N)M$$

is not meaningless if we shift from the usual call-by-name lambda calculus to the call-by-value lambda calculus, where $(\lambda x.N)M$ is not necessarily a redex. In this paper, we make the best of this idea, introducing a type assignment system, that we call ETAS, assigning formulae of Elementary Affine Logic (EAL) to lambda-terms. ETAS enjoys the following remarkable properties:

- Every proof of EAL can be mapped into a type derivation in ETAS.
- (Call-by-value) subject reduction holds.
- Type-inference is decidable.
- Elementary bounds can be given on the length of any reduction sequence involving a typable term. A similar bound holds on the size of terms involved in the reduction.

The basic idea underlying ETAS consists in partitioning premises into three classes, depending on whether they are used once, or more than once, or they are in an intermediate status. We believe this approach can work for other light logics too, and some hints will be given.

The proposed system is the first one satisfying the given requirements for light logics. A notion of typability for lambda calculus has been defined in [5, 6] for EAL, and in [9] for LAL. Type inference has been proved to be decidable. In both cases, however, the notion of typability is not preserved by β-reduction.

The paper is organized as follows: Section 2 recalls some preliminary notions about EAL and lambda calculus, Section 3 introduces ETAS system, Section 4 and 5 explain ETAS main properties, namely complexity bounds and a type inference algorithm. Section 6 presents two possible extensions, allowing to reach completeness for elementary functions, and to apply our idea to other light logics.

2 Preliminaries

In this section we recall the proof calculus for Elementary Affine Logic, Λ^{EA}. Relations with the lambda calculus will be then discussed.

Definition 1. i) The set Λ of terms of the lambda calculus is defined by the grammar $M ::= x \mid MM \mid \lambda x.M$, where $x \in Var$, a countable set of variables.

ii) The grammar generating the set Λ^{EA} of terms of the Elementary Lambda Calculus is obtained from the previous one by adding rules:

$$M ::= !(M)\left[{}^{M}/x, \ldots, {}^{M}/x\right] \mid [M]_{M=x,y}$$

and by constraining all variables to occur at most once.

iii) *EA-types* are formulae of Elementary Affine Logic (hereby EAL), and are generated by the grammar $A ::= \alpha \mid A \multimap A \mid !A$ where α belongs to a countable set of basic type constants. EA-types will be ranged over by A, B, C.

iv) *EA-contexts* are finite subsets of EA-type assignments to variables. Contexts are ranged over by Φ, Ψ. If $\Phi = \{x_1 : A_1, \ldots, x_n : A_n\}$, then $dom(\Phi) = \{x_1, \ldots, x_n\}$. Two contexts are *disjoint* if their domains have empty intersection.

v) The type assignment system $\vdash_{\text{NEAL}}$ assigns EA-types to EA-terms. The system is given in Table 1. With a slight abuse of notation, we will denote by NEAL the set of typable terms in Λ^{EA}.

Both Λ^{EA} and Λ are ranged over by M, N, P, Q. The context should help avoiding ambiguities. Symbol $\equiv$ denotes syntactic identity on terms, modulo names of bound variables and modulo permutation in the list ${}^{M}/x, \cdots, {}^{M}/x$ inside $!(M)\left[{}^{M}/x, \ldots, {}^{M}/x\right]$ and in contracted variables x, y inside $[M]_{M=x,y}$.

Table 1. Type assignment system for EA-terms. Contexts with different names are intended to be disjoint

$$\frac{}{\Phi, x : A \vdash_{\text{NEAL}} x : A}\,A \qquad \frac{\Phi \vdash_{\text{NEAL}} M :!A \quad \Psi, x :!A, y :!A \vdash_{\text{NEAL}} N : B}{\Phi, \Psi \vdash_{\text{NEAL}} [N]_{M=x,y} : B}\,C$$

$$\frac{\Phi, x : A \vdash_{\text{NEAL}} M : B}{\Phi \vdash_{\text{NEAL}} \lambda x.M : A \multimap B}\,I_{\multimap} \qquad \frac{\Phi \vdash_{\text{NEAL}} M : A \multimap B \quad \Psi \vdash_{\text{NEAL}} N : A}{\Phi, \Psi \vdash_{\text{NEAL}} M\ N : B}\,E_{\multimap}$$

$$\frac{\Psi_1 \vdash_{\text{NEAL}} M_1 :!A_1 \quad \cdots \quad \Psi_n \vdash_{\text{NEAL}} M_n :!A_n \quad x_1 : A_1, \ldots, x_n : A_n \vdash_{\text{NEAL}} N : B}{\Phi, \Psi_1, \ldots, \Psi_n \vdash_{\text{NEAL}} !(N)\left[{}^{M_1}/x_1, \ldots, {}^{M_n}/x_n\right] :!B}\,!$$

On Λ, both the call-by-name and the call-by-value β-reduction will be used, according to the following definition.

Definition 2. i) The *call-by-name β-reduction* is the contextual closure of the following rule: $(\lambda x.M)N \to_n M\{N/x\}$, where $M\{N/x\}$ denotes the capture free substitution of N to the free occurrences of x in M;

ii) *Values* are generated by the grammar $V ::= x \mid \lambda x.M$ where x ranges over *Var* and M ranges over Λ. $\mathcal{V}$ is the set of all values. Values are denoted by V, U, W. The *call-by-value* β-reduction is the contextual closure of the following rule: $(\lambda x.M)V \to_v M\{V/x\}$ where V ranges over values.

iii) Let $t \in \{n, v\}$; symbols $\rightarrow_t^+$ and $\rightarrow_t^*$ denote the transitive closure and the symmetric and transitive closure of $\rightarrow_t$, respectively.

A term in Λ^{EA} can be tranformed naturally in a term in Λ by performing the substitutions which are explicit in it, and forgetting the modality !. Formally, the translation function $(\cdot)^* : \Lambda^{EA} \rightarrow \Lambda$ is defined by induction on the structure of EA-terms as follows:

$$\begin{aligned}
(x)^* &= x \\
(\lambda x.M)^* &= \lambda x.(M)^* \\
(MN)^* &= (M)^*(N)^* \\
([M]_{N=x_1,x_2})^* &= (M)^*\{(N)^*/x_1, (N)^*/x_2\} \\
(!(N)\left[{}^{M_1}/x_1, \ldots, {}^{M_n}/x_n\right])^* &= (N)^*\{(M_1)^*/x_1, \ldots, (M_n)^*/x_n\}
\end{aligned}$$

where $M\{{}^{M_1}/x_1, \cdots, {}^{M_n}/x_n\}$ denotes the simultaneous substitution of all free occurrences of x_i by M_i $(1 \leq i \leq n)$.

The map $(\cdot)^*$ easily induces a type-assignment system for pure lambda-calculus: take NEAL and replace every occurrence of a term M by M^* in every rule. Normalization in EAL, however, is different from normalization in lambda-calculus — the obtained system does not even satisfy subject-reduction. Moreover, lambda calculus does not provide any mechanism for sharing: the argument is duplicated as soon as β-reduction fires. This, in turn, prevents from analyzing normalization in the lambda calculus using the same techniques used in logical systems. This phenomenon has catastrophic consequences in the context of Light Affine Logic, where polynomial time bounds cannot be transferred from the logic to pure lambda-calculus [4].

Consider now a different translation $(\cdot)^\# : \Lambda^{EA} \rightarrow \Lambda$:

$$\begin{aligned}
(x)^\# &= x \\
(\lambda x.M)^\# &= \lambda x.(M)^\# \\
(MN)^\# &= (M)^\# \; (N)^\# \\
([N]_{M=x,y})^\# &= \begin{cases} (N)^\#\{M/x, M/y\} & \textit{if } M \textit{ is a variable} \\ (\lambda z.(N)^\#\{z/x, z/y\})(M)^\# & \textit{otherwise} \end{cases} \\
(!(N)\left[{}^{M_1}/x_1, \ldots, {}^{M_n}/x_n\right])^\# &= \begin{cases} (N)^\# \quad \textit{if } n = 0 \\ (!(N)\left[{}^{M_2}/x_2, \ldots, {}^{M_n}/x_n\right])^\#\{M_1/x_1\} \\ \quad \textit{if } n \geq 1 \textit{ and } M_1 \textit{ is a variable} \\ (\lambda x_1.(!(N)\left[{}^{M_2}/x_2, \ldots, {}^{M_n}/x_n\right])^\#)(M_1)^\# \\ \quad \textit{if } n \geq 1 \textit{ and } M_1 \textit{ is not a variable} \end{cases}
\end{aligned}$$

If lambda calculus is endowed by ordinary β-reduction, then the two translations are almost equivalent. Indeed:

Lemma 3. *For every EA-term M, $(M)^\# \rightarrow_n^* (M)^*$.*

Proof. By induction on M.

However, it is not certainly true that $(M)^\# \rightarrow_v^* (M)^*$.

The map $(\cdot)^\#$, differently from $(\cdot)^*$ does not cause an exponential blowup on the length of terms. The *length* $L(M)$ of a term M is defined inductively as follows:

$$\begin{aligned} L(x) &= 1 \\ L(\lambda x.M) &= 1 + L(M) \\ L(M\ N) &= 1 + L(M) + L(N) \end{aligned}$$

The same definition can be extended to EA-terms by way of the following equations:

$$\begin{aligned} L(!\,(M)) &= L(M) + 1 \\ L(!\,(M)\left[{}^{M_1}/x_1, \ldots, {}^{M_n}/x_n\right]) &= L(!\,(M)\left[{}^{M_1}/x_1, \ldots, {}^{M_{n-1}}/x_{n-1}\right]) + L(M_n) + 1 \\ L([M]_{N=x,y}) &= L(M) + L(N) + 1 \end{aligned}$$

Proposition 4. *For every $N \in \Lambda^{EA}$, $L(N^\#) \leq 2L(N)$.*

In the following section, we describe a type-system which types all the terms in $(\mathrm{NEAL})^\#$, satysfing call-by-value subject-reduction and guaranteeing bounds on normalization time.

3 The Elementary Type Assignment System

In this section we will define a type assignment system typing lambda-terms with EAL formulae. We want the system to be *almost* syntax directed, the difficulty being the handling of C and ! rules. This is solved by splitting the context into three parts, the *linear* context, the *modal* context, and the *parking* context. In particular the parking context is used to keep track of premises which must become modal in the future.

Definition 5. i) An EAL formula A is *modal* if $A \equiv !B$ for some B, it is *linear* otherwise.

ii) A context is *linear* if it assigns linear EA-types to variables, while it is *modal* if it assigns modal EA-types to variables. If Φ is a context, Φ^L and Φ^I denote the linear and modal sub-contexts of Φ, respectively.

iii) The Elementary Type Assignment System (*ETAS*) proves statements like $\Gamma \mid \Delta \mid \Theta \vdash M : A$ where Γ and Θ are linear contexts and Δ is a modal context. The rules of the system are shown in Table 2. In what follows, Γ, Δ and Θ will range over linear, modal and parking contexts respectively.

iv) A term $M \in \Lambda$ is *EA-typable* if there are Γ, Δ, A such that $\Gamma \mid \Delta \mid \emptyset \vdash M : A$.

Rules A^L and A^P (see Table 2) are two variations on the classical axiom rule. Notice that a third axiom rule

$$\frac{}{\Gamma \mid x :!A, \Delta \mid \Theta \vdash x :!A}\ A^I$$

is derivable. Abstractions cannot be performed on variables in the parking context. The rule $E_{\multimap}$ is the standard rule for application. Rule ! is derived from the

Table 2. The Elementary Type Assignment System (ETAS). Contexts with different names are intended to be disjoint

$$\frac{}{\Gamma, x : A \mid \Delta \mid \Theta \vdash x : A}\ A^L \qquad \frac{}{\Gamma \mid \Delta \mid x : A, \Theta \vdash x : A}\ A^P$$

$$\frac{\Gamma, x : A \mid \Delta \mid \Theta \vdash M : B}{\Gamma \mid \Delta \mid \Theta \vdash \lambda x.M : A \multimap B}\ I^L_{\multimap} \qquad \frac{\Gamma \mid \Delta, x : A \mid \Theta \vdash M : B}{\Gamma \mid \Delta \mid \Theta \vdash \lambda x.M : A \multimap B}\ I^I_{\multimap}$$

$$\frac{\Gamma_1 \mid \Delta \mid \Theta \vdash M : A \multimap B \quad \Gamma_2 \mid \Delta \mid \Theta \vdash N : A}{\Gamma_1, \Gamma_2 \mid \Delta \mid \Theta \vdash M\ N : B}\ E_{\multimap}$$

$$\frac{\Gamma_1 \mid \Delta_1 \mid \Theta_1 \vdash M : A}{\Gamma_2 \mid !\Gamma_1, !\Delta_1, !\Theta_1, \Delta_2 \mid \Theta_2 \vdash M : !A}\ !$$

one traditionally found in sequent calculi and is weaker than the rule induced by NEAL via $(\cdot)^*$. Nevertheless, it is sufficient for our purposes and (almost) syntax-directed. The definition of an EA-typable term takes into account the auxiliary role of the parking context.

This system does not satisfy call-by-name subject-reduction. Consider, for example, the lambda term $M \equiv (\lambda x.yxx)(wz)$. A typing for it is the following:

$$y : !A \multimap !A \multimap A, w : A \multimap !A, z : A \mid \emptyset \mid \emptyset \vdash M : A$$

$M \rightarrow_n N$, where $N \equiv y(wz)(wz)$ and $y : !A \multimap !A \multimap A, w : A \multimap !A, z : A \mid \emptyset \mid \emptyset \not\vdash N : A$, because rule $E_{\multimap}$ requires the two linear contexts to be disjoint. Note that both $\emptyset \mid \emptyset \mid y : !A \multimap !A \multimap A, w : A \multimap !A, z : A \vdash M : A$ and $\emptyset \mid \emptyset \mid y : !A \multimap !A \multimap A, w : A \multimap !A, z : A \vdash N : A$, but this does not imply N to be EA-typable. Moreover, $\lambda w.M \rightarrow_n \lambda w.N$, but while M can be given type $(A \multimap !A) \multimap A$, N cannot.

The subject reduction problem, however, disappears when switching from call-by-name to call-by-value reduction.

Lemma 6 (Weakening Lemma). *If* $\Gamma_1 \mid \Delta_1 \mid \Theta_1 \vdash M : A$, *then* $\Gamma_1, \Gamma_2 \mid \Delta_1, \Delta_2 \mid \Theta_1, \Theta_2 \vdash M : A$.

Lemma 7 (Shifting Lemma). *If* $\Gamma, x : A \mid \Delta \mid \Theta \vdash M : B$, *then* $\Gamma \mid \Delta \mid x : A, \Theta \vdash M : B$.

Lemma 8 (Substitution Lemma). *Suppose* Γ_1 *and* Γ_2 *are disjoint contexts. Then:*

- *If* $\Gamma_1, x : A \mid \Delta \mid \Theta \vdash M : B$, $\Gamma_2 \mid \Delta \mid \Theta \vdash N : A$ *and* $N \in \mathcal{V}$, *then* $\Gamma_1, \Gamma_2 \mid \Delta \mid \Theta \vdash M\{N/x\} : B$.
- *If* $\Gamma_1 \mid \Delta \mid x : A, \Theta \vdash M : B$, $\Gamma_2 \mid \Delta \mid \Theta \vdash N : A$ *and* $N \in \mathcal{V}$, *then* $\Gamma_1 \mid \Delta \mid \Gamma_2, \Theta \vdash M\{N/x\} : B$.
- *If* $\Gamma_1 \mid \Delta, x : A \mid \Theta \vdash M : B$, $\Gamma_2 \mid \Delta \mid \Theta \vdash N : A$ *and* $N \in \mathcal{V}$, *then* $\Gamma_1, \Gamma_2 \mid \Delta \mid \Theta \vdash M\{N/x\} : B$.

Proof. The first point can be easily proved by induction on the derivation for $\Gamma_1, x : A \mid \Delta \mid \Theta \vdash M : B$ using, in particular, the Weakening Lemma. Indeed, the hypothesis on N is not needed.

Let us prove the second point (by the same induction). The case for A^P can be proved by way of the previous lemmas. $I^L_{\multimap}$ and $I^I_{\multimap}$ are trivial. $E_{\multimap}$ comes directly from the induction hypothesis. ! is very easy, because x cannot appear free in M and so $M\{N/x\}$ is just M.

The third point can be proved by induction, too, but it is a bit more difficult. First of all, observe that A must be in the form $\underbrace{!\ldots!}_{n} C$, with $n \geq 1$. Let us focus on rules $E_{\multimap}$ and ! (the other ones can be handled easily). Notice that the derivation for $\Gamma_2 \mid \Delta \mid \Theta \vdash N : A$ must end with A^L, A^P, $I^L_{\multimap}$ or $I^I_{\multimap}$ (depending on the shape of N), followed by exactly n instances of the ! rule, being it the only non-syntax-directed rule. This implies, in particular, that every variable appearing free in N is in Δ. So the proof follows easily by induction. Using Lemma 7 and Lemma 6, we can use the induction hypothesis and handle the case !. □

Theorem 9 (Call-by-Value Subject Reduction). *$\Gamma \mid \Delta \mid \Theta \vdash M : A$ and $M \rightarrow_v N$ implies $\Gamma \mid \Delta \mid \Theta \vdash N : A$.*

Proof. By the Substitution Lemma. □

We are now going to prove that the set of typable λ-terms coincides with $(\text{NEAL})^{\#}$. To do this we need the following lemma.

Lemma 10 (Contraction Lemma).
i) If $\Gamma \mid \Delta \mid x : A, y : A, \Theta \vdash M : B$, then $\Gamma \mid \Delta \mid z : A, \Theta \vdash M\{z/x, z/y\} : B$
ii) If $\Gamma \mid x : A, y : A, \Delta \mid \Theta \vdash M : B$, then $\Gamma \mid z : A, \Delta \mid \Theta \vdash M\{z/x, z/y\} : B$

Proposition 11. *i) If $\Phi \vdash_{\text{NEAL}} M : A$ then $\Phi^L \mid \Phi^I \mid \emptyset \vdash (M)^{\#} : A$.*
ii) If $\Gamma \mid \Delta \mid \emptyset \vdash M : A$, there is $N \in \Lambda^{EA}$ such that $(N)^{\#} = M$ and $\Gamma, \Delta \vdash_{\text{NEAL}} N : A$.

Proof. i) By induction on the structure of the derivation for $\Phi \vdash_{\text{NEAL}} M : A$. Let us focus on nontrivial cases.

If the last rule used is $E_{\multimap}$, the two premises are $\Phi \vdash_{\text{NEAL}} N : B \multimap C$ and $\Phi_2 \vdash_{\text{NEAL}} P : B$. By induction hypothesis, $\Phi^L_1 \mid \Phi^I_1 \mid \emptyset \vdash (N)^{\#} : B \multimap C$, and $\Phi^L_2 \mid \Phi^I_2 \mid \emptyset \vdash (P)^{\#} : B$ and, by Weakening Lemma, $\Phi^L_1 \mid \Phi^I_1, \Phi^I_2 \mid \emptyset \vdash (N)^{\#} : B \multimap C$, $\Phi^L_2 \mid \Phi^I_1, \Phi^I_2 \mid \emptyset \vdash (P)^{\#} : B$ Rule $E_{\multimap}$ leads to the thesis.

If the last rule used is *contr*, the two premises are $\Phi_1 \vdash_{\text{NEAL}} N :!A$ and $\Phi_2, x :!A, y :!A \vdash_{\text{NEAL}} P : B$. By induction hypothesis, $\Phi^L_1 \mid \Phi^I_1 \mid \emptyset \vdash (N)^{\#} :!A$, $\Phi^L_2 \mid \Phi^I_2, x :!A, y :!A \mid \emptyset \vdash (P)^{\#} : B$. By Contraction Lemma, $\Phi^L_2 \mid \Phi^I_2, z : !A \mid \emptyset \vdash (P)^{\#}\{z/x, z/y\} : B$ and so $\Phi^L_2 \mid \Phi^I_2 \mid \emptyset \vdash \lambda z.(P)^{\#}\{z/x, z/y\} :!A \multimap B$ By rule $E_{\multimap}$ and Weakening Lemma, we finally get $\Phi^L_1, \Phi^L_2 \mid \Phi^I_1, \Phi^I_2 \mid \emptyset \vdash (\lambda z.(P)^{\#}\{z/x, z/y\})(N)^{\#} : B$.

ii) The following, stronger, statement can be proved by induction on π: if $\pi : \Gamma \mid \Delta \mid x_1 : A_1, \ldots, x_n : A_n \vdash M : A$, then there is $N \in \Lambda^{EA}$ such that $(N)^{\#} = M\{x_1/y_1^1, \ldots, x_1/y_1^{m_1}, \ldots, x_n/y_n^1, \ldots, x_n/y_n^{m_n}\}$ and $\Gamma, \Delta, y_1^1 : A_1, \ldots, y_1^{m_1} : A_1, \ldots, y_n^1 : A_n, \ldots, y_n^{m_n} : A_n \vdash_{\mathrm{NEAL}} N : A$. □

We have just established a deep *static* correspondence between NEAL and the class of typable lambda terms. But what about *dynamics*? Unfortunately, the two systems are not bisimilar. Nevertheless, every call-by-value β-step in the lambda calculus corresponds to at least one normalization step in Λ^{EA}. A normalization step in Λ^{EA} is denoted by $\to$ (reduction rules can be found in [10]); $\to^+$ denotes the transitive closure of $\to$.

Proposition 12. *For every $M \in \Lambda^{EA}$, if $(M)^{\#} \to_v N$, then there is $L \in \Lambda^{EA}$ such that $(L)^{\#} = N$ and $M \to^+ L$.*

4 Bounds on Normalization Time

In order to prove elementary bounds on reduction sequences, we need to define a refined measure on lambda terms. We can look at a type derivation $\pi : \Gamma \mid \Delta \mid \Theta \vdash M : A$ as a labelled tree, where every node is labelled by a rule instance. We can give the following definition:

Definition 13. Let $\pi : \Gamma \mid \Delta \mid \Theta \vdash M : A$.

i) A subderivation ρ of π has *level* i if there are i applications of the rule ! in the path from the root of ρ to the root of π.
ii) An occurrence of a subterm N of M has level i in π if i is the maximum level of a subderivation of π having N as subject.
iii) The level $\partial(\pi)$ of π is the maximum level of subderivations of π.

Notice that the so defined level corresponds to the notion of box-nesting depth in proof-nets [2]. The length $L(M)$ of a typable lambda term M does not take into account levels as we have just defined them. The following definitions reconcile them, allowing $L(M)$ to be "split" on different levels.

Definition 14. Let $\pi : \Gamma \mid \Delta \mid \Theta \vdash M : A$.

i) $S(\pi, i)$ is defined by induction on π as follows:
   - If π consists of an axiom, then $S(\pi, 0) = 1$ and $S(\pi, i) = 0$ for every $i \geq 1$;
   - If the last rule in π is $I^I_{\multimap}$ or $I^L_{\multimap}$, then $S(\pi, 0) = S(\rho, 0) + 1$ and $S(\pi, i) = S(\rho, i)$ for every $i \geq 1$, where ρ is the immediate subderivation of π;
   - If the last rule in π is $E_{\multimap}$ then $S(\pi, 0) = S(\rho, 0) + S(\sigma, 0) + 1$ and $S(\pi, i) = S(\rho, i) + S(\sigma, i)$ for every $i \geq 1$, where ρ and σ are the immediate subderivations of π;
   - If the last rule in π is !, then $S(\pi, 0) = 0$ and $S(\pi, i) = S(\rho, i-1)$ for every $i \geq 1$, where ρ is the immediate subderivation of π.
ii) Let n be the level of π. The *size* of π is $S(\pi) = \sum_{i \leq n} S(\pi, i)$.

The following relates $S(\pi)$ to the size of the term π types:

Lemma 15. *Let $\pi : \Gamma \mid \Delta \mid \Theta \vdash M : A$. Then, $S(\pi) = L(M)$.*

Substitution Lemma can be restated in the following way:

Lemma 16 (Substitution Lemma, Revisited).

i) *If* $\pi : \Gamma_1, x : A \mid \Delta \mid \Theta \vdash M : B$, $\rho : \Gamma_2 \mid \Delta \mid \Theta \vdash N : A$ *and* $N \in \mathcal{V}$, *then there is* $\sigma : \Gamma_1, \Gamma_2 \mid \Delta \mid \Theta \vdash M\{N/x\} : B$ *such that* $S(\sigma, i) \leq S(\rho, i) + S(\pi, i)$ *for every* i.

ii) *If* $\pi : \Gamma_1 \mid \Delta \mid x : A, \Theta \vdash M : B$, $\rho : \Gamma_2 \mid \Delta \mid \Theta \vdash N : A$ *and* $N \in \mathcal{V}$, *then there is* $\sigma : \Gamma_1 \mid \Delta \mid \Gamma_2, \Theta \vdash M\{N/x\} : B$ *such that* $S(\sigma, i) \leq S(\pi, i)S(\rho, 0) + S(\pi, i)$ *for every* i.

iii) *If* $\pi : \Gamma_1 \mid \Delta, x : A \mid \Theta \vdash M : B$, $\rho : \Gamma_2 \mid \Delta \mid \Theta \vdash N : A$ *and* $N \in \mathcal{V}$, *then there is* $\sigma : \Gamma_1, \Gamma_2 \mid \Delta \mid \Theta \vdash M\{N/x\} : B$ *such that* $S(\sigma, 0) \leq S(\pi, 0)$ *and* $S(\sigma, i) \leq (\sum_{j \leq i} S(\pi, j))S(\rho, i) + S(\pi, i)$ *for every* $i \geq 1$.

The following can be thought of as a strenghtening of subject reduction and is a corollary of Lemma 16.

Proposition 17. *If* $\pi : \Gamma \mid \Delta \mid \Theta \vdash M : A$, *and* $M \rightarrow_v N$ *by reducing a redex at level* i *in* π, *then there is* $\rho : \Gamma \mid \Delta \mid \Theta \vdash N : A$ *such that*

$$\forall j < i . S(\rho, j) = S(\pi, j)$$
$$S(\rho, i) < S(\pi, i)$$
$$\forall j > i . S(\rho, j) \leq S(\pi, j)(\sum_{k \leq j} S(\pi, k))$$

Proof. Type derivation ρ is identical to π up to level i, so the equality $S(\rho, j) = S(\pi, j)$ holds for all levels $j < i$. At levels $j \geq i$, the only differences between ρ and π are due to the replacement of a type derivation ϕ for $(\lambda x.L)P$ with another type derivation ψ for $L\{P/x\}$. ψ is obtained by Lemma 16. The needed inequalitites follow from the ones in Lemma 16. □

If π is obtained from ρ by reducing a redex at level i as in Proposition 17, then we will write $\pi \rightarrow_v^i \rho$. Consider now a term M and a derivation $\pi : \Gamma \mid \Delta \mid \Theta \vdash M : A$. By Proposition 17, every reduction sequence $M \rightarrow_v N \rightarrow_v L \rightarrow_v \ldots$ can be put in correspondence with a sequence $\pi \rightarrow_v^i \rho \rightarrow_v^j \sigma \rightarrow_v^k \ldots$ (where ρ types N, σ types L, etc.). The following result give bounds on the lengths of these sequences and on the possible growth during normalization.

Proposition 18. *For every* $d \in \mathbb{N}$, *there are elementary functions* $f_d, g_d : \mathbb{N} \rightarrow \mathbb{N}$ *such that, for every sequence*

$$\pi_0 \rightarrow_v^{i_0} \pi_1 \rightarrow_v^{i_1} \pi_2 \rightarrow_v^{i_2} \ldots$$

it holds that

- *For every* $i \in \mathbb{N}$, $\sum_{e \leq d} S(\pi_i, e) \leq f_d(S(\pi_0))$;
- *There are at most* $g_d(S(\pi_0))$ *reduction steps with indices* $e \leq d$.

Theorem 19. *For every* $d \in \mathbb{N}$ *there are elementary functions* $p_d, q_d : \mathbb{N} \rightarrow \mathbb{N}$ *such that whenever* $\pi : \Gamma \mid \Delta \mid \Theta \vdash M : A$, *the length of reduction sequences starting from* M *is at most* $p_{\partial(\pi)}(L(M))$ *and the length of any reduct of* M *is at most* $q_{\partial(\pi)}(L(M))$.

Proof. This is immediate from Proposition 18. □

5 Type Inference

We prove, in a constructive way, that the type inference problem for ETAS is decidable. Namely a type inference algorithm is designed giving, for every lambda term M, a finite set of *principal typings*, from which all and only its typings can be obtained. If this set is empty, then M is not typable. The design of the algorithm is based on the following Generation Lemma.

Lemma 20 (Generation Lemma). *Let* $\Gamma \mid \Delta \mid \Theta \vdash M : A$.

i) Let $M \equiv x$. *If* A *is linear, then either* $\{x : A\} \subseteq \Gamma$ *or* $\{x : A\} \subseteq \Theta$. *Otherwise,* $\{x : A\} \in \Delta$.

ii) Let $M \equiv \lambda x.N$. *Then* A *is of the shape* $\underbrace{!...!}_{n}(B \multimap C)$ $(n \geq 0)$.

- *Let* $n = 0$. *If* B *is linear then* $\Gamma, x : B \mid \Delta \mid \Theta \vdash N : C$, *else* $\Gamma \mid \Delta, x : B \mid \Theta \vdash N : C$.
- *Let* $n > 0$. *Then* $\emptyset \mid \Delta \mid \emptyset \vdash M : A$ *and* $\Gamma' \mid \Delta' \mid \Theta' \vdash N : C$, *where* $\Delta = \underbrace{!...!}_{n}((\Gamma' \cup \Delta' \cup \Theta') - \{x : B\})$.

iii) Let $M \equiv PQ$. *Then* A *is of the shape* $\underbrace{!...!}_{n} B$ $(n \geq 0)$, $\Gamma_1 \mid \Delta' \mid \Theta' \vdash P : C \multimap \underbrace{!...!}_{m} B$ *and* $\Gamma_2 \mid \Delta' \mid \Theta' \vdash Q : C$, *for some* $m \leq n$.

- *If* $n - m = 0$, *then* $\Gamma = \Gamma_1 \cup \Gamma_2$, $\Delta = \Delta'$ *and* $\Theta = \Theta'$.
- *If* $n - m > 0$, *then* $\emptyset \mid \Delta \mid \emptyset \vdash M : A$, *where* $\Delta = \underbrace{!...!}_{n-m}(\Gamma_1 \cup \Gamma_2 \cup \Delta' \cup \Theta')$.

The principal typings are described through the notion of a *type scheme*, which is a variation on the one used in [6] in the context of Λ^{EA} and NEAL. Roughly speaking, a type scheme describes a class of types, i.e. it can be transformed into a type through a suitable notion of a substitution.

Definition 21. i) *Linear type schemes* and *type schemes* are respectively defined by the grammars

$$\mu ::= \alpha \mid \sigma \multimap \sigma$$
$$\sigma ::= \beta \mid \mu \mid !^p \sigma.$$

where the *exponential* p is defined by the grammar

$$p ::= n \mid p + p.$$

α and β respectively belong to $NVar$ and $MVar$, two disjoint countable sets of scheme variables, and n belongs to a countable set of literals. A generic scheme variable is ranged over by ϕ, linear type schemes are ranged over by μ, ν, type schemes are ranged over by σ, τ, ρ, and exponentials are ranged over by p, q, r. Let $\mathcal{T}$ denote the set of type schemes. A type scheme $!^p\sigma$ is a *modal* type scheme.

Table 3. The unification algorithm U

$$\frac{}{U(\phi,\phi)=\langle\emptyset,[]\rangle}\ (U1)\qquad \frac{\alpha \text{ does not occur in } \mu}{U(\alpha,\mu)=\langle\emptyset,[\alpha\mapsto\mu]\rangle}\ (U2)$$

$$\frac{\alpha \text{ does not occur in } \mu}{U(\mu,\alpha)=\langle\emptyset,[\alpha\mapsto\mu]\rangle}\ (U3)\qquad \frac{\beta \text{ does not occur in } \sigma}{U(\beta,\sigma)=\langle\emptyset,[\beta\mapsto\sigma]\rangle}\ (U4)$$

$$\frac{\beta \text{ does not occur in } \sigma}{U(\sigma,\beta)=\langle\emptyset,[\beta\mapsto\sigma]\rangle}\ (U5)$$

$$\frac{U(\mu,\nu)=\langle C,s\rangle}{U(!^{p_1}...!^{p_n}\mu,!^{q_1}...!^{q_m}\nu)=\langle C\cup\{p_1+...+p_n=q_1+...+q_m\},s\rangle}\ (U6)$$

$$\frac{U(\sigma_1,\tau_1)=\langle C_1,s_1\rangle \quad U(s_1(\sigma_2),s_1(\tau_2))=\langle C_2,s_2\rangle}{U(\sigma_1\multimap\sigma_2,\tau_1\multimap\tau_2)=\langle C_1\cup C_2,s_1\circ s_2\rangle}\ (U7)$$

In all other cases, U is undefined: for example both $U(\alpha,\alpha\multimap\beta)$ and $U(!^p\alpha,\sigma\multimap\tau)$ are undefined. $s_1\circ s_2$ is the substitution such that $s_1\circ s_2(\sigma)=s_2(s_1(\sigma))$.

ii) A *scheme substitution* S is a function from type schemes to types, replacing scheme variables in $NVar$ by linear types, scheme variables in $MVar$ by types and literals by natural numbers greater than 0. The application of S to a type scheme is defined inductively as follows:

$$S(\phi)=A \text{ if } [\phi\mapsto A]\in S;$$

$$S(\sigma\multimap\tau)=S(\sigma)\multimap S(\tau);$$

$$S(!^{n_1+...+n_i}\sigma)=\underbrace{!...!}_{q}S(\sigma);$$

where $q=S(n_1)+...+S(n_i)$.

iii) A *scheme basis* is a finite subset of type scheme associations to variables. With an abuse of notation, we will let Ξ,Γ,Δ,Θ range over scheme basis, with the constraint that Γ and Θ denote scheme basis associating non-modal schemes to variables, while Δ denotes a scheme basis associating modal type schemes to variables.

Binary relation $\equiv$ is extended to denote the syntactical identity between both types and type schemes. Making clear what we said before, a type scheme can be seen as a description of the set of all types that can be obtained from it through a scheme substitution. So:

- a linear type scheme describes a set of linear types;
- a modal type scheme describes a subset of modal types;
- a scheme variable in $NVar$ describes the set of all types.

Table 4. The type inference algorithm PT. (two 5-tuples are disjoint if and only if they are built from different scheme variables)

$$PT(x) = \{< x : \alpha; \emptyset; \emptyset; \alpha; \epsilon >, < \emptyset; \emptyset; x : \alpha; \alpha; \epsilon >, < \emptyset; x :!^n \alpha; \emptyset; !^n \alpha; \epsilon >\}$$

$$\begin{array}{ll}
\multicolumn{2}{l}{PT(\lambda x.M) = \{< \Gamma; \Delta; \Theta; \sigma \multimap \tau; C >, < \emptyset; !^m(\Gamma \cup \Delta \cup \Theta); \emptyset; !^m \sigma \multimap \tau; C >|} \\
\quad (< \Gamma, x : \sigma; \Delta; \Theta; \tau; C > \in PT(M)) & \texttt{or} \\
\quad (< \Gamma; \Delta, x : \sigma; \Theta; \tau; C > \in PT(M)) & \texttt{or} \\
\quad (< \Gamma; \Delta; \Theta; \tau; C > \in PT(M) & \texttt{and} \\
\quad \sigma \equiv \alpha \ \ \texttt{and} \ \ x \notin dom(\Gamma) \cup dom(\Delta) \cup dom(\Theta)) \ \} &
\end{array}$$

$$\begin{array}{ll}
\multicolumn{2}{l}{PT(MN) = \{< \Gamma; \Delta; \Theta; \sigma; C >, < \emptyset; !^m(\Gamma \cup \Delta \cup \Theta); \emptyset; !^m \sigma; C >|} \\
\quad < \Gamma_1; \Delta_1; \Theta_1; \sigma_1; C_1 > \in PT(M) & \texttt{and} \\
\quad < \Gamma_2; \Delta_2; \Theta_2; \sigma_2; C_2 > \in PT(N) & \texttt{(disjoint) and} \\
\quad dom(\Gamma_1) \cap dom(\Gamma_2) = \emptyset & \texttt{and} \\
\quad i \neq j \ \texttt{implies} \ dom(\Xi_i) \cap dom(\Xi_j) = \emptyset & \texttt{and} \\
\quad U(\sigma_1, \sigma_2 \multimap \beta) =< s, C' > & (\beta \ \texttt{fresh) and} \\
\quad \sigma = s \circ s_1 \circ ... \circ s_k(\beta) & \\
\quad\ \texttt{where} & \\
\quad U(s(\tau_1^1), s(\tau_2^1)) =< s_1, C_1' > & \texttt{and} \\
\quad U(s_i(\tau_1^i), s_i(\tau_2^i)) =< s_{i+1}, C_{i+1}' > & \texttt{and} \\
\quad x_i \in dom(\Xi_1) \cup dom(\Xi_2), \ x_i : \tau_j^i \in \Xi_j & \texttt{and} \\
\quad \Xi = \{x : s \circ s_1 \circ ... \circ s_k(\tau) \mid x : \tau \in \Xi_j\} & \texttt{and} \\
\quad C = C' \bigcup_{1 \leq i \leq k} C_i' & \\
\multicolumn{2}{l}{(1 \leq i \leq k, \ 1 \leq j \leq 2, \ \Xi \in \{\Gamma, \Delta, \Theta\}, \ \Xi_i \in \{\Gamma_i, \Delta_i, \Theta_i \mid 1 \leq i \leq 2\} \ )\}}
\end{array}$$

In order to define the principal typing, we will use a unification algorithm for type schemes, which is a variant of that defined in [6]. Let $=_e$ be the relation between type schemes defined as follows: $\phi =_e \phi$; $\sigma =_e \sigma'$ and $\tau =_e \tau'$ imply $\sigma \multimap \tau =_e \sigma' \multimap \tau'$; $\sigma =_e \tau$ implies $!^p \sigma =_e !^q \tau$. Roughly speaking, two type schemes are in $=_e$ if and only if they are identical modulo the exponentials.

The unification algorithm, which we will present in SOS style in Table 3, is a function U from $\mathcal{T} \times \mathcal{T}$ to pairs of the shape $\langle C, s \rangle$, where C (the *modality* set) is a set of natural linear constraints in the form $p = q$, where p and q are exponentials, and s is a substitution, replacing scheme variables by type schemes. A set C of linear constraints is *solvable* if there is a scheme substitution S such that, for every constraint $n_1 + ... + n_i = m_1 + ... + m_j$ in C, $S(n_1) + ... + S(n_i) = S(m_1) + ... + S(m_j)$. Clearly the solvability of a set of linear constraints is a decidable problem.

The following two technical lemmas prove that, if $U(\sigma, \tau) = \langle C, s \rangle$, then this result supplies a more general unifier for type schemes (modulo $=_e$) and moreover this can be extended to types.

Lemma 22. *i) (correctness)* $U(\sigma, \tau) = \langle C, s \rangle$ *implies* $s(\sigma) =_e s(\tau)$.
ii) (completeness) $s(\sigma) =_e s(\tau)$ *implies* $U(\sigma, \tau) = \langle C, s' \rangle$ *and* $s = s' \circ s''$, *for some* s''.

The extension to types must take into consideration the set of linear constraints generated by U, which imposes some relations between the number of modalities in different subtypes of the same type.

Lemma 23. *i) (correctness) Let* $U(\sigma, \tau) = \langle C, s \rangle$. *Then, for every scheme solution* S *of* C, $S(s(\sigma)) \equiv S(s(\tau))$.
ii) (completeness) $S(\sigma) \equiv S(\tau)$ *implies* $U(\sigma, \tau) = \langle C, s \rangle$, *and* $S(\sigma) \equiv S'(s(\sigma))$, $S(\tau) \equiv S'(s(\tau))$, *for some* S' *satisfying* C.

The set of principal type schemes of a term is a set of tuples in the form $< \Gamma; \Delta; \Theta; \sigma; C >$, where Γ, Δ, Θ are scheme basis, σ is a type scheme and C is a set of constraints. It is defined in Table 4.

Theorem 24 (Type Inference).
i) (correctness) $< \Gamma; \Delta; \Theta; \sigma; C > \in PT(M)$ *implies that, for every scheme substitution* S *satisfying* C, *for every substitution* s, $S(s(\Gamma)) \mid S(s(\Delta)) \mid S(s(\Theta)) \vdash M : S(s(\sigma))$.
ii) (completeness) $\Gamma \mid \Delta \mid \Theta \vdash M : A$ *implies there is* $< \Gamma'; \Delta'; \Theta'; \sigma; C > \in PT(M)$ *such that* $A = S(\sigma)$ *and* $S(\Xi') \subseteq \Xi$ $(\Xi \in \{\Gamma, \Delta, \Theta\})$, *for some scheme substitution* S *satisfying* C.

Proof. i) By induction on M.
ii) By induction on the derivation proving $\Gamma \mid \Delta \mid \Theta \vdash M : A$, using the Generation Lemma. □

6 Extensions

6.1 Achieving Completeness

The type-system we introduced in this paper is not complete for the class of elementary time functions, at least if we restrict to uniform encodings. One possible solution consists in extending the type system with second order quantification. This, however, would make type inference much harder (if not undecidable). Another approach, consists in extending the language with basic types and constants. In this section, we will sketch one possible extension going exactly in this direction.

Suppose we fix a finite set of free algebras $\mathcal{A} = \{\mathbb{A}_1, \ldots, \mathbb{A}_n\}$. The constructors of $\mathbb{A}_i$ will be denoted as $c^1_{\mathbb{A}_i}, \ldots, c^{k(\mathbb{A}_i)}_{\mathbb{A}_i}$. The arity of constructor $c^j_{\mathbb{A}_i}$ will be denoted as $\mathcal{R}^j_{\mathbb{A}_i}$. The algebra $\mathbb{U}$ of unary integers has two constructors $c^1_{\mathbb{U}}, c^2_{\mathbb{U}}$, where $\mathcal{R}^1_{\mathbb{U}} = 1$ and $\mathcal{R}^1_{\mathbb{U}} = 0$. The languages of types, terms and values are extended by the the following productions

$$A ::= \mathbb{A}_j$$
$$M ::= iter_{\mathbb{A}_j} \mid cond_{\mathbb{A}_j} \mid c^i_{\mathbb{A}_j}$$
$$V ::= iter_{\mathbb{A}_j} \mid cond_{\mathbb{A}_j} \mid c^i_{\mathbb{A}_j} \mid t$$

where $\mathbb{A}_j$ ranges over $\mathcal{A}$, i ranges over $\{1, \ldots, k(\mathbb{A}_j)\}$ and t ranges over free algebra terms. If t is a term of the free algebra $\mathbb{A}$ and $M_1, \ldots, M_{k(\mathbb{A})}$ are terms, then $t\{M_1, \ldots, M_{k(\mathbb{A})}\}$ is defined by induction on t. In particular, $(c^i_{\mathbb{A}} t_1, \ldots, t_{\mathcal{R}^j_{\mathbb{A}_i}})\{M_1, \ldots, M_{k(\mathbb{A})}\}$ will be

$$M_i(t_1\{M_1, \ldots, M_{k(\mathbb{A})}\}) \ldots (t_{\mathcal{R}^j_{\mathbb{A}_i}}\{M_1, \ldots, M_{k(\mathbb{A})}\}).$$

The new constants receive the following types in any context:

$$\mathit{iter}_{\mathbb{A}} : \mathbb{A} \multimap !(\underbrace{A \multimap \ldots \multimap A}_{\mathcal{R}^1_{\mathbb{A}} \ \mathit{times}} \multimap A) \multimap \ldots \multimap !(\underbrace{A \multimap \ldots \multimap A}_{\mathcal{R}^{k(\mathbb{A})}_{\mathbb{A}} \ \mathit{times}} \multimap A) \multimap !A$$

$$\mathit{cond}_{\mathbb{A}} : \mathbb{A} \multimap (\underbrace{\mathbb{A} \multimap \ldots \multimap \mathbb{A}}_{\mathcal{R}^1_{\mathbb{A}} \ \mathit{times}} \multimap A) \multimap \ldots \multimap (\underbrace{\mathbb{A} \multimap \ldots \multimap \mathbb{A}}_{\mathcal{R}^{k(\mathbb{A})}_{\mathbb{A}} \ \mathit{times}} \multimap A) \multimap A$$

$$c^i_{\mathbb{A}} : \underbrace{\mathbb{A} \multimap \ldots \multimap \mathbb{A}}_{\mathcal{R}^i_{\mathbb{A}} \ \mathit{times}} \multimap \mathbb{A}$$

New (call-by-value) reduction rules are the following ones:

$$\mathit{iter}_{\mathbb{A}} t V_1 \ldots V_{k(\mathbb{A})} \rightarrow_v t\{V_1 \ldots V_{k(\mathbb{A})}\}$$
$$\mathit{cond}_{\mathbb{A}} c^i_{\mathbb{A}}(t_1 \ldots t_{\mathcal{R}^i_{\mathbb{A}}}) V_1 \ldots V_{k(\mathbb{A})} \rightarrow_v V_i t_1 \ldots t_{\mathcal{R}^i_{\mathbb{A}}}$$

It is easy to check that lemma 16 continue to be true in the presence of the new constants. Moreover, we can prove the following theorem:

Theorem 25. *There is a finite set of free algebra $\mathcal{A}$ including the algebra $\mathbb{U}$ of unary integers such that for every elementary function $f : \mathbb{N} \rightarrow \mathbb{N}$, there is a term $M_f : \mathbb{U} \rightarrow !^k\mathbb{U}$ such that $M_f \lceil u \rceil \rightarrow^*_v \lceil f(u) \rceil$ (where $\lceil n \rceil$ is the term in $\mathbb{U}$ corresponding to the natural number n).*

6.2 Adapting the System to Other Logics

We believe the approach described in this paper to be applicable to other logics besides elementary affine logic. Two examples are Light Affine Logic [2] and Soft Affine Logic [11]. Light Affine Logic needs two modalities. So, there will be two rules:

$$\frac{\Gamma_1 \mid \Delta_1 \mid \Theta_1 \vdash M : A \quad |\Gamma_1| + |\Delta_1| + |\Theta_1| \leq 1}{\Gamma_2 \mid !\Gamma_1, !\Delta_1, !\Theta_1, \Delta_2 \mid \Theta_2 \vdash M : !A} \; !$$

$$\frac{\Gamma_1, \Gamma_2 \mid \Delta_1, \Delta_2 \mid \Theta_1 \vdash M : A}{\S\Gamma_1, \S\Delta_1, \S\Theta_1, \Gamma_3 \mid !\Gamma_2, !\Delta_2, !\Theta_2, \Delta_3 \mid \Theta_2 \vdash M : \S A} \; \S$$

Soft Affine Logic is even simpler than elementary affine logic: there is just one modality and the context is split in just two sub-contexts. The ! rule becomes:

$$\frac{\Gamma \mid \Delta \vdash M : A}{!\Gamma \mid !\Delta \vdash M : !A} \; !$$

We further need a couple of rules capturing dereliction:

$$\frac{\Gamma \mid x : A, \Delta \vdash M : A}{x :!A, \Gamma \mid \Delta \vdash M : A}\, D^L \qquad \frac{\Gamma \mid x : A, \Delta \vdash M : A}{\Gamma \mid x :!A, \Delta \vdash M : A}\, D^I$$

References

1. Girard, J.Y.: Light linear logic. Information and Computation **143(2)** (1998) 175–204
2. Asperti, A.: Light affine logic. In: Proceedings of the 13th IEEE Syposium on Logic in Computer Science. (1998) 300–308
3. Asperti, A., Roversi, L.: Intuitionistic light affine logic. ACM Transactions on Computational Logic **3(1)** (2002) 137–175
4. Baillot, P., Terui, K.: Light types for polynomial time computation in lambda-calculus. In: Proceedings of the 19th IEEE Syposium on Logic in Computer Science. (2004) 266–275
5. Coppola, P., Martini, S.: Typing lambda terms in elementary logic with linear constraints. In: Proceedings of the 6th International Conference on Typed Lambda-Calculus and Applications. (2001) 76–90
6. Coppola, P., Ronchi della Rocca, S.: Principal typing in elementary affine logic. In: Proceedings of the 7th International Conference on Typed Lambda-Calculus and Applications. (2003) 90–104
7. Terui, K.: Light affine lambda calculus and polytime strong normalization. In: Proceedings of the 16th IEEE Symposium on Logic in Computer Science. (2001) 209–220
8. Terui, K.: Light logic and polynomial time computation. PhD thesis, Keio University (2002)
9. Baillot, P.: Checking polynomial time complexity with types. In: Proceedings of the 2nd IFIP International Conference on Theoretical Computer Science. (2002)
10. Coppola, P., Martini, S.: Optimizing optimal reduction. a type inference algorithm for elementary affine logic. ACM Transactions on Computational Logic (2004) To appear.
11. Baillot, P., Mogbil, V.: Soft lambda-calculus: a language for polynomial time computation. In: Proceedings of the 7th International Conference on Foundations of Software Science and Computational Structures. (2004)

Rank-2 Intersection and Polymorphic Recursion

Ferruccio Damiani*

Dipartimento di Informatica, Università di Torino,
Corso Svizzera 185, I-10149 Torino, Italy
damiani@di.unito.it

Abstract. Let $\vdash$ be a rank-2 intersection type system. We say that a term is $\vdash$-*simple* (or just *simple* when the system $\vdash$ is clear from the context) if system $\vdash$ can prove that it has a simple type. In this paper we propose new typing rules and algorithms that are able to type recursive definitions that are not simple. At the best of our knowledge, previous algorithms for typing recursive definitions in the presence of rank-2 intersection types allow only simple recursive definitions to be typed. The proposed rules are also able to type interesting examples of *polymorphic recursion* (i.e., recursive definitions $\mathsf{rec}\,\{x = e\}$ where different occurrences of x in e are used with different types). Moreover, the underlying techniques do not depend on particulars of rank-2 intersection, so they can be applied to other type systems.

1 Introduction

The Hindley-Milner type system (a.k.a. the ML type system) [5], which is the core of the type systems of modern functional programming languages (like SML, OCaml, and Haskell), has several limitations that prevent safe programs from being typed. In particular, it does not allow different types to be assigned to different occurrences of a formal parameter in the body of a function. To overcome these limitations, various extensions of the ML system based on *universal types* [7, 19], *intersection types* [3, 1], *recursive types*, and combinations of them, have been proposed in the literature.

The system of *rank-2 intersection types* [16, 20, 23, 13, 6] is particularly interesting since it is able to type all ML programs, has the principal pair property (a.k.a. principal typing property [13, 22]), decidable type inference, and the complexity of type inference is of the same order as in ML.

Intersection types are obtained from *simple types* [11] by adding the *intersection type constructor* $\wedge$. A term has type $u_1 \wedge u_2$ (u_1 intersection u_2) if it has both type u_1 and type u_2. For example, the identity function $\lambda x.x$ has both type $\mathsf{int} \to \mathsf{int}$ and $\mathsf{bool} \to \mathsf{bool}$, so it has type $(\mathsf{int} \to \mathsf{int}) \wedge (\mathsf{bool} \to \mathsf{bool})$. Rank-2 intersection types may contain intersections only to the left of a single arrow. Therefore, for instance, $((\mathsf{int} \to \mathsf{int}) \wedge (\mathsf{bool} \to \mathsf{bool})) \to \mathsf{int} \to \mathsf{int}$ is a rank-2

* Partially supported by IST-2001-33477 DART and MIUR cofin'04 EOS.The funding bodies are not responsible for any use made of the results presented here.

P. Urzyczyn (Ed.): TLCA 2005, LNCS 3461, pp. 146–161, 2005.

intersection type (as usual, the arrow type constructor is right associative), while $(((\mathsf{int} \to \mathsf{int}) \wedge (\mathsf{bool} \to \mathsf{bool})) \to \mathsf{int}) \to \mathsf{int}$ is not a rank-2 intersection type.

The problem of typing standard programming language constructs like local definitions, conditional expressions, and recursive definitions without losing the extra information provided by rank-2 intersection is more difficult than one might expect (see, e.g., [12, 13, 21, 6]).

Definition 1 ($\vdash$-Simple Terms). Let $\vdash$ be a rank-2 intersection type system. We say that a term is $\vdash$-*simple* (or just *simple* when the system $\vdash$ is clear from the context) if system $\vdash$ can prove that it has a simple type.

An example of *non-simple* term is $\lambda x.xx$ (which has principal type $((\alpha_1 \to \alpha_2) \wedge \alpha_1) \to \alpha_2$, where α_1, α_2 are type variables).

In previous work [6] we introduced rules and algorithms for typing *non-simple local definitions* (i.e., terms of the shape $\mathsf{let}\, x = e_0 \,\mathsf{in}\, e_1$ where e_0 is non-simple) and *non-simple conditional expressions* (i.e., non-simple terms of the shape $\mathsf{if}\, e_0 \,\mathsf{then}\, e_1 \,\mathsf{else}\, e_2$). In this paper we propose new rules and algorithms for typing *non-simple recursive definitions* (i.e., non-simple terms of the shape $\mathsf{rec}\,\{x = e\}$). At the best of our knowledge, previous algorithms for typing recursive definitions in the presence of rank-2 intersection types [12, 13, 21, 6] allow only simple recursive definitions to be typed.

Note that, the ability of typing non-simple recursive definitions is not, a priori, a fair measure for the expressive power of a system. It fact, it might be possible that a given system could type a term that is non-simple *in the given system* only because the given system somehow prevents the term from having a simple type. In another system that allows only simple terms to be typed, the same term might have a simple type and therefore be simple. When designing the new rules we will be careful to avoid such a pathological situation.

Inferring types for *polymorphic recursion* (i.e., recursive definitions $\mathsf{rec}\,\{x = e\}$ where different occurrences of x in e are used with different types) [17, 18, 10, 15] is a recurring topic on the mailing list of popular typed programming languages (see, e.g., [9] for a discussion of several examples). The rules proposed in this paper are able to type interesting examples of polymorphic recursion. So, besides providing a solution to the problem of finding decidable rules for typing non-simple recursive definitions, the techniques proposed in this paper address also the related topic of polymorphic recursion. Moreover (as we will point out in Section 8), these techniques do not depend on particulars of rank-2 intersection. So they can be applied to other type systems.

Organization of the Paper. Section 2 introduces a small functional programming language, which can be considered the kernel of languages like SML, OCaml, and Haskell. Section 3 introduces some basic definitions. Section 4 presents the rank-2 intersection type system ($\vdash_2$) for the rec-free subset of the language. Section 5 briefly reviews the rules for typing recursive definitions in the presence of rank-2 intersection types that have been proposed in the literature. Section 6 extends $\vdash_2$ with new rules for typing non-simple recursive definitions and Section 7 outlines how to adapt the rules to deal with mutual recursion. We conclude by discussing some further work.

The proofs and an on-line demonstration of a prototype implementation of the typing algorithm are available at the url http://lambda.di.unito.it/pr.

2 A Small ML-Like Language

We consider a quite rich set of constants (that will be useful to formulate the examples considered through the paper) including the booleans, the integer numbers, the constructors for pairs and lists, some logical and arithmetic operators, and the functions for decomposing pairs (fst and snd) and lists (null, hd and tl). The syntax of constants (ranged over by c) is as follows:

$$c ::= \flat \mid \iota \mid \mathsf{pair} \mid \mathsf{nil} \mid \mathsf{cons} \mid \mathsf{not} \mid \mathsf{and} \mid \mathsf{or} \mid + \mid - \mid * \mid = \mid < \mid \mathsf{fst} \mid \mathsf{snd} \mid \mathsf{null} \mid \mathsf{hd} \mid \mathsf{tl}$$

where $\flat$ ranges over booleans (true and false) and ι ranges over integer numbers.

Expressions (ranged over by e) are defined by the pseudo-grammar:

$$e ::= x \mid c \mid \lambda x.e \mid e_1\, e_2 \mid \mathsf{rec}\,\{x = e\} \mid \mathsf{let}\, x = e_0\, \mathsf{in}\, e_1 \mid \mathsf{if}\, e_0\, \mathsf{then}\, e_1\, \mathsf{else}\, e_2,$$

where x ranges over variables. The finite set of the free variables of an expression e is denoted by $\mathrm{FV}(e)$.

3 Basic Definitions

In this section we introduce the syntax of our rank-2 intersection types, together with other basic definitions that will be used in the rest of the paper.

We will be defining several classes of types. The set of *simple types* ($\mathbf{T}_0$), ranged over by u, the set of *rank-1 intersection types* ($\mathbf{T}_1$), ranged over by w, and the set of *rank-2 intersection types* ($\mathbf{T}_2$), ranged over by v, are defined by the pseudo-grammar:

$$\begin{array}{lll} u & ::= \alpha \mid u_1 \to u_2 \mid \mathsf{bool} \mid \mathsf{int} \mid u_1 \times u_2 \mid u\,\mathsf{list} & \text{(simple types)} \\ w & ::= u_1 \wedge \cdots \wedge u_n & \text{(rank-1 types)} \\ v & ::= u \mid w \to v & \text{(rank-2 types)} \end{array}$$

where $n \geq 1$. We have *type variables* (ranged over by α), arrow types, and a selection of *ground types* and *parametric datatypes*. The ground types are bool (the type of booleans) and int (the type of integers). The other types are pair types and list types. Note that $\mathbf{T}_0 = \mathbf{T}_1 \cap \mathbf{T}_2$ (for technical convenience, following [13] and other papers, rank-1 types are not included into rank-2 types).

The constructor $\to$ is right associative, e.g., $u_1 \to u_2 \to u_3$ means $u_1 \to (u_2 \to u_3)$, and the constructors $\times$ and list bind more tightly than $\to$, e.g., $u_1 \to u_2 \times u_3$ means $u_1 \to (u_2 \times u_3)$. We consider $\wedge$ to be associative, commutative, and idempotent. Therefore any type in $\mathbf{T}_1$ can be considered (modulo elimination of duplicates) as a set of types in $\mathbf{T}_0$. The constructor $\wedge$ binds more tightly than $\to$, e.g., $u_1 \wedge u_2 \to u_3$ means $(u_1 \wedge u_2) \to u_3$, and less tightly than $\times$ and list (which can be applied only to simple types).

We assume a countable set of type variables. A *substitution* $\mathbf{s}$ is a function from type variables to simple types which is the identity on all but a finite number of type variables. The application of a substitution $\mathbf{s}$ to a type t, denoted by $\mathbf{s}(t)$, is defined as usual. Note that, since substitutions replace type variables by simple types, we have that $\mathbf{T}_0$, $\mathbf{T}_1$, and $\mathbf{T}_2$ are closed under substitution.

An *environment* T is a set $\{x_1 : t_1, \ldots, x_n : t_n\}$ of assumptions for variables such that every variable x_i $(1 \leq i \leq n)$ can occur at most once in T. The expression $\mathrm{Dom}(T)$ denotes the *domain* of T, which is the set $\{x_1, \ldots, x_n\}$. We write $T, x : t$ for the environment $T \cup \{x : t\}$ where it is assumed that $x \notin \mathrm{Dom}(T)$. The application of a substitution $\mathbf{s}$ to an environment T, denoted by $\mathbf{s}(T)$, is defined as usual.

Definition 2 (Rank-1 Environments). A *rank-1 environment* A is an environment $\{x_1 : w_1, \ldots, x_n : w_n\}$ of rank-1 type assumptions for variables.

Given two rank-1 environments A_1 and A_2, we write $A_1 \wedge A_2$ to denote the rank-1 environment:

$$\begin{array}{l}\{x : w_1 \wedge w_2 \mid x : w_1 \in A_1 \text{ and } x : w_2 \in A_2\} \\ \cup\{x : w_1 \in A_1 \mid x \notin \mathrm{Dom}(A_2)\} \cup \{x : w_2 \in A_2 \mid x \notin \mathrm{Dom}(A_1)\}.\end{array}$$

A *pair* is a formula $\langle A;\, v\rangle$ where A is a rank-1 environment and v is a rank-2 type. Let p range over pairs.

The following relation is fairly standard.

Definition 3 (Pair Specialization Relation $\leq_{\mathbf{spc}}$). The subtyping relations $\leq_1$ $(\subseteq \mathbf{T}_1 \times \mathbf{T}_1)$ and $\leq_2$ $(\subseteq \mathbf{T}_2 \times \mathbf{T}_2)$ are defined by the following rules.

$$(\wedge)\ \frac{\cup_{1\leq i\leq n}\{u_i\} \supseteq \cup_{1\leq j\leq m}\{u'_j\}}{u_1 \wedge \cdots \wedge u_n \leq_1 u'_1 \wedge \cdots \wedge u'_m} \qquad (\text{REF})\ \frac{u \in \mathbf{T}_0}{u \leq_2 u} \qquad (\rightarrow)\ \frac{w' \leq_1 w \quad v \leq_2 v'}{w \rightarrow v \leq_2 w' \rightarrow v'}$$

Given two rank-1 environments A and A' we write $A \leq_1 A'$ to mean that

- $\mathrm{Dom}(A) = \mathrm{Dom}(A')$,[1] and
- for every assumption $x : w' \in A'$ there is an assumption $x : w \in A$ such that $w \leq_1 w'$.

A pair $\langle A;\, v\rangle$ *can be specialized to* $\langle A';\, v'\rangle$ (notation $\langle A;\, v\rangle \leq_{\mathbf{spc}} \langle A';\, v'\rangle$) if $A' \leq_1 \mathbf{s}(A)$ and $\mathbf{s}(v) \leq_2 v'$, for some substitution $\mathbf{s}$.

Example 4. We have $\langle\{y : \beta\};\, \alpha \rightarrow \beta\rangle \leq_{\mathbf{spc}} \langle\{y : \gamma\};\, ((\gamma \rightarrow \gamma) \wedge \gamma) \rightarrow \gamma\rangle$.

Note that the relation $\leq_{\mathbf{spc}}$ is reflexive and transitive.

---

[1] The requirement $\mathrm{Dom}(A) = \mathrm{Dom}(A')$ in the definition of $A \leq_1 A'$ is not present in most other papers. The "usual" definition drops this requirement, thus allowing $\mathrm{Dom}(A) \supseteq \mathrm{Dom}(A')$. We have added such a requirement since it will simplify the presentation of the new typing rules for recursive definitions (in Section 6).

4 Typing the "rec-Free" Fragment of the Language

In this section we introduce the type system $\vdash_2$ for the "rec-free" fragment of the language (i.e., the fragment without recursive definitions). System $\vdash_2$ is just a reformulation of Jim's system $\mathbf{P}_2$ [13].

4.1 System $\vdash_2$

Following Wells [22], in the type inference system $\vdash_2$ we use typing judgements of the shape $\vdash_2 e : \langle A; v\rangle$, instead of the more usual notation $A \vdash_2 e : v$. This slight change of notation will simplify the presentation of the new typing rules for recursive definitions (in Section 6). The judgement $\vdash_2 e : \langle A; v\rangle$ means "e is $\vdash_2$-typable with pair $\langle A; v\rangle$", where

- A is a rank-1 environment containing the type assumptions for the free variables of e, and
- v is a rank-2 type.

In any valid judgement $\vdash_2 e : \langle A; v\rangle$ it holds that $\mathrm{Dom}(A) = \mathrm{FV}(e)$.

The typing rules of system $\vdash_2$ are given in Fig. 2. Rule (SPC), which is the only non-structural rule, allows to specialize (in the sense of Definition 3) the pair inferred for an expression.

c	**type**(c)	c	**type**(c)	c	**type**(c)
$\flat$	bool	not	bool $\to$ bool	fst	$\alpha_1 \times \alpha_2 \to \alpha_1$
ι	int	and, or	bool $\times$ bool $\to$ bool	snd	$\alpha_1 \times \alpha_2 \to \alpha_2$
pair	$\alpha_1 \to \alpha_2 \to (\alpha_1 \times \alpha_2)$	$+, -, *$	int $\times$ int $\to$ int	null	α list $\to$ bool
nil	α list	$=, <$	int $\times$ int $\to$ bool	hd	α list $\to \alpha$
cons	$\alpha \to \alpha$ list $\to \alpha$ list			tl	α list $\to \alpha$ list

Fig. 1. Types for constants

$$(\textsc{Spc})\ \frac{\vdash e : p}{\vdash e : p'} \quad \text{where } p \leq_{\mathbf{spc}} p' \qquad (\textsc{Con})\ \vdash\ annTyc\langle\emptyset; v\rangle \quad \text{where } v = \mathbf{type}(c) \qquad (\textsc{Var})\ \vdash x : \langle\{x : u\}; u\rangle \quad \text{where } u \in \mathbf{T}_0$$

$$(\textsc{App})\ \frac{\vdash e : \langle A; u_1 \wedge \cdots \wedge u_n \to v\rangle \qquad \vdash e_0 : \langle A_1; u_1\rangle \quad \cdots \quad \vdash e_0 : \langle A_n; u_n\rangle}{\vdash e\, e_0 : \langle A \wedge A_1 \wedge \cdots \wedge A_n; v\rangle}$$

$$(\textsc{Abs})\ \frac{\vdash e : \langle A, x : w; v\rangle}{\vdash \lambda x.e : \langle A; w \to v\rangle} \qquad (\textsc{AbsVac})\ \frac{\vdash e : \langle A; v\rangle}{\vdash \lambda x.e : \langle A; u \to v\rangle} \quad \text{where } x \notin \mathrm{FV}(e) \text{ and } u \in \mathbf{T}_0$$

Fig. 2. Typing rules for the rec-free fragment of the language (system $\vdash_2$)

The rule for typing constants, (Con), uses the function **type** (tabulated in Figure 1) which specifies a type for each constant. Note that, by rule (Spc), it is possible to assign to a constant c all the specializations of the pair $\langle\emptyset;\, \mathbf{type}(c)\rangle$.

Since $\vdash_2 e : \langle A;\, v\rangle$ implies $\mathrm{Dom}(A) = \mathrm{FV}(e)$, we have two rules for typing an abstraction $\lambda x.e$, (Abs) and (AbsVac), corresponding to the two cases $x \in \mathrm{FV}(e)$ and $x \notin \mathrm{FV}(e)$. Note that, by rule (Var), it is possible to assume a different simple type for each occurrence of the λ-bound variable.

The rule for typing function application, (App), allows to use a different pair for each expected type of the argument (the operator $\wedge$ on rank-1 environments has been defined immediately after Definition 2).

To save space, we have omitted the typing rule for local definitions, which handles expressions "$\mathsf{let}\, x = e_0 \,\mathsf{in}\, e_1$" like syntactic sugar for "$(\lambda x.e_1)\, e_0$", and the typing rule for for conditional expressions, which handles expressions "$\mathsf{if}\, e_0 \,\mathsf{then}\, e_1 \,\mathsf{else}\, e_2$" like syntactic sugar for the application "$\mathsf{ifc}\, e_0\, e_1\, e_2$", where ifc is a special constant of type $\mathsf{bool} \to \alpha \to \alpha \to \alpha$. Note that, according to these rules, only simple local definitions and conditional expressions can be typed.

4.2 Principal Pairs and Decidability for $\vdash_2$

Definition 5 (Principal Pairs). Let $\vdash$ be a type system with judgements of the shape $\vdash e : p$. A pair p is *principal for a term e* if $\vdash e : p$, and if $\vdash e : p'$ implies $p \leq_{\mathbf{spc}} p'$. We say that system $\vdash$ has the *principal pair property* to mean that every typable term has a principal pair.

System $\vdash_2$ has the principal pair property and is decidable (see, e.g., [13]).

5 Typing Simple Recursive Definition

In this section we briefly recall the typing rules for recursive definitions proposed by Jim [12,13] (see also [6]) which, at the best of our knowledge, are the more powerful rules for typing recursive definitions in presence of rank-2 intersection types that can be found in the literature.

In order to be able to formulate these typing rules we need some auxiliary definitions. The set of *rank-2 intersection type schemes* ($\mathbf{T}_{\forall 2}$), ranged over by vs, is defined by the following pseudo-grammar:

$$vs ::= \forall\overrightarrow{\alpha}.v \qquad \text{(rank-2 schemes)},$$

where $\overrightarrow{\alpha}$ denotes a finite (possibly empty) unordered sequence of distinct type variables $\alpha_1 \cdots \alpha_m$ and $v \in \mathbf{T}_2$. *Free* and *bound* type variables are defined as usual. For every type or scheme $t \in \mathbf{T}_1 \cup \mathbf{T}_2 \cup \mathbf{T}_{\forall 2}$ let $\mathrm{FTV}(t)$ denote the set of free type variables of t. For every scheme $\forall\overrightarrow{\alpha}.v$ it is assumed that $\{\overrightarrow{\alpha}\} \subseteq \mathrm{FTV}(v)$. Moreover, schemes are considered equal modulo renaming of bound type variables. Given a type $v \in \mathbf{T}_2$ and a rank-1 environment A, we write

$\text{Gen}(A, v)$ for the $\forall$-*closure of v in A*, that is the rank-2 scheme $\forall\overrightarrow{\alpha}.v$, where $\overrightarrow{\alpha}$ is the sequence of the type variables in $\text{FTV}(v) - \cup_{x:w\in A}\text{FTV}(w)$.

Definition 6 (Scheme Instantiation Relation). For every rank-2 scheme $\forall\overrightarrow{\alpha}.v$ and for every rank-1 type $u_1 \wedge \cdots \wedge u_n$, let $\forall\overrightarrow{\alpha}.v \leq_{\forall 2,1} u_1 \wedge \cdots \wedge u_n$ mean that, for every $i \in \{1, \ldots, n\}$, $u_i = \mathbf{s}_i(v)$, for some substitution $\mathbf{s}_i$ such that $\mathbf{s}_i(\beta) = \beta$ for all $\beta \notin \overrightarrow{\alpha}$.

Example 7. We have (remember that $\wedge$ is idempotent): $\forall\alpha\beta\gamma.((\alpha \to \beta) \wedge (\beta \to \gamma)) \to \alpha \to \gamma \leq_{\forall 2,1} ((\mathsf{int} \to \mathsf{int}) \to \mathsf{int} \to \mathsf{int}) \wedge ((\mathsf{bool} \to \mathsf{bool}) \to \mathsf{bool} \to \mathsf{bool})$.

We can now present the typing rules. All these rules type recursive definitions $\mathsf{rec}\,\{x = e\}$ by assigning simple types to the occurrences of x in e (each occurrence may be assigned a different simple type). Therefore, they allow only simple (in the sense of Definition 1) *non-vacuous* recursive definitions to be typed (we say that a recursive definition $\mathsf{rec}\,\{x = e\}$ is *vacuous* to mean that $x \notin \text{FV}(e)$). Jim [12] proposed the following rules for typing recursive definitions:[2]

$$(\text{Rec})\ \frac{\vdash e : \langle A, x : w;\ v\rangle}{\vdash \mathsf{rec}\,\{x = e\} : \langle A;\ v\rangle} \quad \text{where } \text{Gen}((A, x : w),\ v) \leq_{\forall 2,1} w$$

$$(\text{RecVac})\ \frac{\vdash e : p}{\vdash \mathsf{rec}\,\{x = e\} : p} \quad \text{where } x \notin \text{FV}(e)$$

These two rules corresponds to the two cases $x \in \text{FV}(e)$ and $x \notin \text{FV}(e)$. Note that the rule for non-vacuous recursion, (Rec), requires that the rank-2 type v assigned to $\mathsf{rec}\,\{x = e\}$ must be such that $\text{Gen}((A, x : w),\ v) \leq_{\forall 2,1} w$. I.e., $\mathbf{s}(v) = u_i$ for some substitution $\mathbf{s}$ and simple type u_i such that $\mathbf{s}(A) = A$ and $w = u_1 \wedge \cdots \wedge u_i \wedge \cdots \wedge u_n$ $(1 \leq i \leq n)$. This implies $\vdash \mathsf{rec}\,\{x = e\} : \langle A;\ u_i\rangle$. Therefore, rule (Rec) allows only simple recursive definitions to be typed. System $\vdash_2$+(Rec) + (RecVac) has the principal pair property and is decidable (see, e.g., [12, 6]).

As pointed out by Jim [13], rule (Rec) might be generalized along the lines of Mycroft's rule (Fix$'$) [18]: just replace the condition $\text{Gen}((A, x : w),\ v) \leq_{\forall 2,1} w$ by the condition $\text{Gen}(A,\ v) \leq_{\forall 2,1} w$. Let us call (Rec$'$) the generalized rule. Rule (Rec$'$) is strictly more powerful than rule (Rec) (see Section 3 of [13] for an example) but, again, it allows only simple recursive definitions to be typed.

Jim [12] proposed also the following rule:[2]

$$(\text{RecInt})\ \frac{\vdash e : \langle A, x : u_1 \wedge \cdots \wedge u_m;\ u_1\rangle \quad \cdots \quad \vdash e : \langle A, x : u_1 \wedge \cdots \wedge u_m;\ u_m\rangle}{\vdash \mathsf{rec}\,\{x = e\} : \langle A;\ u_{i_0}\rangle} \quad \text{where } i_0 \in \{1, \ldots, m\}$$

The decidability of $\vdash_2$+(RecInt) is an open question (there is no obvious way to find an upper bound on the value of m used in the rule) [12]. Note that, since $u_1, \cdots, u_m \in \mathbf{T}_0$ (and, in particular, $u_{i_0} \in \mathbf{T}_0$), also this rule allows only simple recursive definitions to be typed.

---

[2] We still give these rules the original name used in [12], but we adapt them to fit in the type assignment system $\vdash_2$.

6 Typing Non-simple Recursive Definitions

In this section we extend system $\vdash_2$ to type non-simple recursive definitions.

6.1 System $\vdash_2^{\mathrm{P}}$

In order to be able to type non-simple recursive definitions, we propose to adopt the following strategy: allow one to assign to $\mathsf{rec}\,\{x = e\}$ any pair p that can be assigned to e by assuming the pair p itself for x.

To implement the above strategy, we introduce the notion of *pair environment* (taken from [6]).

Definition 8 (Pair Environments). A *pair environment* D is an environment $\{x_1 : p_1, \ldots, x_n : p_n\}$ of pair assumptions for variables such that $\mathrm{Dom}(D) \cap \mathrm{VR}(D) = \emptyset$, where $\mathrm{VR}(D) = \cup_{x:\langle A;\, v\rangle \in D}\mathrm{Dom}(A)$ is the *set of variables occurring in the range of* D. Every pair p occurring in D is implicitly universally quantified over all type variables occurring in p.[3]

The typing rules of system $\vdash_2^{\mathrm{P}}$ (where "P" stands for "polymorphic") are given in Fig. 3. The judgement $D \vdash_2^{\mathrm{P}} e : \langle A;\, v\rangle$ means "e is $\vdash_2^{\mathrm{P}}$-typable in D with pair $\langle A;\, v\rangle$", where

- D is a pair environment specifying pair assumptions for the variables introduced by a rec-binder in the program context surrounding e,
- $\langle A;\, v\rangle$ is the pair inferred for e, where A is a rank-1 environment containing the type assumptions for the free variables of e which are not in $\mathrm{Dom}(D)$, and v is a rank-2 type.

Let D be a pair environment, "$x \notin D$" is short for "$x \notin \mathrm{Dom}(D) \cup \mathrm{VR}(D)$" and $\mathrm{FV}_D(e) = (\mathrm{FV}(e) - \mathrm{Dom}(D)) \cup \mathrm{VR}(\{x : p \in D \mid x \in \mathrm{FV}(e)\})$ is the *set of the free variables of the expression* e *in* D. In any valid judgement $D \vdash_2^{\mathrm{P}} e : \langle A;\, v\rangle$ it holds that $\mathrm{Dom}(D) \cap \mathrm{Dom}(A) = \emptyset$ and $\mathrm{Dom}(A) = \mathrm{FV}_D(e)$.

Rules (Spc), (Con), (Var), (Abs), (AbsVac), and (App) are just the rules of system $\vdash_2$ (in Fig. 2) modified by adding the pair environment D on the left of the typing judgements and, when necessary, side conditions (like "$x \notin \mathrm{Dom}(D)$" in rule (Var)) to ensure that $\mathrm{Dom}(D) \cap \mathrm{Dom}(A) = \emptyset$.

Rule (RecP) allows to assign to a recursive definition $\mathsf{rec}\,\{x = e\}$ any pair p that can be assigned to e by assuming the pair p for x. Note that the combined use of rules (VarP) and (Spc) allows to assign a different specialization of p to each occurrence of x in e.

6.2 On the Expressive Power of System $\vdash_2^{\mathrm{P}}$

System $\vdash_2^{\mathrm{P}}$ is able to type non-simple recursive definitions, as illustrated by the following example (for more interesting examples see http://lambda.di.unito.it/pr).

[3] To emphasize this fact the paper [6] uses *pair schemes*. I.e., formulae of the shape $\forall\overrightarrow{\alpha}.p$, where $\overrightarrow{\alpha}$ is the sequence of *all* the type variables occurring in the pair p.

$$(\textsc{Spc})\ \frac{D \vdash e : p}{D \vdash e : p'} \text{ where } p \leq_{\mathbf{spc}} p' \qquad (\textsc{Con})\ D \vdash c : \langle \emptyset;\ v \rangle \text{ where } v = \mathbf{type}(c) \qquad (\textsc{Var})\ D \vdash x : \langle \{x : u\};\ u \rangle \text{ where } u \in \mathbf{T}_0 \text{ and } x \notin \mathrm{Dom}(D)$$

$$(\textsc{App})\ \frac{D \vdash e : \langle A;\ u_1 \wedge \cdots \wedge u_n \rightarrow v \rangle \qquad D \vdash e_0 : \langle A_1;\ u_1 \rangle \quad \cdots \quad D \vdash e_0 : \langle A_n;\ u_n \rangle}{D \vdash e\, e_0 : \langle A \wedge A_1 \wedge \cdots \wedge A_n;\ v \rangle}$$

$$(\textsc{Abs})\ \frac{D \vdash e : \langle A, x : w;\ v \rangle}{D \vdash \lambda x.e : \langle A;\ w \rightarrow v \rangle} \text{ where } x \notin D \qquad (\textsc{AbsVac})\ \frac{D \vdash e : \langle A;\ v \rangle}{D \vdash \lambda x.e : \langle A;\ u \rightarrow v \rangle} \text{ where } x \notin \mathrm{FV}(e),\ u \in \mathbf{T}_0, \text{ and } x \notin D$$

$$(\textsc{VarP})\ D, x : p \vdash x : p \qquad (\textsc{RecP})\ \frac{D, x : \langle A;\ v \rangle \vdash e : \langle A;\ v \rangle}{D \vdash \mathsf{rec}\,\{x = e\} : \langle A;\ v \rangle} \text{ where } \mathrm{Dom}(A) = \mathrm{FV}_D(\mathsf{rec}\,\{x = e\}) \text{ and } x \notin D$$

Fig. 3. Typing rules of system $\vdash_2^{\mathrm{P}}$

Example 9. The recursive definition $\mathsf{rec}\,\{f = e\}$, where

$$e \;=\; \lambda g\, l.\, \mathsf{if}\ (\mathsf{null}\ l)\ \mathsf{then}\ \mathsf{nil}\ \mathsf{else}\ \mathsf{cons}\ (\mathsf{pair}\ (g\ (\mathsf{hd}\ l)\ 5)\ (g\ y\ \mathsf{true}))\ (f\ g\ (\mathsf{tl}\ l)),$$

is non-simple since it defines a function that uses its parameter g with two different non unifiable types. The following $\vdash_2^{\mathrm{P}}$-typing judgement holds.

$$\emptyset \vdash \mathsf{rec}\,\{f = e\} : \langle \{y : \alpha_2\};\ ((\alpha_1 \rightarrow \mathsf{int} \rightarrow \beta_1) \wedge (\alpha_2 \rightarrow \mathsf{bool} \rightarrow \beta_2)) \rightarrow \alpha_1\ \mathsf{list} \rightarrow (\beta_1 \times \beta_2)\ \mathsf{list} \rangle.$$

System $\vdash_2^{\mathrm{P}}$ has more expressive power than the system $\vdash_2$+(Rec)+(RecVac) of Section 5 (and therefore of system $\mathbf{P}_2^{\mathrm{R}}$ [13, 12]) and of the Milner-Mycroft system [18] (see also [17]), in the sense that the set of typable terms increases, and types express better the behaviour of terms. In particular, the following theorems hold.

Theorem 10. *If* $\vdash_2$+(Rec)+(RecVac) $e : \langle A;\ v \rangle$, *then* $\emptyset \vdash_2^{\mathrm{P}} e : \langle A;\ v \rangle$.

Theorem 11. *If* $\emptyset \vdash e : u$ *is Milner-Mycroft derivable, then* $\emptyset \vdash_2^{\mathrm{P}} e : \langle \emptyset;\ u \rangle$.

6.3 Principal-in-D Pairs and (Un)decidability of $\vdash_2^{\mathrm{P}}$

The following notion of *principal-in-D pair* (taken from [6]) adapts the notion of principal pair (see Definition 5) to deal with the pair environment D.

Definition 12 (Principal-in-D Pairs). Let $\vdash$ be a system with judgements of the shape $D \vdash e : p$. A pair p is *principal-in-D for a term e* if $D \vdash e : p$, and if $D \vdash e : p'$ implies $p \leq_{\mathbf{spc}} p'$. We say that system $\vdash$ has the *principal-in-D pair property* to mean that every typable term has a principal-in-D pair.

We don't know whether system $\vdash_2^{\mathrm{P}}$ has the principal-in-D pair property. The following theorem implies that the restriction of $\vdash_2^{\mathrm{P}}$ which uses only simple types, that we will call $\vdash_0^{\mathrm{P}}$, is undecidable (as is the Milner-Mycroft system [10, 15]). We conjecture that also the whole $\vdash_2^{\mathrm{P}}$ is undecidable.

Theorem 13. *Let e be a* let*-free expression. Then $\emptyset \vdash_0^{\mathrm{P}} e : \langle \emptyset;\, u\rangle$ iff $\emptyset \vdash e : u$ is Milner-Mycroft derivable.*

6.4 Systems $\vdash_2^{\mathrm{P}_k+\text{-}}$ ($k \geq 1$): A Family of Decidable Restrictions of $\vdash_2^{\mathrm{P}}$

By taking inspiration from the idea of iterating type inference (see, e.g., [18, 17]) and by relying on the notion of principal-in-D pair (see Definition 12) we will now design a family of decidable restrictions of rule (RECP).

For every finite set of variables $X = \{x_1, \ldots, x_n\}$ ($n \geq 0$) let

- $\mathsf{P}_X = \{\langle A;\, v\rangle \mid \langle A;\, v\rangle$ is pair such that $\mathrm{Dom}(A) = X\}$, and
- $\mathsf{bot}_X = \langle\{x_1 : \alpha_1, \ldots, x_n : \alpha_n\};\, \alpha\rangle$, where the type variables $\alpha_1, \ldots, \alpha_n, \alpha$ are all distinct.

The relation $\leq_{\mathbf{spc}}$ is a preorder over P_X and, for all pairs $p \in \mathsf{P}_X$, $\mathsf{bot}_X \leq_{\mathbf{spc}} p$.

For every $k \geq 1$, let $\vdash_2^{\mathrm{P}_k}$ be the system obtained from $\vdash_2^{\mathrm{P}}$ by replacing rule (RECP) with the following rule:

$$(\mathrm{RECP}_k)\ \frac{D, x : p_0 \vdash e : p_1 \quad \cdots \quad D, x : p_{k-1} \vdash e : p_k}{D \vdash \mathsf{rec}\,\{x = e\} : p_k}$$

where $x \notin D$, $p_0 = \mathsf{bot}_{\mathrm{FV}(\mathsf{rec}\,\{x=e\})}$, $p_{k-1} = p_k$, and for all $i \in \{1, \ldots, k\}$ p_i is a principal-in-$(D, x : p_{i-1})$ pair for e

(note that $D \vdash_2^{\mathrm{P}_k} e : p$ implies $D \vdash_2^{\mathrm{P}_{k+1}} e : p$). For all $k \geq 1$, system $\vdash_2^{\mathrm{P}_k}$ has the principal-in-D pair property and is decidable — the result follows from Theorem 20 (soundness and completeness of the inference algorithm for $\vdash_2^{\mathrm{P}_k+\mathrm{J}}$, which is an extension of $\vdash_2^{\mathrm{P}_k}$) of Section 6.5. The relation between system $\vdash_2^{\mathrm{P}_k}$ and system $\vdash_2^{\mathrm{P}}$ is stated by the following theorem which, roughly speaking, says that when rule (RECP$_k$) works at all, it works as well as rule (RECP) does.

Theorem 14. *For every $k \geq 1$:*

1. *If $D \vdash_2^{\mathrm{P}_k} e : p$, then $D \vdash_2^{\mathrm{P}} e : p$.*
2. *If e is $\vdash_2^{\mathrm{P}_k}$-typable in D and $D \vdash_2^{\mathrm{P}} e : p$, then $D \vdash_2^{\mathrm{P}_k} e : p$.*

Unfortunately, for every $k \geq 1$, system $\vdash_2^{\mathrm{P}_k}$ is not able to type all the ML-typable recursive definitions (see Example 15 below).

Example 15 (Rule (RECP$_k$) *and the ML rule are incomparable).* The expression $\mathsf{rec}\,\{f = e\}$ of Example 9 in Section 6.2 is non-simple, therefore it is not ML-typable. Since

$$p = \langle\{y : \alpha_2\};\, ((\alpha_1 \to \mathsf{int} \to \beta_1) \wedge (\alpha_2 \to \mathsf{bool} \to \beta_2)) \to \alpha_1\,\mathsf{list} \to (\beta_1 \times \beta_2)\,\mathsf{list}\rangle,$$

is both a principal-in-$\{f : \langle\{y : \alpha_1\};\, \alpha\rangle\}$ and a principal-in-$\{f : p\}$ pair for e in system $\vdash_2^{\mathrm{P}_1}$, we have that p is a principal-in-$\emptyset$ pair for $\mathsf{rec}\,\{f = e\}$ in system $\vdash_2^{\mathrm{P}_k}$ (for all $k \geq 1$).

The expression $\mathsf{rec}\,\{f = e'\}$, where $e' = \lambda g\, y.\, \mathsf{if\ true\ then}\ y\ \mathsf{else}\ g(f\, g\, y)$, is ML-typable with principal pair $\langle\emptyset;\, (\alpha \to \alpha) \to \alpha \to \alpha\rangle$ and is not $\vdash_2^{\mathrm{P}_k}$-typable (for all $k \geq 1$) — in fact, for every $k \geq 1$, the expression e' has principal-in-$\{f : p_{k-1}\}$ pair

$$p_k = \langle \emptyset; ((\alpha_0 \to \alpha_1) \wedge (\alpha_1 \to \alpha_2) \wedge \cdots \wedge (\alpha_{k-1} \to \alpha_k)) \to (\alpha_1 \wedge \alpha_2 \wedge \cdots \wedge \alpha_k) \to \alpha_k \rangle$$

in system $\vdash_2^{\mathrm{P}}$.

Note that $\mathsf{rec}\,\{f = e'\}$ is $\vdash_2^{\mathrm{P}}$-typable with pair $\langle \emptyset; ((\alpha \to \gamma) \wedge (\gamma \to \alpha) \wedge (\alpha \to \beta)) \to (\alpha \wedge \beta \wedge \gamma) \to \beta \rangle$.

We will now show that, for all $k \geq 1$, it is quite easy to modify system $\vdash_2^{\mathrm{P}_k}$ in order to make it to extend the ML system while preserving decidability and principal-in-D pair property. To this aim, we will say that *a typing rule for recursive definitions* (REC_) *is* $\vdash_2^{\mathrm{P}}$*-suitable* to mean that: the system $\vdash_{\bar{2}}$ obtained from $\vdash_2^{\mathrm{P}}$ by replacing rule (RECP) with rule (REC_)

- is a restriction of system $\vdash_2^{\mathrm{P}}$ (i.e., $D \vdash_{\bar{2}} e : \langle A; v \rangle$ implies $D \vdash_2^{\mathrm{P}} e : \langle A; v \rangle$),
- is decidable, and
- has the principal-in-D pair property.

For instance, for every $k \geq 1$, rule (RECP$_k$) is $\vdash_2^{\mathrm{P}}$-suitable. Theorem 14 guarantees that, for all $k \geq 1$, adding to system $\vdash_2^{\mathrm{P}_k}$ a $\vdash_2^{\mathrm{P}}$-suitable rule (REC_) results in a system, denoted by $\vdash_2^{\mathrm{P}_k+-}$, with both decidability and principal-in-D pair property. So, to extend system $\vdash_2^{\mathrm{P}_k}$ to type all the ML typable recursive definitions, we have just to add to system $\vdash_2^{\mathrm{P}_k}$ a $\vdash_2^{\mathrm{P}}$-suitable rule which is at least as expressive as the ML rule for recursive definitions. The simplest way of doing this would be to add (a version, modified to fit into system $\vdash_2^{\mathrm{P}_k}$, of) the ML rule itself:

$$(\mathrm{RECML})\ \frac{D \vdash e : \langle A, x : u;\, u \rangle}{D \vdash \mathsf{rec}\,\{x = e\} : \langle A;\, u \rangle}\ \text{where } x \notin D$$

(producing system $\vdash_2^{\mathrm{P}_k+\mathrm{ML}}$). Another possibility, is to add the following rule

$$(\mathrm{RECJ})\ \frac{D \vdash e : \langle A, x : w;\, v \rangle}{D \vdash \mathsf{rec}\,\{x = e\} : \langle A;\, v \rangle}\ \text{where } \mathrm{Gen}((A, x : w), v) \leq_{\forall 2,1} w \text{ and } x \notin D$$

which corresponds to rule (REC) of Section 5. In this way we obtain a system, $\vdash_2^{\mathrm{P}_k+\mathrm{J}}$, which is more expressive that system $\vdash_2$+(REC)+(RECVAC) of Section 5 (observe that $\vdash_2$+(RECVAC)-typabily implies $\vdash_2^{\mathrm{P}_k}$-typability).

Example 16. The expression $\mathsf{rec}\,\{f = e'\}$ of Example 15, which is not $\vdash_2^{\mathrm{P}_k}$-typable (for all $k \geq 1$), has principal-in-$\emptyset$ pairs $\langle \emptyset; (\alpha \to \alpha) \to \alpha \to \alpha \rangle$ and $\langle \emptyset; ((\alpha \to \alpha) \wedge (\alpha \to \beta)) \to (\alpha \wedge \beta) \to \beta \rangle$ in systems $\vdash_2^{\mathrm{P}_1+\mathrm{ML}}$ and $\vdash_2^{\mathrm{P}_1+\mathrm{J}}$, respectively.

6.5 An Inference Algorithm for $\vdash_2^{\mathrm{P}_k+\mathrm{J}}$ ($k \geq 1$)

The inference algorithm makes use of an algorithm for checking whether the $\leq_{\mathbf{spc}}$ relation (see Definition 3) holds and of an algorithm for finding a most general solution to a $\leq_{\forall 2,1}$*-satisfaction problem* ($\leq_{\forall 2,1}$ is the relation of Definition 6).

Existence of an algorithm for checking whether the $\leq_{\mathbf{spc}}$ relation holds is stated by the following theorem.

Theorem 17 (Decidability of $\leq_{\mathbf{spc}}$). *There is an algorithm that, for every p and p', decides whether $p \leq_{\mathbf{spc}} p'$ holds.*

A $\leq_{\forall 2,1}$-*satisfaction problem* [13, 12] (see also [6]) is a formula $\exists \overrightarrow{\alpha}.P$, where $\overrightarrow{\alpha}$ is a (possibly empty) sequence of type variables occurring free in P, and P is a set in which every element is either: 1) an equality between $\mathbf{T}_0$ types; or 2) an inequality between a $\mathbf{T}_{\forall 2} \cup \mathbf{T}_2$ type and a $\mathbf{T}_1$ type. A substitution $\mathbf{s}$ is a *solution* to $\exists \overrightarrow{\alpha}.P$ if there exists a substitution $\mathbf{s}'$ such that: $\mathbf{s}(\alpha) = \mathbf{s}'(\alpha)$ for all $\alpha \notin \overrightarrow{\alpha}$, $\mathbf{s}'(u_1) = \mathbf{s}'(u_2)$ for every equality $(u_1 = u_2) \in P$, and $\mathbf{s}'(vs) \leq_{\forall 2,1} \mathbf{s}'(w)$ (resp. $\mathbf{s}'(\forall \epsilon.v) \leq_{\forall 2,1} \mathbf{s}'(w)$) for every inequality $(vs \leq w) \in P$ (resp. $(v \leq w) \in P$). We will write $\mathbf{MGS}(\exists \overrightarrow{\alpha}.P)$ for the set of most general solutions to the $\leq_{\forall 2,1}$-satisfaction problem $\exists \overrightarrow{\alpha}.P$ (a $\leq_{\forall 2,1}$-satisfaction problem $\exists \overrightarrow{\alpha}.P$ generalizes unification and, as with unification, most general solutions are not unique). Existence of an algorithm for finding a most general solution to a $\leq_{\forall 2,1}$-satisfaction problem is stated by the following theorem [13, 12] (see also [6]).

Theorem 18. *There is an algorithm that decides, for any $\leq_{\forall 2,1}$-satisfaction problem, whether it is solvable, and, if so, returns a most general solution.*

The inference algorithm is presented in a style favored by the intersection type community. For all $k \geq 1$, we define a function $\mathbf{PP}_k$ which, for every expression e and environment D, returns a set of pairs $\mathbf{PP}_k(D, e)$ such that

- if $\mathbf{PP}_k(D, e) = \emptyset$, then e can not be typed by $\vdash_2^{\mathrm{P}_k + \mathrm{J}}$ w.r.t. D, and
- every element of $\mathbf{PP}_k(D, e)$ is a principal pair for e w.r.t. D.[4]

Definition 19 (The Function $\mathbf{PP}_k$). For every expression e and environment D, the set $\mathbf{PP}_k(D, e)$ is defined by structural induction on e.

- If $e = x$, then
  - If $x : \langle A; v \rangle \in D$ and the substitution $\mathbf{s}$ is a fresh renaming of $\overrightarrow{\alpha} = \mathrm{FTV}(A) \cup \mathrm{FTV}(v)$, then $\langle \mathbf{s}(A); \mathbf{s}(v) \rangle \in \mathbf{PP}_k(D, x)$.
  - If $x \notin \mathrm{Dom}(D)$ and α is a type variable, then $\langle \{x : \alpha\}; \alpha \rangle \in \mathbf{PP}_k(D, x)$.
- If $e = c$ and $\mathbf{type}(c) = v$, then $\langle \emptyset; v \rangle \in \mathbf{PP}_k(D, c)$.
- If $e = \lambda x.e_0$ and $\langle A; v \rangle \in \mathbf{PP}_k(D, e_0)$, then
  - If $x \notin \mathrm{FV}(e_0)$ and α is a fresh type variable, then $\langle A; \alpha \rightarrow v \rangle \in \mathbf{PP}_k(D, \lambda x.e_0)$.
  - If $x \in \mathrm{FV}(e_0)$ and $A = A', x : w$, then $\langle A'; w \rightarrow v \rangle \in \mathbf{PP}_k(D, \lambda x.e_0)$.
- If $e = e_0\, e_1$ and $\langle A_0; v_0 \rangle \in \mathbf{PP}_k(D, e_0)$, then
  - If $v_0 = \alpha$ (a type variable), α_1 and α_2 are fresh type variables, $\langle A_1; v_1 \rangle \in \mathbf{PP}_k(D, e_1)$ is fresh, and $\mathbf{s} \in \mathbf{MGS}(\exists \epsilon.\{v_1 \leq \alpha_1, \alpha = \alpha_1 \rightarrow \alpha_2\}$, then $\langle \mathbf{s}(A_0 \wedge A_1); \mathbf{s}(\alpha_2) \rangle \in \mathbf{PP}_k(D, e_0\, e_1)$.
  - If $v_0 = u_1 \wedge \cdots \wedge u_n \rightarrow v$, for all $i \in \{1, \ldots, n\}$ the pairs $\langle A_i; v_i \rangle \in \mathbf{PP}_k(D, e_1)$ are fresh, and $\mathbf{s} \in \mathbf{MGS}(\exists \epsilon.\{v_i \leq u_i \mid i \in \{1, \ldots, n\}\})$, then $\langle \mathbf{s}(A_0 \wedge A_1 \wedge \cdots \wedge A_n); \mathbf{s}(v) \rangle \in \mathbf{PP}_k(D, e_0\, e_1)$.

---

[4] The set $\mathbf{PP}_k(D, e)$ does not contain all the principal pairs for e w.r.t. D. For instance, for all $k \geq 1$, $\langle \emptyset; (\alpha_1 \wedge \alpha_2) \rightarrow \alpha_1 \rangle$ is a principal-in-$\emptyset$ pair for $\lambda x.x$ in $\vdash_2^{\mathrm{P}_k + \mathrm{J}}$, but $\langle \emptyset; (\alpha_1 \wedge \alpha_2) \rightarrow \alpha_1 \rangle \notin \mathbf{PP}_k(\emptyset, \lambda x.x)$.

– If $e = \mathsf{rec}\,\{x = e_0\}$ and $\langle A;\, v\rangle \in \mathbf{PP}_k(D, e_0)$, then
  - If $x \notin \mathrm{FV}(e_0)$, then $\langle A;\, v\rangle \in \mathbf{PP}_k(D, e)$.
  - If $x \in \mathrm{FV}(e_0)$, then
    * If h is the minimum number in $\{1, \ldots, k\}$ such that $p_0 = \mathsf{bot}_{\mathrm{FV}(e)}$, $p_1 \in \mathbf{PP}_k((D, x : p_0), e_0)$, ..., $p_h \in \mathbf{PP}_k((D, x : p_{h-1}), e_0)$, and $p_h \leq_{\mathbf{spc}} p_{h-1}$, then $p_{h-1} \in \mathbf{PP}_k(D, e)$.
    * Otherwise (if such an h does not exist), if $A = A', x : w$ and $\mathbf{s} \in \mathbf{MGS}(\exists\epsilon.\{\mathrm{Gen}(A', v) \leq w\})$, then $\langle \mathbf{s}(A');\, \mathbf{s}(v)\rangle \in \mathbf{PP}_k(D, e)$.

For every $k \geq 1$, expression e, and environment D, the set $\mathbf{PP}_k(D, e)$ is an equivalence class of pairs modulo renaming of the type variables in a pair. Indeed Definition 19 specifies an inference algorithm: to perform type inference on an expression e w.r.t. the environment D simply follow the definition of $\mathbf{PP}_k(D, e)$, choosing fresh type variables and using the $\leq_2$-satisfaction and $\leq_{\mathbf{spc}}$-checking algorithms as necessary.

Theorem 20 (Soundness and completeness of $\mathbf{PP}_k$ for $\vdash_2^{\mathrm{P}_k+\mathrm{J}}$). *For every $k \geq 1$, expression e, and environment D:*
(Soundness). *If $p \in \mathbf{PP}_k(D, e)$, then $D \vdash_2^{\mathrm{P}_k+\mathrm{J}} e : p$.*
(Completeness). *If $D \vdash_2^{\mathrm{P}_k+\mathrm{J}} e : p'$, then $p \leq_{\mathbf{spc}} p'$ for some $p \in \mathbf{PP}_k(D, e)$.*

7 Typing Non-simple Mutually Recursive Definitions

The results presented in Section 6 can be straightforwardly adapted to mutually recursive definitions. Let $\mathsf{rec}_i\,\{x_1 = e_1, \ldots, x_n = e_n\}$ (where $1 \leq i \leq n$) denote the i-th expression defined by the mutually recursive definition $\{x_1 = e_1, \ldots, x_n = e_n\}$.

Let $\vdash_2^{\mathrm{P2}}$ be the extension of system $\vdash_2^{\mathrm{P}}$ to mutual recursion, obtained by replacing rule (RecP) by the following rule:

$$\text{(RecP2)}\ \frac{\begin{array}{c} D, x_1 : \langle A_1;\, v_1\rangle, \ldots, x_n : \langle A_n;\, v_n\rangle \vdash e_1 : \langle A_1;\, v_1\rangle \\ \cdots \\ D, x_1 : \langle A_1;\, v_1\rangle, \ldots, x_n : \langle A_n;\, v_n\rangle \vdash e_n : \langle A_n;\, v_n\rangle \end{array}}{D \vdash \mathsf{rec}_{i_0}\,\{x_1 = e_1, \ldots, x_n = e_n\} : \langle A_1 \wedge \cdots \wedge A_n;\, v_{i_0}\rangle}$$

where
$i_0 \in \{1, \ldots, n\}$, $x_1, \ldots, x_n \notin D$, and (for all $i \in \{1, \ldots, n\}$)
$$\mathrm{Dom}(A_i) = \mathrm{FV}_D(e_i \underbrace{[x_1 := e_1, \ldots, x_n := e_n] \cdots [x_1 := e_1, \ldots, x_n := e_n]}_{n-1 \text{ times}}) - \{x_1, \ldots, x_n\}$$

The design of decidable systems $\vdash_2^{\mathrm{P2}_k}$, $\vdash_2^{\mathrm{P2}_k+\mathrm{ML}}$, and $\vdash_2^{\mathrm{P2}_k+\mathrm{J}}$, corresponding to the decidable systems $\vdash_2^{\mathrm{P}_k}$, $\vdash_2^{\mathrm{P}_k+\mathrm{ML}}$, and $\vdash_2^{\mathrm{P}_k+\mathrm{J}}$, is straightforward.

8 Conclusion

In this paper we have taken the system of rank-2 intersection type for the λ-calculus and have extended it with a decidable rule for typing non-simple recursive definitions. The new rules can be integrated without problems with the rules for typing non-simple local definitions and conditional expressions that we have proposed in previous work [6].

The technique developed in this paper does not depend on particulars of rank-2 intersection and could therefore be applied to other type systems. To clarify this point, we consider the following definition (taken from [22]):

> A *typing* t for a typable term e is the collection of all the information other than e which appears in the final judgement of a proof derivation showing that e is typable (for instance, in system $\vdash_2$ a typing is a pair $\langle A; v\rangle$).

We can now describe our technique as follows:

1. Take a type system for the λ-calculus, with judgements of the shape $\vdash e : t$ where t mentions exactly the variables in $\mathrm{FV}(e)$ (this requirement is not restrictive, since it is always possible to adjust the judgment and the rules of a type system in order to satisfy it), such that: system $\vdash$ has the principal typing property (which is the property described by Definition 5 by replacing *pair* with *typing* and $\leq_{\mathbf{spc}}$ with a suitable relation for $\vdash$, that we will call $\leq^{\vdash}_{\mathbf{spc}}$); it is decidable to establish whether a typing t_1 can be specialized to a typing t_2 (i.e, whether $t_1 \leq^{\vdash}_{\mathbf{spc}} t_2$ holds); there is a known algorithm that for every term e decides whether e is $\vdash$-typable and, if so, returns a principal typing for e. We also require that system $\vdash$ contains the analogous of rule (SPC) (this additional requirement is not restrictive since, whenever the previous requirements are satisfied, such a rule is admissible).
2. Modify system $\vdash$ by introducing a *typing environment* D (containing typing assumptions for the rec-bound identifiers) and by adding typing rules analogous to (VARP) and (RECP). Let $\vdash^{\mathrm{P}}$ be the resulting system (which has judgements of the shape $D \vdash^{\mathrm{P}} e : t$).
3. Prove that, for every set of variables $X = \{x_1, \ldots, x_n\}$ ($n \geq 0$) the relation $\leq^{\vdash}_{\mathbf{spc}}$ is a preorder over $\mathsf{P}_X = \{t \mid$ the typing t mentions exactly the variables in $X\}$ and there is a known typing $\mathsf{bot}_X \in \mathsf{P}_X$ such that, for all typings $t \in \mathsf{P}_X$, $\mathsf{bot}_X \leq^{\vdash}_{\mathbf{spc}} t$. For every $k \geq 1$, define the analogous of rule (RECP$_k$) and prove the analogous of Theorem 14. Let $\vdash^{\mathrm{P}_k}$ denote the system obtained from $\vdash^{\mathrm{P}}$ by replacing the analogous of rule (RECP) with the analogous of rule (RECP$_k$). System $\vdash^{\mathrm{P}_k}$ is guaranteed to have the principal-in-D typing property (which is the property described by Definition 12 by replacing *pair* with *typing* and $\leq_{\mathbf{spc}}$ with $\leq^{\vdash}_{\mathbf{spc}}$).
4. If necessary, add to $\vdash^{\mathrm{P}_k}$ a $\vdash^{\mathrm{P}}$*-suitable* (the analogous for $\vdash^{\mathrm{P}}$ of the notion of $\vdash^{\mathrm{P}}_2$*-suitable* given in Section 6.4) rule (REC_). Let $\vdash^{\mathrm{P}_k+-}$ denote the resulting system.

The above steps describe a procedure that transforms a type system $\vdash$ (without rules for rec-expressions) enjoying the principal typing property into a system $\vdash^{\mathrm{P}_k+-}$ (with rules for rec-expressions) enjoying the *principal-in-D* (and, in general, not the *principal*) typing property.

It worth examining what happens when the procedure is applied to the system of simple types [11]: the system at step 1 turns out to be $\vdash_0$ (the restriction of

$\vdash_2$ which uses only simple types), the one obtained at step 2 is $\vdash_0^{\mathrm{P}}$, which is essentially a reformulation of the Milner-Mycroft system (see Theorem 13), and the systems obtained at step 4 by adding the ML typing rule for recursion, $\vdash_0^{\mathrm{P}_k+\mathrm{ML}}$, are of intermediate power between the let-free fragments of the ML system and of the Milner-Mycroft system — we believe that the systems $\vdash_0^{\mathrm{P}_k+\mathrm{ML}}$ correspond to the family of abstract interpreters described in [8].

Further work includes, on the one side, designing more expressive decidable extensions of systems $\vdash_2^{\mathrm{P}_k+\mathrm{J}}$ (we are investigating the possibility of integrating techniques from the theory of abstract interpretation [4]). On the other, verifying the applicability of the technique to other type systems, like the system with rank-2 universal and intersection types proposed in [21], System **P** [14], and System E [2].

Acknowledgments. I thank Viviana Bono, Sebastien Carlier, Mario Coppo, Joe Hallet, Assaf Kfoury, Emiliano Leporati, Peter Møller Neergaard, and Joe Wells for discussions on the subject of this paper. I also thank the TLCA'05 referees and the anonymous referees of earlier versions of this paper for many insightful and constructive comments.

References

1. H. P. Barendregt, M. Coppo, and M. Dezani-Ciancaglini. A filter lambda model and the completeness of type assignment. *J. of Symbolic Logic*, 48:931–940, 1983.
2. S. Carlier, J. Polakow, J. B. Wells, and A. J. Kfoury. System E: Expansion variables for flexible typing with linear and non-linear types and intersection types. In *ESOP'04*, volume 2986 of *LNCS*, pages 294–309. Springer, 2004.
3. M. Coppo and M. Dezani-Ciancaglini. An extension of basic functional theory for lambda-calculus. *Notre Dame Journal of Formal Logic*, 21(4):685–693, 1980.
4. P. Cousot. Types as Abstract Interpretations. In *POPL'97*, pages 316–331. ACM, 1997.
5. L. M. M. Damas and R. Milner. Principal type schemas for functional programs. In *POPL'82*, pages 207–212. ACM, 1982.
6. F. Damiani. Rank 2 intersection types for local definitions and conditional expressions. *ACM Trans. Prog. Lang. Syst.*, 25(4):401–451, 2003.
7. J. Y. Girard. *Interpretation fonctionelle et elimination des coupures dans l'aritmetique d'ordre superieur.* PhD thesis, Université Paris VII, 1972.
8. R. Gori and G. Levi. Properties of a type abstract interpreter. In *VMCAI'03*, volume 2575 of *LNCS*, pages 132–145. Springer, 2003.
9. J. J. Hallett and A. J. Kfoury. Programming examples needing polymorphic recursion. In *ITRS'04 (workshop affiliated to LICS'04)*, ENTCS. Elsevier, to appear.
10. F. Henglein. Type inference with polymorphic recursion. *ACM Trans. Prog. Lang. Syst.*, 15(2):253–289, 1993.
11. R. Hindley. *Basic Simple Type Theory.* Number 42 in Cambridge Tracts in Theoretical Computer Science. Cambridge University Press, London, 1997.
12. T. Jim. Rank 2 type systems and recursive definitions. Technical Report MIT/LCS/TM-531, LCS, Massachusetts Institute of Technology, 1995.
13. T. Jim. What are principal typings and what are they good for? In *POPL'96*, pages 42–53. ACM, 1996.

14. T. Jim. A polar type system. In *ICALP Workshops*, volume 8 of *Proceedings in Informatics*, pages 323–338. Carleton-Scientific, 2000.
15. A. J. Kfoury, J. Tiuryn, and P. Urzyczyn. Type reconstruction in the presence of polymorphic recursion. *ACM Trans. Prog. Lang. Syst.*, 15(2):290–311, 1993.
16. D. Leivant. Polymorphic Type Inference. In *POPL'83*, pages 88–98. ACM, 1983.
17. L. Meertens. Incremental polymorphic type checking in B. In *POPL'83*, pages 265–275. ACM, 1983.
18. A. Mycroft. Polymorphic Type Schemes and Recursive Definitions. In *International Symposium on Programming*, volume 167 of *LNCS*, pages 217–228. Springer, 1984.
19. J. C. Reynolds. Towards a Theory of Type Structure. In *Colloque sur la Programmation*, volume 19 of *LNCS*. Springer, 1974.
20. S. van Bakel. *Intersection Type Disciplines in Lambda Calculus and Applicative Term Rewriting Systems.* PhD thesis, Katholieke Universiteit Nijmegen, 1993.
21. S. van Bakel. Rank 2 types for term graph rewriting. In *TIP'02*, volume 75 of *ENTCS*. Elsevier, 2003.
22. J.B. Wells. The essence of principal typings. In *ICALP'02*, volume 2380 of *LNCS*, pages 913–925. Springer, 2002.
23. H. Yokouchi. Embedding a Second-Order Type System into an Intersection Type System. *Information and Computation*, 117:206–220, 1995.

Arithmetical Proofs of Strong Normalization Results for the Symmetric $\lambda\mu$-Calculus

René David and Karim Nour

Laboratoire de Mathématiques,
Université de Savoie,
73376 Le Bourget du Lac, France
{david, nour}@univ-savoie.fr

Abstract. The symmetric $\lambda\mu$-calculus is the $\lambda\mu$-calculus introduced by Parigot in which the reduction rule μ', which is the symmetric of μ, is added. We give *arithmetical* proofs of some strong normalization results for this calculus. We show (this is a new result) that the $\mu\mu'$-reduction is strongly normalizing for the un-typed calculus. We also show the strong normalization of the $\beta\mu\mu'$-reduction for the typed calculus: this was already known but the previous proofs use candidates of reducibility where the interpretation of a type was defined as the fix point of some increasing operator and thus, were highly non arithmetical.

1 Introduction

Since it has been understood that the Curry-Howard isomorphism relating proofs and programs can be extended to classical logic, various systems have been introduced: the λ_c-calculus (Krivine [12]), the λ_{exn}-calculus (de Groote [6]), the $\lambda\mu$-calculus (Parigot [18]), the λ^{Sym}-calculus (Barbanera & Berardi [1]), the λ_Δ-calculus (Rehof & Sørensen [24]), the $\overline{\lambda}\mu\tilde{\mu}$-calculus (Curien & Herbelin [3]), ...

The first calculus which respects the intrinsic symmetry of classical logic is λ^{Sym}. It is somehow different from the previous calculi since the main connector is not the arrow as usual but the connectors *or* and *and*. The symmetry of the calculus comes from the de Morgan laws.

The second calculus respecting this symmetry has been $\overline{\lambda}\mu\tilde{\mu}$. The logical part is the (classical) sequent calculus instead of natural deduction.

Natural deduction is not, intrinsically, symmetric but Parigot has introduced the so called *Free deduction* [17] which is completely symmetric. The $\lambda\mu$-calculus comes from there. To get a confluent calculus he had, in his terminology, to fix the inputs on the left. To keep the symmetry, it is enough to keep the same terms and to add a new reduction rule (called the μ'-reduction) which is the symmetric rule of the μ-reduction and also corresponds to the elimination of a cut. We get then a symmetric calculus that is called the *symmetric $\lambda\mu$-calculus*.

The μ'-reduction has been considered by Parigot for the following reasons. The $\lambda\mu$-calculus (with the β-reduction and the μ-reduction) has good properties : confluence in the un-typed version, subject reduction and strong normalization

P. Urzyczyn (Ed.): TLCA 2005, LNCS 3461, pp. 162–178, 2005.

in the typed calculus. But this system has, from a computer science point of view, a drawback: the unicity of the representation of data is lost. It is known that, in the λ-calculus, any term of type N (the usual type for the integers) is β-equivalent to a Church integer. This no more true in the $\lambda\mu$-calculus and we can find normal terms of type N that are not Church integers. Parigot has remarked that by adding the μ'-reduction and some simplification rules the unicity of the representation of data is recovered and subject reduction is preserved, at least for the simply typed system, even though the confluence is lost.

Barbanera & Berardi proved the strong normalization of the λ^{Sym}-calculus by using candidates of reducibility but, unlike the usual construction (for example for Girard's system F), the definition of the interpretation of a type needs a rather complex fix-point operation. Yamagata [25] has used the same technic to prove the strong normalization of the symmetric $\lambda\mu$-calculus where the types are those of system F and Parigot, again using the same ideas, has extended Barbanera & Berardi's result to a logic with second order quantification. These proofs are thus highly non arithmetical.

We consider here the $\lambda\mu$-calculus with the rules β, μ and μ'. It was known that, for the un-typed calculus, the μ-reduction is strongly normalizing (see [23]) but the strong normalization of the $\mu\mu'$-reduction for the un-typed calculus was an open problem raised long ago by Parigot. We give here a proof of this result. Studying this reduction by itself is interesting since a μ (or μ')-reduction can be seen as a way "to put the arguments of the μ where they are used" and it is useful to know that this is terminating. We also give an *arithmetical* proof of the strong normalization of the $\beta\mu\mu'$-reduction for the simply typed calculus. We finally show (this is also a new result) that, in the un-typed calculus, if $M_1, ..., M_n$ are strongly normalizing for the $\beta\mu\mu'$-reduction, then so is $(x\ M_1\ ...\ M_n)$.

The proofs of strong normalization that are given here are extensions of the ones given by the first author for the simply typed λ-calculus. This proof can be found either in [7] (where it appears among many other things) or as a simple unpublished note on the web page of the first author (`www.lama.univ-savoie.fr/david`).

The same proofs can be done for the $\overline{\lambda}\mu\tilde{\mu}$-calculus and these proofs are, in fact, much simpler for this calculus since some difficult problems that appear in the $\lambda\mu$-calculus do not appear in the $\overline{\lambda}\mu\tilde{\mu}$-calculus: this is mainly due to the fact that, in the latter, there is a right-hand side and a left-hand side (the terms and the environments) whereas, in the $\lambda\mu$-calculus, this distinction is impossible since a term on the right of an application can go on the left of an application after some reductions. The proof of the strong normalization of the $\mu\tilde{\mu}$-reduction can be found in [22]. The proof is done (by using candidates of reducibility and a fix point operator) for a typed calculus but, in fact, since the type system is such that every term is typable, the result is valid for every term. A proof of the strong normalization of the $\overline{\lambda}\mu\tilde{\mu}$-typed calculus (again using candidates of reducibility and a fix point operator) can also be found there. Due to the lack of space, we do not give our proofs of these results here but they will appear in [11].

The paper is organized as follows. In section 2 we give the syntax of the terms and the reduction rules. An arithmetical proof of strong normalization is given in section 3 for the $\mu\mu'$-reduction of the un-typed calculus and, in section 4, for the $\beta\mu\mu'$-reduction of the simply typed calculus. In section 5, we give an example showing that the proofs of strong normalization using candidates of reducibility *must* somehow be different from the usual ones and we show that, in the un-typed calculus, if $M_1, ..., M_n$ are strongly normalizing for the $\beta\mu\mu'$-reduction, then so is $(x\ M_1 ... \ M_n)$. We conclude with some future work.

2 The Symmetric $\lambda\mu$-Calculus

2.1 The Un-typed Calculus

The set (denoted as $\mathcal{T}$) of $\lambda\mu$-terms or simply terms is defined by the following grammar where $x, y, ...$ are λ-variables and $\alpha, \beta, ...$ are μ-variables:

$$\mathcal{E} ::= x \mid \lambda x\mathcal{T} \mid (\mathcal{E}\ \mathcal{T}) \mid \mu\alpha\mathcal{T}$$

$$\mathcal{T} ::= \mathcal{E} \mid (\alpha\ \mathcal{T})$$

Note that we adopt here a more liberal syntax (also called de Groote's calculus) than in the original calculus since we do not ask that a $\mu\alpha$ is immediately followed by a $(\beta\ M)$ (denoted $[\beta]M$ in Parigot's notation). The definition is given here via two sets to ensure that a μ-variable is always applied to exactly one argument.

Definition 1. Let M be a term.

1. $cxty(M)$ is the number of symbols occurring in M.
2. We denote by $N \leq M$ (resp. $N < M$) the fact that N is a sub-term (resp. a strict sub-term) of M.
3. If $\overrightarrow{P}$ is a sequence $P_1, ..., P_n$ of terms, $(M\ \overrightarrow{P})$ will denote $(M\ P_1\ ...\ P_n)$.

2.2 The Typed Calculus

The types are those of the simply typed $\lambda\mu$-calculus i.e. are built from atomic formulas and the constant symbol $\perp$ with the connector $\rightarrow$. As usual $\neg A$ is an abbreviation for $A \rightarrow \perp$.

The typing rules are given by figure 1 below where Γ is a context, i.e. a set of declarations of the form $x : A$ and $\alpha : \neg A$ where x is a λ (or intuitionistic) variable, α is a μ (or classical) variable and A is a formula.

Note that, here, we also have changed Parigot's notation but these typing rules are those of his classical natural deduction. Instead of writing

$$M : (A_1^{x_1}, ..., A_n^{x_n} \vdash B, C_1^{\alpha_1}, ..., C_m^{\alpha_m})$$

we have written

$$x_1 : A_1, ..., x_n : A_n, \alpha_1 : \neg C_1, ..., \alpha_m : \neg C_m \vdash M : B$$

Definition 2. Let A be a type. We denote by $lg(A)$ the number of arrows in A.

$$\frac{}{\Gamma, x : A \vdash x : A}\ ax$$

$$\frac{\Gamma, x : A \vdash M : B}{\Gamma \vdash \lambda x M : A \to B}\ \to_i \qquad \frac{\Gamma \vdash M : A \to B \quad \Gamma \vdash N : A}{\Gamma \vdash (M\ N) : B}\ \to_e$$

$$\frac{\Gamma, \alpha : \neg A \vdash M : \bot}{\Gamma \vdash \mu\alpha M : A}\ \bot_e \qquad \frac{\Gamma, \alpha : \neg A \vdash M : A}{\Gamma, \alpha : \neg A \vdash (\alpha\ M) : \bot}\ \bot_i$$

Fig. 1.

2.3 The Reduction Rules

The cut-elimination procedure (on the logical side) corresponds to the reduction rules (on the terms) given below. There are three kinds of cuts.

- A *logical cut* occurs when the introduction of the connective $\to$ is immediately followed by its elimination. The corresponding reduction rule (denoted by β) is:

$$(\lambda x M\ N) \triangleright M[x := N]$$

- A *classical cut* occurs when $\bot_e$ appears as the left premiss of a $\to_e$. The corresponding reduction rule (denoted by μ) is:

$$(\mu\alpha M\ N) \triangleright \mu\alpha M[\alpha =_r N]$$

  where $M[\alpha =_r N]$ is obtained by replacing each sub-term of M of the form $(\alpha\ U)$ by $(\alpha\ (U\ N))$. This substitution is called a μ-substitution.
- A *symmetric classical cut* occurs when $\bot_e$ appears as the right premiss of a $\to_e$. The corresponding reduction rule (denoted by μ') is:

$$(M\ \mu\alpha N) \triangleright \mu\alpha N[\alpha =_l M]$$

  where $N[\alpha =_l M]$ is obtained by replacing each sub-term of N of the form $(\alpha\ U)$ by $(\alpha\ (M\ U))$. This substitution is called a μ'-substitution.

Remarks

1. It is shown in [18] that the $\beta\mu$-reduction is confluent but neither $\mu\mu'$ nor $\beta\mu'$ is. For example $(\mu\alpha x\ \mu\beta y)$ reduces both to $\mu\alpha x$ and to $\mu\beta y$. Similarly $(\lambda z x\ \mu\beta y)$ reduces both to x and to $\mu\beta y$.
2. The reductions on terms correspond to the elimination of cuts on the proofs.
   - The β-reduction is the usual one.
   - The μ-reduction is as follows. If M corresponds to a proof of $\bot$ assuming $\alpha : \neg(A \to B)$ and N corresponds to a proof of A, then $M[\alpha =_r N]$ corresponds to the proof M of $\bot$ assuming $\alpha : \neg B$ but where, each time we used the hypothesis $\alpha : \neg(A \to B)$ with a proof U of $A \to B$ to get $\bot$, we replace this by the following proof of $\bot$. Use U and N to get a proof of B and then $\alpha : \neg B$ to get a proof of $\bot$.

   - Similarly, the μ'-reduction is as follows. If N corresponds to a proof of $\perp$ assuming $\alpha : \neg A$ and M corresponds to a proof of $A \to B$, then $N[\alpha =_l M]$ corresponds to the proof N of $\perp$ assuming $\alpha : \neg B$ but where, each time we used the hypothesis $\alpha : \neg A$ with a proof U of A to get $\perp$, we replace this by the following proof of $\perp$. Use U and M to get a proof of B and then $\alpha : \neg B$ to get a proof of $\perp$.
3. Unlike for a β-substitution where, in $M[x := N]$, the variable x has disappeared it is important to note that, in a μ or μ'-substitution, the variable α has not disappeared. Moreover its type has changed. If the type of N is A and, in M, the type of α is $\neg(A \to B)$ it becomes $\neg B$ in $M[\alpha =_r N]$. If the type of M is $A \to B$ and, in N, the type of α is $\neg A$ it becomes $\neg B$ in $N[\alpha =_l M]$.

In the next sections we will study various reductions : the $\mu\mu'$-reduction in section 3 and the $\beta\mu\mu'$-reduction in sections 4, 5. The following notions will correspond to these reductions.

Definition 3. Let $\triangleright$ be a notion of reduction and M be a term.

1. The transitive (resp. reflexive and transitive) closure of $\triangleright$ is denoted by $\triangleright^+$ (resp. $\triangleright^*$).
2. If M is in SN i.e. M has no infinite reduction, $\eta(M)$ will denote the length of the longest reduction starting from M and $\eta c(M)$ will denote $(\eta(M), cxty(M))$.
3. We denote by $N \prec M$ the fact that $N \leq M'$ for some M' such that $M \triangleright^* M'$ and either $M \triangleright^+ M'$ or $N < M'$. We denote by $\preceq$ the reflexive closure of $\prec$.

Remarks

- It is easy to check that the relation $\preceq$ is transitive and that $N \preceq M$ iff $N \leq M'$ for some M' such that $M \triangleright^* M'$.
- If $M \in SN$ and $N \prec M$, then $N \in SN$ and $\eta c(N) < \eta c(M)$. It follows that the relation $\preceq$ is an order on the set SN.
- Many proofs will be done by induction on some k-uplet of integers. In this case the order we consider is the lexicographic order.

3 The $\mu\mu'$-Reduction Is Strongly Normalizing

In this section we consider the $\mu\mu'$-reduction, i.e. $M \triangleright M'$ means M' is obtained from M by one step of the $\mu\mu'$-reduction. The main points of the proof of the strong normalization of $\mu\mu'$ are the following.

- We first show (cf. lemma 6) that a μ or μ'-substitution cannot create a μ.
- It is easy to show (see lemma 8) that if $M \in SN$ but $M[\sigma] \notin SN$ where σ is a μ or μ'-substitution, there are an α in the domain of σ and some $M' \prec M$ such that $M'[\sigma] \in SN$ and (say σ is a μ-substitution) $(M'[\sigma]\ \sigma(\alpha)) \notin SN$. This is sufficient to give a simple proof of the strongly normalization of the μ-reduction. But this is not enough to do a proof of the strongly normalization

of the $\mu\mu'$-reduction. We need a stronger (and more difficult) version of this: lemma 9 ensure that, if $M[\sigma] \in SN$ but $M[\sigma][\alpha =_r P] \notin SN$ then the real cause of non SN is, in some sense, $[\alpha =_r P]$.

- Having these results, we show, essentially by induction on $\eta c(M) + \eta c(N)$, that if $M, N \in SN$ then $(M\ N) \in SN$. The point is that there is, in fact, no deep interactions between M and N i.e. in a reduct of $(M\ N)$ we always know what is coming from M and what is coming from N.

Definition 4. – The set of simultaneous substitutions of the form $[\alpha_1 =_{s_1} P_1\ ...,\ \alpha_n =_{s_n} P_n]$ where $s_i \in \{l, r\}$ will be denoted by Σ.

- For $s \in \{l, r\}$, the set of simultaneous substitutions of the form $[\alpha_1 =_s P_1\ ...\alpha_n =_s P_n]$ will be denoted by Σ_s.
- If $\sigma = [\alpha_1 =_{s_1} P_1\ ...,\ \alpha_n =_{s_n} P_n]$, we denote by $dom(\sigma)$ (resp. $Im(\sigma)$) the set $\{\alpha_1,\ ...,\ \alpha_n\}$ (resp. $\{P_1,\ ...,\ P_n\}$).
- Let $\sigma \in \Sigma$. We say that $\sigma \in SN$ iff for every $N \in Im(\sigma)$, $N \in SN$.

Lemma 5. *If $(M\ N) \triangleright^* \mu\alpha P$, then either $M \triangleright^* \mu\alpha M_1$ and $M_1[\alpha =_r N] \triangleright^* P$ or $N \triangleright^* \mu\alpha N_1$ and $N_1[\alpha =_l M] \triangleright^* P$.*

Proof. By induction on the length of the reduction $(M\ N) \triangleright^* \mu\alpha P$. □

Lemma 6. *Let M be a term and $\sigma \in \Sigma$. If $M[\sigma] \triangleright^* \mu\alpha P$, then $M \triangleright^* \mu\alpha Q$ for some Q such that $Q[\sigma] \triangleright^* P$.*

Proof. By induction on M. M cannot be of the form $(\beta\, M')$ or $\lambda x\, M'$. If M begins with a μ, the result is trivial. Otherwise $M = (M_1\ M_2)$ and, by lemma 5, either $M_1[\sigma] \triangleright^* \mu\alpha R$ and $R[\alpha =_r M_2[\sigma]] \triangleright^* P$ or $M_2[\sigma] \triangleright^* \mu\alpha R$ and $R[\alpha =_l M_1[\sigma]] \triangleright^* P$. Look at the first case (the other one is similar). By the induction hypothesis $M_1 \triangleright^* \mu\alpha Q$ for some Q such that $Q[\sigma] \triangleright^* R$ and thus $M \triangleright^* \mu\alpha Q[\alpha =_r M_2]$. Since $Q[\alpha =_r M_2][\sigma] = Q[\sigma][\alpha =_r M_2[\sigma]] \triangleright^* R[\alpha =_r M_2[\sigma]] \triangleright^* P$ we are done. □

Lemma 7. *Assume $M, N \in SN$ and $(M\ N) \notin SN$. Then either $M \triangleright^* \mu\alpha M_1$ and $M_1[\alpha =_r N] \notin SN$ or $N \triangleright^* \mu\beta N_1$ and $N_1[\beta =_l M] \notin SN$.*

Proof. By induction on $\eta(M) + \eta(N)$. Since $(M\ N) \notin SN$, $(M\ N) \triangleright P$ for some P such that $P \notin SN$. If $P = (M'\ N)$ where $M \triangleright M'$ we conclude by the induction hypothesis since $\eta(M') + \eta(N) < \eta(M) + \eta(N)$. If $P = (M\ N')$ where $N \triangleright N'$ the proof is similar. If $M = \mu\alpha M_1$ and $P = \mu\alpha M_1[\alpha =_r N]$ or $N = \mu\beta N_1$ and $P = \mu\beta N_1[\beta =_l M]$ the result is trivial. □

Lemma 8. *Let M be term in SN and $\sigma \in \Sigma_s$ be in SN. Assume $M[\sigma] \notin SN$. Then, for some $(\alpha\, P) \preceq M$, $P[\sigma] \in SN$ and, if $s = l$ (resp. $s = r$), $(\sigma(\alpha)\, P[\sigma]) \notin SN$ (resp. $(P[\sigma]\, \sigma(\alpha)) \notin SN$).*

Proof. We only prove the case $s = l$ (the other one is similar). Let $M_1 \preceq M$ be such that $M_1[\sigma] \notin SN$ and $\eta c(M_1)$ is minimal. By the minimality, M_1 cannot be $\lambda x M_2$ or $\mu\alpha M_2$. It cannot be either $(N_1\ N_2)$ because otherwise, by the minimality, the $N_i[\sigma]$ would be in SN and thus, by lemma 7 and 6, we would have, for example, $N_1 \triangleright^* \mu\alpha N_1'$ and $N_1'[\sigma][\alpha =_r N_2[\sigma]] = N_1'[\alpha =_r N_2][\sigma] \notin SN$ but this contradicts the minimality of M_1 since $\eta(N_1'[\alpha =_r N_2]) < \eta(M_1)$. Then $M_1 = (\alpha\, P)$ and the the minimality of M_1 implies that $P[\sigma] \in SN$. □

Remark
From these results it is easy to prove, by induction on the term, the strong normalization of the μ-reduction. It is enough to show that, if $M, N \in SN$, then $(M\ N) \in SN$. Otherwise, we construct below a sequence (M_i) of terms and a sequence (σ_i) of substitutions such that, for every i, σ_i has the form $[\alpha_1 =_r N, ..., \alpha_n =_r N]$, $M_i[\sigma_i] \notin SN$ and $M_{i+1} \prec M_i \prec M$. The sequence (M_i) contradicts the fact that $M \in SN$. Since $(M\ N) \notin SN$, by lemma 7, $M \triangleright^* \mu\alpha M_1$ and $M_1[\alpha =_r N] \notin SN$. Assume we have constructed M_i and σ_i. Since $M_i[\sigma_i] \notin SN$, by lemma 8, there is $M_i' \prec M_i$ such that $M_i'[\sigma_i] \in SN$ and $(M_i'[\sigma]\ N) \notin SN$. By lemmas 6 and 7, $M_i' \triangleright^* \mu\alpha M_{i+1}$ and $M_{i+1}[\sigma_i + \alpha =_r N] \notin SN$.

In the remark above, the fact that $(M\ N) \notin SN$ gives an infinite μ-reduction in M. This not the same for the the $\mu\mu'$-reduction and, if we try to do the same, the substitutions we get are more complicated. In particular, it is not clear that we get an infinite sequence either of the form $... \prec M_2 \prec M_1 \prec M$ or of the form $... \prec N_2 \prec N_1 \prec N$. Lemma 9 below will give the answer since it will ensure that, at each step, we may assume that the cause of non SN is the last substitution.

Lemma 9. *Let M be a term and $\sigma \in \Sigma_s$. Assume δ is free in M but not free in $Im(\sigma)$. If $M[\sigma] \in SN$ but $M[\sigma][\delta =_s P] \notin SN$, there is $M' \prec M$ and σ' such that $M'[\sigma'] \in SN$ and, if $s = r$, $(M'[\sigma']\ \ P) \notin SN$ and, if $s = l$, $(P\ \ M'[\sigma']) \notin SN$.*

Proof. Assume $s = r$ (the other case is similar). Let $Im(\sigma) = \{N_1, ..., N_k\}$. Assume M, δ, σ, P satisfy the hypothesis. Let $\mathcal{U} = \{U \ / \ U \preceq M\}$ and $\mathcal{V} = \{V \ / \ V \preceq N_i \text{ for some } i\}$. Define inductively the sets Σ_m and Σ_n of substitutions by the following rules:

$\rho \in \Sigma_m$ iff $\rho = \emptyset$ or $\rho = \rho' + [\beta =_r V[\tau]]$ for some $V \in \mathcal{V}$, $\tau \in \Sigma_n$ and $\rho' \in \Sigma_m$

$\tau \in \Sigma_n$ iff $\tau = \emptyset$ or $\tau = \tau' + [\alpha =_l U[\rho]]$ for some $U \in \mathcal{U}$, $\rho \in \Sigma_m$ and $\tau' \in \Sigma_n$

Denote by C the conclusion of the lemma, i.e. there is $M' \prec M$ and σ' such that $M'[\sigma'] \in SN$, and $(M'[\sigma']\ \ P) \notin SN$.
We prove something more general.
(1) Let $U \in \mathcal{U}$ and $\rho \in \Sigma_m$. Assume $U[\rho] \in SN$ and $U[\rho][\delta =_r P] \notin SN$. Then, C holds.
(2) Let $V \in \mathcal{V}$ and $\tau \in \Sigma_n$. Assume $V[\tau] \in SN$ and $V[\tau][\delta =_r P] \notin SN$. Then, C holds.

The conclusion C follows from (1) with M and σ. The properties (1) and (2) are proved by a simultaneous induction on $\eta c(U[\rho])$ (for the first case) and $\eta c(V[\tau])$ (for the second case).

Look first at (1)

- if $U = \lambda x U'$ or $U = \mu\alpha U'$: the result follows from the induction hypothesis with U' and ρ.
- if $U = (U_1\ U_2)$: if $U_i[\rho][\delta =_r P] \notin SN$ for $i = 1$ or $i = 2$, the result follows from the induction hypothesis with U_i and ρ. Otherwise, by lemma 6 and 7, say $U_1 \triangleright^* \mu\alpha U_1'$ and, letting $U' = U_1'[\alpha =_r u_2]$, $U'[\rho][\delta =_r P] \notin SN$ and the result follows from the induction hypothesis with U' and ρ.

- if $U = (\delta\ U_1)$: if $U_1[\rho][\delta =_r P] \in SN$, then $M' = U_1$ and $\sigma' = \rho[\delta =_r P]$ satisfy the desired conclusion. Otherwise, the result follows from the induction hypothesis with U_1 and ρ.
- if $U = (\alpha\ U_1)$: if $\alpha \notin dom(\rho)$ or $U_1[\rho][\delta =_r P] \notin SN$, the result follows from the induction hypothesis with U_1 and ρ. Otherwise, let $\rho(\alpha) = V[\tau]$. If $V[\tau][\delta =_r P] \notin SN$, the result follows from the induction hypothesis with V and τ (with (2)). Otherwise, by lemma 6 and 7, there are two cases to consider.
- $U_1 \rhd^* \mu\alpha_1 U_2$ and $U_2[\rho'][\delta =_r P] \notin SN$ where $\rho' = \rho + [\alpha_1 =_r V[\tau]]$. The result follows from the induction hypothesis with U_2 and ρ'.
- $V \rhd^* \mu\beta V_1$ and $V_1[\tau'][\delta =_r P] \notin SN$ where $\tau' = \tau + [\beta =_l U_1[\rho]]$. The result follows from the induction hypothesis with V_1 and τ' (with (2)).

The case (2) is proved in the same way. Note that, since δ is not free in the N_i, the case $b = (\delta\ V_1)$ does not appear. □

Theorem 10. *Every term is in SN.*

Proof. By induction on the term. It is enough to show that, if $M, N \in SN$, then $(M\ N) \in SN$. We prove something more general: let σ (resp. τ) be in Σ_r (resp. Σ_l) and assume $M[\sigma], N[\tau] \in SN$. Then $(M[\sigma]\ N[\tau]) \in SN$. Assume it is not the case and choose some elements such that $M[\sigma], N[\tau] \in SN$, $(M[\sigma]\ N[\tau]) \notin SN$ and $(\eta(M)+\eta(N), cxty(M)+cxty(N))$ is minimal. By lemma 7, either $M[\sigma] \rhd^* \mu\delta M_1$ and $M_1[\delta =_r N[\tau]] \notin SN$ or $N[\tau] \rhd^* \mu\beta N_1$ and $N_1[\beta =_l M[\sigma]] \notin SN$. Look at the first case (the other one is similar). By lemma 6, $M \rhd^* \mu\delta M_2$ for some M_2 such that $M_2[\sigma] \rhd^* M_1$. Thus, $M_2[\sigma][\delta =_r N[\tau]] \notin SN$. By lemma 9 with M_2, σ and $N[\tau]$, let $M' \prec M_2$ and σ' be such that $M'[\sigma'] \in SN$, $(M'[\sigma']\ N[\tau]) \notin SN$. This contradicts the minimality of the chosen elements since $\eta c(M') < \eta c(M)$. □

4 The Simply Typed Symmetric $\lambda\mu$-Calculus Is Strongly Normalizing

In this section, we consider the simply typed calculus with the $\beta\mu\mu'$-reduction i.e. $M \rhd M'$ means M' is obtained from M by one step of the $\beta\mu\mu'$-reduction. To prove the strong normalization of the $\beta\mu\mu'$-reduction, it is enough to show that, if $M, N \in SN$, then $M[x := N]$ also is in SN. This is done by induction on the type of N. The proof very much looks like the one for the $\mu\mu'$-reduction and the induction on the type is used for the cases coming from a β-reduction. The two new difficulties are the following.

- A β-substitution may create a μ, i.e. the fact that $M[x := N] \rhd^* \mu\alpha P$ does not imply that $M \rhd^* \mu\alpha Q$. Moreover the μ may come from a complicated interaction between M and N and, in particular, the alternation between M and N can be lost. Let e.g. $M = (M_1\ (x\ (\lambda y_1 \lambda y_2 \mu\alpha M_4)\ M_2\ M_3))$ and

$N = \lambda z(z\ N_1)$. Then $M[x := N] \triangleright^* (M_1\ (\mu\alpha M_4'\ M_3)) \triangleright^* \mu\alpha M_4'[\alpha =_r M_3][\alpha =_l M_1]$. To deal with this situation, we need to consider some new kind of $\mu\mu'$-substitutions (see definition 13). Lemma 16 gives the different ways in which a μ may appear. The difficult case in the proof (when a μ is created and the control between M and N is lost) will be solved by using a typing argument.

- The crucial lemma (lemma 18) is essentially the same as the one (lemma 9) for the $\mu\mu'$-reduction but, in its proof, some cases cannot be proved "by themselves" and we need an argument using the types. For this reason, its proof is done using the additional fact that we already know that, if $M, N \in SN$ and the type of N is small, then $M[x := N]$ also is in SN. Since the proof of lemma 19 is done by induction on the type, when we will use lemma 18, the additional hypothesis will be available.

Lemma 11. *1. If $(M\ N) \triangleright^* \lambda xP$, then $M \triangleright^* \lambda y M_1$ and $M_1[y := N] \triangleright^* \lambda xP$.*
2. If $(M\ N) \triangleright^* \mu\alpha P$, then either ($M \triangleright^* \lambda y M_1$ and $M_1[y := N] \triangleright^* \mu\alpha P$) or ($M \triangleright^* \mu\alpha M_1$ and $M_1[\alpha =_r N] \triangleright^* P$) or ($N \triangleright^* \mu\alpha N_1$ and $N_1[\alpha =_l M] \triangleright^* P$).

Proof. (1) is trivial. (2) is as in lemma 5. □

Lemma 12. *Let $M \in SN$ and $\sigma = [x_1 := N_1, ..., x_k := N_k]$. Assume $M[\sigma] \triangleright^* \lambda yP$. Then, either $M \triangleright^* \lambda y P_1$ and $P_1[\sigma] \triangleright^* P$ or $M \triangleright^* (x_i\ \overrightarrow{Q})$ and $(N_i\ \overrightarrow{Q[\sigma]}) \triangleright^* \lambda yP$.*

Proof. By induction on $\eta c(M)$. The only non immediate case is $M = (R\ S)$. By lemma 11, there is a term R_1 such that $R[\sigma] \triangleright^* \lambda z R_1$ and $R_1[z := S[\sigma]] \triangleright^* \lambda yP$. By the induction hypothesis (since $\eta c(R) < \eta c(M)$), we have two cases to consider.

(1) $R \triangleright^* \lambda z R_2$ and $R_2[\sigma] \triangleright^* R_1$, then $R_2[z := S][\sigma] \triangleright^* \lambda yP$. By the induction hypothesis (since $\eta(R_2[z := S]) < \eta(M)$),

- either $R_2[z := S] \triangleright^* \lambda y P_1$ and $P_1[\sigma] \triangleright^* P$; but then $M \triangleright^* \lambda y P_1$ and we are done.
- or $R_2[z := S] \triangleright^* (x_i\ \overrightarrow{Q})$ and $(N_i\ \overrightarrow{Q[\sigma]}) \triangleright^* \lambda yP$, then $M \triangleright^* (x_i\ \overrightarrow{Q})$ and again we are done.

(2) $R \triangleright^* (x_i\ \overrightarrow{Q})$ and $(N_i\ \overrightarrow{Q[\sigma]}) \triangleright^* \lambda z R_1$. Then $M \triangleright^* (x_i\ \overrightarrow{Q}\ S)$ and the result is trivial. □

Definition 13. – An address is a finite list of symbols in $\{l, r\}$. The empty list is denoted by [] and, if a is an address and $s \in \{l, r\}$, $[s :: a]$ denotes the list obtained by putting s at the beginning of a.

- Let a be an address and M be a term. The sub-term of M at the address a (denoted as M_a) is defined recursively as follows : if $M = (P\ Q)$ and $a = [r :: b]$ (resp. $a = [l :: b]$) then $M_a = Q_b$ (resp. P_b) and undefined otherwise.
- Let M be a term and a be an address such that M_a is defined. Then $M\langle a = N\rangle$ is the term M where the sub-term M_a has been replaced by N.
- Let M, N be some terms and a be an address such that M_a is defined. Then $N[\alpha =_a M]$ is the term N in which each sub-term of the form $(\alpha\ U)$ is replaced by $(\alpha\ M\langle a = U\rangle)$.

Remarks and Examples

- Let $N = \lambda x(\alpha\ \lambda y(x\ \mu\beta(\alpha\ y)))$, $M = (M_1\ (M_2\ M_3))$ and $a = [r :: l]$. Then $N[\alpha =_a M] = \lambda x(\alpha\ (M_1\ (\lambda y(x\ \mu\beta(\alpha\ (M_1\ (y\ M_3))))\ M_3)))$.
- Let $M = (P\ ((R\ (x\ T))\ Q))$ and $a = [r :: l :: r :: l]$. Then $N[\alpha =_a M] = N[\alpha =_r T][\alpha =_l R][\alpha =_r Q][\alpha =_r P]$.
- Note that the sub-terms of a term having an address in the sense given above are those for which the path to the root consists only on applications (taking either the left or right son).
- Note that $[\alpha =_{[l]} M]$ is not the same as $[\alpha =_l M]$ but $[\alpha =_l M]$ is the same as $[\alpha =_{[r]} (M\ N)]$ where N does not matter. More generally, the term $N[\alpha =_a M]$ does not depend of M_a.
- Note that $M\langle a = N\rangle$ can be written as $M'[x_a := N]$ where M' is the term M in which M_a has been replaced by the fresh variable x_a and thus (this will be used in the proof of lemma 19) if M_a is a variable x, $(\alpha\ U)[\alpha =_a M] = (\alpha\ M_1[y := U[\alpha =_a M]])$ where M_1 is the term M in which the particular occurrence of x at the address a has been replaced by the fresh name y and the other occurrences of x remain unchanged.

Lemma 14. *Assume $M, N \in SN$ and $(M\ N) \notin SN$. Then, either ($M \triangleright^* \lambda yP$ and $P[y := N] \notin SN$) or ($M \triangleright^* \mu\alpha P$ and $P[\alpha =_r N] \notin SN$) or ($N \triangleright^* \mu\alpha P$ and $P[\alpha =_l M] \notin SN$).*

Proof. By induction on $\eta(M) + \eta(N)$. □

In the rest of this section, we consider the typed calculus. To simplify the notations, we do not write explicitly the type information but, when needed, we denote by type(M) the type of the term M.

Lemma 15. *If $\Gamma \vdash M : A$ and $M \triangleright^* N$ then $\Gamma \vdash N : A$.*

Proof. Straight forward. □

Lemma 16. *Let n be an integer, $M \in SN$, $\sigma = [x_1 := N_1, ..., x_k := N_k]$ where $lg(type(N_i)) = n$ for each i. Assume $M[\sigma] \triangleright^* \mu\alpha P$. Then,*

1. *either $M \triangleright^* \mu\alpha P_1$ and $P_1[\sigma] \triangleright^* P$.*
2. *or $M \triangleright^* Q$ and, for some i, $N_i \triangleright^* \mu\alpha N_i'$ and $N_i'[\alpha =_a Q[\sigma]] \triangleright^* P$ for some address a in Q such that $Q_a = x_i$.*
3. *or $M \triangleright^* Q$, $Q_a[\sigma] \triangleright^* \mu\alpha N'$ and $N'[\alpha =_a Q[\sigma]] \triangleright^* P$ for some address a in Q such that $lg(type(Q_a)) < n$.*

Proof. By induction on $\eta c(M)$. The only non immediate case is $M = (R\ S)$. Since $M[\sigma] \triangleright^* \mu\alpha P$, the application $(R[\sigma]\ S[\sigma])$ must be reduced. Thus there are three cases to consider.

- It is reduced by a μ'-reduction, i.e. there is a term S_1 such that $S[\sigma] \triangleright^* \mu\alpha S_1$ and $S_1[\alpha =_l R[\sigma]] \triangleright^* P$. By the induction hypothesis:
  - either $S \triangleright^* \mu\alpha Q$ and $Q[\sigma] \triangleright^* S_1$, then $M \triangleright^* \mu\alpha Q[\alpha =_l R]$ and $Q[\alpha =_l R][\sigma] \triangleright^* P$.

  - or $S \triangleright^* Q$ and, for some i, $N_i \triangleright^* \mu\alpha N'_i$, $Q_a = x_i$ for some address a in Q and $N'_i[\alpha =_a Q[\sigma]] \triangleright^* S_1$. Then $M \triangleright^* (R\ Q) = Q'$ and letting $b = [r :: a]$ we have $N'_i[\alpha =_b Q'[\sigma]] \triangleright^* P$.
  - or $S \triangleright^* Q$, $Q_a[\sigma] \triangleright^* \mu\alpha N'$ for some address a in Q such that $lg(type(Q_a)) < n$ and $N'[\alpha =_a Q[\sigma]] \triangleright^* S_1$. Then $M \triangleright^* (R\ Q) = Q'$ and letting $b = [r :: a]$ we have $N'[\alpha =_b Q'[\sigma]] \triangleright^* P$ and $lg(type(Q'_b)) < n$.
- It is reduced by a μ-reduction. This case is similar to the previous one.
- It is reduced by a β-reduction, i.e. there is a term U such that $R[\sigma] \triangleright^* \lambda y U$ and $U[y := S[\sigma]] \triangleright^* \mu\alpha P$. By lemma 12, there are two cases to consider.
  - either $R \triangleright^* \lambda y R_1$ and $R_1[\sigma][y := S[\sigma]] = R_1[y := S][\sigma] \triangleright^* \mu\alpha P$. The result follows from the induction hypothesis sine $\eta(R_1[y := S]) < \eta(M)$.
  - or $R \triangleright^* (x_i\ \overrightarrow{R_1})$. Then $Q = (x_i\ \overrightarrow{R_1}\ S)$ and $a = []$ satisfy the desired conclusion since then $lg(type(M)) < n$. □

Definition 17. Let A be a type. We denote by Σ_A the set of substitutions of the form $[\alpha_1 =_{a_1} M_1, ..., \alpha_n =_{a_n} M_n]$ where the type of the α_i is $\neg A$.

Remark
Since in such substitutions the type of the variables changes, when we consider the term $N[\sigma]$ where $\sigma \in \Sigma_A$, we mean that the type of the α_i is A in N i.e. before the substitution. Also note that considering $N[\alpha =_a M]$ implies that the type of M_a is A.

Lemma 18. *Let n be an integer and A be a type such that $lg(A) = n$. Let N, P be terms and $\tau \in \Sigma_A$. Assume that,*

- *for every $M, N \in SN$ such that $lg(type(N)) < n$, $M[x := N] \in SN$.*
- *$N[\tau] \in SN$ but $N[\tau][\delta =_a P] \notin SN$.*
- *δ is free and has type $\neg A$ in N but δ is not free in $Im(\tau)$.*

Then, there is $N' \prec N$ and $\tau' \in \Sigma_A$ such that $N'[\tau'] \in SN$ and $P\langle a = N'[\tau']\rangle \notin SN$.

Proof. Essentially as in lemma 9. Denote by (H) the first assumption i.e. for every $M, N \in SN$ such that $lg(type(N)) < n$, $M[x := N] \in SN$.

Let $\tau = [\alpha_1 =_{a_1} M_1, ..., \alpha_n =_{a_n} M_n]$, $\mathcal{U} = \{U \mid U \preceq N\}$ and $\mathcal{V} = \{V \mid V \preceq M_i$ for some $i\}$. Define inductively the sets Σ_m and Σ_n of substitutions by the following rules:

$\rho \in \Sigma_n$ iff $\rho = \emptyset$ or $\rho = \rho' + [\alpha =_a V[\sigma]]$ for some $V \in \mathcal{V}$, $\sigma \in \Sigma_m$, $\rho' \in \Sigma_n$ and α has type $\neg A$.

$\sigma \in \Sigma_m$ iff $\sigma = \emptyset$ or $\sigma = \sigma' + [x := U[\rho]]$ for some $U \in \mathcal{U}$, $\rho \in \Sigma_n$, $\sigma' \in \Sigma_m$ and x has type A.

Denote by C the conclusion of the lemma. We prove something more general.
(1) Let $U \in \mathcal{U}$ and $\rho \in \Sigma_n$. Assume $U[\rho] \in SN$ and $U[\rho][\delta =_a P] \notin SN$. Then, C holds.
(2) Let $V \in \mathcal{V}$ and $\sigma \in \Sigma_m$. Assume $V[\sigma] \in SN$ and $V[\sigma][\delta =_a P] \notin SN$. Then, C holds.

The conclusion C follows from (1) with N and τ. The properties (1) and (2) are proved by a simultaneous induction on $\eta c(U[\rho])$ (for the first case) and $\eta c(V[\tau])$ (for the second case).

The proof is as in lemma 9. The new case to consider is, for $V[\sigma]$, when $V = (V_1\ V_2)$ and $V_i[\sigma][\delta =_a P] \in SN$.

- Assume first the interaction between V_1 and V_2 is a β-reduction. If $V_1 \triangleright^* \lambda x V_1'$, the result follows from the induction hypothesis with $V_1'[x := V_2][\sigma]$. Otherwise, by lemma 12, $V_1 \triangleright^* (x\ \overrightarrow{W})$. Let $\sigma(x) = U[\rho]$. Then $(U[\rho]\ \overrightarrow{W}[\sigma]) \triangleright^* \lambda y Q$ and $Q[y := V_2[\sigma]][\delta =_a P] \notin SN$. But, since the type of x is A, the type of y is less than A and since $Q[\delta =_a P]$ and $V_2[\sigma][\delta =_a P]$ are in SN this contradicts (H).
- Assume next the interaction between V_1 and V_2 is a μ or μ'-reduction. We consider only the case μ (the other one is similar). If $V_1 \triangleright^* \mu\alpha V_1'$, the result follows from the induction hypothesis with $V_1'[\alpha =_r V_2][\sigma]$. Otherwise, by lemma 16, there are two cases to consider.
- $V_1 \triangleright^* Q$, $Q_c = x$ for some address c in Q and $x \in dom(\sigma)$, $\sigma(x) = U[\rho]$, $U \triangleright^* \mu\alpha U_1$ and $U_1[\rho][\alpha =_c Q[\sigma]][\alpha =_r V_2[\sigma]][\delta =_a P] \notin SN$. Let $V' = (Q\ V_2)$ and $b = l :: c$. The result follows then from the induction hypothesis with $U_1[\rho']$ where $\rho' = \rho + [\alpha =_b V'[\sigma]]$.
- $V_1 \triangleright^* Q$, $Q_c[\sigma][\delta =_a P] \triangleright^* \mu\alpha R$ for some address c in Q such that $lg(type(Q_c)) < n$, $R[\alpha =_c Q[\sigma][\delta =_a P]][\alpha =_r V_2[\sigma][\delta =_a P]] \notin SN$. Let $V' = (Q'\ V_2)$ where Q' is the same as Q but Q_c has been replaced by a fresh variable y and $b = l :: c$. Then $R[\alpha =_b V'[\sigma][\delta =_a P]] \notin SN$. Let R' be such that $R' \prec R$, $R'[\alpha =_b V'[\sigma][\delta =_a P]] \notin SN$ and $\eta c(R')$ is minimal. It is easy to check that $R' = (\alpha\ R'')$, $R''[\alpha =_b V'[\sigma][\delta =_a P]] \in SN$ and $V'[\sigma'][\delta =_a P] \notin SN$ where $\sigma' = \sigma + y := R''[\alpha =_b V'[\sigma]]$. If $V'[\sigma][\delta =_a P] \notin SN$, we get the result by the induction hypothesis since $\eta c(V'[\sigma]) < \eta c(V[\sigma])$. Otherwise this contradicts the assumption (H) since $V'[\sigma][\delta =_a P], R''[\alpha =_b V'[\sigma][\delta =_a P]] \in SN$, $V'[\sigma][\delta =_a P][y := R''[\alpha =_b V'[\sigma][\delta =_a P]]] \notin SN$ and the type of y is less than n.

□

Lemma 19. *If $M, N \in SN$, then $M[x := N] \in SN$.*

Proof. We prove something a bit more general: let A be a type, $M, N_1, ..., N_k$ be terms and $\tau_1, ..., \tau_k$ be substitutions in Σ_A. Assume that, for each i, N_i has type A and $N_i[\tau_i] \in SN$. Then $M[x_1 := N_1[\tau_1], ..., x_k := N_k[\tau_k]] \in SN$. This is proved by induction on $(lg(A), \eta(M), cxty(M), \Sigma\ \eta(N_i), \Sigma\ cxty(N_i))$ where, in $\Sigma\ \eta(N_i)$ and $\Sigma\ cxty(N_i)$, we count each occurrence of the substituted variable. For example if $k = 1$ and x_1 has n occurrences, $\Sigma\ \eta(N_i) = n.\eta(N_1)$.

If M is $\lambda y M_1$ or $(\alpha\ M_1)$ or $\mu\alpha M_1$ or a variable, the result is trivial. Assume then that $M = (M_1\ M_2)$. Let $\sigma = [x_1 := N_1[\tau_1], ..., x_k := N_k[\tau_k]]$. By the induction hypothesis, $M_1[\sigma], M_2[\sigma] \in SN$. By lemma 14 there are 3 cases to consider.

- $M_1[\sigma] \triangleright^* \lambda y P$ and $P[y := M_2[\sigma]] \notin SN$. By lemma 12, there are two cases to consider.

- $M_1 \triangleright^* \lambda y Q$ and $Q[\sigma] \triangleright^* P$. Then $Q[y := M_2][\sigma] = Q[\sigma][y := M_2[\sigma]] \triangleright^* P[y := M_2[\sigma]]$ and, since $\eta(Q[y := M_2]) < \eta(M)$, this contradicts the induction hypothesis.
- $M_1 \triangleright^* (x_i\ \overrightarrow{Q})$ and $(N_i\ \overrightarrow{Q[\sigma]}) \triangleright^* \lambda y P$. Then, since the type of N_i is A, $lg(type(y)) < lg(A)$. But $P, M_2[\sigma] \in SN$ and $P[y := M_2[\sigma]] \notin SN$. This contradicts the induction hypothesis.

– $M_1[\sigma] \triangleright^* \mu\alpha P$ and $P[\alpha =_r M_2[\sigma]] \notin SN$. By lemma 16, there are three cases to consider.

- $M_1 \triangleright^* \mu\alpha Q$ and $Q[\sigma] \triangleright^* P$. Then, $Q[\alpha =_r M_2][\sigma] = Q[\sigma][\alpha =_r M_2[\sigma]] \triangleright^* P[\alpha =_r M_2[\sigma]]$ and, since $\eta(Q[\alpha =_r M_2]) < \eta(M)$, this contradicts the induction hypothesis.
- $M_1 \triangleright^* Q$, $N_i[\tau_i] \triangleright^* \mu\alpha L'$ and $Q_a = x_i$ for some address a in Q such that $L'[\alpha =_a Q[\sigma]] \triangleright^* P$ and thus $L'[\alpha =_b M'[\sigma]] \notin SN$ where $b = (l :: a)$ and $M' = (Q\ M_2)$.
By lemma 6, $N_i \triangleright^* \mu\alpha L$ and $L[\tau_i] \triangleright^* L'$. Thus, $L[\tau_i][\alpha =_b M'[\sigma]] \notin SN$. By lemma 18, there is $L_1 \prec L$ and τ' such that $L_1[\tau'] \in SN$ and $M'[\sigma]\langle b = L_1[\tau']\rangle \notin SN$. Let M'' be M' where the variable x_i at the address b has been replaced by the fresh variable y and let $\sigma_1 = \sigma + y := L_1[\tau']$. Then $M''[\sigma_1] = M'[\sigma]\langle b = L_1[\tau']\rangle \notin SN$.
If $M_1 \triangleright^+ Q$ we get a contradiction from the induction hypothesis since $\eta(M'') < \eta(M)$. Otherwise, M'' is the same as M up to the change of name of a variable and σ_1 differs from σ only at the address b. At this address, x_i was substituted in σ by $N_i[\tau_i)$ and in σ_1 by $L_1[\tau']$ but $\eta c(L_1) < \eta c(N_i)$ and thus we get a contradiction from the induction hypothesis.
- $M \triangleright^* Q$, $Q_a[\sigma] \triangleright^* \mu\alpha L$ for some address a in Q such that $lg(type(Q_a)) < lg(A)$ and $L[\alpha =_a Q[\sigma]] \triangleright^* P$. Then, $L[\alpha =_b M'[\sigma]] \notin SN$ where $b = [l :: a]$ and $M' = (Q\ M_2)$.
By lemma 18, there is an L' and τ' such that $L'[\tau'] \in SN$ and $M'[\sigma]\langle b = L'[\tau']\rangle \notin SN$. Let M'' be M' where the variable x_i at the address b has been replaced by the fresh variable y. Then $M''[\sigma][y := L'[\tau']] = M'[\sigma]\langle b = L'[\tau']\rangle \notin SN$.
But $\eta(M'') \leq \eta(M)$ and $cxty(M'') < cxty(M)$ since, because of its type, Q_a cannot be a variable and thus, by the induction hypothesis, $M''[\sigma] \in SN$. Since $M''[\sigma][y := L'[\tau']] \notin SN$ and $lg(type(L')) < lg(A)$, this contradicts the induction hypothesis.

– $M_2[\sigma] \triangleright^* \mu\alpha P$ and $P[\alpha =_l M_1[\sigma]] \notin SN$. This case is similar to the previous one. □

Theorem 20. *Every typed term is in SN.*

Proof. By induction on the term. It is enough to show that if $M, N \in SN$, then $(M\ N) \in SN$. Since $(M\ N) = (x\ y)[x := M][y := N]$ where x, y are fresh variables, the result follows by applying theorem 19 twice and the induction hypothesis. □

5 Why the Usual Candidates Do Not Work ?

In [21], the proof of the strong normalization of the $\lambda\mu$-calculus is done by using the *usual* (i.e. defined without a fix-point operation) candidates of reducibility. This proof could be easily extended to the symmetric $\lambda\mu$-calculus if we knew the following properties for the un-typed calculus:

1. If N and $(M[x := N]\ \overrightarrow{P})$ are in SN, then so is $(\lambda x M\ N\ \overrightarrow{P})$.
2. If N and $(M[\alpha =_r N]\ \overrightarrow{P})$ are in SN, then so is $(\mu\alpha M\ N\ \overrightarrow{P})$.
3. If $\overrightarrow{P}$ are in SN, then so is $(x\ \overrightarrow{P})$.

These properties are easy to show for the $\beta\mu$-reduction but they were not known for the $\beta\mu\mu'$-reduction.

The properties (1) and (2) are false. Here is a counter-example. Let $M_0 = \lambda x(x\ P\ \underline{0})$ and $M_1 = \lambda x(x\ P\ \underline{1})$ where $\underline{0} = \lambda x \lambda y y$, $\underline{1} = \lambda x \lambda y x$, $\Delta = \lambda x(x\ x)$ and $P = \lambda x \lambda y \lambda z\ (y\ (z\ \underline{1}\ \underline{0})\ (z\ \underline{0}\ \underline{1})\ \lambda d \underline{1}\ \Delta\ \Delta)$. Let $M = \lambda f(f\ (x\ M_1)\ (x\ M_0))$, $M' = \lambda f(f\ (\beta\ \lambda x(x\ M_1))\ (\beta\ \lambda x(x\ M_0)))$ and $N = (\alpha\ \lambda z(\alpha\ z))$. Then,

- $M[x := \mu\alpha N] \in SN$ but $(\lambda x M\ \mu\alpha N) \notin SN$.
- $M'[\beta =_r \mu\alpha N] \in SN$ but $(\mu\beta M'\ \mu\alpha N) \notin SN$.

This comes from the fact that $(M_0\ M_0)$ and $(M_1\ M_1)$ are in SN but $(M_1\ M_0)$ and $(M_0\ M_1)$ are not in SN. More details can be found in [10].

The third property is true and its proof is essentially the same as the one of the strong normalization of $\mu\mu'$. This comes from the fact that, since $(x\ M_1 ... M_n)$ never reduces to a λ, there is no "dangerous" β-reduction. In particular, the β-reductions we have to consider in the proofs of the crucial lemmas, are uniquely those that appear in the reductions $M \preceq M'$. We give this proof below.

Lemma 21. *The term $(x\ M_1\ ...\ M_n)$ never reduces to a term of the form $\lambda y M$.*

Proof. By induction on n. Use lemma 11. □

Definition 22.
- Let $M_1, ..., M_n$ be terms and $1 \leq i \leq n$. Then, the term M in which every sub-term of the form $(\alpha\ U)$ is replaced by $(\alpha\ (x\ M_1\ ...\ M_{i-1}\ U\ M_{i+1}\ ...\ M_n))$ will be denoted by $M[\alpha =_i (M_1\ ...\ M_n)]$.
- We will denote by Σ_x the set of simultaneous substitutions of the form $[\alpha_1 =_{i_1} (M_1^1\ ...\ M_n^1), ..., \alpha_k =_{i_k} (M_1^k\ ...\ M_n^k)]$.

Remark
These substitutions are special cases of the one defined in section 4 (see definition 13). For example $M[\alpha =_2 (M_1\ M_2\ M_3)] = M[\alpha =_l (x\ M_1)][\alpha =_r M_3] = M[\alpha =_a (x\ M_1\ M_2\ M_3)]$ where $a = [l :: r]$.

Lemma 23. *Assume $(x\ M_1\ ...\ M_n) \triangleright^* \mu\alpha M$. Then, there is an i such that $M_i \triangleright^* \mu\alpha P$ and $P[\alpha =_i (M_1\ ...\ M_n)] \triangleright^* M$.*

Proof. By induction on n.
- $n = 1$. By lemma 11, $M_1 \triangleright^* \mu\alpha P$ and $P[\alpha =_l x] = P[\alpha =_1 (M_1)] \triangleright^* M$.
- $n \geq 2$. Assume $(x\ M_1\ ...\ M_{n-1}\ M_n) \triangleright^* \mu\alpha M$. By lemmas 11 and 21,

- either $(x\ M_1\ ...\ M_{n-1}) \triangleright^* \mu\alpha N$ and $N[\alpha =_r M_n] \triangleright^* M$. By the induction hypothesis, there is an i such that $M_i \triangleright^* \mu\alpha P$ and $P[\alpha =_i (M_1\ ...\ M_{n-1})] \triangleright^* N$. Then $P[\alpha =_i (M_1\ ...\ M_{n-1}\, M_n)] = P[\alpha =_i (M_1\ ...\ M_{n-1})][\alpha =_r M_n] \triangleright^* N[\alpha =_r M_n] \triangleright^* M$.
- or $M_n \triangleright^* \mu\alpha N$ and $N[\alpha =_l (x\ M_1\ ...\ M_{n-1})] \triangleright^* M$. Then $N[\alpha =_l (x\ M_1\ ...\ M_{n-1})] = N[\alpha =_n (M_1\ ...\ M_{n-1}\, M_n)] \triangleright^* M$.

□

Lemma 24. *Assume $M_1, ..., M_n \in SN$ and $(x\ M_1\ ...\ M_n) \notin SN$. Then, there is an $1 \leq i \leq n$ such that $M_i \triangleright^* \mu\alpha\, U$ and $U[\alpha =_i (M_1\ ...\ M_n)] \notin SN$.*

Proof. Let k be the least such that $(x\ M_1\ ...\ M_{k-1}) \in SN$ and $(x\ M_1\ ...\ M_k) \notin SN$. By lemmas 14 and 21,

- either $M_k \triangleright^* \mu\alpha U$ and $U[\alpha =_l (x\ M_1\ ...\ M_{k-1})] \notin SN$. Then, $i = k$ satisfies the desired property since $U[\alpha =_k (M_1\ ...\ M_n)] = U[\alpha =_l (x\ M_1\ ...\ M_{k-1})]$ $[\alpha =_r M_{k+1}]...[\alpha =_r M_n]$.
- or $(x\ M_1\ ...\ M_{k-1}) \triangleright^* \mu\alpha P$ and $P[\alpha =_r M_k] \notin SN$. By lemma 23, let $i \leq k-1$ be such that that $M_i \triangleright^* \mu\alpha U$ and $U[\alpha =_i (M_1\ ...\ M_{k-1})] \triangleright^* P$. Then $U[\alpha =_i (M_1\ ...\ M_n)] \notin SN$ since $U[\alpha =_i (M_1\ ...\ M_n)] = U[\alpha =_i (M_1\ ...\ M_{k-1})][\alpha =_r M_k][\alpha =_r M_{k+1}]...[\alpha =_r M_n]$ reduces to $P[\alpha =_r M_k][\alpha =_r M_{k+1}]...[\alpha =_r M_n]$.

□

Lemma 25. *Let M be a term and $\sigma \in \Sigma_x$. If $M[\sigma] \triangleright^* \mu\alpha P$ (resp. $M[\sigma] \triangleright^* \lambda x P$), then $M \triangleright^* \mu\alpha Q$ (resp. $M \triangleright^* \lambda x Q$) for some Q such that $Q[\sigma] \triangleright^* P$.*

Proof. As in lemma 6. □

Lemma 26. *Let M be a term and $\sigma \in \Sigma_x$. Assume δ is free in M but not free in $Im(\sigma)$. If $M[\sigma] \in SN$ but $M[\sigma][\delta =_i (P_1...P_n)] \notin SN$, there is $M' \prec M$ and σ' such that $M'[\sigma'] \in SN$ and $(x\ P_1...P_{i-1}\ M'[\sigma']\ P_{i+1}...P_n) \notin SN$.*

Proof. As in lemma 9. □

Theorem 27. *Assume $M_1, ..., M_n$ are in SN. Then $(x\ M_1\ ...\ M_n) \in SN$.*

Proof. We prove a more general result: Let $M_1, ..., M_n$ be terms and $\sigma_1, ..., \sigma_n$ be in Σ_x. If $M_1[\sigma_1]$, ..., $M_n[\sigma_n] \in SN$, then $(x\ M_1[\sigma_1]\ ...\ M_n[\sigma_n]) \in SN$. The proof is done exactly as in theorem 10 using lemmas 24, 25 and 26. □

6 Future Work

- Parigot has introduced other simplification rules in the $\lambda\mu$-calculus. They are as follows : $(\alpha\ \mu\beta M) \rightarrow_\rho M[\beta := \alpha]$ and, if α is not free in M, $\mu\alpha(\alpha\ M) \rightarrow_\theta M$. It would be interesting to extend our proofs to these reductions. The rule θ causes no problem since it is strongly normalizing and it is easy to see that this rule can be postponed (i.e. if $M \rightarrow^*_{\beta\mu\mu'\rho\theta} M_1$ then $M \rightarrow^*_{\beta\mu\mu'\rho} M_2 \rightarrow^*_\theta M_1$

for some M_2). However it is not the same for the rule ρ which cannot be postponed. Moreover a basic property (if $M[\alpha =_s N] \triangleright^* \mu\beta P$, then $M \triangleright^* \mu\beta Q$ for some Q such that $Q[\alpha =_s N] \triangleright^* P$) used in the proofs is no more true if the ρ-rule is used. It seems that, in this case, the μ can only come either from M or from N i.e. without deep interaction between M and N and thus that our proofs can be extended to this case but, due to the lack of time, we have not been able to check the details.
- We believe that our technique, will allow to give explicit bounds for the length of the reductions of a typed term. This is a goal we will try to manage.

References

1. F. Barbanera and S. Berardi. *A symmetric lambda-calculus for classical program extraction.* In M. Hagiya and J.C. Mitchell, editors, Proceedings of theoretical aspects of computer software, TACS'94. LNCS (789), pp. 495-515. Springer Verlag, 1994.
2. R. Constable and C. Murthy. *Finding computational content in classical proofs.* In G. Huet and G. Plotkin, editors, Logical Frameworks, pp. 341-362, Cambridge University Press, 1991.
3. P.L. Curien and H. Herbelin. *The Duality of Computation.* Proc. International Conference on Functional Programming, September 2000, Montral, IEEE, 2000.
4. J.-Y. Girard. *A new constructive logic: classical logic.* MSCS (1), pp. 255-296, 1991.
5. P. de Groote. *A CPS-translation of the lambda-mu-calculus.* In S. Tison, editor, 19th International Colloquium on Trees in Algebra and Programming, CAAP'94, volume 787 of Lecture Notes in Computer Science, pp 85-99. Springer, 1994.
6. P. de Groote. *A simple calculus of exception handling.* In M. Dezani and G. Plotkin, editors, Second International Conference on Typed Lambda Calculi and Applications, TLCA'95, volume 902 of Lecture Notes in Computer Science, pp. 201-215. Springer, 1995.
7. R. David. *Normalization without reducibility.* Annals of Pure and Applied Logic (107), pp. 121-130, 2001.
8. R. David and K. Nour. *A short proof of the strong normalization of the simply typed $\lambda\mu$-calculus.* Schedae Informaticae n12, pp. 27-34, 2003.
9. R. David and K. Nour. *A short proof of the strong normalization of classical natural deduction with disjunction.* The Journal of Symbolic Logic n 68.4, pp. 1277 - 1288, 2003.
10. R. David and K. Nour. *Why the usual candidates of reducibility do not work for the symetric $\lambda\mu$-calculus.* To appear in ENTCS (2005).
11. R. David and K. Nour. *Arithmetical proofs of the strong normalization of the $\overline{\lambda}\mu\tilde{\mu}$-calculus.* Manuscript 2004.
12. J.-L. Krivine. *Classical logic, storage operators and 2nd order lambda-calculus.* Annals of Pure and Applied Logic (68), pp. 53-78, 1994.
13. C.R. Murthy. *An evaluation semantics for classical proofs.* In Proceedings of the sixth annual IEEE symposium on logic in computer science, pp. 96-107, 1991.
14. K. Nour. *La valeur d'un entier classique en $\lambda\mu$-calcul.* Archive for Mathematical Logic (36), pp. 461-471, 1997.
15. K. Nour. *A non-deterministic classical logic (the $\lambda\mu^{++}$-calculus).* Mathematical Logic Quarterly (48), pp. 357 - 366, 2002.

16. K. Nour and K. Saber. *A semantical proof of the strong normalization theorem of full propositionnal classical natural deduction.* Manuscript (2004).
17. M. Parigot. *Free Deduction: An Analysis of "Computations" in Classical Logic.* Proceedings. Lecture Notes in Computer Science, Vol. 592, Springer, pp. 361-380, 1992.
18. M. Parigot. *$\lambda\mu$-calculus: An algorithm interpretation of classical natural deduction.* Lecture Notes in Artificial Intelligence (624), pp. 190-201. Springer Verlag, 1992.
19. M. Parigot. *Strong normalization for second order classical natural deduction.* In Proceedings, Eighth Annual IEEE Symposium on Logic in Computer Science, pp. 39-46, Montreal, Canada, 19–23 June 1993. IEEE Computer Society Press.
20. M. Parigot. *Classical proofs as programs.* In G. Gottlob, A. Leitsch, and D. Mundici, eds., Proc. of 3rd Kurt Godel Colloquium, KGC'93, vol. 713 of Lecture Notes in Computer Science, pp. 263-276. Springer-Verlag, 1993.
21. M. Parigot. *Proofs of strong normalization for second order classical natural deduction.* Journal of Symbolic Logic, 62 (4), pp. 1461-1479, 1997.
22. E. Polonovsky. *Substitutions explicites, logique et normalisation.* PhD thesis. Paris 7, 2004.
23. W. Py. *Confluence en $\lambda\mu$-calcul.* PhD thesis. University of Chambéry, 1998.
24. N.J. Rehof and M.H. Sørensen. *The λ_Δ-calculus.* In M. Hagiya and J.C. Mitchell, editors, Proceedings of the international symposium on theoretical aspects of computer software, TACS'94, LNCS (789), pp. 516-542. Springer Verlag, 1994.
25. Y. Yamagata. *Strong Normalization of Second Order Symmetric Lambda-mu Calculus.* TACS 2001, Lecture Notes in Computer Science 2215, pp. 459-467, 2001.

Subtyping Recursive Types Modulo Associative Commutative Products

Roberto Di Cosmo[1], François Pottier[2], and Didier Rémy[2]

[1] Université Paris 7
roberto@dicosmo.org
[2] INRIA Rocquencourt
{Francois.Pottier, Didier.Remy}@inria.fr

Abstract. This work sets the formal bases for building tools that help retrieve classes in object-oriented libraries. In such systems, the user provides a query, formulated as a set of class interfaces. The tool returns classes in the library that can be used to implement the user's request and automatically builds the required glue code. We propose subtyping of recursive types in the presence of associative and commutative products—that is, subtyping modulo a restricted form of type isomorphisms—as a model of the relation that exists between the user's query and the tool's answers. We show that this relation is a composition of the standard subtyping relation with equality up to associativity and commutativity of products and we present an efficient decision algorithm for it. We also provide an automatic way of constructing coercions between related types.

1 Introduction

The study of type isomorphisms is concerned with identifying data types by abstracting away from irrelevant details in the syntax of types, or—in other words—irrelevant choices in the representation of data. The basic idea is quite simple: one wishes to identify two data types if data of one type can be transformed into data of the other type without loss of information. Formally speaking, τ_1 and τ_2 are said to be isomorphic if and only if there exist functions $f : \tau_1 \rightarrow \tau_2$ and $g : \tau_2 \rightarrow \tau_1$ that are mutual inverses, in the sense that they make the following diagram commute:

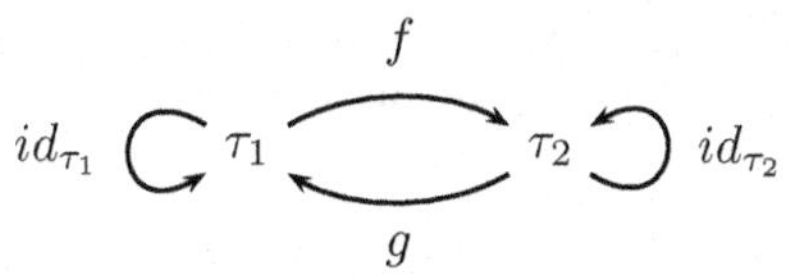

This study has wide ramifications in different research fields, ranging from number theory to category theory, and from λ-calculus to proof theory [14]. In particular, it helps attack some of the problems raised by the growing complexity of today's multi-language code bases. Indeed, the vast majority of currently available search tools suffer from the fact that they only allow *textual* searches of libraries for method or function *names*, while such names are largely arbitrary. An interesting instance of this phenomenon is the ubiquity of the *fold* identifier in ML-like languages, pointed out by Rittri [20].

P. Urzyczyn (Ed.): TLCA 2005, LNCS 3461, pp. 179–193, 2005.

The key idea behind the use of type isomorphisms in information retrieval is to forget about names altogether and to rely on *types* instead. Indeed, a type provides a (possibly partial) specification of a component. Of course, types must be equated up to type isomorphisms, so as to make queries robust against arbitrary choices on the library implementor's part. *Which* type isomorphisms to use depends on the type system, the programming language, and the observational equivalence at hand. A large variety of complete equational theories are known that axiomatize type isomorphisms in various core calculi. Probably best known is the theory of isomorphisms for Cartesian Closed Categories—the models of the simply-typed lambda calculus with products and a unit type [23, 10]:

$$\begin{array}{llll} 1. & \tau \times \tau' = \tau' \times \tau & 5. & \tau \times 1 = \tau \\ 2. & \tau \times (\tau' \times \tau'') = (\tau \times \tau') \times \tau'' & 6. & \tau \to 1 = 1 \\ 3. & (\tau \times \tau') \to \tau'' = \tau \to (\tau' \to \tau'') & 7. & 1 \to \tau = \tau \\ 4. & \tau \to (\tau' \times \tau'') = (\tau \to \tau') \times (\tau \to \tau'') & & \end{array}$$

The type isomorphisms-based approach can help in retrieving complex software components from large libraries of functions [13, 21, 22] or modules [25, 3] and in automatically producing bridge code between different representations of a (possibly recursive) data type in systems like Mockingbird [5, 6]. These active areas are currently attracting the attention of many researchers. Unfortunately, the general problem of characterizing isomorphic types for a full-fledged type system, including sums, products, polymorphic and recursive types—such as that underlying Mockingbird [4, 8]—is extremely complex and remains open; there are, in particular, difficulties with recursive types [1] and with sum types [7]. In view of this difficulty, Jha, Palsberg, and Zhao [19, 18] proposed to study a weak approximation of isomorphisms of recursive types, obtained by viewing products as associative and commutative, which we refer to as AC-equality. This relation may be decided in time $O(N \log N)$, where N is the sum of the sizes of the input types. (The same time bound was obtained by Downey, Sethi and Tarjan [15] for the closely related problem of *symmetric congruence closure*.) AC-equality captures a lot of the inessential syntactic details one wants to get rid of when querying a library. Jha *et al.* propose to view a collection of Java interface declarations as a collection of types, using arrow types to encode method signatures and n-ary products to encode collections of methods or method parameters. Of course, the types thus obtained are recursive, because Java interface declarations may mutually refer to one another. For instance, the Java interfaces:

```
interface I1 {                 interface I2 {
  float m1 (I1 a);               I1 m3 (float a);
    int m2 (I2 a);               I2 m4 (float a);
}                              }
```

may be encoded (forgetting method names) as the mutually recursive types $I_1 = (I_1 \to \mathit{float}) \times (I_2 \to \mathit{int})$ and $I_2 = (\mathit{float} \to I_1) \times (\mathit{float} \to I_2)$. Thus, the notion of AC-equality of recursive types gives rise to a notion of equivalence between (collections of) Java interfaces.

However, AC-equality is not the right relation on types for searching libraries. As noted by Thatté [24], when querying a complex object-oriented library, the actual type of the desired class or interface may be extremely complex, because it lists *all* of (the types of) its methods. As a result, it is not reasonable to require the query (that is, the type provided by the user) to be AC-*equal* to the actual type. Indeed, the user would have to guess the list of (the types of) *all* methods in the class. It is more realistic to allow the user to formulate a query that is only a *supertype* of the actual type, so for instance, a user looking for a collection implementation may formulate the query:

```
public interface SomeCollection {
  public void    add (Object o);
  public void    remove (Object o);
  public boolean contains (Object o);
  public int     size ();
}
```

In the Java standard library, the `Collection` interface has 15 methods. As a result, every class that implements it has at least 15 methods as well, which means that *no* match will be found for this query if types are compared up to AC-equality. The purpose of this paper is to introduce a notion of AC-*subtyping* defined so that the `Collection` interface is an AC-*subtype* of this query. Furthermore, even such a simple notion of isomorphism of recursive types can give rise to very complex conversion functions. As a result, it is quite unrealistic to expect that a user could be satisfied with a mere *true* or *false* answer. A practical search system must be able to generate code for converting between the search result and the search query, as already advocated by Thatté [24].

In this paper, we pursue Thatté's seminal work and give an efficient subtyping algorithm modulo AC for a core language with products, arrows, and recursive types. The algorithm also produces coercion code when it succeeds. We believe that when the language is extended to cover a class-based object-oriented language such as Java, our algorithm could be combined with ideas from Thatté to synthesize adapters for existing classes.

The paper is laid out as follows. §2 gives a comparison with related work and an overview of our results. In §3, we recall a few basic notions about recursive types, as well as Palsberg and Zhao's notion of equality up to associativity and commutativity of products [19]. In §4, we introduce the notion of AC-subtyping and prove that it is a composition of the usual subtyping relation with AC-equality. Then, in §5, we describe an algorithm that decides whether two types are in the subtyping relation modulo associativity and commutativity of products. We establish its correctness and assess its time complexity. In §6, we discuss how to generate code for coercion functions. Throughout the paper, we consider recursive types built out of arrows, products, and the constants $\bot$ and $\top$. In §7, we argue that this simple setting is general enough.

2 Related Work and Overview of Our Results

Two main lines of work are closely related to ours. To our knowledge, Thatté is the first to have put forth a relaxed form of subtyping between recursive types as a model of object-oriented retrieval tools [24]. Without relating to Thatté's work, Palsberg *et al.* have studied efficient algorithms to solve AC-equality of recursive types [19, 18].

By comparison with Thatté's work, we have taken a more foundational approach by working directly with recursive types. We also use co-inductive techniques—which were not yet popular at the time of Thatté's work—to provide an efficient, deterministic decision algorithm that improves over his exponential algorithm (essentially a variant of Amadio and Cardelli's original subtyping algorithm). However, some work remains to be done to specialize our results to classed-based languages and build "adapters", in Thatté's terminology, out of our coercions.

Technically, our co-inductive algorithms share a common ground with the work of Palsberg *et al.* on AC-equality [19]. Indeed, co-induction is a most natural tool for reasoning about recursive types. Unfortunately, many of the well-known algorithmic optimizations (inspired by classic foundational work on finite automata) that are applicable when dealing with equivalence relations [19, 18] break down when dealing with an ordering. This is very well explained by Jha *et al.* [18–Section 6], who describe AC-subtyping, but quickly dismiss it as not amenable to the optimizations used for AC-equality. The authors state that this relation is decidable, but make no effort to give a tight complexity bound or describe an actual decision algorithm. Yet, a naive generalization of Palsberg and Zhao's ideas [19] to the setting of AC-subtyping—as opposed to AC-equality—already leads to a decision procedure whose worst-case time complexity is $O(n^2n'^2d^{5/2})$ (1), where n and n' count the sub-terms of the types that are being compared and d is a bound on the arity of the products involved.

The naive procedure starts from the full relation—a graph with $O(nn')$ edges—and repeatedly removes edges that are found not to be in the AC-subtyping relation. Because it might be necessary to inspect all edges in order to remove only one of them, and because, in the worst case, all edges have to be removed, the procedure might require $O(n^2n'^2)$ edge inspections, each of which happens to require time $O(d^{5/2})$ in the worst case.

In this paper, we improve on this naive procedure by a careful choice of the *order* in which edges must be inspected. The worst-case time complexity of our improved algorithm may be bounded by (1), which shows that it performs no worse than the naive procedure. It may also be bounded by $O(NN'd^{5/2})$ (2), where N and N' are the sizes of the types that are being compared. In practice, N and N' might be significantly less than n^2 and n'^2, respectively. Furthermore, we show that, if the types at hand are not recursive (that is, do not involve cycles), then our algorithm runs in time $O(nn'd^{5/2})$ (3). One may expect the algorithm's performance to degrade gracefully when the types at hand involve few cycles. Last, in §5, we give worst-case complexity bounds analogous to (2) and (3), but where the quantities $O(NN')$ and $O(nn')$ are replaced with the size of a certain graph. Intuition suggests that, in practice, the size of this graph might be significantly less than quadratic. For all these reasons, we expect our algorithm to perform well in practice, whereas an implementation of the naive algorithm would not be realistic—even though, in rare cases, both algorithms may require the same amount of computation.

A mild difference with Palsberg and Zhao [19] is that we allow products to be immediately nested. Indeed, our definition of AC-equality and AC-subtyping is such that flattening nested products is *not* part of equality. That is, if we write $(\tau_1 \times \ldots \times \tau_n)$ for $\Pi_{i=1}^n \tau_i$, then the types $(\tau_1 \times \tau_2 \times \tau_3)$ and $(\tau_1 \times (\tau_2 \times \tau_3))$ are *not* AC-related. If one wishes that these types be identified, one can preprocess the input types by flattening nested products before running our algorithm. (Of course, this is possible only in the absence of infinite products, but this restriction makes practical sense, since "flat" infinite products cannot exist in memory.) However, there are situations where we want to keep these types distinct. For example, products representing persistent database information may be kept nested, as stored on disk, while products used for passing arguments to functions may be flattened.

To sum up, we feel our work is more in line with Thatté's, in that we want to provide a formal basis for *actual* search tools, that need AC-subtyping and the automatic synthesis of the coercions, even if this means giving up the algorithmic optimizations that make deciding an equivalence relation more efficient. Still, identifying types up to AC-equality may remain useful as a preprocessing phase, in order to decrease the number of nodes in the problem that is submitted to the AC-subtyping algorithm.

3 Recursive Types

Recursive types are usually given in concrete syntax as finite systems of contractive type equations, which, according to Courcelle [12], uniquely define regular trees; or as finite terms involving μ binders [16]. The process of unfolding these finite representations gives rise to regular infinite trees.

Definition 1 (Signature). A *signature* is a mapping from *symbols*, written s, to integer *arities*. In this paper, we consider a fixed signature, which consists of a binary symbol $\rightarrow$, a n-ary symbol Π^n for every nonnegative integer n, and the constant symbols $\bot$ and $\top$. ◇

Definition 2 (Path, tree, type). A *path* p is a finite sequence of integers. The empty path is written ϵ and the concatenation of the paths p and p' is written $p \cdot p'$. A *tree* is a partial function τ from paths to symbols whose domain is nonempty and prefix-closed and such that, for every path p in the domain of τ, $p \cdot i \in dom(\tau)$ holds if and only if i is comprised between 1 and the arity of the symbol $\tau(p)$, inclusive. If p is in the domain of τ, then the *subtree* of τ rooted at p, written τ/p, is the partial function $p' \mapsto \tau(p \cdot p')$. A tree is *regular* if and only if it has a finite number of distinct subtrees. (Every finite tree is thus regular.) A *recursive type* (or *type* for short) is a regular tree. We write $\mathcal{T}$ for the set of all types. We write $\bot$ (resp. $\top$) for the tree that maps ϵ to $\bot$ (resp. $\top$). We write $\tau_1 \rightarrow \tau_2$ for the tree that maps ϵ to $\rightarrow$ and whose subtrees rooted at 1 and 2 are τ_1 and τ_2, respectively. We write $\Pi_{i=1}^n \tau_i$ for the tree that maps ϵ to Π^n and whose subtree rooted at i is τ_i for every $i \in \{1, \ldots, n\}$. ◇

There are many ways to present equality of recursive types, ranging from traditional definitions based on finite approximations [2] to more modern co-inductive approaches [9, 11]. Following Brandt and Henglein, we reason in terms of simulations.

Definition 3 (Equality). A binary relation $\mathcal{R} \subseteq \mathcal{T}^2$ is a $=$*-simulation* if and only if it satisfies the following implications:

$$\text{EQ-TOP}\quad \frac{\tau\ \mathcal{R}\ \tau'}{\tau(\epsilon) = \tau'(\epsilon)} \qquad \text{EQ-ARROW}\quad \frac{\tau_1 \rightarrow \tau_2\ \mathcal{R}\ \tau_1' \rightarrow \tau_2'}{\tau_1\ \mathcal{R}\ \tau_1' \qquad \tau_2\ \mathcal{R}\ \tau_2'} \qquad \text{EQ-PI}\quad \frac{\Pi_{i=1}^n \tau_i\ \mathcal{R}\ \Pi_{i=1}^n \tau_i'}{(\tau_i\ \mathcal{R}\ \tau_i')^{i \in \{1,\ldots,n\}}}$$

Equality $=$ is the largest $=$-simulation. ◇

Palsberg and Zhao [19] define equality up to associativity and commutativity of products as follows; see also Downey *et al.* [15–section 4.1]. We write Σ_n^m for the set of all injective mappings from $\{1,\ldots,m\}$ into $\{1,\ldots,n\}$. In particular, Σ_n^n is the set of all permutations of $\{1,\ldots,n\}$.

Definition 4 (AC-Equality). A binary relation $\mathcal{R} \subseteq \mathcal{T}^2$ is a $=_{AC}$-*simulation* if and only if it satisfies the following implications:

$$\textsc{EqAC-Top}\ \frac{\tau \mathrel{\mathcal{R}} \tau'}{\tau(\epsilon) = \tau'(\epsilon)} \qquad \textsc{EqAC-Arrow}\ \frac{\tau_1 \to \tau_2 \mathrel{\mathcal{R}} \tau_1' \to \tau_2'}{\tau_1 \mathrel{\mathcal{R}} \tau_1' \qquad \tau_2 \mathrel{\mathcal{R}} \tau_2'} \qquad \textsc{EqAC-Pi}\ \frac{\Pi_{i=1}^n \tau_i \mathrel{\mathcal{R}} \Pi_{i=1}^n \tau_i'}{\exists \sigma \in \Sigma_n^n \quad (\tau_{\sigma(i)} \mathrel{\mathcal{R}} \tau_i')^{i \in \{1,\ldots,n\}}}$$

AC-Equality $=_{AC}$ is the largest $=_{AC}$-simulation. ◇

Note that a product one of whose components is itself a product is not considered AC-equal to the corresponding "flattened" product. We come back to this point in §7.

4 Subtyping and AC-Subtyping

In this section, we define subtyping of recursive types up to associativity and commutativity of products, and show that it is precisely a composition of the usual subtyping relation with equality up to associativity and commutativity of products.

Let us first define subtyping between recursive types. This requires extending the standard definition of subtyping from the case of binary products [9] to that of n-ary products.

Definition 5 (Subtyping). Let $\leq_0$ be the ordering on symbols generated by the rules:

$$\bot \leq_0 s \qquad s \leq_0 \top \qquad \to\, \leq_0\, \to \qquad \frac{n \geq m}{\Pi^n \leq_0 \Pi^m}$$

A binary relation $\mathcal{R} \subseteq \mathcal{T}^2$ is a $\leq$-*simulation* if and only if it satisfies the following implications:

$$\textsc{Sub-Top}\ \frac{\tau_1 \mathrel{\mathcal{R}} \tau_2}{\tau_1(\epsilon) \leq_0 \tau_2(\epsilon)} \qquad \textsc{Sub-Arrow}\ \frac{\tau_1 \to \tau_2 \mathrel{\mathcal{R}} \tau_1' \to \tau_2'}{\tau_1' \mathrel{\mathcal{R}} \tau_1 \qquad \tau_2 \mathrel{\mathcal{R}} \tau_2'} \qquad \textsc{Sub-Pi}\ \frac{\Pi_{i=1}^n \tau_i \mathrel{\mathcal{R}} \Pi_{i=1}^m \tau_i'}{(\tau_i \mathrel{\mathcal{R}} \tau_i')^{i \in \{1,\ldots,m\}}}$$

Subtyping $\leq$ is the largest $\leq$-simulation. ◇

This definition allows *depth* and *width* subtyping. Depth subtyping refers to the covariance of products. Width subtyping refers to the fact that a product with more components may be a subtype of a product with fewer components. Enabling width subtyping better suits our intended applications. Furthermore, it is possible, if desired, to introduce a distinct family of product constructors, which forbid width subtyping; see §7.

We now define subtyping of recursive types up to associativity and commutativity of products. Its definition relaxes Definition 5 by allowing the components of a product to be arbitrarily permuted. It is given in a slightly generalized style, introducing the notion of simulation *up to* a relation; this helps state the algorithm's invariant in §5.2.

Definition 6 (AC-Subtyping). Let $\mathcal{R} \subseteq \mathcal{T}^2$ and $\mathcal{R}' \subseteq \mathcal{T}^2$ be binary relations. $\mathcal{R}$ is a $\leq_{AC}$*-simulation up to* $\mathcal{R}'$ if and only if the following implications are satisfied:

SUBAC-TOP
$$\frac{\tau_1 \;\mathcal{R}\; \tau_2}{\tau_1(\epsilon) \leq_0 \tau_2(\epsilon)}$$

SUBAC-ARROW
$$\frac{\tau_1 \rightarrow \tau_2 \;\mathcal{R}\; \tau_1' \rightarrow \tau_2'}{\tau_1' \; (\mathcal{R} \cup \mathcal{R}') \; \tau_1 \qquad \tau_2 \; (\mathcal{R} \cup \mathcal{R}') \; \tau_2'}$$

SUBAC-PI
$$\frac{\Pi_{i=1}^{n} \tau_i \;\mathcal{R}\; \Pi_{i=1}^{m} \tau_i'}{\exists \sigma \in \Sigma_n^m \quad (\tau_{\sigma(i)} \; (\mathcal{R} \cup \mathcal{R}') \; \tau_i')^{i \in \{1,\ldots,m\}}}$$

$\mathcal{R}$ is a $\leq_{AC}$*-simulation* if and only if it is a $\leq_{AC}$-simulation up to the empty relation. *AC-Subtyping* $\leq_{AC}$ is the largest $\leq_{AC}$-simulation. ◇

It is known that $=_{AC}$ is a congruence and $\leq$ is an ordering. We show that $\leq_{AC}$ is a preorder, that is, it is reflexive and transitive.

Proposition 7. $\leq_{AC}$ *is a preorder.* ◇

We argue that our definition of subtyping modulo associativity and commutativity of products is natural by establishing that it is a composition of the pre-existing relations $=_{AC}$ and $\leq$. One may hope to prove that $\leq_{AC}$ coincides with $=_{AC} \circ \leq$. However, this does not hold, because the contravariance of the arrow symbol forces $=_{AC}$ to be used on both sides of $\leq$. This is illustrated by the pair $(\Pi^1(\top) \rightarrow \Pi^2(\bot, \top),\ \Pi^2(\bot, \top) \rightarrow \Pi^1(\top))$, which is a member of $\leq_{AC}$, but not a member of $=_{AC} \circ \leq$ or of $\leq \circ =_{AC}$. As a result, $=_{AC}$ must in fact be used on both sides of $\leq$, as stated below.

Theorem 8. *The relations* $\leq_{AC}$ *and* $(=_{AC}) \circ (\leq) \circ (=_{AC})$ *coincide.* ◇

5 Deciding AC-Subtyping

Let us say that a pair of types $p = (\tau, \tau')$ is *valid* if $\tau \leq_{AC} \tau'$ holds and *invalid* otherwise. We now define an algorithm that, given a pair of types $p_0 = (\tau_0, \tau_0')$, determines whether p_0 is valid.

The algorithm's complexity is assessed as a function of the following parameters. Let T and T' be the sets of all subtrees of τ_0 and τ_0', respectively. Let n and n' be the cardinalities of these sets; they are finite. Let us view T and T' as directed graphs, where every tree is a node and there is an edge from τ to τ' labeled i if and only if τ/i is τ'. In other words, there is an edge from every tree to each of its immediate subtrees. Please note that there may be multiple edges, with distinct labels, between τ and τ'. If τ is a node in T or T', let $d(\tau)$ denote its outgoing degree, that is, the arity of the symbol $\tau(\epsilon)$. Let $u(\tau)$ denote its incoming degree, that is, the number of its predecessors in the graph T or T'. We write d for the maximum of $d(\tau)$ when τ ranges over all nodes in T and T'. Last, let N (resp. N') be the *size* of the graph T (resp. T'), where every node and every edge contributes one unit. Please note that we have: $N = \Sigma_{\tau \in T}(1 + u(\tau))$ as well as a similar identity concerning T'.

The algorithm maintains sets of pairs of nodes. We assume that elementary set operations can be performed in constant time. This is indeed possible by using an array of size $O(nn')$, or, more realistically, a hash table.

5.1 First Phase: Exploration

Specification. The first phase of the algorithm consists in constructing a (finite) set U of pairs of types whose validity one must determine in order to be able to tell whether p_0 is valid. The universe U may be defined as the smallest set that contains p_0 and is closed under the following two rules:

$$\textsc{Explore-Arrow}\quad \frac{(\tau_1 \to \tau_2, \tau_1' \to \tau_2') \in U}{(\tau_1', \tau_1) \in U \qquad (\tau_2, \tau_2') \in U} \qquad\qquad \textsc{Explore-Pi}\quad \frac{(\Pi_{i=1}^n \tau_i, \Pi_{j=1}^m \tau_j') \in U}{((\tau_i, \tau_j') \in U)^{i \in \{1,\ldots,n\},\, j \in \{1,\ldots,m\}}}$$

The set $(T \times T') \cup (T' \times T)$ contains p_0 and is closed under these rules. This ensures that U exists and has cardinality $O(nn')$.

We have explained above how to view T and T' as graphs. It is useful to view $(T \times T') \cup (T' \times T)$ as a graph as well. Let there be an (unlabeled) edge from a pair of types p to a pair of types p' if p matches the premise of Explore-Arrow or Explore-Pi while p' matches one of its conclusions. In that case, we also say that p is a *parent* of p'. Then, the exploration phase can be viewed simply as an explicit traversal (and construction) of *part of* the graph $(T \times T') \cup (T' \times T)$, starting from the node p_0. In other words, U is the connected component of p_0 in the directed graph $(T \times T') \cup (T' \times T)$.

The number of nodes in the graph U is clearly bounded by $O(nn')$. Because U is an unlabeled graph, the number of its edges must be bounded by $O(n^2 n'^2)$. This yields $\mathit{size}(U) \leq O(n^2 n'^2)$. Furthermore, because the predecessors of a pair (τ, τ') are pairs of a predecessor of τ and a predecessor of τ', we have $u(\tau, \tau') \leq u(\tau)u(\tau')$. This yields another bound on the size of the graph U:

$$\begin{aligned} \mathit{size}(U) = \Sigma_{(\tau,\tau') \in U}(1 + u(\tau, \tau')) &\leq \Sigma_{\tau \in T,\, \tau' \in T'}(1 + u(\tau)u(\tau')) \\ &\leq (\Sigma_{\tau \in T}(1 + u(\tau)))(\Sigma_{\tau' \in T'}(1 + u(\tau'))) = NN' \end{aligned}$$

In practice, we expect both of these bounds to be pessimistic. In the particular case where the types at hand are not recursive (that is, do not involve cycles) and do not involve any products, the size of U may be bounded by $\min(N, N')$. There is a lot of slack between this optimistic bound and the worst-case bounds given above. It should be interesting to measure the size of U in real-world situations.

Implementation. The graph U can be computed using a simple iterative procedure, as follows.

1. Let $U = \emptyset$ and $W = \{p_0\}$.
2. While W is nonempty, do:
   (a) Take a pair p out of W;
   (b) If $p \in U$, continue at 2;
   (c) Insert p into U;
   (d) If p is of the form $(\tau_1 \to \tau_2, \tau_1' \to \tau_2')$, then insert (τ_1', τ_1) and (τ_2, τ_2') into W;
   (e) If p is of the form $(\Pi_{i=1}^n \tau_i, \Pi_{j=1}^m \tau_j')$,
   then insert every (τ_i, τ_j'), for $i \in \{1, \ldots, n\}$ and $j \in \{1, \ldots, m\}$, into W.

It is clear that this procedure implements the construction of U as specified above. In step 2e, one should remove any duplicate elements from the families $(\tau_i)_{i=1}^n$ and $(\tau_j')_{j=1}^m$ prior to iterating over them. Then, this procedure runs in time $O(\mathit{size}(U)d)$. It is dominated by the running time of the second phase.

5.2 Second Phase: Fixpoint Computation

The idea behind the second phase of the algorithm is to determine the greatest subset of U that is a $\leq_{AC}$-simulation, then to check whether p_0 is a member of it. In order to build this subset, we start from the full relation U, and successively remove pairs that violate SUBAC-TOP, SUBAC-ARROW or SUBAC-PI, until we reach a fixpoint. Whether a pair violates SUBAC-TOP or SUBAC-ARROW may be determined in constant time. However, in the case of SUBAC-PI, the check requires solving a matching problem in a bipartite graph, whose time complexity may be bounded by $O(d^{5/2})$, as we shall see.

A naive procedure begins by iterating once over all pairs, removing those that violate one of the rules; this takes time $O(nn'd^{5/2})$. But one such iteration may not be enough to reach the fixpoint, so the naive procedure repeats this step as many times as required. In the worst case, each step invalidates only one pair, in which case up to $O(nn')$ successive steps are required. Thus, the overall time complexity is $O(n^2n'^2d^{5/2})$. Below, we propose an enhanced approach, whose convergence is faster. Instead of blindly checking every pair at each iteration, we check only the *parents* of pairs that have just been invalidated. Downey, Sethi, and Tarjan exploit the same idea to accelerate the convergence of their congruence closure algorithm [15].

Description. The universe U is now fixed. We maintain three sets W, S, and F, which form a partition of U. The set W is a *worklist* and consists of pairs whose validity remains to be determined. The set S consists of *suspended* pairs, which are conditionally valid: the algorithm maintains the invariant that S is a $\leq_{AC}$-simulation up to W. In other words, a pair S is known to be valid *provided* its (indirect) descendants in W are found to be valid as well. The set F consists of known invalid (*false*) pairs.

When a pair p is found to be invalid, it is moved to the set F and all (if any) of its parents within S are transferred to W for examination. We refer to this auxiliary procedure as *invalidating* p. The time complexity of this procedure is $O(1 + u(p))$, where $u(p)$ is the incoming degree of the pair p in the graph U (see §5.1).

The second phase of the algorithm is as follows.

1. Let $W = U$ and $S = F = \emptyset$.
2. While W is nonempty, do:
   (a) Take a pair p out of W;
   (b) If p is of the form $(\bot, \tau')$ or $(\tau, \top)$, then insert p into S;
   (c) If p is of the form $(\tau_1 \to \tau_2, \tau_1' \to \tau_2')$, then
   if $(\tau_1', \tau_1) \notin F$ and $(\tau_2, \tau_2') \notin F$ then insert p into S else invalidate p;
   (d) If p is of the form $(\Pi_{i=1}^n \tau_i, \Pi_{j=1}^m \tau_j')$, then
   if there exists $\sigma \in \Sigma_n^m$ such that, for all $j \in \{1, \dots, m\}$, $(\tau_{\sigma(j)}, \tau_j') \notin F$ holds, then insert p into S else invalidate p;
   (e) If p satisfied none of the three previous tests, then invalidate p.
3. If $p_0 \notin F$, return *true*, otherwise return *false*.

Correctness. Each iteration of the main loop (step 2) takes a pair p out of W and either inserts it into S or invalidates it. In either case, it is clear that (W, S, F) remains a partition of U.

Let us now check that S remains a $\leq_{AC}$-simulation up to W. If the pair p is inserted into S, then p satisfies SUBAC-TOP, and there exist pairs in $W \cup S$ (that is, outside F)

whose validity is sufficient for p to satisfy SUBAC-ARROW or SUBAC-PI. So, the invariant is preserved. If, on the other hand, the pair p is invalidated, then all of its parents within S are transferred back to W, which clearly preserves the invariant as well.

Last, let us check that F remains a set of invalid pairs only. If the pair p is invalidated at step 2c, then p is invalid, for otherwise, by SUBAC-ARROW, the pairs (τ_1', τ_1) and (τ_2, τ_2') would be valid—but these pairs are members of F, a contradiction. Because p is invalid, inserting it into F preserves the invariant. If the pair p is invalidated at steps 2d or 2e, then p may be shown invalid analogously, using SUBAC-PI or SUBAC-TOP.

When the algorithm terminates, W is empty, so S is a $\leq_{AC}$-simulation, which implies that every member of S is valid. On the other hand, every member of F is invalid. We have established that the result returned in step 3 is correct, as stated below:

Theorem 9. *If the algorithm returns true, then $\tau_0 \leq_{AC} \tau_0'$ holds. If the algorithm returns false, then $\tau_0 \leq_{AC} \tau_0'$ does not hold.* ◇

Termination and Complexity. Invalidating a pair transfers it from W to F. Because pairs are never taken out of F, and because W and F remain disjoint, no pair is ever invalidated twice.

The initial size of W is the number of nodes in U. Furthermore, when a pair p is invalidated, the size of W increases by $u(p)$. Thus, considering that every pair is invalidated at most once, the total number of pairs that are ever taken out of W—that is, the total number of iterations of step 2—is at most

$$(\Sigma_{p \in U} 1) + (\Sigma_{p \in U} u(p)) = \Sigma_{p \in U}(1 + u(p)) \;=\; \mathit{size}(U)$$

Let us now estimate the cost of a single iteration of step 2. In step 2d, determining whether an appropriate σ exists is a matching problem in a bipartite graph with at most $2d$ nodes and d^2 edges. Such a problem can be solved in time $O(d^{5/2})$ using Hopcroft and Karp's algorithm [17]. The cost of invalidating a pair may be viewed as $O(1)$ if we consider that the price for transferring a parent from S to W is paid when that parent is later examined. Thus, the (amortized) cost of a single iteration of step 2 is $O(d^{5/2})$.

Combining these results, we find that the second phase of the algorithm runs in time $O(\mathit{size}(U)d^{5/2})$. This is more expensive that the first phase, so we may state

Theorem 10. *The algorithm runs in time $O(\mathit{size}(U)d^{5/2})$, which is bounded both by $O(NN'd^{5/2})$ and $O(n^2n'^2d^{5/2})$.* ◇

As explained in §5.1, the size of the graph U might be significantly smaller, in practice, than either of NN' and $O(n^2n'^2)$, which is why we give the first complexity bound. The second bound shows that, in the worst case, the algorithm remains linear in each of the sizes of the input types, namely N and N', with additional overhead $O(d^{5/2})$, where d is a bound on the arity of the products involved. The third bound shows that our improved algorithm performs no worse than the naive procedure outlined in §1 and §5.2.

For comparison, Downey *et al.*'s symmetric congruence closure algorithm [15], as well as Jha *et al.*'s decision procedure for AC-equality [18], run in time $O((N + N')\log(N + N'))$. These algorithms compute an *equivalence* relation. This opens the way to a more efficient data representation, where a relation is not stored as a set of pairs but as a partition, and simplifies the matching problem.

5.3 Further Refinements

A cheap refinement consists in modifying the first phase so that it fails as soon as it reaches a pair p that does not satisfy SUBAC-TOP, *provided* the path from p_0 to p never leaves a pair of products—that is, provided the validity of p_0 implies that of p. This helps immediately detect some failures. For this refinement to be most effective, the paths in U where immediate failure may occur should be explored first. One way of achieving this effect is simply to give higher priority to edges that leave a pair of arrows than to edges that leave a pair of products.

A more interesting refinement consists in specifying in what order pairs should be taken out of the worklist W during the second phase. It is more efficient to deal with descendants first and with ancestors last, because dealing with an ancestor too early might be wasted work—we might decide to suspend it and later be forced to transfer it back to the worklist because new information about its descendants has been made available. Of course, because types are recursive, the relation "to be a parent of" is in general only a preorder, not an ordering—that is, the graph U may exhibit cycles.

Let us remark, though, that when U *is* acyclic, it is indeed possible to process pairs in order. This ensures that, when a pair is processed, none of its parents have been processed yet, so all of them must still be in the worklist. Thus, when invalidating a pair, it is no longer necessary to iterate over its parents. In that case, the algorithm's time complexity becomes $O(nodes(U)d^{5/2})$, where $nodes(U)$ counts the nodes of the graph U, but *not* its edges, and is bounded by $O(nn')$.

It is possible to take advantage of this remark even in the presence of cycles. The first phase, upon completion, can be made to produce an explicit representation of the graph U. Determine its strongly connected components and topologically sort them. Then, *remove all edges whose endpoints do not belong to the same component*. The cost of this additional preprocessing is linear in the size of U. Now, run the second phase, one component at a time, in topological order, that is, descendants first and ancestors last. Because of the removed edges, when invalidating a pair p, only the parents of p that belong to the *same* strongly connected component are checked. This is correct because components are being processed in topological order, which ensures that the parents of p that belong to a *distinct* component must still be in the worklist.

The modified algorithm runs in time $O(size(U')d^{5/2})$, where U' is the result of pruning the graph U, that is, of keeping only the edges that participate in a cycle. Thus, its complexity may still be bounded by $O(NN'd^{5/2})$ in the worst case, but this bound gradually decreases down to $O(nn'd^{5/2})$ in the case of nonrecursive types. We conjecture that, in practice, cycles often involve only a fraction of the type structure, so this improvement may be significant.

Searching a Whole Library. For our purposes, a software library is a collection of possibly mutually recursive types, which we may view as a single recursive type τ_L, some distinguished subterms of which form a set T_L. The programmer's query is a possibly recursive type τ_Q. The problem is to find all components in the library that provide (at least) the requested functionality, that is, to find every $\tau \in T_L$ such that $\tau \leq_{AC} \tau_Q$ holds.

One possibility is to run the algorithm with $p_0 = (\tau, \tau_Q)$ successively for every $\tau \in T_L$. However, this is inefficient. Let U_τ denote the universe explored by the algorithm when run with initial pair (τ, τ_Q). Then, the universes $(U_\tau)_{\tau \in T_L}$ might overlap, causing repeated work. It is more efficient to run the algorithm once with *multiple* initial pairs, that is, with the family of initial pairs $(\tau, \tau_Q)_{\tau \in T_L}$. Extending the algorithm to deal with a set of initial pairs $\{p_0, \ldots, p_{k-1}\}$ is immediate; it suffices to define the universe U as the smallest superset of $\{p_0, \ldots, p_{k-1}\}$ that is closed under EXPLORE-ARROW and EXPLORE-PI. By running the algorithm only once, we ensure that the worst-case time complexity is bounded by $O(NN'd^{5/2})$, where N is the size of the library τ_L and N' is the size of the query τ_Q.

In fact, running the algorithm once with a set of initial pairs $\{p_0, \ldots, p_{k-1}\}$ is equivalent to running it k times in succession, supplying the single initial pair p_i to the ith run, *provided* each run starts where the previous left off, that is, re-uses the sets U, S, F computed by the previous run. With this proviso, one may, without loss of efficiency, provide initial pairs to the algorithm one after the other.

This remark leads to an optimization. Imagine that T_L is organized as a graph, with an edge from τ to τ' if and only if $\tau \leq_{AC} \tau'$ holds. (This graph might be built during a preprocessing phase. We may assume that it is acyclic: if it isn't, cycles may be collapsed.) Then, pick a maximal node τ, that is, a node with no successors in the graph. Run the algorithm with initial pair (τ, τ_Q). If τ is found to be comparable with τ_Q, then, by transitivity of $\leq_{AC}$, so is *every predecessor* of τ in the graph. In that case, remove τ *and all of its predecessors* from the graph; otherwise, remove τ alone. Then, pick a maximal node in what remains of the graph, and proceed in the same manner. This approach offers the double advantage of being potentially more efficient and of providing successful answers in groups, where each group contains a distinguished maximal (w.r.t. $\leq_{AC}$) answer to the query and distinct groups contain incomparable answers. We believe that the user should find this behavior natural. The actual efficiency gain remains to be assessed.

One should point out that this optimization is but a simple way of exploiting the fact that $\leq_{AC}$ is transitive. One might wonder whether it is possible to exploit transitivity at the core of the algorithm: for instance, by directly inserting a pair into S, without examining its descendants, if it is a transitive consequence of the pairs that are members of S already. This issue is left for future research.

6 Building Coercions

We now discuss the coercions that witness the relation $\leq_{AC}$, and how to compute them from the simulation discovered by the algorithm, when it succeeds. We follow Brandt and Henglein's presentation [9], but work directly with regular trees, instead of using the μ notation, which allows us to make "fold" and "unfold" coercions implicit.

Definition 11 (Coercions for $\leq_{AC}$). Coercions are defined by the grammar

$$c ::= \iota_\tau \mid f \mid \mathit{fix}\ f.c \mid c \to c' \mid \Pi_i^\sigma c_i \mid \mathit{abort}_\tau \mid \mathit{discard}_\tau \qquad \diamond$$

Most coercion forms are taken from Brandt and Henglein's paper, with the same typing rules [9–figure 6]. Let us recall that a typing judgment is of the form $E \vdash c : \tau \to \tau'$, where the environment E maps coercion variables f to coercion types of the form $\tau \to \tau'$. The one new coercion form is $\Pi_i^\sigma c_i$, whose typing rule is

$$\frac{\sigma \in \Sigma_n^m \qquad (E \vdash c_i : \tau_{\sigma(i)} \to \tau_i')^{i \in \{1,\ldots,m\}}}{E \vdash \Pi_i^\sigma c_i : \Pi_{i=1}^n \tau_i \to \Pi_{i=1}^m \tau_i'}$$

and whose operational meaning is $\lambda p.\Pi_{i=1}^m c_i(\pi_{\sigma(i)}(p))$. If $\tau \leq_{AC} \tau'$ holds, then the algorithm, applied to the pair (τ, τ'), produces a finite $\leq_{AC}$-simulation S that contains (τ, τ'). It is straightforward to turn S into a system of recursive equations that defines one coercion for each pair within S, including, in particular, a coercion of type $\tau \to \tau'$.

Theorem 12. *If $\tau \leq_{AC} \tau'$ holds, there exists a (closed) coercion c s. t. $\vdash c : \tau \to \tau'$.* $\diamond$

The size of the equation associated with (τ, τ') is $O(1 + d(\tau'))$, where $d(\tau')$ is the outgoing degree of the node τ' in the graph T or T'. As a result, the total size of the system of equations is bounded by

$$\begin{aligned}
&O(\Sigma_{\tau\in T, \tau'\in T'}(1 + d(\tau')) + \Sigma_{\tau'\in T', \tau\in T}(1 + d(\tau)))\\
&= O(n(\Sigma_{\tau'\in T'}(1 + d(\tau'))) + n'(\Sigma_{\tau\in T}(1 + d(\tau))))\\
&= O(nN' + n'N)
\end{aligned}$$

The system can be produced in linear time with respect to its size, so the time complexity of producing code for the coercions is $O(nN' + n'N)$. (If one applies Bekič's theorem, as suggested above, then the time and space complexity increases quadratically, but there is no reason to do so in practice.)

It is worth pointing out that not all well-typed coercions have the same operational meaning, and some user interaction is, in practice, necessary to ensure that the coercion code suits the user's needs.

7 Practical Considerations

In practical applications, the language of types is usually much richer than the one considered in this paper. The grammar of types may include a set of atoms (such as *int*, *float*, etc.), equipped with a subtyping relation, and a set of parameterized type constructors. Each of these type constructors may have some contravariant and some covariant parameters, may support or forbid permutations of its parameters, and may support or forbid width subtyping.

Fortunately, it is straightforward to adapt the results of this paper to such an extended language of types. As far as atoms and atomic subtyping are concerned, it suffices to add appropriate clauses to the definition of a $\leq_{AC}$-simulation and to the algorithms for deciding AC-subtyping and building coercions; these new clauses are variations of the existing clauses for $\bot$ and $\top$. As far as parameterized type constructors are concerned, it is enough to extend our definitions by distinguishing four kinds of products that respectively support or forbid parameter permutations and width subtyping. The rules that describe the three new (restricted) kinds of products are special cases of our current rules, since our current product constructor allows both parameter permutations and width subtyping. Then, every parameterized type constructor may be desugared into a combination of atoms, the arrow constructor (which allows encoding contravariance) and the four product constructors.

Our core language is purely functional. However, real-world languages, and object-oriented languages in particular, often have mutable data structures and a notion of object identity. Then, it is important that coercions preserve object identity. One might wish the following property to hold: the program that is linked, using adapters, to a certain library, should have the same semantics as that obtained by linking, without adapters, to a library whose method and class names have been suitably renamed. We believe that, combining our algorithms with the adapter model sketched by Thatté [24], it is possible to achieve such a property. We leave this as future work.

8 Conclusion

We have introduced a notion of subtyping of recursive types up to associativity and commutativity of products. We have justified our definition by showing that this relation is a composition of the usual subtyping relation with Palsberg and Zhao's notion of equality up to associativity and commutativity of products. We have provided an algorithm for deciding whether two types are in the relation. The algorithm's worst-case time complexity may be bounded by $O(NN'd^{5/2})$ and $O(n^2n'^2d^{5/2})$; we believe it will prove fairly efficient in practice. It is straightforward and cheap to produce coercion code when the algorithm succeeds.

We believe this paper may constitute the groundwork for *practical* search tools within libraries of object-oriented code. Indeed, as argued in §1, AC-equality alone is not flexible enough, since it does not allow looking for only a *subset* of the features provided by a library.

References

1. Martín Abadi and Marcelo P. Fiore. Syntactic considerations on recursive types. In *IEEE Symposium on Logic in Computer Science (LICS)*, pages 242–252, July 1996.
2. Roberto M. Amadio and Luca Cardelli. Subtyping recursive types. *ACM Transactions on Programming Languages and Systems*, 15(4):575–631, September 1993.
3. Maria-Virginia Aponte and Roberto Di Cosmo. Type isomorphisms for module signatures. In *Symposium on Programming Language Implementation and Logic Programming (PLILP)*, volume 1140 of *Lecture Notes in Computer Science*, pages 334–346. Springer Verlag, 1996.
4. Joshua Auerbach, Charles Barton, and Mukund Raghavachari. Type isomorphisms with recursive types. Technical Report RC 21247, IBM Yorktown Heights, 1998.
5. Joshua Auerbach and Mark C. Chu-Carrol. The Mockingbird system: a compiler-based approach to maximally interoperable distributed systems. Technical Report RC 20718, IBM Yorktown Heights, 1997.
6. Joshua Auerbach, Mark C. Chu-Carrol, Charles Barton, and Mukund Raghavachari. Mockingbird: Flexible stub generation from pairs of declarations. Technical Report RC 21309, IBM Yorktown Heights, 1998.
7. Vincent Balat, Roberto Di Cosmo, and Marcelo Fiore. Remarks on isomorphisms in typed lambda calculi with empty and sum type. In *IEEE Symposium on Logic in Computer Science (LICS)*, July 2002.
8. Charles M. Barton. M-types and their coercions. Technical Report RC-21615, IBM Yorktown Heights, December 1999.

9. Michael Brandt and Fritz Henglein. Coinductive axiomatization of recursive type equality and subtyping. *Fundamenta Informaticæ*, 33:309–338, 1998.
10. Kim Bruce, Roberto Di Cosmo, and Giuseppe Longo. Provable isomorphisms of types. *Mathematical Structures in Computer Science*, 2(2):231–247, 1992.
11. Felice Cardone. A coinductive completeness proof for the equivalence of recursive types. *Theoretical Computer Science*, 275(1–2):575–587, 2002.
12. Bruno Courcelle. Fundamental properties of infinite trees. *Theoretical Computer Science*, 25(2):95–169, March 1983.
13. Roberto Di Cosmo. Deciding type isomorphisms in a type assignment framework. *Journal of Functional Programming*, 3(3):485–525, 1993.
14. Roberto Di Cosmo. *Isomorphisms of types: from λ-calculus to information retrieval and language design*. Progress in Theoretical Computer Science. Birkhauser, 1995.
15. Peter J. Downey, Ravi Sethi, and Robert Endre Tarjan. Variations on the common subexpression problem. *Journal of the ACM*, 27(4):758–771, October 1980.
16. Vladimir Gapeyev, Michael Levin, and Benjamin Pierce. Recursive subtyping revealed. *Journal of Functional Programming*, 12(6):511–548, 2003.
17. John E. Hopcroft and Richard M. Karp. An $n^{5/2}$ algorithm for maximum matchings in bipartite graphs. *SIAM Journal on Computing*, 2(4):225–231, December 1973.
18. Somesh Jha, Jens Palsberg, and Tian Zhao. Efficient type matching. In *International Conference on Foundations of Software Science and Computation Structures (FOSSACS)*, volume 2303 of *Lecture Notes in Computer Science*, pages 187–204. Springer Verlag, April 2002.
19. Jens Palsberg and Tian Zhao. Efficient and flexible matching of recursive types. *Information and Computation*, 171:364–387, 2001.
20. Mikael Rittri. Using types as search keys in function libraries. *Journal of Functional Programming*, 1(1):71–89, 1991.
21. Mikael Rittri. Retrieving library functions by unifying types modulo linear isomorphism. *RAIRO Theoretical Informatics and Applications*, 27(6):523–540, 1993.
22. Colin Runciman and Ian Toyn. Retrieving re-usable software components by polymorphic type. *Journal of Functional Programming*, 1(2):191–211, 1991.
23. Sergei V. Soloviev. The category of finite sets and cartesian closed categories. *Journal of Soviet Mathematics*, 22(3):1387–1400, 1983.
24. Satish R. Thatté. Automated synthesis of interface adapters for reusable classes. In *ACM Symposium on Principles of Programming Languages (POPL)*, pages 174–187, January 1994.
25. Jeannette M. Wing, Eugene Rollins, and Amy Moormann Zaremski. Thoughts on a Larch/ML and a new application for LP. In *First International Workshop on Larch*, pages 297–312, July 1992.

Galois Embedding from Polymorphic Types into Existential Types

Ken-etsu Fujita

Department of Computer Science, Gunma University,
Kiryu 376-8515, Japan
fujita@cs.gunma-u.ac.jp

Abstract. We show that there exist bijective translations between polymorphic λ-calculus and a subsystem of minimal logic with existential types, which form a Galois connection and moreover a Galois embedding. From a programming point of view, this result means that polymorphic functions can be represented by abstract data types.

1 Introduction

We show that polymorphic types can be interpreted by the use of second order existential types. For this, we prove that there exist bijective translations between polymorphic λ-calculus $\lambda 2$ and a subsystem of minimal logic with existential types, which form a Galois connection and moreover a Galois embedding. From a programming point of view, this result means that polymorphic functions can be represented by abstract data types via embedding.

Peter Selinger [Seli01] has introduced control categories and established an isomorphism between call-by-name and call-by-value $\lambda\mu$-calculi. The isomorphism reveals duality not only on propositional connectives ($\wedge, \vee$) like de Morgan but also on reduction strategies (call-by-name and call-by-value), input-output relations (demand- and data-driven) and inference rules (introduction and elimination).

Philip Wadler [Wad03] introduced the dual calculus in the style of Gentzen's sequent calculus LK, such that the duality explicitly appears on antecedent and succedent in the sequent of the propositional calculus.

Our main interest is a neat connection and proof duality between polymorphic types and existential types. It is logically quite natural like de Morgan's duality, and computationally still interesting, since dual of polymorphic functions with universal type can be regarded as abstract data types with existential type [MP85]. Instead of classical systems like [Pari92], even intuitionistic systems can enjoy that polymorphic types can be interpreted by existential types and vice versa. This interpretation also involves proof duality, such that the universal introduction rule is interpreted by the use of the existential elimination rule, and the universal elimination by the existential introduction. Moreover, we established not only a Galois connection but also a Galois embedding from polymorphic λ-calculus (Girard-Reynolds) into a calculus with existential types.

P. Urzyczyn (Ed.): TLCA 2005, LNCS 3461, pp. 194–208, 2005.

In order to establish such a Galois embedding from polymorphic λ-calculus, we have nontrivial problems to be overcome, contrary to the simply typed case:

(1) What's the target calculus and how to interpret polymorphic functions?
(2) What's the denotation of types and how to obtain commutativity w.r.t. type-substitutions?
(3) How to establish an inverse translation for the completeness?

First, we observe the well-known CPS-translations Plotkin [Plot75] and Hofmann-Streicher [HS97]. The former constitute a sound and complete translation with respect to β-equality, and the latter validates $\beta\eta$-equality as well. Following naïvely the latter translation of the simply typed case, polymorphic functions could be interpreted by the use of strong sum with projections: $[\![\lambda X.M]\!] = \lambda a.(\lambda X.[\![M]\!])(\pi_1 a)(\pi_2 a)$. Then the η-rule for polymorphic functions: $\lambda X.MX \to M$ provided $X \notin FV(M)$ would also be validated. However, from Coquand's analysis [Coq86] on impredicative systems with strong sums, that target calculus became inconsistent.

Terms of polymorphic λ-calculus in Church-style also contain type information, so that we have to give a denotation to types as well. According to [HS97] again, let k be an embedding from classical logic into intuitionistic logic and $*$ be for a continuation space, that is, $A^k = \neg A^*$ together with $X^* = \neg X$ and $(A_1 \Rightarrow A_2)^* = A_1^k \wedge A_2^*$. Then denotation of type A would be naturally defined by $A^\bullet$ such that $A^* = \neg A^\bullet$. Then one has $\neg A^k \leftrightarrow \neg A^\bullet$, i.e., type for denotations is in a sense equal to denotation of types. However, the existence of $A^\bullet$ cannot be guaranteed[1], and we cannot either expect commutativity with respect to type-substitutions like $(A[X := A_1])^* = A^*[X := A_1^\bullet]$. A simple solution is a logically equivalent definition of $*$ such that $(A_1 \Rightarrow A_2)^* = \neg\neg(A_1^k \wedge A_2^*)$, which now preserves type-substitutions. This slight modification leads to change of all the definition of the CPS-translation [HS97, Seli01], and then η-rule would not be valid any more under the modification.

Plotkin's translation [Plot75] was proved complete by the use of the Church-Rosser property of the target. On the other hand, a bijective CPS-translation is studied in [Fuji03] along the definition of [HS97], and the completeness of the translation was syntactically proved by the technique in [SF93] and the heavy use of η-rule of the source calculus, where the target is not Church-Rosser in general. The CPS-translation together with projections makes it possible to execute partial evaluation in the sense that projections over a continuation can be performed even though continuation components are not given. For instance, the translation in [HS97, Seli01] interprets the two $\lambda\mu$-terms [Pari92] $\mu a.[b]z$ and $\lambda x.\mu a.[b]z$ as $\lambda a.zb$ and $\lambda a.(\lambda x.\lambda a.zb)(\pi_1 a)(\pi_2 a) \to_\beta^+ \lambda a.zb$, respectively. Here, the two source terms are extensionally equal. How to distinguish the denotations unless the source calculus is extensional? Our idea is to take a weak form of conjunction elimination, so that `let`-expression blocks or suspends projections until two components of a continuation are, in fact, given. The use of such `let`-expressions (not syntactic sugar) plays an important rôle throughout this paper.

[1] This point was commented by Ryu Hasegawa.

Following the above observation concerning extensionality and polymorphism, this paper handles non-extensional $\lambda 2$ and weak products and sums. This logically uniform approach to $\Rightarrow$ and $\forall$ via `let`-expressions gives a neat correspondence between universal and existential types, including reduction rules. Of course our previous result [Fuji03] in the type free case can also be reformulated more elegantly along this approach with extensionality.

2 Polymorphic λ-Calculus λ2

We give the definition of polymorphic λ-calculus *à la* Church as second order intuitionistic logic, denoted by $\lambda 2$. This calculus is also known as the system F. The syntax of types is defined from type variables denoted by X, using $\Rightarrow$ or $\forall$ over type variables. The syntax of $\lambda 2$-terms is defined from individual variables denoted by x, using term-applications, type-applications or λ-abstractions over individual variables or type variables.

Definition 1 (Types).

$$A ::= X \mid A \Rightarrow A \mid \forall X.A$$

Definition 2 (Pseudo-Terms).

$$\Lambda 2 \ni M ::= x \mid \lambda x\!:\!A.M \mid MM \mid \lambda X.M \mid MA$$

Definition 3 (Reduction Rules).

(β) $(\lambda x\!:\!A.M)M_1 \to M[x := M_1]$
(β_t) $(\lambda X.M)A \to M[X := A]$

The one step reduction relation is denoted by $\to_{\lambda 2}$. We write $\to^{+}_{\lambda 2}$ or $\to^{*}_{\lambda 2}$ to denote the transitive closure or the reflexive and transitive closure of $\to_{\lambda 2}$, respectively. We employ the notation $=_{\lambda 2}$ for the symmetric, reflexive and transitive closure of the one step reduction $\to_{\lambda 2}$ defined above. We write $\equiv$ for a syntactical identity modulo renaming of bound variables. Let R be β or β_t. Then we often write $\to_R$ to denote the corresponding subset of $\to_{\lambda 2}$.

The typing judgement of $\lambda 2$ takes the form of $\Gamma \vdash M : A$, where Γ is a set of declarations in the form of $x : A$ with distinct variables as subjects. A set of free type variables in each predicate of Γ is denoted by $FV(\Gamma)$.

Definition 4 (Type Assignment Rules).

$$\frac{x\!:\!A \in \Gamma}{\Gamma \vdash x : A}$$

$$\frac{\Gamma, x\!:\!A_1 \vdash M : A_2}{\Gamma \vdash \lambda x\!:\!A_1.M : A_1 \Rightarrow A_2}\,(\Rightarrow I) \qquad \frac{\Gamma \vdash M_1 : A_1 \Rightarrow A_2 \quad \Gamma \vdash M_2 : A_1}{\Gamma \vdash M_1 M_2 : A_2}\,(\Rightarrow E)$$

$$\frac{\Gamma \vdash M : A}{\Gamma \vdash \lambda X.M : \forall X.A}\,(\forall I)^{\star} \qquad \frac{\Gamma \vdash M : \forall X.A}{\Gamma \vdash M A_1 : A[X := A_1]}\,(\forall E)$$

where $(\forall I)^{\star}$ denotes the eigenvariable condition $X \notin FV(\Gamma)$.

3 Minimal Logic with Second Order Sum

Next, we introduce the counter calculus $\lambda^{\exists}$ as minimal logic consisting of negations, conjunctions and second order sums. Such a calculus seems to be logically weak and has never been considered as far as we know. However, $\lambda^{\exists}$ turns out strong enough to interpret $\lambda 2$ and interesting to investigate polymorphism.

Definition 5 (Types).

$$A ::= \bot \mid X \mid \neg A \mid A \wedge A \mid \exists X.A$$

Definition 6 (Pseudo-Terms).

$$\begin{aligned}\Lambda^{\exists} \ni M ::= x \mid \lambda x\!:\!A.M \mid MM \\ \mid \langle M, M\rangle \mid \texttt{let}\ \langle x, x\rangle = M\ \texttt{in}\ M \\ \mid \langle A, M\rangle_{\exists X.A} \mid \texttt{let}\ \langle X, x\rangle = M\ \texttt{in}\ M\end{aligned}$$

Definition 7 (Reduction Rules).

(β) $(\lambda x\!:\!A.M)M_1 \to M[x := M_1]$
(η) $\lambda x\!:\!A.Mx \to M$ if $x \notin FV(M)$
($\texttt{let}_\wedge$) $\texttt{let}\ \langle x_1, x_2\rangle = \langle M_1, M_2\rangle\ \texttt{in}\ M \ \to\ M[x_1 := M_1, x_2 := M_2]$
($\texttt{let}_\exists$) $\texttt{let}\ \langle X, x\rangle = \langle A_1, M_2\rangle_{\exists X.A}\ \texttt{in}\ M \ \to\ M[X := A_1, x := M_2]$

A set of free variables in M is denoted by $FV(M)$. A simultaneous substitution for free variables x_1, x_2 or X, x is denoted by $[x_1 := M_1, x_2 := M_2]$ or $[X := A, x := M]$, respectively. We also write $=_{\lambda^{\exists}}$ for the reflexive, symmetric and transitive closure of the one step reduction $\to_{\lambda^{\exists}}$ defined above. We may sometimes omit type annotations from terms.

Definition 8 (Type Assignment Rules).

$$\frac{x\!:\!A \in \Gamma}{\Gamma \vdash x : A}$$

$$\frac{\Gamma, x\!:\!A \vdash M : \bot}{\Gamma \vdash \lambda x\!:\!A.M : \neg A}\ (\neg I) \qquad \frac{\Gamma \vdash M_1 : \neg A \quad \Gamma \vdash M_2 : A}{\Gamma \vdash M_1 M_2 : \bot}\ (\neg E)$$

$$\frac{\Gamma \vdash M_1 : A_1 \quad \Gamma \vdash M_2 : A_2}{\Gamma \vdash \langle M_1, M_2\rangle : A_1 \wedge A_2}\ (\wedge I)$$

$$\frac{\Gamma \vdash M_1 : A_1 \wedge A_2 \quad \Gamma, x_1\!:\!A_1, x_2\!:\!A_2 \vdash M : A}{\Gamma \vdash \texttt{let}\ \langle x_1, x_2\rangle = M_1\ \texttt{in}\ M : A}\ (\wedge E)$$

$$\frac{\Gamma \vdash M : A[X := A_1]}{\Gamma \vdash \langle A_1, M\rangle_{\exists X.A} : \exists X.A}\ (\exists I) \qquad \frac{\Gamma \vdash M_1 : \exists X.A_1 \quad \Gamma, x\!:\!A_1 \vdash M : A}{\Gamma \vdash \texttt{let}\ \langle X, x\rangle = M_1\ \texttt{in}\ M : A}\ (\exists E)^{\star}$$

where $(\exists E)^{\star}$ denotes the eigenvariable condition $X \notin FV(A, \Gamma)$.

4 CPS-Translation and Soundness

For a CPS-translation from λ2-calculus into $\lambda^{\exists}$-calculus, we define an embedding of types (types for denotations of proof terms), denoted by $\neg A^*$, types for continuations, denoted by A^*, and denotation of λ2-types, denoted by $A^\bullet$.

Definition 9 (Types for Continuations). $A^* = \neg A^\bullet$

Definition 10 (Denotation of Types).

(1) $X^\bullet = X$
(2) $(A_1 \Rightarrow A_2)^\bullet = \neg(\neg A_1^* \wedge A_2^*)$
(3) $(\forall X.A)^\bullet = \neg\exists X.A^*$

Remarked that $\neg\neg A^*$ and $\neg A^\bullet$ are intuitionistically equivalent. We may write A° for B such that $A^\bullet \equiv \neg B$ for non-atomic type A. For non-atomic A, $\neg A^*$ and $\neg A^\circ$ are intuitionistically equivalent. We note that $(A_1 \Rightarrow A_2)^\bullet \leftrightarrow \neg\neg(\neg A_1^\bullet \vee A_2^\bullet)$ and $(\forall X.A)^\bullet \leftrightarrow \forall X.\neg\neg A^\bullet$ are intuitionistically provable. Thus the embedding is similar to both Kolmogorov's negative translation and Hofmann-Streicher [HS97].

Lemma 11. (1) *We have* $A^\bullet[X := A_1^\bullet] = (A[X := A_1])^\bullet$.
(2) *We have* $(A[X := A_1])^* = A^*[X := A_1^\bullet]$.

Proof. (1), (2) By induction on the structure of A. □

The definition of denotation of proof terms, denoted by $[\![M]\!]$, is given by induction on the typing derivation of M.

Definition 12 (Denotation of λ2-Terms).

(i) $[\![x]\!] = x \quad \text{if } \Gamma \vdash x : A$
(ii) $[\![\lambda x{:}A_1.M]\!]$
$= \lambda a{:}(A_1 \Rightarrow A_2)^*.a(\lambda k{:}(\neg A_1^* \wedge A_2^*).(\texttt{let}\ \langle x, c\rangle = k\ \texttt{in}\ [\![M]\!]c))$
if $\Gamma \vdash \lambda x{:}A_1.M : A_1 \Rightarrow A_2$
(iii) $[\![M_1 M_2]\!] = \lambda a{:}A_2^*.[\![M_1]\!](\lambda d{:}\neg(\neg A_1^* \wedge A_2^*).d\langle [\![M_2]\!], a\rangle)$
if $\Gamma \vdash M_1 : A_1 \Rightarrow A_2$ and $\Gamma \vdash M_2 : A_1$
(iv) $[\![\lambda X.M]\!] = \lambda a{:}(\forall X.A)^*.a(\lambda k{:}(\exists X.A^*).(\texttt{let}\ \langle X, c\rangle = k\ \texttt{in}\ [\![M]\!]c))$
if $\Gamma \vdash \lambda X.M : \forall X.A$
(v) $[\![MA_1]\!] = \lambda a{:}(A[X := A_1])^*.[\![M]\!](\lambda d{:}(\neg\exists X.A^*).d\langle A_1^\bullet, a\rangle_{\exists X.A^*})$
if $\Gamma \vdash MA_1 : A[X := A_1]$

We may write simply $\langle\langle R, M\rangle\rangle$ for $\lambda d : A^\bullet.d\langle R, M\rangle$, and $\langle\langle R_1, R_2, \ldots, R_n, M\rangle\rangle$ for $\langle\langle R_1, \langle\langle R_2, \ldots, R_n, M\rangle\rangle\rangle\rangle$, where R is either A or M, and $\langle\langle M\rangle\rangle \equiv M$.

The definition above interprets each proof term with type A as a functional element with type $\neg A^*$ (space of denotations of type A), which takes, as an argument, a continuation with type A^*. The cases of application say that continuations are in the form of a pair $\langle\langle [\![M]\!], a\rangle\rangle$ or $\langle\langle A^\bullet, a\rangle\rangle$ consisting of a denotation and a continuation in this order. The cases of λ-abstraction mean that after the interpretation, λ-abstraction is waiting for a first component of a continuation (i.e., a denotation of its argument), and the second component becomes a rest continuation to the result. It should be remarked that $(\forall I)$ and $(\forall E)$ are respectively interpreted by the use of dual $(\exists E)$ and $(\exists I)$, we call proof duality.

Example 13. Let $xM_1 \cdots M_n$ be with type A_{m+1} and A be $A_1 \Rightarrow \cdots \Rightarrow A_{m+1}$:

$$
\begin{aligned}
&[\![\lambda x_1 \!:\! A_1 \ldots \lambda x_m \!:\! A_m . x M_1 \cdots M_n]\!] \\
&\to_\beta^+ \lambda c_0 \!:\! A^*. c_0(\lambda k_1.\ \texttt{let}\ \langle x_1, c_1\rangle = k_1\ \texttt{in} \\
&\qquad\qquad c_1(\lambda k_2.\ \texttt{let}\ \langle x_2, c_2\rangle = k_2\ \texttt{in} \\
&\qquad\qquad \ldots \\
&\qquad\qquad c_{m-1}(\lambda k_m.\ \texttt{let}\ \langle x_m, c_m\rangle = k_m\ \texttt{in}\ x\langle\langle [\![M_1]\!], \ldots, [\![M_n]\!], c_m\rangle\rangle) \ldots)) \\
&\qquad\qquad \text{where } k_i : A_i^k \wedge (A_{i+1} \Rightarrow \cdots \Rightarrow A_{m+1})^*
\end{aligned}
$$

Lemma 14. *We have* $[\![M[x := N]]\!] = [\![M]\!][x := [\![N]\!]]$ *and* $[\![M[X := A]]\!] = [\![M]\!][X := A^\bullet]$.

Proof. By induction on the structure of M together with Lemma 11. □

Proposition 15 (Soundness).

(i) *If we have* $\Gamma \vdash_{\lambda 2} M : A$, *then* $\neg\Gamma^* \vdash_{\lambda^\exists} [\![M]\!] : \neg A^*$.
(ii) *For well-typed* $M_1, M_2 \in \Lambda 2$, *if we have* $M_1 \to_{\lambda 2} M_2$ *then* $[\![M_1]\!] \to_{\lambda^\exists}^+ [\![M_2]\!]$.

Proof. If we have $\Gamma \vdash M : A$, then $\neg\Gamma^* \vdash [\![M]\!] : \neg A^*$ by induction on the derivation together with Definition 12. We show two cases of (1) $\lambda X.M$ and (2) MA.
(1) Suppose the following figure of λ2, where X is never free in the context Γ.

$$\frac{M : A}{\lambda X.M : \forall X.A}\ (\forall I)^\star$$

Then we have the proof figure of $\lambda^\exists$, where the eigenvariable condition of $(\exists E)$ can be guaranteed by that of $(\forall I)$.

$$
\dfrac{[a : (\forall X.A)^*] \quad \dfrac{\dfrac{[k : \exists X.A^*] \quad \dfrac{[\![M]\!] : \neg A^* \quad [c : A^*]}{[\![M]\!]c : \bot}}{\texttt{let}\ \langle X, c\rangle = k\ \texttt{in}\ [\![M]\!]c : \bot}\ (\exists E)^\star}{\lambda k \!:\! (\exists X.A^*).(\texttt{let}\ \langle X, c\rangle = k\ \texttt{in}\ [\![M]\!]c) : \neg\exists X.A^*}}{\dfrac{a(\lambda k \!:\! (\exists X.A^*).(\texttt{let}\ \langle X, c\rangle = k\ \texttt{in}\ [\![M]\!]c)) : \bot}{\lambda a \!:\! (\forall X.A)^*. a(\lambda k \!:\! (\exists X.A^*).(\texttt{let}\ \langle X, c\rangle = k\ \texttt{in}\ [\![M]\!]c)) : \neg(\forall X.A)^*}}
$$

(2) Suppose that

$$\frac{M : \forall X.A}{MA_1 : A[X := A_1]}\ (\forall E)$$

Then we have the following proof figure:

$$\dfrac{[\![M]\!] : \neg(\forall X.A)^* \qquad \dfrac{\dfrac{[d : \neg\exists X.A^*] \qquad \dfrac{[a : (A[X := A_1])^* = A^*[X = A_1^\bullet]]}{\langle A_1^\bullet, a\rangle_{\exists X.A^*} : \exists X.A^*}(\exists I)}{d\langle A_1^\bullet, a\rangle_{\exists X.A^*} : \bot}}{\lambda d{:}(\neg\exists X.A^*).d\langle A_1^\bullet, a\rangle_{\exists X.A^*} : \neg\neg\exists X.A^*}}{\dfrac{[\![M]\!]\langle\langle A_1^\bullet, a\rangle\rangle : \bot}{\lambda a{:}(A[X := A_1])^*.[\![M]\!]\langle\langle A_1^\bullet, a\rangle\rangle : \neg(A[X := A_1])^*}}$$

The other cases for $(\Rightarrow I)$ and $(\Rightarrow E)$ are the same as above.

Next, we can prove that if we have $M_1 \to_{\lambda 2} M_2$ then $[\![M_1]\!] \to_{\lambda^\exists}^+ [\![M_2]\!]$ by induction on the derivation of well-typed terms. We show the case of (3) (β_t) where $\lambda X.M : \forall X.A$.

(3) $[\![(\lambda X.M)A_1]\!]$

$$\begin{aligned}
&= \lambda a{:}(A[X := A_1])^*.\\
&\quad (\lambda a{:}(\forall X.A)^*.a\,(\lambda k{:}(\exists X.A^*).(\mathtt{let}\ \langle X, c\rangle = k\ \mathtt{in}\ [\![M]\!]c)))\,\langle\langle A_1^\bullet, a\rangle\rangle\\
&\to_\beta^+ \lambda a{:}(A[X := A_1])^*.(\mathtt{let}\ \langle X, c\rangle = \langle A_1^\bullet, a\rangle_{\exists X.A^*}\ \mathtt{in}\ [\![M]\!]c)\\
&\to_{\mathtt{let}_\exists} \lambda a{:}(A[X := A_1])^*.[\![M]\!][X := A_1^\bullet]a\\
&= \lambda a{:}(A[X := A_1])^*.[\![M[X := A_1]]\!]a \quad \text{from Lemma 14}\\
&\to_\eta [\![M[X := A_1]]\!]
\end{aligned}$$

□

5 Inverse Translation and Galois Embedding

We introduce a key definition, an inductive generation rule of $\mathcal{R}$ *à la* [SF93], which describes the image of the CPS-translation closed under the reduction rules. We write $R \in \mathcal{R}, \mathcal{R}^\bullet$ for both $R \in \mathcal{R}$ and $R \in \mathcal{R}^\bullet$, and $R_1, \ldots, R_n \in \mathcal{R}$ for $R_i \in \mathcal{R}$ $(1 \le i \le n)$.

Definition 16 (Inductive Generation of $\mathcal{R}$).

1.
$$x \in \mathcal{R}, \mathcal{R}^\bullet \qquad\qquad A^\bullet \in \mathcal{R}^\bullet$$

2.
$$\frac{R \in \mathcal{R} \qquad R_1, \ldots, R_n \in \mathcal{R}^\bullet \qquad a \notin FV(RR_1 \ldots R_n) \quad n \ge 0}{\lambda a.R\langle\langle R_1, \ldots, R_n, a\rangle\rangle \in \mathcal{R}, \mathcal{R}^\bullet}$$

3.
$$\frac{\lambda a.W, R_1 \in \mathcal{R} \qquad R_2, \ldots, R_n \in \mathcal{R}^\bullet \qquad b \notin FV(R_1 \ldots R_n W) \quad n \ge 0}{\lambda b.\langle\langle R_1, \ldots, R_n, b\rangle\rangle(\lambda k.\mathtt{let}\ \langle x, a\rangle = k\ \mathtt{in}\ W) \in \mathcal{R}, \mathcal{R}^\bullet}$$

$$\frac{\lambda a.W \in \mathcal{R} \qquad A_1^\bullet, R_2, \ldots, R_n \in \mathcal{R}^\bullet \qquad b \notin FV(R_2 \ldots R_n W) \quad n \ge 0}{\lambda b.\langle\langle A_1^\bullet, R_2, \ldots, R_n, b\rangle\rangle(\lambda k.\mathtt{let}\ \langle X, a\rangle = k\ \mathtt{in}\ W) \in \mathcal{R}, \mathcal{R}^\bullet}$$

4.

$$\frac{\lambda a.W, R \in \mathcal{R} \qquad R_1, \ldots, R_n \in \mathcal{R}^\bullet \qquad b \notin FV(RR_1 \ldots R_n W) \quad n \geq 0}{\lambda b.(\lambda k.\texttt{let } \langle x, a\rangle = k \texttt{ in } W)\langle R, \langle\langle R_1, \ldots, R_n, b\rangle\rangle\rangle \in \mathcal{R}, \mathcal{R}^\bullet}$$

$$\frac{\lambda a.W \in \mathcal{R} \qquad R_1, \ldots, R_n \in \mathcal{R}^\bullet \qquad b \notin FV(R_1 \ldots R_n W) \quad n \geq 0}{\lambda b.(\lambda k.\texttt{let } \langle X, a\rangle = k \texttt{ in } W)\langle A^\bullet, \langle\langle R_1, \ldots, R_n, b\rangle\rangle\rangle_{\exists X.A^*} \in \mathcal{R}, \mathcal{R}^\bullet}$$

5.

$$\frac{\lambda a.W, R \in \mathcal{R} \qquad R_1, \ldots, R_n \in \mathcal{R}^\bullet \qquad b \notin FV(RR_1 \ldots R_n W) \quad n \geq 0}{\lambda b.(\texttt{let } \langle x, a\rangle = \langle R, \langle\langle R_1, \ldots, R_n, b\rangle\rangle\rangle \texttt{ in } W) \in \mathcal{R}, \mathcal{R}^\bullet}$$

$$\frac{\lambda a.W \in \mathcal{R} \qquad R_1, \ldots, R_n \in \mathcal{R}^\bullet \qquad b \notin FV(R_1 \ldots R_n W) \quad n \geq 0}{\lambda b.(\texttt{let } \langle X, a\rangle = \langle A^\bullet, \langle\langle R_1, \ldots, R_n, b\rangle\rangle\rangle_{\exists X.A^*} \texttt{ in } W) \in \mathcal{R}, \mathcal{R}^\bullet}$$

From the inductive definition above, $R \in \mathcal{R}$ is in the form of either x or $\lambda a.W$ for some W. It is important that terms with the pattern of $\lambda a.W \in \mathcal{R}$ have the form such that the continuation variable a appears exactly once in W (linear continuation), since our source calculus is intuitionistic. To save the space, we omit here the typing rules for $R \in \mathcal{R}$; $\neg\Gamma^* \vdash_{\lambda^\exists} x : \neg A^*$ if $x : \neg A^* \in \neg\Gamma^*$, etc.

Lemma 17 (Subject reduction w.r.t. $\mathcal{R}$). *The category $\mathcal{R}$ is closed under the reduction rules of $\lambda^\exists$.*

Proof. Substitutions associated to the reduction rules are closed with respect to the category. □

Lemma 18 (Subject reduction w.r.t. types). *If we have $R : \neg A^*$ together with $R \to^*_{\lambda^\exists} R_1$, then we also have $R_1 : \neg A^*$.*

Proof. The calculus $\lambda^\exists$ has the subject reduction property. □

Let (η_a^-) be an η-expansion: $R \to \lambda a{:}A^*.Ra$ where $a \notin FV(R)$ and $R \in \mathcal{R}$.

Definition 19 (Universe of the CPS-Translation).

$$Univ \stackrel{\text{def}}{=} \{P \in \Lambda^\exists \mid [\![M]\!] \to^*_{\lambda^\exists \eta_a^-} P \text{ for some well-typed } M \in \Lambda 2\}$$

Proposition 20. *Univ is generated by $\mathcal{R}$, i.e., Univ $\subseteq \mathcal{R}$.*

Proof. For well typed $M \in \Lambda 2$, we have $[\![M]\!] \in \mathcal{R}$, and moreover $\mathcal{R}$ is closed under (η_a^-) and the reduction rules by Lemma 17. □

Lemma 21. *For any $P \in Univ$, we have some Γ and A such that $\neg\Gamma^* \vdash_{\lambda^\exists} P : \neg A^*$.*

Proof. From the definition of *Univ*, Proposition 15 and Lemma 18. □

Following the patterns of $\lambda a.W \in \mathcal{R}$, we now give the definition of the inverse translation $\sharp$ as $(\lambda a.W)^\sharp = W^\sharp$.

Definition 22 (Inverse Translation $\sharp$ for $\mathcal{R}$).

(i) $x^\sharp = x$; $\quad (A^\bullet)^\sharp = A$

(ii) $(R\langle\langle R_1, \ldots, R_n, a\rangle\rangle)^\sharp = R^\sharp R_1^\sharp \ldots R_n^\sharp$

(iii) – $(\langle\langle R_1, \ldots, R_n, a\rangle\rangle(\lambda k{:}(\neg A_1^* \wedge A_2^*).(\texttt{let}\ \langle x, c\rangle = k\ \texttt{in}\ W)))^\sharp$
$= (\lambda x{:}A_1.W^\sharp)R_1^\sharp \ldots R_n^\sharp$

– $(\langle\langle R_1, \ldots, R_n, a\rangle\rangle(\lambda k{:}(\exists X.A^*).(\texttt{let}\ \langle X, c\rangle = k\ \texttt{in}\ W)))^\sharp$
$= (\lambda X.W^\sharp)R_1^\sharp \ldots R_n^\sharp$

(iv) – $((\lambda k{:}(\neg A_1^* \wedge A_2^*).(\texttt{let}\ \langle x, c\rangle = k\ \texttt{in}\ W))\langle R, \langle\langle R_1, \ldots, R_n, a\rangle\rangle\rangle)^\sharp$
$= (\lambda x{:}A_1.W^\sharp)R^\sharp R_1^\sharp \ldots R_n^\sharp$

– $((\lambda k{:}(\exists X.A^*).(\texttt{let}\ \langle X, c\rangle = k\ \texttt{in}\ W))\langle R, \langle\langle R_1, \ldots, R_n, a\rangle\rangle\rangle)^\sharp$
$= (\lambda X.W^\sharp)R^\sharp R_1^\sharp \ldots R_n^\sharp$

(v) – $(\texttt{let}\ \langle x, c\rangle = \langle R, \langle\langle R_1, \ldots, R_n, a\rangle\rangle\rangle\ \texttt{in}\ W)^\sharp$
$= (\lambda x{:}A_1.W^\sharp)R^\sharp R_1^\sharp \ldots R_n^\sharp$ for $R : \neg A_1^*$

– $(\texttt{let}\ \langle X, c\rangle = \langle R, \langle\langle R_1, \ldots, R_n, a\rangle\rangle\rangle\ \texttt{in}\ W)^\sharp$
$= (\lambda X.W^\sharp)R^\sharp R_1^\sharp \ldots R_n^\sharp$

Proposition 23 (Completeness 1). *For any $P \in Univ$, there exist some Γ, A such that $\Gamma \vdash P^\sharp : A$ in $\lambda 2$.*

Proof. From Lemma 21, it is enough to show $\Gamma \vdash_{\lambda 2} P^\sharp : A$ if we have $\neg\Gamma^* \vdash_{\lambda^\exists} P : \neg A^*$. By induction on the length of the derivation $\neg\Gamma^* \vdash_{\lambda^\exists} P : \neg A^*$, following the case analysis on well-typed $P \in \mathcal{R}$. □

Proposition 24. (1) *Let $M \in \Lambda 2$ be well-typed. Then we have that $[\![M]\!]^\sharp \equiv M$.*
(2) *Let $P \in \mathcal{R}$ be well-typed. Then we have that $[\![P^\sharp]\!] \to^*_{\beta\eta_a^-} P$.*
(3) *If $P \in \mathcal{R}$ is a normal form of $\lambda^\exists$, then $P^\sharp$ is a normal form of $\lambda 2$.*

Proof. (1) By induction on the structure of well-typed $M \in \Lambda 2$.
(2) By case analysis on $P \in \mathcal{R}$, following the definition of $\sharp$.
(3) Following case analysis on $P \in \mathcal{R}$.

- Case P of $\lambda a{:}A^*.R\langle\langle R_1, \ldots, R_n, a\rangle\rangle$:
Since P is a normal form of $\lambda^\exists$, we have $R \equiv x$ and R_i is also in normal, to say, R_i^{nf}. Then we have normal $P^\sharp = x(R_1^{nf})^\sharp \ldots (R_n^{nf})^\sharp$.
- Case P of $\lambda a{:}A^*.a(\lambda k.(\texttt{let}\ \langle x, c\rangle = k\ \texttt{in}\ W))$:
Since P is in normal, so is W, to say, W^{nf}. Then we have normal $P^\sharp = \lambda x{:}A_1.(W^{nf})^\sharp$. □

Proposition 25. *We have $Univ = \mathcal{R}$ with respect to well-typed terms.*
Proof. We have $Univ \subseteq \mathcal{R}$ from Proposition 20. Let $P \in \mathcal{R}$ be well-typed. Then $P^\sharp \in \Lambda 2$ is well-typed from the proof of Proposition 23. Proposition 24 implies that $[\![P^\sharp]\!] \to^*_{\beta\eta_a^-} P$, and hence $P \in Univ$. Therefore we have $\mathcal{R} \subseteq Univ$. □

Lemma 26. $(W[a := \langle\langle R_1, \ldots, R_m, b\rangle\rangle])^\sharp = W^\sharp R_1^\sharp, \ldots, R_n^\sharp$ *provided* $a \in FV(W)$.
Proof. Following the case analysis on W. We show one case of $W = aD$ where $D = (\lambda k.\texttt{let}\ \langle x, c\rangle = k\ \texttt{in}\ W')$. Let θ be $[a := \langle\langle R_1, \ldots, R_n, b\rangle\rangle]$. We have $W\theta = (aD)\theta = \langle\langle R_1, \ldots, R_m, b\rangle\rangle D$, and then we have
$(W\theta)^\sharp = (\lambda x.W'^\sharp)R_1^\sharp \ldots R_m^\sharp = W^\sharp R_1^\sharp \ldots R_m^\sharp$. □

Proposition 27 (Completeness 2). *Let* $P, Q \in \mathcal{R}$.

(1) *If* $P \to_\beta Q$ *then* $P^\sharp \equiv Q^\sharp$.
(2) *If* $P \to_\eta Q$ *then* $P^\sharp \equiv Q^\sharp$.
(3) *If* $P \to_{\mathtt{let}_\wedge} Q$ *then* $P^\sharp \to_\beta Q^\sharp$.
(4) *If* $P \to_{\mathtt{let}_\exists} Q$ *then* $P^\sharp \to_{\beta_t} Q^\sharp$.

Proof. By induction on the derivations. The cases (1,2) are straightforward. We show the case of **(4)**:

Let P be $\lambda a.\mathtt{let}\ \langle X, c\rangle = \langle A^\bullet, \langle\langle R_1, \ldots, R_n, a\rangle\rangle\rangle\ \mathtt{in}\ W$.

$$\begin{aligned} P^\sharp &= (\lambda X.W^\sharp)(A^\bullet)^\sharp R_1^\sharp \ldots R_n^\sharp \\ &\to_{\beta_t} W^\sharp[X := A]R_1^\sharp \ldots R_n^\sharp \\ &= (W[X := A^\bullet])^\sharp R_1^\sharp \ldots R_n^\sharp = (W[X := A^\bullet][c := \langle\langle R_1, \ldots, R_n, a\rangle\rangle])^\sharp \end{aligned}$$ □

Theorem 28. (i) $\Gamma \vdash_{\lambda 2} M : A$ *if and only if* $\neg\Gamma^* \vdash_{\lambda\exists} [\![M]\!] : \neg A^*$.
(ii) $P \in Univ$ *if and only if* $\Gamma \vdash_{\lambda 2} P^\sharp : A$ *for some* Γ, A.
(iii) *Let* M_1, M_2 *be well-typed* $\lambda 2$*-terms.*
$M_1 =_{\lambda 2} M_2$ *if and only if* $[\![M_1]\!] =_{\lambda\exists} [\![M_2]\!]$.
In particular, $M_1 \to_{\lambda 2} M_2$ *if and only if* $[\![M_1]\!] \to_\beta^+ \to_{\mathtt{let}} \to_\eta [\![M_2]\!]$.
(iv) *Let* $P_1, P_2 \in Univ$. $P_1 =_{\lambda\exists} P_2$ *if and only if* $P_1^\sharp =_{\lambda 2} P_2^\sharp$.

Proof. (i, ii) From Propositions 15 and 23. (iii, iv) From Propositions 15 and 27. □

Corollary 29. *The inverse translation* $\sharp : Univ \to \Lambda 2$ *is bijective, in the following sense:*

(1) *If we have* $P_1^\sharp =_{\lambda 2} P_2^\sharp$ *then* $P_1 =_{\lambda\exists} P_2$ *for* $P_1, P_2 \in Univ$.
(2) *For any well-typed* $M \in \Lambda 2$*, we have some* $P \in Univ$ *such that* $P^\sharp \equiv M$.

Proof. For (2), we can take P as $[\![M]\!]$ from Proposition 24. □

Definition 30 (Galois Connection). Let $\to_S^*$ and $\to_T^*$ be pre-orders on S and T respectively, and $f : S \to T$ and $g : T \to S$ be maps. Two maps f and g form a Galois connection between S and T whenever $f(M) \to_T^* P$ if and only if $M \to_S^* g(P)$, see also [SW97].

It is known that the definition above is equivalent to the following clauses:

(i) $M \to_S^* g(f(M))$
(ii) $f(g(P)) \to_T^* P$
(iii) $M_1 \to_S^* M_2$ implies $f(M_1) \to_T^* f(M_2)$
(iv) $P_1 \to_T^* P_2$ implies $g(P_1) \to_S^* g(P_2)$

Definition 31 (Galois Embedding). Two maps f and g form a Galois embedding into T if they form a Galois connection and $g(f(M)) \equiv M$.

Theorem 32. *The translations $[\![\ ]\!]$ and $\sharp$ form a Galois connection between $\lambda 2$ and Univ, and moreover, they establish a Galois embedding into Univ.*

Proof. From Propositions 15, 24, and 27. □

It is remarked that a Galois embedding is the dual notion of a reflection: f and g form a reflection in S if they form a Galois connection and $f(g(P)) \equiv P$. In fact, let $M \to^{-} N$ (expansion) be $N \to M$ (reduction). Then $\to^{-*}$ is a pre-order, and $\langle \sharp, [\![\ ]\!], \to^{-*}_{\lambda^\exists}, \to^{-*}_{\lambda 2} \rangle$ forms a reflection.

Let $\sharp Univ$ be $\{P^\sharp \mid P \in Univ\}$. Let $[\![\sharp Univ]\!]$ be $\{[\![M]\!] \mid M \in \sharp Univ\}$.

Corollary 33 (Kernel of $\Lambda 2$). *For any $P \in [\![\sharp Univ]\!]$, we have $P \equiv [\![P^\sharp]\!]$.*

Proof. Let $\Lambda 2$ be a set of well-typed $\lambda 2$-terms. Then we have $\sharp Univ = \Lambda 2$ and $[\![\sharp Univ]\!] = [\![\Lambda 2]\!]$. Hence, any $P \in [\![\Lambda 2]\!]$ is in the form $P \equiv [\![M]\!]$ for some $M \in \Lambda 2$, such that $[\![P^\sharp]\!] \equiv [\![[\![M]\!]^\sharp]\!] \equiv [\![M]\!] \equiv P$. □

Corollary 34 (Normalization of $\Lambda 2$). *The weak normalization of $\lambda 2$ is inherited from that of $\lambda^\exists$. Moreover, the strong normalization of $\lambda 2$ is implied by that of $\lambda^\exists$.*

Proof. The weak normalization of $\lambda 2$ is implied by Theorem 32 ($[\![\ ]\!]$ and $\sharp$ form a Galois connection) together with Proposition 24 (3). The strong normalization of $\lambda 2$ is implied by Proposition 15 (soundness). □

Corollary 35 (Church-Rosser of $\Lambda 2$). *The Church-Rosser property of $\lambda 2$ is inherited from that of $\lambda^\exists$.*

Proof. The Church-Rosser property of $\lambda 2$ is implied by Theorem 32. □

We remark that the system $\lambda^\exists$ can be regarded logically as a subsystem of F, in the sense that the connectives $\wedge$ and $\exists$ together with the reduction rules can be coded by universal types of F [GTL89]. Our result, in turn, means that universal types can be interpreted by the use of existential types. Moreover, proof duality appears in the proof such that $(\forall I) \leftrightarrow (\exists E)$ and $(\forall E) \leftrightarrow (\exists I)$.

6 Proof Duality Between Polymorphic Functions and Abstract Data Types

We discuss the proof duality in detail. If we have $\Gamma \vdash_{\lambda 2} A$ in $\lambda 2$, then classical logic has $A^* \vdash \Gamma^*$. In terms of minimal logic, we can expect that $\neg\Gamma^*, A^* \vdash \bot$. In fact, we obtain $\neg\Gamma^*, a : A^* \vdash_{\lambda^\exists} \underline{\underline{M}} : \bot$ if $\Gamma \vdash_{\lambda 2} M : A$, under the following definition.

Definition 36 (Modified CPS-Translation).

(i) $\underline{\underline{x}} = xa$

(ii) $\underline{\underline{\lambda x{:}A_1.M}} = a(\lambda k{:}(\neg A_1^* \wedge A_2^*).\mathtt{let}\ \langle x, a\rangle = k\ \mathtt{in}\ \underline{\underline{M}})$
for $\lambda x{:}A_1.M : A_1 \Rightarrow A_2$

(iii) $\underline{\underline{M_1 M_2}} = \underline{\underline{M_1}}[a := \langle\langle \lambda a\!:\!A_1^*.\underline{\underline{M_2}}, a\rangle\rangle]$ for $M_2 : A_1$
(iv) $\underline{\underline{\lambda X.M}} = a(\lambda k\!:\!(\exists X.A^*).\mathtt{let}\ \langle X, a\rangle = k\ \mathtt{in}\ \underline{\underline{M}})$ for $\lambda X.M : \forall X.A$
(v) $\underline{\underline{M A_1}} = \underline{\underline{M}}[a := \langle\langle A_1^\bullet, a\rangle\rangle]$

Lemma 37. *Let $M \in \Lambda 2$ be a well-typed term.*

(1) *We have $[\![M]\!]a \to^*_{\beta\eta_a^-} \underline{\underline{M}}$ and $[\![M]\!] \to^*_{\beta\eta_a^-} \lambda a.\underline{\underline{M}}$.*
(2) $[\![M]\!]^\sharp = (\underline{\underline{M}})^\sharp \equiv M$
(3) *If M is a normal form of $\lambda 2$, then $\underline{\underline{M}}$ is a normal form of $\lambda^\exists$ without (η_a).*

Proof. By induction on the structure of M together with Proposition 24. □

The notion of path is defined as in Prawitz [Pra65], and dual path is introduced here to investigate relationship between $\lambda 2$-proofs and $\lambda^\exists$-proofs.

Definition 38 (Path). A sequence consisting of formulae and inference rules $A_1(R_1)A_2(R_2)\ldots A_{n-1}(R_{n-1})A_n$ is defined as a path in the deduction Π of $\lambda 2$, as follows:

(i) A_1 is a top-formula in Π;
(ii) A_i $(i < n)$ is not the minor premise of an application of $(\Rightarrow E)$, and A_{i+1} is the formula occurrence immediately below A_i by an application of (R_i);
(iii) A_n is either a minor premise of $(\Rightarrow E)$ or the end-formula of Π.

Definition 39 (Dual Path). A sequence consisting of formulae and inference rules $A_1(R_1)A_2(R_2)\ldots A_{n-1}(R_{n-1})A_n$ is defined as a dual path in the deduction Σ of $\lambda^\exists$, as follows:

(i) A_1 is a top-formula in Σ;
(ii) A_i $(i < n)$ is not the major premise of an application of $(\neg E)$, and either
1) A_i is not a major premise of $(\wedge E)$ or $(\exists E)$, and A_{i+1} is the formula occurrence immediately below A_i by an application of (R_i), or
2) A_i is the major premise of an application of $(\wedge E)$ or $(\exists E)$, and A_{i+1} is the assumption discharged in Σ by $(\wedge E)$ or $(\exists E)$, to say, (R_i);
(iii) A_n is either a major premise of $(\neg E)$ or the end-formula of Σ.

We write (I) for either $(\Rightarrow I)$ or $(\forall I)$, and (E) for either $(\Rightarrow E)$ or $(\forall E)$. We also define inference rule correspondence as follows: $(\Rightarrow I)^* = (\wedge E)$, $(\Rightarrow E)^* = (\wedge I)$, $(\forall I)^* = (\exists E)$, $(\forall E)^* = (\exists I)$.

Theorem 40 (Proof duality). *Let Π be a normal deduction of $\Gamma \vdash_{\lambda 2} M : A$, and let π be a path $A_1(E_1)A_2(E_2)\ldots A_i(E_i)A_{i+1}(I_{i+1})\ldots A_{n-1}(I_{n-1})A_n$ in the normal deduction. Then, in the deduction of $\neg\Gamma^*, a\!:\!A^* \vdash_{\lambda^\exists} \underline{\underline{M}} : \bot$, there exist dual paths $\pi^d_n, \ldots, \pi^d_{(i+2)}$, as follows:*

$\pi^d_n = A^\circ_n(I_{n-1})^* A^*_{n-1}$,
$\pi^d_{(n-1)} = A^\circ_{n-1}(I_{n-2})^* A^*_{n-2}, \ldots$,
$\pi^d_{(i+3)} = A^\circ_{i+3}(I_{i+2})^* A^*_{i+2}$, *and*
$\pi^d_{(i+2)} = A^\circ_{i+2}(I_{i+1})^* A^*_{i+1}(E_i)^* A^\circ_i(\neg E)\bot(\neg I)A^*_i(E_{i-1})^* A^\circ_{i-1}(\neg E)\bot(\neg I)A^*_{i-1}$
$\ldots(E_1)^* A^\circ_1(\neg E)\bot(\neg I)A^*_1(\neg E)\bot$.

Proof. By induction on the normal derivation of $\Gamma \vdash_{\lambda 2} M : A$.

From Proposition 24, the form of normal $\underline{\underline{M}}$ without (η_a) is described as follows:

$$
\begin{aligned}
\underline{\underline{NF}} ::= {} & xa \\
& \mid a(\lambda k.\mathtt{let}\ \langle \chi, a\rangle = k\ \mathtt{in}\ a(\lambda k.\mathtt{let}\ \langle \chi, a\rangle = k\ \mathtt{in}\ \ldots \\
& \quad a(\lambda k.\mathtt{let}\ \langle \chi, a\rangle = k\ \mathtt{in}\ x\langle\langle \underline{\underline{Nf}}, \ldots, \underline{\underline{Nf}}, a\rangle\rangle)\ldots))
\end{aligned}
$$

where $\underline{\underline{Nf}} ::= A^{\bullet} \mid \lambda a.\underline{\underline{NF}}$, and we write χ for either x or X.

We show here some of the cases:

(1) A_n $(n = i + 1)$ is derived by an elimination rule.

Case of $(\Rightarrow E)$:

From a normal deduction Π, $(B \Rightarrow A_n)$ cannot be derived by an introduction rule:

$$
\frac{\begin{array}{c}\Pi_1\\ M_1 : B \Rightarrow A_n\end{array} \qquad \begin{array}{c}\Pi_2\\ M_2 : B\end{array}}{M_1 M_2 : A_n}\ (\Rightarrow E)
$$

Then we have a dual path π_1^d from $(B \Rightarrow A_n)^*$ to $\bot$, corresponding to the path π_1 to $(B \Rightarrow A_n)$:

$$
\begin{array}{c} a : (B \Rightarrow A_n)^* \\ \Sigma_1 \\ \underline{\underline{M_1}} : \bot \end{array}
\qquad
\begin{array}{c} a : B^* \\ \Sigma_2 \\ \underline{\underline{M_2}} : \bot \end{array}
$$

The figure below says that we have a dual path
$\pi^d = A_n^*(\Rightarrow E)^*(B \Rightarrow A_n)^{\circ}(\neg E)\bot(\neg I)\pi_1^d$:

$$
\begin{array}{c}
\dfrac{\dfrac{[d : \neg(\neg B^* \wedge A_n^*)] \qquad \dfrac{\dfrac{\begin{array}{c}[a : B^*]\\ \Sigma_2 \\ \underline{\underline{M_2}} : \bot\end{array}}{\lambda a.\underline{\underline{M_2}} : \neg B^*}\,(\neg I) \qquad a : A_n^*}{\langle \lambda a.\underline{\underline{M_2}}, a\rangle : \neg B^* \wedge A_n^*}\,(\wedge I)}{d\langle \lambda a.\underline{\underline{M_2}}, a\rangle : \bot}\,(\neg E)}{\langle\langle \lambda a.\underline{\underline{M_2}}, a\rangle\rangle : (B \Rightarrow A_n)^*}\,(\neg I) \\
\Sigma_1[a := \langle\langle \lambda a.\underline{\underline{M_2}}, a\rangle\rangle] \\
\underline{\underline{M_1}}[a := \langle\langle \lambda a.\underline{\underline{M_2}}, a\rangle\rangle] : \bot
\end{array}
$$

(2) A_n $(n > i + 2)$ is derived by an introduction rule.

$$
\dfrac{\dfrac{\begin{array}{c}\Pi_1\\ A_{n-2}\end{array}}{A_{n-1}}\,(I_{n-2})}{M : A_n}\,(I_{n-1})
$$

From the form of normal terms in the dual path corresponding to the I-part of the path to A_n, we have $\underline{\underline{M}} : \bot$ as the following form together with type annotations:

$$a(\lambda k{:}A_n^\circ.\mathtt{let}\ \langle\chi, a{:}A_{n-1}^*\rangle = k\ \mathtt{in}\ a(\lambda k{:}A_{n-1}^\circ.\mathtt{let}\ \langle\chi, a{:}A_{n-2}^*\rangle = k\ \mathtt{in}\ \ldots$$
$$a(\lambda k.\mathtt{let}\ \langle\chi, a\rangle = k\ \mathtt{in}\ x\langle\langle \underline{\underline{Nf}}, \ldots, \underline{\underline{Nf}}, a\rangle\rangle)\ldots))$$

Hence, we have the dual paths $A_n^\circ(I_{n-1})^* A_{n-1}^*$, and at least, $A_{n-1}^\circ(I_{n-2})^* A_{n-2}^*$, which correspond to the tail parts of the path to A_n. □

Let π be a path $A_1(R_1)A_2(R_2)\ldots A_{n-1}(R_{n-1})A_n$. Then we define a sequence of inference rules $|\pi| = (R_1)(R_2)\ldots(R_{n-1})$, and $|\pi|^- = (R_{n-1})\ldots(R_2)(R_1)$. Let π^d be a dual path $A_1(R_1)A_2(R_2)\ldots A_{n-1}(R_{n-1})A_n$. Then we define a sequence of inference rules $\|\pi^d\|$ deleting $(\neg I)$ and $(\neg E)$, as follows:

$$\|\pi^d\| = \begin{cases} \|A_2(R_2)A_3\ldots(R_{n-1})A_n\| & \text{if } (R_1) = (\neg I) \text{ or } (\neg E); \\ (R_1)\|A_2(R_2)A_3\ldots(R_{n-1})A_n\| & \text{otherwise.} \end{cases}$$

We write $|\pi|^- \simeq \|\pi^d\|$ for $|\pi|^- = \|\pi^d\|$ under the correspondence between $(\Rightarrow I)$ and $(\wedge E)$; $(\Rightarrow E)$ and $(\wedge I)$; $(\forall I)$ and $(\exists E)$; $(\forall E)$ and $(\exists I)$.

Corollary 41. *Let Π be a normal deduction of $\Gamma \vdash_{\lambda 2} M : A$, and let π be a path in the normal deduction. Then there exist dual paths $\pi_n^d, \ldots, \pi_{i+2}^d$ in $\neg\Gamma^*, a{:}A^* \vdash_{\lambda^\exists} \underline{\underline{M}} : \bot$, such that $|\pi|^- \simeq \|\pi_n^d\|\ldots\|\pi_{i+2}^d\|$.*

It is remarked that in the simply typed case, the definitions of $[\![\ ]\!]$ and $\underline{\underline{\ \ }}$ can be simplified, so that the theorem above becomes straightforward $|\pi|^- \simeq \|\pi^d\|$.

7 Concluding Remarks

The calculus $\lambda^\exists$ can be regarded as a subsystem of $\lambda 2$, in the sense that $\wedge$ and $\exists$ with reduction rules can be impredicatively coded in $\lambda 2$. We have established a Galois embedding from polymorphic $\lambda 2$ into $\lambda^\exists$, in which proof duality appears such that polymorphic functions with $\forall$-type can be interpreted by abstract data types with $\exists$-type [MP85] and vice versa. Moreover, inference rules in a path of normal deductions of $\lambda 2$ are reversely applied in the corresponding dual paths of $\lambda^\exists$, under the correspondence between $(\forall I)$ and $(\exists E)$; $(\forall E)$ and $(\exists I)$; etc. The involved CPS-translation is similar to that of [Plot75], [HS97], [Seli01] or [Fuji03]. However, relating to extensionality, the case of conjunction-elimination is essentially distinct from them, and this point is important for the completeness. Although none of two through [Plot75], [HS97] and ours in this paper are $\beta\eta$-equal, we remark that they are isomorphic to each other in the simply typed case, from the work on answer type polymorphism by Thielecke [Thie04]. Our definition of the CPS-translation can work even for polymorphic $\lambda\mu$-calculus [Pari92].

After completing this work, Masahito Hasegawa commented another definition of denotation of $\lambda 2$-types such that $(A_1 \Rightarrow A_2)^* = \neg A_1^* \wedge A_1^*$ and $(\forall X.A)^* = \exists X.A^*$, where the denotation of types is syntactically equal to type for continuations. His definition makes every theorem in this paper valid as well, and theorem 40 (proof duality) becomes more natural under this definition. This topics will be discussed in the revised and extended version of this paper. We think that our minimal logic $\lambda^{\exists}$ is interesting to investigate fundamental properties of calculi including the system F, e.g., F-algebras under parametricity, duality between initial and terminal fixed points, etc.

Acknowledgements I am grateful to Thierry Coquand, Peter Dybjer, Masahito Hasegawa, Ryu Hasegawa, Per Martin-Löf and Masahiko Sato for helpful discussions. The author is also grateful to the TLCA '05 programme chair and the referees for their constructive comments. This research has been supported by Grants-in-Aid for Scientific Research (C)(2)14540119, Japan Society for the Promotion of Science and by the Kayamori Foundation of Informational Science Advancement.

References

[Coq86] Th. Coquand: An analysis of Girard's paradox, *Proc. the Annual IEEE Symposium on Logic in Computer Science* (1986) 227–236

[Fuji03] K. Fujita: A sound and complete CSP-translation for $\lambda\mu$-Calculus, Lecture Notes in Computer Science **2701** (2003) 120–134

[GTL89] J-Y. Girard, P. Taylor, and Y. Lafont: *Proofs and Types*, Cambridge University Press (1989)

[HS97] M. Hofmann and T. Streicher: Continuation models are universal for $\lambda\mu$-calculus, *Proc. the 12th Annual IEEE Symposium on Logic in Computer Science* (1997) 387–395

[MP85] J. C. Mitchell and G. D. Plotkin: Abstract types have existential type, *Proc. the 12th Annual ACM Symposium on Principles of Programming Languages* (1985) 37–51

[Pari92] M. Parigot: $\lambda\mu$-Calculus: An Algorithmic Interpretation of Classical Natural Deduction, Lecture Notes in Computer Science **624** (1992) 190–201

[Plot75] G. Plotkin: Call-by-Name, Call-by-Value and the λ-Calculus, *Theoretical Computer Science* **1** (1975) 125–159

[Pra65] D. Prawitz: *Natural Deduction, A Proof Theoretical Study*, Almqvist & Wiksell, Stockholm (1965)

[Seli01] P. Selinger: Control Categories and Duality: on the Categorical Semantics of the Lambda-Mu Calculus, *Math. Struct. in Compu. Science* **11** (2001) 207–260

[SF93] A. Sabry and M. Felleisen: Reasoning about Programs in Continuation-Passing Style, *Lisp and Symbolic Computation: An International Journal* **6** (1993) 289–360

[SW97] A. Sabry and Ph. Wadler: A reflection on call-by-value, *ACM Transactions on Programming Languages and Systems* **19-6** (1997) 916–941

[Thie04] H. Thielecke: Answer type polymorphism in call-by-name continuation passing, Lecture Notes in Computer Science **2986** (2004) 279–293

[Wad03] Ph. Wadler: Call-by-value is dual to call-by-name, *International Conference on Functional Programming*, August 25-29, Uppsala (2003)

On the Degeneracy of Σ-Types in Presence of Computational Classical Logic

Hugo Herbelin

LIX - INRIA-Futurs - PCRI,
École Polytechnique,
F-91128 Palaiseau Cedex
Hugo.Herbelin@inria.fr

Abstract. We show that a minimal dependent type theory based on Σ-types and equality is degenerated in presence of computational classical logic. By computational classical logic is meant a classical logic derived from a control operator equipped with reduction rules similar to the ones of Felleisen's $\mathcal{C}$ or Parigot's μ operators. As a consequence, formalisms such as Martin-Löf's type theory or the (Set-predicative variant of the) Calculus of Inductive Constructions are inconsistent in presence of computational classical logic. Besides, an analysis of the role of the η-rule for control operators through a set-theoretic model of computational classical logic is given.

1 Introduction

1.1 Computational Classical Logic

The `call-with-current-continuation` operator is a construct that has been introduced in Scheme a few decades ago. Numerous variants of the original `call-with-current-continuation` have been considered. Felleisen introduced the operators $\mathcal{C}$, $\mathcal{K}$ and $\mathcal{A}$ and studied calculi based on these operators [4]. The SML language introduced the `callcc` and `throw` operators, all equipped with comparable reduction rules.

Griffin [5] showed that Felleisen's $\mathcal{C}$ operator was typable under some conditions of type $\neg\neg A \to A$ in a simply typed framework, thus extending the Curry-Howard correspondence to classical logic.

Parigot [7] introduced a distinction between the (ordinary) variables and the continuation variables, together with operators μ and brackets, leading to the elegant $\lambda\mu$-calculus. A variant of $\lambda\mu$-calculus based on SML `callcc` (there renamed `catch`) and `throw` has been given in Crolard [3].

Basically, computational classical calculus comes with commutation rules (called structural rules or ζ rules in the context of $\lambda\mu$-calculus), an elimination rule (also called simplification or η_μ rule in the context of $\lambda\mu$-calculus), and an idempotency rule (also called renaming or β_μ rule) .

P. Urzyczyn (Ed.): TLCA 2005, LNCS 3461, pp. 209–220, 2005.

As an introduction to computational classical logic, we here describe $\lambda\mu$-calculus:

$$\begin{array}{lll} t, u ::= \lambda x.t \mid tu \mid x \mid \mu\alpha.c & & \textit{terms} \\ c \quad ::= [\alpha]t & & \textit{commands} \end{array}$$

To express the reduction rules, we need to define the notion of substitution of a continuation variable α by an evaluation context C for commands (i.e. a command with a placeholder $\{\,\}$):

$$\begin{array}{lll} x[C/\alpha] & = x & \\ (\lambda x.t)[C/\alpha] & = \lambda x.(t[C/\alpha]) & \\ (tu)[C/\alpha] & = t[C/\alpha]u[C/\alpha] & \\ (\mu\beta.c)[C/\alpha] & = \mu\beta.(c[C/\alpha]) & \\ ([\alpha]t)[C/\alpha] & = C\{t[C/\alpha]\} & \\ ([\beta]t)[C/\alpha] & = [\beta](t[C/\alpha]) & \alpha \neq \beta \end{array}$$

where x in the second rule and β in the fourth rule are chosen such that no capture of free variables in C happens.

In a call-by-name setting, the reduction rules express as:

$$\begin{array}{lll} (\lambda x.t)u \rightarrow t[u/x] & & \beta \\ (\mu\alpha.c)t \rightarrow \mu\alpha.(c[[\alpha](\{\,\}t)/\alpha]) & & \zeta_{app} \\ [\beta]\mu\alpha.c \rightarrow c[[\beta]\{\,\}/\alpha] & & \beta_\mu \\ \mu\alpha.[\alpha]t \rightarrow t & (\alpha \text{ not free in } t) & \eta_\mu \end{array}$$

Thanks to computational classical logic, classical proofs of simple formulae such as Σ_1^0 formulae eventually normalise to proofs which are (essentially) intuitionistic.

Actually, it is worth to notice that reduction rules close to the rules above were already present in Prawitz' proof of normalisation of the classical extension of natural deduction [9]. What was apparently missing, even after the emergence of the intuitionistic part of the proof-as-program paradigm, was the conviction that they were computationally meaningful in practise.

1.2 Computational Versus Platonistic Classical Logic

We oppose computational classical logic to Platonistic classical logic. In Platonistic classical logic, computationally undecidable properties are transcendentally decided by an oracle which transgresses the infinity of time. A Platonistic interpretation of classical logic is given in Sect. 2.5.

1.3 Classical Logic, Axiom of Choice and Definite Description

The axiom of choice (in its functional form) strongly interacts with classical logic. Coquand [2] showed that their conjunction forces propositions to be embeddable in the booleans, thus forbidding non trivial realisability models of the propositional world. Especially, predicative logics with quantification over functions become impredicative in presence of the axiom of choice in its functional form and classical logic (observation attributed to Spector [11]). Also, logics with non degenerated impredicative sets such as the Calculus of Inductive Constructions are inconsistent in presence of the axiom of choice in its functional form and classical logic.

More precisely, what strongly modifies the semantics of a classical logic is not strictly speaking the (functional form of the) axiom of choice but its underlying principle of definite description (also called axiom of unique choice or function construction principle), as shown by Pottinger [8]. Indeed, the functional form of the axiom of choice in type theory

$$(\forall x : A, \exists y : B, R(x,y)) \to \exists f : A \to B, \forall x : A, R(x, f(x))$$

can be shown equivalent in impredicative type theory to the conjunction of its relational form

$$(\forall x : A, \exists y : B, R(x,y)) \to \exists R' \subset R, \forall x : A, \exists ! y : B, R'(x,y)$$

and of the principle of definite description

$$(\forall x : A, \exists ! y : B, R(x,y)) \to \exists f : A \to B, \forall x : A, R(x, f(x)) \ .$$

In presence of classical logic, the principle of definite description alone is enough to force propositions to be embedded in the booleans.

1.4 Computational Classical Logic and Strong Existential Quantification

Classical logic inherits a computational interpretation through the reduction rules assigned to control operators. The functional form of the axiom of choice also inherits a computational interpretation through the reduction rules of strong existential quantification, which is existential quantification equipped with its first and second projections, the type of the second projection being dependent on the first projection.

It is a natural question to study their interaction at a computational level, knowing that they imply at the logical level the existence of a retraction from propositions to the booleans [2].

The computational analysis of the proof of embedding of the propositions within the booleans shows a failure of subject reduction which is due to the dependency of the type of the second projection of the strong existential in the first projection, making untypable the commutation rule of the control operator used for the interpretation with the second projection of the strong existential.

Subject reduction can be restored to the price of assuming proof-irrelevance. Concurrently, it can be shown that the commutation rule of the control operator used for the interpretation with the first projection itself leads to proof-irrelevance, or, more generally, to the degeneracy of the quantification domain. This is the purpose of the current paper.

2 The Degeneracy of Computationally Classical Type Theory with Σ-Types

In this section, we use the terminology Σ-types to denote indifferently strong existential quantification or usual Σ-types with both projections (also referred to as strong sums).

2.1 A Minimal Logic of Σ-Types and Equality

We consider a type theory TT_Σ based on strong existential quantification (i.e. Σ-types) over a unique domain. We use the variable names x, y, ... to range over the elements of the domain. The syntax of proofs and terms is mutually given by

$$\begin{array}{ll} t, u & ::= x \mid \mathsf{wit}\ \pi \\ \pi & ::= (t, \pi) \mid \mathsf{prf}\ \pi \mid \mathsf{refl} \end{array}$$

The syntax of formulae is given by

$$A, B ::= t = u \mid \Sigma x.A$$

The set $FV(A)$ of free variables of A is defined as usual.
This theory is equipped with a single reduction rule on the language of terms.

$$\mathsf{wit}(t, \pi) \rightarrow t \qquad\qquad (\iota_{\mathsf{wit}})$$

The inference rules are on Fig. 1.

$$\frac{\vdash \pi : A(t)}{\vdash (t, \pi) : \Sigma x.A(x)} \qquad \frac{\vdash \pi : \Sigma x.A(x)}{\vdash \mathsf{prf}\ \pi : A(\mathsf{wit}\ \pi)}$$

$$\frac{t \rightarrow u}{\vdash \mathsf{refl} : t = u} \qquad \frac{\vdash \pi_1 : t = u \qquad \vdash \pi_2 : A(t)}{\vdash \mathsf{subst}\ \pi_1\ \pi_2 : A(u)}$$

Fig. 1. Inference rules of TT_Σ

Proposition 1. *TT_Σ is not degenerated, i.e., for distinct variables x and y, $\nvdash x = y$.*

This is direct by interpreting Σ-types on a domain $\mathcal{D}$ with (at least) two distinct elements $a \neq b$. For distinct elements in $\mathcal{D}$, equality is interpreted as the empty set, otherwise as a singleton set with the unique element interpreting the reflexivity proof. The construction (t, π) is interpreted as pairing and wit and prf as the first and second projections so that wit (t, π) and t are identical through the interpretation and the reflexivity rule is valid.

If our only reduction rule is ι_{wit}, it is because it is enough to infer the results shown in the next subsections. We would have got a better-behaved reduction system by adding the rules $\mathsf{prf}(t,\pi) \rightarrow \pi$ and $\mathsf{subst}\ \pi_1\ (t,\pi_2) \rightarrow (t, \mathsf{subst}\ \pi_1\ \pi_2))$. Moreover, with the premise of the reflexivity rule generalised to the congruent reflexive-symmetric-transitive closure of $\rightarrow$, and the extra rule $\mathsf{subst}\ \mathsf{refl}\ \mathsf{refl} \rightarrow \mathsf{refl}$ added, we would have got normalisability of the proofs, and, as a consequence, the subformula property and a syntactic evidence of the non-derivability of the degeneracy of the domain.

2.2 ... and Its Computationally Classical Extension $TT_{\Sigma}^{\mathsf{cc}}$

We now extend the type theory with classical logic. To allow reasoning by contradiction on a formula A, we add the operator $\mathtt{cc}_k\ \pi$ that tries to prove A under the assumption $k : \neg A$. A contradiction is derived at any point of the derivation by applying the new operator $\mathtt{th}\ k\ \pi$ to any proof π of A in the context $k : \neg A$. We thus extend the syntax of proofs with

$$\pi ::= \ldots \mid \mathtt{cc}_k\ \pi \mid \mathtt{th}\ k\ \pi$$

where k ranges over a set of continuation variables. The operators cc and th are similar to the catch and throw operators studied in Crolard [3]. In terms of the $\lambda\mu$-calculus, $\mathtt{cc}_k\ \pi$ and $\mathtt{th}\ k\ \pi$ are essentially the same as $\mu k.[k]\pi$ and $\mu\_.[k]\pi$ where $\_$ denotes a fresh continuation variables that do not occur in π.

The associated inference rules involved contexts of negated formulae. The rules for cc and th are reminiscent of Peirce's law and negation elimination. The full resulting set of inference rules is given on Fig. 2.

$$\frac{\Gamma \vdash \pi : A(t)}{\Gamma \vdash (t,\pi) : \Sigma x.A(x)} \qquad \frac{\Gamma \vdash \pi : \Sigma x.A(x)}{\Gamma \vdash \mathsf{prf}\ \pi : A(\mathsf{wit}\ \pi)}$$

$$\frac{t \rightarrow u}{\Gamma \vdash \mathsf{refl} : t = u} \qquad \frac{\Gamma \vdash \pi_1 : t = u \quad \Gamma \vdash \pi_2 : A(t)}{\Gamma \vdash \mathsf{subst}\ \pi_1\ \pi_2 : A(u)}$$

$$\frac{\Gamma, k : \neg A \vdash \pi : A}{\Gamma \vdash \mathtt{cc}_k\ \pi : A} \qquad \frac{\Gamma, k : \neg A \vdash \pi : A}{\Gamma, k : \neg A \vdash \mathtt{th}\ k\ \pi : B}$$

Fig. 2. Inference rules of $TT_{\Sigma}^{\mathsf{cc}}$

Since proofs occur in terms and that we want the classical extension to be computational, we also extend the syntax of terms. This extension requires to extend also the syntax of proofs with a construction which actually occurs only as argument of wit in terms.

$$\begin{aligned} t &::= \ldots \mid \mathtt{cc}_k\ t \\ \pi &::= \ldots \mid \mathtt{th}\ k\ t \end{aligned}$$

We want this classical extension to be computational. We add a subset of the standard computation rules for $\mathtt{cc}$ and $\mathtt{th}$ [3], but adapted to Σ-types. It is just enough to be able to derive the degeneracy of the domain.

$$\begin{array}{llll} \mathsf{wit}(\mathtt{cc}_k\ \pi) & \to \mathtt{cc}_k\ \mathsf{wit}(\pi[k(\mathsf{wit}\ \{\})/k]) & & (\zeta_{\mathsf{wit}}) \\ \mathtt{cc}_k\ t & \to t & k \text{ not free in } t & (\eta_{\mathtt{cc}}) \end{array}$$

where $[k(\mathsf{wit}\ \{\})/k]$ denotes the capture-free substitution which replaces every occurrence of $\mathtt{th}\ k\ t$ with $\mathtt{th}\ k\ (\mathsf{wit}\ t)$. Notice that rule $\eta_{\mathtt{cc}}$ is identical to η_μ along the interpretation of $\mathtt{cc}_k\ t$ as $\mu k.[k]t$.

The terms and proofs of $TT_\Sigma^{\mathtt{cc}}$ contain a context binder (the operator $\mathtt{cc}$) but do not include any term or proof binder. Hence, the reduction rules of $TT_\Sigma^{\mathtt{cc}}$ do not commit to a call-by-name or call-by-value discipline of reduction. This is in contrast with $\lambda\mu$-calculus where the presence of a term binder (the λ-abstraction) introduces a critical pair (observable on the redex $(\lambda x.t)(\mu\alpha.c)$) that can be resolved by committing the reduction system either to a call-by-name or a call-by-value discipline.

2.3 Deriving the Collapse of the Quantification Domain

The domain of terms in $TT_\Sigma^{\mathtt{cc}}$ is degenerated. Indeed, we have

Proposition 2. *For any two variables x and y, $x = y$ is derivable in $TT_\Sigma^{\mathtt{cc}}$.*

The proof proceeds as follows.

- First prove $\Sigma z.z = x$ using the artificially classical proof

$$\pi_0 \triangleq \mathtt{cc}_k\ (x, \mathtt{th}\ k\ (x, \mathsf{refl}))\ .$$

- Deduce $\mathsf{wit}\ \pi_0 = x$ whose proof is $\pi_1 \triangleq \mathsf{prf}\ \pi_0$.
- Observe that

$$\begin{array}{lll} \mathsf{wit}\ \pi_0 & \to \mathtt{cc}_k(\mathsf{wit}(x, \mathtt{th}\ k\ \mathsf{wit}(x, \mathsf{refl}))) & (\zeta_{\mathsf{wit}}) \\ & \to \mathtt{cc}_k\ x & (\iota_{\mathsf{wit}}) \end{array}$$

  so that

$$\pi_2 \triangleq \mathsf{subst}\ \mathsf{refl}\ \pi_1$$

  is a proof of $\mathtt{cc}_k\ x = x$.
- Show then $\Sigma z.z = y$ using the artificially classical proof

$$\pi_3 \triangleq \mathtt{cc}_k\ (x, \mathtt{th}\ k\ (y, \mathsf{refl}))\ .$$

- Observe also that

$$\begin{array}{lll} \mathsf{wit}\ \pi_3 & \to \mathtt{cc}_k\ (\mathsf{wit}(x, \mathtt{th}\ k\ \mathsf{wit}(y, \mathsf{refl}))) & (\zeta_{\mathsf{wit}}) \\ & \to \mathtt{cc}_k\ x & (\iota_{\mathsf{wit}}) \end{array}$$

  to conclude that

$$\pi_4 \triangleq \mathsf{subst}\ \mathsf{refl}\ (\mathsf{prf}\ \pi_3)$$

  is a proof of $\mathtt{cc}_k\ x = y$.

– Conclude that
$$\mathsf{subst}\ \pi_3\ \pi_4$$
is a proof of $x = y$.

Notice that we only used the ζ_{wit} and ι_{wit} rules. The next section shows that for typed control operators, one can exhibit a set-theoretic model of the system.

2.4 Explicit Typing of cc and th: System $TT_{\Sigma}^{\mathtt{cc}_T}$

We now consider explicitly typed cc and th. The new syntax of terms is

$$\begin{array}{ll} t,u ::= x \mid \mathsf{wit}\ \pi \mid \mathtt{cc}_k^{x.A} t \\ \pi \quad ::= (t,\pi) \mid \mathsf{prf}\ \pi \mid \mathsf{refl} \mid \mathtt{cc}_{k:\neg A}\ \pi \mid \mathtt{th}_B\ k\ \pi \mid \mathtt{th}_B\ k\ t \end{array}$$

The typing rules are similar: just add the constraint for typing $\mathtt{cc}_{k:\neg A}\ \pi$ that $\neg A$ is the type of k in the context and add the constraint that the type of $\mathtt{th}_B\ k\ \pi$ is B. The new reduction rules now take care of types.

$$\begin{array}{llll} \mathsf{wit}(t,\pi) & \to t & & (\iota_{\mathsf{wit}}) \\ \mathsf{wit}(\mathtt{cc}_{k:\neg\Sigma x.A}\ \pi) & \to \mathtt{cc}_k^{x.A}\mathsf{wit}(\pi[k(\mathsf{wit}\ \{\ \})/k]) & & (\zeta_{\mathsf{wit}}) \\ \mathtt{cc}_k^{x.A}t & \to t & k \text{ not free in } t & (\eta_{\mathtt{cc}}) \end{array}$$

Thanks to the explicit typing, the previous proof of degeneracy do not work any longer. Indeed, the two occurrences of $\mathtt{cc}_k\ x$ now appear as $\mathtt{cc}_k^{z.z=x}x$ and $\mathtt{cc}_k^{z.z=y}x$ so that they are not convertible any more. The next section shows that ι_{wit} and ζ_{wit} together with explicitly typed cc and th do not allow to derive the degeneracy of the quantification domain.

2.5 A Set-Theoretic Model of $TT_{\Sigma}^{\mathtt{cc}_T}$ Without $\eta_{\mathtt{cc}}$

Let $\mathcal{D}$ be a non empty domain and d_0 be an element of $\mathcal{D}$. To distinguish the different roles we give to $\emptyset$, we use the abbreviation $\bullet$ to denote $\emptyset$ when seen as an element rather than as a set. We interpret the formulae of $TT_{\Sigma}^{\mathtt{cc}_T}$ by sets in $\mathcal{T}$ where $\mathcal{T}$ is defined by

$$\begin{array}{ll} \mathcal{T}_0 & = \{\emptyset, \{\bullet\}\} \\ \mathcal{T}_{n+1} & = \{\Sigma_{a\in\mathcal{D}}T_a \mid (T_a)_{a\in\mathcal{D}} \in \mathcal{T}_n^{\mathcal{D}}\} \\ \mathcal{T} & = \bigcup_n \mathcal{T}_n \end{array}$$

where $\Sigma_{a\in\mathcal{D}}T_a = \{(a,p) \mid p \in T_a\}$.

For each inhabited $\Sigma_a T_a$, we let $d_{\Sigma_a T_a}$ be a canonical witness of the set, i.e. a constant in $\mathcal{D}$ such that $T_{d_{\Sigma_a T_a}}$ is inhabited (we need the axiom of choice if the domain is not countable). For empty $\Sigma_a T_a$, we let $d_{\Sigma_a T_a}$ be d_0. To each $T \in \mathcal{T}$, we associate a canonical witness $\epsilon(T)$ (which is the same for all empty T). It is defined by

$$\begin{array}{ll} \epsilon(\emptyset) = \epsilon(\{\bullet\}) = \bullet \\ \epsilon(\Sigma_a T_a) & = (d_{\Sigma_a T_a}, \epsilon(T_{d_{\Sigma_a T_a}})) \end{array}$$

and it satisfies $\epsilon(T) \in T$ for non empty T. We use the letter ρ to denote substitutions from the set of variables of the logic to $\mathcal{D}$. The notation $\rho, (x \leftarrow a)$ denotes the substitution which binds (or rebinds) x to a. For a given substitution ρ, we define the interpretations of terms, proofs and formulae as follows:

$$\begin{array}{ll} [\![x]\!]_\rho & = \rho(x) \\ [\![\mathsf{cc}_k^{x.A}\ t]\!]_\rho & = d_{[\![\Sigma x.A]\!]_\rho} \\ [\![\mathsf{wit}\ \pi]\!]_\rho & = fst([\![\pi]\!]_\rho) \end{array}$$

$$\begin{array}{ll} [\![\mathsf{refl}]\!]_\rho & = \bullet \\ [\![\mathsf{subst}\ \pi_1\ \pi_2]\!]_\rho & = [\![\pi_2]\!]_\rho \\ [\![(t,\pi)]\!]_\rho & = ([\![t]\!]_\rho, [\![\pi]\!]_\rho) \\ [\![\mathsf{prf}\ \pi]\!]_\rho & = snd([\![\pi]\!]_\rho) \\ [\![\mathsf{cc}_k^A\ \pi]\!]_\rho & = \epsilon([\![A]\!]_\rho) \\ [\![\mathtt{th}_B\ k\ \pi]\!]_\rho & = \epsilon([\![B]\!]_\rho) \end{array}$$

$$\begin{array}{lll} [\![t = u]\!]_\rho & = \{\bullet\} & \text{if } [\![t]\!]_\rho = [\![u]\!]_\rho \\ [\![t = u]\!]_\rho & = \emptyset & \text{otherwise} \\ [\![\Sigma x.A(x)]\!]_\rho & = \Sigma_{a \in \mathcal{D}} [\![A(x)]\!]_{\rho,(x \leftarrow a)} & \end{array}$$

Notice that we don't need to define $[\![\mathtt{th}\ k\ t]\!]_\rho$ since this pattern occurs only within proofs π occurring in terms of the form $\mathsf{cc}_k\ (\mathsf{wit}\ (t',\pi))$.

Lemma 3. *The interpretation validates the reduction rules ι_{wit} and ζ_{cc}.*

$$\begin{array}{ll} [\![\mathit{wit}(t,\pi)]\!]_\rho & = [\![t]\!]_\rho \\ [\![\mathit{wit}(\mathsf{cc}_{k:\Sigma x.A(x)}\ \pi)]\!]_\rho & = [\![\mathsf{cc}_k^{x.A(x)}\ \mathit{wit}(\pi[k(\mathit{wit}\ \{\ \})/k])]\!]_\rho \end{array}$$

Moreover,

$$[\![A(x)]\!]_{\rho,(x \leftarrow [\![t]\!]_\rho)} = [\![A(t)]\!]_\rho$$

Proposition 4 (Soundness). *If $\Gamma \vdash \pi : A$ then, forall $\rho \in FV(A) \to \mathcal{D}$, if forall $k_i : \neg A_i$ in Γ, $[\![A_i]\!]_\rho$ is empty, then $[\![\pi]\!]_\rho \in [\![A]\!]_\rho$*

Proof. The proof is by induction.

- If $\Gamma \vdash \mathsf{refl} : t = u$ with $t \to u$ then by validity of the reduction rules, $[\![t]\!]_\rho = [\![u]\!]_\rho$ and $[\![t = u]\!]_\rho = \{\bullet\}$.
- If $\Gamma \vdash (t,\pi) : \Sigma x.A(x)$ with $\Gamma \vdash \pi : A(t)$ then, by induction $[\![\pi]\!]_\rho \in [\![A(t)]\!]_\rho = [\![A(x)]\!]_{\rho,(x \leftarrow [\![t]\!]_\rho)}$, hence $[\![(t,\pi)]\!]_\rho = ([\![t]\!]_\rho, [\![\pi]\!]_\rho) \in [\![\Sigma x.A(x)]\!]_\rho$.
- If $\Gamma \vdash \mathsf{prf}\ \pi : A(\mathsf{wit}\ \pi)$ with $\Gamma \vdash \pi : \Sigma x.A(x)$ then, by induction, we get $[\![\pi]\!]_\rho \in [\![\Sigma x.A(x)]\!]_\rho$, so that there exists c and p such $[\![\pi]\!]_\rho = (c,p)$ and $p \in [\![A(x)]\!]_{\rho,(x \leftarrow c)}$. Since $c = fst([\![\pi]\!]_\rho) = [\![\mathsf{wit}\ \pi]\!]_\rho$, we have $[\![\mathsf{prf}\ \pi]\!]_\rho = snd((c,p)) = p \in [\![A(x)]\!]_{\rho,(x \leftarrow c)} = [\![A(\mathsf{wit}\ \pi)]\!]_\rho$.

- If $\Gamma \vdash \mathsf{subst}\ \pi_1\ \pi_2 : A(u)$ with $\Gamma \vdash \pi_1 : t = u$ and $\Gamma \vdash \pi_2 : A(t)$ then, by induction, $[\![\pi_1]\!]_\rho \in [\![t = u]\!]_\rho$, so that $[\![t = u]\!]_\rho$ is not empty and $[\![t]\!]_\rho = [\![u]\!]_\rho$. Also, $[\![\pi_2]\!]_\rho \in [\![A(t)]\!]_\rho$ so that we have $[\![\mathsf{subst}\ \pi_1\ \pi_2]\!]_\rho = [\![\pi_2]\!]_\rho \in [\![A(t)]\!]_\rho = [\![A(x)]\!]_{\rho,(x\leftarrow[\![t]\!]_\rho)} = [\![A(x)]\!]_{\rho,(x\leftarrow[\![u]\!]_\rho)} = [\![A(u)]\!]_\rho$.
- If $\Gamma \vdash \mathsf{cc}_k\ \pi : A$ with $\Gamma, k : \neg A \vdash \pi : A$ then, $[\![A]\!]_\rho$ is either empty or inhabited. If it is inhabited, then $\epsilon_\rho(A) \in [\![A]\!]_\rho$, hence $[\![\mathsf{cc}_k\ \pi]\!]_\rho \in [\![A]\!]_\rho$. Otherwise, we can apply the induction hypothesis and get $[\![\pi]\!]_\rho \in [\![A]\!]_\rho$, which is contradictory with the assumption that $[\![A]\!]_\rho$ is empty.
- If $\Gamma, k : \neg A \vdash k\pi : B$ with $\Gamma, k : \neg A \vdash \pi : A$ then, by induction, we get $[\![\pi]\!]_\rho \in [\![A]\!]_\rho$ which contradicts the assumption that $[\![A]\!]_\rho$ is empty.

Taking for $\mathcal{D}$ a domain with at least two elements, we get the following corollary.

Corollary 5. *$TT_\Sigma^{\mathsf{cc}_T}$ without the η_{cc} rule is not degenerated, i.e. for distinct variables x and y, we have $\nvdash x = y$.*

2.6 Deriving the Collapse of the Quantification Domain with Explicitly Typed Control Operators

Though $TT_\Sigma^{\mathsf{cc}_T}$ without the η_{cc} rule is not degenerated, it gets degenerated by considering the η_{cc} rule. Indeed, we have again

Proposition 6. *For any two variables x and y, $x = y$ is derivable in $TT_\Sigma^{\mathsf{cc}_T}$.*

The new proof proceeds as follows.

- First prove $\Sigma z.x = z$ using the artificially classical proof
$$\pi_0 \triangleq \mathsf{cc}_{k:\Sigma z.x=z}\ (y, \mathtt{th}\ k\ (x, \mathsf{refl}))\ .$$
- Then observe that
$$\begin{array}{rll} \mathsf{wit}\ \pi_0 & \rightarrow \mathsf{cc}_{k:\Sigma z.x=z}\ (\mathsf{wit}(y, \mathtt{th}\ k\ \mathsf{wit}(x, \mathsf{refl}))) & (\zeta_{\mathsf{wit}}) \\ & \rightarrow \mathsf{cc}_k^{z.x=z} y & (\iota_{\mathsf{wit}}) \\ & \rightarrow y & (\eta_{\mathsf{cc}}) \end{array}$$
- Conclude that
$$\mathsf{subst}\ \mathsf{refl}\ (\mathsf{prf}\ \pi_0)$$
is a proof of $x = y$.

2.7 Inconsistency of Martin-Löf's Type Theory Extended with Computational Classical Logic

Since Martin-Löf's type theory [6] has Σ-types in `Set`, its extension with computational classical logic is inconsistent. We first extend the syntax of terms:

$$t ::= \ldots \mid \mathsf{cc}_k\ t$$

Then, we let $\neg A \triangleq A \to N_0$ and we add the following inference rules:

$$\frac{\begin{array}{c}(k \in \neg A)\\ t \in A\end{array}}{\mathtt{cc}_k\ t \in A} \qquad \frac{\begin{array}{c}(k \in \neg A)\\ t = u \in A\end{array}}{\mathtt{cc}_k\ t = \mathtt{cc}_k\ u \in A}$$

For equality, we restrict the commutation of $\mathtt{cc}$ with the elimination operator E for Σ-types to the *non dependent* case, i.e. to the case where x and y do not occur free in C:

$$\frac{\begin{array}{cc}(k \in \neg(\Sigma x \in A)B(x)) & (x \in A, y \in B(x))\\ t \in (\Sigma x \in A)B(x) & u \in C\end{array}}{\mathtt{E}(\mathtt{cc}_k\ t, (x,y)u) = \mathtt{cc}_k\ (\mathtt{E}(t[k(\mathtt{E}(\{\}, (x,y)u))/k], (x,y)u)) \in C}$$

$$\frac{t \in A \qquad k \text{ not free in } t}{\mathtt{cc}_k\ t = t \in A}$$

Without universes, one can only show that the theory is proof-irrelevant, as enforced by Smith's result on the independence of Peano's fourth axiom in the theory without universes [10]. With one universe, $\neg 0 = 1$ is provable and the computational classical theory is inconsistent.

2.8 Inconsistency of the Set-Predicative Calculus of Inductive Constructions Extended with Computational Classical Logic

Since the Calculus of Inductive Constructions [1] has Σ-types in Set and non degenerated datatypes, its extension with computational classical logic in Set, even in its Set-predicative version that Coq version 8 implements, is inconsistent.

We let $\bot \triangleq \forall C : Set.C$ and $\neg A \triangleq A \to \bot$. To get computational classical logic, the syntax of terms is extended with the following construction

$$t ::= \ldots \mid \mathtt{cc}_{k:\neg A}\ t$$

The new inference rule is

$$\frac{\Gamma, k : \neg A \vdash t : A}{\Gamma \vdash \mathtt{cc}_k\ t : A}$$

And the new set of reduction rules, at least, contains $\eta_{\mathtt{cc}}$ and a commutation rule for *non dependent* case analysis.

$$\begin{array}{l}\mathtt{case}_P\ (\mathtt{cc}_{k:\neg A}\ t)\ \mathtt{of}\ t_1 \ldots t_n\\ \quad \to\ \mathtt{cc}_{k:\neg P}\ (\mathtt{case}_P\ (t[k(\mathtt{case}_P\ \{\}\ \mathtt{of}\ t_1 \ldots t_n)/k])\ \mathtt{of}\ t_1 \ldots t_n)\\ \mathtt{cc}_{k:\neg A}\ t\ \to\ t \qquad\qquad k \text{ not free in } t\end{array}$$

Of course, one would expect of a fully-fledged computationally classical Calculus of Inductive Constructions commutation rules of cc for all kinds of constructors (application, inductive types, constructors of inductive types, ...) and only for a given reduction semantics (call-by-name of call-by-value), so as to preserve confluence. But to get an inconsistency, commutation of cc with case analysis (which is the construction needed for defining wit and prf) is enough.

3 Remarks

3.1 Commutation of cc with Respect to prf

We did not consider the commutation rule of cc with respect to prf though it would be needed for completion of the reduction system. The reason was that it was not necessary in order to derive the degeneracy of the quantification domain of the logic. In fact, the naive formulation of this rule

$$\mathsf{prf}(\mathtt{cc}_k\ \pi) \rightarrow \mathtt{cc}_{k'}\ \mathsf{prf}(\pi[k'(\mathsf{prf}\ \{\ \})/k]) \qquad (\zeta_{\mathsf{prf}})$$

is problematic since it does not satisfy subject reduction. Indeed, if k has type $\Sigma x.A(x)$ on the left-hand-side, then, on the right-hand-side, it maps to a continuation variable k' (we chose a different name to emphasise the difference of types) that cannot be typed consistently in the general case. The binding occurrence of k' is intended to have type $A(\mathsf{wit}(\mathtt{cc}_k\ \pi)$ while each place of the form $\mathtt{th}\ k'\ (\mathsf{prf}\ \pi')$ where it occurs bound expects it to be of type $A(\mathsf{wit}(\mathtt{cc}_k\ \pi')$ for π' a strict subproof of π. There is no reason that each of the $\mathsf{wit}(\mathtt{cc}_k\ \pi')$ (that reduce to $\mathtt{cc}_k^{x.A}\mathsf{wit}(\pi'[k(\mathsf{wit}\ \{\ \})/k]))$, and also $\mathsf{wit}(\mathtt{cc}_k\ \pi)$ (that reduces to $\mathtt{cc}_k^{x.A}\mathsf{wit}(\pi[k(\mathsf{wit}\ \{\ \})/k]))$, all are convertible (and there are effectively not convertible for the degeneracy proofs given in Sect. 2.3 and 2.6).

The mismatch can be solved by inserting a coercion that derives $A(\mathtt{cc}_k^{x.A(x)}\ \pi)$ from $A(t)$ for any A, t and π. It may be worth to notice that along the interpretation in section 2.5 that throws away the argument of each typed cc and see it as an Hilbert-style ϵ operator, the coercion simply corresponds to the characteristic axiom of this ϵ operator.

3.2 Intuitionistic Uses of cc

The degeneracy proof needs that some calls to the continuation variables are done to inhabit a priori non inhabited types, such as $x = y$ for distinct variables x and y.

Since cc can still be interesting from a computational point of view even in an non essentially classical framework (typically to reason intuitionistically on algorithms that "backtracks" thanks to cc), it can be interesting to restrict the call to continuation variables set up by cc only on inhabited types.

By this way, any derivation using cc can trivially be translated into an intuitionistic one: just replace each occurrence of $\mathtt{th}\ k\ t$ of type B by b_0 where b_0 is an inhabitant of B. Hence the logic is non degenerated. The soundness of this replacement remains to be investigated in presence of the (expected) commutation rule ζ_{prf}.

3.3 Axiom of Choice *versus* Principle of Definite Description

For simplicity (since definite existential quantification is heavier to deal with than indefinite existential quantification), we only considered ordinary (indefinite) existential quantification.

However, we believe that the results still hold with $\Sigma!$ instead of Σ. Especially, all witnesses occurring in the proofs we considered were unique witnesses.

Acknowledgements

I thank Freek Wiedijk for helpful discussions on the set-theoretic interpretation of the functional space $\neg\neg A \rightarrow A$.

References

1. The Coq development team: The Coq Proof Assistant Reference Manual, Version 8.0. (2004). Available at http://coq.inria.fr/doc.
2. Coquand, T.: Metamathematical investigations of a calculus of constructions. In Odifreddi, P., ed.: Logic and Computer Science. Apic Series 31. Academic Press (1990) 91–122. Also INRIA Research Report number 1088, sept 1989.
3. Crolard, T.: A confluent lambda-calculus with a catch/throw mechanism. Journal of Functional Programming **9(6)** (1999) 625–647
4. Felleisen, M., Friedman, D.P., Kohlbecker, E., Duba, B.F.: Reasoning with continuations. In: First Symposium on Logic and Computer Science. (1986) 131–141
5. Griffin, T.G.: The formulae-as-types notion of control. In: Conf. Record 17th Annual ACM Symp. on Principles of Programming Languages, POPL '90, San Francisco, CA, USA, 17-19 Jan 1990, ACM Press, New York (1990) 47–57
6. Martin-Löf, P.: Intuitionistic Type Theory. Bibliopolis (1984)
7. Parigot, M.: Lambda-mu-calculus: An algorithmic interpretation of classical natural deduction. In: Logic Programming and Automated Reasoning: International Conference LPAR '92 Proceedings, St. Petersburg, Russia, Springer-Verlag (1992) 190–201
8. Pottinger, G.: Definite descriptions and excluded middle in the theory of constructions (1989). Communication to the TYPES electronic mailing list.
9. Prawitz, D.: Natural Deduction - A Proof-Theoretical Study. Almqvist & Wiksell, Stockholm (1965)
10. Smith, J.M.: The independence of Peano's fourth axiom from Martin-Löf's type theory without universes. Journal of Symbolic Logic **53** (1988) 840–845
11. Spector, C.: Provably recursive functionals of analysis: a consistency proof of analysis by an extension of principles in current intuitionistic mathematics. In: Recursive Function Theory: Proc. Symposia in Pure Mathematics. Volume 5., American Mathematical Society (1962) 1–27

Semantic Cut Elimination in the Intuitionistic Sequent Calculus

Olivier Hermant

Projet LogiCal,
Pôle Commun de Recherche en Informatique du plateau de Saclay, CNRS,
École Polytechnique, INRIA, Université Paris-Sud
ohermant@pauillac.inria.fr
http://pauillac.inria.fr/~ohermant

Abstract. Cut elimination is a central result of the proof theory. This paper proposes a new approach for proving the theorem for Gentzen's intuitionistic sequent calculus LJ, that relies on completeness of the cut-free calculus with respect to Kripke Models. The proof defines a general framework to extend the cut elimination result to other intuitionistic deduction systems, in particular to deduction modulo provided the rewrite system verifies some properties. We also give an example of rewrite system for which cut elimination holds but that doesn't enjoys proof normalization.

Keywords: intuitionistic sequent calculus, Kripke Structure, semantic, deduction modulo, cut admissibility, cut elimination property.

1 Introduction

Since Gentzen's result [1], the cut elimination theorem has been a central result of Proof Theory. Proving the cut elimination theorem is the key to the good properties of deduction systems, such as consistency, or the disjunction and the witness property for the intuitionistic framework. It allows also to prove the decidability of some logical fragments (as the propositional case), and is essential for proving completeness of proof search methods such as tableaux or resolution [2, 3, 4].

Two main approaches can be used to establish the result. One way is a syntactic one, proving termination of a certain cut-elimination process, as in the original proof of Gentzen [1]. A modern way to prove the result uses proof terms [5] and reducibility method.

The other way is to prove the admissibility (or redundancy) of the cut rule [6, 7, 8], proving completeness of the cut-free calculus with respect to some notion of model. This is known since Beth, Hintikka and others [9], and this has been recently used by De Marco and Lipton [10] to prove cut elimination of the Intuitionistic Higher-Order Logic, and by Okada [11] for intuitionistic Linear Logic (first and higher-order).

P. Urzyczyn (Ed.): TLCA 2005, LNCS 3461, pp. 221–233, 2005.

An interesting field of research is to try to understand the links between these two methods. In particular, one may ask if all formalisms verifying cut admissibility are normalizing under proof reduction.

A first difficulty for this study is that intuitionistic logic seems to be a better framework for proof normalization, whereas classical logic is easier to use when dealing with semantic methods. There are two manners to bridge the gap: either study proof normalization for a classical logic, either, as we do here, establish semantic methods for the intuitionistic logic.

In this paper, we thus describe a semantic method to prove cut admissibility in the intuitionistic sequent calculus. Although the result is not new, the method seems not to have been used yet. Moreover, it extends easily to sequent calculus modulo several congruences, as we will see in the last part of the paper. This is an important extension for two reasons. First, it shows cut-elimination for many axiomatic theories, without considering *ad-hoc* axiomatic cuts. Then, Deduction Modulo is a good framework to understand the links between semantic and syntactic approaches, since Dowek and Werner have defined in [5] general syntactic methods for proving termination of proof reduction, based on pre-models and reducibility candidates.

Our model construction is obtained by transforming Gödel's completeness theorem for first-order classical logic. We prove completeness of the cut-free sequent calculus with respect to some notion of model. The construction is similar in many aspects to Gödel's, but differs on several important points. First, we consider here intuitionistic logic instead of classical logic, thus our models will have a different form. Then - and this is the most important point - we consider a *cut-free* calculus. This leads to many technical difficulties. In particular it requires to introduce new definitions of consistency and completeness of a theory.

Unlike classical logic, intuitionistic logic has many different notions of models, among which Kripke Structure [12] and Heyting Algebras [13]. Recently, an extension of Heyting Algebra have been used by De Marco and Lipton [10] to prove cut redundancy for Intuitionistic Higher-Order Sequent Calculus. Okada, in [11], uses phase semantics, that reduce to Heyting Algebra in the Intuitionistic Logic subcase. In this paper, we will use Kripke Structure. We believe that Kripke Structures lead to much simpler proofs, in particular they seem to extend rather straightforwardly techniques already used in classical logic ([14, 8]).

In the last section, we discuss shortly the extension of the result to the Deduction Modulo. An example is given, where the cut-elimination proof appears to be a very simple modification of the former. We also present a terminating, confluent rewrite system such that deduction modulo this rule enjoys cut-elimination, although the cut-elimination process using reduction of proof-terms fails [5].

In the later, we will consider, unless specified, the cut-free intuitionistic sequent calculus, this is the calculus as defined in figure 1 minus the cut rule. In a sequent $\Gamma \vdash P$, Γ is a finite multiset of proposition (a proposition can appear several times). So we can always find a fresh constant (provided the language has a countable set of constants) to introduce in the rules $\forall$-right and $\exists$-left.

$$\frac{}{\Gamma, P \vdash P}\text{axiom} \qquad \frac{\Gamma, P \vdash Q \quad \Gamma \vdash P}{\Gamma \vdash Q}\text{cut}$$

$$\frac{\Gamma, P, P \vdash Q}{\Gamma, P \vdash Q}\text{contr-l} \qquad \frac{}{\Gamma, \bot \vdash Q}\bot\text{-l}$$

$$\frac{\Gamma \vdash Q}{\Gamma, P \vdash Q}\text{weak-l} \qquad \frac{\Gamma \vdash}{\Gamma \vdash P}\text{weak-r}$$

$$\frac{\Gamma, P, Q \vdash R}{\Gamma, P \wedge Q \vdash R}\wedge\text{-l} \qquad \frac{\Gamma \vdash P \quad \Gamma \vdash Q}{\Gamma \vdash P \wedge Q}\wedge\text{-r}$$

$$\frac{\Gamma, P \vdash R \quad \Gamma, Q \vdash R}{\Gamma, P \vee Q \vdash R}\vee\text{-l} \qquad \frac{\Gamma \vdash P}{\Gamma \vdash P \vee Q}\vee\text{-r} \qquad \frac{\Gamma \vdash Q}{\Gamma \vdash P \vee Q}\vee\text{-r}$$

$$\frac{\Gamma \vdash P \quad \Gamma, Q \vdash R}{\Gamma, P \Rightarrow Q \vdash R}\Rightarrow\text{-l} \qquad \frac{\Gamma, P \vdash Q}{\Gamma \vdash P \Rightarrow Q}\Rightarrow\text{-r}$$

$$\frac{\Gamma \vdash P}{\Gamma, \neg P \vdash}\neg\text{-l} \qquad \frac{\Gamma, P \vdash}{\Gamma \vdash \neg P}\neg\text{-r}$$

$$\frac{\Gamma, \{t/x\}P \vdash Q}{\Gamma, \forall x P \vdash Q}\forall\text{-l} \qquad \frac{\Gamma \vdash \{c/x\}P}{\Gamma \vdash \forall x P}\forall\text{-r}, c \text{ fresh constant}$$

$$\frac{\Gamma, \{c/x\}P \vdash Q}{\Gamma, \exists x P \vdash Q}\exists\text{-l}, c \text{ fresh constant} \qquad \frac{\Gamma \vdash \{t/x\}P}{\Gamma \vdash \exists x P}\exists\text{-r}$$

Fig. 1. Deduction rule of intuitionistic sequent calculus (with the cut rule)

These two rules are usually (equivalently) formulated with fresh variables instead of constants. Here we prefer this formulation, that avoid considerations over α-equivalence of propositions.

To recall that we are working in the cut-free sequent calculus, we will write a sequent $\Gamma \vdash^{cf} P$

2 Definitions

In [10], De Marco and Lipton discuss the reason why Henkin's completion process [12] fails when we disallow the use of the cut rule. This is the case because the completion process is done with a heavy use of the cut rule. Then, the authors discard the usual completeness notion, and build downward complete sets (with respect to the subformula property), in defining a very nice tableau construction for intuitionistic logic.

Here, we propose a different approach, that keeps the notion of a complete theory. In fact, we adapt the notion of complete theory to the cut-free calculus in a very simple way. The reader can check that when the cut rule is allowed, the two completeness notions are equivalent. But when it is not, the two notions split.

Our construction, and the completion process that follows have the advantage to preserve the maximality of the constructed theories. Moreover, they stick to more usual completeness construction [12] used to define the semantic of sequent calculi (with the cut rule).

We also need a larger understanding of completeness and consistency, because we are in an intuitionistic framework. So, we are led to define A-consistency and A-completeness, where A is a formula. From these definitions, it becomes simple to prove the completeness theorem, following the lines of Gödel's proof, applying it to Kripke Structures.

Definition 1 (A-Consistency). Let A be a proposition. A set of propositions (theory) Γ is said to be A-consistent iff $\Gamma \nvdash^{cf} A$.

Definition 2 (A-Completeness). Let A be a proposition. A set of propositions (theory) Γ is said to be A-complete iff for any proposition P, either $\Gamma, P \vdash^{cf} A$, or $P \in \Gamma$.

Definition 3 (A-Henkin Witnesses). Let A be a proposition. A set of propositions (theory) Γ is said to admit A-Henkin witnesses if for any proposition of the form $\exists x P$ such that $\Gamma, \exists x P \nvdash^{cf} A$, there exists a constant c such that $\{c/x\}P \in \Gamma$.

These definitions are different from from those used in the classical case [14], because we are now in the intuitionistic framework: in particular, we don't have symmetry between the left and the right parts of a sequent, so we lose symmetry between $\forall$ and $\exists$ quantifiers, and we can't have Henkin witnesses for both of them. Another point is that instead of considering only consistency, we have to consider A-consistency, so sets of propositions become smaller, although they still possess all the good properties we need, as shown in section 3.2

Definition 4 (Kripke Structure).

A Kripke Structure $\mathcal{K}$ is a quadruple $\langle K, \leq, D, \Vdash \rangle$, such that K is a set (the set of nodes, or worlds), $\leq$ is a partial order on K, D a function (called the domain) from K to non empty sets, that is monotone w.r.t. $\leq$ (if $\alpha \leq \beta$ then $D(\alpha) \subseteq D(\beta)$). And $\Vdash$ is a relation between elements $\alpha \in K$ and the closed propositions over $D(\alpha)$, such that:

1. for any $A(x_1, ..., x_n)$ atomic, any worlds $\alpha \leq \beta$, any $a_1, ..., a_n \in D(\alpha)$, $\alpha \Vdash A(a_1, ..., a_n)$ implies $\beta \Vdash A(a_1, ..., a_n)$
2. $\alpha \Vdash A \vee B$ iff $\alpha \Vdash A$ or $\alpha \Vdash B$.
3. $\alpha \Vdash A \wedge B$ iff $\alpha \Vdash A$ and $\alpha \Vdash B$.
4. $\alpha \Vdash A \Rightarrow B$ iff for any $\beta \geq \alpha$, $\beta \Vdash A$ implies $\beta \Vdash B$.
5. $\alpha \Vdash \neg A$ iff for any $\beta \geq \alpha$, $\beta \nVdash A$.
6. $\alpha \Vdash \exists x A$ iff there exists $a \in D(\alpha)$ such that $\alpha \Vdash \{a/x\}A$.
7. $\alpha \Vdash \forall x A$ iff for any $\beta \geq \alpha$, for any $a \in D(\beta)$, $\beta \Vdash \{a/x\}A$.

With respect to Kripke Structures, we should first prove soundness of the Intuitionistic Sequent Calculus *with cut.*

Theorem 5 (Soundness). *Let Γ be a set of propositions, and P be a proposition. If $\Gamma \vdash P$ (with possible use of the cut rule), then for any Kripke Structure $\langle K, \leq, D, \Vdash \rangle$, for any node $\alpha \in K$, if $\alpha \Vdash \Gamma$ then $\alpha \Vdash P$.*
We write $\Gamma \models P$ if P is valid at any node that validates Γ.

Proof. We check that all the derivation rules are valid as in [15]. The result holds also for the cut-free sequent calculus, but this is not relevant here. □

The difficult part is to prove the converse, namely the completeness theorem. In our case, we have to prove completeness of the cut-free calculus with respect to Kripke Structures.

3 Completion of a Theory and Basic Results

First, given a theory $\mathcal{T}$ and a proposition A such that $\mathcal{T}$ is A-consistent, we describe how to get an A-complete, A-consistent set Γ containing $\mathcal{T}$, admitting A-Henkin witnesses. Then, we will describe the properties of Γ.

3.1 Completion

Let $\mathcal{L}$ be a language, $\mathcal{T}$ a theory in $\mathcal{L}$, and A a proposition such that $\mathcal{T} \nvdash^{cf} A$. We consider an infinite set of constants $\mathcal{C}$ disjoint from $\mathcal{L}$, and we define $\mathcal{L}' = \mathcal{L} \cup \mathcal{C}$.

We consider an enumeration of the propositions of $\mathcal{L}'$: $P_0, ..., P_n, ...$ and we let $\Gamma_0 = \mathcal{T}$. We define Γ_n by induction:

- if $\Gamma_n, P_n \nvdash^{cf} A$ and P_n is not of the form $\exists x Q$ we let $\Gamma_{n+1} = \Gamma_n \cup \{P_n\}$.
- if $\Gamma_n, P_n \nvdash^{cf} A$ and P_n is of the form $\exists x Q$, we let $\Gamma_{n+1} = \Gamma_n \cup \{P_n, \{c/x\}Q\}$, where $c \in \mathcal{C}$ is a constant that doesn't occur in Γ_n.
- otherwise we let $\Gamma_{n+1} = \Gamma_n$

Notice that in the first case, if P_n is of the form $\exists x Q$,we have $\Gamma_n, \{c/x\}Q \nvdash^{cf} A$ since c is fresh. So we don't lose the A-consistency of Γ_{n+1}.

Finally, we let $\Gamma = \bigcup_{i=0}^{\infty} \Gamma_i$.

3.2 Properties of the Completed Theory

Proposition 6. *Γ is A-consistent, A-complete, and admits A-Henkin witnesses.*

Proof. Let's see the proof for A-completeness: suppose Γ is not A-complete, so there exists a proposition P such that $\Gamma, P \nvdash^{cf} A$ and $P \notin \Gamma$. By the former enumeration, there exists a n such that $P = P_n$. We have $\Gamma_n \subseteq \Gamma$, so $\Gamma_n, P_n \nvdash^{cf} A$. We get a contradiction, since by construction $P_n \in \Gamma_{n+1} \subseteq \Gamma$.

The two other properties are proved in the same way. □

An important property of any A-consistent, A-complete theory admitting A-Henkin witnesses is that it enjoys some form of the subformula property.

Proposition 7. *Let A be a proposition and Γ an A-complete, A-consistent set of propositions that admits A-Henkin witnesses. Then:*

1. *if $P \wedge Q \in \Gamma$ then $P \in \Gamma$ and $Q \in \Gamma$*
2. *if $P \vee Q \in \Gamma$ then $P \in \Gamma$ or $Q \in \Gamma$*
3. *if $\exists x P \in \Gamma$ then $\{c/x\}P \in \Gamma$ for some c*
4. *if $\forall x P \in \Gamma$ then $\{t/x\}P \in \Gamma$ for any t*
5. *if $P \Rightarrow Q \in \Gamma$ then either $Q \in \Gamma$, either $\Gamma \nvdash^{cf} P$*
6. *if $\neg P \in \Gamma$ then $\Gamma \nvdash^{cf} P$*

7. *if $\Gamma \nvdash^{cf} P \wedge Q$ then $\Gamma \nvdash^{cf} P$ or $\Gamma \nvdash^{cf} Q$*
8. *if $\Gamma \nvdash^{cf} P \vee Q$ then $\Gamma \nvdash^{cf} P$ and $\Gamma \nvdash^{cf} Q$*
9. *if $\Gamma \nvdash^{cf} \exists x P$ then for any term t, $\Gamma \nvdash^{cf} \{t/x\}P$*
10. *if $\Gamma \nvdash^{cf} P \Rightarrow Q$ then $\Gamma, P \nvdash^{cf} Q$*
11. *if $\Gamma \nvdash^{cf} \neg P$ then $\Gamma, P \nvdash^{cf}$*

Proof. It relies essentially on the arguments that Γ is A-complete, A-consistent, admits A-Henkin witnesses, and on the fact that we can use in a reversed way the rules of sequent calculus of figure 1.

Let's see some examples:

- 3 is the A-Henkin witnesses property.
- In 5, $P \Rightarrow Q \in \Gamma$ means in particular that $\Gamma, P \Rightarrow Q \nvdash^{cf} A$. We can not have at the same time $\Gamma, Q \vdash^{cf} A$ and $\Gamma \vdash^{cf} P$ (otherwise we could apply $\Rightarrow$-left rule). So, we have either $Q \in \Gamma$ (by A-completeness), or $\Gamma \nvdash^{cf} P$. □

Notice that there are already links with Kripke Structures in this definition: at point 5, $\Gamma \nvdash^{cf} P$ can be understood as the following: we can (in a richer language) complete Γ in Δ, P-complete, P-consistent, and that admits P-Henkin witnesses, in the same way as in section 3.1. So proposition 7 gives us a very easy way to construct a Kripke Structure, ordered by inclusion. This will be the object of next section.

4 Completeness Theorem and Cut Redundancy

We are now ready to prove the completeness theorem. In fact, we will prove another equivalent formulation.

Theorem 8 (Completeness). *Let $\mathcal{T}$ be a theory and A a proposition, both expressed in some language $\mathcal{L}_0$.*
If $\mathcal{T} \nvdash^{cf} A$ then there exists a Kripke Structure, and a world α such that $\alpha \Vdash \mathcal{T}$ and $\alpha \nVdash A$

Proof. First consider $\mathcal{C}_n$ a countable family of countable sets of new constants. We form the family of languages $\mathcal{L}_{n+1} = \mathcal{L}_n \cup \mathcal{C}_n$.

In the rest of the proof, we consider the Kripke Structure defined as follows:

- $\mathcal{K} = \{\Gamma |$ B-complete, B consistent, B-Henkin, expressed in $\mathcal{L}_i$ for some i and $B \in \mathcal{L}_i\}$

- the order over K, $\leq$ is the large inclusion $\subseteq$
- $\mathcal{D}(\Gamma)$ is the set of closed terms of the language $\mathcal{L}_i$ in which is expressed Γ.
- the forcing relation $\Vdash$ defined by induction on the size of propositions. For atomic propositions we let $\Gamma \Vdash C$ iff $C \in \Gamma$. We extend this forcing relation to non atomic propositions thanks to the clauses $2-7$ of definition 4.
  It still remains to be checked that the first clause of the forcing relation holds: for any atom C, if $\Gamma \Vdash C$, let $\Delta \supseteq \Gamma$, we have to show that $\Delta \Vdash C$. This is immediate since $C \in \Delta$, so we straightforwardly use the forcing relation definition. Finally, we have checked all the clauses, and $\Vdash$ is a forcing relation.

By the completion procedure, we know the existence of a world Γ, expressed in $\mathcal{L}_i$, such that $\mathcal{T} \subset \Gamma$, and Γ is A-consistent, A-complete and admits A-Henkin witnesses. It remains to prove that $\Gamma \Vdash \mathcal{T}$ and $\Gamma \nVdash A$. More generally, we will prove the following:

For any proposition P, for any world Γ, $P \in \Gamma$ implies $\Gamma \Vdash P$ and $\Gamma \nvdash^{cf} P$ implies $\Gamma \nVdash P$.

By an induction on the size of the proposition P:

- the atomic case is immediate: if $A \in \Gamma$ so $\Gamma \Vdash A$. And if $\Gamma \nvdash^{cf} A$, then $A \notin \Gamma$, so by definition of the forcing relation $\Gamma \nVdash A$.
- if $A \vee B \in \Gamma$, we use proposition 7 and get $A \in \Gamma$ or $B \in \Gamma$, hence by induction hypothesis $\Gamma \Vdash A$ or $\Gamma \Vdash B$. Thus $\Gamma \Vdash A \vee B$.
  if $\Gamma \nvdash^{cf} A \vee B$, by proposition 7, we have $\Gamma \nvdash^{cf} A$ and $\Gamma \nvdash^{cf} B$, so by induction hypothesis $\Gamma \nVdash A$ and $\Gamma \nVdash B$, hence $\Gamma \nVdash A \vee B$.
- if $A \Rightarrow B \in \Gamma$, let $\Delta \supseteq \Gamma$. Obviously $A \Rightarrow B \in \Delta$. By proposition 7, either $\Delta \nvdash^{cf} A$, either $B \in \Delta$. If the former holds, by induction hypothesis, we must have $\Gamma \nVdash A$. In the other case, we have $\Delta \Vdash B$ by induction hypothesis. So in both cases: $\Delta \Vdash A$ implies $\Delta \Vdash B$.
  if $\Gamma \nvdash^{cf} A \Rightarrow B$, then by proposition 7, we have $\Gamma, A \nvdash^{cf} B$. Let $\mathcal{L}_j$ the language in which is expressed Γ. By the completion procedure of section 3.1, we can define in the language $\mathcal{L}_{j+1}$ a theory $\Delta \supseteq \Gamma$ that is B-consistent, B-complete and admits B-Henkin witnesses. This Δ is also a world of the Kripke Structure considered. And by induction hypothesis, $\Delta \Vdash A$ and $\Delta \nVdash B$, so we must have $\Gamma \nVdash A \Rightarrow B$.
- if $\exists x P \in \Gamma$, then by the Henkin witnesses property, we have $\{c/x\}P \in \Gamma$, so by induction hypothesis, $\Gamma \Vdash \{c/x\}P$, and then $\Gamma \Vdash \exists x P$.
  if $\Gamma \nvdash^{cf} \exists x P$, then, for any term t, $\Gamma \nvdash^{cf} \{t/x\}P$, by proposition 7. So for any t, $\Gamma \nVdash \{t/x\}P$ by induction hypothesis. Hence $\Gamma \nVdash \exists x P$.
- if $\forall x P \in \Gamma$, then for any $\Delta \supseteq \Gamma$, $\forall x P \in \Delta$, and we use the same arguments as in the previous case to prove that $\Delta \Vdash \{t/x\}P$ for any t. So $\Gamma \Vdash \forall x P$.
  If $\Gamma \nvdash^{cf} \forall x P$, then let $\mathcal{L}_i$ the language of $\Gamma \cup \{\forall x P\}$. Let $c \in \mathcal{C}_i$. c is fresh w.r.t Γ and P by construction of the set $\mathcal{C}_i$. So, we have $\Gamma \nvdash^{cf} \{c/x\}P$. By the completion procedure of 3.1, we get the existence of a world Δ, $\{c/x\}P$-complete, $\{c/x\}P$-consistent admitting P-Henkin witnesses. So by induction hypothesis, $\Delta \nVdash \{c/x\}P$, hence $\Gamma \nVdash \forall x P$.
- the other cases are treated in a similar way. □

As a corollary, we get the cut-elimination theorem:

Theorem 9 (Cut-elimination). *If* $\Gamma \vdash P$, *then* $\Gamma \vdash^{cf} P$.

Proof. Proof: Suppose $\Gamma \vdash P$. By soundness, $\Gamma \models P$, so there is no node α of any Kripke Structure such that $\alpha \Vdash \Gamma$ and $\alpha \nVdash P$. Hence by the completeness theorem, we must have $\Gamma \vdash^{cf} P$. □

5 Adding Rewrite Rules

In this section, we show briefly how the result extends to deduction modulo in a straightforward way, provided the rewrite system verifies some conditions. We recall briefly the context of Deduction Modulo, but we suppose that the reader of this section is familiar with it, or at least with rewrite rules. For further informations, see for example [5, 4].

Definition 10. A term rewrite rule is a pair of terms $l \rightarrow r$ such that all the variables of r appears in l.
A propositional rewrite rule is a pair of propositions $l \rightarrow r$ such that l is atomic and all free variables of r appears in l.

An example of a term rewrite rule is:

$$x \times 0 \rightarrow 0$$

An example of a propositional rewrite rule is:

$$x \times y = 0 \rightarrow (x = 0) \vee (y = 0)$$

In this case, we notice that an atomic proposition can rewrite on a non-atomic proposition.

A rewrite system $\mathcal{R}$ is a set of propositional and term rewrite rules.

The deduction system is transformed in such a way that active propositions should be equal modulo the rewrite system considered. For example the new axiom rule will be:

$$\frac{}{\Gamma, A \vdash_{\mathcal{R}} B} \text{ axiom, with } A \equiv_{\mathcal{R}} B$$

All definitions are transformed in a straightforward way, using cut-free provability modulo the rewrite rules $\vdash_{\mathcal{R}}^{cf}$ instead of cut-free provability $\vdash^{cf}$.

We introduce the notion of the validity of a rewrite system in a Kripke Structure.

Definition 11. A rewrite system $\mathcal{R}$ is valid in a Kripke Structure iff the following property for any world α and propositions A, B holds:

$$\text{if } A \equiv_{\mathcal{R}} B \text{ then } \alpha \Vdash A \Leftrightarrow \alpha \Vdash B$$

When a Kripke Structure validates a rewrite system $\mathcal{R}$, we write the forcing relation $\Vdash_{\mathcal{R}}$.

We check that, given a confluent rewrite system, the proof of soundness theorem (w.r.t. Kripke Structure in which the rewrite system is valid), the completion process of section 3.1, and the proposition 7 still hold.

The only stage that differs from the former proof of the cut-elimination theorem is the construction of the Kripke Structure for A-complete, A-consistent theories that admit A-Henkin witnesses. Indeed, since the expressiveness of deduction modulo goes beyond first-order, we must have a stage in which the logical complexity appears.

So for different kinds of rewrite systems, we will have different model constructions. In some cases, these constructions can directly be derived from that described in section 4, as we will shall see now.

5.1 An Order Condition

We will prove the cut-elimination theorem for all the rewrite systems verifying the following order condition. We consider a confluent rewrite system and a well-founded order $\prec$ such that:

- if $P \rightarrow_{\mathcal{R}} Q$ then $Q \prec P$.
- if A is a subformula of B then $A \prec B$.

This order condition was first introduced by Stuber [3] for proving completeness of Resolution Modulo (ENAR) with respect to Classical Sequent Calculus Modulo. Since we have this order, we can show that the rewrite system is normalizing, in the sense that every term has a normal form.

The Kripke Structure considered is the same as that of the proof of theorem 8, which worlds are A-complete, A-consistent theories that admit A-Henkin witnesses, ordered by inclusion. The only slight difference is in the definition of the forcing relation $\Vdash_{\mathcal{R}}$. We first define it on normal atoms:

$$\Gamma \Vdash_{\mathcal{R}} B \text{ iff } B \in \Gamma$$

We extend $\Vdash_{\mathcal{R}}$ on propositions following clauses $2-7$ of the definition 4, and on non-normal atoms by $\Gamma \Vdash_{\mathcal{R}} B$ if $\Gamma \Vdash_{\mathcal{R}} B \downarrow$. This has to be done simultaneously.

The definition is well founded, since the order is well-founded, and at every step, we decrease the order.

We yet have to check that we really defined a forcing relation. The only point to present a difficulty is the first axiom of a forcing relation. Indeed, if an atom A is non-normal, this is not self-evident to prove that $\Gamma \Vdash_{\mathcal{R}} A$ implies $\Delta \Vdash_{\mathcal{R}} A$ for $\Delta \supseteq \Gamma$. As usual, we have to show a more general result, that for any proposition P, for any $\Delta \supseteq \Gamma$:

$$\Gamma \Vdash_{\mathcal{R}} P \text{ implies } \Delta \Vdash_{\mathcal{R}} P$$

This is done by a straightforward induction over the well-founded order, rewriting non-normal atoms into their normal form. □

Once we have the fact that we really have constructed a Kripke Structure, we remark that this is a Kripke Structure for the rewrite system. This is true by construction on the atoms, and we extend it to any proposition by induction over the proposition structure. □

The last point to prove is that $\Gamma \Vdash_{\mathcal{R}} \Gamma$ and $\Gamma \nVdash_{\mathcal{R}} P$ (when Γ is P-consistent). This is done exactly in the same way as in section 4. □

So, by the very same arguments as in section 4 the cut-elimination theorem holds for confluent rewrite systems compatible with a well-founded order. As an example, the following rewrite system is compatible with such an order:

$$x * y = 0 \rightarrow_{\mathcal{R}} (x = 0) \vee (y = 0)$$
$$x * 0 \rightarrow_{\mathcal{R}} 0$$
$$x + 0 \rightarrow_{\mathcal{R}} x$$

in a general way, all the confluent, terminating, quantifier-free rewrite systems described in [5] are compatible with such an order. Stuber in [3] gives a more detailed example.

5.2 A Non-normalizing Theory

In this section, we transform a result of Dowek and Werner, that found a confluent and terminating rewrite system that doesn't enjoys the cut-elimination property. Here, we exhibit a confluent terminating rewrite system that *enjoys* cut-elimination, but that doesn't have proof normalization.

In [5], a non-normalizing confluent terminating rewrite system is presented. It is defined by the following rule, with $y \simeq z$ standing for $\forall x(y \in x \Rightarrow z \in x)$:

$$R \in R \rightarrow_{\mathcal{R}} \forall y\ (y \simeq R \Rightarrow \neg y \in R)$$

Modulo this rewrite rule, we can prove both sequents $R \in R \vdash^{cf}_{\mathcal{R}}$ and $\vdash^{cf}_{\mathcal{R}} R \in R$, so we can prove, using the cut rule, the sequent $\vdash_{\mathcal{R}}$ (the rewrite system is then inconsistent).

The idea is to modify slightly this rule, to get a consistent rewrite system, that we call $\mathcal{R}$:

$$R \in R \rightarrow_{\mathcal{R}} \forall y(y \simeq R \Rightarrow (y \in R \Rightarrow C)) \tag{1}$$

The same derivations lead this time to proofs of $R \in R \vdash^{cf}_{\mathcal{R}} C$ and of $\vdash^{cf}_{\mathcal{R}} R \in R$. Proof terms are the same as in [5]. These two proofs can be combined with a cut and we get a proof of the sequent $\vdash_{\mathcal{R}} C$. We cannot eliminate the cut by the normalization method, because applying one proof term to the other leads by reductions to the same proof term. And in fact, any reduction-based cut-elimination will fail, since $\vdash^{cf}_{\mathcal{R}} C$ is not provable (what kind of rule could be the first rule, if not the cut rule ?).

So, the rewrite system $\mathcal{R}$ doesn't normalize.

Let's now replace in (1) C by a well-known intuitionistic tautology: $A \Rightarrow A$. We get a new set of rewrite rules $\mathcal{R}^*$. Of course, we can prove $\vdash^{cf}_{\mathcal{R}^*} A \Rightarrow A$

without the cut rule. But the former analysis is still valid, any normalization process fails if we try to eliminate cut from the following proof:

$$\frac{R \in R \vdash^{cf}_{\mathcal{R}^*} A \Rightarrow A \quad \vdash^{cf}_{\mathcal{R}^*} R \in R}{\vdash_{\mathcal{R}^*} A \Rightarrow A} \text{cut}$$

In fact, a normalization procedure can't make the difference between the two rewrite rules (with C and with $A \Rightarrow A$), since proof terms are exactly the same in the two cases.

So this rewrite system doesn't enjoy normalization, however, we here show that it has the cut-elimination property, using the completeness method:

Proposition 12. *The sequent calculus modulo $\mathcal{R}^*$ admits cut.*

Proof. The principle is the same as in previous sections: we first prove the completeness theorem. Given a B-complete, consistent theory Γ, we construct a Kripke Structure that validates $\mathcal{R}^*$, and a node forcing Γ and not forcing B.

The Kripke structure is defined as usual: K is the set of all C-complete, consistent theories admitting C-Henkin witnesses, for some C, both expressed in one of the languages $\mathcal{L}_i$. K is ordered by inclusion, and the domain $D(\Gamma)$ is the closed terms of $\mathcal{L}_i$.
The forcing relation is defined on atoms, no matter whether $\Delta, D \vdash^{cf}_{\mathcal{R}^*}$ or not:

$$\Delta \Vdash D \text{ iff } \Delta \vdash^{cf}_{\mathcal{R}^*} D$$

This is extended over all the propositions. With this method, we are sure that we define a Kripke Structure. We check, as in section 4, that $\Gamma \Vdash \Gamma$ and that $\Gamma \nVdash B$ (when Γ is B-consistent).

It remains yet to prove that we have defined a Kripke Structure for the rewrite rule. All we have to check is that the interpretation of $R \in R$ and of $\forall y(y \simeq R \Rightarrow (y \in R \Rightarrow (A \Rightarrow A)))$ is the same for any world Δ.

Since $\vdash^{cf}_{\mathcal{R}^*} R \in R$, we have for any world $\Delta \Vdash R \in R$ (this is an atomic proposition). It remains to prove that $\Delta \Vdash \forall y(y \simeq R \Rightarrow (y \in R \Rightarrow (A \Rightarrow A)))$.

Let $\Delta' \supseteq \Delta$, and $t \in D(\Delta')$. Moreover, suppose $\Delta' \Vdash t \simeq R$. We now have to prove $\Delta' \Vdash t \in R \Rightarrow (A \Rightarrow A)$. This is trivial since $\Gamma' \Vdash A \Rightarrow A$ for any Γ'. □

So the Kripke Structure constructed is a Kripke Structure for $\mathcal{R}^*$, the completeness theorem is proved and the announced result holds: this rewrite system enjoys cut-elimination. □

The key to understand this result is that while proving the cut-elimination theorem we strongly need a *semantic* information, namely: $A \Rightarrow A$ is an intuitionistic tautology. This information is of course not available when defining a proof reduction process, and when trying to prove the termination of it. Another point that should be stressed is that the cut-free proof has nothing to do with the original proof.

6 Conclusion and Further Work

We have shown how to get the cut-elimination theorem by semantic methods, proving completeness of the cut-free intuitionistic calculus modulo with respect to Kripke Structures. Then we showed how this result extends to Deduction Modulo for an order condition on the rewrite system.

In our study of the links between proof normalization and cut admissibility,we have found a counterexample to the fact that proof normalization is equivalent to the redundancy of the cut rule. In [11], Okada gives a hint about a correspondence between his method (for Higher-Order Logic) and Girard's Reducibility Candidates, but doesn't gives any further information. We think that thanks to our negative result, there is no way to give such a correspondence without giving more information that we get with our model construction.

We should extend the semantic cut-elimination result to other theories modulo, such as the positive theories of [5], or to the formulation of Higher-Order Intuitionistic Sequent Calculus in Deduction Modulo. Then, it seems that one could add positive rules to the order condition, preserving the cut-elimination theorem. Finally, we can try to bridge the gap between semantic and syntactic proofs.

References

1. Gentzen, G.: Untersuchungen über das logische Schliessen. Mathematische Zeitschrift **39** (1934) 176–210, 405–431
2. Bachmair, L., Ganzinger, H.: 11. In: Associative-commutative superposition. Kluwer (1998) 353–397
3. Stuber, J.: A model-based completeness proof of extended narrowing and resolution. In: First International Joint Conference on Automated Reasoning (IJCAR-2001). Volume 2083 of LNCS., Springer (2001) 195–210
4. Dowek, G., Hardin, T., Kirchner, C.: Theorem proving modulo. Journal of Automated Reasoning **31** (2003) 33–72
5. Dowek, G., Werner, B.: Proof normalization modulo. The Journal of Symbolic Logic **68** (2003) 1289–1316
6. Prawitz, D.: Hauptsatz for higher order logic. The Journal of Symbolic Logic **33** (1968) 452–457
7. Takahashi, M.o.: A proof of cut-elimination theorem in simple type-theory. Journal of the Mathematical Society of Japan **19** (1967) 399–410
8. Andrews, P.B.: Resolution in type theory. The Journal of Symbolic Logic **36** (1971) 414–432
9. Troelstra, A.S., Schwichtenberg, H.: Basic Proof Theory. Cambridge University Press (1996)
10. De Marco, M., Lipton, J.: Cut elimination and completeness in church's intuitionistic theory of types. To appear (2003)
11. Okada, M.: A uniform semantic proof for cut-elimination and completeness of various first and higher order logics. Theoretical Computer Science **281** (2002) 471–498
12. Troelstra, A.S.: Metamathematical Investigation of Intuitionistic Arithmetic and Analysis. Springer-Verlag (1973)

13. Rasiowa, H., Sikorski, R.: The mathematics of metamathematics. PWN, Polish Scientific Publishers, Warsaw (1963)
14. Hermant, O.: A model-based cut elimination proof. 2nd St-Petersburg Days of Logic and Computability (2003)
15. Kripke, S.: Semantical analysis of intuitionistic logic. In Crossley, J.N., Dummett, M.A.E., eds.: Formal systems and recursive function. North-Holland (1965) 92–130
16. Troelstra, A.S., van Dalen, D.: Constructivism in Mathematics, An Introduction. North-Holland (1988)
17. Szabo, M.E., ed.: Collected Papers of Gerhard Gentzen. Studies in Logic and the Foundation of Mathematics. North Holland (1969)

The Elimination of Nesting in SPCF

J. Laird

Dept. of Informatics, University of Sussex, UK
jiml@sussex.ac.uk

Abstract. We use a fully abstract denotational model to show that nested function calls and recursive definitions can be eliminated from SPCF (a typed functional language with simple non-local control operators) without losing expressiveness. We describe — via simple typing rules — an *affine* fragment of SPCF in which function nesting and recursion (other than iteration) are not permitted. We prove that this affine fragment is fully expressive in the sense that every term of SPCF is observationally equivalent to an affine term.

Our proof is based on the observation of Longley — already used to prove universality and full abstraction results for models of SPCF — that every type of SPCF is a retract of a first-order type. We describe retractions of this kind which are definable in the affine fragment. This allows us to transform an arbitrary SPCF term into an affine one by mapping it to a first-order term, obtaining an (affine) normal form, and then projecting back to the original type. In the case of finitary SPCF, the retraction is based on a simple induction, which yields bounds for the size of the resulting term. In the infinitary case, it is based on an analysis of the relationship between SPCF definable functions and *strategies* for computing them sequentially.

1 Introduction

One of the important sources of expressive power in functional languages is the *nesting* of function calls, both explicitly, and in recursive definitions. With this expressive power comes subtle and complex behaviour, which complicates the implementation and analysis of functional programs. In this paper, we will show that simple non-local control operators can be used to *eliminate* nesting from functional programs: we show that every program of SPCF (a prototypical functional language with control) is observationally equivalent to a term containing no function-nesting, and in which all loops take the form of iterations.

To highlight the key role that non-local control plays in this result, we observe that a simple example suffices to prove that nesting cannot be eliminated in the purely functional language PCF: there is no term of boolean PCF equivalent to $G(f) = ((f\,\mathtt{tt})\,((f\,\mathtt{ff})\,\mathtt{tt})) : \mathtt{bool}$ which does not contain a nested call to f (for proof see the Appendix). However, in (call-by-name) SPCF we may use control operators to define tests such as $\mathtt{strict}(g)$, which returns $\mathtt{tt}$ if $g : \mathtt{bool} \Rightarrow \mathtt{bool}$ evaluates its argument, and false otherwise, and so define a term equivalent to

P. Urzyczyn (Ed.): TLCA 2005, LNCS 3461, pp. 234–245, 2005.

$G(f)$ without nesting, for example:

```
If strict(f tt)
   then (If ((f ff) tt) then ((f tt) tt) else ((f tt) ff))
   else ((f tt) tt)
```

Formally, we use a simple linear affine typing system to identify a class of SPCF terms which are free of nesting, based on the requirement that in the application of M to N, M and N should not share any free variables. Sharing of variables is permitted in the *sequential composition* of M with N, since evaluation of M is completed before evaluation of N can start. This distinction is the basis of Reynolds' Syntactic Control of Interference typing system for functional languages with state [13], for example. In these settings, affinity is not a reqquireement to use resources at most once, but to use at most one copy of each resource at a time. We may contrast our results with research into type-theories for functional languages and λ-calculi which are used to guarantee polynomial-time normalization of all typable terms [6, 1, 7]. The use of higher-order procedures appears in some senses more constrained in our affine type theory, but it is fully expressive at all types because we allow unlimited sequential uses of procedures, (in particular, we can define all partial recursive first-order functions).

The proof of nesting elimination proceeds via analysis of the fully abstract denotational semantics of SPCF. This can be described in two styles: intensional and extensional. In the intensional presentation [4, 5], types are interpreted as sequential data structures or games, and programs as sequential algorithms or strategies. In the extensional presentation [9], types are interpreted as "bistable biorders" and programs as bistable functions. In this paper, we shall use bistable functions as a simple representation of observational equivalence classes of SPCF programs. We also give a self-contained account of the relationship between bistable functions and evaluation strategies for a small fragment of the SPCF (a general account appears in [10]).

The basis for our proof is the observation by John Longley [11, 12], that in SPCF, the type of first-order functions on the natural numbers is *universal*. That is, for any type T there is an embedding from T to into this type, and a projection back into T, the composition of which is the identity on T. This gives a faithful, internally definable representation of higher-order functionals as first-order functions, which can be thought of as a *compilation* of a functional program down into a low-level representation as a list of numerals $f(0), f(1), \ldots$. The significance for this paper is that (computable) first order functions can always be defined without nesting, and thus we can prove elimination of nesting by developing refined versions of the retractions themselves, which are definable in both finitary and infinitary versions of our affine version of SPCF.

2 SPCF and Its Semantics

SPCF, or sequentially observable PCF [3] is an applied simply-typed λ-calculus (PCF) with a basic form of non-local *control operator* allowing a program to jump back to a declared label, and possibly some unrecoverable errors, (these do not affect our result; we find it useful to include one, called $\top$). Although our version of the language is basically call-by-name, we include types for *strict* (or call-by-value) functions taking ground-type values as arguments. Thus the types of SPCF are given by the following grammar:

$$\sigma, \tau ::= B \mid \sigma^B \mid \sigma \Rightarrow \tau \mid \sigma \times \tau$$

where B is a set of *basic* types of the form $\underline{n}$, where n is a countable cardinal, this being the type of natural numbers less than n (so the type of natural numbers itself is $\underline{\omega}$). A type is *bounded* if its basic subtypes are all finite. The strict function-space $\tau^{\underline{n}}$ may also be thought of as a n-fold product of copies of τ (in the finitary case, it is isomorphic to the corresponding product type).

To the simply-typed λ-calculus with products, we add the following operations and constants:

Sequential Composition. From $M : B$, and $N : \tau^B$, form $M \cdot N : \tau$ which evaluates M to an atomic value and supplies it to N (we may think of this as an infix form of a "case" operator $\mathtt{case} : B \times \tau^B \rightarrow \tau$, which is definable using the standard $\mathtt{If} \ldots \mathtt{then} \ldots \mathtt{else}$, or as call by value application of N to M).

Pattern Matching. From $M : \tau$ and $N : \tau^{\underline{n}}$ form $(M, N) : \tau^{\underline{n+1}}$ — the strict function which evaluates M if its input is 0 or $n \cdot N$ if its input is $n + 1$.

Forcing. A constant $\mathtt{force} : (B \Rightarrow \tau) \Rightarrow \tau^B$ which converts a non-strict (call-by-name) function to a strict function by forcing evaluation of its argument — so $v \cdot (\mathtt{force}\, M) \longrightarrow M\, v$. We will write $\delta x.M$ for $\mathtt{force}\, (\lambda x.M)$.

Error and Divergence. $\top, \bot : \tau$.

Recursion. Fixpoint combinators $Y_\tau : (\tau \Rightarrow \tau) \Rightarrow \tau$ for each type τ.

Iterated Sequential Composition. From $M : \underline{\omega}^{\underline{\omega}}$ form $M^* : \underline{0}^{\underline{\omega}}$. This is expressible in full SPCF as $Y \lambda x.\lambda v.((v \cdot M) \cdot x)$.

Numerals. Constants $\mathtt{0} : \underline{n}$ and $\mathtt{succ} : \underline{n+1}^{\underline{n}}$.

Value Pairing and Projection. From $M : \underline{\omega}$ and $N : \underline{\omega}$ form $M * N : \underline{\omega}$, which evaluates M to v, N to u, and represents the pair of values as e.g. $2^v.(2u + 1)$. The corresponding projections are $\mathtt{fst}, \mathtt{snd} : \underline{\omega}^{\underline{\omega}}$.

Control. A control operator $\mathtt{label} : (\tau^{\underline{n}} \Rightarrow \underline{0}) \Rightarrow \underline{n}$, with which to declare labels to which a program may subsequently jump back. This is a simple form of Cartwright and Felleisen's $\mathtt{catch}$ [3], which sends a functional program strict in its nth argument to the numeral n. Having declared a label k in M with $\mathtt{label}\, \lambda k.M$, whenever we call k with a value v (as $v \cdot k$) we exit M with the value v.

The operational semantics for SPCF programs — closed terms of basic type — is given in Table 1. It is based on *evaluation contexts*, which are given by the grammar:

$E[\cdot] ::=$
$[\cdot] \mid E[\cdot]\, M \mid \mathtt{label}\, E[\_] \mid \lambda k.E[\_] \mid \pi_i\, E[\cdot] \mid E[\_]\cdot M \mid v \cdot E[\_] \mid E[\_] * M \mid v * E[\_]$
(Where a *value* v is a term of the form $0\cdot\mathtt{succ}^n$.) We write $E_k[\_]$ for an evaluation context which does not capture the variable k.

Table 1. "Small-step" operational semantics for SPCF programs

$$
\begin{array}{c}
E[\top] \longrightarrow \top \\
E[(\lambda x.M)\, N] \longrightarrow E[M[N/x]] \\
E[\pi_i(\langle M_1, M_2\rangle)] \longrightarrow E[M_i] \\
E[0 \cdot (M, N)] = E[M] \\
E[(v \cdot \mathtt{succ}) \cdot (M, N)] \longrightarrow E[v \cdot N] \\
E[\mathtt{label}\, \lambda k.E_k[v \cdot k]] \longrightarrow E[v] \\
E[v \cdot (\mathtt{force}\, M)] \longrightarrow E[M\, v] \\
E[Y\, M] \longrightarrow E[M\,(Y\, M)] \\
E[v \cdot M^*] \longrightarrow E[(v \cdot M) \cdot M^*] \\
E[(2^m.2n+1) \cdot \mathtt{fst}] \longrightarrow E[m] \\
E[(2^m.2n+1) \cdot \mathtt{snd}] \longrightarrow E[n].
\end{array}
$$

For a program M we write $M \Downarrow$ if there exists a value v such that $M \twoheadrightarrow v$. We adopt a standard definition of observational equivalence: given terms $M, N : \tau$, $M \simeq N$ if for all compatible program contexts $C[\cdot]$, $C[M] \Downarrow$ if and only if $C[N] \Downarrow$.

2.1 Denotational Semantics of SPCF

We will now briefly describe the fully abstract denotational semantics of SPCF [8, 9] in the category of bistable bicpos and bistable and continuous functions. A bistable bicpo may be presented as a cpo with an equivalence relation (*bistable coherence*); two functions are equivalent essentially if they explore their arguments in the same way, but may fail (either through error or divergence) in different ways.

Definition 1. *A* bistable biorder *consists of a partial order* $(D, \sqsubseteq)$ *and an equivalence relation* $\updownarrow$ *on* D *such that:*

- *$(D, \sqsubseteq)$ has least and greatest elements $\bot, \top$, such that $\bot \updownarrow \top$*
- *for any element a, the equivalence class of a with respect to $\updownarrow$, ordered by $\sqsubseteq$, is a distributive* lattice, *and if $a \updownarrow b$ then $a \wedge b, a \vee b$ are a greatest lower bound and least upper bound for $\{a, b\}$ in $(D, \sqsubseteq)$.*

Given $\sqsubseteq$-directed sets X, Y, we say that $X \updownarrow Y$ if for all $x \in X$ and $y \in Y$ there exists $x' \in X$ and $y' \in Y$ such that $x \sqsubseteq x'$, $y \sqsubseteq y'$ and $x' \updownarrow y'$.

A bistable bicpo *is a bistable biorder D such that $(|D|, \sqsubseteq)$ is a cpo and if $X \updownarrow Y$ then $\bigsqcup X \updownarrow \bigsqcup Y$ and $\bigsqcup X \wedge \bigsqcup Y = \bigsqcup\{x \wedge y \mid x \in X \wedge y \in Y \wedge x \updownarrow y\}$*

A function $f : D \to E$ is *bistable* if its restriction to each $\updownarrow$-equivalence classs is a lattice homomorphism — i.e. if $x \updownarrow y$, then $f(x) \updownarrow f(y)$, $f(x \wedge y) = f(x) \wedge f(y)$ and $f(x \vee y) = f(x) \vee f(y)$.

Proposition 1 ([9, 8]). *Bistable bicpos and bistable and continuous functions form a cpo-enriched CCC.*

Proof. For details, we refer to [9]. The product is defined pointwise, in standard fashion, and the exponential $A \Rightarrow B$ consists of the bistable and continuous functions from A to B, with the extensional (Scott) ordering, and bistable coherence defined by $f \updownarrow g$ if $x \updownarrow y$ implies $f(x) \updownarrow g(y)$, and $f(x) \wedge g(y) = f(y) \wedge g(x)$ and $f(x) \vee g(y) = f(y) \vee g(x)$.

Thus we may interpret the λ-calculus with pairing, and fixpoint combinators, in standard fashion. To interpret the ground types, for each set X we have a "flat" bistable biorder $X_\bot^\top$ consisting of the elements of X, together with $\top$ and $\bot$ elements such that $x \sqsubseteq y$ iff $x = y$ or $x = \bot$ or $y = \top$, and $x \updownarrow y$ iff $x = y$ or $x, y \in \{\top, \bot\}$. We write Σ for $\varnothing_\bot^\top$. The atomic type $\underline{n}$ is intepreted as a $\{i \mid 0 \leq i < n\}_\bot^\top$, and the type $\tau^{\underline{n}}$ as the n-fold product $\Pi_{i<n}[\![T]\!]$. Thus sequential composition is interpreted as composition with the function which sends the numeral i to the ith projection, pattern matching as pairing, and forcing as composition which sends $f : [\![\underline{n}]\!] \rightarrow [\![\tau]\!]$ to $\langle f(i) \mid i \in [\![\underline{n}]\!]\rangle$.

The interpretation of the control operator `label` is based on the observation that bistable and monotone/continuous functions are observably *sequential* in the following sense.

Definition 2. *A function $f : A^n \rightarrow B$ is i-strict if $\pi_i(e) = \top$ implies $f(e) = \top$ and $\pi_i(e) = \bot$ implies $f(e) = \bot$. (So f is simply strict if $f(\top) = \top$ and $f(\bot) = \bot$).*

Proposition 2. *Any strict, bistable and continuous function $f : A^n \rightarrow \Sigma$ is either constant, or i-strict for some unique $i \leq n$.*

Proof. We consider the case $n = 2$, which generalises to arbitrary n. Since f is strict and bistable, $f(\top, \bot) \wedge f(\bot, \top) = f(\langle \top, \bot\rangle \wedge \langle \bot, \top\rangle) = f(\bot, \bot) = \bot$, and similarly $f(\top, \bot) \vee f(\bot, \top) = f(\top, \top) = \top$. Hence either $f(\bot, \top) = \top$ and $f(\top, \bot) = \bot$ — in which case f is right-strict — or $f(\top, \bot) = \top$ and $f(\bot, \top) = \top$ — in which case f is left-strict.

Thus for any biorder A and integer n, we have a strict bistable function `catch` from $A^n \Rightarrow \Sigma$ to $[\![\underline{n}]\!]$ which sends each i-strict function to the value i, and with which we interpret `label`. (In particular, note that $\Sigma^n \Rightarrow \Sigma$ is isomorphic to $[\![\underline{n}]\!]$.) By showing that all compact elements of the model (which is algebraic) are definable, we prove full abstraction.

Theorem 1 ([9]). *$M \simeq N$ if and only if $[\![M]\!] = [\![N]\!]$.*

3 Elimination of Nesting

We capture a class of nesting-free terms of SPCF as a sublanguage ASPCF, defined using simple typing rules based on affine intuitionistic type-theory, for deriving terms in contexts (which are *multisets* of typed variables). Thus a term

Table 2. Typing judgements for ASPCF

$$\frac{}{\Gamma,x{:}\sigma\vdash x{:}\sigma} \qquad \frac{\Gamma,x{:}\sigma\vdash M{:}\tau}{\Gamma\vdash\lambda x.M{:}\sigma\Rightarrow\tau} \qquad \frac{\Gamma\vdash M{:}\sigma\Rightarrow\tau \qquad \Delta\vdash N{:}\sigma}{\Gamma,\Delta\vdash M\ N{:}\tau}$$

$$\frac{}{\Gamma\vdash\mathtt{force}{:}(B\Rightarrow\tau)\Rightarrow\tau^{B}} \qquad \frac{\Gamma\vdash M{:}\sigma \qquad \Gamma\vdash N{:}\sigma^{\underline{n}}}{\Gamma\vdash(M,N){:}\sigma^{\underline{n+1}}} \qquad \frac{\Gamma\vdash M{:}B \qquad \Gamma\vdash N{:}\sigma^{B}}{\Gamma\vdash M\cdot N{:}\sigma}$$

$$\frac{}{\Gamma\vdash\mathtt{label}{:}(\tau^{\underline{n}}\Rightarrow\underline{0})\Rightarrow\underline{n}} \qquad \frac{\Gamma\vdash M{:}\sigma \qquad \Gamma\vdash N{:}\tau}{\Gamma\vdash\langle M,N\rangle{:}\sigma\times\tau} \qquad \frac{\Gamma\vdash M{:}\sigma_1\times\sigma_2}{\Gamma\vdash\pi_i(M){:}\sigma_i}\ i\in\{1,2\}$$

$$\frac{\Gamma\vdash M{:}\underline{\omega} \qquad \Gamma\vdash N{:}\underline{\omega}}{\Gamma\vdash M*N{:}\underline{\omega}} \qquad \frac{}{\Gamma\vdash\mathtt{fst}{:}\underline{\omega}^{\underline{\omega}}} \qquad \frac{}{\Gamma\vdash\mathtt{snd}{:}\underline{\omega}^{\underline{\omega}}}$$

$$\frac{}{\Gamma\vdash 0{:}\underline{n}} \qquad \frac{}{\Gamma\vdash\mathtt{succ}{:}\underline{n+1}^{\underline{n}}} \qquad \frac{}{\Gamma\vdash\top{:}\tau}$$

$$\frac{\Gamma\vdash M{:}\underline{\omega}^{\underline{\omega}}}{\Gamma\vdash M^{*}{:}\underline{0}^{\underline{\omega}}} \qquad \frac{}{\Gamma\vdash\bot{:}\tau}$$

of SPCF is in ASPCF if the judgement $\Gamma \vdash M : T$ is derivable according to the rules in Table 2.

We note that the typing rule for application is *multiplicative* with respect to contexts, whilst all of the others are *additive* — in particular, in the sequential composition, $M\cdot N$, the two terms may share variables, because the computation of M must be completed before the computation of N may commence. If we think of sequential composition as a variant on the conditional in PCF, then this contrasts with the multiplicative rules for `If...then...else` in accounts of linear PCF such as [2]. Instead, our calculus is based on the same typing rules as Syntactic Control of Interference (SCI) [13], in which nesting is excluded because it can lead to *interference* between imperative variables. Note also that the Y combinator is not typable at all in ASPCF — in general, evaluating it violates subject reduction.[1]

3.1 Elimination of Nesting at Bounded Types

We will now show that every term of SPCF of bounded type is contextually equivalent to a term of ASPCF. By Theorem 1, this is equivalent to showing that for every term of SPCF, there is a term of ASPCF with the same denotation. First note that we may replace each instance of the Y combinator on a bounded type with an equivalent Y-free term.

Lemma 1. *For every bounded type τ, there exists n such that $Y \simeq \lambda f.f^n\,\bot$.*

Proof. In the bistable model, $[\![Y]\!]$ is the least upper bound of the chain $\{[\![\lambda f.f^i\,\bot]\!] \mid i \in \mathbb{N}\}$, but since the denotation of $(\tau\Rightarrow\tau)\Rightarrow\tau$ is finite, $[\![Y]\!] = [\![\lambda f.f^n\,\bot]\!]$ for some n, and hence $Y \simeq \lambda f.f^n\,\bot$.

[1] We could resolve this problem by requiring that Y is applied only to *closed* terms, but Y still effectively creates nested calls to its argument.

To eliminate nesting of function calls, we use the notion of *definable retraction.*

Definition 3. *Given types σ, τ, an ASPCF-definable retraction from σ to τ is a pair of terms:* $\mathtt{inj} : \sigma \Rightarrow \tau$ *and* $\mathtt{proj} : \tau \Rightarrow \sigma$ *which denote a retraction — i.e.* $[\![\lambda x : \sigma.\mathtt{proj}(\mathtt{inj}(x))]\!] = [\![\lambda x : \sigma.x]\!]$. *We write $\sigma \trianglelefteq \tau$ if there is a definable retraction from σ to τ ($\sigma \cong \tau$ if it is an isomorphism).*

We now show that that every type is an ASPCF-definable retract of a type of the form $\underline{n}^{\underline{m}}$. The key to our proof is to show that this holds for types of the form $\underline{n}^{\underline{m}} \Rightarrow \underline{0}$, since we can then show that each higher type is a retract of one at lower order, using the fact that the relation $\trianglelefteq$ forms a precongruence on types.

Lemma 2. *If $\tau_1 \trianglelefteq \tau_2$ and $\sigma_1 \trianglelefteq \sigma_2$, then $\sigma_1^B \trianglelefteq \sigma_2^B$, $\sigma_1 \times \tau_1 \trianglelefteq \sigma_2 \times \tau_2$, and $\sigma_1 \Rightarrow \tau_1 \trianglelefteq \sigma_2 \Rightarrow \tau_2$*

Proof. For example, the terms $\lambda fx.\mathtt{inj}_\tau\ (f\ (\mathtt{proj}_\sigma\ x)$ and $\lambda fx.\mathtt{proj}_\tau\ (f\ (\mathtt{inj}_\sigma x))$ define a retraction from $\sigma_1 \Rightarrow \tau_1$ to $\sigma_2 \Rightarrow \tau_2$.

Given elements $e \in A^n$, and $a \in A$, let $e\lfloor a \rfloor_i \in A^{n+1}$ denote the *insertion* of a at position i in e — i.e. $\pi_0(e) \times \ldots \times \pi_{i-1}(e) \times a \times \pi_i(e) \times \ldots \times \pi_{n-1}(e)$. For any $j < n$, let $\lceil e \rceil_j$ denote the tuple obtained by removing the jth element of e — i.e. $\pi_0(e) \times \ldots \times \pi_{j-1}(e) \times \pi_{j+1}(e) \times \ldots \times \pi_{n-1}(e)$.

The corresponding ASPCF terms $\mathtt{insert}_m(x, y, z)$ and $\mathtt{remove}(x, y)$ denoting the functions sending $\langle e, i, j \rangle$ to $e\lfloor i \rfloor_j$, and $\langle e, j \rangle$ to $\lceil e \rceil_j$ are readily definable.

Lemma 3. *For any $n > 0$, $\underline{n}^{m+1} \Rightarrow \underline{0} \trianglelefteq \underline{m+1} \times (\underline{n}^m \Rightarrow \underline{0})^n$.*

Proof. The strict map in from $[\![\underline{n}]\!]^{m+1} \Rightarrow \Sigma$ to $[\![\underline{m+1}]\!] \times ([\![\underline{n}]\!]^m \Rightarrow \Sigma)^n$ which sends each i-strict function f to $\langle i, \langle \lambda x.f(x\lfloor j \rfloor_i) \mid j < n \rangle\rangle$ is the denotation of the term

$$\lambda f.(\mathtt{label}\ f) \cdot \delta j.\langle j, \delta k.\lambda x.f\ \mathtt{insert}(x, k, j)\rangle$$

The strict map out from $[\![\underline{m+1}]\!] \times ([\![\underline{n}]\!]^m \Rightarrow \Sigma)^n$ to $[\![\underline{n}]\!]^{m+1} \Rightarrow \Sigma$ such that $\mathsf{out}(\langle i, \langle g_j \mid j < n \rangle\rangle)(e) = \top$ iff $\pi_i(e) = \top$, or $\pi_i(e) = j$ and $g_j(\lceil e \rceil_i) = \top$, is definable as

$$\lambda xy.\pi_1(x) \cdot \delta i.i \cdot y \cdot \delta j.((j \cdot \pi_2(x))\ \mathtt{remove}(y, i))$$

Moreover, for all f, $\mathsf{out}(\mathsf{in}(f)) = f$: this holds by strictness if f is constant, otherwise, suppose f is i-strict. Then for any e, if $\mathsf{out}(\mathsf{in}(f))(e) = \top$ then $\mathsf{out}(\langle i, \langle \lambda x.f(x\lfloor j \rfloor_i) \mid j < n \rangle = \top$ and $\pi_i(e) = \top$ (and hence $f(e) = \top$ by i-strictness) or $\pi_i(e) = j$ and $f(\lceil e \rceil_i \lfloor j \rfloor_i) = f(e) = \top$. Similarly, if $(\mathsf{out}(\mathsf{in}(e)) = \bot$, then $f(e) = \bot$ and so $\mathsf{out}(\mathsf{in}(f)) = f$ as required.

Corollary 1. *For $n > 0$, $\underline{n}^{\underline{m}} \Rightarrow \underline{0} \trianglelefteq \underline{m}^{\underline{n}^m . m}$*

Proof. By induction on m, for which the base case is trivial. For the inductive case, $\underline{n}^{\underline{m+1}} \Rightarrow \underline{0} \trianglelefteq \underline{m+1} \times (\underline{n}^{\underline{m}} \Rightarrow \underline{0})^{\underline{n}} \trianglelefteq \underline{m+1} \times (\underline{m}^{\underline{n}^m . m})^{\underline{n}} \trianglelefteq \underline{m+1} \times \underline{m+1}^{\underline{n}^{m+1} . m} \trianglelefteq \underline{m+1}^{\underline{n}^{m+1} . (m+1)}$.

Lemma 4. *For any m, $\underline{0}^{\underline{m}} \Rightarrow \underline{n} \cong \underline{m+n}$.*

Proof. In the bistable model we have $[\![\underline{0}^{\underline{m}} \Rightarrow \underline{n}]\!] \cong \Sigma^m \Rightarrow \Sigma^n \Rightarrow \Sigma \cong \Sigma^{m+n} \Rightarrow \Sigma \cong [\![\underline{m+n}]\!]$. The defining terms for the isomorphism are $\lambda f.\mathtt{label}\ \lambda k.(f\ (\delta x.(x+n)\cdot k))\cdot k$ and $\lambda x.\lambda y.\mathtt{label}\ \lambda k.x\cdot(0\cdot y,(1\cdot y,(\ldots(m\cdot y,k)\ldots)))$

Proposition 3. *For every bounded type τ there exist integers $n(\tau), m(\tau)$ such that $\tau \trianglelefteq \underline{n(\tau)}^{\underline{m(\tau)}}$.*

Proof. By induction on type-structure: for example, if $\tau = \rho \Rightarrow \sigma$, then $\rho \Rightarrow \sigma \trianglelefteq \underline{n(\rho)}^{\underline{m(\rho)}} \Rightarrow \underline{n(\sigma)}^{\underline{m(\sigma)}}$
$\cong \underline{n(\rho)}^{\underline{m(\rho)}} \Rightarrow (\underline{0}^{\underline{n(\sigma)}} \Rightarrow \underline{0})^{\underline{m(\sigma)}}$
$\cong (\underline{0}^{\underline{n(\sigma)}} \Rightarrow \underline{n(\rho)}^{\underline{m(\rho)}} \Rightarrow \underline{0})^{\underline{m(\sigma)}}$
$\trianglelefteq (\underline{0}^{\underline{n(\sigma)}} \Rightarrow \underline{m(\rho)}^{\underline{n(\rho)^{m(\rho)}.m(\rho)}})^{\underline{m(\sigma)}}$
$\cong \underline{(n(\sigma)+m(\rho))}^{\underline{n(\rho)^{m(\rho)}.m(\rho).m(\sigma)}}$.

Theorem 2. *Every SPCF term of bounded type is equivalent to a term of ASPCF.*

Proof. Given any (closed) SPCF term $M:\tau$, by Proposition 3 there exist n, m such that $\tau \trianglelefteq \underline{n}^{\underline{m}}$. $[\![\mathtt{inj} M]\!]$ is a m-tuple of elements of $[\![\underline{n}]\!]$ and is therefore definable as a term N of ASPCF (a tuple composed of numerals, $\top$, and $\bot$). Hence M is observationally equivalent to the ASPCF term $\mathtt{proj}\ N$.

3.2 Unbounded SPCF: Recursion Versus Iteration

We now extend our results to prove eliminability of nesting over unbounded types. In addition to eliminating explicit instances of nesting, we now need to remove those which are introduced by the Y combinator: we will show that we can eliminate both in favour of *iteration*. We first note that (in combination with the surjective pairing operation $\_ * \_$, this is sufficient to define all partial recursive functions — for example, the minimization $\mu x.M(x) = 0$ is represented as $\mathtt{label}\ k.0\cdot(\delta y.y\cdot(\delta x.M)\cdot((y\cdot k),\delta w.(y\cdot \mathtt{succ})))^*$. We also note that we may use surjective pairing to represent a finite list of numerals $n_1,\ldots,n_k$ uniquely as the numeral $n_1 * (n_2 * \ldots * (n_k * 0))$.

As in the bounded case, we show expressiveness of ASPCF by proving that every type has an ASPCF-definable retraction into a universal type, in this case the type $\underline{\omega}^{\underline{\omega}}$ of infinite (lazy) lists of natural numbers, or strict partial functions from $\mathbb{N}$ to $\mathbb{N}$. The proof is based on an ASPCF-definable retraction $\underline{\omega}^{\underline{\omega}} \Rightarrow \underline{0} \trianglelefteq \underline{\omega}^{\underline{\omega}}$. In SPCF, such a retraction can be defined as the fixpoint of a series of approximants defined using the terms given in Lemma 3. However, this requires the use of recursion. Our definition of the required retraction using only iteration is based on representing bistable functions from $(\mathbb{N}_\bot^\top)^\omega$ to Σ as *strategies* for the first player in a two-player game in which players alternately choose natural numbers (or terminate the game by choosing $\top$ or $\bot$). Thus we define a strategy to be a partial function $\sigma : (\mathbb{N} \times \mathbb{N})^* \rightarrow \mathbb{N}_\bot^\top$ giving the first player's response to each finite sequence of pairs of moves. A bistable function $f : (\mathbb{N}_\bot^\top)^\omega \Rightarrow \Sigma$ is represented as a strategy for sequentially evaluating its application to an argument; the first player chooses a component of the argument, the second player must return the value of that component, then the first player chooses another component and so on. Note that a strategy may contain responses for positions which are not reachable in the evaluatation of a function. (Since the representation is used to define a retraction rather than an isomorphism.)

Definition 4. *Given a pair of natural numbers i, j, and a tuple $e \in (\mathbb{N}_\bot^\top)^\omega$, let $e[i,j]$ denote the tuple obtained by* substuting *j for the ith element of e. A finite sequence $s \in (\mathbb{N} \times \mathbb{N})^*$ acts on the tuple $e \in (\mathbb{N}_\bot^\top)^\omega$ as the corresponding series of substitutions — i.e. we define $e[s] \in \mathbb{N}_\bot^\top$ by induction: $e[\varepsilon] = e$ and $e[s(i,j)] = e[s][i,j]$.*

Thus we define a strategy for each bistable function $f : (\mathbb{N}_\bot^\top)^\omega \rightarrow \Sigma$: $\mathsf{strat}(f)(s) = \mathsf{catch}(\lambda e. f\ (e[s]))$.

From each strategy κ, we may recover a function $\mathsf{fun}(\kappa) : (\mathbb{N}_\bot^\top)^\omega \rightarrow \Sigma$ by reconstructing a series of *sequentializations* for each argument.

Definition 5. *Given a strategy κ and an element $e \in (\mathbb{N}_\bot^\top)^\omega$, we define a series of elements $\mathsf{seq}_i(\kappa, e)$ in $((\mathbb{N} \times \mathbb{N})^*)_\bot^\top$*
$\mathsf{seq}_0(\kappa, e) = \varepsilon$
$\mathsf{seq}_{n+1}(\kappa, e) = \top$, *if* $\mathsf{seq}_n(\kappa, e) = \top$, *or* $\mathsf{seq}_n(\kappa, e) = s$ *and* $\kappa(s) = \top$ *or* $\kappa(s) = i$ *and* $\pi_i(e) = \top$,
$\mathsf{seq}_{n+1}(\kappa, e) = s(i,j)$ *if* $\mathsf{seq}_n(\kappa, e) = s$, $\kappa(\mathsf{seq}_n(\kappa, e)) = i$ *and* $\pi_i(e) = j$. $\mathsf{seq}_{n+1}(s) = \bot$, *otherwise.*

Thus we define $\mathsf{fun}(\kappa) : (\mathbb{N}_\bot^\top)^\omega \rightarrow \Sigma$:
$\mathsf{fun}(\kappa)(e) = \top$ *if there exists n such that* $\mathsf{seq}_n(\kappa, e) = \top$,
$\mathsf{fun}(\kappa)(e) = \bot$, *otherwise.*

Lemma 5. *For any f,* $\mathsf{fun}(\mathsf{strat}(f)) = f$.

Proof. We show by straightforward induction that if $s = \mathsf{seq}_n(\kappa, e)$, then $e[s] = e$. So suppose $\mathsf{fun}(\mathsf{strat}(f))(e) = \top$. Then there exists n such that $\mathsf{seq}_n(\mathsf{strat}(f), e) = s$, and either $\mathsf{strat}(f)(s) = \top$, or $\mathsf{strat}(f)(s) = i$, and $\pi_i(e) = \top$. In the former case, we have $\top = (\lambda x. f(x[s]))\ \bot = f(\bot[s]) \sqsubseteq f(e[s]) = f(e)$. In the latter case $\lambda x. f(x[s])$ is i-strict, and $\pi_i(e) = \top$, and so $\top = (\lambda x. f(x[s]))\ e = f(e[s]) = f(e)$.

To prove the converse, we first observe that if $\mathsf{strat}(f)(s) = i$, then there is no pair of the form (i,j) already ocurring in s. Therefore, if $\mathsf{seq}_{n+1}(\mathsf{strat}(f), e) = s(i,j)$, then $\bot[s] < \bot[s(i,j)]$. So if e is compact, then there exists n such that $\mathsf{seq}_n(\mathsf{strat}(f), e) = \top$, or $\mathsf{seq}_n(\mathsf{strat}(f), e) = \bot$, since otherwise $\bot[\mathsf{seq}_n(\mathsf{strat}(f), e)]$ forms a strictly increasing infinite sequence of elements bounded above by e, contradicting compactness of e.

Now suppose $f(e) = \top$. Then there exists a compact $e' \sqsubseteq e$ such that $f(e') = \top$. By compactness of e', there exists (a smallest) n such that $\mathsf{seq}_{n+1}(\mathsf{strat}(f), e') = \top$, or $\mathsf{seq}_{n+1}(\mathsf{strat}(f), e) = \bot$. In the former case, $\mathsf{fun}(\mathsf{strat}(f))(e) = \top$ as required. In the latter case, $\mathsf{seq}_n(\mathsf{strat}(f), e') = s$ and either $\mathsf{strat}(f)(s) = \bot$ —

but then $f(e') = f(e'[s]) \sqsubseteq f(\top[s]) = (\lambda x.f(x[s])\,\top = \bot$, which is a contradiction — or else $\mathsf{strat}(f)(s) = i$, and $\pi_i(e') = \bot$ — but then $\lambda x.f(x[s])$ is i-strict but $\lambda x.f(x[s])\,e' = f(e') = \top$, which is also a contradiction.

We may prove directly that strat and fun are bistable functions (the general relationship between strategies and bistable functions is studied in [10]) but here it suffices to observe that they are definable in ASPCF. For any strategy κ, let $\overline{\kappa}$ be the strict function from $\mathbb{N}$ to $\mathbb{N}_\bot^\top$ obtained by precomposing κ with the projection from $\mathbb{N}$ to $(\mathbb{N} \times \mathbb{N})^*$ corresponding to the representation of finite sequences of pairs as elements of $\mathbb{N}$.

Proposition 4. *The map sending f to $\overline{\mathsf{strat}(f)}$ is an ASPCF definable retraction.*

Proof. Assuming an equality test $M = N : \underline{2}$ which returns 0 if M and N evaluate to the same numeral, and 1 otherwise, we define:
$\mathtt{strat} = \lambda f.\delta i.\mathtt{label}\,\lambda k.f\;(\delta j.\mathtt{label}\,\lambda l.\mathtt{subs}(i,j,k,l))$
where
$\mathtt{subs}(i,j,k,l) = i\cdot(j\cdot k, (\mathtt{succ}\cdot\delta v.((v\cdot\mathtt{fst})\cdot\mathtt{fst} = j)\cdot(((v\cdot\mathtt{fst})\cdot\mathtt{snd})\cdot l, \delta x.v\cdot\mathtt{snd})))^*$.
$\mathtt{fun} = \lambda xy.0\cdot(\delta u.u\cdot x\cdot(\delta v.v\cdot y\cdot(\delta w.(v * w) * u)))^*$.

It is straightforward to prove that $[\![\mathtt{strat}]\!](f) = \overline{\mathsf{strat}(f)}$ and $[\![\mathtt{fun}]\!](\overline{\kappa}) = \mathsf{fun}(\kappa)$ by showing that $\delta j.\mathtt{label}\,\lambda l.\mathtt{subs}(i,j,k,l)$ computes the substitution of the (coded) sequence i into an element of $(\mathbb{N}_\bot^\top)^\omega$, and jumps to k when it has finished, and that n-fold iteration of $\delta u.u\cdot x\cdot(\delta v.v\cdot y\cdot(\delta w.(v*w)*u))$ in fun computes seq_n.

Proposition 5. *Every type of unbounded SPCF is an ASPCF-definable retract of $\underline{\omega}^{\underline{\omega}}$.*

Proof. This follows precisely the proof of Proposition 3, replacing the finite bounds with ω in each case.

Theorem 3. *Every SPCF term M is observationally equivalent to a term of ASPCF.*

Proof. As in the finite case, we apply the definable retraction, to obtain an element $\mathtt{inj}([\![M]\!])$ of $(\mathbb{N}_\bot^\top)^\omega$, corresponding to a function from $\mathbb{N}$ to $\mathbb{N}_\bot^\top$. At this point, we may appeal to the Church-Turing thesis. This function is clearly effectively computable (by the associated term $[\![\mathtt{inj}\,M]\!]$ of SPCF) and is therefore representable as a program $N : \underline{\omega}^{\underline{\omega}}$ of (first-order) ASPCF[2]. Hence M is observationally equivalent to the ASPCF term $\mathtt{proj}\,M$.

To give a more constructive proof, it would be necessary to give a translation from SPCF programs into ASPCF. This can be done either by directly describing

[2] We may choose either of two ways to incorporate $\top$ into the notion of partial recursive function — either as a unrecoverable error (in which case the partial recursive functions correspond to the first-order SPCF-computable functions) or by encoding $\mathbb{N}_\bot^\top$ in $\mathbb{N}_\bot$ by representing $\top$ as a natural number.

a compilation of SPCF into its first-order fragment (see e.g. [14]) or else by a representation of (an effective version of) the denotational semantics. Another possibility would be to use the retractions of SPCF types into $\underline{\omega}^{\underline{\omega}}$ to define a λ-algebra of ASPCF terms [12].

4 Conclusions

In this paper, we have described an example of the use of a denotational model to eliminate nesting in an applied λ-calculus with control operators. It remains to be seen whether this result has any application in the design, implementation or analysis of functional programming languages. In general, elimination of nesting will reduce the space required for program evaluation in a stack-based implementation, since the size of the allocation stack for an ASPCF program can be bounded in the size of the types of the variables. However, this comes at the cost of increase in the size of the program itself (unless the original program is unnecessarily large). Similarly, with regard to time-efficiency, we may observe that optimal reduction techniques such as graph reduction are much easier to apply to terms without nesting, but this must be set against their increased size. One possibility would be to apply de-nesting locally, to eliminate particular nested calls or recursive definitions, as these may only occur in a small fragment of a program.

If the priority is reasoning correctly about programs, rather than evaluating them efficiently, then ASPCF does appear to offer potential advantages. For example, much of the difficulty of the higher-order matching problem stems from the presence of nesting; we are investigating a simple procedure for solving it in ASPCF.

The nesting elimination results for the bounded and unbounded languages may be contrasted in the following respect. In the bounded case, we can normalize the de-nested program, removing all trace of the original; for instance, we can derive bounds on the size of the de-nested program from its type, based on the bounds for the size of the first-order type of which it is a retract in Proposition 3 (essentially, a tower of exponentials proportional in height to the depth of the type). In the unbounded case, a de-nested program will contain a representation of the original program, together with a compiler from SPCF into (first-order) ASPCF. Thus any evaluation or analysis of the de-nested program may be viewed as operating on the original program via this compilation.

In the presence of effects, such as state, which allow nested function calls to be observed, de-nesting is not possible in the strong sense described here (up to observational equivalence). On the other hand, access to state allows many functions to be written more efficiently without nesting — for example, the retractions defined in this paper. By adding control operators to Reynolds' (basic) SCI, for example, we arrive at a language which is at least as expressive as SPCF (since it contains ASPCF), but retains the advantage of using state in an interference-controlled form.

References

1. A. Asperti. Light affine logic. In *Proceedings of LICS '98*. IEEE press, 1998.
2. T. Braüner. *An axiomatic approach to adequacy*. PhD thesis, BRICS, 1996.
3. R. Cartwright and M. Felleisen. Observable sequentiality and full abstraction. In *Proceedings of POPL '92*, 1992.
4. R. Cartwright, P.-L. Curien and M. Felleisen. Fully abstract semantics for observably sequential languages. *Information and Computation*, 1994.
5. P.-L. Curien. On the symmetry of sequentiality. In *Mathematical Foundations of Computer Science*, number 802 in LNCS. Springer, 1993.
6. A. Scedrov J.-Y. Girard and P. Scott. Bounded linear logic: A modular approach to polynomial-time computability. *Theoretical Computer Science*, 97:1–66, 1992.
7. Y. Lafont. Soft linear logic and polynomial time. *Theoretical Computer Science*, 2004. To appear.
8. J. Laird. Bistability: an extensional characterization of sequentiality. In *Proceedings of CSL '03*, number 2803 in LNCS. Springer, 2003.
9. J. Laird. Bistability: A sequential domain theory. Available from http://www.cogs.susx.ac.uk/users/jiml, 2004.
10. J. Laird. Locally boolean domains. To appear in *Theoretical Computer Science*, 2005.
11. J. Longley. The sequentially realizable functionals. *Annals of Pure and Applied Logic*, 1998.
12. J. Longley. Universal types and what they are good for. In *Domain Theory, Logic and Computation: Proceedings of the 2nd International Symposium on Domain Theory*. Kluwer, 2004.
13. J. Reynolds. Syntactic control of interference. In *Conf. Record 5th ACM Symposium on Principles of Programming Languages*, pages 39–46, 1978.
14. Jon G. Riecke. *The Logic and Expressibility of Simply-Typed Call-by-Value and Lazy Languages*. PhD thesis, Massachusetts Institute of Technology, 1991. Available as technical report MIT/LCS/TR-523 (MIT Laboratory for Computer Science).

Appendix

Here we sketch a proof that nesting is not eliminable in PCF by showing that there is no term of boolean PCF which is equivalent to $G(f) = ((f\ \mathtt{tt})\ ((f\ \mathbf{ff})\ \mathtt{tt})))$, and free of nesting (i.e. typable in ASPCF).

Lemma 6. *Any nesting free term $F(f : \mathtt{bool} \Rightarrow \mathtt{bool})$ of boolean PCF is not (PCF) observationally equivalent to $G(f)$.*

Proof. (sketch) We may assume that F is of the form $\mathtt{If}\ ((f\ s_1)\ s_2)\ \mathtt{then}\ t_1\ \mathtt{else}\ t_2$, since it is straightforward to show that every term is equivalent to one in such a form to such a form. Moreover, since F contains no nestings, s_1 and s_2 are closed terms, and we may therefore assume that they are either $\mathtt{tt}$, $\mathbf{ff}$ or $\bot$. We show by case analysis that there is always a term $N : \mathtt{bool} \Rightarrow \mathtt{bool} \Rightarrow \mathtt{bool}$ such that $G(N) \Downarrow$, and $F(N) \not\Downarrow$. (So it suffices to consider cases in which s_1 and s_2 are non-$\bot$.)

- If $s_1 = \mathbf{ff}$, then let $N = \lambda xy.\mathtt{If}\ x\ \mathtt{then}\ \mathtt{tt}\ \mathtt{else}\ \bot$.
- If $s_1 = \mathtt{tt}$ and $s_2 = \mathtt{tt}$, then let $N = \lambda xy.\mathtt{If}\ x\ \mathtt{then}\ (\mathtt{If}\ y\ \mathtt{then}\ \bot\ \mathtt{else}\ \mathtt{tt})\ \mathtt{else}\ \mathbf{ff}$.
- If $s_1 = \mathtt{tt}$ and $s_2 = \mathbf{ff}$, then let $N = \lambda xy.\mathtt{If}\ x\ \mathtt{then}\ (\mathtt{If}\ y\ \mathtt{then}\ \mathtt{tt}\ \mathtt{else}\ \bot)\ \mathtt{else}\ \mathtt{tt}$.

Naming Proofs in Classical Propositional Logic

François Lamarche[1] and Lutz Straßburger[2]

[1] LORIA & INRIA-Lorraine, Projet Calligramme,
615, rue du Jardin Botanique, 54602 Villers-lès-Nancy — France
http://www.loria.fr/~lamarche
[2] Universität des Saarlandes, Informatik — Programmiersysteme,
Postfach 15 11 50, 66041 Saarbrücken — Germany
http://www.ps.uni-sb.de/~lutz

Abstract. We present a theory of proof denotations in classical propositional logic. The abstract definition is in terms of a semiring of weights, and two concrete instances are explored. With the Boolean semiring we get a theory of classical proof nets, with a geometric correctness criterion, a sequentialization theorem, and a strongly normalizing cut-elimination procedure. This gives us a "Boolean" category, which is not a poset. With the semiring of natural numbers, we obtain a sound semantics for classical logic, in which fewer proofs are identified. Though a "real" sequentialization theorem is missing, these proof nets have a grip on complexity issues. In both cases the cut elimination procedure is closely related to its equivalent in the calculus of structures.

1 Introduction

Finding a good way of naming proofs in classical logic—a good theory of proof terms, or proof nets, or whatever—is a notoriously difficult question, and the literature about it is already quite large, and still increasing.

Other logics have been helped enormously by the presence of good semantics, where by semantics we mean mathematical objects that have an independent existence from syntax. Linear logic was found through the observation of the category of coherence spaces and linear maps. For intuitionistic logic, it has been obvious for a long time that all it takes to give an interpretation of formulas and proofs à la Brouwer-Heyting-Kolmogorov-Curry-Howard is a bi-cartesian closed category... and cartesian closed categories abound in nature.

But if we try to extend naively these semantics to classical logic, it is well-known that everything collapses to a poset (a Boolean algebra, naturally) and we are back to the old semantics of provability. Clearly something has to be weakened, if we ever want classical logic to have a meaning beyond syntax. Very recently, it was found [17] that a class of algebras from geometry permits relevant interpretations of classical proofs; in addition proposals for abstract categorical frameworks has been made; the one in [10, 11] is based on the proof nets of [24] (which avoids poset collapse is by not identifying arrow composition with cut-

P. Urzyczyn (Ed.): TLCA 2005, LNCS 3461, pp. 246–261, 2005.

elimination), and the one in [9] extends the tradition of "coherence" results in category theory, which predates linear logic by decades.

Let us describe succinctly the view when this problem is approached from the other end, that of syntax. We use the sequent calculus as our main proof paradigm, but what we say is presented so as to apply to natural deduction as well. It is well known that problems begin when a proof contains redundancies and has to be normalized. Let us represent this situation in the following manner

$$\mathsf{cut}\,\dfrac{\begin{array}{c}\pi_1\\ \vdash \Gamma, A\end{array} \qquad \begin{array}{c}\pi_2\\ \vdash \bar{A}, \Delta\end{array}}{\vdash \Gamma, \Delta} \quad .$$

Here, we use one-sided *notation* for sequents for the sake of generality, and an expression like A could be a formula with some polarity information added, instead of just a formula. The π_1 and π_2 represent the proofs that led to the sequents: they could be sequent calculus trees, proof terms or proof nets. Similarly, the expression $\bar{A}$ is a *formal negation* for A; this notation could be used for instance in a natural deduction context like the $\lambda\mu$-calculus [22], where the "cut" inference above would just be a substitution of a term into another, the negated $\bar{A}$ meaning that it is on the side of the input/premises/λ-variables. But nonetheless the following have for a long time been identified as Desirable Features:

1. $\bar{A}$ is the *logical* negation of A,
2. $\bar{\bar{A}}$ is *structurally equivalent (isomorphic)* to A.

These additional symmetries simplify life enormously, allowing things like structural de Morgan duals. The second feature will not happen, for example, when negation is an introduced symbol, as in the case for two-sided sequent calculi or the $\lambda\mu$-calculus (for which the first feature does not hold either).

The problem of cut-elimination (or normalization) is encapsulated in two cases, called weakening-weakening and contraction-contraction in [12], which hereafters will be written as weak-weak and cont-cont:

$$\mathsf{cut}\,\dfrac{\mathsf{weak}\,\dfrac{\begin{array}{c}\pi_1\\ \vdash \Gamma\end{array}}{\vdash \Gamma, A} \qquad \mathsf{weak}\,\dfrac{\begin{array}{c}\pi_2\\ \vdash \Delta\end{array}}{\vdash \bar{A}, \Delta}}{\vdash \Gamma, \Delta} \qquad \text{and} \qquad \mathsf{cut}\,\dfrac{\mathsf{cont}\,\dfrac{\begin{array}{c}\pi_1\\ \vdash \Gamma, A, A\end{array}}{\vdash \Gamma, A} \qquad \mathsf{cont}\,\dfrac{\begin{array}{c}\pi_2\\ \vdash \bar{A}, \bar{A}, \Delta\end{array}}{\vdash \bar{A}, \Delta}}{\vdash \Gamma, \Delta} \quad .$$

It is well known [13, 12] that both reductions cannot be achieved without choosing a side, and that the outcome is very much dependent on that choice.

The most standard way to resolve these dilemmas is to introduce asymmetry in the system (if it is not already there), by the means of polarity information on the formulas, and using this to dictate the choices. Historically, the first approaches to polarization were closely aligned on the premiss/conclusion duality we have mentioned. One reason for this is that they were derived from double-negation style translations of classical logic into intuitionistic logic. If a classical proof can be turned into an intuitionistic one, then in every sequent in the history of that proof there will be a special formula: the conclusion of the corresponding intuitionistic sequent. This is what is done, for example, *mutatis mutandis*, in the $\lambda\mu$-calculus.

This left-right asymmetry is also at the bottom of Coquand's game semantics [6], where it translates as the two players.

In [12] Girard presented System LC, where the sequents have *at most* one special formula. Not only are there both positive and negative formulas—this time an arbitrary number of each—but in addition there is a *stoup*, which is either empty or contains *one* formula, which has to be positive. Then when a choice has to be made at normalization time, the presence or absence of the positive formula in the stoup is used in addition to the polarity information. This calculus has very nice properties; in particular both Desirable Features above are present. System LC was discovered by the means of a translation into a bi-cartesian closed category $\mathscr{C}$, but something much weaker can be used. Our story would be over if everything had been solved by that approach; but semantic cut-elimination (composition of denotations of proofs) is not associative here in general; this is shown by a case analysis on the polarities. Thus normal forms are still dependent somehow on the history of the proof's construction. Viewed from another angle this says that the category $\mathscr{C}$ cannot *inherently* be a model for classical logic (composition in categories is associative...), it is more a *vehicle for a translation.*

This direction of research has nonetheless been extremely fruitful. It has given a systematic analysis of translations of classical logic into linear logic [7]. Moreover LC's approach to polarities was extended to the formulation of polarized logic LLP [19]. It has the advantage of a much simpler theory of proof nets (e.g., for boxes) and produces particularly perspicuous translations of more traditional logics. This new proof net syntax has been used to represent proofs in LC [19] and the $\lambda\mu$-calculus [20].

Let us go back to the weak-weak and cont-cont problems. It is well-known (e.g., [8]) that one way of solving weak-weak is to permit the system to have a mix rule. As for the cont-cont problem, the proof formalism of the calculus of structures [15, 2] has permitted the emergence of a novel solution: through the use of deep inference a proof can always be transformed into one whose only contractions are made on *constants and atomic formulas.*

In this paper we exploit these two ideas to construct two systems of proof denotations for classical logic, which are at the border of syntax and semantics, and which possess both Desirable Features as well as one of the main features of proof nets, since a proof of a formula is represented as a graph structure on on its set of atoms, the edges being directly related to the axioms of a corresponding sequent proof. But other standard features of non-multiplicative proof nets (boxes and explicit contraction links) are absent—we hasten to say that it has been shown in [16] that multiplicative-additive linear logic can be presented in the same manner as we do, strictly as additional structure on the atomic formulas, without explicit contractions. The most important of the two systems here is the first one; it benefits from a full completeness theorem—in other words, a correctness criterion and a sequentialization theorem—and so it can be used directly to represent proofs, without recourse to other syntactical formalisms. Moreover strong normalization holds, in the most general sense. The other system conveys both more and less information at the same time: the number of times an axiom link is used in a proof is counted, but since we do not have (as of yet) a sequentialization theorem, it is closer to a semantics, in particular to the Geometry of Interaction. Issues of normalization are much more delicate in this latter system, but it has a definite interest from the point of view of complexity.

One important aspect of the first system is that it seems to contradict some widely held ideas about proof terms: it is a collection of term-like objects (nets) with a notion of composition (cut) and for which we have a strong normalization theorem. But it cannot be said to come from the Curry-Howard tradition. In other words the cut-elimination procedure cannot be used as a paradigm of computation. There is more research to be done on this issue. It could be that polarities also introduce another distinction: that between data and program.

Remarkably the idea of using axiom links to capture a proof in classical logic (including the correctness criterion!) has been around since Andrews' paper of 1976 [1], and his use of the term "essence of a proof" clearly shows that he understood what was at stake. But since he was working on proof search, he never explored the possibility of *composing* these "essences". The idea of keeping all axiom links that appear in a sequent proof is already present in Buss' *logical flow graphs* [3, 4].

2 Cut Free Proof Nets for Classical Propositional Logic

Let $\mathscr{A} = \{a, b, \dots\}$ be an arbitrary set of atoms, and let $\bar{\mathscr{A}} = \{\bar{a}, \bar{b}, \dots\}$ the set of their duals. The set of CL-*formulas* is defined as follows:

$$\mathscr{F} ::= \mathscr{A} \mid \bar{\mathscr{A}} \mid \mathbf{t} \mid \mathbf{f} \mid \mathscr{F} \wedge \mathscr{F} \mid \mathscr{F} \vee \mathscr{F} \quad .$$

We will use A, B, ... to denote formulas. The elements of the set $\{\mathbf{t}, \mathbf{f}\}$ are called *constants*. A formula in which no constants appear is called a CL_0-*formula*. *Sequents*, denoted by Γ, Δ, ..., are finite lists of formulas, separated by comma.

In the following, we will consider formulas as binary trees (and sequents as forests), whose leaves are decorated by elements of $\mathscr{A} \cup \bar{\mathscr{A}} \cup \{\mathbf{t}, \mathbf{f}\}$, and whose inner nodes are decorated by $\wedge$ or $\vee$. Given a formula A or a sequent Γ, we write $\mathscr{L}(A)$ or $\mathscr{L}(\Gamma)$, respectively, to denote its set of leaves.

For defining proof nets, we start with a commutative semiring of *weights* $(W, 0, 1, +, \cdot)$. That is, $(W, 0, +)$ is a commutative monoid structure, $(W, 1, \cdot)$ is another commutative monoid structure, and we have the usual distributivity laws $x \cdot (y + z) = (x \cdot y) + (x \cdot z)$ and $0 \cdot x = 0$. This abstraction layer is just there to ensure a uniform treatment for the two cases that we will encounter in practice, namely $W = \mathbb{N}$ (the semiring of the natural numbers with the usual operations), and $W = \mathbb{B} = \{0, 1\}$ (the Boolean semiring, where addition is disjunction, i.e.,

$1+1=1$, and multiplication is conjunction). There are two additional algebraic properties that we will need:

$$v+w=0 \ \text{ implies } \ v=w=0 \tag{1}$$

$$v \cdot w=0 \ \text{ implies } \ \text{either } v=0 \text{ or } w=0 \quad . \tag{2}$$

These are obviously true in both concrete cases. No other structure or property on $\mathbb{B}$ and $\mathbb{N}$ is needed, and thus other choices for W can be made. They all give sound semantics, but completeness (or sequentialization) is another matter.

2.1 Definition. Given W and a sequent Γ, a *W-linking for Γ* is a function $P\colon \mathscr{L}(\Gamma)\times\mathscr{L}(\Gamma)\to W$ which is symmetrical (i.e., $P(x,y)=P(y,x)$ always), and such that whenever $P(x,y)\neq 0$ for two leaves, then one of the following three cases holds:

0. one of x and y is decorated by an atom a and the other by its dual $\bar{a}$,
1. $x=y$ and it is decorated by $\mathbf{t}$, or
2. one of x and y is decorated by $\mathbf{t}$ and the other by $\mathbf{f}$.

A *W-pre-proof-net*[1] (or shortly *W-prenet*) consists of a sequent Γ and a linking P for it. It will be denoted by $P \rhd \Gamma$. If $W=\mathbb{B}$ we say it is a *simple pre-proof-net* (or shortly *simple prenet*).

In what follows, we will simply say prenet, if no semiring W is specified.

If we choose $W=\mathbb{B}$, a linking is just an ordinary, undirected graph structure on $\mathscr{L}(\Gamma)$, with an edge between x and y when $P(x,y)=1$. An example is

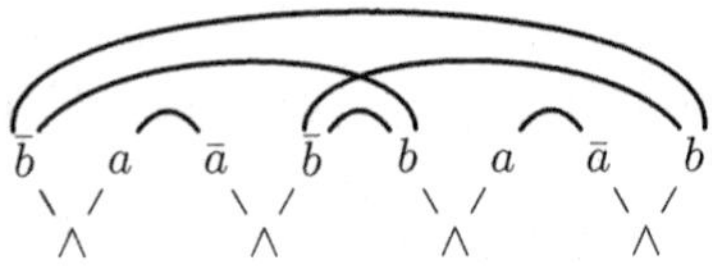

(3)

To save space that example can also be written as

$$\{\,\bar{b}_1\frown b_5\,,\,\bar{b}_1\frown b_8\,,\,\bar{b}_4\frown b_5\,,\,\bar{b}_4\frown b_8\,,\,a_2\frown \bar{a}_3\,,\,a_6\frown \bar{a}_7\,\}\rhd \bar{b}_1\wedge a_2, \bar{a}_3\wedge \bar{b}_4, b_5\wedge a_6, \bar{a}_7\wedge b_8\ ,$$

where the set of linked pairs is written explicitly in front of the sequent. Here we use the indices only to distinguish different atom occurrences (i.e., a_3 and a_6 are not different atoms but different occurrences of the same atom a).

For more general cases of W, we can consider the edges to be decorated with elements of $W\setminus\{0\}$. When $P(x,y)\neq 0$ we say that x and y are *linked*. Here is an example of an $\mathbb{N}$-prenet:

$$\{\,\mathbf{t}_1\overset{2}{\frown}\mathbf{t}_1\,,\,a_4\overset{3}{\frown}\bar{a}_5\,,\,\mathbf{t}_7\frown\mathbf{t}_7\,,\,\mathbf{t}_7\frown\mathbf{f}_8\,\}\rhd \mathbf{t}_1\vee(a_2\wedge\mathbf{t}_3),(a_4\vee(\bar{a}_5\vee\mathbf{f}_6))\wedge(\mathbf{t}_7\vee\mathbf{f}_8)\ . \tag{4}$$

As before, no link means that the value is 0. Furthermore, we use the convention that a link without value means that the value of the linking is 1. When drawing

[1] What we call *pre-proof-net* is in the literature often called a *proof structure*.

$\mathbb{N}$-prenets as graphs (i.e., the sequent forest plus linking), we will draw n links between two leaves x and y, if $P(x, y) = n$. Although this might be a little cumbersome, we find it more intuitive. Example (4) is then written as

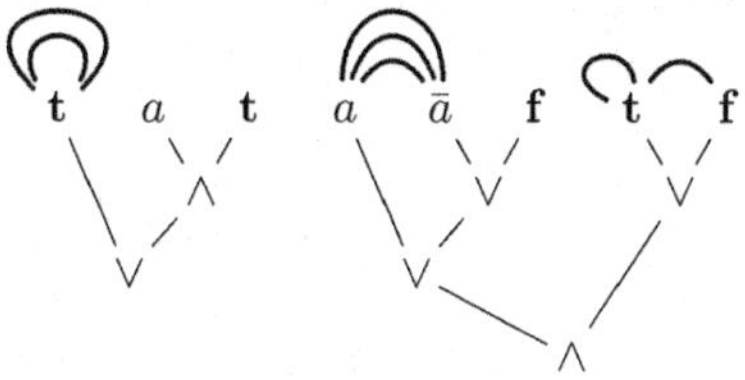

(5)

Now for some more notation: let $P \triangleright \Gamma$ be a prenet and $L \subseteq \mathscr{L}(\Gamma)$ an arbitrary subset of leaves. There is always a $P|_L : L \times L \to W$ which is obtained by restricting P on the smaller domain. But L also determines a subforest $\Gamma|_L$ of Γ, in the manner that all elements of L are leaves of $\Gamma|_L$, and an inner node s of Γ is in $\Gamma|_L$ if *one or two* of its children is in $\Gamma|_L$. Thus $\Gamma|_L$ is something a bit more general than a "subsequent" or "sequent of subformulas", since some of the connectors are allowed to be unary, although still labeled by $\wedge$ and $\vee$. Let $\Gamma' = \Gamma|_L$. Then not only is Γ' determined by L, but the converse is also true: $L = \mathscr{L}(\Gamma')$. We will say that $P|_L \triangleright \Gamma'$ is a *sub-prenet* of $P \triangleright \Gamma$, although it is not *strictu sensu* a prenet. Since this sub-prenet is entirely determined by Γ', we can also write it as $P|_{\Gamma'} \triangleright \Gamma'$ without mentioning L any further.

On the set of W-linkings we define the following operations. Let $P : L \times L \to W$ and $Q : M \times M \to W$ be two W-linkings.

- If $L = M$ we define the *sum* $P + Q$ to be the pointwise sum $(P+Q)(x, y) = P(x, y) + Q(x, y)$. When $W = \mathbb{B}$ this is just the union of the two graphs.
- If $L \subseteq M$ we define the *extension* $P{\uparrow}^M$ *of* P *to* M as the binary function on M which is equal to $P(x, y)$ when both x and y are in L and zero elsewhere. Most of the times we will write $P{\uparrow}^M$ simply as P.
- If L and M are disjoint, we define the *disjoint sum* $P \oplus Q$ on the disjoint union[2] $L \uplus M$ as $P \oplus Q = P{\uparrow}^{L \uplus M} + Q{\uparrow}^{L \uplus M}$.

2.2 Definition. A *conjunctive resolution* of a prenet $P \triangleright \Gamma$ is a sub-prenet $P|_{\Gamma'} \triangleright \Gamma'$ where Γ' has been obtained by deleting one child subformula for every conjunction node of Γ (i.e., in $P|_{\Gamma'} \triangleright \Gamma'$ every $\wedge$-node is unary).

2.3 Definition. A W-prenet $P \triangleright \Gamma$ is said to be *correct* if for every one of its conjunctive resolutions $P|_{\Gamma'} \triangleright \Gamma'$ the W-linking $P|_{\Gamma'}$ is not the zero function. A *W-proof-net* (or shortly *W-net*) is a correct W-prenet. A correct $\mathbb{B}$-prenet is also called a *simple net.*

Both examples shown so far are correct: (3) is a $\mathbb{B}$-net as well as an $\mathbb{N}$-net; (5) is an $\mathbb{N}$-net. Notice that the definition of correctness does not take the exact values of the weights into account, only the presence ($P(x, y) \neq 0$) or absence

[2] If L and M are not actually disjoint, we can rename one of the sets to ensure that they are.

$(P(x,y) = 0)$ of a link. Notice also that correctness is a monotone property because of Axiom (1): if $P \rhd \Gamma$ is correct then $P + Q \rhd \Gamma$ is also correct.

The terms "linking" and "resolution", as well as the $\rhd$-notation, have been lifted directly from the work on multiplicative additive (MALL) proof nets of [16], and we use them in the same way, for the same reasons. In fact, there is a remarkable similarity between the MALL correctness criterion therein—when restricted to the purely additive case—and ours (which is essentially the same as Andrews' [1]); this clearly deserves further investigation.

3 Sequentialization

Figure 1 shows how sequent proofs are mapped into prenets. The sequent system we use contains the multiplicative versions of the $\wedge$- and $\vee$-rules, the usual axioms for identity (reduced to atoms and constants) and truth, as well as the rules of exchange, weakening, contraction, and mix. We call that system CL (for Classical Logic). We use three minor variations: $\mathsf{CL_0}$ where the only axiom available is $\mathsf{id_0}$, involving only atoms, $\mathsf{CL_1}$ which allows in addition the axiom $\mathbf{t}_1$, and $\mathsf{CL_2}$ which allows all three axioms. In the case of $\mathsf{CL_0}$ we consider only $\mathsf{CL_0}$-formulas, and in $\mathsf{CL_1}$ and $\mathsf{CL_2}$ we consider all CL-formulas. When we write just CL we mean $\mathsf{CL_2}$.

There are two rules that are not strictly necessary from the point of view of provability, namely mix and $\mathsf{id_2}$. Thus, although we do not get more tautologies by including these rules in the system, we get *more proofs*. These new proofs are needed in order to make cut elimination confluent (mix), and get identity proofs in the logic with units ($\mathsf{id_2}$), thus allowing us to construct a category. It is only one more example of the extreme usefulness of completions in mathematics: adding stuff can make your life simpler.

Let us now explain the translation from $\mathsf{CL_i}$ sequent proofs to prenets. We should have a notion of $\mathsf{CL_i}$-prenet for any one of $\mathsf{i} = 0, 1, 2$, and Definition 2.1 has been designed to produce them automatically: a $\mathsf{CL_i}$-prenet is one where conditions $0, \ldots, \mathsf{i}$ hold in that definition.

$$\mathsf{id_0}\,\frac{}{\{a \frown \bar{a}\} \rhd a, \bar{a}} \qquad \mathbf{t}_1\,\frac{}{\{\mathbf{t} \frown \mathbf{t}\} \rhd \mathbf{t}} \qquad \mathsf{id_2}\,\frac{}{\{\mathbf{f} \frown \mathbf{t}\} \rhd \mathbf{f}, \mathbf{t}}$$

$$\vee\,\frac{P \rhd A, B, \Gamma}{P \rhd A \vee B, \Gamma} \qquad \wedge\,\frac{P \rhd \Gamma, A \quad Q \rhd B, \Delta}{P \oplus Q \rhd \Gamma, A \wedge B, \Delta} \qquad \mathsf{exch}\,\frac{P \rhd \Gamma, A, B, \Delta}{P \rhd \Gamma, B, A, \Delta}$$

$$\mathsf{weak}\,\frac{P \rhd \Gamma}{P \rhd A, \Gamma} \qquad \mathsf{cont}\,\frac{P \rhd A, A, \Gamma}{P' \rhd A, \Gamma} \qquad \mathsf{mix}\,\frac{P \rhd \Gamma \quad Q \rhd \Delta}{P \oplus Q \rhd \Gamma, \Delta}$$

Fig. 1. Translation of cut free sequent calculus proofs into prenets

The construction is done inductively on the size of the proof. In the two rules for disjunction and exchange, nothing happens to the linking. In the case of weakening we apply the extension operation to P. In the mix and $\wedge$ rules we get the linking of the conclusion by forming the disjoint sum of the linkings of the premises. Therefore, the only rule that deserves further explanation is contraction. Consider the two sequents $\Delta' = A, \Gamma$ and $\Delta = A, A, \Gamma$, where Δ is obtained from Δ' by duplicating A. Let $p\colon \mathscr{L}(\Delta) \to \mathscr{L}(\Delta')$ be the function that identifies the two occurrences of A. We see in particular that for any leaf $x \in \mathscr{L}(\Delta')$, the inverse image $p^{-1}\{x\}$ has either one or two elements. Given $P \rhd \Delta$ let us define the linking P' for Δ' as

$$P'(x,y) \quad = \sum_{\substack{z \in p^{-1}\{x\} \\ w \in p^{-1}\{y\}}} P(z,w) \quad .$$

3.1 Theorem. (Soundness). *Given any W as above, any $\mathsf{i} \in \{0,1,2\}$ and a sequent proof in $\mathsf{CL_i}$, the construction above yields a correct W-prenet.*

Proof. The proof is an easy induction and will be left to the reader for the time being. Notice that we need Axiom (1) for the contraction rule, but not (2). □

We say a prenet is *sequentializable* if it can be obtained from a sequent calculus proof via this translation. Theorem 3.1 says that every sequentializable prenet is a net.

3.2 Theorem. (Sequentialization). *For any $\mathsf{i} \in \{0,1,2\}$, a simple $\mathsf{CL_i}$-net (i.e., $W = \mathbb{B}$) is sequentializable in $\mathsf{CL_i}$.*

Proof. We proceed by induction on the size of the sequent (i.e., the number of $\wedge$-nodes, $\vee$-nodes, and leaves in the sequent forest). Consider a simple net $P \rhd \Delta$. We have the following cases:

- If Δ contains a formula $A \vee B$, then we can apply the $\vee$-rule, and proceed by induction hypothesis.
- If Δ contains a formula $A \wedge B$, i.e., $\Delta = \Gamma, A \wedge B$, then we can form the three simple nets $P' \rhd \Gamma, A$ and $P'' \rhd \Gamma, B$ and $P \rhd \Gamma, A, B$, where $P' = P|_{\Gamma,A}$ and $P'' = P|_{\Gamma,B}$. All three of them are correct, quite obviously. Therefore, we can apply the induction hypothesis to them. Now we apply the $\wedge$-rule twice to get $P' \oplus P'' \oplus P \rhd \Gamma, \Gamma, \Gamma, A \wedge B, A \wedge B$. To finally get $P \rhd \Gamma, A \wedge B$, we only need a sufficient number of contractions (and exchanges).
  Let us make two remarks about that case:
  - If $P \rhd \Gamma, A \wedge B$ contains no link between A and B, i.e., $P|_{A,B} = P|_A \oplus P|_B$, then we do not need the net $P \rhd \Gamma, A, B$, and can instead proceed by a single use of the $\wedge$-rule, followed by contractions.
  - This is the only case where the fact that $W = \mathbb{B}$ is needed.
- If $\Delta = \Gamma, A$, such that $P = P|_\Gamma$, i.e., the formula A does not take part in the linking P, then we can apply the weakening rule and proceed by induction hypothesis.
- The only remaining case is where all formulas in Δ are atoms, negated atoms, or constants. Then the sequent proof is obtained by a sufficient number of instances of the axioms $\mathsf{id_0}$, $\mathsf{t_1}$, $\mathsf{id_2}$, and the rules cont, exch, and mix. □

$$
\begin{array}{rc}
\mathsf{id}^4 & \overline{} \\
\mathsf{s}^4 & \dfrac{[\bar b, b] \wedge [\bar b, b] \wedge [\bar b, b] \wedge [\bar b, b]}{[\bar b \wedge \bar b, b, b] \wedge [\bar b \wedge \bar b, b, b]} \\
\mathsf{s}^2 & \dfrac{}{[\bar b \wedge \bar b, \bar b \wedge \bar b, [b, b] \wedge [b, b]]} \\
\mathsf{m} & \dfrac{}{[[\bar b, \bar b] \wedge [\bar b, \bar b], [b, b] \wedge [b, b]]} \\
\mathsf{cont}^4 & \dfrac{}{[\bar b \wedge \bar b, b \wedge b]} \\
\mathsf{id}^2 & \dfrac{}{[\bar b \wedge [a, \bar a] \wedge \bar b, b \wedge [a, \bar a] \wedge b]} \\
\mathsf{s}^4 & \dfrac{}{[\bar b \wedge a, \bar a \wedge \bar b, b \wedge a, \bar a \wedge b]}
\end{array}
$$

$$
\mathsf{cont}^3\,\dfrac{\mathsf{exch}^5\,\dfrac{\wedge\,\dfrac{\mathsf{weak}\,\dfrac{\mathsf{id}\,\dfrac{}{\vdash \bar a, a}}{\vdash \bar a, a, a} \qquad \wedge\,\dfrac{\mathsf{id}\,\dfrac{}{\vdash \bar a, a} \qquad \mathsf{weak}\,\dfrac{\mathsf{id}\,\dfrac{}{\vdash \bar a, a}}{\vdash \bar a, \bar a, a}}{\vdash \bar a, a \wedge \bar a, \bar a, a}}{\vdash \bar a, a, a \wedge \bar a, a \wedge \bar a, \bar a, a}}{\vdash \bar a, \bar a, a \wedge \bar a, a \wedge \bar a, a, a}}{\vdash \bar a, a \wedge \bar a, a}
$$

Fig. 2. Left: (3) in the calculus of structures **Right:** A "fake" church numeral

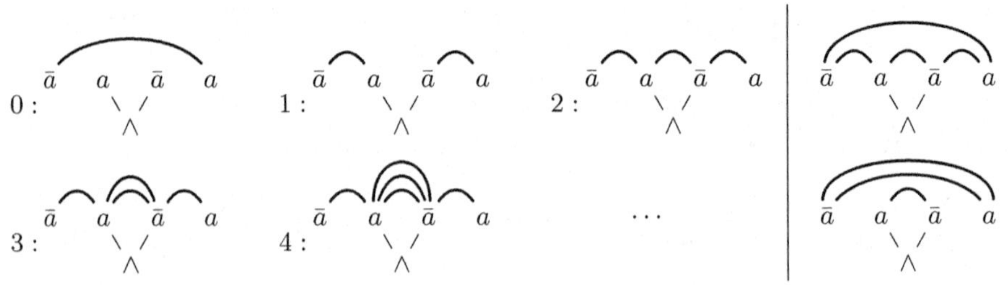

Fig. 3. Left: Church numerals as $\mathbb{N}$-nets **Right:** "Fake" Church numerals

Note that the particular sequent system CL is only needed for obtaining the completeness, i.e., sequentialization, of $\mathbb{B}$-nets. For obtaining the soundness result, any sequent system for classical propositional logic (with the identity axiom reduced to atomic form) can be used. Moreover, this is not restricted to sequent calculus. We can also start from resolution proofs (as done in [1]), tableau proofs, Hilbert style proofs, etc.

Whereas $\mathbb{B}$-nets only take into account *whether* a certain axiom link is used in the proof, $\mathbb{N}$-nets also count *how often* it is used. Therefore, $\mathbb{N}$-nets can be used for investigating certain complexity issues related to the size of proofs, e.g., the exponential blow-up usually related to cut elimination. This is not visible for $\mathbb{B}$-nets, where the size of a proof net is always quadratic in the size of the sequent. It should not come as a surprise that finding a fully complete correctness criterion for $\mathbb{N}$-nets is much harder. One reason is the close connection to the NP vs. co-NP problem [5]. Moreover, there are correct $\mathbb{N}$-nets for which no corresponding sequent proof exists, for example (3) seen as an $\mathbb{N}$-net, but which can be represented in other formalisms, for example the calculus of structures [15, 2]). Because of the conflation of sequents and formulas into a single kind of syntactic expression, we can write the proof that is shown on the left of Figure 2, and whose translation into $\mathbb{N}$-nets is exactly (3)—To save space we did in the figure several steps in one. For example id^4 stands for four applications of the identity rule.

To give some more examples, consider the sequent $\vdash \bar a, a \wedge \bar a, a$. This is equivalent to the formula $(a \to a) \to (a \to a)$ modulo some applications of associativity and commutativity (here $\to$ stands for implication). Hence, the proofs of that sequent can be used to encode the Church numerals. Figure 3 shows on the left the encodings of the numbers 0 to 4 as $\mathbb{N}$-nets. Observe that using $\mathbb{B}$-nets, we can distinguish only the numbers 0, 1, and 2, because all numbers ≥ 2 are collapsed. Note that there are also proofs of that sequent that do not encode a numeral. There are two examples on the right of Figure 3. The top one is obtained by simply mixing together the two proofs 0 and 2. One of the arguments for not having the mix rule in a system is that it causes types (resp. formulas) to be inhabited by more terms (resp. proofs) than the intended ones. However, we would like to stress the (well-known) fact, that this phenomenon is by no means caused by the mix rule, as the bottom "fake" numeral in Figure 3 shows, which comes from the mix-free sequent proof on the right of Figure 2.

4 Proof Nets with Cuts

A *cut* is a formula $A \Phi \bar{A}$, where Φ is called the *cut connective*, and where the function $\overline{(-)}$ is defined on formulas as follows (with a trivial abuse of notation):

$$\bar{a} = \bar{a}\,, \quad \bar{\bar{a}} = a\,, \quad \bar{\mathbf{t}} = \mathbf{f}\,, \quad \bar{\mathbf{f}} = \mathbf{t}\,, \quad \overline{(A \wedge B)} = \bar{A} \vee \bar{B}\,, \quad \overline{(A \vee B)} = \bar{A} \wedge \bar{B}\,.$$

A *sequent with cuts* is a sequent where some of the formulas are cuts. But cuts are not allowed to occur inside formulas, i.e., all Φ-nodes are roots. A *prenet with cuts* is a prenet $P \rhd \Gamma$, where Γ may contain cuts. The Φ-nodes have the same geometric behavior as the $\wedge$-nodes. Therefore the correctness criterion has to be adapted only slightly:

4.1 Definition. A *conjunctive resolution* of a prenet $P \rhd \Gamma$ with cuts is a sub-prenet $P|_{\Gamma'} \rhd \Gamma'$ where Γ' has been obtained by deleting one child subformula for every $\wedge$-node and every Φ-node of Γ.

4.2 Definition. A W-prenet $P \rhd \Gamma$ with cuts is said to be *correct* if for every one of its conjunctive resolutions $P|_{\Gamma'} \rhd \Gamma'$ the W-linking $P|_{\Gamma'}$ is not the zero function. A *W-net with cuts* is a correct W-prenet with cuts.

An example of a correct net with cuts (taken from [12]):

(6)

In the translation from sequent proofs containing the cut rule into prenets with cuts, the cut is treated as follows:

$$\mathsf{cut}\,\frac{\Gamma, A \quad \bar{A}, \Delta}{\Gamma, \Delta} \quad \rightsquigarrow \quad \mathsf{cut}\,\frac{P \rhd \Gamma, A \quad Q \rhd \bar{A}, \Delta}{P \oplus Q \rhd \Gamma, A \Phi \bar{A}, \Delta}\,.$$

Here the cut connective is used to keep track of the cuts in the sequent proof. To the best of our knowledge the use of a special connective for cut comes from [23] (see also [16]).

In order to simplify the presentation and maintain the similarity between cut and conjunction, our sequent calculus allows contraction to be applied to cut formulas. This slightly unconventional rule is used only for obtaining a generic proof of sequentialization; in no way does it affect the other results (statements or proofs) in the rest of this paper.

The generalization of soundness and completeness is now immediate:

4.3 Theorem. (Soundness). *For any W and any $\mathsf{i} \in \{0, 1, 2\}$, a sequentializable W-prenet in $\mathsf{CL_i}$ with cuts is correct.*

4.4 Theorem. (Sequentialization). *For any $\mathsf{i} \in \{0, 1, 2\}$, a $\mathbb{B}$-net in $\mathsf{CL_i}$ with cuts is sequentializable in $\mathsf{CL_i} + \mathsf{cut}$.*

5 Cut Elimination

Cut elimination in CL-nets has much in common with multiplicative proof nets. The cut-reduction step on a compound formula is exactly the same:

$$P \rhd (A \wedge B) \Diamond (\bar{A} \vee \bar{B}), \Gamma \;\rightarrow\; P \rhd A \Diamond \bar{A}, B \Diamond \bar{B}, \Gamma$$

and so it does not affect the linking itself (although we have to show it preserves correctness). The really interesting things happen in the atomic case, which this time splits in two: atomic formulas or constants. Here cut elimination means "counting paths through the cuts". Let us illustrate the idea by an example:

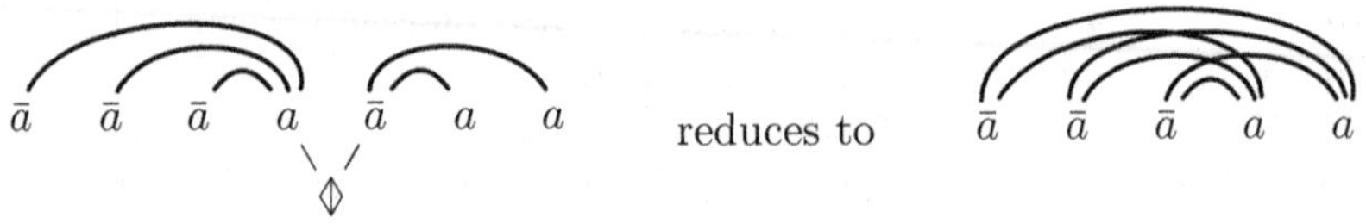

More generally, if some weights are different from 1, we multiply them:

$$\{ \bar{a}_1 \overset{p}{\frown} a_4 , \bar{a}_2 \overset{q}{\frown} a_4 , \bar{a}_3 \overset{r}{\frown} a_4 , \bar{a}_5 \overset{m}{\frown} a_6 , \bar{a}_5 \overset{n}{\frown} a_7 \} \rhd \bar{a}_1, \bar{a}_2, \bar{a}_3, a_4 \Diamond \bar{a}_5, a_6, a_7$$
$$\rightarrow \{ \bar{a}_1 \overset{pm}{\frown} a_6 , \bar{a}_1 \overset{pn}{\frown} a_7 , \bar{a}_2 \overset{qm}{\frown} a_6 , \bar{a}_2 \overset{qn}{\frown} a_7 , \bar{a}_3 \overset{rm}{\frown} a_6 , \bar{a}_3 \overset{rn}{\frown} a_7 \} \rhd \bar{a}_1, \bar{a}_2, \bar{a}_3, a_6, a_7 .$$

In the case of constants we have for example (here two cuts are reduced):

$$\{ \mathbf{t}_1 \overset{p}{\frown} \mathbf{t}_1 , \mathbf{f}_2 \overset{q}{\frown} \mathbf{t}_3 , \mathbf{f}_4 \overset{r}{\frown} \mathbf{t}_5 \} \rhd \mathbf{t}_1 \Diamond \mathbf{f}_2, \mathbf{t}_3 \Diamond \mathbf{f}_4, \mathbf{t}_5 \quad \rightarrow \quad \{ \mathbf{t}_5 \overset{pqr}{\frown} \mathbf{t}_5 \} \rhd \mathbf{t}_5 \quad .$$

To understand certain subtleties let us consider

$$\{ \bar{a}_1 \overset{p}{\frown} a_4 , \bar{a}_1 \overset{q}{\frown} a_2 , a_2 \overset{r}{\frown} \bar{a}_3 , \bar{a}_3 \overset{s}{\frown} a_4 \} \rhd \bar{a}_1, a_2 \Diamond \bar{a}_3, a_4 \quad \rightarrow \quad \{ \bar{a}_1 \overset{z}{\frown} a_4 \} \rhd \bar{a}_1, a_4 \quad .$$

What is the value of z? We certainly cannot just take $q \cdot s$, we also have to add p. But the question is what happens to r, i.e., is the result $z = p + qs$ or $z = p + q \cdot (1 + r) \cdot s = p + qs + qrs$ or even $z = p + q \cdot (1 + r + r^2 + r^3 + \cdots) \cdot s$? All choices lead to a sensible theory of cut elimination, but here we only treat the first, simplest case: we drop r. In [18], this property is called *loop-killing.*

Let us now introduce some notation. Given $P \rhd \Gamma$ and $x, y, u_1, u_2, \ldots, u_n \in \mathscr{L}(\Gamma)$, with n even, we write $P(x \frown u_1 \cdot u_2 \frown u_3 \cdot \ldots \cdot u_n \frown y)$ as an abbreviation for $P(x, u_1) \cdot P(u_2, u_3) \cdot \ldots \cdot P(u_n, y)$. In addition we define

$$P(x \rceil u_1 \cdot u_2 \frown u_3 \cdot \ldots \cdot u_n \rceil y) = \begin{cases} P(x \frown u_1 \cdot u_2 \frown u_3 \cdot \ldots \cdot u_n \frown y) + P(x \frown u_n \cdot \ldots \cdot u_3 \frown u_2 \cdot u_1 \frown y) & \text{if } y \neq x \\ P(x \frown u_1 \cdot u_2 \frown u_3 \cdot \ldots \cdot u_n \frown u_n) + P(x \frown u_n \cdot \ldots \cdot u_3 \frown u_2 \cdot u_1 \frown u_1) & \text{if } y = x \end{cases}$$

Notice that in both cases one of the summands is always zero, and that the second case applies only when x is a $\mathbf{t}$ and a $\mathbf{t}_1$-axiom is involved. We now can define cut reduction formally for a single atomic cut:

$$P \rhd u \Diamond v, \Gamma \;\rightarrow\; Q \rhd \Gamma \;, \text{ where } Q(x, y) = P(x, y) + P(x \rceil u \cdot v \rceil y)$$

for all $x, y \in \mathscr{L}(\Gamma)$, and where u is labelled by an arbitrary atom or constant, and v by its dual. But we can go further and do *simultaneous reduction* on a set of atomic cuts:

$$P \rhd u_1 \Diamond v_1, u_2 \Diamond v_2, \ldots, u_n \Diamond v_n, \Gamma \;\rightarrow\; Q \rhd \Gamma \quad , \tag{7}$$

where each u_i labelled by an arbitrary atom or constant, and v_i by its dual. For defining Q, we need the following notion:
A *cut-path between x and y* in a net $P \rhd \Delta$ with $x, y \in \mathscr{L}(\Delta)$ is an expression of the form $x \frown w_1 \cdot z_1 \frown w_2 \cdot z_2 \frown w_3 \cdot \ldots \cdot z_k \frown y$ where $w_i \Diamond z_i$ are all *distinct* atomic cuts in Δ, and such that $P(x \rceil w_1 \cdot z_1 \frown w_2 \cdot z_2 \frown w_3 \cdot \ldots \cdot z_k \rceil y) \neq 0$. For a set S of atomic cuts in Δ, the cut-path is *covered by S* if all the $w_i \Diamond z_i$ are in S, and it *touches* S if at least one of the $w_i \Diamond z_i$ is in S. The Q in (7) is now given by

$$Q(x, y) = P(x, y) + \sum_{\{x \frown w_1 \cdot z_1 \frown w_2 \cdot \ldots \cdot z_k \frown y\}} P(x \rceil w_1 \cdot z_1 \frown w_2 \cdot \ldots \cdot z_k \rceil y) \quad ,$$

where the sum ranges over all cut-paths covered by $\{u_1 \Diamond v_1, u_2 \Diamond v_2, \ldots, u_n \Diamond v_n\}$.

5.1 Lemma. *Let $P \rhd \Delta$ be a W-prenet in* $\mathsf{CL_i}$*, and let $P \rhd \Delta \rightarrow P' \rhd \Delta'$. Then $P' \rhd \Delta'$ is also in* $\mathsf{CL_i}$*. Furthermore, if $P \rhd \Delta$ is correct, then $P' \rhd \Delta'$ is also correct.*

The proof is an ordinary case analysis, and it is the only place where Axiom (2) is used. The next observation is that there is no infinite sequence $P \rhd \Gamma \rightarrow P' \rhd \Gamma' \rightarrow P'' \rhd \Gamma'' \rightarrow \cdots$, because in each reduction step the size of the sequent (i.e., the number of $\wedge$, $\vee$ and $\Diamond$-nodes) is reduced. Therefore:

5.2 Lemma. *The cut reduction relation $\to$ is terminating.*

Let us now attack the issue of confluence. Obviously we only have to consider atomic cuts; let us begin when two singleton cuts: $P \rhd a_i \between \bar{a}_j, a_h \between \bar{a}_k, \Gamma$ are reduced. If the first cut is reduced, we get $P' \rhd a_h \between \bar{a}_k, \Gamma$, where $P'(x,y) = P(x,y) + P(x \rceil a_i \cdot \bar{a}_j \rceil y)$. Then reducing the second cut gives us $Q_1 \rhd \Gamma$, where $Q_1(x,y) = P'(x,y) + P'(x \rceil a_h \cdot \bar{a}_k \rceil y)$. An easy computation shows that

$$Q_1(x,y) = P(x,y) + P(x \rceil a_i \cdot \bar{a}_j \rceil y) + P(x \rceil a_h \cdot \bar{a}_h \rceil y) + P(x \rceil a_i \cdot \bar{a}_j \frown a_k \cdot \bar{a}_h \rceil y) + \\ P(x \rceil a_h \cdot \bar{a}_k \frown a_i \cdot \bar{a}_j \rceil y) + P(x \rceil a_i \cdot \bar{a}_j \frown a_h \cdot \bar{a}_k \frown a_i \cdot \bar{a}_j \rceil y) \quad . \tag{8}$$

Reducing the two cuts in the other order yields $Q_2 \rhd \Gamma$, where

$$Q_2(x,y) = P(x,y) + P(x \rceil a_i \cdot \bar{a}_j \rceil y) + P(x \rceil a_h \cdot \bar{a}_k \rceil y) + P(x \rceil a_i \cdot \bar{a}_j \frown a_k \cdot \bar{a}_h \rceil y) + \\ P(x \rceil a_h \cdot \bar{a}_k \frown a_i \cdot \bar{a}_j \rceil y) + P(x \rceil a_h \cdot \bar{a}_k \frown a_i \cdot \bar{a}_j \frown a_h \cdot \bar{a}_k \rceil y) \quad . \tag{9}$$

We see that the last summand is different in the two results. But if we reduce both cuts simultaneously, we get $Q \rhd \Gamma$, where

$$Q(x,y) = P(x,y) + P(x \rceil a_i \cdot \bar{a}_j \rceil y) + P(x \rceil a_h \cdot \bar{a}_k \rceil y) + \\ P(x \rceil a_i \cdot \bar{a}_j \frown a_k \cdot \bar{a}_h \rceil y) + P(x \rceil a_h \cdot \bar{a}_k \frown a_i \cdot \bar{a}_j \rceil y) \quad . \tag{10}$$

Now the troublesome summand is absent. There are also good news: In the case of $\mathbb{B}$-nets we have that $Q = Q_1 = Q_2$. The reason is that if in either Q_1 or Q_2 the last summand is 1, then at least one of the other summands is also 1. This ensures that the whole sum is 1, because of idempotency of addition. Therefore:

5.3 Lemma. *On $\mathbb{B}$-prenets the cut reduction relation $\to$ is locally confluent.*

Lemmas 5.1–5.3 together give us immediately:

5.4 Theorem. *On $\mathbb{B}$-nets cut elimination via $\to$ is strongly normalizing. The normal forms are cut free $\mathbb{B}$-nets.*

Note that we do *not* have this result for general W.

Let us compare our cut elimination with other (syntactic) cut elimination procedures for classical propositional logic. In the case of $\mathbb{B}$-nets, the situation is quite similar to the sequent calculus: the main differences is that we do not lose any information in the weak-weak case, although we lose some information of a numeric nature in the cont-cont case.

In the case of $\mathbb{N}$-nets, the situation is very different. Let us use (6) for an example. The sequent calculus cut elimination needs to duplicate either the right-hand side proof or the left-hand side proof. The two possible outcomes, together with their presentation as $\mathbb{N}$-nets, are shown in Figure 4, where the ▼ stand for contractions[3]. However, in our setting, the result of eliminating the cut in (6) is always (3), whether we are in $\mathbb{B}$-nets or in $\mathbb{N}$-nets.

[3] This idea of using explicit contraction nodes was sketched in [12] and is carried out in detail in [24].

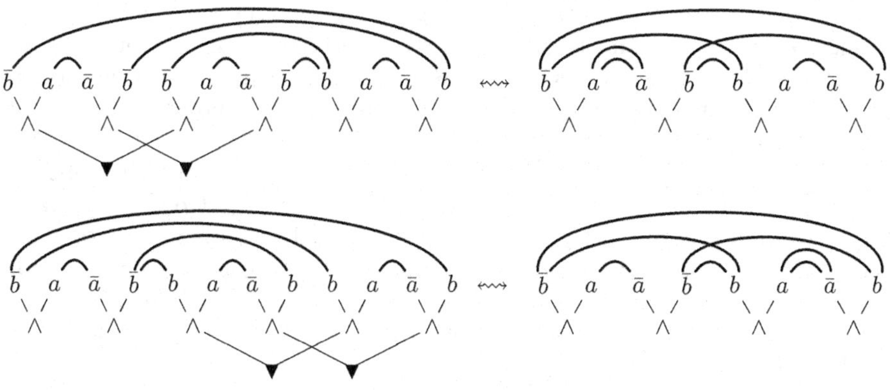

Fig. 4. The two different results of applying *sequent calculus cut elimination* to the proof (6). **Left:** Written as Girard/Robinson proof-net. **Right:** Written as $\mathbb{N}$-proof-net

Although for $\mathbb{N}$-nets the cut elimination operation does not have a close relationship to the sequent calculus, there is a good correspondence with cut elimination in the calculus of structures, when done via splitting [14].

We do not have confluence in general, but at least, given a sequent with cuts, there is a "most canonical" way of obtaining a cut-free proof net: do simultaneous elimination of all the cuts at once.

6 A Bit of Abstract Nonsense

For $\mathsf{i} \in \{0, 2\}$, let $\mathsf{CL}_\mathsf{i}^{\mathbb{B}}$ denote the category whose objects are the CL_i-formulas and whose arrows are the cut-free $\mathbb{B}$-nets (in CL_i) that have two (ordered) conclusions: $P \rhd \bar{A}, B$ is a map from A to B. The composition of two maps $P \rhd \bar{A}, B$ and $Q \rhd \bar{B}, C$ is given by eliminating the cut on $P \oplus Q \rhd \bar{A}, B \Diamond \bar{B}, C$. The associativity of that operation is a direct consequence of Theorem 5.4. In $\mathsf{CL}_0^{\mathbb{B}}$ and $\mathsf{CL}_2^{\mathbb{B}}$ there is an obvious identity map for every object. $\mathsf{CL}_1^{\mathbb{B}}$ is not a category because it does not have identities: this is easy to check for $\mathbf{t}$.

Given a general W, it is not certain that we can adapt the construction [10] to get a category, where the objects would be the CL_i-formulas but where the arrows would be the two-conclusion W-nets *in which atomic cuts may be present.* One of the main points of that construction is that it allows the definition of an enrichment in posets—more correctly, sup-semilattices—where bigger nets for that order are nets that have more cuts. But then in our case there is always a naturally defined commutative monoid "enrichment", given by pointwise sum of nets, which is the corresponding structure.

In what follows we will sketch the axiomatic structure that the $\mathsf{CL}_\mathsf{i}^{\mathbb{B}}$ possess, allowing comparison with the categorical formalisms that have been recently proposed. It is not hard to show that we do get a *-autonomous category, with the expected interpretation (tensor is $\wedge$, the involution is $\overline{(-)}$, etc.); but not one that has units in general (new developments on the concept of unitless autonomous category can be found in [18]). This makes our semantics rather similar to [10, 11] (which, as we have said, is based on a rather different notion of proof net). But it does not seem that the categories proposed in [9] can be *-autonomous without being posets.

In the case of $\mathsf{CL}_2^{\mathbb{B}}$, the $\wedge$ does have a unit $\mathbf{t}$ of some sort, but the standard unit laws are not exactly true: there is a natural map $\lambda_A \colon \mathbf{t} \wedge A \to A$, (and thus, because of the symmetry, a $\rho_A \colon A \wedge \mathbf{t} \to A$) and they obey the "standard diagram" [21–p. 159], *but they are not isomorphisms.* Instead λ only has a right inverse $\lambda^*_A \colon A \to \mathbf{t} \wedge A$, with $\lambda_A \circ \lambda^*_A = 1_A$. It is not hard to generalize the notion of symmetric monoidal category to accommodate that situation; this includes a suitable coherence theorem.

But naturally our categories have more: there is diagonal map $\Delta_A \colon A \to A \wedge A$, and the counit map $!_A \colon A \to \mathbf{t}$ which exists in $\mathsf{CL}_2^{\mathbb{B}}$ and which can be replaced for $\mathsf{CL}_0^{\mathbb{B}}$ by the usual projection map $A \wedge X \to X$, which is natural in X. Thus we can say that every object is equipped with a $\wedge$-comonoid structure (and by duality a $\vee$-monoid structure), when these notions are adapted to fit the absence of real units to $\wedge, \vee$. All the recent proposals for "Boolean" categories have this structure; it is by now clear that the reason that we do not have collapse to a poset is that *the families* $(\Delta_A)_A$ *and* $(!_A)_A$ *are not natural.* Some additional important equations on the interaction between the *-autonomous and the monoid-comonoid structure are in [18]; a general "covariant" treatment of these issues is in [9].

Our logic gives us a natural map $\mathrm{mix}_{A,B} : A \wedge B \to A \vee B$. Thus given any pair of parallel maps $f, g \colon A \to B$ we can construct (see also [9]) $f + g = \nabla_B \circ (f \vee g) \circ \mathrm{mix}_{A,A} \circ \Delta_A$.[4] It is then easy to check that this operation is commutative and associative. (But in general it does not give us an enrichment of $\mathsf{CL}_{\mathsf{i}}^{\mathbb{B}}$ over the category of commutative semigroups.) Thus the sum of linkings (see Section 2) can be recovered through the categorical axioms. Since $W = \mathbb{B}$ here the additional axiom $f + f = f$ of idempotency holds; thus in this case every hom-set does have a sup-semilattice structure.

References

1. Peter B. Andrews. Refutations by matings. *IEEE Transactions on Computers*, C-25:801–807, 1976.
2. Kai Brünnler and Alwen Fernanto Tiu. A local system for classical logic. In *LPAR 2001*, volume 2250 of *L*, pages 347–361. Springer-Verlag, 2001.
3. Samuel R. Buss. The undecidability of k-provability. *Annals of Pure and Applied Logic*, 53:72–102, 1991.
4. Alessandra Carbone. Interpolants, cut elimination and flow graphs for the propositional calculus. *Annals of Pure and Applied Logic*, 83:249–299, 1997.

[4] It has recently been shown that the semilattice enrichment mentioned above can also be obtained that way [11].

5. Stephen A. Cook and Robert A. Reckhow. The relative efficiency of propositional proof systems. *The Journal of Symbolic Logic*, 44(1):36–50, 1979.
6. Thierry Coquand. A semantics of evidence for classical arithmetic. *The Journal of Symbolic Logic*, 60(1):325–337, 1995.
7. V. Danos, J.-B. Joinet, and H. Schellinx. A new deconstructive logic: Linear logic. *The Journal of Symbolic Logic*, 62(3):755–807, 1997.
8. Kosta Došen. Identity of proofs based on normalization and generality. *The Bulletin of Symbolic Logic*, 9:477–503, 2003.
9. Kosta Došen and Zoltan Petrić. *Proof-Theoretical Coherence.* KCL Publications, London, 2004.
10. Carsten Führmann and David Pym. On the geometry of interaction for classical logic (extended abstract). In *LICS 2004*, pages 211–220, 2004.
11. Carsten Führmann and David Pym. Order-enriched categorical models of the classical sequent calculus. 2004.
12. Jean-Yves Girard. A new constructive logic: Classical logic. *Mathematical Structures in Computer Science*, 1:255–296, 1991.
13. Jean-Yves Girard, Yves Lafont, and Paul Taylor. *Proofs and Types.* Cambridge Tracts in Theoretical Computer Science. Cambridge University Press, 1989.
14. Alessio Guglielmi. A system of interaction and structure, 2002. To appear in *ACM Transactions on Computational Logic.* On the web at: http://www.ki.inf.tu-dresden.de/~guglielm/Research/Gug/Gug.pdf.
15. Alessio Guglielmi and Lutz Straßburger. Non-commutativity and MELL in the calculus of structures. In Laurent Fribourg, editor, *Computer Science Logic, CSL 2001*, volume 2142 of *LNCS*, pages 54–68. Springer-Verlag, 2001.
16. Dominic Hughes and Rob van Glabbeek. Proof nets for unit-free multiplicative-additive linear logic. In *LICS 2003*, pages 1–10. 2003.
17. J. Martin E. Hyland. Abstract interpretation of proofs: Classical propositional calculus. In *CSL 2004*, volume 3210 of *LNCS*, pages 6–21. Springer-Verlag, 2004.
18. François Lamarche and Lutz Straßburger. Constructing free Boolean categories, 2005. Submitted.
19. Olivier Laurent. *Etude de la Polarisation en Logique.* PhD thesis, Univ. Aix-Marseille II, 2002.
20. Olivier Laurent. Polarized proof-nets and $\lambda\mu$-calculus. *Theoretical Computer Science*, 290(1):161–188, 2003.
21. Saunders Mac Lane. *Categories for the Working Mathematician.* Number 5 in Graduate Texts in Mathematics. Springer-Verlag, 1971.
22. Michel Parigot. $\lambda\mu$-calculus: An algorithmic interpretation of classical natural deduction. In *LPAR 1992*, volume 624 of *LNAI*, pages 190–201, 1992.
23. Christian Retoré. Pomset logic: A non-commutative extension of classical linear logic. In *TLCA 1997*, volume 1210 of *LNCS*, pages 300–318, 1997.
24. Edmund P. Robinson. Proof nets for classical logic. *Journal of Logic and Computation*, 13:777–797, 2003.

Reducibility and $\top\top$-Lifting for Computation Types

Sam Lindley and Ian Stark*

Laboratory for Foundations of Computer Science
School of Informatics, The University of Edinburgh, Scotland
{Ian.Stark, Sam.Lindley}@ed.ac.uk

Abstract. We propose $\top\top$-*lifting* as a technique for extending operational predicates to Moggi's monadic computation types, independent of the choice of monad. We demonstrate the method with an application to Girard-Tait reducibility, using this to prove strong normalisation for the computational metalanguage λ_{ml}. The particular challenge with reducibility is to apply this semantic notion at computation types when the exact meaning of "computation" (stateful, side-effecting, nondeterministic, etc.) is left unspecified. Our solution is to define reducibility for *continuations* and use that to support the jump from value types to computation types. The method appears robust: we apply it to show strong normalisation for the computational metalanguage extended with sums, and with exceptions. Based on these results, as well as previous work with local state, we suggest that this "leap-frog" approach offers a general method for raising concepts defined at value types up to observable properties of computations.

1 Introduction

Moggi's computational metalanguage λ_{ml} is a typed calculus for describing programming languages with real-world features like exceptions, nondeterminism and side-effects. It refines the pure simply-typed lambda-calculus by explicitly distinguishing *values* from *computations* in the type system: for each type A of values, there is a type TA of programs that compute a value of type A. The calculus specifies that the type constructor T be a *strong monad*, which is enough to support a wide range of notions of computation [5, 21, 22, 33].

In this paper we present $\top\top$-*lifting*: a method for reasoning about properties of computations in λ_{ml}, independent of the underlying monad, by raising up concepts defined explicitly on values.

We demonstrate the technique with a type-directed proof of strong normalisation for λ_{ml}, extending Girard-Tait reducibility to handle computation types. We also apply it to some extensions of λ_{ml}, and observe that $\top\top$-lifting gives a smooth treatment of reducibility for commuting conversions.

Section 2 provides a brief review of the computational metalanguage and related systems. Reduction in λ_{ml} properly extends that in the simply-typed lambda-calculus, with three reductions specific to computations. One of these, $T.assoc$, is a commuting

* Research supported by an EPSRC Advanced Research Fellowship

P. Urzyczyn (Ed.): TLCA 2005, LNCS 3461, pp. 262–277, 2005.

conversion; another, $T.\beta$, involves substituting one term within another; which may make a term grow larger, and create subterms not present before. As usual with these kinds of reduction, the consequence is that straightforward induction over the structure of terms or types is not enough to prove termination of λ_{ml} reduction.

In earlier work, Benton et al. proved strong normalisation for λ_{ml} terms by translating them into a lambda-calculus with sums, and then invoking Prawitz's result for that system [4]. Our alternative is to use $\top\top$-lifting to give a standalone proof of strong normalisation, inductively on the structure of λ_{ml} types.

Section 3 sets out the details. We define an auxiliary notion of *reducibility* at every type, that is linked to strong normalisation but amenable to induction over the structure of types. This is a standard technique from the lambda-calculus: roughly, reducibility is the logical predicate induced by strong normalisation at ground types. We show that all reducible terms are strongly normalising, and go on to prove the fundamental theorem of logical relations, that in fact all definable terms are reducible.

The challenge, and the chief technical contribution of this paper, is to find a suitable definition for reducibility at computation types. Some such definition is essential, as the type constructor T is intentionally left unspecified. A first informal attempt might be to echo the definition for functions, and look at the immediate application of a computation:

(Bad 1) Term M of type TA is reducible if for all reducible N of type TB, the term $let\, x \Leftarrow M\ in\ N$ is reducible.

This is not inductive over types, as the definition of reducibility at type TA depends on reducibility at type TB, which may be more complex. We can try to patch this:

(Bad 2) Term M of type TA is reducible if for all strongly normalising N of type TB, the term $let\, x \Leftarrow M\ in\ N$ is strongly normalising.

However, this turns out to be too weak to prove properties of M in richer contexts like $let\, y \Leftarrow (let\, x \Leftarrow (-)\ in\ N)\ in\ P$. Examining the structure of these, we define a *continuation* K as a nested sequence of $let\, x_i {\Leftarrow} (-)\ in\ N_i$, and use these for our definition of reducibility:

(Good 1) Term M of type TA is reducible if for all reducible continuations K, the application K @ M is strongly normalising.

Here application means pasting term M into the hole $(-)$ within K. Of course, we now have to define reducibility for continuations:

(Good 2) Continuation K accepting terms of type TA is reducible if for all reducible V of type A, the application K @ $[V]$ is strongly normalising.

The term $[V]$ is the trivial computation returning value V. By moving to the simpler value type A we avoid a potential circularity, and so get a notion of reducibility defined by induction on types. What is more, the characterisation by continuations is strong enough to treat both the commuting conversion $T.assoc$ and substitution in $T.\beta$, and the strong normalisation proof goes through without undue difficulty.

Looking beyond reducibility, this jump over continuations offers a quite general method to raise concepts from value type A up to computation type TA, whether or not we know the nature of T. Suppose that we write $K \top M$ when K applied to M is strongly normalising, and for any predicate $\phi \subseteq A$ define in turn:

$$\phi^{\top} = \{ K \mid K \top [V] \text{ for all } V \in \phi \}$$
$$\phi^{\top\top} = \{ M \mid K \top M \text{ for all } K \in \phi^{\top} \} \subseteq TA\,.$$

This is our operation of $\top\top$-lifting: to take a predicate ϕ on value type A and return another $\phi^{\top\top}$ on the computation type TA, by a "leap-frog" over $\phi^{\top}$ on continuations. One informal view of this is that continuations K represent possible observations on terms, and $\phi^{\top\top}$ lifts ϕ to computations based on their observable behaviour.

We believe that the use of $\top\top$-lifting in the metalanguage λ_{ml} is original. It was inspired by similar constructions applied to specific notions of computation; it is also related to Pitts's $\top\top$-closure, and that in turn has analogues in earlier work on reducibility. Section 5.1 discusses this further.

In Sect. 4 we demonstrate $\top\top$-lifting for reducibility in some variations of λ_{ml}; treating sums, exceptions, and Moggi's λ_c. For each case we vary our notion of continuation, but leave the definition of $(-)^{\top\top}$ unchanged. Notably, this includes the commuting conversions introduced by sums. Section 5 discusses rèlated work, and concludes with some possible future directions.

2 The Computational Metalanguage

We start with a standard simply-typed lambda-calculus with ground type 0, product $A \times B$ and function space $A \to B$ for all types A and B. The *computational metalanguage* extends this with a type constructor T and two term constructions:

- For each A there is a type TA, of computations that return an answer in A.
- The *lifted* term $[M]$ is the computation which simply returns the answer M.
- The *composition* term $let\ x \Leftarrow M\ in\ N$ denotes computing M, binding the answer to x and then computing N.

Fig. 1 presents typing[1] and reduction rules for this language λ_{ml}. It corresponds to Moggi's λML_T [21]. In categorical terms, this is the internal language for a cartesian closed category with a strong monad T. More concretely, it is also what lies behind the use of monads in the Haskell programming language, where T is any type constructor in the `Monad` class and the term formers are `return M` for lifting and `do {x<-M; N}` for composition [24].

Often we do not require the full power of λ_{ml}, and there are two common simplifications: first, that all functions must return computations, thus having type $A \to TB$; and second, that this is the only place where T can occur. These constrain the calculus to represent computations and only computations, disallowing *pure* functions

[1] Our presentation of typing follows Girard et al. [14], in that we assume a global assignment of types to variables. This is in contrast to typing "à la Curry" and typing "à la Church" [2], which use local *typing contexts*.

of type $A \to B$ as well as *metacomputations* like those with type $TA \to TB$ and $T(TA)$.

With both of these restrictions in place we obtain the sub-calculus λ_{ml*}. This contains the call-by-value embedding [16] of the simply-typed lambda-calculus into the computational metalanguage; with the attention on functions of type $A \to TB$ embodying call-by-value semantics.

It turns out that the terms of λ_{ml*} are so constrained that we can dispense with explicit lifting and computation types, replacing them by a simple syntactic separation of values V from non-values M. This leaves only the *let*-construction, and we have a subset λ_{c*} of Moggi's computational lambda-calculus λ_c [20]. Sabry and Wadler discuss in detail the correspondences between λ_{ml}, λ_{ml*}, λ_{c*} and λ_c [28]. Our results on λ_{ml} apply directly to its restriction λ_{ml*}; however, λ_c has extra reduction rules, and in Sect. 4.3 we give a ⊤⊤-lifting approach to cover these too.

The reductions for λ_{ml} appear in the last part of Fig. 1. These extend those for the simply-typed lambda-calculus with three reductions that act only on terms of computation type: $T.\beta$, $T.\eta$ and $T.assoc$. Before looking more closely at these three, we review some relevant properties of typed reduction, and the notion of strong normalisation.

Proposition 1. *Reduction in the computational metalanguage preserves types and is itself preserved under substitution.*

(i) *If* $M : A$ *and* $M \to M'$ *then* $M' : A$.
(ii) *If* $M \to M'$ *then* $M[x := N] \to M'[x := N]$.

Proof. Induction on the derivation of $M : A$ and the structure of M respectively. □

Definition 2. *A term M in some calculus is* strongly normalising *(it is* SN*) if there is no infinite reduction sequence $M \to M_1 \to \cdots$. In this case we write $max(M)$ for the length of the longest reduction sequence starting from M. A calculus itself is strongly normalising if every term in it is strongly normalising.*

We use the results of Prop. 1 repeatedly in the proofs for Sect. 3, and also the following:

Corollary 3. *If the λ_{ml} term $M[x := N]$ is strongly normalising, then so is M.*

Proof. By contradiction, from Prop. 1(ii): suppose M has some infinite reduction sequence $M \to M_1 \to \cdots$; then so does $M[x := N] \to M_1[x := N] \to \cdots$. If $M[x := N]$ has no such sequence, then neither does M and both are SN. □

It is standard that under β-reduction the untyped lambda-calculus is not strongly normalising. For example, the term $\Omega = (\lambda x.xx)(\lambda x.xx)$ β-reduces to itself, leading to the infinite reduction sequence $\Omega \to_\beta \Omega \to_\beta \ldots$. On the other hand, the simply-typed lambda-calculus is strongly normalising with respect to β-reduction [14]: in particular, Ω has no simple type.

We shall be investigating strong normalisation with the additional terms and reductions of λ_{ml} from Fig. 1. The reductions to watch are $T.\beta$ and $T.assoc$: like $\to.\beta$, a $T.\beta$ step performs substitution, and so may enlarge the term at hand; while $T.assoc$ is a *commuting conversion*, also termed a *permutation* or *permutative conversion*.

Syntax

$$\begin{array}{llcl} \text{Types} & A, B & ::= & 0 \mid A \to B \mid A \times B \mid TA \\ \text{Terms} & L, M, N, P & ::= & x^A \mid \lambda x^A.M \mid MN \mid \langle M, N\rangle \mid \pi_1(M) \mid \pi_2(M) \\ & & & \mid [M] \mid \mathit{let}\, x^A \Leftarrow M \,\mathit{in}\, N \end{array}$$

Typing

$$\frac{M : B}{\lambda x^A.M : A \to B} \qquad \frac{M : A \to B \quad N : A}{MN : B} \qquad \frac{M : A \quad N : B}{\langle M, N\rangle : A \times B}$$

$$\frac{}{x^A : A} \qquad \frac{M : A}{[M] : TA} \qquad \frac{M : TA \quad N : TB}{\mathit{let}\, x^A \Leftarrow M \,\mathit{in}\, N : TB} \qquad \frac{M : A_1 \times A_2}{\pi_i(M) : A_i}\ i = 1, 2$$

Reductions

$$\begin{array}{lrcll} \to.\beta & (\lambda x.M)N & \longrightarrow & M[x := N] & \\ \to.\eta & \lambda x.Mx & \longrightarrow & M & \text{if } x \notin fv(M) \\ \times.\beta i & \pi_i(\langle M_1, M_2\rangle) & \longrightarrow & M_i & i = 1, 2 \\ \times.\eta & \langle \pi_1(M), \pi_2(M)\rangle & \longrightarrow & M & \\ T.\beta & \mathit{let}\, x \Leftarrow [N] \,\mathit{in}\, M & \longrightarrow & M[x := N] & \\ T.\eta & \mathit{let}\, x \Leftarrow M \,\mathit{in}\, [x] & \longrightarrow & M & \\ T.\mathit{assoc} & \mathit{let}\, y \Leftarrow (\mathit{let}\, x \Leftarrow L \,\mathit{in}\, M) \,\mathit{in}\, N & \longrightarrow & \mathit{let}\, x \Leftarrow L \,\mathit{in}\, (\mathit{let}\, y \Leftarrow M \,\mathit{in}\, N) & \text{if } x \notin fv(N) \end{array}$$

Fig. 1. The computational metalanguage λ_{ml}

Commuting conversions are so named for their transforming action, via the Curry-Howard isomorphism, on derivation trees in natural deduction (indeed, the counterpart in logic of $T.assoc$ is described in [4]). They also arise when the lambda-calculus is extended with sums, and are known for the issues they can cause in proofs over reduction systems. Prawitz originally addressed this in [27]; see [17] for a discussion and further references. As we shall see below, ⊤⊤-lifting uses structured continuations to perform proof over commuting conversions.

3 Reducibility

We present ⊤⊤-lifting with the concrete example of a proof of strong normalisation in λ_{ml}, by extending the type-directed reducibility approach originally due to Tait [29]. We follow closely the style of Girard et al. [14–Chap. 6]; although in this short presentation we focus on the proof parts specific to λ_{ml}, with full details appearing elsewhere [19]. As explained earlier, the key step is to find an appropriate definition of reducibility for computation types, which we do by introducing a mechanism for managing continuations.

3.1 Continuations

Informally, a continuation should capture how the result of a computation might be used in a larger program. Our formal definition is structured to support inductive proof about these uses.

- A *term abstraction* $(x)N$ of type $TA \multimap TB$ is a computation term N of type TB with a distinguished free variable x of type A.
- A *continuation* K is a finite list of term abstractions, with length $|K|$.

$$K ::= \mathit{Id} \mid K \circ (x)N \qquad\qquad \begin{aligned} |\mathit{Id}| &= 0 \\ |K \circ (x)N| &= |K| + 1 \end{aligned}$$

- Continuations have types assigned using the following rules:

$$\mathit{Id} : TA \multimap TA \qquad\qquad \frac{(x)N : TA \multimap TB \qquad K : TB \multimap TC}{K \circ (x)N : TA \multimap TC}\ .$$

- We apply a continuation of type $TA \multimap TB$ to a computation term M of type TA by wrapping M in *let*-statements that use it:

$$\begin{aligned} \mathit{Id} \mathbin{@} M &= M \\ (K \circ (x)N) \mathbin{@} M &= K \mathbin{@} (\mathit{let}\, x \Leftarrow M \;\mathit{in}\; N) \end{aligned}$$

  Notice that when $|K| > 1$ this is a nested stack of computations, not simple sequencing: i.e.

$$\mathit{let}\, x_1 \Leftarrow (\mathit{let}\, x_2 \Leftarrow (\ldots (\mathit{let}\, x_n \Leftarrow M \;\mathit{in}\; N_n)) \ldots \mathit{in}\; N_2) \;\mathit{in}\; N_1$$

  rather than

$$\mathit{let}\, x_1 \Leftarrow M_1 \;\mathit{in}\; \mathit{let}\, x_2 \Leftarrow M_2 \;\mathit{in} \ldots \mathit{in}\; \mathit{let}\, x_n \Leftarrow M_n \;\mathit{in}\; N\ .$$

  Although these two are interconvertible by a sequence of $T.assoc$ rewrites, we cannot identify them while we are looking to confirm strong normalisation in the presence of substituting rewrites like $\rightarrow.\beta$ and $T.\beta$.
  In fact, it is exactly this nesting structure that we use to tackle $T.assoc$ in our key Lemma 7; essentially, the stack depth of a continuation tracks the action of the commuting conversion.
- We define a notion of reduction on continuations:

$$\begin{aligned} K \rightarrow K' \quad &\overset{def}{\iff} \quad \forall M\,.\, K \mathbin{@} M \rightarrow K' \mathbin{@} M \\ &\iff \quad K \mathbin{@} x \rightarrow K' \mathbin{@} x \end{aligned}$$

  where the second equivalence follows from Prop. 1(ii). A continuation K is *strongly normalising* if all reduction sequences starting from K are finite; and in this case we write $max(K)$ for the length of the longest.

Lemma 4. *If $K \to K'$, for continuations K and K', then $|K'| \leq |K|$.*

Proof. Suppose $K = Id \circ (x_1)N_n \circ \cdots \circ (x_n)N_n$. Then its application $K @ x = let\, x_1 \Leftarrow (\ldots (let\, x_n \Leftarrow x\; in\; N_n) \ldots)\; in\; N_1$ and there are only two reductions that might change the length of K.

- $T.\eta$ where $N_i = [x_i]$ for some i. Then $K \to K'$ where $K' = Id \circ (x_1)N_1 \circ \cdots \circ (x_{i-1})N_{i-1} \circ (x_{i+1})N_{i+1} \circ \cdots \circ (x_n)N_n$ and $|K'| = |K| - 1$.
- $T.assoc$ may occur at position i for $1 \leq i < n$ to give $K' = (x_1)N_1 \circ \cdots \circ (x_{i-1})N_i \circ (x_{i+1})(let\, x_i \Leftarrow N_{i+1}\; in\; N_i) \circ (x_{i+2})N_{i+2} \circ \cdots \circ (x_n)N_n$. Again $|K'| = |K| - 1$.

Hence $|K'| \leq |K|$ as required. □

3.2 Reducibility and Neutrality

Figure 2 defines two sets by induction on the structure of types: reducible terms red_A of type A, and reducible continuations $\mathsf{red}_A^\top$ of type $TA \multimap TB$ for some B. As described in the introduction, for computations we use $\mathsf{red}_{TA} = \mathsf{red}_A^{\top\top}$.

We also need to classify some terms as *neutral*; we do this by decomposing every reduction into a rewrite context with a hole that must be plugged with a term of a particular form (see Fig. 2 again). From this we define:

- Term M is *active* if $R[M]$ is a redex for at least one of the rewrite contexts.
- Term M is *neutral* if $R[M]$ is not a redex for any of the rewrite contexts.

The neutral terms are those of the form x, MN, $\pi_1(M)$ and $\pi_2(M)$; i.e. computation types add no new neutral terms. The basic properties of reducibility now follow (**CR 1**)–(**CR 4**) of [14].

Theorem 5. *For every term M of type A, the following hold.*

(i) *If $M \in \mathsf{red}_A$, then M is strongly normalising.*
(ii) *If $M \in \mathsf{red}_A$ and $M \to M'$, then $M' \in \mathsf{red}_A$.*
(iii) *If M is neutral, and whenever $M \to M'$ then $M' \in \mathsf{red}_A$, then $M \in \mathsf{red}_A$.*
(iv) *If M is neutral and normal (has no reductions) then $M \in \mathsf{red}_A$.*

Proof. Part (iv) is a trivial consequence of (iii), so we only need to prove (i)–(iii), which we do by induction over types. The proof for ground, function and product types proceeds as usual [14]. Here we expand the details for computation types:

(i) Say $M \in \mathsf{red}_{TA}$. By the induction hypothesis (i), for every $N \in \mathsf{red}_A$ we have that N is SN, and so $[N]$ is too. This is enough to show that $Id : TA \multimap TA$ is in $\mathsf{red}_A^\top$, and so $Id @ M = M$ is SN as required.
(ii) Suppose $M \in \mathsf{red}_{TA}$ and $M \to M'$. For all $K \in \mathsf{red}_A^\top$, application $K @ M$ is SN, and $K @ M \to K @ M'$; thus $K @ M'$ is SN and $M' \in \mathsf{red}_{TA}$ as required.
(iii) Take $M : TA$ neutral with $M' \in \mathsf{red}_{TA}$ whenever $M \to M'$. We have to show that $K @ M$ is SN for each $K \in \mathsf{red}_A^\top$. First, we have that $K @ [x]$ is SN, as $x \in \mathsf{red}_A$ by the induction hypothesis (iv). Hence K itself is SN, and we can work by induction on $max(K)$.

Reducibility for terms and continuations

$M \in \mathsf{red}_0$	if the ground term M is strongly normalising
$F \in \mathsf{red}_{A \to B}$	if $FM \in \mathsf{red}_B$ for all $M \in \mathsf{red}_A$
$P \in \mathsf{red}_{A \times B}$	if $\pi_1(P) \in \mathsf{red}_A$ and $\pi_2(P) \in \mathsf{red}_B$
$M \in \mathsf{red}_{TA}$	if $K \mathbin{@} M$ is strongly normalising for all $K \in \mathsf{red}_A^\top$
$K \in \mathsf{red}_A^\top$	if $K \mathbin{@} [N]$ is strongly normalising for all terms $N \in \mathsf{red}_A$.

Reduction	Rewrite context	Active term
$\to.\beta$	$-N$	$\lambda x.M$
$\to.\eta$	$-$	$\lambda x.Mx$
$\times.\beta i$	$\pi_i(-)$	$\langle M, N \rangle$
$\times.\eta$	$-$	$\langle \pi_1(M), \pi_2(M) \rangle$
$T.\beta$	$let\ x \Leftarrow -\ in\ M$	$[N]$
$T.\eta$	$let\ x \Leftarrow M\ in\ -$	$[x]$
$T.assoc$	$let\ y \Leftarrow -\ in\ N$	$let\ x \Leftarrow L\ in\ M$

Fig. 2. Reducibility and neutrality for λ_{ml}

Application $K \mathbin{@} M$ may reduce as follows:

- $K \mathbin{@} M'$, where $M \to M'$, which is SN as $K \in \mathsf{red}_A^\top$ and $M' \in \mathsf{red}_{TA}$.
- $K' \mathbin{@} M$, where $K \to K'$. For any $N \in \mathsf{red}_A$, $K \mathbin{@} [N]$ is SN as $K \in \mathsf{red}_A^\top$; and $K \mathbin{@} [N] \to K' \mathbin{@} [N]$, so $K' \mathbin{@} [N]$ is also SN. From this we have $K' \in \mathsf{red}_A^\top$ with $max(K') < max(K)$, so by the induction hypothesis $K' \mathbin{@} M$ is SN.

There are no other possibilities as M is neutral. Hence $K \mathbin{@} M$ is strongly normalising for every $K \in \mathsf{red}_A^\top$, and so $M \in \mathsf{red}_{TA}$ as required. □

3.3 Reducibility Theorem

We show that all terms are reducible, and hence strongly normalising, by induction on their syntactic structure. This requires an appropriate lemma for each term constructor. Here we set out proofs for the new constructors associated with computation: lifting $[-]$ and *let*. The other cases follow as usual from the properties of Thm. 5, and are set out in [19].

Lemma 6. *Lifting preserves reducibility: if term* $P \in \mathsf{red}_A$ *then* $[P] \in \mathsf{red}_{TA}$.

Proof. For any continuation $K \in \mathsf{red}_A^\top$, the application $K \mathbin{@} [P]$ is SN, as $P \in \mathsf{red}_A$; and so $[P] \in \mathsf{red}_{TA}$. □

We next wish to show that formation of *let*-terms preserves reducibility. That will be Lemma 8, but we first need a result on the strong normalisation of *let*-terms in context.

This is the key component of our overall proof, and is where our attention to the stack-like structure of continuations pays off: the challenging case is the commuting conversion $T.assoc$, which does not change its component terms; but it does alter the continuation stack length, and this gives enough traction to maintain the induction proof.

Lemma 7. *Let $P : A$ be a term, $(x)N : TA \multimap TB$ a term abstraction, and $K : TB \multimap TC$ a continuation, such that both P and $K @ (N[x := P])$ are strongly normalising. Then $K @ (let\, x \Leftarrow [P]\, in\, N)$ is strongly normalising.*

Proof. We show by induction on $|K| + max(K @ N) + max(P)$ that the reducts of $K @ (let\, x \Leftarrow [P]\, in\, N)$ are all SN. The interesting reductions are as follows:

- $T.\beta$ giving $K @ (N[x := P])$, which is SN by hypothesis.
- $T.\eta$ when $N = [x]$, giving $K @ [P]$. But $K @ [P] = K @ (N[x := P])$, which is again SN by hypothesis.
- $T.assoc$ in the case where $K = K' \circ (y)M$ with $x \notin fv(M)$; giving the reduct $K' @ (let\, x \Leftarrow [P]\, in\, (let\, y \Leftarrow N\, in\, M))$. We aim to apply the induction hypothesis with K' and $(let\, y \Leftarrow N\, in\, M)$ for K and N, respectively. Now

$$\begin{aligned} K' @ ((let\, y \Leftarrow N\, in\, M)[x := P]) &= K' @ (let\, y \Leftarrow N[x := P]\, in\, M) \\ &= K @ (N[x := P]) \end{aligned}$$

which is SN by hypothesis. Also

$$|K'| + max(K' @ (let\, y \Leftarrow N\, in\, M)) + max(P) < |K| + max(K @ N) + max(P)$$

as $|K'| < |K|$ and $(K' @ (let\, y \Leftarrow N\, in\, M)) = (K @ N)$. This last equality explains our use of $max(K @ N)$; it remains fixed under $T.assoc$, unlike $max(K)$ and $max(N)$. Applying the induction hypothesis gives that $K' @ (let\, x \Leftarrow [P]\, in\, (let\, y \Leftarrow N\, in\, M))$ is SN as required.

Other reductions are confined to K, N or M, and can be treated by the induction hypothesis, decreasing either $max(K @ N)$ or $max(M)$. □

We are now in a position to prove that composing computations in let-terms preserves reducibility.

Lemma 8. *If $M \in \mathsf{red}_{TA}$ and $(x)N : TA \multimap TB$ has $N[x := P] \in \mathsf{red}_{TB}$ for all $P \in \mathsf{red}_A$, then $(let\, x \Leftarrow M\, in\, N) \in \mathsf{red}_{TB}$.*

Proof. Given a continuation $K \in \mathsf{red}_B^\top$, we must show that $K @ (let\, x \Leftarrow M\, in\, N)$ is SN. Now for any $P \in \mathsf{red}_A$, application $K @ (N[x := P])$ is SN, as $K \in \mathsf{red}_B^\top$ and $N[x := P] \in \mathsf{red}_{TB}$ by hypothesis. But P is also SN, by Thm. 5(i), and so Lemma 7 shows that $K @ (let\, x \Leftarrow [P]\, in\, N)$ is SN too. This proves that $(K \circ (x)N) \in \mathsf{red}_A^\top$, so applying it to $M \in \mathsf{red}_{TA}$ gives that $K @ (let\, x \Leftarrow M\, in\, N)$ is SN as required. □

We finally reach the desired theorem via a stronger result on substitutions into open terms.

Theorem 9. *Let $M : B$ be some term with free variables $x_1 : A_1, \dots, x_k : A_k$. Then for any $N_1 \in \mathsf{red}_{A_1}, \dots, N_k \in \mathsf{red}_{A_k}$ we have $M[x_1 := N_1, \dots, x_k := N_k] \in \mathsf{red}_B$.*

Proof. By induction on the structure of the main term. For computation terms we have:

- $[P]$, where $P : A$. By the induction hypothesis $P[\boldsymbol{x} := \boldsymbol{N}] \in \mathsf{red}_A$, and by Lemma 6 we get $[P][\boldsymbol{x} := \boldsymbol{N}] = [P[\boldsymbol{x} := \boldsymbol{N}]] \in \mathsf{red}_{TA}$ as required.
- $let\, x \Leftarrow L\, in\, M$, where $L : TC$ and $M : TB$. The induction hypothesis is that $L[\boldsymbol{x} := \boldsymbol{N}] \in \mathsf{red}_{TC}$, and $M[\boldsymbol{x} := \boldsymbol{N}, x := P] \in \mathsf{red}_{TA}$ for all $P \in \mathsf{red}_C$. Lemma 8 gives $(let\, x \Leftarrow L\, in\, M)[\boldsymbol{x} := \boldsymbol{N}] = let\, x \Leftarrow L[\boldsymbol{x} := \boldsymbol{N}]\, in\, M[\boldsymbol{x} := \boldsymbol{N}] \in \mathsf{red}_{TA}$. □

Theorem 10. *Each λ_{ml} term $M : A$ is in red_A, and hence strongly normalising.*

Proof. Apply Thm. 9 with $N_i = x_i$, where $x_i \in \mathsf{red}_{A_i}$ by Thm. 5(iv). This tells us that $M \in \mathsf{red}_A$, and by Thm. 5(i) also strongly normalising. □

4 Extensions

In this section we apply ⊤⊤-lifting to reducibility in some extensions of λ_{ml}: with sum types, with exceptions; and in the computational lambda-calculus λ_c. Both sums and exceptions have existing normalisation results in the standard lambda-calculus (for example, [11] and [18–Thm. 6.1]); we know of no prior proofs for them in λ_{ml}. More important, though, is to see how ⊤⊤-lifting adapts to these features. The key step is to extend our formalized continuations with new kinds of observation. Once this is done, we can use these to lift predicates to computation types. The case of reducibility, and hence a proof of strong normalisation, then goes through as usual. Here we can only summarize, and full details appear in [19].

4.1 Reducibility for Sums

Prawitz first showed how to extend reducibility to sums [27]. His method is quite intricate: for a term M of sum type to be reducible, not only must the immediate subterms of M be reducible, but also a certain class of subterms of M' must be reducible whenever M reduces to M'. We avoid this complexity by defining reducibility for sums as we do for computations, by a leap-frog over continuations.

We begin by extending λ_{ml} with sum types and a *case* construct where each branch must be a computation (we later lift this constraint):

$$\frac{M : A}{\iota_1(M) : A + B} \qquad \frac{M : B}{\iota_2(M) : A + B}$$

$$\frac{M : A + B \quad N_1 : TC \quad N_2 : TC}{case\ M\ of\ \iota_1(x_1{}^A) \Rightarrow N_1 \mid \iota_2(x_2{}^B) \Rightarrow N_2 : TC}$$

To record possible observations of sum terms, we introduce *sum continuations*:

$$S ::= K \circ \langle (x_1)N_1, (x_2)N_2 \rangle$$

$$(K \circ \langle (x_1)N_1, (x_2)N_2 \rangle) \mathbin{@} M \;=\; K \mathbin{@} (case\ M\ of\ \iota_1(x_1) \Rightarrow N_1 \mid \iota_2(x_2) \Rightarrow N_2).$$

We can now define reducibility for sum continuations, and thence for sums.

- Sum continuation $S : A + B \multimap TC$ is in $\mathsf{red}^{\top}_{A+B}$ if:
  - $S \mathbin{@} (\iota_1(M))$ is strongly normalising for all $M \in \mathsf{red}_A$ and
  - $S \mathbin{@} (\iota_2(N))$ is strongly normalising for all $N \in \mathsf{red}_B$.
- Sum term $P : A + B$ is in red_{A+B} if $S \mathbin{@} P$ is strongly normalising for all $S \in \mathsf{red}^{\top}_{A+B}$.

This is then sufficient to prove strong normalisation for λ_{ml} with sums in the manner of Sect. 3.3.

To apply this to a more general *case* construction, we can move to *frame stacks*: nested collections of elimination contexts for any type constructor [26]. Frame stacks generalise continuations, and we have been able to use them to give a leap-frog definition of reducibility not just for computations, but also for sums, products and function types. This in turn gives a proof of strong normalisation for λ_{ml} with full sums, as well as the simply-typed lambda-calculus with sums [19–§3.5].

One special case of this brings us full circle: λ_{ml} trivially embeds into the simply-typed lambda-calculus with *unary* sums.

$$[M] \longmapsto \iota(M) \qquad\qquad let\, x \Leftarrow M\, in\, N \longmapsto case\, M\, of\, \iota(x) \Rightarrow N$$

The two languages are essentially the same, except that λ_{ml} has tighter typing rules and admits fewer reductions. Frame stacks and $\top\top$-reducibility then provide strong normalisation for both calculi.

4.2 Reducibility for Exceptions

Benton and Kennedy propose a novel syntax for incorporating exceptions into λ_{ml}, which they use within the SML.NET compiler [9]. They combine exceptions and *let* into the single construction $try\, x^A \Leftarrow M\, in\, N\, unless\, H$. This first evaluates M, then binds the result to x and evaluates N; unless an exception was raised in M, in which case it evaluates the *handler* H instead. The control flow of $try\text{-}in\text{-}unless$ strictly extends the classic $try\text{-}catch$ metaphor: for more on this see [9]; and also the rationale [10] for a similar recent extension of exception handling in the Erlang programming language.

Here we take exceptions E ranging over some fixed (possibly infinite) set; this is necessary to ensure termination [18]. A handler $H : TB$ is then a list of pairs (E, P) of exceptions and computations of type TB: evaluation picks the first pair that matches the exception to be handled; unmatched exceptions are re-raised. Typing rules are:

$$\frac{}{raise(E) : TA} \qquad\qquad \frac{M : TA \quad N : TB \quad H : TB}{try\, x^A \Leftarrow M\, in\, N\, unless\, H : TB}\,.$$

The original *let* is now a special case of *try*, with empty handler: $let\, x \Leftarrow M\, in\, N = try\, x \Leftarrow M\, in\, N\, unless\, \{\}$. Notice that we are not fixing our choice of monad T; it must support exceptions, but it may incorporate other effects too.

For $\top\top$-lifting in this calculus, we generalise continuations to cover the new observable behaviour of exception raising, by associating a handler to every step of the continuation.

$$K ::= Id \mid K \circ \langle (x)N, H\rangle$$
$$(K \circ \langle (x)N, H\rangle) \mathbin{@} M = K \mathbin{@} (try\, x \Leftarrow M\, in\, N\, unless\, H)$$

We now say that continuation K is in $\mathsf{red}_A^{\top}$ if:

- $K \mathbin{@} [V]$ is strongly normalising for all $N \in \mathsf{red}_A$; and in addition
- $K \mathbin{@} (raise(E))$ is strongly normalising for all exceptions E.

Building ⊤⊤-reducibility on this is enough to give strong normalisation for λ_{ml} with exceptions, with a proof in the style of Sect. 3.3.

4.3 Reducibility for the Computational Lambda-Calculus

Strong normalisation for λ_{ml} immediately gives strong normalisation for the subcalculus λ_{ml*} described in Sect. 2. However, despite the close correspondence between λ_{ml*} and λ_c, explored in [28], we do not immediately get strong normalisation for λ_c. This is because of two additional reduction rules in λ_c:

$$\begin{array}{llcll} let.1 & PM & \longrightarrow & let\, x \Leftarrow P\, in\, xM & \text{if } x \notin fv(M) \\ let.2 & VQ & \longrightarrow & let\, y \Leftarrow Q\, in\, Vy & \text{if } y \notin fv(V) \end{array}$$

where P, Q range over non-values, and V ranges over values.

We can adapt our proof, again using continuations in a leap-frog definition of reducibility:

Ground value	$V \in \mathsf{red}_0$	if V is strongly normalising
Function value	$V \in \mathsf{red}_{A\to B}$	if, for all $M \in \mathsf{red}_A \cup \mathsf{red}_A^{\top\top}$, $VM \in \mathsf{red}_B^{\top\top}$
Continuation	$K \in \mathsf{red}_A^{\top}$	if, for all $V \in \mathsf{red}_A$, $K \mathbin{@} V$ is strongly normalising
Non-value	$P \in \mathsf{red}_A^{\top\top}$	if, for all $K \in \mathsf{red}_A^{\top}$, $K \mathbin{@} P$ is strongly normalising

The distinction between values and non-values is crucial. There is no explicit computation type constructor in λ_c, but non-values are always computations. Thus red_A is reducible values of type A, and $\mathsf{red}_A^{\top\top}$ is reducible non-values of type A, playing the role of red_{TA}. This ⊤⊤-reducibility leads as before to a proof of strong normalisation for λ_c, accounting for both additional reductions.

5 Conclusion

We have presented the leap-frog method of ⊤⊤-lifting as a technique for raising operational predicates from type A to type TA, based on the observable behaviour of terms. This is independent of the nature of computations T, and introduces the opportunity of proof by induction on the structure of continuations.

As a concrete example, we demonstrated ⊤⊤-lifting in a definition of reducibility for λ_{ml}, and thence a type-directed proof of strong normalisation. We have also applied this to some extensions of λ_{ml}, addressing in particular the robustness of the method in treating systems with commuting conversions.

In this final section we expand on the relation to other work on this topic, and comment on some possibilities for future research.

5.1 Related Work

We believe that our use of $\top\top$-lifting for computation types in λ_{ml} is new. It is, however, inspired by similar constructions applied to specific notions of computation. Pitts and Stark [25] apply the method to give a structurally inductive characterisation of observational equivalence for a functional language with local state. They then use this to validate certain proof techniques for reasoning about dynamically-allocated reference cells. Direct validation of these techniques had proved fruitless, because even though the precise form of computational effects was known — non-termination, state, and dynamic allocation — the interaction between them was intractable.

In [26], Pitts employs $\top\top$-*closure* to define an operational form of relational parametricity for a polymorphic PCF. Here the computational effect is nontermination, and $(-)^{\top\top}$ leads to an operational analogue of the semantic concept of "admissible" relations. Abadi in [1] investigates further the connection between $\top\top$-closure and admissibility.

The notion of $\top\top$-closed is different from our lifting: it expresses a property of a set of terms at a single type, whereas we lift a predicate ϕ on terms of type A to $\phi^{\top\top}$ on terms of a different type TA. However, the concept is clearly related, and the closure operation makes some appearance in the literature on reducibility, in connection with *saturation* and *saturated* sets of terms. Loosely, saturation is the property one wishes candidates for reducibility to satisfy; and this can sometimes be expressed as $\top\top$-closure. Examples include Girard's reducibility candidates for linear logic [13–pp. 72–73] and Parigot's work on $\lambda\mu$ and classical natural deduction [23–pp. 1469–1471]. For Girard the relevant continuations are the linear duals $A^{\perp}$, while for Parigot they are applicative contexts, lists of arguments in normal form $\mathcal{N}^{<\omega}$. We conjecture that in their style our $\top\top$-lifting could be presented as an insertion $\{ [V] \mid V : \mathrm{red}_A \}$ followed by saturation (although we then lose the notion of reducible continuations).

Melliès and Vouillon use *biorthogonality* in their work on ideal models for types; this is a closure operation based on an orthogonality relation matching our $K \top M$ [31, 32]. They make a case for the importance of orthogonality, highlighting the connection to reducibility. They also deconstruct contexts into frame stacks for finer analysis: elsewhere, Vouillon notes the correspondence between different forms of continuation and possible observations [30].

There are evident echoes of continuation-passing style in the leap-frog character of $\top\top$-lifting; and its independence from the choice of monad recalls Filinski's result that composable continuations can simulate all definable monads [12]. The apparent connection here is appealing, but we have not been able to make any formal link.

Goubault-Larrecq et al. investigate logical relations for computation types, proposing a distributivity law that these should satisfy [15]. They give a number of examples of logical relations lifted to specific monads; and, again, their chosen relation for the continuations monad has a similar structure to our $\top\top$-lifting.

As mentioned in the introduction, existing proofs of strong normalisation for λ_{ml} are based on translations into other calculi that are already known to be strongly normalising. We have said how Benton et al., working from a logical perspective, used a translation into a lambda-calculus with sums [4]. In a report on *monadic type systems* — a generalisation of pure type systems and the computational metalanguage — Barthe et al. [3] prove strong normalisation by translation into a lambda-calculus with an extra reduction β'. Finally, Hatcliff and Danvy [16] state that T-reductions are strongly normalising, although they do not indicate a specific proof method.

5.2 Further Work

Subsequent to the work described here, we have developed a *normalisation by evaluation* algorithm for λ_{ml}, which we prove correct using the strong normalisation result. Normalisation by evaluation (NBE) then leads to further results on the theory of λ_{ml}: namely, that convertibility of terms is decidable, and reduction is confluent. This is described in detail in the first author's PhD thesis [19], which implements NBE for the version of λ_{ml} used as an intermediate language in the SML.NET compiler [7, 8], and evaluates its performance compared to conventional rewriting.

There is an extensive and growing body of work on the problem of normalisation for many varieties of typed lambda-calculi, with reducibility as just one approach. Joachimski and Matthes have proposed an alternative induction method, that characterises the strongly normalisable terms in a calculus [17]. This is proof-theoretically simpler, and it would be interesting to see how this applies to computation types in λ_{ml}. Their method covers sum types, commuting conversions and, most interestingly for us, *generalized applications* of the form $s(t, y.r)$. These have some resemblance to our decomposition of continuations: here $y.r$ is a term abstraction, to which will be passed the result of applying function s to argument t.

The broader test for ⊤⊤-lifting is to investigate its application to other predicates or relations on λ_{ml} terms. Ultimately we want to make precise, and confirm, the informal conjecture of Kennedy and Benton that $(-)^{\top\top}$ captures "observation": if ϕ is some predicate on values, then $\phi^{\top\top}$ is a "best observable approximation" to it on computations [6].

References

[1] M. Abadi. ⊤⊤-closed relations and admissibility. *Math. Struct. Comp. Sci.*, 10(3):313–320, 2000.

[2] H. P. Barendregt. Lambda calculi with types. In *Handbook of Logic in Computer Science*, vol. II, pp. 118–309. OUP, 1992.

[3] G. Barthe, J. Hatcliff, and P. Thiemann. Monadic type systems: Pure type systems for impure settings. In *Proc. HOOTS II*, ENTCS 10. Elsevier, 1997.

[4] P. N. Benton, G. Bierman, and V. de Paiva. Computational types from a logical perspective. *J. Funct. Prog.*, 8(2):177–193, 1998.

[5] P. N. Benton, J. Hughes, and E. Moggi. Monads and effects. In *Applied Semantics; Advanced Lectures*, LNCS 2395, pp. 42–122. Springer-Verlag, 2002.

[6] P. N. Benton and A. Kennedy. Personal communication, December 1998.

[7] P. N. Benton, A. Kennedy, and G. Russell. Compiling Standard ML to Java bytecodes. In *Proc. ICFP '98*. ACM Press, 1998.

[8] P. N. Benton, A. Kennedy, C. Russo, and G. Russell. The SML.NET compiler. Available at http://www.cl.cam.ac.uk/Research/TSG/SMLNET/.

[9] P. N. Benton and A. J. Kennedy. Exceptional syntax. *J. Funct. Prog.*, 11(4):395–410, 2001.

[10] R. Carlsson, B. Gustavsson, and P. Nyblom. Erlang's exception handling revisited. In *Proc. ERLANG '04*, pp. 16–26. ACM Press, 2004.

[11] P. de Groote. On the strong normalisation of intuitionistic natural deduction with permutation-conversions. *Inf. & Comp.*, 178(2):441–464, 2002.

[12] A. Filinski. Representing monads. In *Conf. Record POPL '94*, pp. 446–457. ACM Press, 1994.

[13] J.-Y. Girard. Linear logic. *Theor. Comp. Sci.*, 50(1):1–102, 1987.

[14] J.-Y. Girard, Y. Lafont, and P. Taylor. *Proofs and Types*. CUP, 1989.

[15] J. Goubault-Larrecq, S. Lasota, and D. Nowak. Logical relations for monadic types. In *Proc. CSL '02*, pp. 553–568, 2002.

[16] J. Hatcliff and O. Danvy. A generic account of continuation-passing styles. In *Conf. Record POPL '94*, pp. 458–471. ACM Press, 1994.

[17] F. Joachimski and R. Matthes. Short proofs of normalization. *Arch. Math. Log.*, 42(1):58–87, 2003.

[18] M. Lillibridge. Unchecked exceptions can be strictly more powerful than call/cc. *Higher-Order & Symb. Comp.*, 12(1):75–104, 1999.

[19] S. Lindley. *Normalisation by Evaluation in the Compilation of Typed Functional Programming Languages*. PhD thesis, U. Edinburgh, 2005.

[20] E. Moggi. Computational lambda-calculus and monads. In *Proc. LICS '89*, pp. 14–23. IEEE Comp. Soc. Press, 1989.

[21] E. Moggi. Notions of computation and monads. *Inf. & Comp.*, 93(1):55–92, 1991.

[22] J. Newburn. All about monads, v1.1.0. http://www.nomaware.com/monads.

[23] M. Parigot. Proofs of strong normalisation for second order classical natural deduction. *J. Symb. Log.*, 62(4):1461–1479, 1997.

[24] S. Peyton Jones, editor. *Haskell 98 Language and Libraries: The Revised Report*. CUP, 2003.

[25] A. Pitts and I. Stark. Operational reasoning for functions with local state. In *Higher Order Operational Techniques in Semantics*, pp. 227–273. CUP, 1998.

[26] A. M. Pitts. Parametric polymorphism and operational equivalence. *Math. Struct. Comp. Sci.*, 10:321–359, 2000.

[27] D. Prawitz. Ideas and results in proof theory. In *Proc. 2nd Scand. Log. Symp.*, Stud. Log. Found. Math. 63, pp. 235–307. North Holland, 1971.

[28] A. Sabry and P. Wadler. A reflection on call-by-value. *ACM Trans. Prog. Lang. Syst.*, 19(6):916–941, 1997.

[29] W. W. Tait. Intensional interpretations of functionals of finite type I. *J. Symb. Log.*, 32(2):198–212, 1967.

[30] J. Vouillon. Subtyping union types. In *Proc. CSL '04*, LNCS 3210, pp. 415–429. Springer-Verlag, 2004.

[31] J. Vouillon and P.-A. Melliès. Recursive polymorphic types and parametricity in an operational framework. Submitted for publication, 2004.

[32] J. Vouillon and P.-A. Melliès. Semantic types: a fresh look at the ideal model for types. In *Conf. Record POPL '04*, pp. 52–63. ACM Press, 2004.

[33] P. Wadler. Monads for functional programming. In *Advanced Functional Programming*, LNCS 925, pp. 24–52. Springer-Verlag, 1995.

Privacy in Data Mining Using Formal Methods

Stan Matwin[1,2], Amy Felty[1], István Hernádvölgyi[3], and Venanzio Capretta[4]

[1] SITE, University of Ottawa, Canada
{stan, afelty}@site.uottawa.ca
[2] Institute of Computer Science, Polish Academy of Sciences, Warsaw, Poland
[3] Siemens PSE, Hungary
istvan.hernadvolgyi@siemens.com
[4] Department of Mathematics and Statistics,
University of Ottawa, Canada
venanzio.capretta@mathstat.uottawa.ca

Abstract. There is growing public concern about personal data collected by both private and public sectors. People have very little control over what kinds of data are stored and how such data is used. Moreover, the ability to infer new knowledge from existing data is increasing rapidly with advances in database and data mining technologies. We describe a solution which allows people to take control by specifying constraints on the ways in which their data can be used. User constraints are represented in formal logic, and organizations that want to use this data provide formal proofs that the software they use to process data meets these constraints. Checking the proof by an independent verifier demonstrates that user constraints are (or are not) respected by this software. Our notion of "privacy correctness" differs from general software correctness in two ways. First, properties of interest are simpler and thus their proofs should be easier to automate. Second, this kind of correctness is stricter; in addition to showing a certain relation between input and output is realized, we must also show that only operations that respect privacy constraints are applied during execution. We have therefore an intensional notion of correctness, rather that the usual extensional one. We discuss how our mechanism can be put into practice, and we present the technical aspects via an example. Our example shows how users can exercise control when their data is to be used as input to a decision tree learning algorithm. We have formalized the example and the proof of preservation of privacy constraints in Coq.

1 Introduction

Privacy is one of the main concerns expressed about modern computing, especially in the Internet context. People and groups are concerned by the practice of gathering information without explicitly informing the individuals that data about them is being collected. Oftentimes, even when people are aware that their information is being collected, it is used for purposes other than the ones stated at collection time. The last concern is further aggravated by the power of modern database and data mining operations which allow inferring, from combined data sets, knowledge of which the person is not aware, and would have never consented to generating and disseminating. People have no ownership of their own data: it is not easy for someone to exclude themselves from, e.g.

P. Urzyczyn (Ed.): TLCA 2005, LNCS 3461, pp. 278–292, 2005.

direct marketing campaigns, where the targeted individuals are selected by data mining models.

This state of affairs has been amply observed by the legal community, particularly by the segment of it interested in human rights [EPI05]. One of the main concepts that has emerged from research on societal and legal aspects of privacy is the idea of Use Limitation Principle (ULP). That principle states that the data should be used only for the explicit purpose for which it has been collected. It has been noted, however, that "...[ULP] is perhaps the most difficult to address in the context of data mining or, indeed, a host of other applications that benefit from the subsequent use of data in ways never contemplated or anticipated at the time of the initial collection." [IPC98]. A special case of the ULP is the principle of opting out vs. opting in: in most cases one needs to limit explicitly the access to one's data: this approach is called "opting-out". It is widely felt (e.g. [Rie01]) that a better approach would be opting-in, where data could only be collected with an explicit consent for the collection and specific usage from the data owner.

In this paper, we propose and prototype a novel approach which gives an individual the *ownership* of her data: a person may express permissions stating the purposes for which the data may or may not be used. We show a mechanism by which such permissions can be reinforced in a data mining environment. The core of this approach is the use of formal methods for proving properties of programs. We use a theorem prover with a highly expressive logic – the Coq Proof Assistant [Coq03]. This system provides a high degree of power and flexibility for constructing proofs and it is widely used to develop formal proofs of correctness of software. We are able to express data mining programs directly in the logic of the theorem prover, and express privacy properties easily. In the spectrum from less formal to more formal, this kind of system is on the formal end, meaning that the method is more rigorous than many others and thus can provide a higher degree of assurance of correctness than less formal methods. This high degree of assurance is not without cost, of course; the price that must be paid for it is that more work must be done to apply such methods. Proofs can be difficult to construct and require a high degree of interaction and knowledge on the part of the user. We address this issue by modularizing our programs and proofs. In particular, we structure the code so that for each data mining algorithm we consider, we filter out the difficult part of the proof so that it can be done once and for all by an expert, and isolate the code that is likely to change so that the lemmas that are required for this code are straightforward and easy to prove. It should be possible to simplify the task of proving such lemmas even further by exploiting the similarities of such lemmas, and designing algorithms to help automate their proofs.

One aspect that sets privacy verification apart from customary algorithm correctness is that privacy concerns put constraints on the operation of the program. A traditional correctness requirement states a relation between the input and the output of an algorithm and verification consists of proving that the particular software realizes this relation. In our case, the requirement is not on the input-output relation but on the operations that the algorithm performs while running: we impose that no privacy violating operation can be executed. Traditionally, two programs are considered logically equivalent if they implement the same input-output relation; therefore if one of the two satisfies a specification, so does the other. However, we want to discriminate programs on the basis of *how* they process their input into output. In order to realize such discrimination while at the same time preserving the classical logical understanding of functions, we decided to overload the output produced by the program so that a trace of the potentially privacy-breaking operations is preserved in the result.

More specifically, we start from the Weka repository of Java code which implements a variety of data mining algorithms [WF99]. We modify this code to include checks that the privacy constraints that we allow users to specify are met. We also restructure the code to help facilitate proving properties of it. We write it in the functional programming language of Coq, taking care to ensure that the part of the code which checks that users' privacy constraints are met is clearly identifiable. It is this part of the code that we need the flexibility to change. In particular, we want to consider a possibly large variety of privacy constraints, and so we must be able to modify the code as we modify or add new constraints. In general, the lemmas required of this added privacy-checking code will be considerably simpler than lemmas that will be needed about the algorithm as a whole.

This work extends earlier work, which outlined the main ideas and began with a simple algorithm as an example [FM02]. This first example was a program to perform a database join operation, and accommodated users who requested that their data not be used in such an operation. Here we consider a significantly more complex algorithm – a decision tree learning algorithm, we illustrate our method of structuring programs and proofs to tackle the complexity of using formal methods, and we provide a deeper analysis of the issues that arise in making this work practical.

The remainder of this paper is organized as follows: we describe the architecture of our approach, show that it has the desired properties, illustrate how it applies to the learning of decision trees, present the formalization of a particular privacy property, and discuss the acceptance and implementation of our general approach.

2 Architecture

In order to describe the architecture of our approach, let us introduce the players that participate in privacy-conscious data mining:

User C is a consumer or a citizen wishing to state her permissions with respect to her data as it is involved in different data mining processes. Specifying permissions could be as simple as choosing options, both positive and negative, from some fixed set. Data miner Org is an organization involved in processing the data about a number of Cs. D denotes the database schemata of the databases representing that data, while A denotes a set of data mining algorithms that Org runs on the data. B denotes the binaries of the software implementation of A. Data mining software developer Dev develops software S (source code) implementing A. Dev provides Orgs with B. $Veri$ is an independent, generally trusted organization that verifies that C's permissions are respected by Org in the course of the normal operation of Org. Observe that no single player owns all the data.

Our main idea is as follows. User C sets permissions $P_C(D, A)$: what can and cannot be done with her data D by an algorithm in A. Any claim that software S respects these permissions can be stated as a theorem $T(P_C, S)$ about S. Proof $R(P_C, S)$ of this theorem can be checked: if the proof holds, then the program S has the property of respecting P_C. $Veri$ checks both that $R(P_C, S)$ is a proof of $T(P_C, S)$, and that the binary software B run by Org is a compiled form of S. (For example, $Veri$ could compare the hashed result of compilation of S with hashed B, so that $Veri$ needs no access to B, just to its hashed form.)

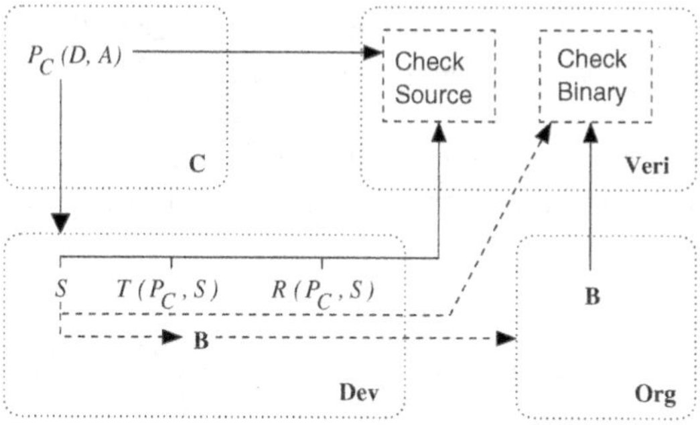

Fig. 1. Architectural diagram of the proposed method

Graphically, we present this architecture in Fig. 1. Arrows pointing from within a box representing player X to a box representing player Y show that X makes an object at the beginning of the arrow available to Y. For instance, an organization on behalf of consumers makes the set of permissions $P_C(D, A)$ from which each individual C can make choices available to Dev and $Veri$. The dashed line between S and B represents the verifiable link that B is the executable of S. As can be seen from this diagram, the architecture has the following properties:

- The user decides what is and what is not permitted to happen with the data. In that sense, a user's data belong to her.
- Users' permissions are verifiably enforced: it can be proven that the data mining software respects them (or not). Consequently, it can be proven as well that the declared use of the data is adhered to, as long as Org respects the proposed architecture. In that sense, ULP becomes verifiable as well.
- The scheme is robust against cheating by Dev or Org. Dev cannot present a proof of a theorem other than $T(P_C, S)$ because $Veri$ recreates the statement of this theorem from P_C and S. Org cannot run binaries of anything other than S (about which $Veri$ can verify that it satisfies permissions) as $Veri$ can verify the B is indeed a binary version of that S.

3 Example

The decision tree learning algorithm we use is the basic ID3 algorithm from [Mit97]. Decision trees classify examples by following, for a given example, a path from the root to a leaf. This path is determined by the values of the attributes of a given example. The leaf on that path gives the class of the example. Decision tree induction algorithms, such as ID3, take as input examples described by their attributes; each example comes with its class. The output of a decision tree induction algorithm is a decision tree like the one shown in Fig. 2. Among many possible decision trees consistent with the input, ID3 chooses heuristically the one with the highest expected accuracy on unseen data – this will be the best tree. We began by implementing this algorithm in Java. Similar, though somewhat more complex versions can be found in the Weka code. We also implemented the same algorithm in the functional programming language SML because it is a smaller step to go from SML to Coq. To illustrate, we apply our program to fictitious data about loan applications. In that data, people are represented by (among other things) their earnings to expenses ratio, whether or not they live in a single dwelling, and whether they live in the suburbs or in the inner city. The tree produced by ID3 from this dataset is shown in Fig. 2.

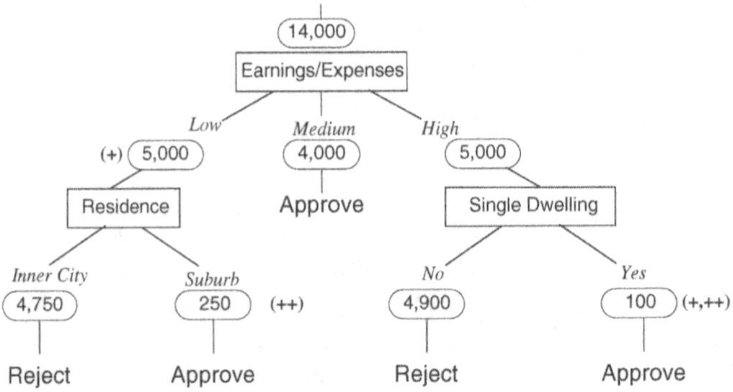

Fig. 2. Example Decision Tree

We have added numbers to each node, indicating the number of training examples considered. For example, the entire training set contains 14,000 records, of which 5,000 are passed on and used to build the tree rooted at the high ratio branch.

Users concerned with privacy may want to restrict how their data is used in training sets to build decision trees. In a typical data mining application the learned decision tree is just a symbolic structure, disconnected from the data used to build its nodes. Business analysts will typically inspect the tree and decide that they are interested in individuals represented by some nodes in the tree, e.g. the rightmost leaf in Fig. 2 (people with high disposable income and likely owning property might be selected for a direct marketing campaign of a life insurance policy, or for a tax audit). Analysts will then perform what is called *data drilling*, i.e. they will request full access to the data subset that resulted in the tree leaf. In such a context, users may want to specify that they do not want their data to be used to build any part of the decision tree unless there is some minimum number of training examples used to build that part of the tree. This may protect them from being singled out or uniquely identified with the condition leading to the leaf in which they find themselves. The ID3 algorithm can be modified to stop building parts of the tree where such constraints are violated. We made this modification, and added two constraints to the data: one of the "single dwelling" loan applicants requires at least 500 people in the training set, and another with the low ratio value requires at least 6,000. The tree resulting from our modified algorithm is the same as Fig. 2 without the branches below the nodes marked with (+). Thus, in the new tree, the low ratio and single dwelling branches will result in no decision. It would be easy, and probably more desirable, to modify the tree so that such branches give some default decision. We leave out this kind of detail when we discuss the proof below.

Data miners might consider such user-imposed constraints to be too restrictive. One alternative is to continue building the tree, and to prune only the leaf node that contains the person whose constraints are violated. Suppose in our example, the person who requires at least 6,000 people in the training set lives in the suburbs. The tree obtained by removing subtrees below nodes marked (++) is the tree obtained from this version of the algorithm. (There is no change to the single dwelling branch in this case.) As before, we will want to modify the two branches that are pruned to give some default decision instead of no decision at all.

These two versions of the algorithm hint at some of the trade-offs and compromises needed between data miners and customers. Instead of discussing this further, we simply note here that (as discussed later), for practical purposes it will be necessary to design a user-friendly language in which users can express constraints. In such a language, we can have a variety of options including the two just discussed here, thus providing increased flexibility.

To obtain an implementation of the ID3 algorithm in Coq's functional language, we began with a direct translation from the SML code and then modified it to use recursion in a style that is more amenable to Coq's reasoning power. Our implementation is modular. We first present a general tree-building procedure that does not depend on specifics such as how to determine the labels of the children of each node or which privacy constraints must be checked. This implementation structure allows us to structure the proof so that we can exploit general mathematical properties of our tree data structures as well as general properties of functions which process such trees.

As mentioned above, we need to overload the output of the algorithm to obtain a trace of the possibly privacy-infringing operations. In the example, the original algorithm produces a search tree that does not contain information about the training data used in its construction. We modify it by labeling each node of the tree with the set of corresponding training data. In this way, the privacy constraints can be verified directly on the output tree. This information can (and should) be discarded before using the tree. This operation can be part of a post-processing phase that also includes replacing branches that give no decision with default decisions as discussed above. We present the algorithm and discuss the formal proof development showing that this code satisfies the required privacy constraints in the next section.

4 The Formal Development

Coq implements the Calculus of Inductive Constructions (CIC), a powerful higher-order logic. In its theory, data types and logical propositions are represented with the same formalism. There are two sorts of types, **Set** for data structures and **Prop** for propositions. An element A : **Set** is a type whose terms are elements of the corresponding data structure. An element P : **Prop** is a type whose terms are proofs of the corresponding proposition.

The type constructors on **Set** (and **Prop**) are: function types (implication) $A \to B$, with abstraction denoted by $[x : A]b$ and application by $(f\ a)$; binary cartesian products $A \times B$ (conjunction $A \wedge B$); binary disjoint unions $A + B$ (disjunction $A \vee B$); and dependent products $(x : A)B$ (universal quantification $\forall x : A.P(x)$).

Two very important constructs of Coq are inductive and coinductive definitions. The notation to define them is similar, but there are deep differences in their meaning. Below left is the general form of the declaration of an inductive or coinductive type:

(Co)Inductive A : **Set**	Inductive nat : **Set**	CoInductive conat : **Set**
$a_0 : (\Gamma_0)A$	0 : nat	0 : conat
$\vdots$	S : nat $\to$ nat	S : conat $\to$ conat
$a_n : (\Gamma_n)A$		

In the general form, the symbols Γ_i represent sequences of argument assumptions. This declaration introduces a new **Set**, A; its elements are constructed by applying the constructors a_i to elements satisfying the assumptions Γ_i. The Γ_is can contain occurrences of A itself, provided that they respect a positivity restriction [CP90, PM93]. In this case the elements of A can be constructed recursively. For example, the set nat defined in the middle above contains natural numbers represented as 0, $(S\ 0)$, $(S\ (S\ 0))$, etc.

Coinductive types are defined in an almost identical way and are subject to the same positivity restrictions [Gim98]: The difference between the two constructs is that the recursive elements of an inductive type must be well-founded, while those of a coinductive type are allowed to be infinitely descending. For example, in the set conat defined on the right above, it is possible to construct a term consisting in a infinite sequence of applications of the S constructor: $(S\ (S\ (S\ \cdots)))$, which is not allowed for nat.

Inductive and Coinductive definitions can be given for elements of **Prop** as well; and the definition of (co)inductive dependent types and predicates is allowed.

The definition of the type for trees is one of the delicate points in the development. We have adopted an implementation methodology that consists of adapting the data types to the structure of the algorithms to be verified. This implementation philosophy has proved very effective in previous work [BC01, MM04, BC04] and it greatly simplifies the representation of algorithms and the verification of their properties.

To see how this methodology is applied in our case, consider the following informal description of the algorithm: The input is a database, that is a list of records, d, representing the input training data. If the privacy restriction is not satisfied by d (e.g. d is too small), then the construction of the tree is blocked at this node and the node itself gives a default result. On the other hand, if d satisfies the privacy restriction, a node is created and d is partitioned into subsets that will be used to build the children of that node. The children are determined by choosing the attribute that results in the best classifier. A list of databases is obtained by dividing d into equivalence classes, one for each value of this attribute, and a new branch of the tree is created for each element of this list.

This is a top-down construction: The tree is constructed starting from its root node by specifying the branches at each stage. This is typical of coinductively constructed trees, because we cannot be sure *a priori* that the constructed tree is well-founded (it can be proved *a posteriori* in our case). On the other hand, inductive trees are characterized by a bottom-up construction in which the subtrees have to be defined first and the main tree is built from them.

Therefore, the natural definition of $\mathsf{Tree}(A)$, for any $A : \mathbf{Set}$, would be:

$$\begin{array}{l} \mathsf{CoInductive}\ \mathsf{Tree}(A) : \mathbf{Set} \\ \quad \mathsf{node} : A \to \mathsf{list}(\mathsf{Tree}(A)) \to \mathsf{Tree}(A) \end{array}$$

This says that a tree consists of a node with a label of type A and a list of subtrees. Unfortunately, this definition is rejected by the type system of Coq, because the assumption $\mathsf{list}(\mathsf{Tree}(A))$ does not satisfy the positivity condition. This condition states that the type that we are defining ($\mathsf{Tree}(A)$ in our case) can appear in the assumptions of a constructor only in a positive position, that is, either by itself or as the result type of a functional construction. Here it appears inside the $\mathsf{list}()$ constructor and it is therefore rejected. This in spite of the fact that such a definition is sound.

We worked around this limitation of Coq by an alternative definition:

$$\begin{array}{l} \mathsf{CoInductive}\ \mathsf{Tree}(A) : \mathbf{Set} \\ \quad \mathsf{pure\_node} : A \to \mathsf{Tree}(A) \\ \quad \mathsf{add\_child} : \mathsf{Tree}(A) \to \mathsf{Tree}(A) \to \mathsf{Tree}(A) \end{array}$$

The idea here is that we first generate a node ($\mathsf{pure\_node}\ a$), with label a and no branches, and then add the subtrees one by one using the constructor add_child (i.e. ($\mathsf{add\_child}\ c\, t$) adds a new child c to existing tree t). In presenting Coq terms in this section, for readability, we often leave type parameters and arguments implicit. (For example, the parameter $[A : \mathbf{Set}]$ is left out of the above $\mathsf{Tree}(A)$ definition and argument A is left out when we write ($\mathsf{pure\_node}\ a$) instead of ($\mathsf{pure\_node}\ A\ a$).) Clearly, all trees that could be constructed by the previous (rejected) definition can be defined in this new format. We can actually define a function node that performs the task that we required of the constructor in the original definition, and just forget about the roundabout way we defined trees:

$$\begin{array}{l} \mathsf{Fixpoint}\ \mathsf{node}\ [a : A; lt : (\mathsf{list}(\mathsf{Tree}(A)))] : \mathsf{Tree}(A) := \\ \quad \mathsf{Cases}\ lt\ \mathsf{of} \\ \quad\quad \mathsf{nil} \Rightarrow (\mathsf{pure\_node}\ a) \\ \quad\quad (\mathsf{cons}\ t\ lt') \Rightarrow (\mathsf{add\_child}\ t\ (\mathsf{node}\ a\ lt')) \\ \quad \mathsf{end} \end{array}$$

The keyword Fixpoint indicates a recursive definition on terms of inductive type. In this case, the function node is defined by recursion on the list lt. The Cases construction analyzes the structure of lt (it is either an empty list, nil, or a non-empty list with head t and tail lt'), and uses the function node recursively on the tail of a non-empty list.

However, now it is possible to construct anomalous trees that did not exist earlier: The constructor add_child can be recursively applied infinitely many times to generate a node with infinitely many branches. The existence of these pathological trees does not influence in any way the functioning of the algorithm or the proof of correctness.

For coinductive types, there is a construction for recursive definitions similar to Fixpoint, the operation CoFixpoint. The difference is in the criteria that the definition must satisfy: In a Fixpoint definition the recursive calls must be performed on structurally smaller objects; in a CoFixpoint definition there is no restriction on the recursive calls, but the operation must be *guarded*, that is, it must guarantee that for every input, it generates a term with a constructor at its head. For a formal definition of the syntactic conditions for Fixpoint and CoFixpoint see [Coq93, Gim94].

However, we chose a different (equivalent) way to define recursive functions on a coinductive type. We exploit instead the categorical characterization of coinductive types as terminal coalgebras [Hag87] (for a type-theoretic introduction, see also Chapter 3 of [Cap02]; for a comparison of the two approaches, see [Gim94]). A coalgebra, in our case, is a pair consisting of a set A and a function $f : A \rightarrow \mathsf{list}(A)$. Terminality of the coinductive type means that for every coalgebra there exists a function $(\mathsf{coalgebra\_tree}\ f) : A \rightarrow \mathsf{Tree}(A)$. Intuitively, given an element $a : A$, the term $(\mathsf{coalgebra\_tree}\ f\ a)$ is the tree with root node labeled by a and subtrees recursively constructed by applying $(\mathsf{coalgebra\_tree}\ f)$ to every element of $(f\ a)$. The operator coalgebra_tree can easily be defined by CoFixpoint:

```
CoFixpoint coalgebra_tree_list : (A → list(A)) → A → list(A) → Tree(A) :=
  [f, a, l] Cases l of
          nil ⇒ (pure_node a)
          (cons b l') ⇒ (add_child (coalgebra_tree_list f b (f b))
                                   (coalgebra_tree_list f a l'))
      end
Definition coalgebra_tree : (A → list(A)) → A → Tree(A) :=
  [f, a](coalgebra_tree_list f a (f a))
```

Notice that in the CoFixpoint definition of coalgebra_tree_list the recursive calls are performed on arguments that are not necessarily structurally simpler than the original input, but they are *guarded* by the application of the constructor add_child which ensures that the construction of the tree proceeds by at least one step. The Definition keyword introduces a (non-recursive) definition in Coq.

We first define a general decision-tree-building procedure that does not depend on the specific data used by the ID3 algorithm. In particular, we assume the existence of the following parameters with their types, but assume nothing about their implementations: $A : \mathbf{Set}$; $\mathsf{children\_list} : A \rightarrow \mathsf{list}(A)$; $\mathsf{constraint} : A \rightarrow \mathsf{bool}$; $\mathsf{dummy} : A$. Node labels will be elements of type A. The children_list function, given an input a, will determine the elements of type A that will be used to construct the children of a node labelled with a. The children of a node are uniquely determined by the label, and there are never two nodes with the same label in any decision tree. The constraint predicate identifies the subset of A that satisfies a particular property, left unspecified here. It returns a boolean value true or false. Finally, dummy is an unspecified default value of type A. Given these parameters, Fig. 3 contains the general implementation of decision_tree. The first definition is a general filter function which, given an input list, replaces every element a that doesn't meet the constraint $(f\ a)$ with some default value z. The secure_children function uses this filter function on the list obtained by calling children_list. The function secure_tree calls coalgebra_tree with secure_children as its argument function. Thus we

```
Fixpoint filter [z : A; f : A → bool; l : list(A)] : list(A) :=
  Cases l of
    nil ⇒ nil
    (cons a l') ⇒ if (f a)
                  then (cons a (filter z f l'))
                  else (cons z (filter z f l'))
  end
Definition secure_children A → list(A) :=
  [a](filter A dummy constraint (children_list a))
Definition secure_tree : A → Tree(A) :=
  [a](coalgebra_tree A secure_children a)
Definition decision_tree : A → Tree(A) :=
  [a]if (constraint a) then (secure_tree a) else (pure_node dummy)
```

Fig. 3. The General Decision Tree Algorithm in Coq

define it by using the characterization of the coinductive type Tree(A) as a terminal coalgebra. The top-level decision_tree function calls secure_tree, but first checks to see that the initial input meets the required constraint. If not, a degenerate tree of one node with a dummy label is returned.

To instantiate the parameters and specialize this algorithm to ID3, we need several definitions. We begin by using Coq's built-in arrays and lists to represent the input training data. A record is represented as an array of fixed size. Each position in the array contains a particular field, and we assume the fields are in the same order in each record in the training data. The training data is a list of such records. Defining an array in Coq requires the type and number of fields. We leave these unspecified here. They are formal parameters to our program, which we call Field and numFields. For simplicity we assume that all fields have the same type (i.e. all possible field contents can be encoded as elements of type Field). We define our array and lists as follows:

```
Definition Record := array(numFields, Field)
Definition DB := list(Record)
```

A privacy constraint is associated with each record. We represent this association as a function min_data : Record → nat. For a record r : Record, (min_data r) specifies the minimum number of records that must be present in a node of the decision tree for the algorithm to be allowed to proceed. This number could, for example, be stored as one of the fields in r, and then min_data would be the function that extracts the value of this field. Fig. 4 contains the implementation of several functions we will need. The first two functions define the code that checks whether privacy is respected for all the records in the database. The first function, min_data_check checks that all records in a certain database have a privacy specification smaller than a given bound. In the second function, privacy_constraint, we just require that the boolean relation min_data_check is satisfied when n is the size of the database.

```
Fixpoint min_data_check [db : DB; n : nat] : bool :=
  Cases db of
    nil ⇒ true
    (cons r db') ⇒ ((min_data r) ≤ n and (min_data_check db' n))
  end
Definition privacy_constraint : DB → bool :=
  [db](min_data_check db (length db))
Definition leaf_db : DB → bool :=
  [db](length (partitioning_functions db)) ≤ 1
Definition id3_children : DB → list(DB) :=
  [db]if (leaf_db db) then nil else (partitions db)
```

Fig. 4. Functions Specific to the ID3 Algorithm

We leave out the part of the ID3 algorithm that determines how to partition the training data by choosing the attribute that results in the best classifier. The details have no bearing on the privacy issue. We just assume the existence of the following function:

$$\text{partitioning\_functions} : \text{DB} \rightarrow \text{list}(\text{Record} \rightarrow \text{bool})$$

Given a database db : DB, (partitioning_functions db) returns a list of boolean predicates over Record. Each predicate selects a particular equivalence class.

For our proof, we need no information about this function other than its type. (For example, we do not even need to know that each predicate selects a subset of db that is disjoint from all others.) If there is only one equivalence class, the ID3 algorithm builds a leaf node and stops. The function leaf_db in Fig. 4 tests for this case by checking the length of the list returned by partitioning_functions. When there is more than one equivalence class, we must compute the partitions of db. We can easily define a function that does so according to the predicates returned by partitioning_functions:

$$\text{partitions} : \text{DB} \rightarrow \text{list}(\text{DB})$$

We omit the definition. This function is used by id3_children in Fig. 4, which first tests whether or not this partitioning should be done by calling leaf_db. In the true case, since there will be no children, the empty list is returned.

The ID3 algorithm is then obtained by instantiating the parameters introduced above. First, we instantiate A with DB. Thus, we store at each node the actual subset of the training data used to build the subtree below the node. (Note that our trees do not store labels such as "Approve", "Reject", or "Single Dwelling" as used in Fig. 2. They are not important for constructing or using the tree.) To complete the algorithm, we instantiate children_list with id3_children, constraint with privacy_constraint, and dummy with null_data. We define null_data to be an empty list of training data. This is the label used for nodes which do not meet the required privacy constraints. Let id3_decision_tree be the name of the version of the decision_tree function with parameters instantiated in this way.

To implement the version of the algorithm that keeps more nodes and eliminates only the leaves marked with (++), the only change needed is to instantiate the constraint parameter with the following code:

$$\text{Definition leaf\_privacy\_constraint} : \text{DB} \rightarrow \text{bool} :=$$
$$[db](\text{leaf\_db } db) \text{ implies } (\text{min\_data\_check } db \ (\text{length } db))$$

instead of instantiating with privacy_constraint.

The following definition of the predicate privacy_pred expresses what it means for user constraints to be satisfied by source code S.

$$\text{Definition privacy\_pred} := [S : \text{DB} \rightarrow \text{Tree(DB)}]$$
$$\forall db_0, db_1 : \text{DB}.(\text{In\_tree } db_1 \ (S \ db_0))$$
$$\rightarrow \forall r : \text{Record}.(\text{In } r \ db_1) \rightarrow (\text{min\_data } r) \preccurlyeq (\text{length } db_1)$$

The predicate $(\text{In\_tree } db_1 \ (S \ db_0))$ expresses the fact that the database db_1 is the label of a node of the tree generated by S for the training set db_0. The predicate says that if r is one of the records in db_1 then the privacy restriction is satisfied, that is, the number of records in db_1, $(\text{length } db_1)$, is at least the minimum limit specified for r, $(\text{min\_data } r)$. We use the symbol $\preccurlyeq$ for the logical version of the order relation to distinguish it from the boolean version used in the algorithm.

Note here that S is a formal parameter. The theorem that is written $T(P_C, S)$ is obtained in this case by the application (privacy_pred id3_decision_tree). The heart of the proof of this theorem is a series of lemmas showing that $(\text{privacy\_constraint } a) = \mathit{true}$ is an invariant of all nodes a created by the id3_decision_tree program. The main theorem follows fairly directly from this property. The version of the algorithm that uses leaf_privacy_constraint instead of privacy_constraint requires only minor modifications to two lemmas and their proofs. The whole proof development, including definitions, lemmas, and proofs, is roughly 500 lines of Coq script.

5 Discussion and Conclusion

Let us turn our attention to some of the practical aspects of the approach we are proposing. These include the additional effort (human and computational) needed to perform data mining compared to the current practice; the question of access of the players to the information proprietary to other players; and the limitations of the approach.

Firstly, as already mentioned, proving the theorem $T(P_C, S)$ is hard, but this needs to be done only once. We envisage that Dev will perform this as part of the documentation activities. The proof $R(P_C, S)$ must be checked by $Veri$. This check can be performed automatically. Instead of being done exhaustively, it can be done at random times, similarly to industrial quality control. Finally, a computational overhead of the software modified so that permissions are checked during execution of B is linear in the number of Cs whose privacy is checked.

Secondly, let us see in more detail what kind of access different players need to have to software belonging to other players. It is access to S that is difficult in practice: for obvious reasons Devs will be reluctant to let other parties read the source code of Dev's proprietary software. We believe that these concerns can be addressed by carefully analyzing and constraining the access process, and engineering it so that the source code is only accessed by programs and never by humans. For instance, $Veri$ needs access to S when checking proof R, but that can be done in Dev's environment, by an applet or other non-intrusive mechanism for which it is known that it does not export any information outside that environment.

Let us now look at some issues related to the language in which Cs express their permissions of P_C. The first question is the issue of names of database fields – how would C know what names of the database fields are needed to describe her permissions? We can see this answered when universal XML standards will normalize the names of fields in large databases. Alternatively, one can envisage the disclosure of field names by Orgs participating in the proposed scheme.

Finally, the language of P_Cs also limits our approach to data properties that can be expressed syntactically in formal logic. This does not take into account data dependencies that may be true in a given domain and exploited by Orgs that have that domain knowledge. It may be possible to deduce information from decision trees that is not covered by privacy constraints. An example from the real world of deductions from data is *mortgage redlining*. This is a name for a discrimination technique that has been used in the past by some US lenders to exclude mortgage loan applicants based on race and ethnic criteria. Racial redlining has been ruled illegal some years ago, but many (see [USC98]) allege that lenders use other "attributes" of loan applicants that the lenders know correlate highly with race, such as a combination of the geographic info (e.g. ZIP indicating inner city) with household income. This results in the same effect as racial redlining, and shows the limitation of "syntactic" privacy permissions that can be sidetracked by having the knowledge of deep relationships between attributes. This is the case in our example with the loan data and the resulting decision tree in Fig. 2: while grouping people by race may be forbidden by law, lenders may know that following the inner city path in the tree may practically identify racial minorities. In general, it is important that users be given as much information as possible about what their chosen privacy constraints cover, and what they don't.

Most related work on addressing privacy problems in the data mining context [AS00, ESAG02, Iye02] approaches the problem by applying data transformations that perturb values of individual data records, changing the "sensitive" fields (e.g. salary information). While the value of an individual perturbed field becomes useless, a reconstruction procedure estimates the original distribution, so that a modified decision tree induction algorithm gives results close to those that would be obtained on the original, unperturbed database. Another branch of this research looks at the privacy aspects when the data is split either vertically [VC02] (i.e. attributes are partitioned, and one party knows only a given partition and does not wish to share the values of these attributes with other parties, while all attributes are needed for data mining), or horizontally [KC02] (i.e. the database is partitioned into subsets of records, one party knows only the records in its partition and does not wish to share these records with other parties, while all records are needed for data mining). None of this work, however, offers any tools to address the ULP.

A variety of approaches to the privacy problem introduce formal models which can serve as a starting point for verifying privacy policies. One example, which does begin to address the ULP, is a language based approach which builds information-flow into the types of a simplified version of Java [HA04]. Although this work does not address data mining in particular, it may be possible to integrate this kind of approach with ours to improve the scope of privacy concerns that can be enforced.

A wealth of future work is ahead of us. A user-friendly permission language for P_Cs, easy to handle by an average person, needs to be designed. As suggested earlier, it could initially have the form of a set of options from which C would choose her permissions, both negative and positive. Tools for proof development that can ease proof construction in this domain need to be designed. Our current work includes experimenting with the Krakatoa approach [MPMU04] which allows us to work more directly with the Weka Java code, avoiding the step of translating code into Coq. We hope this approach will also provide better automation of proofs. Also, the approach presented here can be combined with the data perturbation method mentioned earlier [AS00]. In our framework, one could prove that the perturbation techniques are in fact applied to the data during data mining. Finally, we need to experiment with a specific dataset used by an organization which will accept to act as the first Org, and a Dev who will provide access to his S on the basis described above.

Acknowledgments

The authors acknowledge the support of the Natural Sciences and Engineering Research Council of Canada, and Communications and Information Technology Ontario. We also thank Guillaume Dufay for useful discussions.

References

[AS00] R. Agrawal and R. Srikant. Privacy-preserving data mining. In W. Chen, J. F. Naughton, and P. A. Bernstein, editors, *2000 ACM SIGMOD International Conference on Management of Data*, pages 439–450. ACM, May 2000.

[BC01] Ana Bove and Venanzio Capretta. Nested general recursion and partiality in type theory. In Richard J. Boulton and Paul B. Jackson, editors, *Theorem Proving in Higher Order Logics: 14th International Conference, TPHOLs 2001*, volume 2152 of *Lecture Notes in Computer Science*, pages 121–135. Springer-Verlag, 2001.

[BC04] Ana Bove and Venanzio Capretta. Modelling general recursion in type theory. To appear in *Mathematical Structures in Computer Science*. Available at http://www.science.uottawa.ca/~vcapr396/, 2004.

[Cap02] Venanzio Capretta. *Abstraction and Computation*. PhD thesis, Computing Science Institute, University of Nijmegen, 2002.

[Coq93] Thierry Coquand. Infinite objects in type theory. In Henk Barendregt and Tobias Nipkow, editors, *Types for Proofs and Programs. International Workshop TYPES'93*, volume 806 of *Lecture Notes in Computer Science*, pages 62–78. Springer-Verlag, 1993.

[Coq03] Coq Development Team. The Coq Proof Assistant reference manual: Version 7.4. Technical report, INRIA, 2003.

[CP90] Thierry Coquand and Christine Paulin. Inductively defined types. In P. Martin-Löf, editor, *Proceedings of Colog '88*, volume 417 of *Lecture Notes in Computer Science*. Springer-Verlag, 1990.

[EPI05] EPIC. Electronic Privacy Information Center. http://www.epic.org/, 2005.

[ESAG02] A. Evfimievski, R. Srikant, R. Agrawal, and J. Gehrke. Privacy preserving mining of association rules. In *Eighth ACM SIGKDD International Conference on Knowledge Discovery in Databases and Data Mining*, July 2002.

[FM02] Amy Felty and Stan Matwin. Privacy-oriented data mining by proof checking. In *Sixth European Conference on Principles of Data Mining and Knowledge Discovery*, volume 2431 of *Lecture Notes in Computer Science*, pages 138–149. Springer-Verlag, August 2002.

[Gim94] Eduardo Giménez. Codifying guarded definitions with recursive schemes. In Peter Dybjer, Bengt Nordström, and Jan Smith, editors, *Types for Proofs and Programs. International Workshop TYPES '94*, volume 996 of *Lecture Notes in Computer Science*, pages 39–59. Springer-Verlag, 1994.

[Gim98] Eduardo Giménez. A Tutorial on Recursive Types in Coq. Technical Report 0221, Unité de recherche INRIA Rocquencourt, May 1998.

[HA04] Katia Hayati and Martín Abadi. Language-based enforcement of privacy policies. In *Proceedings of Privacy Enhancing Technologies Workshop (PET 2004)*, 2004.

[Hag87] Tatsuya Hagino. A typed lambda calculus with categorical type constructors. In D. H. Pitt, A. Poigné, and D. E. Rydeheard, editors, *Category Theory and Computer Science*, volume 283 of *Lecture Notes in Computer Science*, pages 140–157. Springer-Verlag, 1987.

[IPC98] IPCO. Data mining: Staking a claim on your privacy, Information and Privacy Commissioner/Ontario. http://www.ipc.on.ca/scripts/index.asp?action=31&-P_ID=11387&N_ID=1&PT_ID=11351&U_ID=0, January 1998.

[Iye02] Vijay S. Iyengar. Transforming data to satisfy privacy constraints. In *Eighth ACM SIGKDD International Conference on Knowledge Discovery in Databases and Data Mining*, pages 279–287, July 2002.

[KC02] Murat Kantarcioglu and Chris Clifton. Privacy-preserving distributed mining of association rules on horizontally partitioned data. In *The ACM SIGMOD Workshop on Research Issues in Data Mining and Knowledge Discovery (DMKD'2002)*, June 2002.

[Mit97] Tom M. Mitchell. *Machine Learning*. McGraw Hill, 1997.

[MM04] Conor McBride and James McKinna. The view from the left. *Journal of Functional Programming*, 14(1):69–111, 2004.

[MPMU04] Claude Marché, Christine Paulin-Mohring, and Xavier Urbain. The Krakatoa tool for certification of Java/JavaCard programs annotated in JML. *Journal of Logic and Algebraic Programming*, 58(1–2):89–106, January–March 2004.

[PM93] C. Paulin-Mohring. Inductive Definitions in the System Coq - Rules and Properties. In M. Bezem and J.-F. Groote, editors, *Proceedings of the conference Typed Lambda Calculi and Applications*, volume 664 of *Lecture Notes in Computer Science*, 1993. LIP research report 92-49.

[Rie01] D. G. Ries. Protecting consumer online privacy – an overview. http://www.pbi.org/-Goodies/privacy/privacy_ries.htm, May 2001.

[USC98] USCM. Mayors attack urban redlining, mortgage discrimination, The US Conference of Mayors. http://www.usmayors.org/uscm/news/press_releases/press-_archive.asp?doc_id=98, 1998.

[VC02] Jaideep Vaidya and Chris Clifton. Privacy preserving association rule mining in vertically partitioned data. In *Eighth ACM SIGKDD International Conference on Knowledge Discovery in Databases and Data Mining*, July 2002.

[WF99] I. H. Witten and E. Frank. *Data Mining: Practical Machine Learning Tools and Techniques with Java Implementations*. Morgan Kaufmann, 1999.

L^3: A Linear Language with Locations

Greg Morrisett[1], Amal Ahmed[1], and Matthew Fluet[2]

[1] Harvard University
{greg, amal}@eecs.harvard.edu
[2] Cornell University
fluet@cs.cornell.edu

Abstract. We explore foundational typing support for *strong updates* — updating a memory cell to hold values of unrelated types at different points in time. We present a simple, but expressive type system based upon standard linear logic, one that also enjoys a simple semantic interpretation for types that is closely related to models for spatial logics. The typing interpretation is strong enough that, in spite of the fact that our core calculus supports shared, mutable references and cyclic graphs, every well-typed program terminates.

We then consider extensions needed to make our calculus expressive enough to serve as a model for languages with ML-style references, where the capability to access a reference cell is unrestricted, but strong updates are disallowed. Our extensions include a `thaw` primitive for temporarily re-gaining the capability to perform strong updates on unrestricted references.

1 Introduction

The goal of this work is to explore foundational typing support for *strong updates*. In type systems for imperative languages, a strong update corresponds to changing the type of a mutable object whenever the contents of the object is changed. As an example, consider the following code fragment written with SML syntax:

```
1.  let val r = ref () in
2.      r := true;
3.      if (!r) then r := 42 else r := 15;
4.      !r + 12
5.  end
```

At line 1, we create a ref cell `r` whose contents are initialized with `unit`. At line 2, we change the contents so that `r` holds a `bool`. Then at line 3, we change the contents of `r` again, this time to `int`. In spite of the fact that at different program points `r` holds values of different, incompatible types, there is nothing in the program that will cause a run-time type error.[1] This is because subsequent reads of the reference are type-compatible with the immediately preceding writes.

[1] We assume that values are represented uniformly so that, for instance, unit, booleans, and integers all take up one word of storage.

P. Urzyczyn (Ed.): TLCA 2005, LNCS 3461, pp. 293–307, 2005.

Unfortunately, most imperative languages, including SML and Java, do not support strong updates. For instance, SML rejects the above program because it requires that reference cells hold values of exactly one type. The reason for this is that tracking the current type of a reference cell at each program point is hindered by the potential for aliasing. Consider, the following function:

```
1.  fun f (r1: int ref, r2: int ref): int =
2.    (r1 := true;
3.     !r2 + 42)
```

In order to avoid a typing error, this function can only be called in contexts where `r1` and `r2` are different ref cells. The reason is that if we passed the same cell for each formal argument, then the update on line 2 should change not only the type of `r1` but also the type of `r2`, causing a type error to occur at line 3.

Thus, any type system that supports strong updates needs some control over aliasing. In addition, it is clear that the hidden side-effects of a function, such as the change in type to `f`'s first argument in the example above, must be reflected in the interface of the function to achieve modular type-checking. In short, strong updates seem to need a lot of technical machinery to ensure soundness and reasonable accuracy.

Lately, there have been a number of languages, type systems, and analyses that have supported some form of strong updates. The Vault language [1, 2] was designed for coding low-level systems code, such as device drivers. The ability to track strong updates was crucial for ensuring that driver code respected certain protocols. Typed Assembly Language [3, 4] used strong updates to track the types of registers and stack slots. More recently, Foster and Aiken have presented a flow-sensitive qualifier system for C, called CQUAL [5], which uses strong updates to track security-relevant properties in legacy C code.

Vault, later versions of TAL, and CQUAL all based their support for strong updates and alias control on the *Alias Types* formalism of Smith, Walker, and Morrisett [6]. Though Alias Types were proven sound in a syntactic sense, we lacked an understanding of their *semantics*. Furthermore, Vault, TAL, and CQUAL added a number of new extensions that were not handled by Alias Types. For instance, the `restrict` operator of CQUAL is unusual in that it allows a computation to temporarily gain exclusive ownership of a reference cell and perform strong updates, in spite of the fact that there may be unknown aliases to the object.

In this paper, we re-examine strong updates from a more foundational standpoint. In particular, we give an alternative formulation of Alias Types in the form of a core calculus based on standard linear logic, which yields an extremely clean semantic interpretation of the types that is directly related to the semantic model of the logic of Bunched Implications (BI) [7]. We show that our core calculus is sound and that every well-typed program terminates, in spite of the fact that the type system supports first-class, shared, mutable references with strong updates. We then show how the calculus can be extended to support a combination of ML-style references with uncontrolled aliasing and a `restrict`-like primitive for temporarily gaining exclusive ownership over such references to support strong updates. We do not envision the core calculi presented here to be used by end programmers. Instead, we intend these calculi to be expressive enough to serve as a target language for more palatable surface languages. Proofs of theorems, as well as extended discussion, examples, and related work, can be found in a companion technical report [8].

2 Core $\mathbf{L}^3$

Linear types, which are derived from Girard's linear logic [9], have proven useful for modeling imperative programming languages in a functional setting [10, 11]. For instance, the Clean programming language [12] relies upon a form of linearity (or uniqueness) to ensure equational reasoning in the presence of mutable data structures (and other effects such as IO). The intuitive understanding is that a linear object cannot be duplicated, and thus there are no aliases to the object, so it is safe to perform updates in-place while continuing to reason equationally.

Though a linear interpretation of reference cells supports strong updates, it is too restrictive for many, if not most, realistic programs. What is needed is some way to support the controlled duplication of references to mutable objects, while supporting strong updates. One approach, suggested by Alias Types, is to separate the typing components of a mutable object into two pieces: a *pointer* to the object, which can be freely duplicated, and a *capability* for accessing the contents of the object. The type of the capability records the current type of the contents of the object and must remain linear to ensure the soundness of strong updates.

In this section, we present a different formulation of Alias Types based on a relatively standard call-by-value linear lambda calculus; we name our calculus $\mathbf{L}^3$(*Linear Language with Locations*). In $\mathbf{L}^3$, capabilities are explicit and first-class, which makes it simple to support inductively defined data structures. Furthermore, as in Alias Types, $\mathbf{L}^3$ supports multiple pointers to a given mutable object as well as strong updates. Somewhat surprisingly, the core language retains a simple semantics, which, for instance, allows us to prove that well-typed programs terminate. Thus, we believe that $\mathbf{L}^3$ is an appropriate foundation for strong updates in the presence of sharing.

2.1 Syntax

The syntax for core $\mathbf{L}^3$ is as follows:

$$
\begin{array}{rrl}
\textit{Locs} & \eta & ::= \ell \mid \rho \qquad \ell \in \textit{LocConsts} \qquad \rho \in \textit{LocVars} \\
\textit{Types} & \tau & ::= \mathbf{1} \mid \tau_1 \otimes \tau_2 \mid \tau_1 \multimap \tau_2 \mid\, !\tau \mid \mathsf{Ptr}\,\eta \mid \mathsf{Cap}\,\eta\,\tau \mid \forall\rho.\tau \mid \exists\rho.\tau \\
\textit{Exprs} & e & ::= \langle\rangle \mid \mathtt{let}\ \langle\rangle = e_1\ \mathtt{in}\ e_2 \mid \langle e_1, e_2\rangle \mid \mathtt{let}\ \langle x, y\rangle = e_1\ \mathtt{in}\ e_2 \mid \\
& & \quad x \mid \lambda x.\, e \mid e_1\, e_2 \mid\, !v \mid \mathtt{let}\ !x = e_1\ \mathtt{in}\ e_2 \mid \mathtt{dup}\, e \mid \mathtt{drop}\, e \mid \\
& & \quad \mathtt{ptr}\,\ell \mid \mathtt{cap}\,\ell \mid \mathtt{new}\, e \mid \mathtt{free}\, e \mid \mathtt{swap}\, e_1\, e_2 \mid \\
& & \quad \Lambda\rho.\, e \mid e\,[\eta] \mid \ulcorner\eta, e\urcorner \mid \mathtt{let}\ \ulcorner\rho, x\urcorner = e_1\ \mathtt{in}\ e_2 \\
\textit{Values} & v & ::= \langle\rangle \mid \langle v_1, v_2\rangle \mid x \mid \lambda x.\, e \mid\, !v \mid \mathtt{ptr}\,\ell \mid \mathtt{cap}\,\ell \mid \Lambda\rho.\, e \mid \ulcorner\eta, v\urcorner
\end{array}
$$

Most of the types, expressions, and values are based on a traditional, call-by-value, linear lambda calculus. In the following sections, we will explain the bits that are new or different.

$$Stores\ \sigma ::= \{\ell_1 \mapsto v_1, \ldots, \ell_n \mapsto v_n\}$$

$$(\textsf{let-bang})\ (\sigma, \texttt{let}\ !x = !v\ \texttt{in}\ e) \longmapsto (\sigma, e[v/x]) \qquad (\textsf{dup})\ (\sigma, \texttt{dup}\,!v) \longmapsto (\sigma, \langle !v, !v\rangle)$$

$$(\textsf{drop})\ (\sigma, \texttt{drop}\,!v) \longmapsto (\sigma, \langle\,\rangle) \qquad (\textsf{new})\ (\sigma, \texttt{new}\,v) \longmapsto (\sigma \uplus \{\ell \mapsto v\}, \ulcorner \ell, \langle \texttt{cap}\,\ell, !(\texttt{ptr}\,\ell)\rangle \urcorner)$$

$$(\textsf{free})\ (\sigma \uplus \{\ell \mapsto v\}, \texttt{free}\,\ulcorner \ell, \langle \texttt{cap}\,\ell, !(\texttt{ptr}\,\ell)\rangle \urcorner) \longmapsto (\sigma, \ulcorner \ell, v \urcorner)$$

$$(\textsf{swap})\ (\sigma \uplus \{\ell \mapsto v_1\}, \texttt{swap}\,(\texttt{ptr}\,\ell)\,\langle \texttt{cap}\,\ell, v_2\rangle) \longmapsto (\sigma \uplus \{\ell \mapsto v_2\}, \langle \texttt{cap}\,\ell, v_1\rangle)$$

Fig. 1. Core $\mathbf{L}^3$– Selected Operational Semantics

Types. The types $\mathbf{1}$, $\tau_1 \otimes \tau_2$, $\tau_1 \multimap \tau_2$, and $!\tau$ are those found in the linear lambda calculus. The first three types are linear and must be eliminated exactly once. The pattern matching expression forms $\texttt{let}\ \langle\,\rangle = e_1\ \texttt{in}\ e_2$ and $\texttt{let}\ \langle x, y\rangle = e_1\ \texttt{in}\ e_2$ are used to eliminate unit ($\mathbf{1}$) and tensor products ($\otimes$) respectively. As usual, a linear function $\tau_1 \multimap \tau_2$ is eliminated via application. The "of course" type $!\tau$ can be used to relax the linear restriction. A value of type $!\tau$ may be explicitly duplicated ($\texttt{dup}\,e$) or dropped ($\texttt{drop}\,e$). To put it another way, *weakening* and *contraction* of unrestricted $!\tau$ values is explicit, rather than implicit.

As mentioned earlier, we break a mutable object into two components: pointers ($\textsf{Ptr}\,\eta$) to the object's location and a capability ($\textsf{Cap}\,\eta\,\tau$) for accessing the contents of the location. The link between these two components is the location's name: either a location constant ℓ or a location variable ρ. Location constants (e.g., physical memory addresses) are used internally by our operational semantics, but are not allowed in source programs. Instead, source programs manipulate location variables, which abstract over location constants. We use the meta-variable η to range over both location constants and location variables. Note that location variables ρ may be bound in types and expressions and alpha-convert, while location constants ℓ do not.

As noted above, we wish to allow the pointer to a location to be freely duplicated and discarded, but we must treat the capability as a linear value. This will be consistent with our semantic interpretation of types, which will establish that $!(\textsf{Ptr}\,\eta)$ is inhabited, while $!(\textsf{Cap}\,\eta\,\tau)$ is uninhabited.

Abstraction over locations within types are given by the universal $\forall\rho.\tau$ and existential $\exists\rho.\tau$ types. Values of universal type must be instantiated and values of existential type must be opened.

Expressions and Operational Semantics. Figure 1 gives the small-step operational semantics for core $\mathbf{L}^3$ as a relation between configurations of the form (σ, e), eliding some of the more obvious transitions. In the configuration, σ is a global store that maps locations to closed values; note that a closed value has no free variables or location variables, but may have arbitrary location constants—even locations not in the domain of σ. The notation $\sigma_1 \uplus \sigma_2$ denotes the disjoint union of the stores σ_1 and σ_2; the operation is undefined when the domains of

σ_1 and σ_2 are not disjoint. We use evaluation contexts E (not shown) to lift the primitive rewriting rules to a left-to-right, inner-most to outer-most, call-by-value interpretation of the language.

Our calculus adopts many familiar terms from the linear lambda calculus. We already explained the introduction and elimination forms for unit, tensor products, and functions; their semantics is straightforward.

There are expression forms for both the pointer to a location ($\mathtt{ptr}\,\ell$) and the capability for a location ($\mathtt{cap}\,\ell$). However, neither expression form is available in source programs.

The expressions $\mathtt{new}\,e$ and $\mathtt{free}\,e$ perform the complementary actions of allocating and deallocating mutable references in the global store. $\mathtt{new}\,e$ evaluates e to a value, allocates a fresh (unallocated) location ℓ storing the value, and returns the pair $\langle \mathtt{cap}\,\ell, !(\mathtt{ptr}\,\ell)\rangle$ in an existential package that hides the particular location ℓ. The static semantics will ensure that the type of $\mathtt{cap}\,\ell$ "knows" the type of the value stored at ℓ. $\mathtt{free}\,e$ performs the reverse. It evaluates e to the pair $\langle \mathtt{cap}\,\ell, !(\mathtt{ptr}\,\ell)\rangle$, deallocates the location ℓ, and returns the value previously stored at ℓ. We remark that deallocation can result in dangling pointers to a location, but that since the (unique) capability for that location is destroyed, those pointers can never be dereferenced.

The expression $\mathtt{swap} e_1 e_2$ combines the operations of dereferencing and updating a mutable reference. Using swap instead of dereference and update ensures that resources are not duplicated [13]. Thus, swap is the appropriate primitive to ensure the linearity of resources. The first expression evaluates to a pointer $\mathtt{ptr}\,\ell$ and the second to a pair $\langle \mathtt{cap}\,\ell, v_2\rangle$. The operation then swaps v_2 for v_1 where v_1 is the value stored at ℓ, and returns $\langle \mathtt{cap}\,\ell, v_1\rangle$. Again, the static semantics will ensure that the type of the input $\mathtt{cap}\,\ell$ "knows" the type of v_1 and the type of the output $\mathtt{cap}\,\ell$ "knows" the type of v_2.

It is easily seen that the $\mathtt{cap}\,\ell$ terms have no operational significance; they could be erased without affecting our ability to evaluate the program.

Finally, there are introduction and elimination forms for universal and existential location quantification. The expression $\Lambda\rho.\,e$ provides universal abstraction over a location and is eliminated with an explicit application of the form $e\,[\eta]$. The expression form $\ulcorner\eta, e\urcorner$ (read "pack η in e") has the type $\exists\rho.\tau$ when e has the type τ with η substituted for ρ. The package can be opened with the expression form $\mathtt{let}\ \ulcorner\rho, x\urcorner = e_1\ \mathtt{in}\ e_2$.

2.2 Static Semantics

The type system for $\mathbf{L}^3$ must ensure that critical resources, such as capabilities, are not duplicated or dropped. Our type system is based on the linear lambda calculus and is thus relatively simple.

$\mathbf{L}^3$ typing judgments have the form $\Delta; \Gamma \vdash e : \tau$ where the contexts Δ and Γ are defined as follows:

$$\textit{Location Contexts}\ \Delta ::= \bullet \mid \Delta, \rho \qquad \textit{Value Contexts}\ \Gamma ::= \bullet \mid \Gamma, x{:}\tau$$

Thus, Δ is used to track the set of location variables in scope, whereas Γ, as usual, is used to track the set of variables (and their types) in scope. We consider

$\boxed{\Delta; \Gamma \vdash e : \tau}$

$$(\mathsf{Bang})\ \frac{\Delta; \Gamma \vdash v : \tau \qquad |\Gamma| = \bullet}{\Delta; \Gamma \vdash !v : !\tau}$$

$$(\mathsf{Let\text{-}Bang})\ \frac{\Delta; \Gamma_1 \vdash e_1 : !\tau_1 \qquad \Delta; \Gamma_2, x{:}\tau_1 \vdash e_2 : \tau_2}{\Delta; \Gamma_1 \boxplus \Gamma_2 \vdash \mathtt{let}\ !x = e_1\ \mathtt{in}\ e_2 : \tau_2}$$

$$(\mathsf{Dup})\ \frac{\Delta; \Gamma \vdash e : !\tau}{\Delta; \Gamma \vdash \mathtt{dup}\, e : !\tau \otimes !\tau} \qquad (\mathsf{Drop})\ \frac{\Delta; \Gamma \vdash e : !\tau}{\Delta; \Gamma \vdash \mathtt{drop}\, e : \mathbf{1}}$$

$$(\mathsf{New})\ \frac{\Delta; \Gamma \vdash e : \tau}{\Delta; \Gamma \vdash \mathtt{new}\, e : \exists\rho.(\mathsf{Cap}\ \rho\ \tau \otimes !(\mathsf{Ptr}\ \rho))}$$

$$(\mathsf{Free})\ \frac{\Delta; \Gamma \vdash e : \exists\rho.(\mathsf{Cap}\ \rho\ \tau \otimes !(\mathsf{Ptr}\ \rho))}{\Delta; \Gamma \vdash \mathtt{free}\, e : \exists\rho.\tau}$$

$$(\mathsf{Swap})\ \frac{\Delta; \Gamma_1 \vdash e_1 : \mathsf{Ptr}\ \rho \qquad \Delta; \Gamma_2 \vdash e_2 : \mathsf{Cap}\ \rho\ \tau_1 \otimes \tau_2}{\Delta; \Gamma_1 \boxplus \Gamma_2 \vdash \mathtt{swap}\ e_1\ e_2 : \mathsf{Cap}\ \rho\ \tau_2 \otimes \tau_1}$$

$$\begin{array}{lll} \bullet \boxplus \bullet & = \bullet & \\ (\Gamma_1, x{:}\tau) \boxplus \Gamma_2 & = (\Gamma_1 \boxplus \Gamma_2), x{:}\tau & (x \notin dom(\Gamma_2)) \\ \Gamma_1 \boxplus (\Gamma_2, x{:}\tau) & = (\Gamma_1 \boxplus \Gamma_2), x{:}\tau & (x \notin dom(\Gamma_1)) \end{array} \qquad \begin{array}{lll} |\bullet| & = \bullet & \\ |\Gamma, x{:}!\tau| & = |\Gamma| & \\ |\Gamma, x{:}\tau| & = |\Gamma|, x{:}\tau & (\tau \neq !\tau') \end{array}$$

Fig. 2. Core $\mathbf{L}^3$– Selected Static Semantics

contexts to be ordered lists of assumptions. There may be at most one occurrence of a location variable ρ in Δ and, similarly, at most one occurrence of a variable x in Γ.

As is usual in a linear setting, our type system relies upon an operator $\Gamma_1 \boxplus \Gamma_2 = \Gamma$ that splits the assumptions in Γ between the contexts Γ_1 and Γ_2. Splitting the context is necessary to ensure that a given resource is used by at most one sub-expression. Note that $\boxplus$ splits all assumptions, even those of !-type. However, recall that contraction and weakening is supported for !-types through explicit operations.

Figure 2 presents the typing rules for $\mathbf{L}^3$, eliding the normal rules for a linear lambda calculus. The (Bang) rule uses an auxiliary function $|\cdot|$ on contexts to extract the linear components. The rule requires that $|\Gamma|$ is empty. This ensures that the value v can be freely duplicated and discarded, without implicitly duplicating or discarding linear assumptions.

Note that there are no rules for $\mathtt{ptr}\ \ell$ or $\mathtt{cap}\ \ell$, as these expression forms are not present in the surface language. Likewise, all of the rules are given in terms of location variables ρ and not in terms of location constants ℓ. Instead, the (New), (Free), and (Swap) rules act as introduction and elimination rules for $\mathsf{Ptr}\ \rho$ and $\mathsf{Cap}\ \rho\ \tau$ types. Both (New) and (Free) operate on existentially

$$
\begin{aligned}
\mathcal{V}[\![\mathbf{1}]\!] &= \{(\{\}, \langle\rangle)\} \\
\mathcal{V}[\![\tau_1 \otimes \tau_2]\!] &= \{(\sigma_1 \uplus \sigma_2, \langle v_1, v_2\rangle) \mid (\sigma_1, v_1) \in \mathcal{V}[\![\tau_1]\!] \wedge (\sigma_2, v_2) \in \mathcal{V}[\![\tau_2]\!]\} \\
\mathcal{V}[\![\tau_1 \multimap \tau_2]\!] &= \{(\sigma_2, \lambda x.\, e) \mid \forall \sigma_1, v_1.\ (\sigma_1, v_1) \in \mathcal{V}[\![\tau_1]\!] \wedge \sigma_1 \uplus \sigma_2 \text{ defined} \Rightarrow \\
&\qquad (\sigma_1 \uplus \sigma_2, e[v_1/x]) \in \mathcal{C}[\![\tau_2]\!]\} \\
\mathcal{V}[\![!\tau]\!] &= \{(\{\}, !v) \mid (\{\}, v) \in \mathcal{V}[\![\tau]\!]\} \\
\mathcal{V}[\![\mathsf{Ptr}\,\ell]\!] &= \{(\{\}, \mathtt{ptr}\,\ell)\} \\
\mathcal{V}[\![\mathsf{Cap}\,\ell\,\tau]\!] &= \{(\sigma \uplus \{\ell \mapsto v\}, \mathsf{cap}\,\ell) \mid (\sigma, v) \in \mathcal{V}[\![\tau]\!]\} \\
\mathcal{V}[\![\forall \rho.\tau]\!] &= \{(\sigma, \Lambda\rho.\, e) \mid \forall \ell.\ (\sigma, e[\ell/\rho]) \in \mathcal{C}[\![\tau[\ell/\rho]]\!]\} \\
\mathcal{V}[\![\exists \rho.\tau]\!] &= \{(\sigma, \ulcorner \ell, v \urcorner) \mid (\sigma, v) \in \mathcal{V}[\![\tau[\ell/\rho]]\!]\}
\end{aligned}
$$

$$
\begin{aligned}
\mathcal{C}[\![\tau]\!] = \{(\sigma_s, e_s) \mid \forall \sigma_r.\ \sigma_s \uplus \sigma_r \text{ defined} \Rightarrow \\
\exists n, \sigma_f, v_f.\ (\sigma_s \uplus \sigma_r, e_s) \longmapsto^n (\sigma_f \uplus \sigma_r, v_f) \wedge (\sigma_f, v_f) \in \mathcal{V}[\![\tau]\!]\}
\end{aligned}
$$

$$
\begin{aligned}
\mathcal{S}[\![\bullet]\!]\delta &= \{(\{\}, \emptyset)\} \\
\mathcal{S}[\![\Gamma, x{:}\tau]\!]\delta &= \{(\sigma \uplus \sigma_x, \gamma[x \mapsto v_x]) \mid (\sigma, \gamma) \in \mathcal{S}[\![\Gamma]\!]\delta \wedge (\sigma_x, v_x) \in \mathcal{V}[\![\delta(\tau)]\!]\}
\end{aligned}
$$

$$
[\![\Delta; \Gamma \vdash e : \tau]\!] = \forall \delta, \sigma, \gamma.\ dom(\delta) = dom(\Delta) \wedge (\sigma, \gamma) \in \mathcal{S}[\![\Gamma]\!]\delta \Rightarrow (\sigma, \gamma(\delta(e))) \in \mathcal{C}[\![\delta(\tau)]\!]
$$

Fig. 3. Core **L**^{3}– Semantic Interpretations

quantified capability/pointer pairs, which hides the location constant present in the operational semantics. Note that (Swap) maintains the linear invariant on capabilities by consuming a value of type $\mathsf{Cap}\,\rho\,\tau_1$ and producing a value of type $\mathsf{Cap}\,\rho\,\tau_2$.

2.3 Examples and Discussion

This core language is expressive enough to approximate the examples given in Section 1. A linear reference can be viewed as a value of type

$$\mathsf{LRef}\ \tau \equiv \exists \rho.(\mathsf{Cap}\ \rho\ \tau \otimes !\mathsf{Ptr}\ \rho),$$

and we can lift the primitive swap to update a reference with

```
lrswap ≡ λr:LRef τ. λx:τ'.
          let ⌜ρ, cp⌝ = r in                 # cp:Cap ρ τ ⊗ !Ptr ρ
          let ⟨c0, p0⟩ = cp in               # c0:Cap ρ τ, p0:!Ptr ρ
          let ⟨p1, p2⟩ = dup p0 in           # p1:!Ptr ρ, p2:!Ptr ρ
          let !p2' = p2 in                   # p2':Ptr ρ
          let ⟨c1, y⟩ = swap p2' ⟨c0, x⟩ in  # c1:Cap ρ τ', y:τ
          ⟨⌜ρ, ⟨c1, p1⟩⌝, y⟩
```

However, by keeping $\mathsf{Cap}\rho\tau$ and $!\mathsf{Ptr}\rho$ packaged together, we lose any benefits of making $\mathsf{Ptr}\rho$ unrestricted. See the technical report [8] for an extended example, demonstrating the power of treating capabilities and pointers separately.

2.4 Semantic Interpretations

In this section, we give semantic interpretations to types and prove that the typing rules of Section 2.2 are sound with respect to these interpretations. We have also sketched a conventional syntactic proof of soundness, but found a semantic interpretation more satisfying for a few reasons. First, while shared $\mathtt{ptr}\ell$ values can be used to create cyclic pointer graphs, the linearity of $\mathtt{cap}\,\ell$ values prevents the construction of recursive functions through the standard "back-patching" technique. (The extension in Section 3 will relax this restriction, giving rise to a more powerful language.) Hence, our core language has the property that every well-typed term terminates, just as in the linear lambda calculus without references [14]. Our semantic proof captures this property in the definition of the types, whereas a syntactic approach is too weak to show that this property holds. Second, the semantic approach avoids the need to define typing rules for various intermediate structures including stores. Rather, stores consistent with a particular type will be incorporated into the semantic interpretation of the type. Finally, the semantic interpretation will allow us some extra flexibility when we consider extensions to the language in the next section.

Figure 3 gives our semantic interpretations of types as values ($\mathcal{V}[\![\tau]\!]$), types as computations ($\mathcal{C}[\![\tau]\!]$), contexts as substitutions ($\mathcal{S}[\![\Gamma]\!]$), and finally a semantic interpretation of typing judgments. We remark that these definitions are well-founded since the interpretation of a type is defined in terms of the interpretations of strictly smaller types.

For any closed type τ, we choose its semantic value interpretation $\mathcal{V}[\![\tau]\!]$ to be a set (i.e., unary logical relation) of tuples of the form (σ, v), where v is a closed value and σ a store. We can think of σ as the "exclusive store" of the value, corresponding to the portion of the store over which the value has exclusive rights. This exclusivity is conveyed by the linear $\mathsf{Cap}\ell\tau$ type, whose interpretation demands that σ includes ℓ and maps it to a value of the appropriate type. This corresponds to the primitive "points-to" relation in BI.

The definition of $\mathcal{C}[\![\tau]\!]$ combines both termination and type preservation. A starting store and expression (σ_s, e_s) is a member of $\mathcal{C}[\![\tau]\!]$ if for every disjoint (rest of the) store σ_r, a finite number of reductions leads to a final store and value (σ_f, v_f) that is a member of $\mathcal{V}[\![\tau]\!]$ and leaves σ_r unmodified. Notice that the computation interpretation corresponds to the frame axiom of BI, whereas the interpretation of linear implication is, as expected, in correspondence with BI's magic wand.

The semantic interpretation of a typing judgment $[\![\Delta; \Gamma \vdash e : \tau]\!]$ is a logical formula asserting that for all substitutions δ and γ and all stores σ compatible with Δ and Γ, $(\sigma, \gamma(\delta(e)))$ is a member of the interpretation of $\delta(\tau)$ as a computation.

Theorem 1 (Core $\mathbf{L}^3$ Soundness). *If* $\Delta; \Gamma \vdash e : \tau$, *then* $[\![\Delta; \Gamma \vdash e : \tau]\!]$.

As an immediate corollary, for any well-typed closed expression e of type τ, we know that evaluating $(\{\}, e)$ terminates with a configuration (σ, v) in the value interpretation of τ. Another interesting corollary is that if we run any closed, well-typed term of base type (e.g., $\mathbf{1}$), then the resulting store will be empty. Thus, the expression will be forced to free any locations that it creates before terminating.

3 Extended L^3

Thus far, our language only supports linear capabilities. While this gives us the ability to do strong updates, and the separation of pointers and capabilities allows us to build interesting store graphs, we still cannot simulate ML-style references, which are completely unrestricted. Such references are strictly more powerful than the linear references considered in the previous sections. Although an ML-style reference requires the cell to hold values of exactly one type, this is sufficient for building recursive computations. For example, we can write a divergent expression as follows:

```
1.  let val r = ref (fn () => ())
2.      val g = fn () => (!r) ()
3.  in  r := g;
4.      g ()
5.  end
```

The unrestricted nature of ML-style references is crucial in this example: the reference `r` (holding a function of type `unit -> unit`), is used both in `g`'s closure (line 2) and in the assignment at line 3.

In this section, we consider some minimal extensions needed for unrestricted references. At the same time, we are interested in modeling more recent languages, such as CQUAL, that support regaining (if only temporarily) a unique capability on an unrestricted reference so as to support strong updates.

One approach to modeling ML-style references is to add a new kind of unrestricted capability, with its own version of `swap`. To ensure soundness, the new swap would require that the value being swapped in to the location have the same type as the value currently in the location. This would ensure that the other capabilities for the location remained consistent with the current world. That is, unrestricted capabilities must have types that are *frozen* throughout their lifetime. An unrestricted, frozen capability could be created from a normal, linear capability. However, there could be no support for destroying a frozen location since this would invalidate the other capabilities for that location.

These additions to the language would be relatively straightforward, but we are also interested in supporting strong updates for unrestricted references. The extensions described below are inspired by CQUAL's `restrict` operator in that they allow an unrestricted, frozen capability to be temporarily "thawed" to a linear capability. This allows us to perform strong updates on the location.

In fact, these extensions obviate the need for a new `swap` on frozen capabilities – only thawed (linear) capabilities permit a swap, regardless of whether the content's type changes. Hence, the process of thawing a location demands exclusive access and the programmer must present evidence that no other frozen capability for the same location is currently thawed. In our extended language, this evidence is a value representing a proof that no other thawed location aliases the location on which we would like to do strong updates. There are many possible ways to prove such a fact, based on types or regions or some other partitioning of objects. Here, we do not commit to a particular logic so that the framework

$$\textit{Frozen Stores } \phi ::= \{\ell_1 \mapsto v_1, \ldots, \ell_n \mapsto v_n\}$$

$$(\mathsf{freeze})\ (\phi, \sigma \uplus \{\ell \mapsto !v\}, \mathtt{freeze}\langle \mathtt{cap}\ell, \mathtt{thwd}L\rangle v') \longmapsto (\phi \uplus \{\ell \mapsto !v\}, \sigma, \langle !(\mathtt{frzn}\ell), \mathtt{thwd}L\rangle)$$

$$(\mathsf{thaw})\ (\phi \uplus \{\ell \mapsto !v\}, \sigma, \mathtt{thaw}\ \langle !(\mathtt{frzn}\ \ell), \mathtt{thwd}\ L\rangle\ v') \longmapsto (\phi, \sigma \uplus \{\ell \mapsto !v\}, \langle \mathtt{cap}\ \ell, \mathtt{thwd}\ (L \uplus \{\ell\})\rangle)$$

$$(\mathsf{refreeze})\ (\phi, \sigma \uplus \{\ell \mapsto !v\}, \mathtt{refreeze}\ \langle \mathtt{cap}\ \ell, \mathtt{thwd}\ (L \uplus \{\ell\})\rangle) \longmapsto (\phi \uplus \{\ell \mapsto !v\}, \sigma, \langle !(\mathtt{frzn}\ \ell), \mathtt{thwd}\ L\rangle)$$

Fig. 4. Extended $\mathbf{L}^3$– Additional Operational Semantics

can be used in various settings. Rather, we use our semantic interpretation of types to specify a general condition so that admissible rules can be added to the type system without re-proving soundness.

A thawed location can also be "re-frozen" in our extended language. This is meant to re-enable access to the location along a different frozen capability. Note that it would be unsound to freeze a thawed location at a type other than the original frozen type, because other frozen capabilities expect the location to hold a value of the original type. Therefore, we provide a separate operation that requires the original type to be re-established when we re-freeze. Together, thawing and re-freezing a location correspond to the lexically-scoped `restrict` of CQUAL. However, we are not limited to the last-in-first-out thawing and re-freezing imposed by a lexically-scoped discipline, and, indeed, there is no real requirement that a thawed location ever be re-frozen.

Finally, because frozen capabilities are unrestricted, we will require a frozen location to hold a value of !-type. This prevents a program from discarding a linear value by placing the (one and only) reference to the value in a frozen location and then discarding all capabilities to access the location.

3.1 Changes to Support the Extensions

The syntactic changes to support the extensions described above are as follows:

$$L \in \mathcal{P}(\textit{LocConsts}) \qquad \textit{Thawed Contexts } \theta ::= \bullet \mid \theta, \eta{:}\tau$$
$$\textit{Types } \tau ::= \ldots \mid \mathsf{Frzn}\ \eta\ \tau \mid \mathsf{Thwd}\ \theta \mid \mathsf{Notin}\ \eta\ \theta$$
$$\textit{Exprs } e ::= \ldots \mid \mathtt{freeze}\ e_1\ e_2 \mid \mathtt{thaw}\ e_1\ e_2 \mid \mathtt{refreeze}\ e \mid \mathtt{frzn}\ \ell \mid \mathtt{thwd}\ L$$
$$\textit{Values } v ::= \ldots \mid \mathtt{frzn}\ \ell \mid \mathtt{thwd}\ L$$

The extended language is evaluated in the presence of a *frozen store* ϕ, which contains type-invariant mutable references, and the *linear store* σ. Figure 4 gives the small-step operational semantics for extended $\mathbf{L}^3$ as a relation between configurations of the form (ϕ, σ, e), where the two stores are necessarily disjoint. All of the operational semantics rules of core $\mathbf{L}^3$ carry over to the extended language by passing ϕ along unmodified. (However, note that (new) must choose a fresh location not in the domain of either ϕ or σ.) The static semantics for the extended language consist of all the rules for the core language and the rules given in Figure 5.

$\boxed{\Delta; \Gamma \vdash e : \tau}$

$$(\mathsf{Freeze})\ \frac{\Delta; \Gamma_1 \vdash e_1 : \mathsf{Cap}\ \rho\ !\tau \otimes \mathsf{Thwd}\ \theta \qquad \Delta; \Gamma_2 \vdash e_2 : \mathsf{Notin}\ \rho\ \theta}{\Delta; \Gamma_1 \boxplus \Gamma_2 \vdash \mathtt{freeze}\ e_1\ e_2 : !(\mathsf{Frzn}\ \rho\ !\tau) \otimes \mathsf{Thwd}\ \theta}$$

$$(\mathsf{Thaw})\ \frac{\Delta; \Gamma_1 \vdash e_1 : !(\mathsf{Frzn}\ \rho\ !\tau) \otimes \mathsf{Thwd}\ \theta \qquad \Delta; \Gamma_2 \vdash e_2 : \mathsf{Notin}\ \rho\ \theta}{\Delta; \Gamma_1 \boxplus \Gamma_2 \vdash \mathtt{thaw}\ e_1\ e_2 : \mathsf{Cap}\ \rho\ !\tau \otimes \mathsf{Thwd}\ (\theta, \rho{:}!\tau)}$$

$$(\mathsf{Refreeze})\ \frac{\Delta; \Gamma \vdash e : \mathsf{Cap}\ \rho\ !\tau \otimes \mathsf{Thwd}\ (\theta, \rho{:}!\tau)}{\Delta; \Gamma \vdash \mathtt{refreeze}\ e : !(\mathsf{Frzn}\ \rho\ !\tau) \otimes \mathsf{Thwd}\ \theta}$$

Fig. 5. Extended **L**^{3}– Additional Static Semantics

The type $\mathsf{Frzn}\,\eta\,\tau$ is the type of a frozen capability for location η which in turn holds a value of type τ. The (internal) term $\mathtt{frzn}\,\ell$ represents such a capability. We allow frozen capabilities to occur under the !-constructor, and thus they can be both duplicated and forgotten.

The type $\mathsf{Notin}\,\eta\,\theta$ represents a proof that the location η is not in the thawed context θ. As presented, our language has no terms of this type. Rather, our intention is that the type should only be inhabited by some value when indeed, the given location is not in the locations given by θ. For instance, in the next section, we will make use of a constant $\mathtt{void}_\eta$, which we could add to the language as a proof of the trivial fact that for all locations η, $\mathsf{Notin}\ \eta\ \bullet$.

A value of type $\mathsf{Thwd}\,\theta$ is called a *thaw token* and is used to record the current set of frozen locations that have been thawed, as well as their original types. The term $\mathtt{thwd}\,L$ is used to represent a thaw token. In a given program, there will be at most one thaw token value that must be effectively threaded through the execution. Thus, $\mathsf{Thwd}\ \theta$ values must be treated linearly. An initial thaw token of type $\mathsf{Thwd}\ \bullet$ is made available at the start of a program's execution.

The `thaw` operation takes as its first argument a pair of a frozen capability for a location ($!\mathsf{Frzn}\,\eta\,\tau$) and the current thaw token ($\mathsf{Thwd}\,\theta$). The second argument is a proof that the location has not already been thawed ($\mathsf{Notin}\eta\theta$). The operation returns a linear capability ($\mathsf{Cap}\,\eta\,\tau$) and a new thaw token of type $\mathsf{Thwd}\ (\theta, \eta{:}\tau)$. In thawing a location, the operational semantics transfers the location from the frozen store to the linear store. This is a technical device that keeps the current state of a location manifest in the semantics; a real implementation would maintain a single, global store with all locations.

The `refreeze` operation takes a linear capability of type $\mathsf{Cap}\,\eta\,\tau$ and a thaw token of type $\mathsf{Thwd}\ (\theta, \eta{:}\tau)$ and returns a frozen capability with type $!\mathsf{Frzn}\ \eta\ \tau$ and the updated thaw token of type $\mathsf{Thwd}\ \theta$. Note that to re-freeze, the type of the capability's contents must match the type associated with the location in the thaw token.

Finally, a frozen capability of type $!\mathsf{Frzn}\,\eta\,\tau$ is created with the `freeze` operation. The first argument to `freeze` is a pair of a linear capability for a location ($\mathsf{Cap}\ \eta\ \tau$) and the current thaw token ($\mathsf{Thwd}\ \theta$). The other argument is a value of type $\mathsf{Notin}\ \eta\ \theta$ ensuring that the location being frozen is not in the current thawed set; thawed locations must be re-frozen to match the type of any frozen aliases. Note that `freeze` returns the thaw token unchanged.

Both `freeze` and `refreeze` have the operational effect of moving a location from the linear store to the frozen store.

3.2 Examples and Discussion

The extended language is now expressive enough to encode the example given at the beginning of this section. An ML-style reference can be viewed as a value of type:

$$\mathsf{Ref}\ !\tau \equiv\ !\exists\rho.(!\mathsf{Frzn}\ \rho\ !\tau \otimes !\mathsf{Ptr}\ \rho).$$

Next, we need to give `read` and `write` operations on references. We consider a simple scenario in which a frozen capability is thawed exactly for the duration of a `read` or `write`; hence, we will assume that the thaw token has type $\mathsf{Thwd}\ \bullet$ at the start of the operation and we will return the thaw token with this type at the conclusion of the operation. Recall that we take $\mathtt{void}_\eta$ as a constant term of type $\mathsf{Notin}\ \eta\ \bullet$, which suffices given our assumed type of the thaw token.

$$\begin{array}{rl}
\mathtt{read} \equiv & \lambda \mathtt{r}^!{:}\mathsf{Ref}\ !\tau.\ \lambda \mathtt{t}^0{:}\mathsf{Thwd}\ \bullet\ . \\
& \mathtt{let}\ \ulcorner\rho, \langle \mathtt{f}_a^!, \mathtt{l}^! \rangle\urcorner = \mathtt{r}\ \mathtt{in} \\
& \mathtt{let}\ \langle \mathtt{c}^1, \mathtt{t}^1 \rangle = \mathtt{thaw}\ \langle \mathtt{f}_a, \mathtt{t}^0 \rangle\ \mathtt{void}_\rho\ \mathtt{in} \\
& \mathtt{let}\ \langle \mathtt{c}^2, \mathtt{x}^! \rangle = \mathtt{swap}\ \mathtt{l}\ \langle \mathtt{c}^1, \langle\rangle \rangle\ \mathtt{in} \\
& \mathtt{let}\ \langle \mathtt{c}^3, \langle\rangle \rangle = \mathtt{swap}\ \mathtt{l}\ \langle \mathtt{c}^2, \mathtt{x} \rangle\ \mathtt{in} \\
& \mathtt{let}\ \langle \mathtt{f}_b^!, \mathtt{t}^2 \rangle = \mathtt{refreeze}\ \langle \mathtt{c}^3, \mathtt{t}^1 \rangle\ \mathtt{in} \\
& \langle \mathtt{x}, \mathtt{t}^2 \rangle
\end{array}
\qquad
\begin{array}{rl}
\mathtt{write} \equiv & \lambda \mathtt{r}^!{:}\mathsf{Ref}\ !\tau.\ \lambda \mathtt{z}^!{:}!\tau.\ \lambda \mathtt{t}^0{:}\mathsf{Thwd}\ \bullet\ . \\
& \mathtt{let}\ \ulcorner\rho, \langle \mathtt{f}_a^!, \mathtt{l}^! \rangle\urcorner = \mathtt{r}\ \mathtt{in} \\
& \mathtt{let}\ \langle \mathtt{c}^1, \mathtt{t}^1 \rangle = \mathtt{thaw}\ \langle \mathtt{f}_a, \mathtt{t}^0 \rangle\ \mathtt{void}_\rho\ \mathtt{in} \\
& \mathtt{let}\ \langle \mathtt{c}^2, \mathtt{x}^! \rangle = \mathtt{swap}\ \mathtt{l}\ \langle \mathtt{c}^1, \mathtt{z} \rangle\ \mathtt{in} \\
& \mathtt{let}\ \langle \mathtt{f}_b^!, \mathtt{t}^2 \rangle = \mathtt{refreeze}\ \langle \mathtt{c}^2, \mathtt{t}^1 \rangle\ \mathtt{in} \\
& \mathtt{t}^2
\end{array}$$

It is easy to see how these operations can be combined to reconstruct the divergent computation presented at the beginning of this section by "back-patching" an unrestricted reference.

3.3 Semantic Interpretations

As the extended $\mathbf{L}^3$ is strictly more powerful that the core language given previously, the semantic interpretation given in Section 2.4 will not suffice as a model. We describe the essential intuitions underlying our semantic interpretation here; details are given in the technical report [8].

Our model for extended $\mathbf{L}^3$ is based on the indexed model of general references by Ahmed, Appel, and Virga [15] where the semantic interpretation of a (closed) type $\mathcal{V}[\![\tau]\!]$ is a set of triples of the form (k, Ψ, v). Here k is a natural number (called the *approximation index*), Ψ is a store typing that maps locations to (the interpretation of) their designated types, and v is a value. Intuitively, $(k, \Psi, v) \in \mathcal{V}[\![\tau]\!]$ says that in any computation running for no more than k steps, v cannot be distinguished from values of type τ. Furthermore, Ψ need only specify the types of locations to approximation $k-1$ — it suffices to know the type of each store location for $k-1$ steps to determine that v has type τ for k steps. This ensures that the model is well-founded.

For any closed type τ in extended $\mathbf{L}^3$, its semantic interpretation $\mathcal{V}[\![\tau]\!]$ is a set of tuples of the form $(k, \Psi, \zeta, \sigma, v)$. Here k is the approximation index; Ψ is a store typing that maps frozen locations (including locations that are currently thawed) to the semantic interpretations of their frozen types (to approximation $k-1$); v is a value. As for core $\mathbf{L}^3$, we consider σ to be the exclusive store of the value v. The lifted thaw set $\zeta \in \mathcal{P}(LocConsts)_\bot$ denotes either the set of currently thawed locations (if v has exclusive rights to the thaw token) or $\bot$ (if v has no such rights).

We define $\mathcal{V}[\![\mathsf{Thwd}\ \theta]\!]$ as the set of all tuples of the form $(k, \Psi, L, \{\}, \mathtt{thwd}\, L)$ such that the type of every currently thawed location ($\ell \in L$) in θ is consistent (to approximation k) with the type of the location in Ψ. This ensures that when we move a location from the linear store back to the frozen store, we end up with a frozen store where every location contains the type mandated by Ψ.

In order to track how far "out of synch" the frozen store ϕ is with respect to the frozen store typing Ψ, we define the relation $\phi :_k \Psi \setminus \zeta$. Informally, this says that the frozen store ϕ is well-typed with respect to the store typing Ψ modulo the current set of thawed locations ζ — that is, the contents of locations in the frozen store must have the types specified by Ψ, but the contents of thawed locations do not have to have the types mandated by Ψ.

As for core $\mathbf{L}^3$, we have established the following theorem which shows the soundness of the typing rules with respect to the model.

Theorem 2 (Extended $\mathbf{L}^3$ Soundness). *If* $\Delta; \Gamma \vdash e : \tau$, *then* $[\![\Delta; \Gamma \vdash e : \tau]\!]$.

4 Related Work

A number of researchers have noted that linearity and strong updates can be used to effectively manage memory (c.f. [13, 16, 17, 18]). Our work is complementary, in the sense that it provides a foundational standpoint for expressing such memory management in the presence of both linear and unrestricted data.

Our core $\mathbf{L}^3$ language is most directly influenced by Alias Types [6]. Relative to that work, the main contributions of our core language are (a) a simplification of the typing rules by treating capabilities as first-class linear objects, and (b) a model for the types that makes the connections with models for spatial logics clear. Of course, the extended version of $\mathbf{L}^3$ goes well beyond what Alias Types provided, with its support for thawing and re-freezing locations. As noted earlier, these primitives are inspired by the lexically-scoped `restrict` of CQUAL [5], though they are strictly more powerful.

The work of Boyland et al. [19] considers another application of capabilities as a means to regulate sharing of mutable state. In their untyped calculus, every pointer is annotated with a set of capabilities, which are checked at each read or write through the pointer. Asserting capabilities revokes them from aliasing pointers, which can stall the abstract machine by removing necessary rights for future pointer accesses. They leave as an open problem the specification of policies and type-systems to ensure that execution does not get stuck.

The Vault programming language [1] extended the ideas of the Capability Calculus [20] and Alias Types to enforce type-state protocols. As far as we are aware, there is no published type soundness proof of Vault's type system. Later work [2] added the `adoption` and `focus` constructs. The former takes linear references to an adoptee and an adopter, returning a non-linear reference to the adoptee, while the latter construct temporarily linear view of an adopted object, suitable for accessing linear components. We are confident that it will be possible to extend $\mathbf{L}^3$ to handle these features.

There has been a great deal of work on adapting some notion of linearity to real programming languages. Examples include ownership types [21], uniqueness types [12, 22, 23], confinement types [24, 25], and roles [26]. Each of these mechanisms is aimed at supporting local reasoning in the presence of aliasing and updates. Most of these approaches relax the strong requirements of linearity to make programming more convenient. We believe that $\mathbf{L}^3$ could provide a convenient foundation for modeling many of these features, because we have made the distinction between a reference and a capability to use the reference.

A more distantly related body of work is the typing of process calculi [27, 28]. Here, a kind of strong update is allowed in the type of channels, where a single communication port can be used for sending values of different types. While a connection with linearity has been established [29], the intuition seems to be more closely related to type-states than to strong updates. A potentially fruitful direction for future work would be to investigate both the application of process types to this work and to extend this work to apply in a concurrent setting.

5 Future Work

A key open issue is what logic to use for proving that it is safe to thaw a given location. For instance, one could imagine a logic that allows us to conclude two locations do not alias because their types are incompatible. In CQUAL, locations are placed in different conceptual regions, and the regions are used to abstract sets of thawed locations.

Another open issue is how to lift the ideas in $\mathbf{L}^3$ to a surface level language. Clearly, explicitly threading linear capabilities and a thaw token through a computation is too painful to contemplate. We are currently working on adapting ideas from indexed monads and type-and-effects systems to support implicit threading of these mechanisms.

References

1. DeLine, R., Fähndrich, M.: Enforcing high-level protocols in low-level software. In: PLDI. (2001)
2. Fähndrich, M., DeLine, R.: Adoption and focus: Practical linear types for imperative programming. In: PLDI. (2002)
3. Morrisett, G., Walker, D., Crary, K., Glew, N.: From System F to typed assembly language. TOPLAS **21** (1999) 528–569
4. Morrisett, G., Crary, K., Glew, N., Walker, D.: Stack-based typed assembly language. JFP **12** (2002) 43–88
5. Aiken, A., Foster, J.S., Kodumal, J., Terauchi, T.: Checking and inferring local non-aliasing. In: (PLDI). (2003)

6. Smith, F., Walker, D., Morrisett, G.: Alias types. In: (ESOP). (2000)
7. Ishtiaq, S., O'Hearn, P.: BI as an assertion language for mutable data structures. In: (POPL). (2001)
8. Ahmed, A., Fluet, M., Morrisett, G.: $\mathbf{L}^3$: A linear language with locations. Technical Report TR-24-04, Harvard University (2004)
9. Girard, J.Y.: Linear logic. Theoretical Computer Science **50** (1987) 1–102
10. Wadler, P.: Linear types can change the world! In: Programming Concepts and Methods. (1990)
11. O'Hearn, P.W., Reynolds, J.C.: From Algol to polymorphic linear lambda-calculus. Journal of the ACM **47** (2000) 167–223
12. Plasmeijer, R., van Eekelen, M. Keep it clean: a unique approach to functional programming. ACM SIGPLAN Notices **34** (1999) 23–31
13. Baker, H.: Lively linear LISP—look ma, no garbage. ACM SIGPLAN Notices **27** (1992) 89–98
14. Benton, P.N.: Strong normalisation for the linear term calculus. JFP **5** (1995) 65–80
15. Ahmed, A., Appel, A.W., Virga, R.: An indexed model of impredicative polymorphism and mutable references. Available at `http://www.cs.princeton.edu/~appel/papers/impred.pdf` (2003)
16. Hofmann, M.: A type system for bouned space and functional in-place update. In: (ESOP). (2000)
17. Cheney, J., Morrisett, G.: A linearly typed assembly language. Technical Report 2003-1900, Cornell University (2003)
18. Aspinall, D., Compagnoni, A.: Heap bounded assembly language. Journal of Automated Reasoning **31** (2003) 261–302
19. Boyland, J., Noble, J., Retert, W.: Capabilities for aliasing: A generalization of uniqueness and read-only. In: (ECOOP). (2001)
20. Walker, D., Crary, K., Morrisett, G.: Typed memory management in a calculus of capabilities. TOPLAS **24** (2000) 701–771
21. Boyapati, C., Sălcianu, A., Beebee, W., Rinard, M.: Ownership types for safe region-based memory management in real-time Java. In: (PLDI). (2003)
22. Clarke, D., Wrigstad, T.: External uniqueness is unique enough. In: (ECOOP). (2003)
23. Hicks, M., Morrisett, G., Grossman, D., Jim, T.: Experience with safe manual memory-management in Cyclone. In: (ISMM). (2004)
24. Grothoff, C., Palsberg, J., Vitek, J.: Encapsulating objects with confined types. In: (OOPSLA). (2001)
25. Vitek, J., Bokowski, B.: Confined types in Java. Software – Practice and Experience **31** (2001) 507–532
26. Kuncak, V., Lam, P., Rinard, M.: Role analysis. In: (POPL). (2002)
27. Igarashi, A., Kobayashi, N.: A generic type system for the Pi-calculus. In: (POPL). (2001)
28. Takeuchi, K., Honda, K., Kubo, M.: An interaction-based language and its typing system. In: Proc. Parallel Architectures and Languages Europe. (1994)
29. Kobayashi, N., Pierce, B.C., Turner, D.N.: Linearity and the Pi-Calculus. TOPLAS **21** (1999) 914–947

Binding Signatures for Generic Contexts*

John Power and Miki Tanaka**

School of Informatics, University of Edinburgh,
King's Buildings, Edinburgh EH9 3JZ, Scotland
Tel: +44 131 650 5159
ajp@inf.ed.ac.uk
miki.tanaka@ed.ac.uk

Abstract. Fiore, Plotkin and Turi provided a definition of binding signature and characterised the presheaf of terms generated from a binding signature by an initiality property. Tanaka did for linear binders what Fiore et al did for cartesian binders. They used presheaf categories to model variable binders for contexts, with leading examples given by the untyped ordinary and linear λ-calculi. Here, we give an axiomatic framework that includes their works on cartesian and linear binders, and moreover their assorted variants, notably including the combined cartesian and linear binders of the Logic of Bunched Implications. We provide a definition of binding signature in general, extending the previous ones and yielding a definition for the first time for the example of Bunched Implications, and we characterise the presheaf of terms generated from the binding signature. The characterisation requires a subtle analysis of a strength of a binding signature over a substitution monoidal structure on the presheaf category.

1 Introduction

There have been numerous recent attempts to provide category theoretic models of binders for cartesian contexts, as for instance in the λ-calculus [2, 3, 4]. The idea is to replace calculi such as the λ-calculus by syntax that is invariant under α-conversion and is supported by a body of category theory. Conceptually, the easiest and most direct approach was that of Fiore, Plotkin and Turi. Their work was modified by Tanaka to model binders for linear contexts as for instance in the linear λ-calculus [15]. Before one can model binders, one must first model substitution, as the concept of binding is derived from that of substitution. So, in the light of Fiore et al and Tanaka's work, Power adumbrated an axiomatic account of substitution to include cartesian, linear, and mixed contexts, as appear

* This work has been done with the support of EPSRC grants GR/N64571/01 and GR/586372/01, A Theory of Effects for Programming Languages.
** Currently at National Institute of Information and Communications Technology, 4-2-1 Nukui-Kitamachi, Koganei, Tokyo 184-8795, Japan. Tel:+81 42 327 5782, miki.tanaka@nict.go.jp

P. Urzyczyn (Ed.): TLCA 2005, LNCS 3461, pp. 308–323, 2005.

for instance in the Logic of Bunched Implications [14]; and Power and Tanaka together resolved the relevant details [11, 13, 16]. With an axiomatic account of substitution in hand, one seeks an axiomatic account of binders, and that is the purpose of this paper, developing and correcting the ideas outlined in [11].

In the light of the axiomatic account, Fiore et al's analysis of substitution may be seen as follows. Start with the trivial one object category 1 and freely add finite products. That yields the category Set_f^{op}, which they denoted by $\mathbb{F}^{op}$ and which modelled contexts for them: they only considered untyped binders, so they modelled a context by a natural number. They then considered the presheaf category $[\mathbb{F}, Set]$. For X in $[\mathbb{F}, Set]$, they regarded $X(n)$ as a set of terms, modulo α-conversion, containing at most n variables. They described a monoidal structure on $[\mathbb{F}, Set]$ to model substitution, with finite products extending from $\mathbb{F}^{op}$ to $[\mathbb{F}, Set]$ to model pairing. Tanaka's analysis was similar.

We axiomatised all this in [13], allowing us to include Fiore et al and Tanaka's work, as well as accounting for corresponding structure in studies such as that of the Logic of Bunched Implications [14]. Finite product structure corresponds to a pseudo-monad T_{fp} on Cat. The presheaf construction $[\mathcal{C}^{op}, Set]$ may be characterised as the free colimit completion of $\mathcal{C}$, and so, except for a size question, amounts to giving another pseudo-monad T_{coc} on Cat, a pseudo-monad for cocomplete categories. There is a canonical pseudo-distributive law of T_{fp} over T_{coc}, allowing one to compose, yielding a pseudo-monad structure on $T_{coc}T_{fp}$. One can then use results about the combination that hold for axiomatic reasons for any pseudo-monad S and T, and any pseudo-distributive law $ST \rightarrow TS$ of S over T. In particular, it follows that there is a canonical substitution monoidal structure on the presheaf category, as the latter is of the form $T1$ for the pseudo-monad on Cat determined by the composite $T_{coc}S$, and S-structure lifts to the presheaf category also for axiomatic reasons.

Having modelled substitution and pairing, Fiore et al moved onto binding signatures. In the absence of binders, a signature would consist of a set of operations O together with a function $ar : O \longrightarrow \mathbb{N}$ sending each operation to an arity. But if one does have binders, one needs more sophistication in the arities as one wants not only a natural number but an account of the number of variables to be bound. Ultimately, Fiore et al defined a binding signature to be a set O of operations together with a function $ar : O \longrightarrow \mathbb{N}^*$. Their leading example was the untyped λ-calculus

$$M ::= x \mid \lambda x.M \mid MM$$

which has two operators, one for lambda and one for application, with arities $\langle 1 \rangle$, and $\langle 0, 0 \rangle$ respectively: λ-abstraction has one argument and binds one variable, and application has two arguments and binds no variables.

Having defined the notion of binding signature, they defined the presheaf of terms generated by a binding signature: it forms a presheaf rather than a set as one must parametrise by the number of variables that are to be bound. They then characterised the presheaf of terms generated by a signature Σ as the initial Σ-monoid, where a Σ-monoid was defined to consist of a Σ-structure to model application of an element of Σ to a putative term, together with a monoid structure to model substitution, satisfying a natural and simple coherence condition. The central proposition they needed in order to make that characterisation provided a canonical strength for the endofunctor on $[\mathbb{F}, Set]$ generated by Σ, with respect to the substitution monoidal structure, over any pointed object

$$\Sigma X \bullet Y \longrightarrow \Sigma(X \bullet Y)$$

Tanaka's definition of signature was identical, and it was a more straightforward construction of the strength relative to pointed objects and hence a more clear proof of the corresponding characterisation of the presheaf of terms.

Here, we axiomatise that work. Our axiomatisation also provides an account of binders in the Logic of Bunched Implications, hence for its associated $\alpha\lambda$-calculus. The axiomatisation is necessarily subtle: for Fiore et al and Tanaka, the number of binders determines an arity, but that is not the case for the Logic of Bunched Implications, which has both a linear binder and a cartesian binder, and hence it is not the case in general. So one needs more subtle definitions of signature and arity in order to include such examples, and one correspondingly needs more care in providing the requisite strength and the characterisation of the presheaf of terms generated by a signature. That in turn requires a closer examination than previously needed of the substitution monoidal structure, which we give in Section 3. The central definition of the paper is that of a binding signature in Section 4, with the central examples arising from cartesian binders, linear binders, and the mixed binders of the Logic of Bunched Implications also in Section 4. The central proof is the construction of the strength with respect to the substitution monoidal structure in Section 5, and the central theorem is the characterisation of the presheaf of terms in Section 6. Section 2 is essential to make the paper comprehensible.

2 Pseudo-Distributive Laws for Context Manipulation

The notion of pseudo-monad on *Cat* is a variant of the notion of monad on *Cat*. For space reasons, we shall not define pseudo-monads, their 2-categories of pseudo-algebras, etcetera, here, beyond remarking that they are the definitive variant of the notions of monad, algebra, etcetera, that respect natural transformations and for which equalities in the various axioms are systematically replaced by coherent isomorphisms [13, 16].

Example 1. Let T_{fp} denote the pseudo-monad on *Cat* for small categories with finite products. The 2-category *Ps*-T_{fp}-*Alg* has objects given by small categories with finite products, maps given by functors that preserve finite products in the usual sense, i.e., up to coherent isomorphism, and 2-cells given by all natural transformations. So *Ps*-T_{fp}-*Alg* is the 2-category *FP*. The category $T_{fp}(X)$ is the free category with finite products on X. Taking $X = 1$, the category $T_{fp}(X)$ is given, up to equivalence, by Set_f^{op}, which is denoted as $\mathbb{F}^{op}$ by Fiore et al [2].

Example 2. Let T_{sm} denote the pseudo-monad on *Cat* for small symmetric monoidal categories. The 2-category $Ps\text{-}T_{sm}\text{-}Alg$ has objects given by small symmetric monoidal categories, maps given by strong symmetric monoidal functors, i.e., functors together with data and axioms to the effect that the symmetric monoidal structure is preserved up to coherent isomorphism, and 2-cells given by all symmetric monoidal natural transformations, i.e., those natural transformations that respect the symmetric monoidal structure. Therefore, $Ps\text{-}T_{sm}\text{-}Alg$ is the 2-category $SymMon_{str}$ and $T_{sm}(X)$ is the free symmetric monoidal category on X. Taking $X = 1$, it follows, up to equivalence, that $T_{sm}(X)$ is the category $\mathbb{P}^{op}$ of finite sets and permutations used by Tanaka [15].

Example 3. Combining the first two examples by taking the sum of pseudo-monads, we may consider the pseudo-monad T_{BI} on *Cat* for small symmetric monoidal categories with finite products. The 2-category $Ps\text{-}T_{BI}\text{-}Alg$ has objects given by small symmetric monoidal categories with finite products, maps given by strong symmetric monoidal functors that preserve finite products, and 2-cells given by all symmetric monoidal natural transformations. This structure is the free category on 1 independently generated by finite-product and symmetric monoidal structures used in the Logic of Bunched Implications [14]. The objects of $T_{BI}(X)$ where $X = 1$ are precisely the *bunches* of Bunched Implications.

Example 4. For size reasons, there is no interesting pseudo-monad on *Cat* for cocomplete categories: small cocomplete categories are necessarily preorders, and the free large cocomplete category on a small category does not lie in *Cat*. But there are well-studied techniques to deal with that concern [16], allowing us safely to ignore it here. Assuming we do that, there is a pseudo-monad T_{coc} for cocomplete categories. For any small category X, the category $T_{coc}(X)$ is given by the presheaf category $[X^{op}, Set]$. This construction is fundamental to all of Fiore et al, Tanaka, and Pym [2, 14, 15]. Its universal property was not considered by them, but, as we shall see in Section 3, it explains why the substitution monoidal structures are definitive.

Definition 1. Given a 2-category $\mathbb{C}$ and pseudo-monads $(S, \mu^S, \eta^S, \tau^S, \lambda^S, \rho^S)$ and $(T, \mu^T, \eta^T, \tau^T, \lambda^T, \rho^T)$ on $\mathbb{C}$, a *pseudo-distributive law* $(\delta, \overline{\mu}^S, \overline{\mu}^T, \overline{\eta}^S, \overline{\eta}^T)$ of S over T consists of

- a pseudo-natural transformation $\delta : ST \to TS$
- invertible modifications

$$\begin{array}{ccccc} S^2T & \xrightarrow{S\delta} & STS & \xrightarrow{\delta S} & TS^2 \\ {\scriptstyle \mu^S T}\downarrow & & \Downarrow \overline{\mu}^S & & \downarrow{\scriptstyle T\mu^S} \\ ST & & \xrightarrow[\delta]{} & & TS \end{array} \qquad \begin{array}{ccccc} ST^2 & \xrightarrow{\delta T} & STS & \xrightarrow{T\delta} & T^2S \\ {\scriptstyle S\mu^T}\downarrow & & \Downarrow \overline{\mu}^T & & \downarrow{\scriptstyle \mu^T S} \\ ST & & \xrightarrow[\delta]{} & & TS \end{array}$$

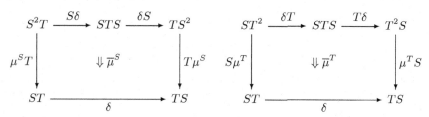

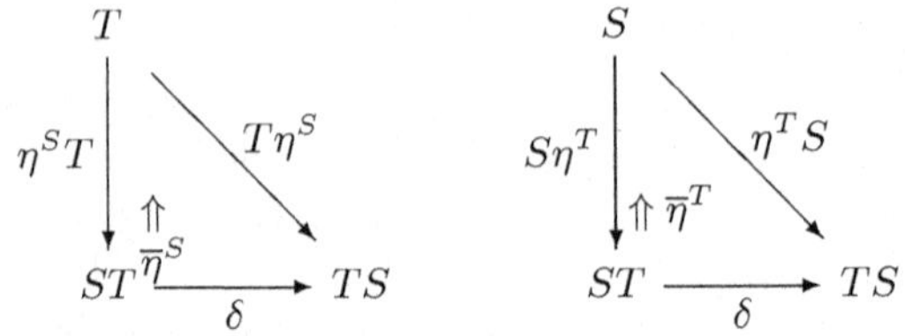

subject to ten coherence axioms [13, 16].

By a *lifting* of a pseudo-monad T to the 2-category *Ps-S-Alg* of pseudo-algebras for a pseudo-monad S, we mean a pseudo-monad $\widetilde{T}$ on the 2-category *Ps-S-Alg* such that $U_S\widetilde{T} = TU_S$, and similarly for the other data, where U_S is the forgetful 2-functor for the pseudo-monad S.

Theorem 1 ([13, 16]). *To give a pseudo-distributive law $\delta : ST \longrightarrow TS$ of pseudo-monads on Cat is equivalent to giving a lifting of the pseudo-monad T to a pseudo-monad $\widetilde{T}$ on Ps-S-Alg.*

Theorem 2 ([13, 16]). *Given a pseudo-distributive law $\delta : ST \longrightarrow TS$ of pseudo-monads on Cat*

- *the pseudo-functor TS acquires the structure for a pseudo-monad, with multiplication given by*

$$TSTS \xrightarrow{T\delta S} TTSS \xrightarrow{\mu^T\mu^S} TS$$

- *Ps-TS-Alg is canonically isomorphic to Ps-$\widetilde{T}$-Alg*
- *the object $TS1$ has both canonical pseudo-S-algebra and pseudo-T-algebra structures on it.*

Theorem 2 yields a selection of pseudo-monads by combining our first three examples with the fourth. The central result that makes all the examples work is as follows.

Proposition 1 ([13]). *The pseudo-monad for free cocompletions lifts from Cat to $SymMon_{str}$.*

Example 5. Applying Theorems 1 and 2 and Proposition 1 to T_{fp} and T_{coc}, one obtains the pseudo-monad $T_{coc}T_{fp}$ with $T_{coc}T_{fp}(1)$ being equivalent to $[\mathbb{F}, Set]$, which was Fiore et al's category for cartesian variable binding [2].

Example 6. Applying Theorems 1 and 2 and Proposition 1 to T_{sm} and T_{coc}, one obtains the pseudo-monad $T_{coc}T_{sm}$ with $T_{coc}T_{sm}(1)$ equivalent to $[\mathbb{P}, Set]$, which was Tanaka's category for linear variable binding.

Example 7. Applying Theorems 1 and 2 and Proposition 1 twice to T_{BI} and T_{coc} yields a composite pseudo-monad with $T_{coc}T_{BI}(1)$ given by the functor category $[(T_{BI}1)^{op}, Set]$. The combination of T_{BI} and T_{coc} is implicit in the Logic of Bunched Implications; presheaf categories such as $[(T_{BI}1)^{op}, Set]$ appear explicitly there [14].

3 Monoidal Structure for Substitution

In this section, given a pseudo-monad T on Cat, we describe a canonical monoidal structure $\bullet$ on the category $T1$, then give a general calculation of $\bullet$ when T is of the form $T_{coc}S$. When S is T_{fp}, that yields Fiore et al's substitution monoidal structure, and likewise for Tanaka when S is T_{sm}. The substitution monoidal structure on $T_{coc}T_{BI}(1)$ does not seem to appear explicitly in the literature on Bunched Implications but it is implicit there.

A *pseudo-strength* for a pseudo-monad $(T, \mu, \eta, \tau, \lambda, \rho)$ on a 2-category $\mathbb{C}$ consists of a pseudo-natural transformation with components

$$t_{X,Y} : TX \times Y \longrightarrow T(X \times Y)$$

and invertible modifications that correspond to the four axioms for an ordinary strength, subject to ten coherence axioms listed in [16]. Every pseudo-monad on Cat gives rise to a pseudo-strength, with $t_{X,Y}$ defined by Currying

$$Y \longrightarrow [X, X \times Y] \xrightarrow{T} [TX, T(X \times Y)]$$

The rest of the data for pseudo-naturality arises from pseudo-functoriality of T, as do two of the structural modifications. The other two structural modifications arise from the pseudo-naturality of μ and η.

Theorem 3 ([13, 16]). *Given a pseudo-monad T on Cat, the category $T1$ has a canonical monoidal structure with multiplication $\bullet$ defined by using the pseudo-strength induced by T as follows:*

$$\bullet : T1 \times T1 \xrightarrow{t_{1,T1}} T(1 \times T1) \xrightarrow{\cong} T^2 1 \xrightarrow{\mu_1} T1$$

and with unit given by

$$\eta_1 : 1 \longrightarrow T1$$

The associativity and unit isomorphisms are generated by those for the multiplication and unit of T together with those of the pseudo-strength. Moreover, the multiplication $\bullet : T1 \times T1 \to T1$ is a pseudo-map of T-algebras in its first variable, i.e., there is a coherent isomorphism

$$\begin{array}{ccccc}
T^2 1 \times T1 & \xrightarrow{t_{T1,T1}} & T(T1 \times T1) & \xrightarrow{T\bullet} & T^2 1 \\
\downarrow{\scriptstyle \mu \times id} & & \cong & & \downarrow{\scriptstyle \mu} \\
T1 \times T1 & & \xrightarrow[\bullet]{\hspace{6em}} & & T1
\end{array}$$

Example 8. Consider the pseudo-monad $T_{coc}T_{fp}$ on Cat. By Example 5, the category $T_{coc}T_{fp}(1)$ is equivalent to $[\mathbb{F}, Set]$. So, by Theorem 3, $[\mathbb{F}, Set]$ acquires a canonical monoidal structure. By the last line of the theorem, for every object Y of $[\mathbb{F}, Set]$, the functor $- \bullet Y : [\mathbb{F}, Set] \longrightarrow [\mathbb{F}, Set]$ is a pseudo-map of $T_{coc}T_{fp}$-algebras, and so preserves both colimits and finite products. Since every functor $X : F \longrightarrow Set$ is a colimit of representables, and every object of $\mathbb{F}^{op}$ is a finite product of copies of the generating object 1, which in turn is the unit of the tensor $\bullet$, it follows that we can calculate $X \bullet Y$ as a canonical coequaliser of the form

$$(X \bullet Y)m = (\coprod_{n \in N} Xn \times (Ym)^n)/\!\sim$$

where the equivalence relation $\sim$ is induced by arrows of $\mathbb{F}$ [2], yielding exactly Fiore et al's construction of a substitution monoidal structure.

Example 9. Consider the pseudo-monad $T_{coc}T_{sm}$ on Cat. By Example 6, the category $T_{coc}T_{sm}(1)$ is equivalent to $[\mathbb{P}, Set]$. Applying the same argument as in the previous example, we can calculate $X \bullet Y$ and check that it agrees with Tanaka's construction of a substitution monoidal structure, namely

$$(X \bullet Y)m = (\coprod_{n \in N} Xn \times (Y^{(n)})m)/\!\sim$$

where $Y^{(n)}$ denotes the n-fold tensor product in $[\mathbb{P}, Set]$ of Y, using the convolution symmetric monoidal product of $[\mathbb{P}, Set]$: that convolution symmetric monoidal product is exactly the lifting to $[\mathbb{P}, Set]$ of the canonical symmetric monoidal product of $\mathbb{P}^{op}$, which is, in turn, the free symmetric monoidal category on 1, i.e., $T_{sm}(1)$. The reason one still sees a product in this formula is because, conceptually, it plays the role of the Xn-fold sum of copies of $Y^{(n)}m$ here rather than that of a product. The equivalence relation $\sim$ is induced by permutations, similarly to the case of the previous example.

Generalising from these examples and using the final clause of Theorem 3, we can give an axiomatic formula for $X \bullet Y$ for objects X and Y of $T_{coc}S(1)$ for any pseudo-monad S and pseudo-distributive law of S over T_{coc}. An object of $S1$ is given by a sophisticated sort of word of copies of 1 as we shall explain. But $1 \bullet Y$ must always be isomorphic to Y. So the final clause of Theorem 3 tells us that, if we express X as a colimit of words of copies of 1, the object $X \bullet Y$ is given by replacing each copy of 1 in that colimit of words by an occurrence of Y. The details are as follows.

Given an arbitrary pseudo-monad S on Cat, let (A, a) be (part of) an arbitrary pseudo-S-algebra, and let α be an object of the category Sk for any small category k, in particular for any natural number. The idea is to use such an α to specify how each argument should be arranged when constructing an operation with k arguments. The object α induces a functor $\overline{\alpha}_A : A^k \to A$ from A^k to A as follows:

$$A^k \cong A^k \times 1 \xrightarrow{S \times \alpha} (SA)^{Sk} \times Sk \xrightarrow{ev_\alpha} SA \xrightarrow{a} A$$

This construction is a routine extension of the idea that every algebra for a (finitary) monad on Set supports a semantics for every operation of the Lawvere theory corresponding to the monad [10, 12]. It is exploited in the modelling of computational effects in [9].

The construction is pseudo-functorial, i.e., given a pseudo-map $(f, \bar{f})$ of algebras, the diagram

$$\begin{array}{ccc} A^k & \xrightarrow{f^k} & B^k \\ {\scriptstyle \overline{\alpha}_A}\downarrow & & \downarrow{\scriptstyle \overline{\alpha}_B} \\ A & \xrightarrow[f]{} & B \end{array}$$

commutes up to coherent isomorphism.

Applying Theorem 2 to the case of T being T_{coc}, and so $TS(1)$ being the category $[(S1)^{op}, Set]$, which we denote by $\widehat{S1}$ in the rest of the paper, we may conclude the following:

Proposition 2. *Given a pseudo-distributive law of S over T_{coc}, the category $\widehat{S1}$ has a canonical pseudo-S-algebra structure on it, and, for any α in Sk,*

$$\begin{array}{ccc} (S1)^k & \xrightarrow{\mathcal{Y}^k} & \widehat{S1}^k \\ {\scriptstyle \overline{\alpha}_{S1}}\downarrow & & \downarrow{\scriptstyle \overline{\alpha}_{\widehat{S1}}} \\ S1 & \xrightarrow[\mathcal{Y}]{} & \widehat{S1} \end{array}$$

commutes up to coherent isomorphism.

This proposition allows us to give the characterisation of $\bullet$ that we seek. The characterisation uses the concept of a *coend* [7], which is a kind of colimit, so can generally be expressed as a coequaliser of a coproduct. Fiore et al and Tanaka's descriptions of $X \bullet Y$ were exactly calculations of coends.

Theorem 4. *Given a pseudo-monad S on Cat and a pseudo-distributive law of S over T_{coc}, and given X, Y in $\widehat{S1}$, one can calculate the value of $X \bullet Y$ at an object c of $S1$ as*

$$(X \bullet Y)c = \int^{c' \in S1} Xc' \times (\overline{c'}_{\widehat{S1}}(Y))c \tag{1}$$

Proof. It follows from the Yoneda lemma (see for instance [6]) that X is the colimit of representables

$$X- = \int^{c' \in S1} Xc' \times (S1)(-, c') \tag{2}$$

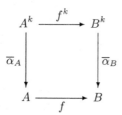

But $c' = \overline{c'}_{S1}(1)$, so by Proposition 2 we have

$$X- = \int^{c' \in S1} Xc' \times \overline{c'}_{\widehat{S1}}(S1)(-,1) \quad (3)$$

But $- \bullet Y$ is a map of pseudo-$T_{coc}S$-algebras, hence a map of pseudo-T_{coc}-algebras and a map of pseudo-S-algebras by Theorem 2. So $- \bullet Y$ respects both $\overline{-}$ and all colimits. Moreover, $(S1)(-,1)$, or equivalently $\mathcal{Y}(1)$, is the unit of $\bullet$, so $(S1)(-,1) \bullet Y$ is isomorphic to Y. So, replacing each occurrence of $(S1)(-,1)$ in Equation (3) by Y, we have the result.

Example 10. Applying Theorem 4 to $T_{coc}T_{BI}$, one obtains a formula for $X \bullet Y$ of the form

$$(X \bullet Y)b = \int^{b' \in T_{BI}1} Xb' \times (Y^{(b')})b$$

where $Y^{(b')}$ represents a b'-bunch of copies of the object Y of $[(T_{BI}1)^{op}, Set]$.

4 Binding Signatures

In this section, generalising the work of both Fiore et al and Tanaka, we give an axiomatic formulation of the notion of a binding signature. Fiore et al and Tanaka each defined a binding signature to consist of a set of operations O together with an arity function $a : O \to \mathbb{N}^*$. Supposing for simplicity they had just one operation with arity $(n_i)_{1 \leq i \leq k}$, the functor they would generate (in Fiore et al's setting) would send X to

$$(\partial^{n_1} X) \times \cdots \times (\partial^{n_k} X)$$

where ∂X was defined to be $X(1+-)$, giving a mathematical formulation of the idea of binding over one variable. Of course, $\partial^n X$, which was therefore $X(n+-)$, allowed the formulation of the idea of binding over n variables. But that is not subtle enough in more complex binding situations such as that of Bunched Implications, which has two sorts of binders: a linear binder and a non-linear binder. A finite sequence of natural numbers does not specify which sort of binder is to be used, and in what combination are the binders to be used. So, in order to capture examples in which one has more than one sort of binder, we need a more refined definition of binding signature to that used by Fiore et al and Tanaka.

Their definition of binding signature essentially contains two pieces of data: for each i, each n_i tells you how many times to apply $X(1+-)$, and k tells you how many such $X(n_i+-)$ need to be multiplied. Their use of k is fine as it tells us the number of arguments, but we need more specificity in regard to their n_i, as we need to allow a choice of which sort of binder is to be specified by each of the natural numbers. We also need to allow a choice in how the arguments are combined: Fiore et al implicitly use $\times$, Tanaka implicitly uses $\otimes$, and Bunched Implications could use a combination. These considerations ultimately led us to the following definition.

Definition 2. For a pseudo-monad S on Cat, a *binding signature* $\Sigma = (O, a)$ is a set of operations O together with an arity function $a : O \to Ar_S$ where an element $(k, \alpha, (\alpha_i)_{1\leq i\leq k})$ of Ar_S consists of a natural number k, an object α of the category Sk, and, for $1 \leq i \leq k$, an object α_i of the category $S2$.

The reason that we choose α_i's to be objects of $S2$ rather than $S1$ is, technically, that the binary operator $+$, for example, is generated by a map in the Lawvere theory, i.e., by an object of $S2$, whereas the unary operator $1 + -$ is not. So $+$ has strong uniformity properties with respect to algebras and maps of algebras that $1 + -$ does not have. And, intuitively, the two arguments of such a binary α must correspond to the number of bound variables and that of free variables. For the cases that there is no binding, only the second argument is significant, reflecting the fact that only free variables are present.

With the definition of signature in hand, we can induce a signature endofunctor, as they did, and we can then speak of algebras for the endofunctor.

Proposition 3. *Each binding signature Σ induces an endofunctor on $\widehat{S1}$ that sends X to*

$$\coprod_{\substack{o\in O \\ a(o)=(k,\alpha^o,(\alpha_i^o)_{1\leq i\leq k})}} \overline{\alpha^o}_{\widehat{S1}}(X(\overline{\alpha_1^o}\,_{S1}(1,-)),\ldots,X(\overline{\alpha_k^o}\,_{S1}(1,-)))$$

The functor constructed in the proposition agrees with the functors Fiore et al and Tanaka generated from their signatures; and the category Σ-Alg of algebras for the functor agrees with their constructions too. Following Fiore et al, we overload notation by denoting both the signature and the functor it generates by Σ. Even when one restricts to the examples of $S = T_{fp}$ and $S = T_{sm}$, our definition of binding signature is more general than those of Fiore et al and Tanaka: their k and our k agree, their n_i amount to canonical choices of α_i for us, and there is a canonical choice of α incorporated into their choice of k.

Example 11. Let S be T_{fp}, i.e., consider Fiore et al's cartesian binders. Our k is their k. Our α is the object of $T_{fp}k$ generating the functor

$$[\mathbb{F}, Set]^k \longrightarrow [\mathbb{F}, Set]$$

defining the k-fold product. And, where they have n_i, our α_i is the object of $T_{fp}2$ generating the functor

$$\overline{\alpha_i}_{\mathbb{F}} : \mathbb{F}^2 \longrightarrow \mathbb{F}$$

that sends a pair (x, y) to $(n_i \times x) + y$.

In particular, the untyped λ-calculus

$$M ::= x \mid \lambda x.M \mid MM$$

has two operators, one with arity, in Fiore et al's terms, given by $\langle 1\rangle$, and the other with arity $\langle 0,0\rangle$. Let 2 be defined to have elements x and y. Then, in our terms, for the first operator, i.e., for the λ-operator, $k=1$, $\alpha \in T_{fp}(1)$ is 1, and α_1 is the element $x \times y$ of $T_{fp}(2)$. For the latter, i.e., for application, $k=2$, α is the element $x \times y$ of $T_{fp}(2)$, and both α_i's are given by y seen as an element of $T_{fp}(2)$.

Example 12. Let S be T_{sm}, i.e., consider Tanaka's linear binders in [15]. Our k is her k. Our α is the object of $T_{sm}k$ generating the functor

$$[\mathbb{P}, Set]^k \longrightarrow [\mathbb{P}, Set]$$

defining the k-fold tensor product. And, where Tanaka has n_i, our α_i is the object of $T_{sm}2$ generating the functor

$$\overline{\alpha_i}_{\mathbb{P}} : \mathbb{P}^2 \longrightarrow \mathbb{P}$$

that sends a pair (x,y) to $(n_i \times x) \otimes y$.

In particular, the untyped linear λ-calculus

$$M ::= x \mid \lambda_l x.M \mid M@M$$

has two operators, which except for the routine replacement of product by tensor, have exactly the same arities as those for the ordinary λ-calculus as above. So, in our terms the signature for the linear λ-calculus is exactly the same as that for the λ-calculus except for the routine replacement of product by tensor.

Example 13. Let S be T_{BI}, i.e., the pseudo-monad for bunches as in the Logic of Bunched Implications. For this example, we no longer have a uniform choice of α and α_i as we must allow a choice between the product and the tensor product. Consider the untyped $\alpha\lambda$-calculus [14] (we replace Pym's α by λ_l in order to avoid overloading of notation)

$$M ::= x \mid \lambda x.M \mid \lambda_l x.M \mid MM \mid M@M$$

It has binding signature $\Sigma_{BI} = (O_{BI}, a : O_{BI} \rightarrow Ar_{BI})$ given by four operators with arities $(1,1,x \times y)$, $(1,1,x \otimes y)$, $(2, x \times y, (y,y))$ and $(2, x \otimes y, (y,y))$ respectively, where x and y are the generators of 2, and hence objects of $T_{BI}(2)$.

5 A Strength for a Signature

The central abstract result that allowed Fiore et al, then Tanaka, to chacterise the presheaf of terms generated by a signature as initial algebra semantics involved the description of a canonical strength (see Section 3 of [2] and Lemma 3.1(2) of [15]). So in this section, we show that in our axiomatic setting, for any signature, the functor Σ has a canonical strength

$$\Sigma X \bullet Y \longrightarrow \Sigma(X \bullet Y)$$

with respect to $\bullet$, for pointed objects Y. The strength we describe here agrees with those given by Fiore et al and Tanaka, albeit subject to effort to check the details. The point will denote an assignment, i.e., a given evaluation of variables.

Generalising Fiore et al's use of the functor $1+-$ and Tanaka's use of $1\otimes -$, our axiomatic definition of a binding signature gave us objects α of $S2$, and hence binary operations $\overline{\alpha}$. We therefore need to consider endofunctors of the form $\overline{\alpha}_{S1}(b,-)$ on $S1$ where b is 1.

Lemma 1. *Let S be a pseudo-monad on Cat, let $\alpha \in S2$, $b, c \in S1$, and let (A, a) be an S-algebra. Then for any $x \in A$,*

$$\overline{\overline{\alpha}_{S1}(b,c)}_A x = \overline{\alpha}_A(\overline{b}_A(x), \overline{c}_A(x))$$

functorially in x.

Proof.

$$\overline{\overline{\alpha}_{S1}(b,c)}_A x = a \circ Sx \circ \mu_1 \circ S(b,c)(\alpha)$$

and

$$\begin{aligned}\overline{\alpha}_A(\overline{b}_A(x), \overline{c}_A(x)) &= a \circ S(a \circ Sx(b), a \circ Sx(c))(\alpha)\\ &= a \circ S(a \circ Sx \circ (b,c))(\alpha)\\ &= a \circ Sa \circ S^2x \circ S(b,c)(\alpha)\\ &= a \circ \mu_A \circ S^2x \circ S(b,c)(\alpha)\\ &= a \circ Sx \circ \mu_1 \circ S(b,c)(\alpha)\end{aligned}$$

all functorially in x.

Observe also that when $\alpha = 1 \in S1$, we have $\overline{1}_A = id_A$.

Proposition 4. *Each $\alpha \in S2$ induces a canonical natural transformation*

$$X(\overline{\alpha}_{S1}(1,-)) \bullet Y \longrightarrow (X \bullet Y)(\overline{\alpha}_{S1}(1,-))$$

Proof. By Theorem 4, we need to give a natural transformation whose component at $d \in S1$ is of the form

$$\int^{c' \in S1} X(\overline{\alpha}_{S1}(1,c')) \times (\overline{c'}_{\widehat{S1}}(Y))d \longrightarrow \int^{c'' \in S1} Xc'' \times (\overline{c''}_{\widehat{S1}}(Y))(\overline{\alpha}_{S1}(1,d))$$

Putting, $c'' = \overline{\alpha}_{S1}(1,c')$, it suffices, subject to suitable naturality, to give a function

$$(\overline{c'}_{\widehat{S1}}(Y))d \longrightarrow (\overline{\overline{\alpha}_{S1}(1,c')}_{\widehat{S1}}(Y))(\overline{\alpha}_{S1}(1,d)) \tag{4}$$

But by Lemma 1 with $b = 1$, $c = c'$ and $A = \widehat{S1}$, we have

$$\overline{\overline{\alpha}_{S1}(1,c')}_{\widehat{S1}}(Y) = \overline{\alpha}_{\widehat{S1}}(Y, \overline{c'}_{\widehat{S1}}(Y))$$

So to give the requisite function (4) is equivalent to giving a function of the form

$$(\overline{c'}_{\widehat{S1}}(Y))d \longrightarrow (\overline{\alpha}_{\widehat{S1}}(Y, \overline{c'}_{\widehat{S1}}(Y)))(\overline{\alpha}_{S1}(1,d)) \tag{5}$$

which in turn, by applying the Yoneda Lemma applied to both the domain and codomain, is equivalent to giving a function of the form:

$$\widehat{S1}(S1(-,d), \overline{c'}_{\widehat{S1}}(Y)) \longrightarrow \widehat{S1}(S1(-, \overline{\alpha}_{S1}(1,d)), (\overline{\alpha}_{\widehat{S1}}(Y, \overline{c'}_{\widehat{S1}}(Y)))) \tag{6}$$

But by Proposition 2, given a pair $(1, d)$ of objects of $S1$, one has

$$S1(-, \overline{\alpha}_{S1}(1,d)) \cong \overline{\alpha}_{\widehat{S1}}(S1(-,1), S1(-,d))$$

So, letting g be a natural transformation from $S1(-,d)$ to $\overline{c'}_{\widehat{S1}}(Y)$, the composite

$$\begin{array}{c} \overline{\alpha}_{\widehat{S1}}(S1(-,1), S1(-,d)) \\ \Big\downarrow {\scriptstyle \overline{\alpha}_{\widehat{S1}}(S1(-,1), g)} \\ \overline{\alpha}_{\widehat{S1}}(S1(-,1), \overline{c'}_{\widehat{S1}}(Y)) \\ \Big\downarrow \\ \overline{\alpha}_{\widehat{S1}}(Y, \overline{c'}_{\widehat{S1}}(Y)) \end{array}$$

where the first map is given by functoriality of $\overline{\alpha}_{\widehat{S1}}$ and the second is given by the point of Y, yields a function of the form (6), and thus the construction, which is natural in g, yields the function required in (4).

Theorem 5. *There is a canonical strength of the endofunctor Σ over $\bullet$*

$$\Sigma X \bullet Y \longrightarrow \Sigma(X \bullet Y)$$

for pointed objects Y.

Proof. By Theorem 3, for any pseudo-monad T on Cat, the functor defined by $\bullet : T1 \times T1 \longrightarrow T1$ is a T-algebra map in its first variable. Taking T to be $T_{coc}S$, by Theorem 2, we have the pseudo-monad for cocomplete categories with S-structure, subject to a coherence condition. So $\bullet$ must preserve both coproducts and S-structure in its first variable. So we have a canonical isomorphism from

$$\Sigma X \bullet Y = \left(\coprod_{\substack{o \in O \\ a(o)=(k,\alpha^o,(\alpha^o_i)_{1 \le i \le k})}} \overline{\alpha^o}_{\widehat{S1}}(X(\overline{\alpha^o_1}_{S1}(1,-)), \ldots, X(\overline{\alpha^o_k}_{S1}(1,-))) \right) \bullet Y$$

to

$$\coprod_{\substack{o \in O \\ a(o)=(k,\alpha^o,(\alpha^o_i)_{1 \le i \le k})}} \overline{\alpha^o}_{\widehat{S1}}(X(\overline{\alpha^o_1}_{S1}(1,-)) \bullet Y, \ldots, X(\overline{\alpha^o_k}_{S1}(1,-)) \bullet Y)$$

So, applying Proposition 4 multiple times, we are done.

6 Initial Algebra Semantics

Fiore et al and Tanaka's initial algebra semantics follow directly from their instances of Theorem 5. So we simply emulate their constructions here, subject to correcting a tiny error in the first (they forgot the point), to characterise the presheaf of terms generated by a binding signature in general here. We proceed from Theorem 5 as follows.

Corollary 1. *For any binding signature Σ, if T_Σ is the free monad generated by Σ on the category $T_{coc}S(1) = [(S1)^{op}, Set]$, it follows that T_Σ has a canonical strength over pointed objects with respect to $\bullet$.*

By a variant of Theorem 3, a strength for any monad on a monoidal closed category (over pointed objects) yields a canonical monoid structure on the free algebra on 1. So we have:

Corollary 2. *For any binding signature Σ, the object $T_\Sigma(1)$ of $[(S1)^{op}, Set]$ has a canonical monoid structure on it.*

And from this, we can deduce, at this level of generality, the initial algebra semantics of Fiore et al and Tanaka as follows:

Definition 3. Let F be an endofunctor with a strength over pointed objects on a monoidal closed category $(C, \cdot, I)$. An *F-monoid* (X, μ, ι, h) consists of a monoid (X, μ, ι) in C and an F-algebra (X, h) such that the diagram

$$\begin{array}{ccccc} F(X) \cdot X & \xrightarrow{t_{X,X}} & F(X \cdot X) & \xrightarrow{F\mu} & FX \\ {\scriptstyle h \cdot X}\downarrow & & & & \downarrow{\scriptstyle h} \\ X \cdot X & & \xrightarrow[\mu]{\qquad\qquad} & & X \end{array}$$

commutes.

F-monoids form a category with maps given by maps in C that preserve both the F-algebra structure and the monoid structure.

Theorem 6. *For any binding signature Σ, the object $T_\Sigma(1)$ of the category $[(S1)^{op}, Set]$ together with its canonical Σ-algebra structure and monoid structure forms the initial Σ-monoid.*

That is the final theorem in Tanaka's paper and one of the two equivalent versions of the final section of Fiore et al's paper.

7 Further Work

Although we have studied syntax, we have not given a general syntax in this paper. So an obvious question to address now is to provide syntax that corresponds to at least a class of the structures we have described here, enough to include at least Fiore et al's analysis, Tanaka's linear variable binders, and the mixed variable binders of the Logic of Bunched Implication.

It seems unlikely that there is a syntax to be found at the full generality of this paper. But there seems likely to be something interesting at a level of generality that is included in that of this paper and extends the three leading classes of examples. The notion of a pseudo-commutative monad [5] may be relevant.

Further, the analysis of this paper should be extended to consider variable binding in a typed setting: everything in this paper has been based on an untyped setting. Fiore [1] and more recently and extensively Miculan and Scagnetto [8] have begun to address types, and their approaches may fit directly within the structures advocated here. But it may ultimately prove more useful to focus on a pseudo-distributive law for 2-monads on Cat^X, given a set of types X: it is unclear yet.

Some of the development of binders has involved the use of sheaves rather than presheaves, e.g., in [3]. Sheaves appear for example if one wants to justify decidable equality of variables, which $[\mathbb{F}, Set]$ does not support. So, in due course, we plan to extend the pseudo-monadic approach of this paper to cover sheaves too: in principle, we are optimistic about that as the category of sheaves is also given by a free cocompletion, one that respects some existing colimiting structure.

Also note that [4] studies logical principles on binding structures. Accordingly, we too would like to extend our approach to incorporate logical principles such as induction over higher-order terms.

References

1. M. Fiore, Semantic analysis of normalisation by evaluation for typed lambda calculus. In *Proc. PPDP 02*, ACM Press, 2002, 26–37.
2. M. Fiore, G. Plotkin, and D. Turi. Abstract syntax and variable binding. In *Proc. LICS 99*, pages 193–202. IEEE Press, 1999.
3. M. Gabbay and A. M. Pitts. A new approach to abstract syntax involving binders. In *Proc. LICS 99*, pages 214–224. IEEE Press, 1999.
4. M. Hofmann, Semantical analysis of higher-order abstract syntax. In *Proc. LICS 99*, IEEE Press, 1999, 204–213.
5. M. Hyland and A. J. Power. Pseudo-commutative monads and pseudo-closed 2-categories. *J. Pure and Applied Algebra* 175:141–185, 2002.
6. G. M. Kelly. *Basic Concepts of Enriched Category Theory, London Math. Soc. Lecture Notes Series 64* Cambridge University Press, 1982.
7. S. Mac Lane. *Categories for the Working Mathematician.* Springer-Verlag, 1971.
8. M. Miculan and I. Scagnetto, A framework for typed HOAS and semantics. In *Proc. PPDP 2003, ACM Press*, pages 184–194, 2003.
9. G. D. Plotkin and A. J. Power. Algebraic Operations and Generic Effects. In *Proc. MFCSIT 2000, Applied Categorical Structures* 11, 2003, 69–94.
10. A. J. Power. Enriched Lawvere theories. *Theory and Applications of Categories*, 6:83–93, 1999.

11. A. J. Power. A Unified Category-Theoretic Approach to Variable Binding. In *Proc. MERLIN 2003, ACM Digital Library*, 2003.
12. A. J. Power. Countable Lawvere theories and Computational Effects. Submitted.
13. A. J. Power and M. Tanaka. Pseudo-Distributive Laws and Axiomatics for Variable Binding. Submitted.
14. D. Pym. *The Semantics and Proof Theory of the Logic of Bunched Implications, Applied Logic Series.* Kluwer, 2002.
15. M. Tanaka. Abstract syntax and variable binding for linear binders. In *Proc. MFCS 2000, LNCS 1893*, pages 670–679, 2000.
16. M. Tanaka. Pseudo-Distributive Laws and a Unified Framework for Variable Binding. Edinburgh Ph.D. thesis, 2004.

Proof Contexts with Late Binding

Virgile Prevosto[1] and Sylvain Boulmé[2]

[1] Max-Planck Institut für Informatik,
Stuhlsatzenhausweg 85 – 66123 Saarbrücken – Germany
prevosto@mpi-sb.mpg.de
[2] LSR-IMAG,
681, rue de la Passerelle BP-72 – 38402 St-Martin D'Hères – France
Sylvain.Boulme@imag.fr

Abstract. The FOCAL language (formerly FoC) allows one to incrementally build modules and to formally prove their correctness. In this paper, we present two formal semantics for encoding FOCAL constructions in the COQ proof assistant. The first one is implemented in the FOCAL compiler to have the correctness of FOCAL libraries verified with the COQ proof-checker. The second one formalizes the FOCAL structures and their main properties as COQ terms (called mixDrecs). The relations between the two embeddings are examined in the last part of the paper.

1 Introduction

As software applications are growing in size and complexity, it becomes necessary to provide strong, machine-checked guarantees of their correctness. FOCAL is a language (formerly called FoC) initially designed to develop certified computer algebra libraries. In short, a component of a FOCAL library can mix abstract specifications, implementations of operations and proofs that the implementations satisfy their specifications. FOCAL encourages a development process by refinement: concrete implementation can be derived step-by-step from abstract specifications. The validity of each step is bound to various constraints. Some of them can be checked by the compiler, but others lead to proof obligations. These proof obligations can be discharged by an automatic prover or directly by the developer. In FOCAL, refinement is realized through a kind of inheritance mechanism. The correctness of the libraries is verified with the COQ proof assistant [21].

This paper introduces two semantics for the FOCAL constructions. The first one is a *very shallow embedding* into COQ using mainly λ-abstractions. This semantics reflects the current implementation of the FOCAL compiler. However, it is purely operational and does not take into account the global structure of FOCAL libraries. We have defined a denotational semantics that associates to each component of a FOCAL library a COQ type called *mixDrec*. These mixDrecs allow us to state formally in the COQ logic the main properties of these structures. In this paper, we examine the relations between these two semantics.

P. Urzyczyn (Ed.): TLCA 2005, LNCS 3461, pp. 324–338, 2005.

Let us now introduce a flavor of the main FOCAL concepts. The building blocks of a computer algebra library are algebraic structures. At first glance, an algebraic structure can be seen as a set of functions (and constants, *i.e.* functions with 0 argument) and properties. For instance, a group is built upon a carrier set, **rep**. It has a binary operation over **rep**, *plus*, which is associative and has a neutral element 0. It also provides a unary operation *opp* such that $plus(x, opp(x)) = 0$ etc. As we may notice from this example, each component of such a structure must be expressed in a certain context, where some other elements are present. For instance, *plus* or 0 can only be introduced after **rep** has been specified. This can be captured by the notion of *dependent records* [7, 15, 6], that is records in which the type of each field might depend on the preceding ones. With such a construction, the notion of group is simply a record type, which can be informally represented as

$$\left\{\begin{array}{l} \mathbf{rep}\ :Set \\ plus\ :\mathbf{rep} \rightarrow \mathbf{rep} \rightarrow \mathbf{rep} \\ assoc{:}\forall x, y, z \in \mathbf{rep}, \\ \qquad\qquad plus(x,plus(y,z)) = plus(plus(x,y),z) \\ \qquad\qquad\qquad \ldots \end{array}\right\}$$

A given group, such as $(\mathbb{Z}, +, 0, -)$, is a particular instance of this type.

While these records can specify single mathematical structures, they do not capture the relations between them. Indeed, once we have groups, we can add a new operation *mult* (together with its properties) to obtain rings. Then it is possible to define integral domains as a special kind of rings with some additional properties. Thus record types must be extensible.

Furthermore, it is often possible to define some operations at an abstract level. For instance, subtraction can be derived from *plus* and *opp* for any group ($x - y = plus(x, opp(y))$), and by extension for any structure deriving from the groups, such as rings and domains: its definition can be given together with the specification of groups, and reused in any instance of a structure deriving from groups, as well as proofs of its properties (for instance $x - y = opp(y - x)$). Such refinements from one structure into another are very similar to the *inheritance* notion in Object-Oriented Programming (OOP).

In order to increase efficiency of programs, it is often interesting to refine a definition when deriving a new structure. If we want to implement $\mathbb{Z}/_{2\mathbb{Z}}$ with booleans, the generic definition of subtraction may be replaced by *xor*, and all other components of this structure have to use this new definition. This concept is known in OOP as *late binding*. However, on the contrary to OOP, definitions represent here (proofs of) theorems as well as functions. Mixing redefinitions with proofs and dependent types is the main issue of FOCAL inheritance semantics.

This paper is divided as follows. First, we present in the next section the main constructions of the FOCAL language. Then, we propose an embedding of these constructions in COQ, which is used to ensure the correctness of the proofs made within FOCAL (section 3). Section 4 introduces *mixDrecs*, which can be seen as partially defined (dependent) records, and hence constitute a good representation of mathematical structures. Last, sections 5 and 6 show the conformance of respectively the FOCAL language and its translation into COQ with respect to the mixDrecs model.

2 The Focal Language

2.1 Presentation

The main goal of the FoC project[1] was to design a new language for computer algebra having both a clear semantics and an efficient implementation – *via* a translation to OCAML. The resulting language incorporates functional and some restricted object-oriented features. For the certification part, the language provides means for the developers to write formal specifications and proofs of their programs and to have them verified with COQ. The FOCAL library, mostly developed by Rioboo [5, 18], implements mathematical structures up to multivariate polynomial rings with performances comparable to the best CAS in existence.

Designing our own language allows us to express more easily than in a general purpose language some very important concepts of computer algebra, and in particular the *carrier type* of a structure. We have also restricted object-oriented features to what was strictly necessary and avoided constructions which would have hindered our intention to prove the correctness of programs [4].

2.2 Main Constructions of the Language

We describe here informally the main features of the language, and give an overview of its syntax. More in-depth descriptions can be found in [17, 22].

Species. The main nodes of the FOCAL hierarchy are called **species**. They can be compared to the *classes* of an object-oriented language. Each species is composed of *methods*, identified by their names. A method can be either *declared* or *defined*. Declared methods represent the primitive operations of the structure, as well as its specifications. Defined methods represent all the operations that have received an implementation so far, and all theorems that have been proved. Moreover, we distinguish three kinds of methods:

Carrier: It is the type of the elements manipulated by the algebraic structure. A declared carrier is an abstract data type. A defined carrier is bound to a concrete type. For instance, polynomials may be represented by a list of pairs, the first component being the degree and the second one the coefficient.

Programming Methods: They represent the constants and the operators of the structure. Declared methods of this category are simply signatures. The definitions are written in a language close to the functional core of ML.

Logical Methods: Such methods represent the properties of the programming methods. Following the Curry-Howard isomorphism, the type of such a method is a statement, while its body (when it is defined) is a proof.

[1] `http://focal.inria.fr`

To give an example of FOCAL syntax, we express below the specification of groups seen in section 1 as a species (due to space constraints, the statements of the properties are given informally in a comment):

```
species group =
  rep;
  sig plus in rep → rep → rep;
  property assoc: (* x+(y+z)=(x+y)+z *);
  sig opp in rep → rep; sig zero in rep;
  property plus_opp: (* -(x+y)=(-y)+(-x) *);
  property opp_opp: (* -(-x)=x *);
  let minus(x,y)= plus(x,opp(y));
  let id(x)=minus(x,zero); ...
  theorem minus_opp: (* x-y=-(y-x) *)
   proof: by plus_opp, opp_opp def minus;
end
```

First, there is the declaration of the abstract carrier **rep**. Then we give the **sig**nature of *plus*, a binary operation over **rep**. After that, we state a logical **property** over *plus* (namely that it is associative). In addition, we declare a unary operation *opp* together with some of its properties. We also *define* (through the **let** keyword) new operations, *minus*, from *plus* and *opp*, and *id* from *minus* and *zero*. In addition, we state a **theorem** about *minus* which can be derived from the properties of *plus* and *opp* and the definition of *minus*.

Inheritance. the species *group* above is defined "from scratch", by providing the complete list of its methods. It is also possible to build species using *inheritance.* A new species may inherit the declarations and definitions of one or several species. For instance, given a species *monoid* with an associative operation *mult* and a neutral element *one*, we can define the species ring as follows:

```
species ring inherits group, monoid =
  property distrib: (* x*(y+z)=(x*y)+(x*z) *);
  let zero = minus(one, one); ...
end
```

The new species can use all the methods of its parents, regardless of their origin. It can declare new methods (such as *distrib*) or directly define them, provide a definition for previously declared methods (such as *zero*), or even redefine methods. On the other hand, the type of the methods (or their statement in the case of logical methods) must remain the same. This constraint guarantees that if a species s_2 inherits from a species s_1, then any instance of s_2 is also an instance of s_1. Similarly, in case of multiple inheritance, the methods with a same name in the two parents must have the same type. If several methods are defined, we select the definition coming from the rightmost species in the **inherits** clause. This is also true for the carrier, whose implicit name is **rep**.

Collections and Interfaces. The *interface* of a species s is obtained by hiding the body of all defined methods of s (while keeping the corresponding declarations). It can be seen as the type of s. All implementations of s must adhere to this interface, while they are free to modify some of the definitions of s. A **collection** is an instance of a completely defined species (*i.e.* in which every method is defined). Users of a collection access it only through its interface.

2.3 Dependencies

A method m_1 of a species s can *depend* on a method m_2 of s. The *group* species gives various examples of dependencies:

- The declaration of *plus* depends on **rep**.
- The statement of *assoc* depends on **rep** and *plus*.
- The body of *minus* depends on *plus* and *opp*, and also implicitly on **rep**, since some subexpressions have type **rep**. Its type (**rep** → **rep** → **rep** as it can be inferred by the compiler), depends only on **rep**.
- *id* depends on *minus*, *zero* (and **rep**).
- The statement of *minus_opp* depends on *minus*, *opp*, and **rep**. The proof itself depends in addition on *plus_opp* and *opp_opp*, and on the *definition* of *minus*.

As shown by this last example, we have two kinds of dependencies. There is a *decl-dependency* on x when we need to rely on the declaration of x (*i.e.* its type or its statement). There is a *def-dependency* on x if we need to unfold its exact definition in order to type-check an expression.

A def-dependency may occur not only in the body of a method, but also in the statement of a property or of a theorem. In this case, it is not possible to extract an interface for the species. Consider for instance the following code:

species *bad* =
  rep = *int*;
  property *id*: **all** x **in rep**, *equal*(*int_plus*(x,0),x);
end

The statement of *id* can only be well-typed in a context where **rep** is bound to the *int* type. Otherwise, it is not even possible to type-check the expression *int_plus*(x,0). Allowing such def-dependencies in types would have a major drawback with respect to redefinition. For instance, redefining **rep** requires at least to remove completely the methods with a def-dependency upon it in their type, such as *id*, because their type could not be type-checked anymore. But then, the resulting species does not offer the same functionalities as its parent (*id* does not exist anymore). To avoid this problem, FOCAL does not allow species without a correct interface: species such as *bad* are rejected.

2.4 Inheritance Resolution and Normal Form

If we redefine a method x, all methods that def-depend upon x are no longer accurate, so that we have to erase their definition. In [17] and [16], Doligez and

Prevosto describe an algorithm that performs inheritance resolution and takes into account def-dependencies. They use the following notations:

- The *decl*-dependencies of a method x in a species s are written $\lfloor x \rceil_s$.
- The *def*-dependencies of a method x in a species s are written $\llbracket x \rrbracket_s$.
- Last, it is required that any species s can be put in *normal form*.

A species in normal form has no **inherits** clause, and its methods are ordered according to their dependencies. Namely, a method can only depend on the preceding ones. Hence, a species in normal form is nothing more than an ordered sequence of methods. It is unique modulo reordering of independent methods. In this paper, we will sometimes implicitly identify such a sequence with a species.

Given a species defined by **species** s **inherits** $s_1, \ldots, s_n = \phi_1 \ldots \phi_m$ **end**, the main properties of the algorithm are the following:

1. If the algorithm succeeds then its result $norm(s)$ is in normal form.
2. If a normal form equivalent to s exists then the algorithm succeeds.
3. $norm(s)$ contains the *newest* definition of each method x. This is the last definition of name x found, starting from $norm(s_1)$ and ending with ϕ_m.
4. Only a minimum set of definitions is erased: for each method x declared in $norm(s)$ but defined in one of the s_i, there exists $y \in \llbracket x \rrbracket_{s_i}$, such that y is only declared in $norm(s)$, or the definition of y is not the same in s and s_i.

3 Minimal Environment and Method Generators

Dependencies also play an important role during the translation of a species s in the Coq language. Each method x of s introducing a new definition is transformed into a well-typed Coq-term. In addition, we want to reuse this term in any species or collection deriving from s (in which x is neither redefined nor erased), *and* the names of $\lfloor x \rceil_s$ to be bound to the newest definitions available, hence emulating a late-binding mechanism. The main issue is that a definition can not come alone. Indeed, we have to take dependencies into account and to provide a whole environment in which the definition can be type-checked. For instance, if we consider again the *group* species, the theorem *minus_opp* has to be verified in an environment containing at least the following methods:

rep; **sig** *plus* **in rep** → **rep** → **rep**; **sig** *opp* **in rep** → **rep**;
property *plus_opp*: ...; **property** *opp_opp*: ...;
let *minus* $(x,y) = plus(x, opp(y))$;

Indeed, *minus_opp* def-depends upon *minus* and decl-depends upon *plus_opp* and *opp_opp*. Then in order to define minus (and to state *plus_opp* and *opp_opp* by the way) we have to include the declarations of *plus* and *opp*. Last, **rep** must also be present, since all the functions manipulate elements of the carrier type.

To achieve that, the *decl*-dependencies of x can be replaced by abstractions. This leads to the notion of *method generators*. To obtain the method x for a given collection, we only have to apply the generator of x to the appropriate methods. In our example, we can apply the generator of *minus_opp* to any implementation of **rep**, *plus* and *opp*, together with proofs of *plus_opp* and *opp_opp*.

By definition, *def*-dependencies can not be abstracted. We must put their definition in the environment. These definitions have themselves their own environment constraints: if $y \in \llbracket x \rrbracket_s$, the method generator must be abstracted with respect to the methods of $\wr y \int_s$, so that we can generate y itself.

In order to properly tackle this issue, we introduce the notion of *minimal environment* in which x can be defined. It is denoted by $s \Cap x$, and corresponds to the smallest subset of $norm(s)$ which is needed to both type-check x *and* have a well formed typing context. The formal definition of $s \Cap x$ relies on the notion of *visible universe* $\mid x \mid$ of a method x. It is the list of method names that will occur in $s \Cap x$. Namely, with $<_s^{def}$ the transitive closure of $\llbracket \cdot \rrbracket_s$ and $\mathcal{T}_s(x)$ denoting the type (or the statement for logical methods) of x in the species s, we have

Definition 1 (Visible Universe).

$$\frac{y \in \wr x \int_s}{y \in \mid x \mid} \qquad \frac{y <_s^{def} x}{y \in \mid x \mid} \qquad \frac{z <_s^{def} x \qquad y \in \wr z \int_s}{y \in \mid x \mid} \qquad \frac{z \in \mid x \mid \qquad y \in \wr \mathcal{T}_s(z) \int_s}{y \in \mid x \mid}$$

In the following, we write $norm(s)$ as an ordered list of methods Φ, where Φ is defined inductively as either the empty list $\emptyset$ or a non-empty list $\{y : \tau = e; \Phi'\}$. In this last case, τ is a type associated to the field name y, and e is $\perp$ when y is only declared, or else a term corresponding to the definition of y.

Definition 2 (Minimal Environment). *The minimal environment is defined with the following rules:*

$$\emptyset \Cap x = \emptyset \qquad \frac{y \notin \mid x \mid \qquad \Phi \Cap x = \Sigma}{\{y : \tau = e; \Phi\} \Cap x = \Sigma} \qquad \frac{y <_s^{def} x \qquad \Phi \Cap x = \Sigma}{\{y : \tau = e; \Phi\} \Cap x = \{y : \tau = e; \Sigma\}}$$

$$\frac{y \in \mid x \mid \qquad y \not<_s^{def} x \qquad \Phi \Cap x = \Sigma}{\{y : \tau = e; \Phi\} \Cap x = \{y : \tau = \perp; \Sigma\}}$$

On the Coq side, the method generator is obtained by mapping any declaration of $s \Cap x$ to a λ-abstraction, and any definition to a local binding, obtained by applying the corresponding method generator to the appropriate variables. In [16], we have shown that such a method generator is a well-typed Coq term. For instance, the method generators corresponding to the *minus*, *id* and *minus_opp* methods of our *group* species would be the following:

```
Definition minus_gen:=
  fun(rep: Set)⇒ fun(plus: rep → rep → rep)⇒ fun (opp: rep → rep)⇒
    fun (x,y:rep) ⇒ plus(x,opp(y)).
Definition minus_opp_gen:=
  fun(rep:Set)⇒ fun (plus:rep → rep → rep)⇒ fun (opp: rep → rep)⇒
    let minus = (minus_gen rep plus opp) in
      fun (plus_opp: ...) ⇒ ...
Definition id_gen:=
  fun(rep:Set)⇒ fun(zero:rep)⇒ fun(minus: rep → rep → rep)⇒
    fun (x:rep) ⇒ minus(x,zero).
```

minus_gen is simply an abstraction over *rep*, *plus* and *opp*. *minus_opp_gen* contains in addition a definition of *minus*, obtained by applying *minus_gen* to the appropriate representations of *rep*, *plus* and *opp* in the context of the theorem generator. *id_gen* is abstracted with respect to *minus* and *zero*. Since it does not rely on the definition of *minus*, there is no need to call *minus_gen*.

4 MixDrecs

Method generators provide a convenient way to represent the method definitions of a species s in COQ, and to reuse the corresponding code in each implementation of s. However this translation gives us only a set of method generators: we do not have any representation of s itself, nor of its relations with the other species. In his PhD [4], Boulmé verifies that relations between species can be described in COQ (and are thus compatible with the COQ logic, the calculus of inductive constructions). He proposes COQ constructions to represent species. This section presents these structures and their main properties using human-friendly notations (roughly speaking, inference rules below correspond to inductive definitions in COQ). The whole COQ development is available at `http://www-lsr.imag.fr/Les.Personnes/Sylvain.Boulme/focal.html`

4.1 Dependent Records

Collections can be represented as records, while their interface can be represented as a record type. Given a (countably infinite) set *Lab* of field names, a record is a function (with a finite domain of definition) which associates a definition to a field name. A record signature associates a type to a field name.

Definition 3 (Drecord Signature).

$$\mathit{Rec} : \mathrm{List}(\mathit{Lab}) \rightarrow \mathit{Type} \qquad \frac{\textsc{Esig}}{\{\}_{\mathrm{s}} : \mathit{Rec}_{\emptyset}} \qquad \frac{\textsc{Csig} \quad T : \mathit{Type} \quad a \notin l \quad F : T \rightarrow \mathit{Rec}_l}{\{a : T; F\}_{\mathrm{s}} : \mathit{Rec}_{a;l}}$$

The function F in CSIG expresses the dependencies of the remaining signature with respect to a. We build then a signature from right to left, that is, following the terminology of [15], right associative records. The definition of a Drecord follows the same rules, with the difference that the field a is now bound to an expression and not only to a type. The main operations over signatures are:

- A sub-signature relation between two signatures, noted $s_1 :\succ s_2$ [2], which says that s_1 contains *at least* all the fields of s_2 with the same type, but not necessarily in the same order. Two *independent* fields can indeed be swapped.
- Single inheritance corresponds to the extension of a given signature s with new fields. These new fields can depend on the fields of s and thus are appended at the end of the signature.

[2] $:\succ$ corresponds to the usual subtyping relation $<$, but the direction of the relation makes "bigger" the signature which has more fields.

– Multiple inheritance corresponds to the fusion of two signatures s_1 and s_2, provided that the common fields have the same type in both signatures.

4.2 Partially Defined Drecords: MixDrecs

To represent *species*, we must be able to *mix* declared and defined fields. This is done in a structure called *MixDrec*. A mixDrec is a tree whose nodes are:

– Empty nodes, forming the leafs of the tree.
– Abstract nodes, corresponding to declared fields. An abstract node contains a name and its type, and has one son.
– Manifest nodes, corresponding to defined fields. Such a node contains a name x , its type and its definition. It has two sons. In the first one, x is abstracted, *i.e.* we only know its type. In the second one, we have access to the definition of x. Both sons contain the same fields in the same order, but some abstract nodes of the first son may be defined in the second. Intuitively, it corresponds to def-dependencies over x.

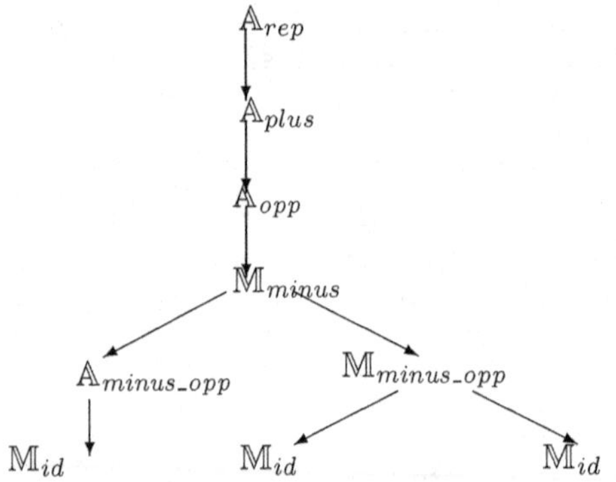

Fig. 1. Tree-structure of a mixDrec

As an example, figure 1 represents the structure of the MixDrec representing groups, with $\mathbb{A}$ being abstract nodes and $\mathbb{M}$ manifest nodes. Due to lack of space, empty nodes (leafs of the tree) have been omitted, as well as some abstract fields. In this figure, the first three nodes are abstract. The fourth one is defined and has two sons. In the left-hand side, we do not take into account the definition of *minus*. Thus, *minus_opp* must also be abstracted, because of its def-dependency. On the other hand, *id*, which has only a decl-dependency upon *minus*, can be defined. On the right-hand side, we know the definition of *minus*. *minus_opp* can thus be defined. Since *id* does not depend upon *minus_opp*, both sons of $\mathbb{M}_{minus\_opp}$ are manifest nodes containing the definition of *id*.

More formally, the type of mixDrecs has three parameters: a list l of field names, a tree-structure p of type Pre_l (defined figure 2) and a Drecord signature S of type Rec_l, which associates a type to each field. A mixDrec M of structure p and signature S is denoted as $M : Mix_{S,p}$ (l is kept implicit). The definition of this type is mutually recursive with the definition of the relation $\gg$ which expresses that a mixDrec is a more defined view of another one. In particular, if m_1 and m_2 are respectively the left and right son of a manifest node, we must have $m_2 \gg m_1$. Inference rules for Pre_l, $M : Mix_{S,p}$ and $\gg$ are described in figure 2. The side condition for the typing rule of a manifest node captures the notion of balanced mixDrec given in [16]. Intuitively, it says that $(f\ x)$ is the most defined view of m when a is abstract.

$$\frac{}{\emptyset_p : Pre_\emptyset} \qquad \frac{a \notin l \qquad p : Pre_l}{\mathbb{A}\; p : Pre_{a;l}} \qquad \frac{a \notin l \qquad p_1 : Pre_l \qquad p_2 : Pre_l}{\mathbb{M}\; p_1\; p_2 : Pre_{a;l}}$$

$$\frac{}{\{\!\{\}\!\} : Mix_{\{\}_s,\emptyset_p}} \qquad \frac{f : \Pi x : T.Mix_{(F\ x),p}}{\{\!\{a : T; f\}\!\} : Mix_{\{a:T;F\}_s,\mathbb{A}p}}$$

$$\frac{x : T \qquad \begin{array}{c} f : \Pi x : T.Mix_{(F\ x),p_1} \\ m : Mix_{(F\ x),p_2} \end{array} \qquad m > (f\ x)}{\{\!\{a : T = x; f; m\}\!\} : Mix_{\{a:T;F\}_s,\mathbb{M}p_1p_2}} \quad \begin{array}{l} \forall f' : \Pi x : T.Mix_{(F\ x),p_1}, \\ m > (f'\ x) \Rightarrow f\ x > f'\ x \end{array}$$

$$\frac{}{\{\!\{\}\!\} > \{\!\{\}\!\}} \qquad \frac{\forall y : T,\ f_1\ y > f_2\ y}{\{\!\{a : T; f_1\}\!\} > \{\!\{a : T; f_2\}\!\}} \qquad \frac{m > (f_1\ x) \qquad \forall y : T,\ f_1\ y > f_2\ y}{\{\!\{a : T = x; f_1; m\}\!\} > \{\!\{a : T; f_2\}\!\}}$$

$$\frac{m_1 > m_2 \qquad \forall y : T,\ f_1\ y > f_2\ y}{\{\!\{a : T = x; f_1; m_1\}\!\} > \{\!\{a : T = x; f_2; m_2\}\!\}}$$

Fig. 2. types of mixDrecs

4.3 Operations on MixDrecs

The two main operations on mixDrecs are the embedding of a mixDrec M of signature s in a sub-signature s' of s, $\Uparrow_{s'} M$, and the fusion of two mixDrecs M_1 and M_2 sharing the same signature, $M_1 \oplus M_2$.

$\Uparrow_{s'} M$ is defined by induction on the derivation of $s' :\succ s$. Basically, we add the fields of s' that are not present in s as abstract nodes, and reorder the fields of s according to s' order.

To compute $M_1 \oplus M_2$, we traverse both structures, and consider the corresponding nodes of each side. The definitions of M_1 have precedence over the one of M_2. In other words, if x is defined in both M_1 and M_2 we take the definition of M_1 and follow the left son of the manifest node in M_2 since we provide a new definition: on this branch, fields with a def-dependency on x are abstract.

But even if the node of the first mixDrec is abstract, it might not be possible to use a definition provided by the second mixDrec. Indeed, we have to take into account possible def-dependencies with respect to previously considered fields. For instance, if we take the two mixDrecs:

$$M_1 = \{\!\{a : T_1 = e_1; \lambda a : T_1. \{\!\{b : T_2\}\!\}; \{\!\{b : T_2 = e_2\}\!\}\}\!\}$$

$$M_2 = \left\{\!\!\left\{ \begin{array}{c} a : T_1 = e_1';\ \lambda a : T_1. \{\!\{b : T_2 = e_2'\}\!\};\\ \{\!\{b : T_2 = e_2'\}\!\} \end{array} \right\}\!\!\right\}$$

then $M_1 \oplus M_2$ is equal to

$$M = \{\!\{a : T_1 = e_1; \lambda a : T_1. \{\!\{b : T_2\}\!\}; \{\!\{b : T_2 = e_2\}\!\}\}\!\}$$

and not to the mixDrec M' obtained by comparing the nodes of M_1 and M_2 placed in the same position:

$$M' = \left\{\!\!\left\{ a : T_1 = e_1;\ \lambda a : T_1 . \begin{array}{c} \{\!\{ b : T_2 = e_2' \}\!\} ; \\ \{\!\{ b : T_2 = e_2 \}\!\} \end{array} \right\}\!\!\right\}$$

Indeed, M' has two different definitions for the field b and thus is not well-formed.

To take into account the global structure of the mixDrecs, Boulmé introduces a list of booleans, the *control list*, indicating for each field whether it is possible or not to take the definition of the mixDrec on the right. Briefly, for a given field x, the corresponding element of the control list is *true* if x is abstract in the rightmost branch of M_1 and defined in M_2, and *false* otherwise, as it is the case for b in the previous example.

5 From Species to MixDrecs

We have just seen two semantics of FOCAL libraries. The *mixDrecs* semantics formalizes the notion of species. The *method generator* semantics provides a light way to express the environment in which each proof obligation of the FOCAL library can be verified with COQ. In the next sections, we examine the relations between these two semantics.

5.1 Plain Translation

A species s put in normal form $norm(s)$ can be directly translated into a mix-Drec, $\ll s \gg$. Whenever there is a defined method x in $norm(s)$, we compute the left son of the corresponding node in $\ll s \gg$ by erasing the definitions that def-depend upon x. The structure of such a mixDrec, $\mathbb{P}(s)$, is defined the same way. It is also possible to derive a signature of Drecord from s, $[\![s]\!]$, by taking the types of the methods in the order given by $norm(s)$

Theorem 1. $\ll s \gg$: $Mix_{[\![s]\!],\mathbb{P}(s)}$ *Moreover, the names of the fields of* $\ll s \gg$ *are exactly the names of the methods of* $norm(s)$.

Proof. By induction on the number of methods of $norm(s)$. □

5.2 Inheritance

Let s_1 be a well-formed species and take $M_1 = \ll s_1 \gg$ the mixDrec associated to its normal form. Let s_2 be a well-formed species defined by

$$\textbf{species } s_2 \textbf{ inherits } s_1 = \phi_1 \ldots \phi_n \textbf{ end}$$

The following properties have been proved in [16]:

Lemma 1. $[\![s_2]\!] :\succ [\![s_1]\!]$

Theorem 2 (Correctness of single inheritance). *With the above notations, the following equality holds:* $\ll s_2 \gg \oplus \left(\Uparrow_{[\![s_2]\!]} tomix s_1\right) = \ll s_2 \gg$

Intuitively, this theorem states that in the single inheritance case, the inheritance resolution algorithm conforms to the mixDrecs semantics: the fusion of $\ll s_2 \gg$ and the embedding of $\ll s_1 \gg$ does not add any definition that existed in s_1 and has been erased during inheritance resolution.

Theorem 3 (Correctness of multiple inheritance). *Let* s *be defined as* **species** s **inherits** $s_1, s_2 =$ **end**. *Then*

$$\ll s \gg = (\Uparrow_{[\![s]\!]} \ll s_2 \gg) \oplus (\Uparrow_{[\![s]\!]} \ll s_1 \gg)$$

6 Method Generators and MixDrecs

First, we define paths inside a MixDrec $\mathcal{M}$ as usual: a path p is a sequence of 0 and 1 of length smaller than the depth of $\mathcal{M}$.

Definition 4 (Definition Contexts). *Let* $\mathcal{M}$ *be a mixDrec, and* p *a path. The* context *associated to* p*, noted* $\Gamma_p(\mathcal{M})$ *is defined according to the following rules:*

$$\begin{array}{ll}
\Gamma_\emptyset(\mathcal{M}) & = \{\!\!\}\\
\Gamma_{0;p'}(\{\!\!\{x : T = e; f; m\}\!\!\}) & = \{\!\!\{x : T; \lambda x.\Gamma_{p'}(f\ x)\}\!\!\}\\
\Gamma_{0;p'}(\{\!\!\{x : T; f\}\!\!\}) & = \{\!\!\{x : T; \lambda x.\Gamma_{p'}(f\ x)\}\!\!\}\\
\Gamma_{1;p'}(\{\!\!\{x : T = e; f; m\}\!\!\}) & = \{\!\!\{x : T = e; \lambda x.\Gamma_{p'}(f\ x); \Gamma_{p'}(m)\}\!\!\}\\
\Gamma_{1;p'}(\{\!\!\{x : T; f\}\!\!\}) & = \{\!\!\{x : T; \lambda x.\Gamma_{p'}(f\ x)\}\!\!\}
\end{array}$$

Let x *be the last field of* $\Gamma_p(\mathcal{M})$. *If* x *is defined in* $\Gamma_p(\mathcal{M})$, *we say that* p *is a* definition path *of* x*, and* $\Gamma_p(\mathcal{M})$ *is a* definition context *of* x *in* $\mathcal{M}$.

Lemma 2. *Given a mixDrec* $\mathcal{M}$ *and a defined field* x *of* $\mathcal{M}$*, let* $\leadsto^{\mathcal{M}}(x)$ *be the* minimal definition path *of* x *in* $\mathcal{M}$ *according to the lexicographic ordering over paths. We write* $\Gamma(\mathcal{M}) \vdash x$ *for* $\Gamma_{\leadsto^{\mathcal{M}}(x)}(\mathcal{M})$. *If a field* y *is defined in* $\Gamma(\mathcal{M}) \vdash x$*,* y *is also defined in any definition context associated to* x *in* $\mathcal{M}$.

In addition, we define an equivalence relation $\leftrightarrow$ over mixDrecs, such that two well-formed mixDrecs defining the same fields but in different order are equivalent. $\leftrightarrow$ can be seen as an extension of the congruence associated to the $:\succ$ relation over signatures to the mixDrecs. Given a species s and a defined method x, we can find a mixDrec $\mathcal{M}$ equivalent to $\ll s \gg$, such that $\Gamma(\mathcal{M}) \vdash x$ is equal to $\ll s \Cap x \gg$, and the depth of x in $\mathcal{M}$ is minimal for the whole equivalence class. This shows that $s \Cap x$ is minimal according to mixDrecs semantics: method generators can be extracted from the mixDrecs by selecting the appropriate path.

Theorem 4. *Let* $\mathcal{T}_s(x)$ *and* $\mathcal{B}_s(x)$ *be the type and the body of* x *in* s*, and* $\gamma_s(x) = \ll s \Cap x; x : \mathcal{T}_s(x) = \mathcal{B}_s(x) \gg$. *There exists a mixDrec* $\mathcal{M}$ *such that*

1. $\mathcal{M} \leftrightarrow \Gamma(\ll s \gg) \vdash x$
2. $\Gamma(\mathcal{M}) \vdash x = \gamma_s(x)$
3. $\forall m$, such that $m \leftrightarrow \Gamma(\ll s \gg) \vdash x$, *the depth of* x *in* $\mathcal{M}$ *is less than or equal to the depth of* x *in* m.

Proof. First, we use the rules of $\leftrightarrow$ to build $\mathcal{M}$ such that it is equivalent to $\Gamma(\ll s \gg) \vdash x$, and then prove that it verifies the two other properties. The construction itself is based on the fact that if y_1 and y_2 are two consecutive fields of $\Gamma(\ll s \gg) \vdash x$, such that y_1 is not in $\mid x \mid$, while y_2 is in $\mid x \mid \cup \{x\}$, then it is possible to swap the two elements. We perform recursively all such permutations, until no one is possible (since the depth of the methods of $\mid x \mid$ strictly decrease at each step, this always terminates).

Then by definition, all the fields of $\mathcal{M}$ preceding x are in $\mid x \mid$ (otherwise, we could make an exchange), and their relative order is preserved. Moreover, it follows from the preceding lemma that the only manifest nodes of $\Gamma\,(\ll s \gg) \vdash x$ correspond to the def-dependencies of x, that is the methods defined in $s \Cap x$: $\Gamma\,(\mathcal{M}) \vdash x = \gamma_s(x)$. Last, by induction on the derivation of $y \in\mid x \mid$, it is impossible to swap x with any of the y in $\mid x \mid$. □

7 Related Work

The very idea of mixDrecs can be viewed as an extension of de Bruijn's telescopic mappings [7], in which the context is formed of definitions as well as of abstractions. Roughly, telescopes can be seen as an embedding of contexts as λ-terms, in which each type can depend on the preceding abstractions. More generally, different formalisms have been designed to deal with "incomplete" terms. In particular, the λc calculus [3] offers a very flexible approach in which holes (similar to the declared methods of FOCAL), can be manipulated as normal λ variables, thanks to new binders. Similar approaches have been proposed in particular by Sato, Sakurai and Kameyama [20], Sands [19], and Mason [12]. Last, Lee and Friedman [11] uses contexts of lambda calculus to obtain a notion of separate compilation, the distinguished free variables of a term being the names of the values that must be given by the context. However, none of these calculi deal explicitly with redefinition, a crucial point in FOCAL inheritance resolution.

Pollack [15] and Betarte [2] have given their own embedding of dependent records in Type Theory. Both provide operations to extend existing signatures with new abstract fields, quite similar to the one that have been presented in section 4. Recently, Coquand, Pollack and Takeyama [6] have also presented a notion of records in which some fields can be defined, as in MixDrecs. However, they do not seem to look toward a computational counterpart such as the FOCAL translation into OCAML, so that they do not deal with redefinitions either. This applies also to the definition of records given by Kopylov [10], which is based on the notion of intersection types. On the other hand, a formalization of late binding with specifications and proofs in the proof assistant LEGO is given in [9]. However, they seem to restrict the theorems that can be proved inside a class in order to avoid issues related to def-dependencies.

On the programming side, mixDrecs can be related to the mixin modules of Ancona and Zucca [1], and to their implementation as an extension of the module system of OCAML [8]. Mixins can be seen as structure mixing some features of modules (and in particular type definitions and abstraction), and classes (inheritance). In [13], the νobj calculus introduces dependent types in an object-oriented language. In this approach, classes can have type components. Hence, on the contrary to mixins, νobj adds module features to objects. However, both of them deal mainly with functions. Thus, they do not address the issues specific to properties and theorems, and in particular the notion of def-dependency.

FOCAL programming features have been partly inspired by the "*compiler of computer algebra libraries*" Axiom and its successor Aldor. In order to integrate deduction steps in the system, Thompson and Poll propose in [23, 14] to extend the type system of Aldor with dependent types and properties. However, their project seems to be in a quite initial stage.

8 Perspectives

During the implementation of the FOCAL library [22], some constructions have been provided inside the FOCAL compiler in addition to the core FOCAL methods presented here. Some work is needed to incorporate these constructions at a theoretical level. First, it is often interesting to be able to define "local" methods. Such methods are only visible to the other methods of the species in which they are defined. They can be treated as normal methods provided dependencies upon such method are flagged as def-dependencies (as if their definition was in-lined everywhere). On the mixDrec side, there is nothing to handle them, though.

It would also be convenient to rename some methods during inheritance. For instance, monoids could declare a generic operation *op*, which would be called *plus* for abelian groups, and *mult* in rings. This has not been implemented yet, but since method generators and Drecords signatures implement dependencies by λ-abstractions, renaming might reduce to alpha-conversion.

The most important extension is the possibility to define inner collections inside a species by using **self**, the species currently defined to instantiate the parameters of a given species. This construction is translated to OCAML, and a restricted version has been studied formally (in particular with respect to dependencies analysis) in [16], but the general case as well as the translation into COQ need to be investigated.

9 Conclusion

In this paper, we have presented two embeddings of the main FOCAL constructions into COQ. The first one, which uses "simple" terms made of abstractions and local bindings, provides an efficient encoding, as the produced terms are quite easily type-checked by COQ, while *method generators* let us reuse as much code as possible. On the contrary, *mixDrecs* are a very heavy encoding, but they preserve the structure of the species and the relation between them. Moreover, we have seen that the treatment of inheritance is the same in both embeddings, and that method generators can be extracted from mixDrecs.

Acknowledgment

The authors wish to thank Thérèse Hardin and the anonymous referees for their helpful remarks on earlier versions of this paper.

References

[1] D. Ancona and E. Zucca. An algebra of mixin modules. In *WADT'97*, volume 1376 of *LNCS*, 1998.
[2] G. Betarte. *Dependent Record Types and Formal Abstract Reasoning: Theory and Practice.* PhD thesis, University of Göteborg, 1998.
[3] M. Bognar and R. de Vrijer. A calculus of lambda calculus contexts. *Journal of Automated Reasoning*, 27(1), 2001.
[4] S. Boulmé. *Spécification d'un environnement dédié à la programmation certifiée de bibliothèques de Calcul Formel.* Thèse de doctorat, Université Paris 6, 2000. `http://www-lsr.imag.fr/Les.Personnes/Sylvain.Boulme/pub/sbthese.ps.gz`.
[5] S. Boulmé, Th. Hardin, and R. Rioboo. Some hints for polynomials in the Foc project. In *Proc. Calculemus*, 2001.
[6] T. Coquand, R. Pollack, and M. Takeyama. A logical framework with dependently typed records. In *Typed Lambda Calculus and Applications, TLCA'03*, volume 2701 of *LNCS*, 2003.
[7] N. G. de Bruijn. Telescopic mappings in typed λ-calculus. *Information and Computation*, 91(2), 1991.
[8] T. Hirschowitz and X. Leroy. Mixin modules in a call-by-value setting. In *ESOP*, volume 2305 of *LNCS*, 2002.
[9] Martin Hofmann et al. Inheritance of proofs. *TAPOS*, 4(1):51–69, 1998.
[10] A. Kopylov. Dependent intersection: A new way of defining records in type theory. In *LICS*, 2003.
[11] S. Lee and D. P. Friedman. Enriching the lambda calculus with contexts: Toward a theory of incremental program construction. In *Proceedings of ICFP*, ACM SIGPLAN notices, 1996.
[12] I. A. Mason. Computing with contexts. *Higher-Order and Symbolic Computation*, 12, 1999.
[13] M. Odersky, V. Cremet, C. Röckl, and M. Zenger. A nominal theory of objects with dependent types. In *FOOL 10*, 2003.
[14] E. Poll and S. Thompson. Integrating Computer Algebra and Reasoning through the Type System of Aldor. In *FROCOS*, volume 1794 of *LNCS*, 2000.
[15] R. Pollack. Dependently typed records for representing mathematical structures. In *TPHOLs*, volume 1869 of *LNCS*, 2000.
[16] V. Prevosto. *Conception et Implantation du langage FoC pour le développement de logiciels certifiés.* Thèse de doctorat, Université Paris 6, 2003. `http://www.mpi-sb.mpg.de/~prevosto/papiers/these.ps.gz`.
[17] V. Prevosto and D. Doligez. Inheritance of algorithms and proofs in the computer algebra library foc. *Journal of Automated Reasoning*, 29(3-4), 2002.
[18] R. Rioboo. *Programmer le calcul formel, des algorithmes à la sémantique.* Habilitation, Université Paris 6, 2002.
[19] D. Sands. Computing with contexts: A simple approach. In *Second Workshop on Higher-Order Operational Techniques in Semantics*, volume 10 of *ENTCS*, 1997.
[20] M. Sato, T. Sakurai, and Y. Kameyama. A simply typed context calculus with first-class environments. *J. of Functional and Logic Programming*, 2002(4), 2002.
[21] The Coq Development Team. *The Coq Proof Assistant Reference Manual Version 8.0.* INRIA-Rocquencourt, 2004.
[22] The Focal development team. *Focal, version 0.2 Tutorial and reference manual.* LIP6 – INRIA – CNAM, 2004. `http://modulogic.inria.fr/focal/download/`.
[23] S. Thompson. Logic and Dependent Types in the Aldor Computer Algebra System. In *Proc. Calculemus*, 2000.

The ∇-Calculus. Functional Programming with Higher-Order Encodings*

Carsten Schürmann, Adam Poswolsky, and Jeffrey Sarnat

Department of Computer Science, Yale University,
51 Prospect St. New Haven, CT, 06511, USA
{carsten, poswolsky, sarnat}@cs.yale.edu

Abstract. Higher-order encodings use functions provided by one language to represent variable binders of another. They lead to concise and elegant representations, which historically have been difficult to analyze and manipulate.

In this paper we present the ∇-calculus, a calculus for defining general recursive functions over higher-order encodings. To avoid problems commonly associated with using the same function space for representations and computations, we separate one from the other. The simply-typed λ-calculus plays the role of the representation-level. The computation-level contains not only the usual computational primitives but also an embedding of the representation-level. It distinguishes itself from similar systems by allowing recursion under representation-level λ-binders while permitting a natural style of programming which we believe scales to other logical frameworks. Sample programs include bracket abstraction, parallel reduction, and an evaluator for a simple language with first-class continuations.

1 Introduction

Higher-order abstract syntax refers to the technique of using a meta-language, or logical framework, to encode an object language in such a way that variables of the object language are represented by the variables of the logical framework. This deceptively simple idea has far reaching consequences for the design of languages that aim to manipulate these encodings. On one hand, higher-order encodings are often very concise and elegant since they take advantage of common concepts and operations automatically provided by the logical framework, including variable renaming, capture avoiding substitutions, and hypothetical judgments. On the other hand, higher-order encodings are not inductive in the usual sense, which means that they are difficult to analyze and manipulate.

Many attempts have been made to integrate advanced encoding techniques into functional programming languages. FreshML [GP99] supports implicit variable renaming for first-order encodings. The modal λ-calculus supports primitive

* This research has been funded by NSF grants CCR-0325808 and CCR-0133502.

P. Urzyczyn (Ed.): TLCA 2005, LNCS 3461, pp. 339–353, 2005.

recursion over higher-order encodings via an iterator. However, function definition via iteration is naturally limited [SDP01].

In this paper, we present the ∇-calculus, a step towards integrating logical frameworks into functional programming. It supports *general* recursive functions over higher-order encodings without burdening the representational expressiveness of the logical framework. The ∇-calculus distinguishes itself from similar systems by allowing recursion under representation-level λ-binders while permitting a natural style of programming, which we believe scales to other logical frameworks.

To avoid problems commonly associated with using the same function space for representations and computations, we separate one from the other. The simply-typed λ-calculus plays the role of the representation-level and provides a function space enabling higher-order encodings. A second simply-typed language plays the role of the computation-level. It provides embeddings of the higher-order encodings, function definition by cases, and insurances for safe returns from computation under representation-level λ-binders.

The resulting system allows us, for example, to write computation-level functions that recurse over the usual higher-order encoding of the untyped λ-calculus (see Example 2). It is general enough to permit case analysis over any object of any representation-level type. In the accompanying Technical Report [SPS04] the reader may find a wide collection of examples, such as translation to de Bruijn indices, parallel reduction, and an evaluator for a simple language with first-class continuations. A prototype implementation [PS05] of the ∇-calculus, including a type-checker, an interactive runtime-system, and a collection of examples is available from the website `http://www.cs.yale.edu/~delphin`.

This paper is organized as follows. We explain the use of the simply-typed λ-calculus as a logical framework in Section 2. We introduce the ∇-calculus in Section 3. It is divided into several subsections describing the conventional features of the ∇-calculus and those constructs that facilitate programming with higher-order encodings. The static and operational semantics of the ∇-calculus are given in Section 4, while the meta-theoretic properties of the calculus are discussed and analyzed in Section 5. We assess results and discuss related and future work in Section 6.

2 The Simply-Typed Logical Framework

We choose the simply-typed λ-calculus as our logical framework, which is expressive enough to permit interesting higher-order encodings.

$$\begin{array}{lll}
\text{Types:} & A, B & ::= a \mid A \rightarrow B \\
\text{Objects:} & M, N & ::= x \mid c \mid \lambda x : A.\, M \mid M\ N \\
\text{Signatures:} & \Sigma & ::= \cdot \mid \Sigma, a : \mathit{type} \mid \Sigma, c : A \\
\text{Contexts:} & \Gamma & ::= \cdot \mid \Gamma, x : A
\end{array}$$

We use a for type constants, c for object constants, and x for variables. We assume that constants and variables are declared at most once in a signature and context, respectively. To maintain this invariant, we tacitly rename bound variables and use capture-avoiding substitutions. The typing judgments for objects and signatures are standard. Type-level and term-level constants must be declared in the signature.

Definition 1 (Typing Judgment). *$\Gamma \vdash_\Sigma M : A$ is defined by the following rules:*

$$\frac{\Gamma(x) = A}{\Gamma \vdash_\Sigma x : A}\,\mathsf{ofvar} \qquad \frac{\Sigma(c) = A}{\Gamma \vdash_\Sigma c : A}\,\mathsf{ofconst}$$

$$\frac{\Gamma, x : A \vdash_\Sigma M : B}{\Gamma \vdash_\Sigma \lambda x : A.\, M : A \to B}\,\mathsf{oflam} \qquad \frac{\Gamma \vdash_\Sigma M : A \to B \quad \Gamma \vdash_\Sigma N : A}{\Gamma \vdash_\Sigma M\, N : B}\,\mathsf{ofapp}$$

To avoid clutter we omit the subscript Σ when convenient. Our notion of definitional equality is obtained by taking the reflexive, transitive, and symmetric closure of β- and η-conversion [Coq91]. We write $\Gamma \vdash M \equiv N : A$ if and only if M is $\beta\eta$-equivalent to N and both have type A. For every well-typed object M of type A, there exists a unique β-normal, η-long term M' such that $\Gamma \vdash M \equiv M' : A$. We refer to M' as being canonical, which we denote as $\Gamma \vdash M' \Uparrow A$.

Throughout this paper, our examples will use encodings of natural numbers, first-order logic, and the untyped λ-calculus. An encoding consists of a signature and a representation function, which maps elements from our domain of discourse into canonical forms in our logical framework. We say that an encoding is *adequate* if the representation function is an isomorphism.

In all of the examples below, the signatures for our encoding are listed in italics and our translation functions $\ulcorner - \urcorner$ are defined by the given sets of equations. For example, natural numbers are represented by the type *nat* where $\ulcorner 0 \urcorner = z$ and $\ulcorner n+1 \urcorner = s\,\ulcorner n \urcorner$.

Example 1 (First-order logic with equality). Terms $t ::= x$ and first-order formulas $F ::= \forall x.\, F \mid F_1 \supset F_2 \mid \neg F \mid t_1 = t_2$ are represented as objects of type i and type o, respectively, in a signature that also includes the following declarations:

$$\begin{array}{rl} \ulcorner \forall x.\, F \urcorner = \mathit{forall}\ (\lambda x : i.\, \ulcorner F \urcorner) & \mathit{forall} : (i \to o) \to o \\ \ulcorner \neg F \urcorner = \mathit{neg}\, \ulcorner F \urcorner & \mathit{neg}\ \ : o \to o \\ \ulcorner F_1 \supset F_2 \urcorner = \mathit{impl}\, \ulcorner F_1 \urcorner \ulcorner F_2 \urcorner & \mathit{impl}\ : o \to o \to o \\ \ulcorner t_1 = t_2 \urcorner = \mathit{eq}\, \ulcorner t_1 \urcorner \ulcorner t_2 \urcorner & \mathit{eq}\ \ \ : i \to i \to o \\ \ulcorner x \urcorner = x & \end{array}$$

Example 2 (Untyped λ-expressions). Untyped λ-expressions $e ::= x \mid \mathbf{lam}\ x.\, e \mid e_1\, e_2$ are encoded as follows:

$$\begin{array}{rl} & \mathit{exp}\ : \mathit{type} \\ \ulcorner \mathbf{lam}\ x.\, e \urcorner = \mathit{lam}\ (\lambda x : \mathit{exp}.\, \ulcorner e \urcorner) & \mathit{lam} : (\mathit{exp} \to \mathit{exp}) \to \mathit{exp} \\ \ulcorner e_1\, e_2 \urcorner = \mathit{app}\, \ulcorner e_1 \urcorner \ulcorner e_2 \urcorner & \mathit{app} : \mathit{exp} \to \mathit{exp} \to \mathit{exp} \\ \ulcorner x \urcorner = x & \end{array}$$

The encodings of first-order formulas and untyped λ-expressions use functions to encode variable binders. Because little meaningful analysis can be done on variables in our logical framework, the only interesting operation that can be performed on a variable is substitution. Thus, it is most helpful to think of a term of type $A \to B$ not as representing a computation, but as representing a term of type B that has a hole of type A.

We demonstrate the formulation of an adequacy theorem. Each case can be proven by a straightforward induction.

Theorem 1 (Adequacy of *exp*). *Adequacy holds for our representation of untyped λ-expressions.*

1. *If e is an expression with free variables among $x_1, \dots, x_n$, then $x_1 : exp, \dots, x_n : exp \vdash \ulcorner e \urcorner \Uparrow exp$.*
2. *If $x_1 : exp, \dots, x_n : exp \vdash M \Uparrow exp$ then $M = \ulcorner e \urcorner$ for some expression e with free variables among $x_1, \dots, x_n$.*
3. *$\ulcorner - \urcorner$ is a bijection between expressions and canonical forms where $\ulcorner [e'/x]e \urcorner = [\ulcorner e' \urcorner / x] \ulcorner e \urcorner$.* □

3 The ∇-Calculus

The representation-level type *exp* is not inductive because the constructor *lam* : $(exp \to exp) \to exp$ has a negative occurrence [PM93] of *exp*. This property has far reaching consequences for the design of the ∇-calculus, which needs to provide a notion of computation general enough to handle higher-order datatypes of this kind. We offer the ability to recurse under λ-binders and consider cases over functions of type $exp \to exp$ while continuing to guarantee the adequacy of the encoding. Allowing for this, as well as general recursive computation, can be seen as the main contributions of this work.

In the ∇-calculus, computation-level functions can be defined by cases and alternations instead of explicit λ-binders. Computation-level expressions and types are summarized in Figure 1 and explained in the remainder of this section.

3.1 Function Definition by Cases and Recursion

In the ∇-calculus, we draw a separating line between the levels of representation and computation. Representation-level types such as *nat* and *exp* are *injected*

$$
\begin{array}{lrl}
\text{Types:} & \tau, \sigma ::= & \langle A \rangle \mid \tau \Rightarrow \sigma \mid \Box \tau \\
\text{Expressions:} & e, f ::= & u \mid \langle M \rangle \mid e_1 \mapsto_\tau e_2 \mid \epsilon x : A.\, e \mid \epsilon u \in \tau.\, e \\
 & & \mid e_1 \cdot e_2 \mid (e_1 \mid e_2) \mid \text{fix } u \in \tau.\, e \\
 & & \mid \nu x : A.\, e \mid \text{pop } e \mid \nabla x : A.\, e
\end{array}
$$

Fig. 1. Syntactic categories of the ∇-calculus

into computation-level types $\langle nat \rangle$ and $\langle exp \rangle$. Likewise, representation-level constants, such as $(s\ z)$ and $lam\ (\lambda x : exp.\, x)$, are injected into computation-level terms $\langle s\ z \rangle$ and $\langle lam\ (\lambda x : exp.\, x) \rangle$. There are no user defined datatypes on the computation-level; all type and constant declarations must be done at the representation-level.

Example 3 (Addition). We define the addition function *plus* and its representation in the ∇-calculus as follows:

$$\begin{array}{ll} plus\ z\ y \quad = y & \text{fix}\ plus \in \langle nat \rangle \Rightarrow \langle nat \rangle \Rightarrow \langle nat \rangle. \\ plus\ (s\ x)\ y = s\ (plus\ x\ y) & \quad \epsilon y : nat.\, \langle z \rangle \mapsto \langle y \rangle \mapsto \langle y \rangle \\ & \quad \mid\ \epsilon x : nat.\, \langle s\ x \rangle \mapsto \epsilon y : nat. \\ & \qquad\quad \langle y \rangle \mapsto \langle s \rangle \circ (plus \cdot \langle x \rangle \cdot \langle y \rangle) \end{array}$$ □

The recursion operator is conventional. In later examples we will omit it for the sake of readability. Alternation, "|", separates cases that may be chosen for evaluation. It binds more tightly than the recursion operator fix $u \in \tau.\, e$, but not as tightly as any of the other operators. Individual cases are of the form $e_1 \mapsto_\tau e_2$, where e_1 can be thought of as a guard. Only when such a case is applied to an object equivalent to e_1 (as defined in Section 4.2) is e_2 evaluated. In particular, if e_1 is a value of type $\langle A \rangle$, then our notion of equality is given by our logical framework's notion of definitional equality. We refer to e_1 as the *pattern* and e_2 as the *body* of the case. The index τ states the type of the pattern, but is usually omitted when the type of the pattern can be easily inferred. In conventional programming languages, variables that occur in patterns are implicitly declared, whereas in the ∇-calculus they must be declared explicitly by $\epsilon x : A.\, e$ for reasons explained in Section 3.2. A similar declaration for the computation-level $\epsilon u \in \tau.\, e$ permits higher-order functions and is discussed in detail in the accompanying Technical Report [SPS04]. Application in the ∇-calculus is written as $e_1 \cdot e_2$ in order to avoid confusion with representation-level application, which is expressed via juxtaposition. The notation $e_1 \circ e_2$ is syntactic sugar that lifts representation-level application to the computation-level.

$$e_1 \circ_{A,B} e_2 = (\epsilon x : A \to B.\, \langle x \rangle \mapsto_{\langle A \to B \rangle} \epsilon y : A.\, \langle y \rangle \mapsto_{\langle A \rangle} \langle x\ y \rangle) \cdot e_1 \cdot e_2$$

We refer to $\circ$ without type annotations because they are easily inferable.

3.2 Traversal of λ-Binders

Next, we explain the operators ν and pop from Figure 1. Recall the encoding of first-order logic from Example 1. As an example, we consider Kolmogorov's double-negation interpretation, which transforms formulas from classical logic into intuitionistic logic in the following way:

$$\begin{array}{ll} dneg\ (eq\ t_1\ t_2) & = neg\ (neg\ (eq\ t_1\ t_2)) \\ dneg\ (impl\ F_1\ F_2) & = neg\ (neg\ (impl\ (dneg\ F_1)\ (dneg\ F_2))) \\ dneg\ (neg\ F) & = neg\ (neg\ (neg\ (dneg\ F))) \\ dneg\ (forall\ F) & = neg\ (neg\ (forall\ F')) \\ & \quad \text{where } F'\ x = dneg\ (F\ x) \\ & \quad \text{for some new parameter } x : i \end{array}$$

In the last case *dneg* must recurse on the body F of the *forall* term, which is a representation-level function of type $i \to o$. Since F is definitionally equivalent to a canonical term that starts with a λ-binder, we strip away the λ-binder by applying F to some new parameter x before invoking *dneg*. The result of the computation depends on x and is hence written as $F'\ x$, where F' is a representation-level function of type $i \to o$.

The first three cases of *dneg* can be implemented in the ∇-calculus with constructs we have already introduced. As for the *forall* case, we need to add new constructs to our language. We feel that there are several interesting possibilities worth considering. One possibility would be to introduce a computation-level operator $\hat{\lambda}$, which lifts representation-level abstraction to the computation-level in much the same way that the syntactic-sugar $\circ$ lifts representation-level application. In this case, we could write the *forall* case as

$$\epsilon F : i \to o.\, \langle \mathit{forall}\ F \rangle \mapsto \langle \mathit{neg} \rangle \circ (\langle \mathit{neg} \rangle \circ (\langle \mathit{forall} \rangle \circ (\hat{\lambda} x : i.\, \mathit{dneg} \cdot \langle F\ x \rangle)))$$

where the subterm $(\hat{\lambda} x : i.\, \mathit{dneg} \cdot \langle F\ x \rangle)$ has type $\langle i \to o \rangle$. In principle this is a possible solution. Adequacy is preserved because although the body of $\hat{\lambda}$ may diverge or get stuck, any value it computes must be of the form $\langle M \rangle$. However, $\hat{\lambda}$ is too limited for our purposes because it always returns a representation-level function, even if the desired result is of a base type (see Example 4 below). Meta-ML [TS00] employs a construct similar to $\hat{\lambda}$.

Another possibility is to add an explicit parameter introduction operator $\bar{\nu}$

$$\begin{aligned} \epsilon F : i \to o.\, \langle \mathit{forall}\ F \rangle \mapsto\ & \bar{\nu} x : i. \\ & \text{case } \mathit{dneg} \cdot \langle F\ x \rangle \\ & \quad \text{of } \epsilon F' : i \to o.\, \langle F'\ x \rangle \mapsto \langle \mathit{neg}\ (\mathit{neg}\ (\mathit{forall}\ F')) \rangle \end{aligned}$$

where we write "case e_1 of e_2" as syntactic sugar for "$e_2 \cdot e_1$". In contrast to $\hat{\lambda}$, the type of the subterm starting with $\bar{\nu}$ is $\langle o \rangle$. Since the recursive call results in a value of type $\langle o \rangle$, and *forall* requires a value of type $i \to o$, we need a way to turn the result into a value of type $\langle i \to o \rangle$. Furthermore, because this value escapes x's declaration, it should not contain any free occurrences of x. Ideally, higher-order pattern matching would yield F', which is the result of abstracting all occurrences of x from the result of the recursive call. But there is no guarantee that this will succeed, because F' is declared within the scope of x. For example, if $\mathit{dneg} \cdot \langle F\ x \rangle$ returns $\langle \mathit{neg}(\mathit{neg}(\mathit{eq}\ x\ x)) \rangle$, then $F' = (\lambda y : i.\, \mathit{neg}(\mathit{neg}(\mathit{eq}\ x\ x)))$ and $F' = (\lambda y : i.\, \mathit{neg}(\mathit{neg}(\mathit{eq}\ y\ y)))$ are among the possible solutions to this matching problem. To remedy this, F' can be declared outside of the scope of x, and thus could not possibly be instantiated with a term containing x:

$$\begin{aligned} \epsilon F : i \to o.\, \langle \mathit{forall}\ F \rangle \mapsto\ & \epsilon F' : i \to o. \\ & \bar{\nu} x : i. \text{case } \mathit{dneg} \cdot \langle F\ x \rangle \text{ of } \langle F'\ x \rangle \mapsto \langle \mathit{neg}\ (\mathit{neg}\ (\mathit{forall}\ F')) \rangle \end{aligned}$$

In this case, the only solution is $F' = (\lambda y : i.\, \mathit{neg}(\mathit{neg}(\mathit{eq}\ y\ y)))$, which illustrates the necessity of explicit ϵ-declarations. However, we do not include $\bar{\nu}$ in the ∇-calculus since, as we have seen, it allows us to write functions that let parameters escape their scope.

Instead, we do include two operators and one new type constructor that can be found in Figure 1. The operator ν is similar to $\bar{\nu}$ in that it introduces new parameters, but different because it statically requires that these parameters cannot extrude their scope. The operator "pop" provides such guarantees. These guarantees are communicated through the type $\Box\tau$, which pop introduces and ν eliminates. The complete function *dneg* is given below.

$$
\begin{aligned}
dneg\ :\ & \langle o \rangle \Rightarrow \langle o \rangle \\
= & \ \epsilon t_1 : i.\, \epsilon t_2 : i.\, \langle eq\ t_1\ t_2 \rangle \mapsto \langle neg\ (neg\ (eq\ t_1\ t_2)) \rangle \\
| & \ \epsilon F_1 : o.\, \epsilon F_2 : o. \\
& \quad \langle imp\ F_1\ F_2 \rangle \mapsto \langle neg \rangle \circ (\langle neg \rangle \circ (\langle imp \rangle \circ (dneg \cdot \langle F_1 \rangle) \circ (dneg \cdot \langle F_2 \rangle))) \\
| & \ \epsilon F : o.\, \langle neg\ F \rangle \mapsto \langle neg \rangle \circ (\langle neg \rangle \circ (\langle neg \rangle \circ (dneg \cdot \langle F \rangle))) \\
| & \ \epsilon F : i \to o.\, \langle forall\ F \rangle \mapsto \epsilon F' : i \to o. \\
& \quad \nu x : i.\, \text{case}\ dneg \cdot \langle F\ x \rangle\ \text{of}\ \langle F'\ x \rangle \mapsto \text{pop}\ \langle neg\ (neg\ (forall\ F')) \rangle
\end{aligned}
$$

The body of the ν is of type $\Box\langle o \rangle$; the $\Box$ ensures that whatever value this expression evaluates to does not contain x. The body of pop has type $\langle o \rangle$ because it neither contains x nor any ϵ-quantified variable that may depend on x. Thus, the subexpression "pop $\langle forall\ F' \rangle$" introduces type $\Box\langle o \rangle$. A precise type theoretic definition and analysis of the $\Box$ type will be given in Section 4.

3.3 Pattern-Matching Parameters

Finally, we turn to the last unexplained operator from Figure 1, the ∇-operator, which is used to match parameters introduced by ν.

Example 4 (Counting variable occurrences). Consider a function that counts the number of occurrences of bound variables in an untyped λ-expression from Example 2.

$$
\begin{aligned}
cntvar\ (x) &= (s\ z)\ \text{where}\ x : exp\ \text{is a parameter} \\
cntvar\ (app\ e_1\ e_2) &= plus\ (cntvar\ e_1)\ (cntvar\ e_2) \\
cntvar\ (lam\ e) &= cntvar\ (e\ x)\ \text{for some new parameter}\ x : exp
\end{aligned}
$$

The first of the three cases corresponds to the parameter case that matches *any* parameter of type *exp* regardless of where and when it was introduced. Formally, we use the ∇-operator to implement this case.

$$
\begin{aligned}
cntvar\ :\ & \langle exp \rangle \Rightarrow \langle nat \rangle \\
= & \ \nabla x : exp.\, \langle x \rangle \mapsto \langle s\ z \rangle \\
| & \ \epsilon e_1 : exp.\, \epsilon e_2 : exp. \\
& \quad \langle app\ e_1\ e_2 \rangle \mapsto plus \cdot (cntvar \cdot \langle e_1 \rangle) \cdot (cntvar \cdot \langle e_2 \rangle) \\
| & \ \epsilon e : exp \to exp.\, \langle lam\ e \rangle \mapsto \epsilon n : nat. \\
& \quad \nu x : exp.\, (\langle n \rangle \mapsto \text{pop}\ \langle n \rangle) \cdot (cntvar \cdot \langle e\ x \rangle)
\end{aligned}
$$

□

Notice that, in the above example, if we were to replace the ∇ with ϵ, it would still be possible for *cntvar* to return correct answers, since $\epsilon x : exp$ can match any expression of type *exp* including parameters; however, it would also be possible for *cntvar* to always return $\langle s\ z \rangle$ for the same reason.

Example 5 (Combinators). The combinators $c ::= \mathbf{S} \mid \mathbf{K} \mid \mathbf{MP}\ c_1\ c_2$ are represented as objects of type *comb* as follows:

$$\begin{array}{rlrl} \ulcorner\mathbf{K}\urcorner &= K & K &: comb \\ \ulcorner\mathbf{S}\urcorner &= S & S &: comb \\ \ulcorner\mathbf{MP}\ c_1\ c_2\urcorner &= MP\ \ulcorner c_1\urcorner\ulcorner c_2\urcorner & MP &: comb \rightarrow comb \rightarrow comb \end{array}$$

Any simply-typed λ-expression from Example 2 can be converted into a combinator in a two-step algorithm. The first step is called bracket abstraction, or *ba*, which converts a parametric combinator (a representation-level function of type $comb \rightarrow comb$) into a combinator with one less parameter (of type *comb*). If M has type $comb \rightarrow comb$ and N has type *comb* then $\langle MP\rangle \circ (ba \cdot \langle M\rangle) \circ \langle N\rangle$ results in a term that is equivalent to $\langle MN\rangle$ in combinator logic.

$$\begin{array}{l} ba\ (\lambda x : comb.\, x) = MP\ (MP\ S\ K)\ K \\ ba\ (\lambda x : comb.\, z) = MP\ K\ z \text{ where } z : comb \text{ is a parameter} \\ ba\ (\lambda x : comb.\, K) = MP\ K\ K \\ ba\ (\lambda x : comb.\, S) = MP\ K\ S \\ ba\ (\lambda x : comb.\, MP\ (c_1\ x)\ (c_2\ x)) = MP\ (MP\ S\ (ba\ c_1))\ (ba\ c_2) \end{array}$$

Formally ba is implemented as follows:

$$\begin{array}{l} ba\ :\ \langle comb \rightarrow comb\rangle \Rightarrow \langle comb\rangle \\ \quad = \langle \lambda x : comb.\, x\rangle \mapsto \langle MP\ (MP\ S\ K)\ K\rangle \\ \quad\ \mid \nabla z : comb.\, \langle \lambda x : comb.\, z\rangle \mapsto \langle MP\ K\ z\rangle \\ \quad\ \mid \langle \lambda x : comb.\, K\rangle \mapsto \langle MP\ K\ K\rangle \\ \quad\ \mid \langle \lambda x : comb.\, S\rangle \mapsto \langle MP\ K\ S\rangle \\ \quad\ \mid \epsilon c_1 : comb \rightarrow comb.\, \epsilon c_2 : comb \rightarrow comb. \\ \qquad \langle \lambda x : comb.\, MP\ (c_1\ x)\ (c_2\ x)\rangle \mapsto \\ \qquad\quad \langle MP\rangle \circ (\langle MP\rangle \circ \langle S\rangle \circ (ba \cdot \langle c_1\rangle)) \circ (ba \cdot \langle c_2\rangle) \end{array}$$

The first two cases of *ba* illustrate how to distinguish x, which is to be abstracted, from parameters that are introduced in the function *convert*, which we discuss next. The function *convert* traverses λ-expressions and uses *ba* to convert them into combinators.

$$\begin{array}{l} convert\ (y\ z) = z \text{ where } y : comb \rightarrow exp \text{ and } z : comb \text{ are parameters} \\ convert\ (app\ e_1\ e_2) = MP\ (convert\ e_1)\ (convert\ e_2) \\ convert\ (lam\ e) = ba\ c \text{ where } c\ z = convert\ (e\ (y\ z)) \\ \qquad\qquad\qquad\qquad\quad \text{and } y : comb \rightarrow exp \\ \qquad\qquad\qquad\qquad\quad \text{and } z : comb \text{ are parameters} \end{array}$$

The last case illustrates how a parameter of functional type may introduce information to be used when the parameter is matched. Rather than introduce a parameter x of type *exp*, we introduce a parameter of type $comb \rightarrow exp$ that carries a combinator as "payload." In our example, the payload is another parameter $z : comb$, the image of x under *convert*. This technique is applicable to a wide range of examples (see the Technical Report [SPS04] for details). We formalize *convert* below:

$$\begin{aligned}
convert\ :\ & \langle exp\rangle \Rightarrow \langle comb\rangle \\
= & \nabla y : comb \to exp.\, \nabla z : comb.\, \langle y\ z\rangle \mapsto \langle z\rangle \\
& \mid \epsilon e_1 : exp.\, \epsilon e_2 : exp. \\
& \quad \langle app\ e_1\ e_2\rangle \mapsto \langle MP\rangle \circ (convert \cdot \langle e_1\rangle) \circ (convert \cdot \langle e_2\rangle) \\
& \mid \epsilon e : exp \to exp.\, \langle lam\ e\rangle \mapsto \epsilon c : comb \to comb. \\
& \quad \nu y : comb \to exp.\, \nu z : comb. \\
& \quad\quad \text{case } convert \cdot \langle e\ (y\ z)\rangle \text{ of } \langle c\ z\rangle \mapsto \text{pop}\ (\text{pop}\ (ba \cdot \langle c\rangle)) \qquad \square
\end{aligned}$$

We summarize a few of the most important properties of the ∇-operator. First, it is intuitively appealing to have one base case (the ∇-case) for each class of parameters, because what happens in these cases is uniquely defined in one place. Second, payload carrying parameters permit sophisticated base cases, which simplify the reading of a program because all information shared between the introduction and matching of parameters must be made explicit.

4 Semantics

The operators ν and pop have guided the design of the static and operational semantics of the ∇-calculus. To reiterate, once a parameter is introduced by a ν, all other declarations that take place within its scope may depend on the new parameter. As we will see, pop statically ensures that an expression is valid outside ν's scope by discarding all declarations since the last parameter introduction in a manner reminiscent of popping elements off a stack. The ambient environment is therefore formally captured in form of *scope stacks*. A scope consists of two parts: The context Γ (defined in Section 2), which summarizes all object-level declarations $x : A$, and the context Φ, which summarizes all meta-level declarations $u \in \tau$.

$$\text{Meta Contexts: } \Phi ::= \cdot \mid \Phi, u \in \tau$$

$$\text{Scope Stacks: } \Omega ::= \cdot \mid \Omega, (\Gamma; \Phi)$$

We refer to the top and second-from-top elements of Ω as the *current* and *previous* scopes, respectively. The scope stack Ω grows monotonically, which means that the current scope always extends the previous scope.

4.1 Static Semantics

We define the typing judgment $\Omega \vdash e \in \tau$ by the rules depicted in Figure 2. Many of the rules are self-explanatory. All rules except for tpnew and tppop touch only the current scope. For example, tpvar relates variables and types, whereas tpinj enforces that only representation-level objects valid in the current scope can be lifted to the computation-level. For functions, tpfun indicates that the pattern must be of the argument type, whereas the body must be of the result type. Variables that may occur in patterns must be declared by a preceding $\epsilon x : A$,

$$\frac{\Phi(u) = \tau}{\Omega, (\Gamma; \Phi) \vdash u \in \tau}\,\mathsf{tpvar} \qquad \frac{\Gamma \vdash M : A}{\Omega, (\Gamma; \Phi) \vdash \langle M \rangle \in \langle A \rangle}\,\mathsf{tpinj}$$

$$\frac{\Omega \vdash e_1 \in \tau \quad \Omega \vdash e_2 \in \sigma}{\Omega \vdash e_1 \mapsto_\tau e_2 \in \tau \Rightarrow \sigma}\,\mathsf{tpfun} \qquad \frac{\Omega, (\Gamma; \Phi, u \in \tau) \vdash e \in \tau}{\Omega, (\Gamma; \Phi) \vdash \text{fix } u \in \tau.\, e \in \tau}\,\mathsf{tpfix}$$

$$\frac{\Omega, (\Gamma, x : A; \Phi) \vdash e \in \tau}{\Omega, (\Gamma; \Phi) \vdash \epsilon x : A.\, e \in \tau}\,\mathsf{tptheobj} \qquad \frac{\Omega, (\Gamma; \Phi, u \in \tau) \vdash e \in \tau}{\Omega, (\Gamma; \Phi) \vdash \epsilon u \in \tau.\, e \in \tau}\,\mathsf{tpthemeta}$$

$$\frac{\Omega \vdash e_1 \in \sigma \Rightarrow \tau \quad \Omega \vdash e_2 \in \sigma}{\Omega \vdash e_1 \cdot e_2 \in \tau}\,\mathsf{tpapp} \qquad \frac{\Omega \vdash e_1 \in \tau \quad \Omega \vdash e_2 \in \tau}{\Omega \vdash (e_1 \mid e_2) \in \tau}\,\mathsf{tpalt}$$

$$\frac{\Omega \vdash e \in \tau}{\Omega, (\Gamma; \Phi) \vdash \text{pop } e \in \Box\tau}\,\mathsf{tppop} \qquad \frac{\Omega, (\Gamma; \Phi), (\Gamma, x : A; \Phi) \vdash e \in \Box\tau}{\Omega, (\Gamma; \Phi) \vdash \nu x : A.\, e \in \tau}\,\mathsf{tpnew}$$

$$\frac{\Omega, (\Gamma, x : A; \Phi) \vdash e \in \tau}{\Omega, (\Gamma; \Phi) \vdash \nabla x : A.\, e \in \tau}\,\mathsf{tpnabla}$$

Fig. 2. The static semantics of the ∇-calculus

$\epsilon u \in \tau$, or $\nabla x : A$ declaration, which will be recorded in the current scope by tptheobj, tpthemeta, and tpnabla respectively. The rules tpapp, tpalt, and tpfix are standard. The tppop rule is the introduction rule for $\Box\tau$. The expression pop e is valid if e is valid in the previous scope. The corresponding elimination rule is tpnew. The expression $\nu x : A.\, e$ has type τ when e is of type $\Box\tau$ in the properly extended scope stack.

4.2 Operational Semantics

Computation level function application in the ∇-calculus is more demanding than the usual substitution of an argument for a free variable. It relies on the proper instantiation of all ϵ- and ∇-bound variables that occur in the function's pattern. Perhaps not surprisingly, the behavior of our calculus depends on when these instantiations are committed. For example,

$$(\epsilon f \in \langle nat \rangle \Rightarrow \langle nat \rangle.\, f \mapsto plus \cdot (f \cdot \langle z \rangle) \cdot (f \cdot \langle s z \rangle)) \cdot (\epsilon n : nat.\, \langle n \rangle \mapsto \langle n \rangle)$$

may either return $s\ z$ under a call-by-name semantics, or no solution at all under a call-by-value semantics because $n : nat$ may be instantiated either by z or $s\ z$ but not both. Consequently, our calculus adopts a call-by-name evaluation strategy. We can define computational-level λ-abstraction "lambda $u \in \tau.\, e$" as syntactic sugar for $(\epsilon u \in \tau.\, u \mapsto e)$ and "let $u \in \tau = e_1$ in e_2 end" as syntactic sugar for $((\epsilon u \in \tau.\, u \mapsto e_2)\ e_1)$.

Definition 2 (Values). *The set of values of the ∇-calculus is defined as follows.*

$$\textit{Values: } v ::= \langle M \rangle \mid \text{pop } e \mid e_1 \mapsto_\tau e_2$$

$$\frac{\Omega \vdash e_1 \equiv e_1' \in \tau}{\Omega \vdash (e_1 \mapsto_\tau e_2) \cdot e_1' \to e_2}\ \mathsf{redbeta} \qquad \frac{}{\Omega \vdash \nu x : A.\, \mathrm{pop}\ e \to e}\ \mathsf{rednupop}$$

$$\frac{}{\Omega \vdash (e_1 \mid e_2) \to e_1}\ \mathsf{redalt}_1 \qquad \frac{}{\Omega \vdash (e_1 \mid e_2) \to e_2}\ \mathsf{redalt}_2$$

$$\frac{\Gamma \vdash M : A}{\Omega, (\Gamma; \cdot) \vdash \epsilon x : A.\, e \to [M/x]e}\ \mathsf{redsome} \qquad \frac{\Omega \vdash f \in \tau}{\Omega \vdash \epsilon u \in \tau.\, e \to [f/u]e}\ \mathsf{redsomeM}$$

$$\frac{\Gamma(y) = A}{\Omega, (\Gamma; \cdot) \vdash \nabla x : A.\, e \to [y/x]e}\ \mathsf{rednabla} \qquad \frac{}{\Omega \vdash \mathrm{fix}\ u \in \tau.\, e \to [\mathrm{fix}\ u \in \tau.\, e/u]e}\ \mathsf{redfix}$$

$$\frac{\Omega \vdash e_1 \to e_1'}{\Omega \vdash e_1 \cdot e_2 \to e_1' \cdot e_2}\ \mathsf{redfun} \qquad \frac{\Omega, (\Gamma; \cdot), (\Gamma, x : A; \cdot) \vdash e \to e'}{\Omega, (\Gamma; \cdot) \vdash \nu x : A.\, e \to \nu x : A.\, e'}\ \mathsf{rednew}$$

Fig. 3. Small-step semantics (Reductions)

$$\frac{\Gamma \vdash M \equiv N : A}{\Omega, (\Gamma; \cdot) \vdash \langle M \rangle \equiv \langle N \rangle \in \langle A \rangle}\ \mathsf{eqinjV} \qquad \frac{\Omega \vdash e_1 \equiv e_2 \in \tau}{\Omega, (\Gamma; \cdot) \vdash \mathrm{pop}\ e_1 \equiv \mathrm{pop}\ e_2 \in \Box\tau}\ \mathsf{eqpopV}$$

$$\frac{\Omega \vdash e_1 \to^* e_1' \quad \Omega \vdash e_2 \to^* e_2' \quad \Omega \vdash e_1' \equiv e_2' \in \tau}{\Omega \vdash e_1 \equiv e_2 \in \tau}\ \mathsf{eqR}\ \text{ where } \tau = \langle A \rangle \text{ or } \Box\tau'$$

$$\frac{}{\Omega \vdash e \equiv e \in \tau_1 \Rightarrow \tau_2}\ \mathsf{eqfun}$$

Fig. 4. Small-step semantics (Equality)

The operational semantics of the ∇-calculus combines a system of reduction rules of the form $\Omega \vdash e \to e'$ with an equivalence relation on meta-level expressions $\Omega \vdash e \equiv e' \in \tau$. We give the reduction rules in Figure 3 where we write $\to^*$ for the reflexive, transitive closure of $\to$. The equality rules are depicted in Figure 4. During runtime, all ϵ-quantified variables are instantiated with concrete objects, so evaluation always takes place in a scope stack of the form $\Omega ::= \cdot \mid \Omega, (\Gamma; \cdot)$, where Γ contains only ν-quantified parameter declarations.

The rules in Figure 3 are organized into three parts. The top part shows the essential reduction rules redbeta and rednupop. The rule rednupop states that it is unnecessary to traverse into a new scope to return an expression that is valid in the previous scope.

Among the second block of rules, redalt_1 and redalt_2 express a nondeterministic choice in the control flow. Similarly, redsome and redsomeM express a nondeterministic choice of instantiations. The abbreviations f/u and M/x stand for single-point substitutions that can easily be expanded into simultaneous substitutions given in Definition 3. During evaluation, the current scope only contains parameters introduced by ν, and thus rednabla expresses a nondeterministic choice of parameters. Finally, redfix implements the unrolling of the recursion operator.

The bottom two rules are necessary to give us a congruence closure for reductions on ∇-expressions. Because the ∇-calculus is call-by-name, we do not evaluate e_2 in the rule redfun. Finally, rednew reduces under the ν after appropriately copying and extending the current scope.

Our notion of equivalence is type-directed. For functions, this is decided only by syntactic equality, as shown by rule eqfun in Figure 4. For all other types, we give two rules: the rule ending in V refers to the case where the left and right hand side are already values, while the rule ending in R is used when further reduction steps are required on either side.

5 Meta Theory

We study the meta-theory of the ∇-calculus culminating in the type-preservation theorem, which entails that parameters cannot escape their scope.

Substituting for ϵ and ∇-bound variables is essential for defining the operational meaning of our expressions. In this section we elaborate on object-level and meta-level substitutions, as well as substitution stacks, which are defined on scope stacks. As is standard, we make our substitutions capture avoiding by tacitly renaming variable names.

Definition 3 (Substitutions).

$$\begin{array}{ll} \textit{Object-Level Substitutions:} & \gamma ::= \cdot \mid \gamma, M/x \\ \textit{Meta-Level Substitutions:} & \varphi ::= \cdot \mid \varphi, f/u \\ \textit{Substitution Stacks:} & \omega ::= \cdot \mid \omega, (\gamma; \varphi) \end{array}$$

We define the meaning of the three typing judgments for substitutions $\Gamma \vdash \gamma : \Gamma'$, $\Omega \vdash \phi : \Phi$, and $\Omega \vdash \omega \in \Omega'$ in Figure 5. The domains of the substitutions are Γ', Φ, and Ω', respectively, and the codomains of the substitutions are Γ, Ω, and Ω, respectively. The definition of substitution application is given in Figure 6.

We write $\Gamma < \Gamma'$ if Γ' strictly extends Γ, and $\Phi \leq \Phi'$, if $\Phi = \Phi'$ or $\Phi < \Phi'$.

Definition 4 (Well-Formed Context Stacks). *We say that a context stack Ω is well-formed if the proposition $\vdash \Omega$ ok can be proved using the following rules of inference*

$$\frac{}{\vdash \cdot \ \mathsf{ok}}\ \mathsf{okempty} \qquad \frac{}{\vdash \cdot, (\Gamma; \Phi)\ \mathsf{ok}}\ \mathsf{okinit} \qquad \frac{\vdash \Omega, (\Gamma; \Phi)\ \mathsf{ok} \quad \Gamma < \Gamma' \quad \Phi \leq \Phi'}{\vdash \Omega, (\Gamma; \Phi), (\Gamma'; \Phi')\ \mathsf{ok}}\ \mathsf{oknew}$$

The following substitution lemma is the key lemma for proving type preservation.

Lemma 1 (Substitution). *If $\Omega \vdash e \in \tau$, Ω ok, Ω' ok and $\Omega' \vdash \omega \in \Omega$ then $\Omega' \vdash [\omega]e \in \tau$.*

$$\frac{}{\Gamma \vdash \cdot : \cdot}\ \mathsf{tpEObjS} \qquad \frac{\Gamma \vdash M : A \quad \Gamma \vdash \gamma : \Gamma'}{\Gamma \vdash (\gamma, M/x) : (\Gamma', x : A)}\ \mathsf{tpIObS}$$

$$\frac{}{\Omega \vdash \cdot : \cdot}\ \mathsf{tpEMetaS} \qquad \frac{\Omega \vdash f \in \tau \quad \Omega \vdash \varphi : \Phi}{\Omega \vdash (\varphi, f/u) : (\Phi, u \in \tau)}\ \mathsf{tpIMetaS}$$

$$\frac{}{\Omega \vdash \cdot : \cdot}\ \mathsf{tpEStackS} \qquad \frac{\Gamma \vdash \gamma : \Gamma' \quad \Omega, (\Gamma; \Phi) \vdash \varphi : \Phi' \quad \Omega \vdash \omega : \Omega'}{\Omega, (\Gamma; \Phi) \vdash \omega, (\gamma; \varphi) : \Omega', (\Gamma', \Phi')}\ \mathsf{tpIStackS}$$

Fig. 5. The static semantics of substitutions

$$\begin{aligned}
[\gamma, M/x]x &= M \\
[\gamma, M/x]y &= [\gamma]y \\
[\gamma]c &= c \\
[\gamma](N_1\ N_2) &= ([\gamma]N_1)\ ([\gamma]N_2) \\
[\gamma](\lambda x : A.\, N) &= \lambda x : A.\, [\gamma, x/x]N
\end{aligned}$$

$$\begin{aligned}
[\varphi, e/u]u &= e \\
[\varphi, e/u]v &= [\varphi]v
\end{aligned}$$

$$\begin{aligned}
[\omega, (\gamma; \varphi)]u &= [\varphi]u \\
[\omega, (\gamma; \varphi)]\langle N \rangle &= \langle [\gamma]N \rangle \\
[\omega, (\gamma; \varphi)](\text{pop } e) &= \text{pop } [\omega]e \\
[\omega](e_1 \mapsto_\tau e_2) &= ([\omega]e_1) \mapsto_\tau ([\omega]e_2) \\
[\omega](e_1 \cdot e_2) &= ([\omega]e_1) \cdot ([\omega]e_2) \\
[\omega](e_1 \mid e_2) &= ([\omega]e_1 \mid [\omega]e_2) \\
[\omega, (\gamma; \varphi)](\text{fix } u \in \tau.\, e) &= \text{fix } u \in \tau.\, [\omega, (\gamma; \varphi, u/u)]e \\
[\omega, (\gamma; \varphi)](\epsilon x : A.\, e) &= \epsilon x : A.\, [\omega, (\gamma, x/x; \varphi)]e \\
[\omega, (\gamma; \varphi)](\epsilon u \in \tau.\, e) &= \epsilon u \in \tau.\, [\omega, (\gamma; \varphi, u/u)]e \\
[\omega, (\gamma; \varphi)](\nabla x : A.\, e) &= \nabla x : A.\, [\omega, (\gamma, x/x; \varphi)]e \\
[\omega, (\gamma; \varphi)](\nu x : A.\, e) &= \nu x : A.\, [\omega, (\gamma; \varphi), (\gamma, x/x; \varphi)]e
\end{aligned}$$

Fig. 6. Substitution Application

Proof. By induction on the structure of $\Omega \vdash e \in \tau$. See the Technical Report [SPS04] for details.

We are now ready to prove the type preservation theorem.

Theorem 2 (Type Preservation). *If* $\vdash \Omega$ ok *and* $\Omega \vdash e \in \tau$ *and* $\Omega \vdash e \rightarrow e'$ *then* $\Omega \vdash e' \in \tau$.

Proof. By induction on the structure of $\Omega \vdash e \rightarrow e'$. See the Technical Report [SPS04] for details.

As a corollary we obtain the property that parameters cannot escape their scope.

Corollary 1 (Scope Preservation). *If* $\vdash \Omega, (\Gamma; \cdot)$ ok *and* $\Omega, (\Gamma; \cdot) \vdash e \in \Box\tau$ *and* $\Omega, (\Gamma; \cdot) \vdash e \rightarrow^* v$ *and* v *is a value then* $v = \text{pop } e'$ *and* $\Omega \vdash e' \in \tau$.

In future work, we will investigate further meta-theoretical properties of the ∇-calculus, such as progress and termination. Neither of these two properties is satisfied without additional side conditions on the typing rules.

6 Conclusion

In this paper we have presented the ∇-calculus. We allow for evaluation under λ-binders, pattern matching against parameters, and programming with higher-order encodings. The ∇-calculus has been implemented as a stand-alone programming language, called ELPHIN [PS05]. The ∇-calculus solves many problems associated with programming with higher-order abstract syntax. We allow for, and can usefully manipulate, datatype declarations whose constructor types make reference to themselves in negative positions while maintaining a closed description of the functions. Many examples, such as parallel reduction and an evaluator for a simple language with first-class continuations can be found in the Technical Report [SPS04].

The ∇-calculus is the result of many years of design, originally inspired by an extension to ML proposed by Dale Miller [Mil90], the type theory $\mathcal{T}_\omega^+$ [Sch01], and Hofmann's work on higher-order abstract syntax [Hof99]. A predecessor to this work is the modal λ-calculus with iterators [SDP01], which separates representation-level from computation-level functions via a modality within one single λ-calculus. We conjecture that any function written in the modal λ-calculus with iterators can also be expressed in the ∇-calculus, the reverse, of course, does not hold.

Closely related to our work are programming languages with freshness [GP99], which provide a built-in α-equivalence relation for first-order encodings but provide neither $\beta\eta$ nor any support for higher-order encodings. Also closely related to the ∇-calculus are meta-programming languages, such as MetaML [TS00], which provide hierarchies of computation levels, but do not single out a particular level for representation. Many other attempts have been made to combine higher-order encodings and functional programming, in particular Honsell, Miculan, and Scagnetto's embedding of the π-calculus in Coq[HMS01], and Momigliano, Amber, and Crole's Hybrid system [MAC03].

In future work, we plan to extend the ∇-calculus to a dependently-typed logical framework, add polymorphism to the computation-level, and study termination and progression.

Acknowledgments. We would like to thank Henrik Nilsson, Simon Peyton-Jones, and Valery Trifonov, and Hai Fang for comments on earlier drafts of this paper.

References

[Coq91] Thierry Coquand. An algorithm for testing conversion in type theory. In Gérard Huet and Gordon Plotkin, editors, *Logical Frameworks*, pages 255–279. Cambridge University Press, 1991.

[GP99] Murdoch Gabbay and Andrew Pitts. A new approach to abstract syntax involving binders. In G. Longo, editor, *Proceedings of the 14th Annual Symposium on Logic in Computer Science (LICS'99)*, pages 214–224, Trento, Italy, July 1999. IEEE Computer Society Press.

[HMS01] Furio Honsell, Marino Miculan, and Ivan Scagnetto. π-calculus in (Co)inductive-type theory. *Theoretical Computer Science*, 253(2):239–285, 2001.

[Hof99] Martin Hofmann. Semantical analysis for higher-order abstract syntax. In G. Longo, editor, *Proceedings of the 14th Annual Symposium on Logic in Computer Science (LICS'99)*, pages 204–213, Trento, Italy, July 1999. IEEE Computer Society Press.

[MAC03] Alberto Momigliano, Simon Ambler, and Roy Crole. A definitional approach to primitive recursion over higher order abstract syntax. In Alberto Momigliano and Marino Miculan, editors, *Proceedings of the Merlin Workshop*, Uppsala, Sweden, June 2003. ACM Press.

[Mil90] Dale Miller. An extension to ML to handle bound variables in data structures: Preliminary report. In *Proceedings of the Logical Frameworks BRA Workshop*, Nice, France, May 1990.

[PM93] Christine Paulin-Mohring. Inductive definitions in the system Coq: Rules and properties. In M. Bezem and J.F. Groote, editors, *Proceedings of the International Conference on Typed Lambda Calculi and Applications*, pages 328–345, Utrecht, The Netherlands, March 1993. Springer-Verlag LNCS 664.

[PS05] Adam Poswolsky and Carsten Schürmann. Elphin user's manual. Technical report, Yale University, 2005. To appear. See also `http://www.cs.yale.edu/~delphin`.

[Sch01] Carsten Schürmann. Recursion for higher-order encodings. In Laurent Fribourg, editor, *Proceedings of the Conference on Computer Science Logic (CSL 2001)*, pages 585–599, Paris, France, August 2001. Springer Verlag LNCS 2142.

[SDP01] Carsten Schürmann, Joëlle Despeyroux, and Frank Pfenning. Primitive recursion for higher-order abstract syntax. *Theoretical Computer Science*, (266):1–57, 2001.

[SPS04] Carsten Schürmann, Adam Poswolsky, and Jeffrey Sarnat. The ∇-calculus. Functional programming with higher-order encodings. Technical Report YALEU/DCS/TR-1272, Yale University, October 2004.

[TS00] Walid Taha and Tim Sheard. MetaML: Multi-stage programming with explicit annotations. *Theoretical Computer Science*, 248(1-2), 2000.

A Lambda Calculus for Quantum Computation with Classical Control

Peter Selinger and Benoît Valiron

Department of Mathematics and Statistics,
University of Ottawa,
Ottawa, Ontario K1N 6N5, Canada
tucosidzia i jeszaca

Abstract. The objective of this paper is to develop a functional programming language for quantum computers. We develop a lambda calculus for the classical control model, following the first author's work on quantum flow-charts. We define a call-by-value operational semantics, and we give a type system using affine intuitionistic linear logic. The main results of this paper are the safety properties of the language and the development of a type inference algorithm.

1 Introduction

The objective of this paper is to develop a functional programming language for quantum computers. Quantum computing is a theory of computation based on the laws of quantum physics, rather than of classical physics. Quantum computing has become a fast growing research area in recent years. For a good introduction, see e.g. [9, 10].

Due to the laws of quantum physics, there are only two kinds of basic operations that one can perform on a quantum state, namely *unitary transformations* and *measurements*. Many existing formalisms for quantum computation put an emphasis on the former, i.e., a computation is understood as the evolution of a quantum state by means of unitary gates. Measurements are usually performed at the end of the computation, and outside of the formalism. In these models, a quantum computer is considered as a purely quantum system, i.e., without any classical parts. One example of such a model is the quantum Turing machine [3, 6], where the entire machine state, including the tape, the finite control, and the position of the head, is assumed to be in quantum superposition. Another example is the quantum lambda calculus of van Tonder [14, 15], which is a higher-order, purely quantum language without an explicit measurement operation.

On the other hand, one might imagine a model of a quantum computer where unitary operations and measurements can be interleaved. One example is the so-called *QRAM model* of Knill [8], which is also described by Bettelli, Calarco and Serafini [4]. Here, a quantum computer consists of a classical computer connected to a quantum device. In this configuration, the operation of the machine is controlled by a classical program which emits a sequence of instructions to the quantum device for performing measurements and unitary operations. In such a model, the control structures of the machine are classical, and only the data being operated upon is quantum. This situation is summarized by the slogan "quantum data, classical control" [12]. Several programming languages have been proposed to deal with such a model [4, 11]. The present paper is based on the work of [12].

P. Urzyczyn (Ed.): TLCA 2005, LNCS 3461, pp. 354–368, 2005.

In this paper, we propose a *higher-order* quantum programming language, i.e., one in which functions can be considered as data. A program is a lambda term, possibly with some quantum data embedded inside. The basic idea is that lambda terms encode the control structure of a program, and thus, they would be implemented classically, i.e., on the classical device of the QRAM machine. However, the data on which the lambda terms act is possibly quantum, and is stored on the QRAM quantum device.

Because our language combines classical and quantum features, it is natural to consider two distinct basic data types: a type of *classical bits* and a type of *quantum bits.* They behave very differently. For instance, a classical bit can be copied as many times as needed. On the other hand, a quantum bit cannot be duplicated, due to the well-known *no cloning property* of quantum states [9, 10]. However, quantum data types are very powerful, due to the phenomena of quantum superposition and entanglement.

The semantics described in this paper is operational; a program is an abstract machine with reductions rules. The reduction rules are probabilistic.

Some care is needed when defining a type system for higher-order quantum functions. This is because the question of whether a function is duplicable or not cannot be directly seen from the types of its arguments or of its value, but rather it depends on the types of any free variables occurring in the function definition. As it turns out, the appropriate type system for higher-order quantum functions in our setting is affine intuitionistic linear logic.

We also address the question of finding a type inference algorithm. Using the remark that a linear type is a decoration of an intuitionistic one, we show that the question of deciding whether or not a program is valid can be reduced to the question of finding an intuitionistic type for it and to explore a finite number of linear decorations for the type.

This work is based on the second author's Master's thesis [13].

2 Quantum Computing Basics

We briefly recall the basic definitions of quantum computing; please see [9, 10] for a complete introduction to the subject. The basic unit of information in quantum computation is a quantum bit or *qubit*. The state of a single qubit is a a normalized vector of the 2-dimensional Hilbert space $\mathbb{C}^2$. We denote the standard basis of $\mathbb{C}^2$ as $\{|0\rangle, |1\rangle\}$, so that the general state of a single qubit can be written as $\alpha|0\rangle + \beta|1\rangle$, where $|\alpha|^2 + |\beta|^2 = 1$.

The state of n qubits is a normalized vector in $\otimes_{i=1}^n \mathbb{C}^2 \cong \mathbb{C}^{2^n}$. We write $|xy\rangle = |x\rangle \otimes |y\rangle$, so that a standard basis vector of $\mathbb{C}^{2^n}$ can be denoted $|\ulcorner i \urcorner^n\rangle$, where $\ulcorner i \urcorner^n$ is the binary representation of i in n digits, for $0 \leqslant i < 2^n$. As a special case, if $n = 0$, we denote the unique standard basis vector in $\mathbb{C}^1$ by $|\rangle$.

The basic operations on quantum states are unitary operations and measurements. A unitary operation maps an n-qubit state to an n-qubit state, and is given by a unitary $2^n \times 2^n$-matrix. It is common to assume that the computational model provides a certain set of built-in unitary operations, including for example the *Hadamard gate* H and the *controlled not-gate* $CNOT$, among others:

$$H = \frac{1}{\sqrt{2}}\begin{pmatrix} 1 & 1 \\ 1 & -1 \end{pmatrix}, \qquad CNOT = \begin{pmatrix} 1&0&0&0 \\ 0&1&0&0 \\ 0&0&0&1 \\ 0&0&1&0 \end{pmatrix}.$$

The measurement acts as a projection. When a qubit $\alpha|0\rangle + \beta|1\rangle$ is measured, the observed outcome is a classical bit. The two possible outcomes 0 and 1 are observed with probabilities $|\alpha|^2$ and $|\beta|^2$, respectively. Moreover, the state of the qubit is affected by the measurement, and collapses to $|0\rangle$ if 0 was observed, and to $|1\rangle$ if 1 was observed. More generally, given an n-qubit state $|\phi\rangle = \alpha_0|0\rangle \otimes |\psi_0\rangle + \alpha_1|1\rangle \otimes |\psi_1\rangle$, where $|\psi_0\rangle$ and $|\psi_1\rangle$ are normalized $(n-1)$-qubit states, then measuring the leftmost qubit results in the answer i with probability $|\alpha_i|^2$, and the resulting state will be $|i\rangle \otimes |\psi_i\rangle$.

3 The Untyped Quantum Lambda Calculus

3.1 Terms

Our language uses the notation of the intuitionistic lambda calculus. For a detailed introduction to the lambda calculus, see e.g. [2]. We start from a standard lambda calculus with booleans and finite products. We extend this language with three special quantum operations, which are *new*, *meas*, and built-in unitary gates. *new* maps a classical bit to a quantum bit. *meas* maps a quantum bit to a classical bit by performing a measurement operation; this is a probabilistic operation. Finally, we assume that there is a set $\mathcal{U}^n$ of built-in n-ary unitary gates for each n. We use the letter U to range over built-in unitary gates. Thus, the syntax of our language is as follows:

$$\begin{array}{llll} \mathit{Term} & M, N, P & ::= & x \mid MN \mid \lambda x.M \mid \mathit{if}\ M\ \mathit{then}\ N\ \mathit{else}\ P \mid 0 \mid 1 \mid \mathit{meas} \\ & & & \mid \mathit{new} \mid U \mid * \mid \langle M, N\rangle \mid \mathit{let}\ \langle x, y\rangle = M\ \mathit{in}\ N, \end{array}$$

We follow Barendregt's convention for identifying terms up to α-equivalence. We also sometimes use the shorthand notation $\langle M_1, \ldots, M_n\rangle = \langle M_1, \langle M_2, \ldots\rangle\rangle$.

3.2 Programs

The reader will have noticed that we have not provided a syntax for constant quantum states such as $\alpha|0\rangle + \beta|1\rangle$ in our language. One may ask why we did not allow the insertion of quantum states into a lambda term, such as $\lambda x.(\alpha|0\rangle + \beta|1\rangle)$. The reason is that, in the general case, such a syntax would be insufficient. Consider for instance the lambda term $(\lambda y.\lambda f.fpy)(q)$, where p and q are entangled quantum bits in the state $|pq\rangle = \alpha|00\rangle + \beta|11\rangle$. Such a state cannot be represented locally by replacing p and q with some constant qubit expressions. The non-local nature of quantum states thus forces us to introduce a level of indirection into the representation of a state of a quantum program.

Definition 1. A *program state* is represented by a triple $[Q, L, M]$, where

- Q is a normalized vector of $\otimes_{i=0}^{n-1}\mathbb{C}^2$, for some $n \geqslant 0$
- M is a lambda term,
- L is a function from W to $\{0, \ldots, n-1\}$, where $FV(M) \subseteq W \subseteq \mathcal{V}_{term}$. L is also called the *linking function* or the *qubit environment*.

The purpose of the linking function is to assign specific free variables of M to specific quantum bits in Q. The notion of α-equivalence extends naturally to programs, for instance, the states $[|1\rangle, \{x \mapsto 0\}, \lambda y.x]$ and $[|1\rangle, \{z \mapsto 0\}, \lambda y.z]$ are equivalent. The set of program states, up to α-equivalence, is denoted by $\mathbb{S}$.

Convention 1. In order to simplify the notation, we will often use the following convention: we use p_i to denote the free variable x such that $L(x) = i$. A program $[Q, L, M]$ is abbreviated to $[Q, M']$ with $M' = M[p_{i_1}/x_1] \dots [p_{i_n}/x_n]$, where $i_k = L(x_k)$.

3.3 Linearity

An important well-formedness property of quantum programs is that quantum bits should always be *uniquely referenced*: roughly, this means that no two variable occurrences should refer to the same physical quantum bit. The reason for this restriction is the well-known no-cloning property of quantum physics, which states that a quantum bit cannot be duplicated: there exists no physically meaningful operation which maps an arbitrary quantum bit $|\phi\rangle$ to $|\phi\rangle \otimes |\phi\rangle$.

Syntactically, the requirement of unique referencing translates into a *linearity condition*: A lambda abstraction $\lambda x.M$ is called *linear* if the variable x is used at most once during the evaluation of M. A well-formed program should be such that quantum data is only used linearly; however, classical data, such as ordinary bits, can of course be used non-linearly. Since the decision of which subterms must be used linearly depends on type information, we will not formally enforce any linearity constraints until we discuss a type system in Section 4; nevertheless, we will assume that all our untyped examples are well-formed in the above sense.

3.4 Evaluation Strategy

As is usual in defining a programming language, we need to settle on a reduction strategy. The obvious candidates are call-by-name and call-by-value. Because of the probabilistic nature of measurement, the choice of reduction strategy affects the behavior of programs, not just in terms of efficiency, but in terms of the actual answer computed. We demonstrate this in an example. Let **plus** be the boolean addition function, which is definable as $\mathbf{plus} = \lambda xy.\, \mathit{if}\ x\ \mathit{then}\ (\mathit{if}\ y\ \mathit{then}\ 0\ \mathit{else}\ 1)\ \mathit{else}\ (\mathit{if}\ y\ \mathit{then}\ 1\ \mathit{else}\ 0)$. Consider the term $M = (\lambda x.\mathbf{plus}\ x\ x)(\mathit{meas}(H(\mathit{new}\ 0)))$.

Call-by-value. Reducing this in the empty environment, using the call-by-value reduction strategy, we obtain the following reductions:

$$\begin{array}{l}
\longrightarrow_{CBV} [|0\rangle, (\lambda x.\mathbf{plus}\ x\ x)(\mathit{meas}(H\ p_0))] \\
\longrightarrow_{CBV} [\frac{1}{\sqrt{2}}(|0\rangle + |1\rangle), (\lambda x.\mathbf{plus}\ x\ x)(\mathit{meas}\ p_0)] \\
\longrightarrow_{CBV} \begin{cases} [\,|0\rangle, (\lambda x.\mathbf{plus}\ x\ x)(0)] \\ [\,|1\rangle, (\lambda x.\mathbf{plus}\ x\ x)(1)] \end{cases} \longrightarrow_{CBV} \begin{cases} [\,|0\rangle, \mathbf{plus}\ 0\ 0] \\ [\,|1\rangle, \mathbf{plus}\ 1\ 1] \end{cases} \longrightarrow_{CBV} \begin{cases} [\,|0\rangle, 0] \\ [\,|1\rangle, 0] \end{cases}
\end{array}$$

each with a probability of $1/2$. Thus, under call-by-value reduction, this program produces the boolean value 0 with probability 1. Note that we have used Convention 1 for writing these program states.

Call-by-name. Reducing the same term under the call-by-name strategy, we obtain in one step $[\,|\rangle, \mathbf{plus}\ (\mathit{meas}(H(\mathit{new}\ 0)))\ (\mathit{meas}(H(\mathit{new}\ 0)))]$, and then with probability $1/4$, $[\,|01\rangle, 1\,]$, $[\,|10\rangle, 1\,]$, $[\,|00\rangle, 0\,]$ or $[\,|11\rangle, 0\,]$. Therefore, the boolean output of this function is 0 or 1 with equal probability.

Mixed strategy. Moreover, if we mix the two reduction strategies, the program can even reduce to an ill-formed term. Namely, reducing by call-by-value until $[\frac{1}{\sqrt{2}}(|0\rangle + |1\rangle), (\lambda x.\mathbf{plus}\ x\ x)(meas\ p_0)]$, and then changing to call-by-name, we obtain in one step the term $[\frac{1}{\sqrt{2}}(|0\rangle+|1\rangle), (\mathbf{plus}\ (meas\ p_0)\ (meas\ p_0)]$, which is not a valid program since there are 2 occurrences of p_0.

In the remainder of this paper, we will only consider the call-by-value reduction strategy, which seems to us to be the most natural.

3.5 Probabilistic Reduction Systems

In order to formalize the operational semantics of the quantum lambda calculus, we need to introduce the notion of a probabilistic reduction system.

Definition 2. A *probabilistic reduction system* is a tuple $(X, U, R, prob)$ where X is a set of *states*, $U \subseteq X$ is a subset of *value states*, $R \subseteq (X \setminus U) \times X$ is a set of *reductions*, and $prob : R \to [0,1]$ is a *probability function*, where $[0,1]$ is the real unit interval. Moreover, we impose the following conditions:

- For any $x \in X$, $R_x = \{ x' \mid (x, x') \in R \}$ is finite.
- $\sum_{x' \in R_x} prob(x, x') \leqslant 1$

We call $prob$ the one-step reduction, and denote $x \longrightarrow_p y$ to be $prob(x,y) = p$. Let us extend $prob$ to the n-step reduction

$$prob^0(x,y) = \begin{cases} 0 \text{ if } & x \neq y \\ 1 \text{ if } & x = y \end{cases}$$
$$prob^1(x,y) = \begin{cases} prob(x,y) \text{ if } & (x,y) \in R \\ 0 & \text{else} \end{cases}$$
$$prob^{n+1}(x,y) = \sum_{z \in R_x} prob(x,z) prob^n(z,y),$$

and the notation is extended to $x \longrightarrow_p^n y$ to mean $prob^n(x,y) = p$.

We say that y is *reachable in one step with non-zero probability* from x, denoted $x \longrightarrow_{>0} y$ when $x \longrightarrow_p y$ with $p > 0$. We say that y is *reachable with non-zero probability* from x, denoted $x \longrightarrow^*_{>0} y$ when there exists n such that $x \longrightarrow_p^n y$ with $p > 0$.

We can then compute the probability to reach $u \in U$ from x: It is a function from $X \times U$ to $\mathbb{R}$ defined by $prob_U(x,u) = \sum_{n=0}^{\infty} prob^n(x,u)$. The total probability for reaching U from x is $prob_U(x) = \sum_{n=0}^{\infty} \sum_{u \in U} prob^n(x,u)$.

On the other hand, there is also the probability to *diverge* from x, or never reaching anything. This value is $prob_\infty(x) = \lim_{n\to\infty} \sum_{y \in X} prob^n(x,y)$.

Lemma 1. *For all* $x \in X$, $prob_U(x) + prob_\infty(x) \leqslant 1$.

We define the *error probability of* x to be the number $prob_{err}(x) = 1 - prob_U(x) - prob_\infty(x)$.

Definition 3. We can define a notion of equivalence in X:

$$x \approx y \quad \text{iff} \quad \forall u \in U \begin{cases} prob_U(x,u) = prob_U(y,u) \\ prob_\infty(x) = prob_\infty(y) \end{cases}$$

Definition 4. In addition to the notion of reachability with non-zero probability, there is also a weaker notion of reachability, given by R: We will say that y is *reachable* from x if xRy. By the properties of $prob$, $x \longrightarrow_{>0} y$ implies $x \rightsquigarrow y$ with $x \rightsquigarrow y$ for xRy. Let us denote by $\longrightarrow^*$ the relation such that $x \rightsquigarrow^* y$ iff there exists n such that $xR^n y$, with R^n defined as the n-th composition of R. Similarly, $x \longrightarrow^*_{>0} y$ implies $x \rightsquigarrow^* y$.

Definition 5. In a probabilistic reduction system, a state x is called an *error-state* if $x \notin U$ and $\sum_{x' \in X} prob(x, x') < 1$. An element $x \in X$ is *consistent* if there is no error-state e such that $x \rightsquigarrow^* e$.

Lemma 2. *If x is consistent, then $prob_{err}(x) = 0$. The converse is false.*

Remark 1. We need the weaker notion of reachability $x \rightsquigarrow^* y$, in addition to reachability with non-zero probability $x \longrightarrow_{>0}{}^* y$, because a null probability of getting a certain result is not an absolute warranty of its impossibility. In the QRAM, suppose we have a qubit in state $|0\rangle$. Measuring it cannot theoretically yield the value 1, but in practice, this might happen with small probability, due to imprecision of the physical operations and decoherence. Therefore, when we prove type safety (see Theorem 2), we will use the stronger notion. In short: a type-safe program should not crash, even in the event of random QRAM errors.

3.6 Operational Semantics

We will define a probabilistic call-by-value reduction procedure for the quantum lambda calculus. Note that, although the reduction itself is probabilistic, the choice of which redex to reduce at each step is deterministic.

Definition 6. A *value* is a term of the following form:

$$Value \quad V, W \quad ::= \quad x \mid \lambda x.M \mid 0 \mid 1 \mid meas \mid new \mid U \mid * \mid \langle V, W \rangle.$$

The set of *value states* is $\mathbb{V} = \{[Q, L, V] \in \mathbb{S} \mid V \in Value\}$.

The reduction rules are shown in Table 1, where we have used Convention 1 to shorten the description of states. We write $[Q, L, M] \longrightarrow_p [Q', L', M']$ for a single-step reduction of states which takes place with probability p. In the rule for reducing the term $U\langle p_{j_1}, \ldots, p_{j_n}\rangle$, U is an n-ary built-in unitary gate, $j_1, \ldots, j_n$ are pairwise distinct, and Q' is the quantum state obtained from Q by applying this gate to qubits $j_1, \ldots, j_n$. In the rule for measurement, $|Q_0\rangle$ and $|Q_1\rangle$ are normalized states of the form $|Q_0\rangle = \sum_j \alpha_j |\phi_j^0\rangle \otimes |0\rangle \otimes |\psi_j^0\rangle$ and $|Q_1\rangle = \sum_j \beta_j |\phi_j^1\rangle \otimes |1\rangle \otimes |\psi_j^1\rangle$, where ϕ_j^0 and ϕ_j^1 is an i-qubit state (so that the measured qubit is the one pointed to by p_i). In the rule for for new, Q is an n-qubit state, so that $Q \otimes |i\rangle$ is an $(n+1)$-qubit state, and p_n refers to its rightmost qubit.

We define a weaker relation $\rightsquigarrow$. This relation models the transformations that can happen in the presence of decoherence and imprecision of physical operations. We define $[Q, M] \rightsquigarrow [Q', M']$ to be $[Q, M] \longrightarrow_p [Q', M']$, even when $p = 0$, plus the additional rule, if Q and Q' are vectors of equal dimensions: $[Q, M] \rightsquigarrow [Q', M]$.

Lemma 3. *Let $prob$ be the function such that for $x, y \in \mathbb{S}$, $prob(x, y) = p$ if $x \longrightarrow_p y$ and 0 else. Then $(\mathbb{S}, \mathbb{V}, \rightsquigarrow, prob)$ is a probabilistic reduction system.* □

This probabilistic reduction system has error states, for example, $[Q, H(\lambda x.x)]$ or $[Q, U\langle p_0, p_0\rangle]$. Such error states correspond to run-time errors. In the next section, we introduce a type system designed to rule out such error states.

Table 1. Reductions rules of the quantum lambda calculus

$$[Q, (\lambda x.M)V] \longrightarrow_1 [Q, M[V/x]]$$

$$\frac{[Q, N] \longrightarrow_p [Q', N']}{[Q, MN] \longrightarrow_p [Q', MN']}$$

$$\frac{[Q, M] \longrightarrow_p [Q', M']}{[Q, MV] \longrightarrow_p [Q', M'V]}$$

$$\frac{[Q, M_1] \longrightarrow_p [Q', M_1']}{[Q, \langle M_1, M_2\rangle] \longrightarrow_p [Q', \langle M_1', M_2\rangle]}$$

$$\frac{[Q, M_2] \longrightarrow_p [Q', M_2']}{[Q, \langle V_1, M_2\rangle] \longrightarrow_p [Q', \langle V_1, M_2'\rangle]}$$

$$[Q, \mathit{if}\ 0\ \mathit{then}\ M\ \mathit{else}\ N] \longrightarrow_1 [Q, N]$$

$$[Q, \mathit{if}\ 1\ \mathit{then}\ M\ \mathit{else}\ N] \longrightarrow_1 [Q, M]$$

$$[Q, U\langle p_{j_1}, \ldots, p_{j_n}\rangle] \longrightarrow_1 [Q', \langle p_{j_1}, \ldots, p_{j_n}\rangle]$$

$$[\alpha|Q_0\rangle + \beta|Q_1\rangle, \mathit{meas}\ \ p_i] \longrightarrow_{|\alpha|^2} [|Q_0\rangle, 0]$$

$$[\alpha|Q_0\rangle + \beta|Q_1\rangle, \mathit{meas}\ \ p_i] \longrightarrow_{|\beta|^2} [|Q_1\rangle, 1]$$

$$[Q, \mathit{new}\ \ 0] \longrightarrow_1 [Q \otimes |0\rangle, p_n]$$

$$[Q, \mathit{new}\ \ 1] \longrightarrow_1 [Q \otimes |1\rangle, p_n]$$

$$\frac{[Q, P] \longrightarrow_p [Q', P']}{[Q, \mathit{if}\ P\ \mathit{then}\ M\ \mathit{else}\ N] \longrightarrow_p [Q', \mathit{if}\ P'\ \mathit{then}\ M\ \mathit{else}\ N]}$$

$$\frac{[Q, M] \longrightarrow_p [Q', M']}{[Q, \text{let}\ \langle x_1, x_2\rangle = M\ \text{in}\ N] \longrightarrow_p [Q', \text{let}\ \langle x_1, x_2\rangle = M'\ \text{in}\ N]}$$

$$[Q, \text{let}\ \langle x_1, x_2\rangle = \langle V_1, V_2\rangle\ \text{in}\ N] \longrightarrow_1 [Q, N[V_1/x_1, V_2/x_2]]$$

4 The Typed Quantum Lambda-Calculus

We will now define a type system designed to eliminate all run-time errors arising from the reduction system of the previous section. We need base types (such as *bit* and *qbit*), function types, and product types. In addition, we need the type system to capture a notion of duplicability, as discussed in Section 3.3. We follow the notation of linear logic [7]. By default, a term of type A is assumed to be non-duplicable, and duplicable terms are given the type $!A$ instead. Formally, the set of types is defined as follows, where α ranges over a set of type constants and X ranges over a countable set of type variables:

$$\mathit{qType} \quad A, B \quad ::= \quad \alpha \mid X \mid\ !A \mid (A \multimap B) \mid \top \mid (A \otimes B)$$

Note that, because all terms are assumed to be non-duplicable by default, the language has a linear function type $A \multimap B$ and a linear product type $A \otimes B$. This reflects the fact that there is in general no canonical diagonal function $A \to A \otimes A$. Also, $\top$ is the linear unit type. This will be made more formal in the typing rules below. We write $!^n A$ for $!!!\ldots!!A$, with n repetitions of $!$. We also write A^n for the n-fold tensor product $A \otimes \ldots \otimes A$.

4.1 Subtyping

The typing rules will ensure that any value of type $!A$ is duplicable. However, there is no harm in using it only once; thus, such a value should also have type A. For this reason, we define a subtyping relation $<:$ as follows:

$$\frac{}{\alpha <: \alpha}\ (ax) \quad \frac{}{X <: X}\ (var) \quad \frac{}{\top <: \top}\ (\top) \quad \frac{A <: B}{!A <: B}\ (D) \quad \frac{!A <: B}{!A <: !B}\ (!)$$

$$\frac{A_1 <: B_1 \quad A_2 <: B_2}{A_1 \otimes A_2 <: B_1 \otimes B_2}\ (\otimes) \quad \frac{A <: A' \quad B <: B'}{A' \multimap B <: A \multimap B'}\ (\multimap)$$

Lemma 4. *For types A and B, if $A <: B$ and $(m = 0) \vee (n \geqslant 1)$, then $!^n A <: !^m B$.* □

Notice that one can rewrite types using the notation:

$$qType \quad A, B \quad ::= \quad !^n\alpha \mid !^n X \mid !^n(A \multimap B) \mid !^n\top \mid !^n(A \otimes B)$$

with $n \in \mathbb{N}$. Using the overall condition on n and m that $(m = 0) \vee (n \geqslant 1)$, the rules can be re-written as:

$$\frac{}{!^n X <: !^m X}\ (var_2) \quad \frac{}{!^n\alpha <: !^m\alpha}\ (\alpha) \quad \frac{}{!^n\top <: !^m\top}\ (\top)$$

$$\frac{A_1 <: B_1 \quad A_2 <: B_2}{!^n(A_1 \otimes A_2) <: !^m(B_1 \otimes B_2)}\ (\otimes) \quad \frac{A <: A' \quad B <: B'}{!^n(A' \multimap B) <: !^m(A \multimap B')}\ (\multimap_2)$$

The two sets of rules are equivalent.

Lemma 5. *The rules of the second set are reversible.* □

Lemma 6. *$(qType, <:)$ is reflexive and transitive. If we define an equivalence relation $\doteqdot$ by $A \doteqdot B$ iff $A <: B$ and $B <: A$, $(qType/\doteqdot, <:)$ is a poset.* □

Lemma 7. *If $A <: !B$, then there exists C such that $A = !C$.* □

Remark 2. The subtyping rules are a syntactic device, and are not intended to catch all plausible type isomorphisms. For instance, the types $!A \otimes !B$ and $!(A \otimes B)$ are not subtypes of each other, although an isomorphism between these types is easily definable in the language.

4.2 Typing Rules

We need to define what it means for a quantum state $[Q, L, M]$ to be well-typed. It turns out that the typing does not depend on Q and L, but only on M. We introduce typing judgments of the form $\Delta \rhd M : B$. Here M is a term, B is a *qType*, and Δ is a typing context, i.e., a function from a set of variables to *qType*. As usual, we write $|\Delta|$ for the domain of Δ, and we denote typing contexts as $x_1{:}A_1, \ldots, x_n{:}A_n$. As usual, we write $\Delta, x{:}A$ for $\Delta \cup \{x{:}A\}$ if $x \notin |\Delta|$. Also, if $\Delta = x_1{:}A_1, \ldots, x_n{:}A_n$, we write $!\Delta = x_1{:}!A_1, \ldots, x_n{:}!A_n$. A typing judgement is called *valid* if it can be derived from the rules in Table 2.

The typing rule (ax) assumes that to every constant c of the language, we have associated a fixed type A_c. The types A_c are defined as follows:

$$A_0 = !bit \qquad A_{new} = !(bit \multimap qbit)$$
$$A_1 = !bit \qquad A_{meas} = !(qbit \multimap !bit) \qquad A_U = !(qbit^n \multimap qbit^n)$$

Table 2. Typing rules

$$\frac{A <: B}{\Delta, x{:}A \rhd x : B}\ (ax_1) \qquad \frac{A_c <: B}{\Delta \rhd c : B}\ (ax_2)$$

$$\frac{\Gamma_1, !\Delta \rhd P : bit \quad \Gamma_2, !\Delta \rhd M : A \quad \Gamma_2, !\Delta \rhd N : A}{\Gamma_1, \Gamma_2, !\Delta \rhd \mathit{if}\ P\ \mathit{then}\ M\ \mathit{else}\ N : A}\ (\mathit{if})$$

$$\frac{\Gamma_1, !\Delta \rhd M : A \multimap B \quad \Gamma_2, !\Delta \rhd N : A}{\Gamma_1, \Gamma_2, !\Delta \rhd MN : B}\ (\mathit{app})$$

$$\frac{x{:}A, \Delta \rhd M : B}{\Delta \rhd \lambda x.M : A \multimap B}\ (\lambda_1) \qquad \begin{array}{c}\text{If } FV(M) \cap |\Gamma| = \emptyset\text{:}\\ \dfrac{\Gamma, !\Delta, x{:}A \rhd M : B}{\Gamma, !\Delta \rhd \lambda x.M : !^{n+1}(A \multimap B)}\end{array}\ (\lambda_2)$$

$$\frac{!\Delta, \Gamma_1 \rhd M_1 : !^n A_1 \quad !\Delta, \Gamma_2 \rhd M_2 : !^n A_2}{!\Delta, \Gamma_1, \Gamma_2 \rhd \langle M_1, M_2\rangle : !^n(A_1 \otimes A_2)}\ (\otimes.I) \qquad \frac{}{\Delta \rhd * : !^n\top}\ (\top)$$

$$\frac{!\Delta, \Gamma_1 \rhd M : !^n(A_1 \otimes A_2) \quad !\Delta, \Gamma_2,\ x_1{:}!^n A_1,\ x_2{:}!^n A_2 \rhd N : A}{!\Delta, \Gamma_1, \Gamma_2 \rhd \text{let } \langle x_1, x_2\rangle = M \text{ in } N : A}\ (\otimes.E)$$

Note that we have given the type $!(bit \multimap qbit)$ to the term new. Another possible choice would have been $!(!bit \multimap qbit)$, which makes sense because all classical bits are duplicable. However, since $!(bit \multimap qbit) <: !(!bit \multimap qbit)$, the second type is less general, and can be inferred by the typing rules.

Note that, if $[Q, L, M]$ is a program state, the term M need not be closed; however, all of its free variables must be in the domain of L, and thus must be of type $qbit$. We therefore define:

Definition 7. A program state $[Q, L, M]$ is *well-typed of type* B if $\Delta \rhd M : B$ is derivable, where $\Delta = \{x{:}\ qbit \mid x \in FV(M)\}$. In this case, we write $[Q, L, M] : B$.

Note that the type system enforces that variables holding quantum data cannot be duplicated; thus, $\lambda x.\langle x, x\rangle$ is not a valid term of type $qbit \multimap qbit \otimes qbit$. On the other hand, we allow variables to be discarded freely. Other approaches are also possible, for instance, Altenkirch and Grattage [1] propose a syntax that allows duplication but restricts discarding of quantum values.

4.3 Example: Quantum Teleportation

Let us illustrate the quantum lambda calculus and the typing rules with an example. The following is an implementation of the well-known quantum teleportation protocol (see e.g. [9]). The purpose of the teleportation protocol is to send a qubit from location A to location B, using only classical communication and a pre-existing shared entangled quantum state. In fact, this can be achieved by communicating only the content of two classical bits.

In terms of functional programming, the teleportation procedure can be seen as the creation of two non-duplicable functions $f : qbit \multimap bit \otimes bit$ and $g : bit \otimes bit \multimap qbit$, such that $f \circ g(x) = x$ for an arbitrary qubit x.

We start by defining the following functions **EPR** : $!(\top \multimap (qbit \otimes qbit))$, **BellMeasure** : $!(qbit \multimap (qbit \multimap bit \otimes bit))$, and **U** : $!(qbit \multimap (bit \otimes bit \multimap qbit))$:

$$
\begin{aligned}
\mathbf{EPR} &= \lambda x.CNOT\langle H(new\,0), new\,0\rangle,\\
\mathbf{BellMeasure} &= \lambda q_2.\lambda q_1.(let\ \langle x,y\rangle = CNOT\langle q_1,q_2\rangle\ in\ \langle\ meas(Hx), meas\,y\rangle,\\
\mathbf{U} &= \lambda q.\lambda\langle x,y\rangle.if\,x\,then\ (if\ y\ then\ U_{11}q\ else\ U_{10}q)\\
&\qquad\qquad\qquad\qquad else\ (if\ y\ then\ U_{01}q\ else\ U_{00}q),
\end{aligned}
$$

where

$$
U_{00} = \begin{pmatrix} 1\,0 \\ 0\,1 \end{pmatrix}, U_{01} = \begin{pmatrix} 0\,1 \\ 1\,0 \end{pmatrix}, U_{10} = \begin{pmatrix} 1 & 0 \\ 0 & -1 \end{pmatrix}, U_{11} = \begin{pmatrix} 0 & 1 \\ -1 & 0 \end{pmatrix}.
$$

The function **EPR** creates an entangled state $\frac{1}{\sqrt{2}}(|00\rangle + |11\rangle)$. The function **BellMeasure** performs a so-called Bell measurement, and the function **U** performs a unitary correction on the qubit q depending on the value of two classical bits. We can now construct a pair of functions $f : qbit \multimap bit \otimes bit$ and $g : bit \otimes bit \multimap qbit$ with the above property by the following code:

$$
\begin{aligned}
&let\ \langle x,y\rangle{=}\mathbf{EPR}\,*\\
&\ in\ let\ f\ = \mathbf{BellMeasure}\ x\\
&\quad in\ let\ g\ = \mathbf{U}\ y.\\
&\quad in\ \langle f,g\rangle.
\end{aligned}
$$

The functions f and g thus created do indeed have the desired property that $f \circ g(x) = x$, where x is any qubit. Note that, since f and g depend on the state of the qubits x and y, respectively, these functions cannot be duplicated, which is reflected in the fact that the types of f and g do not contain a top-level "!".

4.4 Properties of the Type System

We derive some basic properties of the type system.

Definition 8. We extend the subtyping relation to contexts by writing $\Delta <: \Delta'$ if $|\Delta'| = |\Delta|$ and for all x in $|\Delta'|$, $\Delta_f(x) <: \Delta'_f(x)$.

Lemma 8. *1. If $x \notin FV(M)$ and $\Delta, x{:}A \rhd M{:}B$, then $\Delta \rhd M{:}B$.*
2. If $\Delta \rhd M{:}A$, then $\Gamma, \Delta \rhd M{:}A$.
3. If $\Gamma <: \Delta$ and $\Delta \rhd N : A$ and $A <: B$, then $\Gamma \rhd N : B$.

The next lemma is crucial in the proof of the substitution lemma. Note that it is only true for a value V, and in general fails for an arbitrary term M.

Lemma 9. *If V is a value and $\Delta \rhd V : !A$, then for all $x \in FV(V)$, there exists some $U \in qType$ such that $\Delta(x) = !U$.*

Proof. By induction on V.

- If V is a variable x, then the last rule in the derivation was $\dfrac{B <: !A}{\Delta', x : B \rhd x : !A}$. Since $B <: !A$, B must be exponential by Lemma 7.
- If V is a constant c, then $FV(V) = \emptyset$, hence the result holds vacuously.
- If $V = \lambda x.M$, the only typing rule that applies is (λ_2), and $\Delta = \Gamma, !\Delta'$ with $FV(M) \cap |\Delta'| = \emptyset$. So every $y \in FV(M)$ except maybe x is exponential. Since $FV(\lambda x.M) = (FV(M) \setminus \{x\})$, this suffices.
- The remaining cases are similar. □

Lemma 10 (Substitution). *If V is a value such that $\Gamma_1, !\Delta, x{:}A \rhd M : B$ and $\Gamma_2, !\Delta \rhd V : A$, then $\Gamma_1, \Gamma_2, !\Delta \rhd M[V/x] : B$.*

Corollary 1. *If $\Gamma_1, !\Delta, x{:}A \rhd M : B$ and $\Gamma_2, !\Delta \rhd V : !^n A$, then $\Gamma_1, \Gamma_2, !\Delta \rhd M[V/x] : B$.*

Proof. From Lemma 10 and Lemma 8(3).

Remark 3. We note that all the usual rules of affine intuitionistic linear logic are derived rules of our type system, *except* for the general promotion rule. However, the promotion rule is derivable when V is a *value*:

$$\frac{!\Gamma \rhd V : A}{!\Gamma \rhd V : !A}.$$

4.5 Subject Reduction and Progress

Theorem 1 (Subject Reduction). *Given $[Q, L, M] : B$ and $[Q, L, M] \rightsquigarrow^* [Q', L', M']$, then $[Q', L', M'] : B$.*

Proof. It suffices to show this for $[Q, L, M] \longrightarrow_p [Q', L', M']$, and we proceed by induction on the rules in Table 1. The rule $[Q, (\lambda x.M)V] \longrightarrow_1 [Q, M[V/x]]$ and the rule for "let" use the substitution lemma. The remaining cases are direct applications of the induction hypothesis. □

Theorem 2 (Progress). *Let $[Q, L, M] : B$ be a well-typed program. Then $[Q, L, M]$ is not an error state in the sense of Definition 5. In particular, either $[Q, L, M]$ is a value, or else there exist some state $[Q', L', M']$ such that $[Q, L, M] \longrightarrow_p [Q', L', M']$. Moreover, the total probability of all possible single-step reductions from $[Q, L, M]$ is 1.*

Corollary 2. *Every sequence of reductions of a well-typed program either converges to a value, or diverges.*

The proof of the Progress Theorem is similar to the usual proof, with two small differences. The first is the presence of probabilities, and the second is the fact that M is not necessarily closed. However, all the free variables of M are of type *qbit*, and this property suffices to prove the following lemma, which generalizes the usual lemma on the shape of closed well-typed values:

Lemma 11. *Suppose $\Delta = x_1{:}qbit, \dots, x_n{:}qbit$, and V is a value. If $\Delta \rhd V : A \multimap B$, then V is new, $meas$, U, or a lambda abstraction. If $\Delta \rhd V : A \otimes B$, then $V = \langle V_1, V_2 \rangle$. If $\Delta \rhd V : bit$, then $V = 0$ or $V = 1$.*

Proof of the Progress Theorem. By induction on M. The claim follows immediately in the cases when M is a value, or when M is a left-hand-side of one of the rules in Table 1 that have no hypotheses. Otherwise, using Lemma 11, M is one of the following: PN, NV, $\langle N, P\rangle$, $\langle V, N\rangle$, $\mathit{if}\ N\ \mathit{then}\ P\ \mathit{else}\ Q$, $\mathit{let}\ \langle x, y\rangle{=}N\ \mathit{in}\ P$, where N is not a value. In this case, the free variables of N are still all of type $qbit$, and by induction hypothesis, the term $[Q, L, N]$ has reductions with total probability 1, and the rules in Table 1 ensure that the same is true for $[Q, L, M]$. □

5 Type Inference Algorithm

It is well-known that in the simply-typed lambda calculus, as well as in many programming languages, satisfy the *principal type property*: every untyped expression has a most general type, provided that it has any type at all. Since most principal types can usually be determined automatically, the programmer can be relieved from the need to write any types at all.

In the context of our quantum lambda calculus, it would be nice to have a type inference algorithm; however, the principal type property fails due to the presence of exponentials $!A$. Not only can an expression have several different types, but in general none of the types is "most general". For example, the term $M = \lambda xy.xy$ has possible types $T_1 = (A \multimap B) \multimap (A \multimap B)$ and $T_2 = !(A \multimap B) \multimap !(A \multimap B)$, among others. Neither of T_1 and T_2 is a substitution instance of the other, and in fact the most general type subsuming T_1 and T_2 is $X \multimap X$, which is not a valid type for M. Also, neither of T_1 and T_2 is a subtype of the other, and the most general type of which they are both subtypes is $(A \multimap B) \multimap !(A \multimap B)$, which is not a valid type for M.

In the absence of the principal type property, we need to design a type inference algorithm based on a different idea. The approach we follow is the one suggested by V. Danos, J.-B. Joinet and H. Schellinx [5]. The basic idea is to view a linear type as a "decoration" of an intuitionistic type. Our type inference algorithm is based on the following technical fact, given below: if a given term has an intuitionistic type derivation π, then it is linearly typable if and only if there exists a linear type derivation which is a decoration of π. Typability can therefore be decided by first doing intuitionistic type inference, and then checking finitely many possible linear decorations.

5.1 Skeletons and Decorations

The class of *intuitionistic types* is

$$iType \quad U, V \quad ::= \quad \alpha \mid X \mid (U \Rightarrow V) \mid (U \times V) \mid \top$$

where α ranges over the type constants and X over the type variables.

To each $A \in qType$, we associate its *type skeleton* ${}^{\dagger}A \in iType$, which is obtained by removing all occurrences of "!". Conversely, every $U \in iType$ can be lifted to some ${}^{\clubsuit}U \in qType$ with no occurrences of "!". Formally:

Definition 9. Define functions $\dagger : qType \to iType$ and $\clubsuit : iType \to qType$ by:

$$\begin{array}{ll} {}^{\dagger}!^n\alpha = \alpha, \quad {}^{\dagger}!^nX = X, \quad {}^{\dagger}!^n\top = \top, & {}^{\clubsuit}\alpha = \alpha, \quad {}^{\clubsuit}X = X, \quad {}^{\clubsuit}\top = \top, \\ {}^{\dagger}!^n(A \multimap B) = {}^{\dagger}A \Rightarrow {}^{\dagger}B, & {}^{\clubsuit}(U \Rightarrow V) = {}^{\clubsuit}U \multimap {}^{\clubsuit}V, \\ {}^{\dagger}!^n(A \otimes B) = {}^{\dagger}A \times {}^{\dagger}B, & {}^{\clubsuit}(U \times V) = {}^{\clubsuit}U \otimes {}^{\clubsuit}V. \end{array}$$

Lemma 12. *If $A <: B$, then ${}^\dagger A = {}^\dagger B$. If $U \in iType$, then $U = {}^{\dagger\clubsuit}U$.*

Writing $\Delta \blacktriangleright M : U$ for a typing judgement of the simply-typed lambda calculus, we can extend the notion of skeleton to contexts, typing judgments, and derivations as follows:

$$\begin{aligned} {}^\dagger\{x_1{:}A_1, \dots, x_n{:}A_n\} &= \{x_1{:}{}^\dagger A_1, \dots, x_n{:}{}^\dagger A_n\} \\ {}^\dagger(\Delta \rhd M : A) &= ({}^\dagger\Delta \blacktriangleright M : {}^\dagger A). \end{aligned}$$

From the rules in Table 2, it is immediate that if $\Delta \rhd M : A$ is a valid typing judgment in the quantum lambda-calculus, then ${}^\dagger(\Delta \rhd M : A) = ({}^\dagger\Delta \blacktriangleright M : {}^\dagger A)$ is a valid typing judgment in the simply-typed lambda-calculus.

We now turn to the question of how an intuitionistic typing derivation can be "decorated" with exponentials to yield a valid quantum typing derivation. These decorations are going to be the heart of the quantum type inference algorithm.

Definition 10. Given $A \in qType$ and $U \in iType$, we define the *decoration* $U \looparrowright A \in qType$ *of* U *along* A by

1. $U \looparrowright !^n A = !^n(U \looparrowright A)$,
2. $(U \Rightarrow V) \looparrowright (A \multimap B) = (U \looparrowright A \multimap V \looparrowright B)$,
3. $(U \times V) \looparrowright (A \otimes B) = (U \looparrowright A \otimes V \looparrowright B)$, and in all other cases:
4. $U \looparrowright A = {}^\clubsuit U$.

The following lemma is the key to the quantum type inference algorithm:

Lemma 13. *If M is well-typed in the quantum lambda-calculus with typing judgment $\Gamma \rhd M : A$, then for any valid typing judgment $\Delta \blacktriangleright M : U$ in simply-typed lambda-calculus with $|\Delta| = |\Gamma|$, the typing judgment $\Delta \looparrowright \Gamma \rhd M : U \looparrowright A$ is valid in the quantum lambda-calculus.*

5.2 Elimination of Repeated Exponentials

The type system in Section 4 allows types with repeated exponentials such as $!!A$. While this is useful for compositionality, it is not very convenient for type inference. We therefore consider a reformulation of the typing rules which only requires single exponentials.

Lemma 14. *The following are derived rules of the type system in Table 2, for all $\tau, \sigma \in \{0, 1\}$.*

$$\frac{!\Delta, \Gamma_1 \rhd M_1 : !A_1 \quad !\Delta, \Gamma_2 \rhd M_2 : !A_2}{!\Delta, \Gamma_1, \Gamma_2 \rhd \langle M_1, M_2\rangle : !(!^\tau A_1 \otimes !^\sigma A_2)} \ (\otimes.I')$$

$$\frac{!\Delta, \Gamma_1 \rhd M : !(!^\tau A_1 \otimes !^\sigma A_2) \quad !\Delta, \Gamma_2,\ x_1{:}!A_1,\ x_2{:}!A_2 \rhd N : A}{!\Delta, \Gamma_1, \Gamma_2 \rhd \mathit{let}\ \langle x_1, x_2\rangle = M\ \mathit{in}\ N : A} \ (\otimes.E')$$

Lemma 15. *If M is typable in the quantum lambda calculus by some derivation π, then M is typable in the system with the added rules $(\otimes.I')$ and $(\otimes.E')$, by a derivation π' using no repeated exponentials. Moreover, ${}^\dagger\pi' = {}^\dagger\pi$.* □

5.3 Description of the Type Inference Algorithm

To decide the typability of a given term M, first note the following: if M is not typable in simply-typed lambda calculus, then M is not quantum typable. On the other hand, suppose M admits a typing judgment $\Gamma \blacktriangleright M : U$ in the simply-typed lambda calculus, say with typing derivation π. Moreover, suppose without loss of generality that the derivation π uses no dummy variables, i.e., each sequent $\Gamma' \blacktriangleright M' : U'$ of π satisfies $|\Gamma'| = FV(M')$. Then by the proof of Lemma 13, M is quantum typable if and only if M has a quantum derivation whose skeleton is π. Thus we can perform type inference in the quantum lambda-calculus in two steps:

1. Find an intuitionistic typing derivation π, if any, using no dummy variables.
2. Find a decoration of π which is a valid quantum typing derivation, if any.

Step (1) is known to be decidable. For step (2), note that by Lemma 15, it suffices to consider decorations of π without repeated exponentials. Since there are only finitely many such decorations, the typability of M is clearly a decidable problem. Also note that if the algorithm succeeds, then it returns a possible type for M. However, it does not return a description of all possible types.

It should further be noted that the space of all decorations of π, while exponential in size, can be searched efficiently by solving a system of constraints. More precisely, if we create a boolean variable for each place in the type derivation which potentially can hold a "!", then the constraints imposed by the linear type system can all be written in the form of implications $x_1 \wedge \ldots \wedge x_n \Rightarrow y$, where $n \geqslant 0$, and negations $\neg z$. It is well-known that such a system can be solved in polynomial time in the number of variables and clauses, which is in turns polynomial in the size of the type derivation. Note, however, that the size of the type derivation need not be polynomial in the size of the term M, as the type of M can be of exponential size in the worst case.

6 Conclusion and Further Work

In this paper, we have defined a higher-order quantum programming language based on a linear typed lambda calculus. Compared to the quantum lambda calculus of van Tonder [14, 15], our language is characterized by the fact that it contains classical as well as quantum features; for instance, we provide classical datatypes and measurements as a primitive feature of our language. Moreover, we provide a subject reduction result and a type inference algorithm. As the language shows, linearity constraints do not just exist at base types, but also at higher types, due to the fact that higher-order function are represented as closures which may in turns contain embedded quantum data. We have shown that affine intuitionistic linear logic provides the right type system to deal with this situation.

There are many open problems for further work. An interesting question is whether the syntax of this language can be extended to include recursion. Another question is to study extensions of the type system, for instance with additive types as in linear logic. One may also study alternative reduction strategies. In this paper, we have only considered the call-by-value case; it would be interesting to see if there is a call-by-name equivalent of this language. Finally, another important open problem is to find a good denotational semantics for a higher order quantum programming language. One approach for finding such a semantics is to extend the framework of Selinger [12] and to identify an appropriate higher-order version of the notion of a superoperator.

References

1. T. Altenkirch and J. Grattage. A functional quantum programming language. Available from arXiv:quant-ph/0409065, 2004.
2. H. P. Barendregt. *The Lambda-Calculus, its Syntax and Semantics*, volume 103 of *Studies in Logic and the Foundation of Mathematics*. North Holland, second edition, 1984.
3. P. Benioff. The computer as a physical system: A microscopic quantum mechanical Hamiltonian model of computers as represented by Turing machines. *Journal of Statistical Physics*, 22:563–591, 1980.
4. S. Bettelli, T. Calarco, and L. Serafini. Toward an architecture for quantum programming. *The European Physical Journal D*, 25(2):181–200, August 2003.
5. V. Danos, J.-B. Joinet, and H. Schellinx. On the linear decoration of intuitionistic derivations. *Archive for Mathematical Logic*, 33:387–412, 1995.
6. D. Deutsch. Quantum theory, the Church-Turing principle and the universal quantum computer. *Proceedings of the Royal Society of London. Series A, Mathematical and Physical Sciences*, 400(1818):97–117, July 1985.
7. J.-Y. Girard. Linear logic. *Theoretical Computer Science*, 50(1):1–101, 1987.
8. E. Knill. Conventions for quantum pseudocode. Technical Report LAUR-96-2724, Los Alamos National Laboratory, 1996.
9. M. A. Nielsen and I. L. Chuang. *Quantum Computation and Quantum Information*. Cambridge University Press, 2002.
10. J. Preskill. Lecture notes for Physics 229, quantum computation. Available from http://www.theory.caltech.edu/people/preskill/ph229/#lecture, 1999.
11. J. W. Sanders and P. Zuliani. Quantum programming. In R. Backhouse and J. N. Oliveira, editors, *Mathematics of Program Construction: 5th International Conference*, volume 1837 of *Lecture Notes in Computer Science*, pages 80–99, Ponte de Lima, Portugal, July 2000. Springer-Verlag.
12. P. Selinger. Towards a quantum programming language. *Mathematical Structures in Computer Science*, 14(4):527–586, 2004.
13. Benoît Valiron. A functional programming language for quantum computation with classical control. Master's thesis, University of Ottawa, September 2004.
14. A. van Tonder. Quantum computation, categorical semantics and linear logic. On arXiv: quant-ph/0312174, 2003.
15. A. van Tonder. A lambda calculus for quantum computation. *SIAM Journal of Computing*, 33(5):1109–1135, 2004. Available from arXiv:quant-ph/0307150.

Continuity and Discontinuity in Lambda Calculus

Paula Severi and Fer-Jan de Vries

Department of Mathematics and Computer Science,
University of Leicester, University Road,
Leicester, LE1 7RH, UK

Abstract. This paper studies continuity of the normal form and the context operators as functions in the infinitary lambda calculus. We consider the Scott topology on the cpo of the finite and infinite terms with the prefix relation. We prove that the only continuous parametric trees are Böhm and Lévy–Longo trees. We also prove a general statement: if the normal form function is continuous then so is the model induced by the normal form; as well as the converse for parametric trees. This allows us to deduce that the only continuous models induced by the parametric trees are the ones of Böhm and Lévy–Longo trees. As a first application, we prove that there is an injective embedding from the infinitary lambda calculus of the $\infty\eta$-Böhm trees in D_∞. As a second application, we study the relation between the Scott topology on the prefix relation and the tree topologies. This allows us to prove that the only parametric tree topologies in which all context operators are continuous and the approximation property holds are the ones of Böhm and Lévy–Longo. As a third application, we give an explicit characterisation of the open sets of the Böhm and Lévy–Longo tree topologies.

1 Introduction

The study of the infinitary lambda calculi has focused on confluence and normalisation [4, 9, 10, 11, 12, 16, 15] and sequentiality [5]. In this paper we will look at another property of these calculi, namely *continuity*.

Our starting point are lambda calculi that extend finite lambda calculus with infinite terms and transfinite reduction. The β and η reduction rules apply to infinite terms in much the same way as they apply to finite terms. However, characteristic for these calculi is that they contain a $\perp$-rule that maps a certain set $\mathcal{U}$ of meaningless terms to $\perp$. Without such an addition the extension of finite lambda calculus with infinite terms and reductions immediately would result in loss of confluence [9]. All infinite calculi that we consider have the same set of finite and infinite terms $\Lambda_\perp^\infty$. The variation comes from the choice of the set $\mathcal{U}$ and the strength of extensionality.

Figure 1 summarises the infinitary lambda calculi studied so far [4, 9, 10, 12, 16, 15]. An interesting aspect of infinitary lambda calculus is the possibility of capturing the notion of tree (such as Böhm and Lévy–Longo trees) as a normal

P. Urzyczyn (Ed.): TLCA 2005, LNCS 3461, pp. 369–385, 2005.

REDUCTION RULES	NORMAL FORMS	NF
Beta and Bottom for terms without tnf	Berarducci trees	$\mathsf{BeT} = \mathsf{T}_{\overline{\mathcal{T}}}$
Beta and Bottom for terms without whnf	Lévy–Longo trees	$\mathsf{LT} = \mathsf{T}_{\overline{\mathcal{W}}}$
Beta and Bottom for terms without hnf	Böhm trees	$\mathsf{BT} = \mathsf{T}_{\overline{\mathcal{H}}}$
Beta, Bottom parametric on $\mathcal{U}$	Parametric trees	$\mathsf{T}_{\mathcal{U}}$
Beta, Bottom for terms w.o. hnf and Eta	η-Böhm trees	$\eta\mathsf{BT}$
Beta, Bottom for terms w.o. hnf and EtaBang	$\infty\eta$-Böhm trees	$\infty\eta\mathsf{BT}$

Fig. 1. Infinitary Lambda Calculi

form. These trees were originally defined for finite lambda terms only, but in the infinitary lambda calculus we can also consider normal forms of infinite terms. The three infinitary lambda calculi mentioned in the first three rows of Figure 1 capture the well-known cases of Böhm, Lévy–Longo and Berarducci trees [4, 9, 10]. In the fourth row, there is an uncountable class of infinitary lambda calculi with a $\perp$-rule parametrised by a set $\mathcal{U}$ of meaningless terms [11, 12]. By changing the parameter set $\mathcal{U}$ of the $\perp$-rule, we obtain different infinitary lambda calculi. If $\mathcal{U}$ is the set of terms without head normal form, we capture the notion of Böhm tree. If $\mathcal{U}$ is the set of terms without weak head normal form we obtain the Lévy–Longo trees. And if $\mathcal{U}$ is the set of terms without top head normal form to $\perp$, we recover the Berarducci trees. The infinitary lambda calculus sketched in the one but last row incorporates the η-rule [16]. This calculus captures the notion of η-Böhm tree. The last row in Figure 1 mentions the infinitary lambda calculus incorporating the $\eta!$-rule, a strengthened form of the η-rule [15]. The normal forms in this calculus capture the notion of $\infty\eta$-Böhm trees.

When the infinite extensions are confluent and normalising (normal forms can now be infinite too!) they induce a function $\mathsf{NF} : \Lambda^{\infty}_{\perp} \to \Lambda^{\infty}_{\perp}$ mapping a term to its unique normal form. The normal form functions NF induce models of the finite lambda calculus: just interpret a term M by its normal form $\mathsf{NF}(M)$ and application $M \cdot N$ of two terms M and N by $\mathsf{NF}(MN)$.

It is natural to compare terms, in particular normal forms, by the prefix relation $\preceq$. When terms are represented as trees, prefixes of a tree are obtained by pruning some of its subtrees and replacing them by $\perp$. Whereas application in the model of Böhm trees is well-known to be continuous with respect to the Scott topology induced by the prefix relation, it is perhaps less well-known that in case of the model of Berarducci trees, the normal form function $\mathsf{BeT} : \Lambda^{\infty}_{\perp} \to \Lambda^{\infty}_{\perp}$ and the application operator are not even monotone [8]. For the models induced by

NF, it makes sense to study continuity of all context operators and this includes not only the application operator but also the abstraction.

In this paper we will make a systematic study of continuity of the following two functions and the relation between them:

- the normal form functions NF with respect to the Scott topology on $(\Lambda^{\infty}_{\perp}, \preceq)$ and
- the context operators $\lambda\!\!\lambda M \in \mathsf{NF}(\Lambda^{\infty}_{\perp}).\mathsf{NF}(C[M]) : \mathsf{NF}(\Lambda^{\infty}_{\perp}) \to \mathsf{NF}(\Lambda^{\infty}_{\perp})$ in the models induced by NF.

We first prove that the only continuous parametric tree functions are the ones that correspond to Böhm and Lévy–Longo trees. We also show that the η and $\infty\eta$-Böhm tree functions are not continuous.

We also study the relation between continuity of NF and continuity of the context operators in the models induced by NF. We prove that if NF is continuous then so is the model induced by NF; as well as the converse when NF is a parametric tree. This allows us to deduce that the only continuous models induced by the parametric trees are the ones of Böhm and Lévy–Longo trees.

As a first application of our results on continuity, we show that there is an injective embedding from the infinitary lambda calculus of $\infty\eta$-Böhm trees in Scott's models D_{∞}. We use the fact that the model induced by BT is continuous to prove that the interpretation on D_{∞} extended to infinite terms is homomorphic with the abstraction and the application.

As a second application, we study the relation between the Scott topology on the prefix relation and the tree topologies. We prove that the only parametric tree topologies that make all context operators continuous and in which the approximation property holds are the ones of Böhm and Lévy–Longo. Continuity of the finite context operators $\lambda\!\!\lambda M \in \Lambda.C[M] : \Lambda \to \Lambda$ in the Böhm and Lévy–Longo tree topologies is proved in [2, 14] using the labelled reduction. We show that it can also be deduced from confluence via the infinitary lambda calculus

As a third application, we define the notion of NF-topology and prove that the BT-topology and the LT-topology coincide with the old notions of Böhm and Lévy–Longo tree topologies.

2 Infinite Lambda Calculus

We will now briefly recall some notions and facts of infinite lambda calculus from our earlier work [9, 10, 12, 16, 15]. We assume familiarity with basic notions and notations from [2].

Let Λ be the set of λ-terms and $\Lambda_{\perp}$ be the set of finite λ-terms with $\perp$ given by the inductive grammar:

$$M ::= \perp \mid x \mid (\lambda x M) \mid (MM)$$

where x is a variable from some fixed set of variables $\mathcal{V}$. We follow the usual conventions on syntax. Terms and variables will respectively be written with (super- and subscripted) letters M, N and x, y, z. Terms of the form $(M_1 M_2)$

and $(\lambda x M)$ will respectively be called applications and abstractions. A context $C[\ ]$ is a term with a hole in it, and $C[M]$ denotes the result of filling the hole by the term M, possibly by capturing some free variables of M.

The set $\Lambda_{\perp}^{\infty}$ of finite and infinite λ-terms is defined by coinduction using the same grammar as for $\Lambda_{\perp}$. This set contains the three sets of Böhm, Lévy–Longo and Berarducci trees. In [10, 11, 12], an alternative definition of the set $\Lambda_{\perp}^{\infty}$ is given using a metric. The coinductive and metric definitions are equivalent [3]. In this paper we consider only one set of λ-terms, namely $\Lambda_{\perp}^{\infty}$, in contrast to the formulations in [10, 11] where several sets (which are all subsets of $\Lambda_{\perp}^{\infty}$) are considered. The paper [12] shows that the infinitary lambda calculi can be formulated using a common set $\Lambda_{\perp}^{\infty}$, confluence and normalisation still hold since the extra terms added by the superset $\Lambda_{\perp}^{\infty}$ are meaningless and equated to $\perp$.

Many notions of finite lambda calculus apply and/or extend more or less straightforwardly to the infinitary setting. The main idea which goes back to Dershowitz e.a. in [7] is that reduction sequences can be of any transfinite ordinal length α: $M_0 \to M_1 \to M_2 \to \ldots M_\omega \to M_{\omega+1} \to \ldots M_{\omega+\omega} \to M_{\omega+\omega+1} \to \ldots M_\alpha$. This makes sense if the limit terms $M_\omega, M_{\omega+\omega}, \ldots$ in such sequence are all equal to the corresponding Cauchy limits, $\lim_{\beta \to \lambda} M_\beta$, in the underlying metric space for any limit ordinal $\lambda \leq \alpha$. If this is the case, the reduction is called *Cauchy converging.* We need the stronger concept of a *strongly converging* reduction that in addition satisfies that the depth of the contracted redexes goes to infinity at each limit term: $\lim_{\beta \to \lambda} d_\beta = \infty$ for each limit ordinal $\lambda \leq \alpha$, where d_β is the depth in M_β of the reduced redex in $M_\beta \to M_{\beta+1}$. Note that any finite reduction is strongly converging.

We use the following notation:

1. $M \to N$ denotes a one step reduction from M to N;
2. $M \twoheadrightarrow N$ denotes a finite reduction from M to N;
3. $M \twoheadrightarrow\!\!\!\!\rightarrow N$ denotes a strongly converging reduction from M to N.

We define several rules used to define different infinite lambda calculi. The β, η and η^{-1}-rules are extensions of the rules for finite lambda calculus to infinite terms. The $\eta!$-rule does not appear in the finite lambda calculus. The $\perp$-rule is parametric on a set $\mathcal{U} \subset \Lambda^{\infty}$ of meaningless terms [11, 12] where Λ^{∞} is the set of terms in $\Lambda_{\perp}^{\infty}$ that do not contain $\perp$.

The notions of head normal form, weak head normal form and top normal form are defined as follows:

1. A head normal form (hnf) is a term of the form $\lambda x_1 \ldots x_n . y M_1 \ldots M_k$.
2. A weak head normal form (whnf) is either a hnf or an abstraction $\lambda x.M$.
3. A top normal form (tnf) is either a whnf or an application (MN) if there is no P such that $M \twoheadrightarrow_\beta \lambda x.P$.

We define the following sets:

$$\begin{aligned}
\mathcal{H} &= \{M \in \Lambda^{\infty} \mid M \twoheadrightarrow_\beta N \text{ and } N \text{ in head normal form}\} \\
\mathcal{W} &= \{M \in \Lambda^{\infty} \mid M \twoheadrightarrow_\beta N \text{ and } N \text{ in weak head normal form}\} \\
\mathcal{T} &= \{M \in \Lambda^{\infty} \mid M \twoheadrightarrow_\beta N \text{ and } N \text{ in top normal form}\}
\end{aligned}$$

Instances of $\mathcal{U} \subseteq \Lambda^\infty$ are $\overline{\mathcal{H}}$, $\overline{\mathcal{W}}$ and $\overline{\mathcal{T}}$ the respective complements of $\mathcal{H}$, $\mathcal{W}$ and $\mathcal{T}$. Since the $\bot$-rule is parametric, each set $\mathcal{U}$ of meaningless terms gives a different infinitary lambda calculus $\lambda^\infty_{\beta\bot}$.

Definition 1. We define the following rewrite rules on $\Lambda^\infty_\bot$:

$$(\lambda x.M)N \to M[x := N] \quad (\beta) \qquad \frac{M[\bot := \Omega] \in \mathcal{U}}{M \to \bot}\ (\bot) \qquad \frac{x \notin FV(M)}{\lambda x.Mx \to M}\ (\eta)$$

$$\frac{x \notin FV(M)}{M \to \lambda x.Mx}\ (\eta^{-1}) \qquad \frac{x \twoheadrightarrow_{\eta^{-1}} N \quad x \notin FV(M)}{\lambda x.MN \to M}\ (\eta!)$$

In this paper we need various rewrite relations constructed from these rules on the set $\Lambda^\infty_\bot$. These are defined in the standard way, eg. $\to_{\beta\bot\eta!}$ is the smallest binary relation containing the β, $\bot$ and $\eta!$-rules which is closed under contexts. Variations on the reduction rules will give rise to different calculi (see Figure 1). The resulting infinite lambda calculus $(\Lambda^\infty_\bot, \to_\rho)$ we will denote by λ^∞_ρ for any $\rho \in \{\beta\bot, \beta\bot\eta, \beta\bot\eta!\}$.

Definition 2. 1. We say that a term M in λ^∞_ρ is in *ρ-normal form* if there is no N in λ^∞_ρ such that $M \to_\rho N$.
2. We say that λ^∞_ρ is *confluent* (*Church-Rosser*) if $(\Lambda^\infty_\bot, \twoheadrightarrow_\rho)$ satisfies the *diamond property*, i.e. ${}_\rho\twoheadleftarrow \circ \twoheadrightarrow_\rho \subseteq \twoheadrightarrow_\rho \circ {}_\rho\twoheadleftarrow$.
3. We say that λ^∞_ρ is *normalising* if for all $M \in \Lambda^\infty_\bot$ there exists an N in ρ-normal form such that $M \twoheadrightarrow_\rho N$.
4. Let α be an ordinal. We say that λ^∞_ρ is *α-compressible* if for all M, N such that $M \twoheadrightarrow_\rho N$ there exists a strongly converging reduction sequence from M to N of length at most α.

Theorem 3. *[10, 11, 12] The calculi $\lambda^\infty_{\beta\bot}$ with a parametric $\bot$-rule on the set $\mathcal{U}$ are confluent, normalising, ω-compressible and satisfy postponement of $\bot$ over β.*

In [12], confluence of the parametric calculi is proved for any Cauchy converging reduction, not only strongly converging ones.

Theorem 4. *[16, 15] The infinite lambda calculi of $\infty\eta$-Böhm and η-Böhm trees are confluent and normalising.*

Assumption. In the rest of the paper whenever we refer to the function $\mathsf{NF} : \Lambda^\infty_\bot \to \Lambda^\infty_\bot$, we are assuming that the infinitary lambda calculus in question is confluent and normalising and that NF is the function that maps a term to its unique normal form.

3 Equality Induced by the Normal Form

The theory given by NF is the set $\mathsf{Eq}(\mathsf{NF}) = \{(M, N) \in \Lambda^\infty_\bot \times \Lambda^\infty_\bot \mid \mathsf{NF}(M) = \mathsf{NF}(N)\}$. Figure 1 shows an order between the calculi. On the first row we see the smallest theory of λ-terms given by the equality of Berarducci trees and in the last row we see the largest theory given by equality of $\infty\eta$-Böhm trees. Hence,

$$\mathsf{Eq}(\mathsf{BeT}) \subset \mathsf{Eq}(\mathsf{LT}) \subset \mathsf{Eq}(\mathsf{BT}) \subset \mathsf{Eq}(\eta\mathsf{BT}) \subset \mathsf{Eq}(\infty\eta\mathsf{BT})$$

Note that $\mathcal{T} \supset \mathcal{W} \supset \mathcal{H}$ and $\overline{\mathcal{T}} \subset \overline{\mathcal{W}} \subset \overline{\mathcal{H}}$.

Lemma 5. *Let $\mathcal{U}$ be a set of meaningless terms satisfying the axioms of [11, 12]. If the theory $\mathsf{Eq}(\mathsf{T}_{\mathcal{U}})$ is consistent then $\overline{\mathcal{T}} \subseteq \mathcal{U} \subseteq \overline{\mathcal{H}}$.*

Proof. By the axioms of meaningless terms [11, 12], we know that $\overline{\mathcal{T}} \subseteq \mathcal{U}$. Suppose now towards a contradiction that there exists $M \in \mathcal{U}$ such that $M \notin \overline{\mathcal{H}}$. Then M has a head normal form. Suppose $M = \lambda x_1 \ldots x_n.yP_1 \ldots P_k$. Once more applying the axioms of meaningless terms, we have that $(Mx_1 \ldots x_n)[y := \lambda y_1 \ldots y_k.P] \twoheadrightarrow_\beta P \in \mathcal{U}$ for any $P \in \Lambda^\infty_\bot$. It follows that all terms $P \in \Lambda^\infty_\bot$ have the same normal form and hence the theory is not consistent.

As a consequence of the previous lemma, any consistent theory of parametric trees lays between the theories of Berarducci and Böhm trees:

$$\mathsf{Eq}(\mathsf{BeT}) \subseteq \mathsf{Eq}(\mathsf{T}_{\mathcal{U}}) \subseteq \mathsf{Eq}(\mathsf{BT})$$

Theorem 6. *The class of parametric trees is uncountable.*

Proof. For each subset X of the set of finite closed β-normal forms, we define a set $\mathcal{U}_X$ as follows:

$$\mathcal{U}_X = \{M \in \Lambda^\infty \mid M \twoheadrightarrow_\beta RP_1 \ldots P_n, n \in \omega,\ R \in \overline{\mathcal{T}} \text{ and } P_1, \ldots, P_n \in X\}$$

It is possible to prove that the set $\mathcal{U}_X$ satisfies the axioms of [11, 12].

4 Truncation and Preorders

In this section we define the notion of truncation and some preorders used in this paper. In the next section we will use truncations instead of approximants to prove continuity.

Definition 7. Let $M \in \Lambda^\infty_\bot$.

1. We define the truncation of M at depth n, denoted as M^n, as the result of replacing in M all subterms at depth n by $\bot$.
2. The truncation of the normal form of M at depth n is denoted by $\mathsf{NF}^n(M)$.

The following lemma is proved by induction on the depth of the hole in the context.

Lemma 8. *Let $C[M] \in \Lambda^\infty_\bot$ and d the depth of the hole in C. If $n > d$ then $(C[M])^n = C^n[M^{n-d}]$. Otherwise $C[M]^n = C^n$ is a term without a hole in it.*

Definition 9. Let $M, N \in \Lambda_{\perp}^{\infty}$. We say that M is a prefix of N (we write $M \preceq N$) if M is obtained from N by replacing some subterms of N by $\perp$

The pair $(\Lambda_{\perp}^{\infty}, \preceq)$ is an algebraic cpo. The compact elements are the finite λ-terms. In particular, truncations of terms are compact. We denote the supremum of a directed subset X of $(\Lambda_{\perp}^{\infty}, \preceq)$ by $\bigsqcup X$. In the particular case of Böhm trees, the pair $(\mathsf{BT}(\Lambda_{\perp}^{\infty}), \preceq)$ is isomorphic to $(\mathcal{B}, \subseteq)$ where $\mathcal{B}$ is the set of Böhm–like trees and $\subseteq$ is the prefix relation on trees [2].

Definition 10. Let $M, N \in \Lambda_{\perp}^{\infty}$.

1. We say that $M \preceq_{fin} N$ if M is the result of replacing a finite number of subterms of N by $\perp$.
2. Let $\mathsf{NF} : \Lambda_{\perp}^{\infty} \to \Lambda_{\perp}^{\infty}$. Then, $M \preceq_{\mathsf{NF}} N$ if $\mathsf{NF}(M) \preceq \mathsf{NF}(N)$.
3. $M \preceq_{\eta^{-1}} N$ if $\mathsf{BT}(M) \twoheadrightarrow_{\eta^{-1}} P \preceq Q \;{}_{\eta^{-1}}\!\twoheadleftarrow \mathsf{BT}(N)$ for P, Q in $\beta\perp$-normal form.
4. We say that $M \subseteq_{h_f} N$ if for all finite contexts C, if $C[M]$ β-reduces to a head normal form then so does $C[N]$.
5. We say that $M \subseteq_{h} N$ if for all (finite or infinite) contexts C, if $C[M]$ β-reduces to a head normal form then so does $C[N]$.

The relation $\preceq_{\mathsf{NF}}$ is a preorder, i.e. it is reflexive and transitive. It is also a partial order if restricted to the set of normal forms, i.e. it is antisymmetric.

Definition 11. We say that NF quasi-preserves $\preceq_{fin}$ if $\mathsf{NF}(M) \preceq \mathsf{NF}(N)$ for all $M \preceq_{fin} N$.

5 Continuity of the Normal Form Function NF

We will now consider the Scott topology on the cpo $(\Lambda_{\perp}^{\infty}, \preceq)$ and study continuity of the normal form function $\mathsf{NF} : \Lambda_{\perp}^{\infty} \to \Lambda_{\perp}^{\infty}$. We prove that the only parametric trees satisfying continuity are BT and LT.

We give some counterexamples against continuity of the normal form function:

Counterexample 12. The map $\mathsf{NF} : \Lambda_{\perp}^{\infty} \to \Lambda_{\perp}^{\infty}$ is not continuous in $(\Lambda_{\perp}^{\infty}, \preceq)$ in the following cases:

1. Case $\mathsf{NF} = \mathsf{BeT}$. We show that BeT is not monotone in $(\Lambda_{\perp}^{\infty}, \preceq)$. Take $M = \perp y$, $N = (\lambda x.\perp)y$. Then $M \preceq N$ but $\mathsf{NF}(M) \not\preceq \mathsf{NF}(N)$.

2. Case $\mathsf{NF} = \{\eta\mathsf{BT}, \infty\eta\mathsf{BT}\}$. We show that $\eta\mathsf{BT}$ and $\infty\eta\mathsf{BT}$ are not monotone. Take $M = \lambda x.y\perp$ and $N = \lambda x.yx$. Then $M \preceq N$ but $\mathsf{NF}(M) \not\preceq \mathsf{NF}(N)$.

3. Case $\mathsf{NF} = \mathsf{T}_{\overline{\mathcal{O}}}$ and $\overline{\mathcal{O}} = \overline{\mathcal{W}} \cup \{M \in \Lambda^{\infty} \mid M \twoheadrightarrow_{\beta} \lambda x_1 \ldots x_n.N \text{ and } N \in \overline{\mathcal{W}}\}$. Then $\mathsf{T}_{\overline{\mathcal{O}}}$ is monotone but it is not continuous. The infinite sequence of abstractions $\mathsf{O} = \lambda x_1 x_2 \ldots$ is in normal form but the truncations $\mathsf{O}^n = \lambda x_1 \ldots x_n.\perp$ reduce to $\perp$ for all n. Hence $\bigsqcup_{n\in\omega} \mathsf{O}^n = \mathsf{O} = \mathsf{NF}(\mathsf{O}) \neq \bigsqcup_{n\in\omega} \mathsf{NF}(\mathsf{O}^n) = \perp$.

Definition 13. We say that the truncations are NF-increasing if there exists m such that $M \to_\rho N$ implies $M^{n+m} \succeq_{\mathsf{NF}} N^n$ for all n.

Lemma 14. *Let λ^∞_ρ be ω-compressible. If the truncations are* NF*-increasing then for all n there exists l such that $\mathsf{NF}^n(P) \preceq_{\mathsf{NF}} P^{n+l}$.*

Proof. By confluence, normalisation and ω-compression for λ^∞_ρ, there exists a strongly convergent reduction sequence of length ω from P to $\mathsf{NF}(P)$:

$$P = P_0 \to_\rho P_1 \to_\rho P_2 \ldots \mathsf{NF}(P)$$

Since this reduction sequence is strongly convergent, there exists P_i such that $\mathsf{NF}^n(P) = (P_i)^n$. Since the truncations are NF-increasing, we construct the following (finite) chain from P^{n+l} to $\mathsf{NF}^n(P)$:

$$P^{n+im} = (P_0)^{n+im} \succeq_{\mathsf{NF}} (P_1)^{n+(i-1)m} \ldots \succeq_{\mathsf{NF}} (P_{i-1})^{n+m} \succeq_{\mathsf{NF}} (P_i)^n = \mathsf{NF}^n(P)$$

Taking $l = im$ we have that $\mathsf{NF}^n(P) \preceq_{\mathsf{NF}} P^{n+l}$.

Lemma 15. *Let $P, Q \in \Lambda^\infty_\perp$. Then, $P^n[x := Q^n] \succeq (P[x := Q])^n$.*

This is proved by induction on the number of symbols of P^n.

Lemma 16. *If $\mathsf{T}_\mathcal{U}$ quasi-preserves $\preceq_{fin}$ then the truncations are $\mathsf{T}_\mathcal{U}$-increasing.*

Proof. Suppose $M \to_\perp \perp$. We have that $M^n \succeq_{\mathsf{T}_\mathcal{U}} \perp$. Suppose $M = C[(\lambda x.P)Q] \to_\beta C[P[x := Q]] = N$. Let d be the position of the hole in $C[\ ]$ and $k = n - d > 0$.

$$\begin{aligned}
(C[(\lambda x.P)Q])^{n+2} &= C^{n+2}[(\lambda x.P^k)Q^{k+1}] && \text{by Lemma 8} \\
&\to_\beta C^{n+2}[P^k[x := Q^{k+1}]] \\
&\succeq C^n[P^k[x := Q^k]] \\
&\succeq C^n[(P[x := Q])^k] && \text{by Lemma 15} \\
&= (C[P[x := Q]])^n && \text{by Lemma 8}
\end{aligned}$$

Since $\beta\perp$ is confluent (Theorem 4) and $\mathsf{T}_\mathcal{U}$ quasi-preserves $\preceq_{fin}$,

$$(C[(\lambda x.P)Q])^{n+2} \succeq_{\mathsf{T}_\mathcal{U}} (C[P[x := Q]])^n$$

Definition 17. Let σ be a function from positions of $\perp$'s to $\Lambda^\infty_\perp$. We define M^σ as the result of replacing $\perp$'s in M by the corresponding terms given by σ.

Lemma 18. *Let $M, N \in \Lambda^\infty_\perp$. Then, $M \preceq N$ if and only if $M^\sigma = N$ for some σ.*

Lemma 19. *Let σ be a function from positions of $\perp$'s to $\Lambda^\infty_\perp$. If $M \twoheadrightarrow_\beta N$ then there exists σ' such that $M^\sigma \twoheadrightarrow_\beta N^{\sigma'}$.*

This is proved by induction on the length of the reduction sequence from M to N.

Theorem 20. BT *and* LT *are monotone in* $(\Lambda_\perp^\infty, \preceq)$.

Proof. Let $M, N \in \Lambda_\perp^\infty$ such that $M \preceq N$. We prove that $\mathsf{BT}(M) \preceq \mathsf{BT}(N)$. By normalisation of $\beta\perp$ and postponement of $\perp$ over β (Theorem 4 and Theorem 3), we have that there exists P such that $M \twoheadrightarrow_\beta P \twoheadrightarrow_\perp \mathsf{BT}(M)$. By Lemma 19 we have that $N = M^\sigma \twoheadrightarrow_\beta P^{\sigma'}$. We prove that for all n, $\mathsf{BT}^n(P) \preceq \mathsf{BT}^n(P^{\sigma'})$ by induction on n. Suppose $n = h + 1$. We have three cases:

1. Case $P = \perp$. Then $\mathsf{BT}^n(P) = \perp \preceq \mathsf{BT}^n(P^{\sigma'})$.
2. Case $P = \lambda x_1 \dots x_n.y\ Q_1 \dots Q_k$.
   Then $\mathsf{BT}^n(P) = \lambda x_1 \dots x_n.y\ \mathsf{BT}^{h_1}(Q_1) \dots \mathsf{BT}^{h_k}(Q_k)$. It follows by induction hypothesis that $\mathsf{BT}^{h_i}(Q_i) \preceq \mathsf{BT}^{h_i}(Q_i^{\sigma_{h_i}})$. Hence $P^n \preceq_{\mathsf{BT}} (P^{\sigma'})^n$.
3. Case $P = \lambda x_1 \dots x_n.(\lambda y.R)SQ_1 \dots Q_k$. Since $P \twoheadrightarrow_\perp \mathsf{BT}(M)$, P cannot have head normal form. Hence $\mathsf{BT}^n(P) = \perp \preceq \mathsf{BT}^n(P^{\sigma'})$.

This proof can be easily adapted to Lévy–Longo trees with some minor adjustments.

Corollary 21. *The functions* BT *and* LT *are continuous in* $(\Lambda_\perp^\infty, \preceq)$.

Proof. By Theorem 20, we have that $\bigcup_{n\in\omega} \mathsf{BT}(M^n) \preceq \mathsf{BT}(M)$. The truncations are BT-increasing by Theorem 20 and Lemma 16. The calculus of Böhm trees is ω-compressible by Theorem 3. Hence, we have that:

$$\begin{aligned}
\mathsf{BT}(M) &= \textstyle\bigcup_{n\in\omega} \mathsf{BT}^n(M) \\
&= \textstyle\bigcup_{n\in\omega} \mathsf{BT}(\mathsf{BT}^n(M)) && \text{because } \mathsf{BT}^n(M) \text{ is in normal form} \\
&\preceq \textstyle\bigcup_{n\in\omega} \mathsf{BT}(M^n) && \text{by Lemma 14}
\end{aligned}$$

The same proof works for LT.

We prove that the only parametric tree functions $\mathsf{T}_\mathcal{U} : \Lambda_\perp^\infty \to \Lambda_\perp^\infty$ satisfying continuity are the Böhm tree function and the Lévy–Longo tree function.

Theorem 22. *If* $\mathsf{T}_\mathcal{U} : \Lambda_\perp^\infty \to \Lambda_\perp^\infty$ *is continuous then* $\mathsf{T}_\mathcal{U} = \mathsf{BT}$ *or* $\mathsf{T}_\mathcal{U} = \mathsf{LT}$.

Proof. By Lemma 5, we have that $\overline{\mathcal{T}} \subseteq \mathcal{U} \subseteq \overline{\mathcal{H}}$. We prove that $\mathcal{U} = \overline{\mathcal{H}}$ or $\mathcal{U} = \overline{\mathcal{W}}$.

Suppose that $M \in \overline{\mathcal{W}} - \overline{\mathcal{T}}$. We can also suppose that $M \in \mathsf{BeT}(\Lambda_\perp^\infty)$ because $\overline{\mathcal{T}} \subseteq \mathcal{U}$ and $\mathsf{T}_\mathcal{U}(\mathsf{BeT}(M)) = \mathsf{T}_\mathcal{U}(M)$ by confluence of $\beta\perp$. We have two cases:

1. Let $M = \perp P_k \dots P_1$ and $N = (\lambda x_1 \dots x_k.\perp)P_k \dots P_1$. Since $\mathsf{T}_\mathcal{U}$ is monotone and $M \preceq N$, we have that $\mathsf{T}_\mathcal{U}(M) \preceq \mathsf{T}_\mathcal{U}(N) = \perp$. Hence $M \in \mathcal{U}$.
2. Let $M = (((\dots P_3)P_2)P_1)$. Then, $\mathsf{T}_\mathcal{U}(M) = \bigcup_{n\in\omega} \mathsf{T}_\mathcal{U}(M^n) = \perp$. Hence $M \in \mathcal{U}$.

Hence, we have that $\overline{\mathcal{W}} - \overline{\mathcal{T}} \subseteq \mathcal{U}$ and also $\overline{\mathcal{W}} \subseteq \mathcal{U}$. Suppose now that $\overline{\mathcal{W}} \subset \mathcal{U} \subseteq \overline{\mathcal{H}}$. Then there exists $M \in \mathcal{U}$ such that $M \in \overline{\mathcal{H}} - \overline{\mathcal{W}}$. We prove that $\overline{\mathcal{H}} - \overline{\mathcal{W}} \subseteq \mathcal{U}$ and hence $\mathcal{U} = \overline{\mathcal{H}}$. We can suppose that the terms in $\overline{\mathcal{H}} - \overline{\mathcal{W}}$ are in $\mathsf{LT}(\Lambda_\perp^\infty)$ and then they are either of the form $\lambda x_1 \dots \lambda x_k.\perp$ or $\lambda x_1 x_2 x_3 \dots$. We have two cases:

1. Let $M = \lambda x_1 \ldots \lambda x_k.\bot$ for some k.

$$\begin{aligned} \mathsf{T}_{\mathcal{U}}(\lambda x.\bot) &= \mathsf{T}_{\mathcal{U}}(Mx_1 \ldots x_{k-1}) && \text{because } Mx_1 \ldots x_{k-1} \twoheadrightarrow_\beta \lambda x.\bot \\ &= \mathsf{T}_{\mathcal{U}}(\bot x_1 \ldots x_{k-1}) && \text{because } M \in \mathcal{U} \\ &= \bot && \text{because } \overline{\mathcal{W}} \subseteq \mathcal{U} \end{aligned}$$

   Then, we also have that $\mathsf{T}_{\mathcal{U}}(\lambda x_1 \ldots x_n.\bot) = \bot$ for all n. Since $\mathsf{T}_{\mathcal{U}}$ is continuous, we also have that $\mathsf{T}_{\mathcal{U}}(\lambda x_1 x_2 \ldots) = \bot$.
2. Let $M = \lambda x_1 x_2 \ldots$. Then $\bot = \mathsf{T}_{\mathcal{U}}(M) \succeq \mathsf{T}_{\mathcal{U}}(M^n) = \lambda x_1 \ldots x_n.\bot$ for all n.

6 Models Induced by NF

In this section we define the model induced by NF and give a notion of continuity for these models.

Definition 23. The model induced by NF, denoted by $\mathcal{M}(\mathsf{NF})$, is the applicative structure $(\mathsf{NF}(\Lambda^\infty_\bot), \,.\,, [\![\,]\!])$ defined as follows:

1. $M.N = \mathsf{NF}(MN)$ for all $M, N \in \mathsf{NF}(\Lambda^\infty_\bot)$,
2. $[\![M]\!]_\sigma = \mathsf{NF}(M^\sigma)$ for all $M \in \Lambda$ and where M^σ is the simultaneous substitution of all free variables of M by σ.

By Theorem 6, the class of models induced by the parametric trees is uncountable.

It is easy to prove that $\mathcal{M}(\mathsf{NF})$ is indeed a λ-model of the finite lambda calculus using confluence and normalisation (see Definition 5.3.2 in [2]).

We consider the prefix relation $\preceq$ on $\mathsf{NF}(\Lambda^\infty_\bot)$. For $\mathsf{NF} \in \{\mathsf{BT}, \mathsf{LT}, \mathsf{BeT}, \infty\eta\mathsf{BT}, \eta\mathsf{BT}\}$, the pair $(\mathsf{NF}(\Lambda^\infty_\bot), \preceq)$ is a cpo. We can deduce that the set of normal forms is closed under directed suprema by showing first that a redex in a term should also be present in some finite prefix. In general, the pair $(\mathsf{NF}(\Lambda^\infty_\bot), \preceq)$ may not be a cpo:

Counterexample 24. We show an example of a pair $(\mathsf{T}_{\mathcal{U}}(\Lambda^\infty_\bot), \preceq)$ which is not a cpo. Let $\mathsf{I} = \lambda x.x$ and $\mathsf{K} = \lambda xy.x$. We consider the infinite term $\mathsf{K}^\infty = ((\ldots \mathsf{K})\mathsf{K})\mathsf{I})$. The set $\mathcal{K} = \overline{\mathcal{T}} \cup \{M \in \Lambda^\infty \mid M \twoheadrightarrow_\beta \mathsf{K}^\infty\}$ satisfies the axioms of [11, 12] and, then, $\mathsf{T}_{\mathcal{K}} : \Lambda^\infty_\bot \to \Lambda^\infty_\bot$ is a parametric tree function. The term K^∞ is a redex but none of its prefixes contain any redex. The pair $(\mathsf{T}_{\mathcal{K}}(\Lambda^\infty_\bot), \preceq)$ is not a cpo because the set $X = \{{\mathsf{T}_{\mathcal{K}}}^n(\mathsf{K}^\infty) \mid n \in \omega\} \subset \mathsf{T}_{\mathcal{K}}(\Lambda^\infty_\bot)$ but $\mathsf{K}^\infty = \bigcup X \notin \mathsf{T}_{\mathcal{K}}(\Lambda^\infty_\bot)$.

For the models induced by NF, it makes sense to define a notion of continuity that considers all context operators and not only the application. In particular, we can consider the abstraction operator as a function in the model, i.e. $\mathsf{abs}(M) = \mathsf{NF}(\lambda x.M)$ for $M \in \mathsf{NF}(\Lambda^\infty_\bot)$.

Definition 25. Let $C[\,]$ be a context in $\Lambda^\infty_\bot$. The context operator $C[\,]$ restricted to NF is the function $\lambda\!\!\lambda M {\in} \mathsf{NF}(\Lambda^\infty_\bot).\mathsf{NF}(C[M]) : \mathsf{NF}(\Lambda^\infty_\bot) \to \mathsf{NF}(\Lambda^\infty_\bot)$.

Definition 26. $\mathcal{M}(\mathsf{NF})$ is continuous if the following holds:

1. $(\mathsf{NF}(\Lambda^{\infty}_{\bot}), \preceq)$ is a cpo,
2. the context operators $C[\,]$ restricted to NF are continuous in the Scott topology on the cpo $(\mathsf{NF}(\Lambda^{\infty}_{\bot}), \preceq)$ for all context $C[\,] \in \Lambda^{\infty}_{\bot}$.
3. the approximation property holds: $\mathsf{NF}(M) = \bigcup_{n\in\omega} \mathsf{NF}(\mathsf{NF}^n(M))$ for $M \in \Lambda^{\infty}_{\bot}$.

Counterexample 27. We give examples against continuity of $\mathcal{M}(\mathsf{NF})$:

1. Case $\mathsf{NF} = \mathsf{BeT}$. The application is not monotone, though the abstraction is continuous. Take $M = \bot$, $N = \lambda x.\bot$ and $P = y$. Then $M \preceq N$ but $M \cdot P \not\preceq N \cdot P$. The approximation property holds since $\mathsf{BeT}^n(M)$ is in normal form for all n.
2. Case $\mathsf{NF} = \{\eta\mathsf{BT}, \infty\eta\mathsf{BT}\}$. Neither the abstraction nor the application operators are monotone:
   (a) Take $M = y\bot$ and $N = yx$. Then $M \preceq N$ but $\mathsf{abs}(M) \not\preceq \mathsf{abs}(N)$.
   (b) Take $M = \lambda zx.zx\bot$, $N = \lambda zx.zxx$ and $P = \lambda x.y$. Then $M \preceq N$ but $M \cdot P \not\preceq N \cdot P$.

   Note that in this case the approximation property does not hold.
3. Case $\mathsf{NF} = \mathsf{T}_{\overline{\mathcal{O}}}$ and $\overline{\mathcal{O}} = \overline{\mathcal{W}} \cup \{M \in \Lambda^{\infty} \mid M \twoheadrightarrow_{\beta} \lambda x_1 \ldots x_n.N \text{ and } N \in \overline{\mathcal{W}}\}$. The abstraction and the application are not continuous:
   (a) Take $\mathsf{O} = \lambda x_1 x_2 \ldots$. Then $\mathsf{O} = \mathsf{abs}(\mathsf{O}) \neq \bigcup_{n\in\omega} \mathsf{abs}(\mathsf{O}^n) = \lambda x.\bot$.
   (b) Take $\mathsf{fix} = \lambda f.f(f(\ldots))$ and $\mathsf{K} = \lambda xy.x$. Then $\mathsf{O} = \mathsf{fix}\cdot\mathsf{K} \neq \bigcup_{n\in\omega} \mathsf{fix}^n\cdot\mathsf{K} = \bot$.

   Note that in this case the approximation property does not hold.

We recall a notion of continuous λ-model defined by Welch to deduce that all fixed point operators are equal in the model [2]. For models induced by NF, this result can be deduced instead from confluence and normalisation since the normal form of a fixed point operator is $\lambda f.f(f(\ldots))$.

Definition 28. An applicative continuous λ-model is a structure $(X, \cdot, \sqsubseteq)$ such that:

1. $(X, \sqsubseteq)$ is a cpo,
2. the operation $\cdot$ is continuous in the Scott topology on the cpo $(X, \sqsubseteq)$ and
3. the approximation property holds for Böhm trees on finite λ-terms: $[\![M]\!] = \bigsqcup\{[\![\mathsf{BT}^n(M)]\!] \mid n \in \omega\}$, for all $M \in \Lambda$.

According to Definition 28, the model induced by BT is the only one from Figure 1 which is applicative continuous. None of the remaining trees satisfy the third clause. By replacing BT by the general form NF, we got the third clause in Definition 26.

7 Continuity of the Context Operators

In this section we study continuity of $\mathcal{M}(\mathsf{NF})$ in relation to continuity of NF. We prove that if NF is continuous in $(\Lambda_\perp^\infty, \preceq)$ then so is $\mathcal{M}(\mathsf{NF})$; and the converse for $\mathsf{NF} = \mathsf{T}_\mathcal{U}$. This allows us to deduce that the only continuous models induced by the parametric trees are $\mathcal{M}(\mathsf{BT})$ and $\mathcal{M}(\mathsf{LT})$.

Theorem 29. *If* NF *is continuous in* $(\Lambda_\perp^\infty, \preceq)$ *then*

1. $(\mathsf{NF}(\Lambda_\perp^\infty), \preceq)$ *is an algebraic cpo.*
2. *The Scott topology on* $(\mathsf{NF}(\Lambda_\perp^\infty), \preceq)$ *is the subset topology and the quotient topology by* NF. *In other words, it is initial for the inclusion and final for* NF.
3. *If* $f : \Lambda_\perp^\infty \to \Lambda_\perp^\infty$ *is continuous in* $(\Lambda_\perp^\infty, \preceq)$ *then* $\mathsf{NF} \circ f_{\restriction \mathsf{NF}(\Lambda_\perp^\infty)}$ *is continuous in* $(\mathsf{NF}(\Lambda_\perp^\infty), \preceq)$.

Proof. 1. This follows from Proposition 1.2.21 in [2]. Because $\mathsf{NF}(\Lambda_\perp^\infty)$ is a retract of $\Lambda_\perp^\infty$, the set $\mathsf{NF}(\Lambda_\perp^\infty)$ of normal forms is closed under directed suprema. It is also easy to see that it is algebraic. The compact elements in $(\mathsf{NF}(\Lambda_\perp^\infty), \preceq)$ are the finite normal forms.
2. See Proposition 5.0.11 in [17].
3. Let f be continuous in $(\Lambda_\perp^\infty, \preceq)$. Since $\mathsf{NF} : \Lambda_\perp^\infty \to \Lambda_\perp^\infty$ is continuous, then so is the inclusion $\mathsf{inc} : \mathsf{NF}(\Lambda_\perp^\infty) \to \Lambda_\perp^\infty$. Then, $\mathsf{NF} \circ f_{\restriction \mathsf{NF}(\Lambda_\perp^\infty)} = \mathsf{NF} \circ f \circ \mathsf{inc}$ is composition of continuous functions.

Theorem 30. *If* NF *is continuous in* $(\Lambda_\perp^\infty, \preceq)$ *then so is* $\mathcal{M}(\mathsf{NF})$.

Proof. The first clause in Definition 26 is Theorem 29 part 1. For the second clause, since $C[\bigcup X] = \bigcup C[X]$, we have that $\lambda\!\!\lambda M \in \Lambda_\perp^\infty . C[M] : \Lambda_\perp^\infty \to \Lambda_\perp^\infty$ is continuous in $(\Lambda_\perp^\infty, \preceq)$ and, then, we apply Theorem 29 part 3. For the third clause, we have that $X = \{\mathsf{NF}^n(M) \mid n \in \omega\}$ is a directed set and $\mathsf{NF}(M) = \mathsf{NF}(\mathsf{NF}(M)) = \bigcup_{n \in \omega} \{\mathsf{NF}(\mathsf{NF}^n(M)) \mid n \in \omega\}$.

The converse holds for the parametric trees:

Theorem 31. *If* $\mathcal{M}(\mathsf{T}_\mathcal{U})$ *is continuous then so is* $\mathsf{T}_\mathcal{U} : \Lambda_\perp^\infty \to \Lambda_\perp^\infty$.

Proof. It is enough to prove that $\mathsf{T}_\mathcal{U}$ quasi-preserves $\preceq_{fin}$. In that case, $\mathsf{T}_\mathcal{U}(M^n) \preceq \mathsf{T}_\mathcal{U}(M)$, by Lemma 16 the truncations are $\mathsf{T}_\mathcal{U}$-increasing and then we have that:

$$\begin{aligned} \mathsf{T}_\mathcal{U}(M) &= \textstyle\bigcup_{n \in \omega} \mathsf{T}_\mathcal{U}(\mathsf{T}_\mathcal{U}^n(M)) \\ &\preceq \textstyle\bigcup_{n \in \omega} \mathsf{T}_\mathcal{U}(M^n) \qquad \text{by Lemma 14} \end{aligned}$$

We now prove that $\mathsf{T}_\mathcal{U}$ quasi-preserves $\preceq_{fin}$. Let $P \preceq_{fin} Q$. We do induction on the number n of subterms that are replaced by $\perp$ in Q. The case $n = 1$ is $P = C[\perp]$ and $Q = C[M]$. Since all context operators are monotone, $\mathsf{T}_\mathcal{U}(C[\perp]) \preceq \mathsf{T}_\mathcal{U}(C[M]) = \mathsf{T}_\mathcal{U}(C[\mathsf{NF}(M)])$. The case $n > 0$ is similar.

Theorem 32. $\mathcal{M}(\mathsf{BT})$ *and* $\mathcal{M}(\mathsf{LT})$ *are the only continuous models induced by parametric trees.*

Proof. By Corollary 21, Theorem 22 and Theorem 31.

8 An Embedding from $\infty\eta\mathsf{BT}(\Lambda_\perp^\infty)$ in D_∞

In this section we use the fact that $\mathcal{M}(\mathsf{BT})$ is continuous to prove that the interpretation on D_∞ extended to infinite terms is homomorphic with the application and the abstraction. We can, then, show that there is an injective embedding from the infinitary lambda calculus of $\infty\eta$-Böhm trees in D_∞.

Using the Approximation Theorem [19] we extend the interpretation to infinite terms as follows: $[\![M]\!] = \sqcup\{[\![\mathsf{BT}^n(M)]\!] \mid n \in \omega\}$ for an infinite term M.

Lemma 33. *Let $M, N \in \Lambda_\perp^\infty$.*

1. *If $\mathsf{BT}(M) \preceq \mathsf{BT}(N)$ then $D_\infty \models M \sqsubseteq N$.*
2. *If $\mathsf{BT}(M) \twoheadrightarrow_{\eta^{-1}} \mathsf{BT}(N)$ then $D_\infty \models M = N$.*

The first part is proved using the Characterisation Theorem on finite terms. For the second part, we have to re-do some work and prove a similar statement to Proposition 19.1.13 in [2] for infinite $\beta\perp$-normal forms.

Lemma 34. $[\![C[M]]\!] = \sqcup\{[\![C[\mathsf{BT}^n(M)]]\!] \mid n \in \omega\}$

Proof. By Theorem 32, we have that $\lambda\!\!\lambda M \in \mathsf{BT}(\Lambda_\perp^\infty).\mathsf{BT}(C[M])$ is continuous. Hence,

1. $C[\mathsf{BT}^n(M)] \preceq_{\mathsf{BT}} C[M]$ by monotonicity.
2. for all n there exists k such that $\mathsf{BT}^n(C[M]) \preceq_{\mathsf{BT}} C[\mathsf{BT}^k(M)]$ because the truncations are compact in $(\mathsf{BT}(\Lambda_\perp^\infty), \preceq)$.

By Lemma 33, $[\![C[\mathsf{BT}^n(M)]]\!] \sqsubseteq [\![C[M]]\!]$ and $[\![\mathsf{BT}^n(C[M])]\!] \sqsubseteq [\![C[\mathsf{BT}^k(M)]]\!]$.

The following lemma is a triviality in the finite lambda calculus but for the infinite case we need to prove it and use continuity.

Lemma 35. *Let $M, N \in \Lambda_\perp^\infty$.*

1. $[\![(MN)]\!] = [\![M]\!].[\![N]\!]$.
2. $[\![(\lambda x.M)]\!] = \lambda^G d \in D_\infty.[\![M]\!]_{\rho(x:=d)}$.

Proof. Using Lemma 34.

Lemma 36. *If $D_\infty \models M \sqsubseteq N$ then $D_\infty \models C[M] \sqsubseteq C[N]$.*

Proof. This is proved by induction on the position of the hole in C using Lemma 35.

Lemma 37. *Let $M \in \Lambda_\perp^\infty$. Then $[\![M]\!] = \perp$ iff M has no head normal form.*

Proof. Using the Characterisation Theorem on finite terms.

Theorem 38 (Characterisation Theorem extended to infinite terms).
The following statements are equivalent for terms M, N in $\Lambda_\perp^\infty$:

1. $M \preceq_{\eta^{-1}} N$.
2. $D_\infty \models M \sqsubseteq N$.
3. $M \subseteq_h N$.
4. $M \subseteq_{h_f} N$.

Proof. $(1 \Rightarrow 2)$ follows from Theorem 33. We prove $(2 \Rightarrow 3)$. By Lemma 36, $D_\infty \models C[M] \sqsubseteq C[N]$. Hence, by Lemma 37, if $C[M]$ has head normal form, so does $C[N]$.
$(3 \Rightarrow 4)$ is trivial. $(4 \Rightarrow 1)$ follows by applying the Böhm-out technique to $\preceq_{\eta^{-1}}$ and it is rather long, though the use of commutation properties of the reductions helps to make it shorter than the proof found in [2] for the finite lambda calculus.

Remark 39. As a consequence of Theorem 38, the interpretation function $[\![\ ]\!]$ is an injective embedding from $\infty\eta\mathsf{BT}(\Lambda_\perp^\infty)$ to D_∞. The following example shows that it is not surjective, i.e. D_∞ contains more elements than $\infty\eta\mathsf{BT}(\Lambda_\perp^\infty)$.

We define $M_0 = y\perp$ and $M_n = \lambda x_1 \ldots x_n.y(x_1 x_2 \ldots x_n \perp) x_1 x_2 \ldots x_n$. Clearly $X = \{M_n \mid n \in \omega\}$ is directed in $(\Lambda_\perp^\infty, \preceq_{\eta^{-1}})$ and so is $[\![X]\!] = \{[\![M_n]\!] \mid n \in \omega\}$ in D_∞ by the Characterisation Theorem. The supremum of $[\![X]\!]$ exists in D_∞ but not in $\Lambda_\perp^\infty$.

9 Tree Topologies

In this section we study the relation between the Scott topology on the prefix relation and the tree topologies. This allows us to deduce that the only parametric tree topologies that make all context operators continuous and in which the approximation property holds are the ones of Böhm and Lévy–Longo. We also give an alternative proof of continuity of the context operator with respect to the Böhm and Lévy–Longo tree topologies on the set of finite lambda terms via the infinitary lambda calculus [2, 14].

The (Böhm) tree topology is defined in [2] as the initial topology for $\mathsf{BT}_{\restriction\Lambda} : \Lambda \to \mathsf{BT}(\Lambda_\perp^\infty)$ where $\mathsf{BT}(\Lambda_\perp^\infty)$ is considered with the Scott topology on the prefix relation. By just replacing BT by NF, we get the following two notions of tree topologies:

Definition 40. Suppose that $(\mathsf{NF}(\Lambda_\perp^\infty), \preceq)$ is a cpo. We consider the Scott topology on $(\mathsf{NF}(\Lambda_\perp^\infty), \preceq)$.

1. The tree topology on $\Lambda_\perp^\infty$ is the initial topology for $\mathsf{NF} : \Lambda_\perp^\infty \to \mathsf{NF}(\Lambda_\perp^\infty)$.
2. The tree topology on Λ is the initial topology for $\mathsf{NF}_{\restriction\Lambda} : \Lambda \to \mathsf{NF}(\Lambda_\perp^\infty)$.

Remark 41. 1. The open sets in the tree topology on $\Lambda_\perp^\infty$ are of the form $\mathsf{NF}^{-1}(O)$ with O open in $\mathsf{NF}(\Lambda_\perp^\infty)$. They are closed under $=_{\mathsf{NF}}$.

2. The tree topology on Λ is the subspace topology of the tree topology on $\Lambda_\perp^\infty$.

In the following lemma, the function NF might not be continuous in $(\Lambda_\perp^\infty, \preceq)$.

Lemma 42. *Suppose* $(\mathsf{NF}(\Lambda_\perp^\infty), \preceq))$ *is a cpo.*

1. *The inclusion* $\mathsf{inc} : \mathsf{NF}(\Lambda_\perp^\infty) \to \Lambda_\perp^\infty$ *is a continuous function from the Scott topology on* $(\mathsf{NF}(\Lambda_\perp^\infty), \preceq)$ *to the tree topology on* $\Lambda_\perp^\infty$.
2. *Let* $f : \Lambda_\perp^\infty \to \Lambda_\perp^\infty$ *be a function such that* $\mathsf{NF} \circ f = \mathsf{NF} \circ f \circ \mathsf{NF}$
   (a) *The function* f *is continuous in the tree topology on* $\Lambda_\perp^\infty$ *if and only if* $\mathsf{NF} \circ f_{\restriction \mathsf{NF}(\Lambda_\perp^\infty)} : \mathsf{NF}(\Lambda_\perp^\infty) \to \mathsf{NF}(\Lambda_\perp^\infty)$ *is continuous in the Scott topology on* $(\mathsf{NF}(\Lambda_\perp^\infty), \preceq))$.
   (b) *Suppose* $f_{\restriction \Lambda} : \Lambda \to \Lambda$. *If* $f : \Lambda_\perp^\infty \to \Lambda_\perp^\infty$ *is continuous in the tree topology on* $\Lambda_\perp^\infty$ *then* $f_{\restriction \Lambda} : \Lambda \to \Lambda$ *is continuous in the tree topology on* Λ.

Proof. 1. An open set in the tree topology on $\Lambda_\perp^\infty$ is of the form $\mathsf{NF}^{-1}(O)$ with O open in $(\mathsf{NF}(\Lambda_\perp^\infty), \preceq))$. Then, $\mathsf{inc}^{-1}(\mathsf{NF}^{-1}(O)) = \{M \in \mathsf{NF}(\Lambda_\perp^\infty) \mid M \in \mathsf{NF}^{-1}(O)\} = \{M \in \mathsf{NF}(\Lambda_\perp^\infty) \mid \mathsf{NF}(M) \in O\} = O$ because $\mathsf{NF}(M) = M$ for all $M \in \mathsf{NF}(\Lambda_\perp^\infty)$.

2. (a) ($\Rightarrow$). Let f be continuous in the tree topology on $\Lambda_\perp^\infty$. Then, $\mathsf{NF} \circ f_{\restriction \mathsf{NF}(\Lambda_\perp^\infty)} = \mathsf{NF} \circ f \circ \mathsf{inc}$ is composition of continuous functions.
($\Leftarrow$). Let $\mathsf{NF} \circ f_{\restriction \mathsf{NF}(\Lambda_\perp^\infty)}$ be continuous. Then $\mathsf{NF} \circ f_{\restriction \mathsf{NF}(\Lambda_\perp^\infty)} \circ \mathsf{NF} : \Lambda_\perp^\infty \to \mathsf{NF}(\Lambda_\perp^\infty)$ is a continuous function from the tree topology to $(\mathsf{NF}(\Lambda_\perp^\infty), \preceq))$. We know that $\mathsf{NF} \circ f_{\restriction \mathsf{NF}(\Lambda_\perp^\infty)} \circ \mathsf{NF} = \mathsf{NF} \circ f \circ \mathsf{NF} = \mathsf{NF} \circ f$. By Proposition 5.0.2 [17], we have that f is continuous in the tree topology on $\Lambda_\perp^\infty$.
(b) Any open set in the tree topology on Λ is of the form $\mathsf{NF}^{-1}(O) \cap \Lambda$. Then $f_{\restriction \Lambda}^{-1}(\mathsf{NF}^{-1}(O) \cap \Lambda) = f^{-1}(\mathsf{NF}^{-1}(O)) \cap \Lambda$ is open in the tree topology on Λ.

Theorem 43.

1. *The Böhm and Lévy–Longo tree topologies are the only parametric tree topologies on the set* $\Lambda_\perp^\infty$ *that satisfies the following two conditions:*
   (a) *continuity of all context operators* $⅄M \in \Lambda_\perp^\infty.C[M] : \Lambda_\perp^\infty \to \Lambda_\perp^\infty$ *and*
   (b) *the approximation property, i.e.* $\mathsf{NF}(M) = \bigsqcup_{n \in \omega} \mathsf{NF}(\mathsf{NF}^n(M))$ *for* $M \in \Lambda_\perp^\infty$.
2. *The finite context operators* $⅄M \in \Lambda.C[M] : \Lambda \to \Lambda$ *are continuous in the Böhm and Lévy–Longo tree topologies on* Λ.

Proof. They follow from Lemma 42 and Theorem 32.

Continuity of the finite context operators with respect to the Böhm tree topology on Λ is proved in [2] and with respect to the Lévy–Longo tree topology on Λ is proved in [14] along the lines of [2]. The proof in [2] uses the notion of approximants (approximants are finite $\beta\perp$-normal forms) and essentially the following proposition (called *syntactic continuity* in [1]): *For all finite* $\beta\perp$*-normal form* P *such that* $P \preceq_{\mathsf{BT}} C[M]$ *there exists* N *in finite* $\beta\perp$*-normal form such that* $N \preceq_{\mathsf{BT}} M$ *and* $C[N] \preceq_{\mathsf{BT}} N$. This proposition has been proved using a variety of methods by Wadsworth [18], Lévy [13] and Welch [20]. Our proof (Theorem 43 part 2) uses the continuity of NF and properties of initial and final topologies.

10 The NF-Topology

We will now give an explicit characterisation of the open sets in the Böhm and Lévy–Longo tree topologies.

Definition 44. A subset O of $\Lambda_\perp^\infty$ is an open set in the NF-topology provided

1. O is open in the Scott topology of $(\Lambda_\perp^\infty, \preceq)$ and
2. O is closed under $=_{\mathsf{NF}}$.

It is easy to see that the NF-topology makes the normal form NF and the context operators continuous.

Lemma 45. *Suppose that* $\mathsf{NF} : \Lambda_\perp^\infty \to \Lambda_\perp^\infty$ *is continuous in* $(\Lambda_\perp^\infty, \preceq)$*. Then the tree topology is exactly the set of open sets of* $(\Lambda_\perp^\infty, \preceq)$ *closed under* $=_{\mathsf{NF}}$.

Proof. Since the tree topology is initial for NF, the open sets of the tree topology are open in $(\Lambda_\perp^\infty, \preceq)$. They are also closed under $=_{\mathsf{NF}}$.
Let O be an open set in $(\Lambda_\perp^\infty, \preceq)$ closed under $=_{\mathsf{NF}}$. Then, $O = \mathsf{NF}^{-1}(\mathsf{NF}(O))$. Since the Scott topology on $(\mathsf{NF}(\Lambda_\perp^\infty), \preceq)$ is final for NF, $\mathsf{NF}(O)$ is open in $\mathsf{NF}(\Lambda_\perp^\infty)$ and hence $O = \mathsf{NF}^{-1}(\mathsf{NF}(O))$ is open in the tree topology.

Corollary 46. *The* BT*-topology and* LT*-topology coincide with the Böhm and Lévy–Longo tree topologies respectively.*

Proof. This follows from Corollary 21 and Lemma 45.

Unfortunately, the BeT-topology coincides with the LT-topology. In general, the $\mathsf{T}_{\mathcal{U}}$-topology is either the BT-topology or the LT-topology.

Acknowledgements. We thank Vincent van Oostrom and the referees for their useful comments, Mariangiola Dezani-Ciancaglini for her knowledge and inspiration, Simona Ronchi della Rocca for telling us the solution of a key exercise in [2] and Alexander Kurz for interesting discussions on coinduction.

References

1. R. M. Amadio and P.-L. Curien. *Domains and Lambda-Calculi.* Cambridge University Press, Cambridge, 1998.
2. H.P. Barendregt. *The Lambda Calculus: Its Syntax and Semantics.* North-Holland, Amsterdam, Revised edition, 1984.
3. M. Barr. Terminal coalgebras for endofunctors on sets. *Theoretical Computer Science*, 114(2):299–315, 1999.
4. A. Berarducci. Infinite λ-calculus and non-sensible models. In *Logic and algebra (Pontignano, 1994)*, pages 339–377. Dekker, New York, 1996.
5. I. Bethke, J.W. Klop, and R. de Vrijer. Descendants and origins in term rewriting. *Information and Computation*, 159:59–124, 2000.

6. M. Coppo, M. Dezani-Ciancaglini, and M. Zacchi. Type theories, normal forms, and D_∞-lambda-models. *Information and Computation*, 72(2):85–116, 1987.
7. N. Dershowitz, S. Kaplan, and D. Plaisted. Rewrite, rewrite, rewrite, rewrite, rewrite, ... *Theoretical Computer Science*, 83(1):71–96, 21 June 1991.
8. M. Dezani-Ciancaglini, P. Severi, and F.J. de Vries. Infinitary lambda calculus and discrimination of Berarducci trees. *Theoretical Computer Science*, 298(2):275–302, 2003.
9. J.R. Kennaway, J.W. Klop, M. Sleep, and F.J. de Vries. Infinite lambda calculus and Böhm models. In *Rewriting Techniques and Applications*, volume 914 of *LNCS*, pages 257–270. Springer-Verlag, 1995.
10. J.R. Kennaway, J.W. Klop, M. Sleep, and F.J. de Vries. Infinitary lambda calculus. *Theoretical Computer Science*, 175(1):93–125, 1997.
11. J.R. Kennaway, V. van Oostrom, and F.J. de Vries. Meaningless terms in rewriting. *J. Funct. Logic Programming*, Article 1:35 pp, 1999.
12. J.R. Kennaway and F.J. de Vries. Infinitary rewriting. In Terese, editor, *Term Rewriting Systems*, volume 55 of *Cambridge Tracts in Theoretical Computer Science*, pages 668–711. Cambridge University Press, 2003.
13. J.-J. Lévy. An algebraic interpretation of the $\lambda\beta K$-calculus, and an application of a labelled λ-calculus. *Theoretical Computer Science*, 2(1):97–114, 1976.
14. C.-H. L. Ong. *The lazy lambda calculus:an investigation into the foundations of functional programming.* PhD thesis, University of Cambridge, 1992.
15. P. Severi and F.J. de Vries. A lambda calculus for D_∞. Technical report, University of Leicester, 2002.
16. P. Severi and F.J. de Vries. An extensional Böhm model. In *Rewriting Techniques and Applications*, volume 2378 of *LNCS*, pages 159–173. Springer-Verlag, 2002.
17. M. Smyth. Topology. In S. Abramsky, D. M. Gabbay, and T. S. E. Maibaum, editors, *Handbook of Logic in Computer Science*, volume 1, pages 641–762. Oxford University Press, Oxford, 1993.
18. C. P. Wadsworth. *Semantics and Pragmatics of the Lambda-calculus.* PhD thesis, Oxford University, 1971.
19. C. P. Wadsworth. Approximate reduction and lambda calculus models. *SIAM Journal on Computing*, 7(3):337–356, 1978.
20. P. Welch. Continuous semantics and inside out reductions. In C. Böhm, editor, *Lambda Calculus and Computer Science Theory*, volume 37 of *LNCS*, pages 122–146. Springer-Verlag, 1975.

Call-by-Name and Call-by-Value as Token-Passing Interaction Nets

François-Régis Sinot*

LIX, École Polytechnique, 91128 Palaiseau, France
frs@lix.polytechnique.fr

Abstract. Two common misbeliefs about encodings of the λ-calculus in interaction nets (INs) are that they are good only for strategies that are not very well understood (e.g. optimal reduction) and that they always have to deal in a complex way with *boxes*. In brief, the theory of interaction nets is more or less disconnected from the standard theory: we can do things in INs that we cannot do with terms, which is true [5, 10]; and we cannot do in INs things that can easily be done with terms. This paper contributes to fighting this misbelief by showing that the standard call-by-name and call-by-value strategies of the λ-calculus are encoded in interaction nets in a very simple and extensible way, and in particular that these encodings do not need any notion of box. This work can also be seen as a first step towards a generic approach to derive graph-based abstract machines.

1 Introduction

Interaction nets (INs) [9] are a graphical paradigm of distributed computation that makes all the steps in a computation explicit and expressed uniformly in the same formalism. Reduction in interaction nets is local and strongly confluent, hence reductions can take place in any order, even in parallel (see [17]). These properties make interaction nets well-suited as an intermediate formalism in the implementation of programming languages.

Indeed, interaction nets have their origins in linear logic [6], but have been most successfully used in the implementation of optimal reduction in the λ-calculus, starting from Lamping [10], Gonthier, Abadi and Lévy [8], Asperti et al. [1] to the recent work of van Oostrom et al. [19]. There have also been several other efficient (non-optimal) implementations of the λ-calculus, for instance Mackie [15, 16].

All of the above encodings of the λ-calculus have in common that a β-redex is always translated to an active pair (i.e. a redex in interaction nets), hence, paradoxically, while all reductions are equivalent, there is still the need for an external interpreter to find the redexes and manage them, which is typically implemented

* Projet Logical, Pôle Commun de Recherche en Informatique du plateau de Saclay, CNRS, École Polytechnique, INRIA, Université Paris-Sud.

P. Urzyczyn (Ed.): TLCA 2005, LNCS 3461, pp. 386–400, 2005.

by maintaining a stack of redexes [17]. The fact that different β-reductions may be interleaved also has the nasty consequence that the encodings need to simulate *boxes* in a more or less complex and costly way (see [10, 8, 13, 15, 16] for various types of such encodings). This reveals two common misbeliefs about interaction nets for λ-calculus: they are good only to express strategies that we cannot write in a term-like framework, and consequently that we do not understand very well, and they always need a complex mechanism to manage boxes. This paper intends to fight these two misbeliefs. More precisely, we will present encodings of the call-by-name and call-by-value strategies of the λ-calculus in interaction nets. These encodings are based on the idea of a single evaluation token, which is a standard interaction agent, walking through the term as an evaluation function would do. They are thus very natural and easy to understand.

An implementation of the λ-calculus on a sequential machine has whatsoever to perform reductions in a certain order (i.e. to follow a strategy), hence it is meaningful to give up the redex-to-redex translation in interaction nets. This has actually been done in Lippi's work [12, 11]. Lippi gives an implementation of left reduction in interaction nets, and goes even further by describing the Krivine machine in interaction nets. However, his work is based on notions of coding and decoding which makes the overall presentation difficult to understand and he does not make clear the notion of evaluation token hidden in his encoding. In particular, he does not extend his presentation to call-by-value, which indeed seems difficult with his presentation.

In contrast, our presentation is more simple and uniform: it is based on the simple idea of a single evaluation token walking through the representation of the term exactly as a functional evaluator would do, going down on recursive calls and up when exiting the recursive calls. This approach is very simple and is indeed a good alternative to working with terms, since it allows to abstract away from syntactical details such as α-conversion. Moreover it is very easily extended from call-by-name to call-by-value.

We thus provide new graph-based abstract machines for call-by-name and call-by-value, with the peculiarity that the structure of the term itself is used instead of a stack or a heap in traditional abstract machine. Moreover, our approach is so simple that there is some serious hope it can be extended to more interesting strategies. It is also nice from a theoretical point of view to (try to) bridge the gap between optimal reduction and call-by-name/value by providing a (more) uniform framework.

The idea of a token walking through a graph is superficially reminiscent of the geometry of interaction (GoI) [7], which has been used to implement call-by-name [14] and call-by-value [3] abstract machines. However, the details of the approach are quite different. In particular, the GoI machines avoid as much as possible to modify the graph, thus they have less freedom in the strategy. For instance, call-by-value is obtained at the price of a greater complexity. While it is relatively clear that the GoI machines can be formalised in our framework (i.e. by making the token explicit and encoding the stack with interaction agents), this does not seem to lead to a better understanding of the GoI machines (in particular to a possibly more satisfactory call-by-value machine).

Our approach is also reminiscent of continuation-passing style (CPS) transformation [18], in the sense that we simulate an evaluation strategy by forbidding certain reductions until something triggers them (the token or the continuation). However, a CPS transformation followed by a traditional encoding in interaction nets would certainly not allow to get rid of boxes, although only one β-reduction would be allowed at a time. In this respect, our framework is thus more satisfactory; it also seems easier to extend to other strategies.

The rest of this paper is structured as follows. In Section 2, we recall some background on interaction nets. In Section 3, we give the full details of our approach in the case of call-by-name for closed terms. Sections 4 and 5 adapt the presentation respectively to closed call-by-value and to open terms. Finally, we conclude in Section 6.

2 Interaction Nets

A system of interaction nets [9] is specified from a set Σ of symbols, and a set $\mathcal{R}$ of interaction rules. Each symbol $\alpha \in \Sigma$ has an associated (fixed) *arity*. An occurrence of a symbol $\alpha \in \Sigma$ will be called an *agent*. If the arity of α is n, then the agent has $n+1$ *ports*: a distinguished one called the *principal port* depicted by an arrow, and n *auxiliary ports* labelled $x_1, \ldots, x_n$ corresponding to the arity of the symbol. Such an agent will be drawn in the following way:

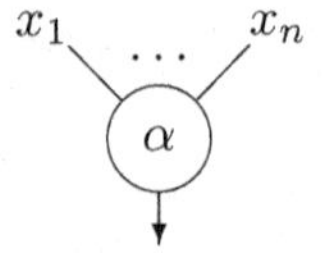

Intuitively, a net N built on Σ is a graph (not necessarily connected) with agents at the vertices. The edges of the graph connect agents together at the ports such that there is only one edge at every port. The ports of an agent that are not connected to another agent are called free. There are two special instances of a net: a wiring (no agents) and the empty net; the extremes of wirings are also called free ports.

An interaction rule $((\alpha, \beta) \Longrightarrow N) \in \mathcal{R}$ replaces a pair of agents $(\alpha, \beta) \in \Sigma \times \Sigma$ connected together on their principal ports (this is called an *active pair* or *redex*), by a net N. Rules must satisfy two conditions: all free ports are preserved during reduction (reduction is local, i.e. only the part of the net involved in the rewrite is modified), and there is at most one rule for each pair of agents. The following diagram shows the format of interaction rules (N can be any net built from Σ).

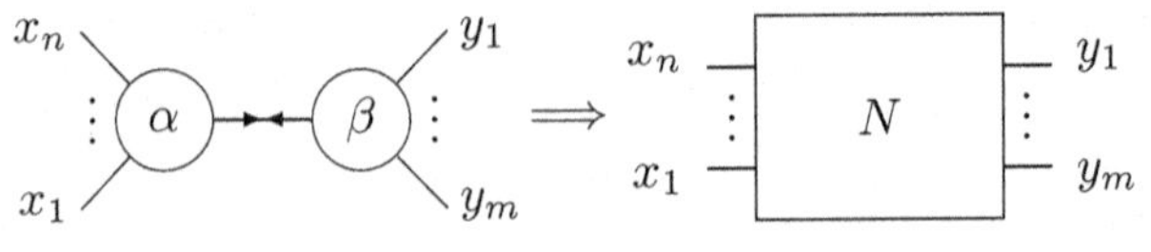

We use the notation $\Longrightarrow$ for the one step reduction relation and $\Longrightarrow^*$ for its transitive and reflexive closure. If a net does not contain any active pairs then we say that it is in normal form. One-step reduction ($\Longrightarrow$) satisfies the diamond property, and thus we obtain a very strong notion of confluence. Indeed, all reduction sequences are permutation equivalent and standard results from rewriting theory tell us that weak and strong normalisation coincide (if one reduction sequence terminates, then all reduction sequences terminate).

3 Call-by-Name

In this section, we give an encoding of the call-by-name strategy of the λ-calculus in interaction nets. We present the strategy with inductive rules, in a big-step style, and the first step in our encoding is to derive a more fine-grained rewrite system. In this section, we only consider closed terms (i.e. terms without free variables). Open terms will be dealt with in Section 5.

3.1 Preliminaries

We assume basic knowledge of the λ-calculus; we refer the reader to [2] for more details. To fix notations, the set Λ of λ-terms is defined by:

$$t, u ::= x \mid \lambda x.t \mid t\ u$$

where x ranges over a set of variables. Terms are considered modulo α-conversion i.e. renaming of bound variables. We denote by $\mathsf{fv}(t)$ the set of free variables of a term t.

This set is equipped with the rewrite relation:

$$(\beta) \qquad (\lambda x.t)\ u \to_\beta t\{x := u\}$$

where $t\{x := u\}$ denotes t where all occurrences of x are replaced by u, without name capture. We write $\to_\beta$ for one-step reduction and $\to_\beta^*$ for its reflexive transitive closure.

We call weak head normal forms (whnf) terms of the form $\lambda x.t$ or $x\ t_1 \ldots t_n$. Note that closed whnf are only terms of the form $\lambda x.t$. We say that v is a weak head normal form of t if v is a weak head normal form and $t \to_\beta^* v$.

3.2 Big-Step Style

The call-by-name strategy for closed λ-terms is specified by the following evaluation rules, as found in various textbooks:

$$\frac{}{\lambda x.t \Downarrow \lambda x.t} \qquad \frac{t \Downarrow \lambda x.t' \quad t'\{x := u\} \Downarrow v}{t\ u \Downarrow v}$$

This is in fact the inductive definition of an evaluation function (also known as big-step semantics), rather than a strategy: we take a λ-term t as input and we inductively find v such that $t \Downarrow v$, then v is the unique weak head normal form of t (provided it exists) obtained by the call-by-name strategy, but the reduction path is not visible at the top-level.

Too much is hidden in these rules for a direct encoding in interaction nets. In the rule for application, we call the procedure recursively on the left term, and then we have to return to this application somehow. In a functional programming setting, this is done automatically, but this is not a free operation: when a function is entered, the current environment is saved on the stack; when it returns, this information is popped down from the stack. We will thus formalise the call-by-name strategy in a small-step style, so as to be more explicit about the control flow and to facilitate the encoding in interaction nets.

3.3 Small-Step Style

We want to replace the previous inductive rules by a first-order rewrite system but we also want to be as explicit about the evaluation order as in the previous system. We thus enrich the syntax of terms with two unary symbols $\Downarrow$ (corresponding to evaluation) and $\Uparrow$ (corresponding to the evaluation function returning) and define the following rewrite system:

$$\begin{array}{lll} \Downarrow \lambda x.t & \to & \Uparrow \lambda x.t \\ \Downarrow (t\ u) & \to & (\Downarrow t)\ u \\ (\Uparrow \lambda x.t)\ u & \to & \Downarrow t\{x := u\} \end{array}$$

Although we do not want to get into any details, it is clear how the small-step system is derived from the big-step one. In the particular case of call-by-name, omitting the symbol $\Uparrow$ gives an equivalent system (this is exactly tail-recursion optimisation), but we prefer to include it already; this point will be discussed again in Section 4. Also note that, as far as we know, such a simple small-step presentation of call-by-name has not been made before; usual small-step presentations of call-by-name and call-by-value rely on inductive rules allowing reductions in a certain class of contexts, hence do not make explicit the flow of evaluation contrary to our presentation, which is crucial for the encoding into interaction nets. In some sense, our presentation is intermediate between traditional small-step semantics (which separate as much as possible reduction and strategy) and abstract machines (which may involve complex data structures). We call this presentation the *token-passing semantics* of call-by-name.

A λ-term t is always in normal form with respect to this system, and so is $\Uparrow t$. To evaluate t, we have to start reduction from $\Downarrow t$.

First note that a reduction always involves a $\Downarrow$ or $\Uparrow$, hence, by the following proposition, there is always at most one redex in a term obtained from reduction of $\Downarrow t$. Thus the control flow is really made explicit at the syntactic level.

Proposition 1. *If $\Downarrow t \to^* u$, then there exists exactly one occurrence of $\Downarrow$ or $\Uparrow$ in u.*

Proof. By induction. The first two rules are easy. In the last rule, the right hand-side may have zero or more than one occurrences of u, but u has no occurrence of $\Downarrow$ or $\Uparrow$ by the induction hypothesis. □

The two systems correspond to each other in the following sense:

Proposition 2. $t \Downarrow v \iff \Downarrow t \to^* \Uparrow v$

Proof. $\Rightarrow$ By induction:

- $\lambda x.t \Downarrow \lambda x.t$ and indeed $\Downarrow \lambda x.t \to \Uparrow \lambda x.t$
- if $t\ u \Downarrow v$, then there exists t' such that $t \Downarrow \lambda x.t'$ and $t'\{x := u\} \Downarrow v$. By induction, $\Downarrow t \to^* \Uparrow \lambda x.t'$ and $\Downarrow t'\{x := u\} \to^* \Uparrow v$, hence:
  $\Downarrow (t\ u) \to (\Downarrow t)\ u \to^* (\Uparrow \lambda x.t')\ u \to \Downarrow t'\{x := u\} \to^* \Uparrow v$

$\Leftarrow$ The first part of the proposition (already proved) allows to state the following lemma: if t is a λ-term and t has a whnf, then there exists v such that $\Downarrow t \to^* \Uparrow v$ and v is a whnf (consequence of classical theorems on call-by-name). Then we can proceed by induction:

- $\Downarrow \lambda x.t \to \Uparrow \lambda x.t$ and indeed $\lambda x.t \Downarrow \lambda x.t$
- $\Downarrow (t\ u) \to (\Downarrow t)\ u$. By the lemma, if t has a whnf, there exists $\lambda x.t'$ (remember that all terms are closed), such that $\Downarrow t \to^* \Uparrow \lambda x.t'$. Moreover, $t \Downarrow \lambda x.t'$ by induction. Then $(\Uparrow \lambda x.t')\ u \to \Downarrow t'\{x := u\}$ and a similar argument (lemma and induction) allows to conclude. If t of $t'\{x := u\}$ does not have a whnf, the proposition is trivially true (we do not reach a term of the form $\Uparrow v$). □

Hence the given rewrite system faithfully corresponds to the call-by-name strategy. This step is crucial, as the interaction net encoding will closely follow the small-step style system. Also remark that the method used here is very general.

3.4 Encoding of Terms

The translation $\mathcal{T}(\cdot)$ of λ-terms into interaction nets is very natural. We basically represent terms by their syntax tree, where we group together several occurrences of the same variable by agents c (corresponding to copy) and bind them to their corresponding λ node (this is sometimes referred to as a *backpointer*). The nodes for application and abstraction are agents λ and a with three ports; their principal port is directed towards the root of the term. Note that in traditional encodings, the application agent looks towards its left, so that interaction with an abstraction is always possible. Here, on the contrary, terms are translated to *packages* [12] and in particular there will be no spontaneous reduction, something will have to trigger them: the *evaluation token*.

Variables. In this section, we consider only closed terms (open terms will be dealt with in Section 5), hence variables are not translated as such. They will simply be represented by edges between their binding λ and their grouped occurrence in the body of the abstraction, as explained below.

Application. The translation $\mathcal{T}(t\ u)$ of an application $t\ u$ is simply an agent a of arity 2 pointing to the root, with $\mathcal{T}(t)$ and $\mathcal{T}(u)$ linked to its auxiliary ports. If t and u share common free variables, then c agents (representing copy) collect these together pairwise so that a single occurrence of each free variable occurs amongst the free edges (only one such copy is represented on the figure).

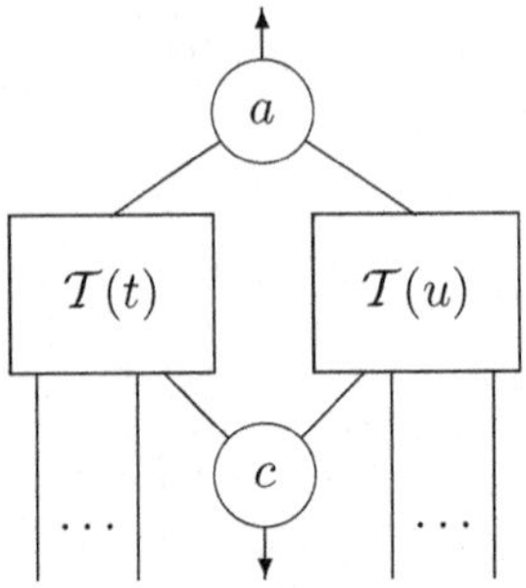

Abstraction. If $\lambda x.t$ is an abstraction, $\mathcal{T}(\lambda x.t)$ is obtained by introducing an agent λ, and simply linking its right auxiliary port to $\mathcal{T}(t)$ and its left one to the unique wire corresponding to x in $\mathcal{T}(t)$. If x does not appear in t, then the left port of the agent λ is linked to an agent ϵ.

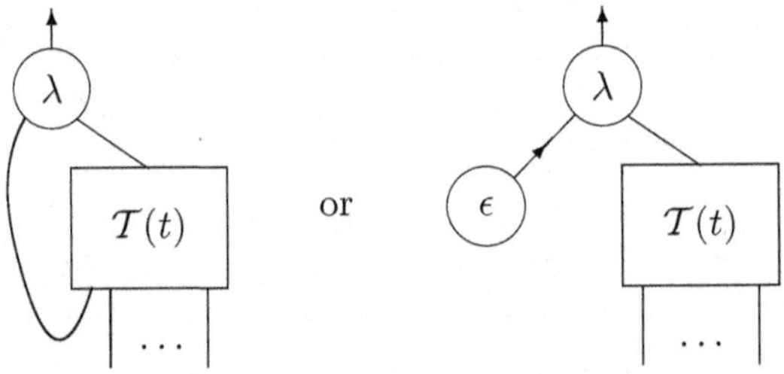

To sum up, we represent λ-terms in a very natural way. In particular, there is no artifact to simulate boxes. Another point worth noticing is that, because of the explicit link between a variable and its binding λ, α-conversion comes from free, as it is often the case in graphical representations of the λ-calculus. So far, we only introduced agents λ and a strictly corresponding to the λ-calculus, as well as agents ϵ and c for the explicit resource managements necessary (and desirable: we do not want to hide such important things) in interaction nets. Also remark that the translation of a term has no active pair, hence is in normal form, whatever the interaction rules we allow. Moreover, it has exactly one principal port, at the root.

3.5 Evaluation by Interaction

We introduce two new unary agents $\Downarrow$ and $\Uparrow$. To evaluate a closed λ-term t with call-by-name, we simply build the following net, that we will denote $\Downarrow \mathcal{T}(t)$.

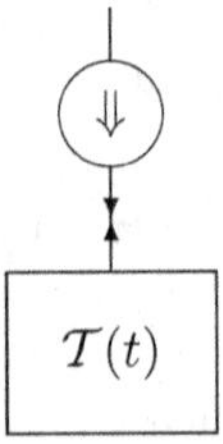

$\Uparrow \mathcal{T}(t)$ will be a net built in the same way, but with a $\Uparrow$ agent instead, with its principal port directed towards the root. In particular, $\Uparrow \mathcal{T}(t)$ is always a net in normal form.

The interaction rules will follow as closely as possible the rewrite system of Section 3.3. The first one is easy; when the evaluation token reaches a λ, it may begin to return:

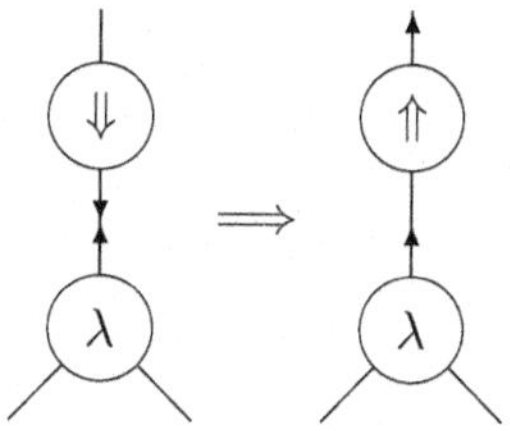

The second one is still simple, but slightly more subtle:

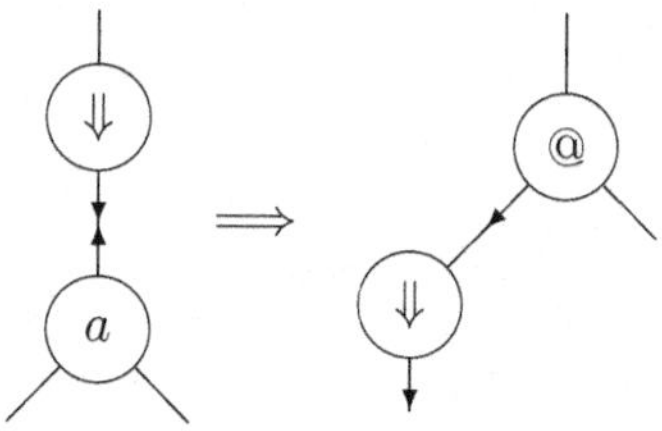

When the evaluation token reaches an application agent, we change the agent a to an agent @ still representing application, but no longer looking at its root but to the left, towards the propagated evaluation agent, waiting until it returns.

Finally, when the agent $\Uparrow$ returns from a successful evaluation to a @, then we know for sure that there is a λ just behind the $\Uparrow$, so the agent $\Uparrow$ may safely disappear, at least if λ and @ promise to create it again later. In a sense, it does not disappear, it just hides in the @ agent.

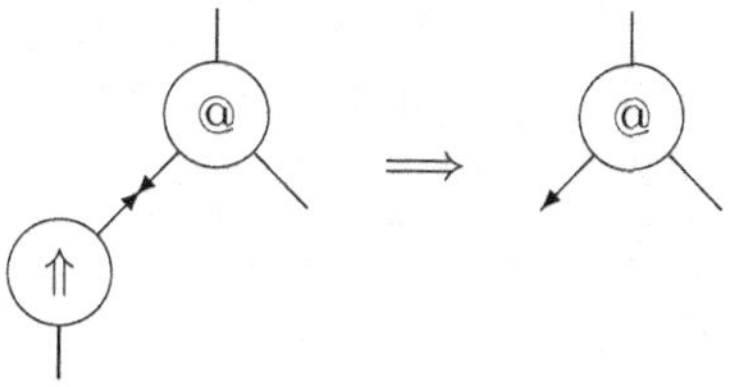

From the previous rule, it is obvious that the agent $\Uparrow$ is in fact useless. However this is the key to the generality of the translation, because we could have a different agent in the right hand-side. In particular, we will see that it is not useless for call-by-value. It is also interesting to note how striking it is in our framework that the agent $\Uparrow$ is useless, which corresponds to tail-recursion optimisation. The framework we propose is so simple that clever optimisations become obvious, hence this is indeed a good intermediate step between the inductive-style definition of a strategy and its implementation as an abstract machine.

Now that the way is free between the @ and the λ, we may let them interact as usual, except that we create a new $\Downarrow$ token. We thus link together the variable port of the λ to the argument port of the @, which initiates the substitution. In brief, we follow exactly the rewrite system, except that we need two steps instead of one.

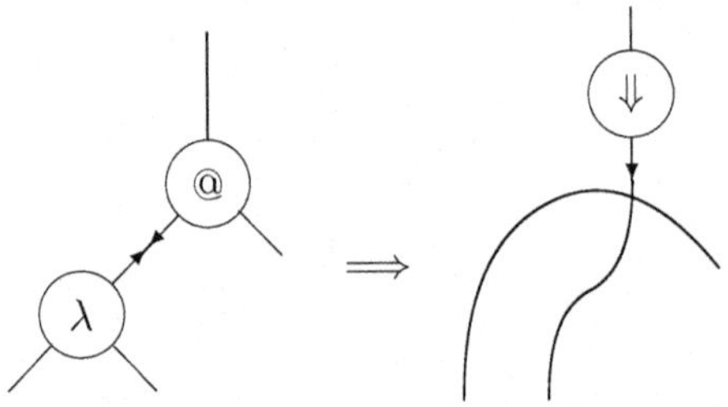

The core of the interaction net machine for call-by-name thus needs only four interaction rules, and no encoding of boxes.

3.6 Resource Management

The explicit resource management typical of interaction nets is done by the agents ϵ, c and δ. The auxiliary agent δ is introduced to duplicate abstractions, as explained below. The agent ϵ erases any agent and propagates according to the following schema (where α represents any agent):

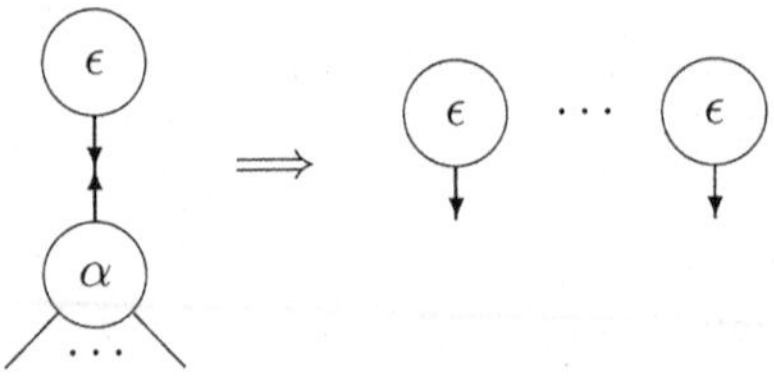

In general, the agent c duplicates any agent it meets. To duplicate an abstraction, we need an auxiliary agent δ that will also duplicate any agent, but will stop the copy when it meets another δ agent. Note that an agent c will thus never interact with another agent c. Here, α represents any agent except λ.

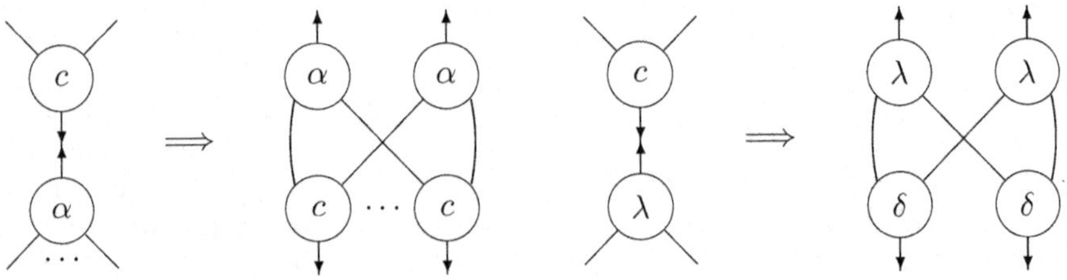

The agent δ duplicates any agent, except itself. If it interacts with itself, it just annihilates. Here, α represents any agent except δ.

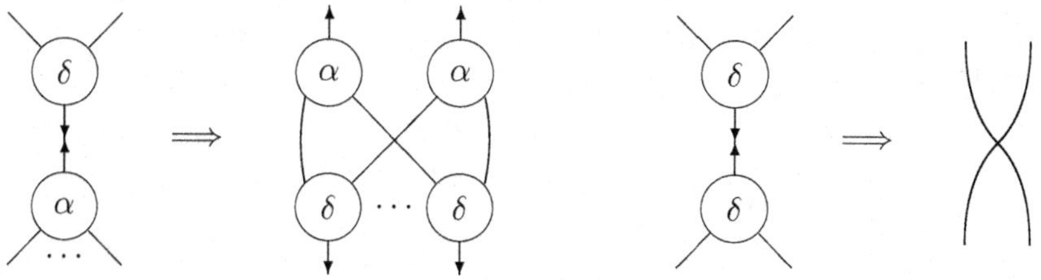

Classical results on packages [12] allow to state the two following properties:

Proposition 3. – *If t is a closed λ-term, then:*

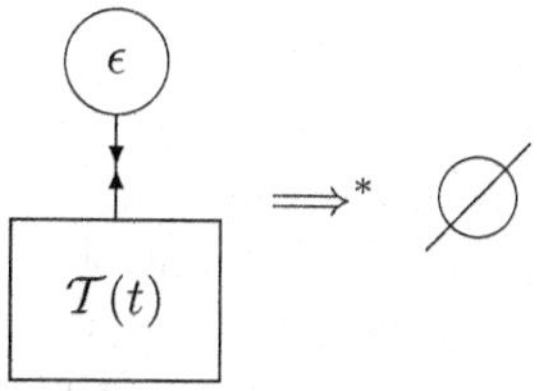

(where the right hand-side of the rule denotes the empty net).
– *If t is a closed λ-term, then:*

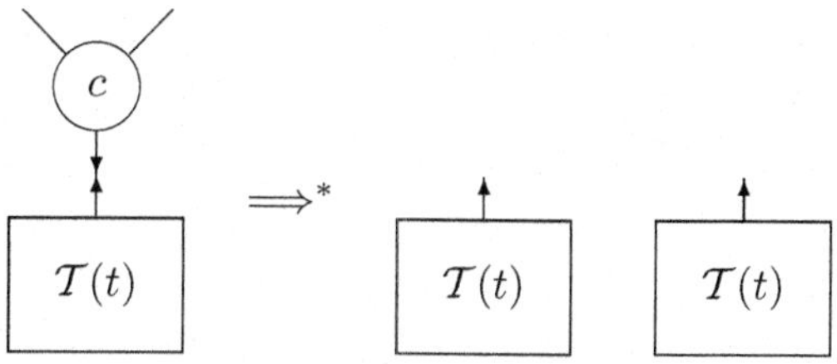

3.7 Properties

In a net obtained starting from $\Downarrow \mathcal{T}(t)$, there may be several redexes involving c's, δ's or ϵ's, however, we have the following result.

Proposition 4. *If $\Downarrow \mathcal{T}(t) \Longrightarrow^* N$ then in N, there is exactly one occurrence of $\Downarrow$, $\Uparrow$ or of a $\lambda-@$ active pair.*

Proof. By induction, using the rules. □

Proposition 5. $t \Downarrow v \Longleftrightarrow \Downarrow \mathcal{T}(t) \Longrightarrow^* \Uparrow \mathcal{T}(v)$

Proof. It is clear that the interaction rules closely follow the rewrite rules of Section 3.3 (using Proposition 3 for non-linear substitutions), then Proposition 2 allows to conclude. □

4 Call-by-Value

In this section, we show that we can very easily adapt the previous presentation to closed call-by-value. We follow the same organisation as Section 3, showing only the differences. In this section again, all terms are closed.

The call-by-value strategy for closed λ-terms is inductively defined by the following set of evaluation rules:

$$\frac{}{\lambda x.t \Downarrow \lambda x.t} \qquad \frac{t \Downarrow \lambda x.t' \quad u \Downarrow v' \quad t'\{x := v'\} \Downarrow v}{t\ u \Downarrow v}$$

We may derive a small-step presentation of the strategy in a similar fashion as in Section 3. Here is the *token-passing semantics* of call-by-value:

$$\begin{array}{lcl} \Downarrow \lambda x.t & \rightarrow & \Uparrow \lambda x.t \\ \Downarrow (t\ u) & \rightarrow & (\Downarrow t)\ u \\ (\Uparrow t)\ u & \rightarrow & t\ (\Downarrow u) \\ (\lambda x.t)\ (\Uparrow u) & \rightarrow & \Downarrow t\{x := u\} \end{array}$$

Here the role of $\Uparrow$ is more complex than with call-by-name: when the function part of an application is evaluated, the control is transferred to the argument. Then, when the argument is evaluated, β-reduction may be performed.

We have a similar property of simulation (the proof is also similar).

Proposition 6. $t \Downarrow v \Longleftrightarrow \Downarrow t \rightarrow^* \Uparrow v$

Some interaction rules have to change a bit, according to the small-step style system. When the left term of an application returns after evaluation, we no longer perform a β-reduction right after. Instead, we turn to evaluating the argument:

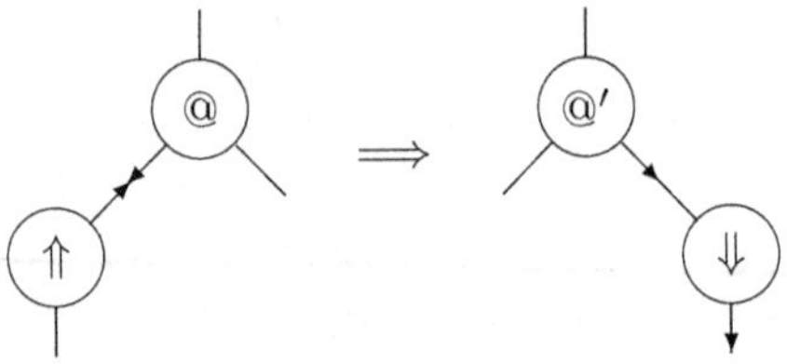

We introduce a new application agent @′ whose job is to wait until the argument of the application is evaluated. When it is, then again, we know for sure that there is a λ waiting at the left, so we may transform the agent into @ to allow the β-reduction to take place:

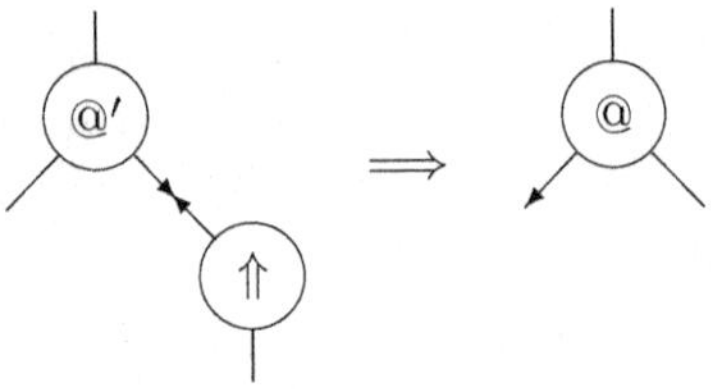

The other rules stay the same. Again, we have (the proof is easily adapted):

Proposition 7. $t \Downarrow v \Longleftrightarrow \Downarrow \mathcal{T}(t) \Longrightarrow^* \Uparrow \mathcal{T}(v)$

To sum up, our presentation allow to adapt very easily from call-by-name to call-by-value, contrary to previous related works. There is no reason to think this approach cannot be adapted beyond to other strategies, or in a more general framework than the λ-calculus.

This interaction system is very faithful to what a sequential evaluation function would probably do. In particular, the agent $\Uparrow$ is necessary, because we have to manage explicitly the control flow in a sequential way.

Of course, interaction nets allow to evaluate the function and the argument of an application in parallel. Keeping the control flow explicit, we have to synchronise on the application node when both evaluations are completed. The system is obtained from the same rules as above, except that we replace the interaction rule $\Downarrow - a$ by:

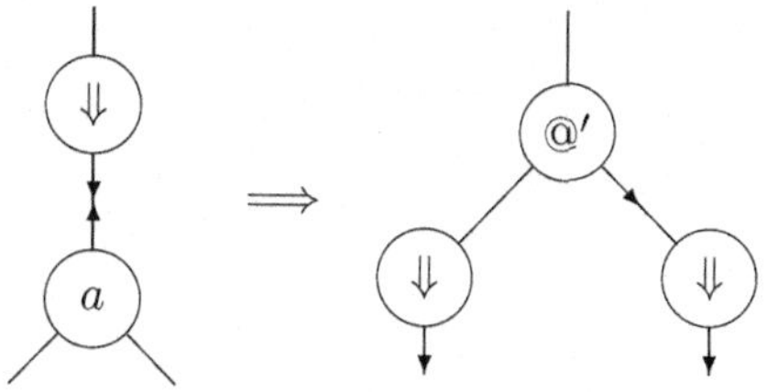

Now in this system, it is again clear that the agent $\Uparrow$ is useless: there is no true need to synchronise both evaluations, and a β-reduction may occur even if evaluation of the argument is not yet completed.

But that is not our point. We prefer the version with sequential, explicit control (i.e. with a unique evaluation token) because it is really closer to an abstract machine: it is very easily implementable on a sequential machine, which is what we often have in practice, and does not need an external mechanism to manage a stack of active pairs.

5 Handling Open Terms

For completeness, we show how to deal with open terms. There is no difficulty, and no new idea. The presentation is done in a modular way: we only say what should be added or changed to the presentations of closed call-by-name and call-by-value to deal with open terms.

Evaluation to weak head normal form of open terms using call-by-name or call-by-value is done by adding to the corresponding system the following rules:

$$\frac{}{x \Downarrow x} \qquad \frac{t \Downarrow x}{t\ u_1 \ldots u_n \Downarrow x\ u_1 \ldots u_n}$$

Or, in a small-steps fashion (keeping the other rules):

$$\begin{array}{lcl} \Downarrow x & \to & \Uparrow x \\ (\Uparrow x)\ u & \to & \Uparrow (x\ u) \\ (\Uparrow (v\ w))\ u & \to & \Uparrow (v\ w\ u) \end{array}$$

On the interaction nets side, it is clear that free variables will have to interact with the evaluation token, hence we cannot just represent them by a wire.

A term t with $\mathsf{fv}(t) = \{x_1, \ldots, x_n\}$ will be translated as a net $\mathcal{T}(t)$ with the root edge at the top, and n free edges marked by an agent v, corresponding to the free variables:

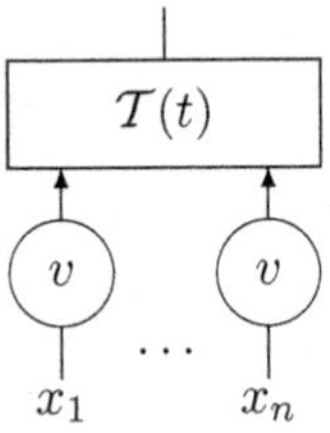

Variables. To sum up, if t is a variable x bound by a λ, then $\mathcal{T}(t)$ is just a wire (left). If it is free in the term, then $\mathcal{T}(t)$ is an agent v (right).

The systems for call-by-name and call-by-value are obtained by adding the two following rules, where we introduce a new agent $\Uparrow_o$ which is essentially the same as $\Uparrow$ but which remembers that the term under it is of the form $x\ t_1 \ldots t_n$ and not $\lambda x.t$. We have to introduce such an agent only because of the restriction to binary left hand-side in interaction nets (there is no deep reason behind).

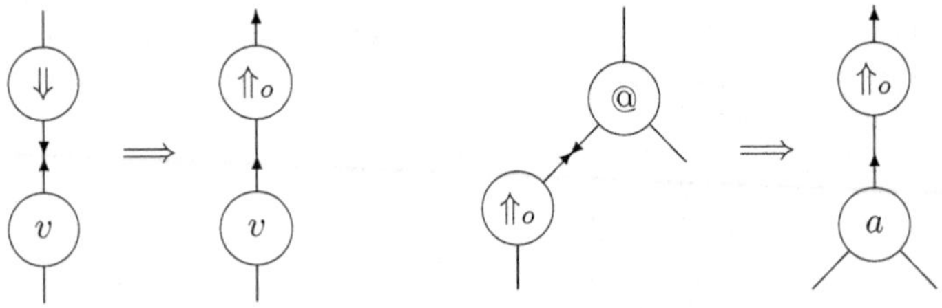

In call-by-value, we also have to eliminate a possible $\Uparrow_o$ appearing to the right of an application. In this case, $\Uparrow_o$ is indeed redundant with $\Uparrow$, hence the rule is the same:

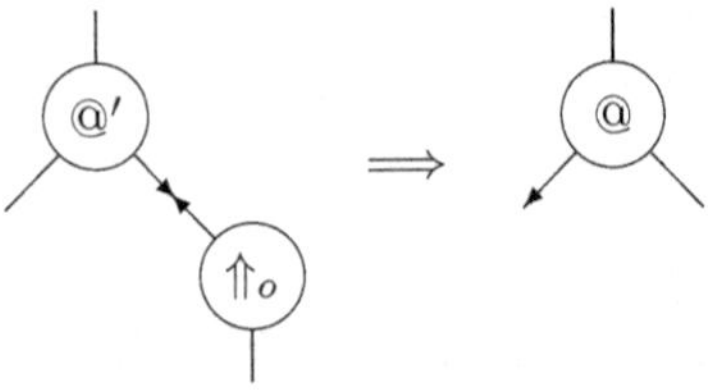

Finally, it may now happen that, in the course of the duplication of an abstraction, a δ agent meets a v agent. Then it is safer to transform it back to a c agent:

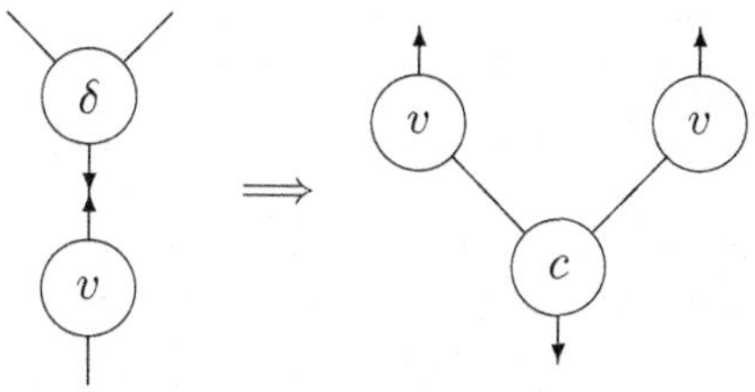

A similar result then holds (for open call-by-name and open call-by-value):

Proposition 8. $t \Downarrow v \Longleftrightarrow \Downarrow \mathcal{T}(t) \Longrightarrow^* \Uparrow \mathcal{T}(v)$ *or* $\Uparrow_o \mathcal{T}(v)$

6 Conclusion

We have presented a simple and extensible approach to express call-by-name and call-by-value in interaction nets. The approach is so simple that it is indeed a good alternative to working with terms, with the advantages of seeing graphically what is going on, of α-conversion for free and of explicit status and cost for the operations of substitution and copying.

Moreover, our interaction nets lie in a particular subclass of *token-passing interaction nets* that is not fully studied here, which seems very easy to implement on a sequential machine, without the usual overheads of looking for a redex and managing a stack of these. Full study of these aspects is left as future work.

We would also like to extend our approach to closed reduction [4] in order to derive an interaction nets based abstract machine for this efficient strategy.

The question whether our approach can benefit to the optimal strategy is still open. Boxes are certainly necessary, since β-reductions have to be interleaved, but controlling more tightly the evaluation flow might still be useful.

References

1. A. Asperti, C. Giovannetti, and A. Naletto. The Bologna optimal higher-order machine. *Journal of Functional Programming*, 6(6):763–810, Nov. 1996.
2. H. P. Barendregt. *The Lambda Calculus: Its Syntax and Semantics*, volume 103 of *Studies in Logic and the Foundations of Mathematics*. North-Holland Publishing Company, second, revised edition, 1984.
3. M. Fernández and I. Mackie. Call-by-value lambda-graph rewriting *without rewriting*. In *Proceedings of the International Conference on Graph Transformations (ICGT'02)*, volume 2505 of *Lecture Notes in Computer Science*, Barcelona, 2002. Springer-Verlag.
4. M. Fernández, I. Mackie, and F.-R. Sinot. Closed reduction: Explicit substitutions without alpha-conversion. *Mathematical Structure in Computer Science*. to appear.
5. J. Field. On laziness and optimality in lambda interpreters: Tools for specification and analysis. In *Conference Record of the 17th Annual ACM Symposium on Principles of Programming Languages (POPL '90)*, pages 1–15, San Francisco, CA, USA, Jan. 1990. ACM Press.

6. J.-Y. Girard. Linear Logic. *Theoretical Computer Science*, 50(1):1–102, 1987.
7. J.-Y. Girard. Geometry of interaction I: Interpretation of system F. In C. Bonotto, R. Ferro, S. Valentini, and A. Zanardo, editors, *Logic Colloquium '88*, pages 221–260. North-Holland, 1989.
8. G. Gonthier, M. Abadi, and J.-J. Lévy. The geometry of optimal lambda reduction. In *Proceedings of the 19th ACM Symposium on Principles of Programming Languages (POPL'92)*, pages 15–26. ACM Press, Jan. 1992.
9. Y. Lafont. Interaction nets. In *Proceedings of the 17th ACM Symposium on Principles of Programming Languages (POPL'90)*, pages 95–108. ACM Press, Jan. 1990.
10. J. Lamping. An algorithm for optimal lambda calculus reduction. In *Proceedings of the 17th ACM Symposium on Principles of Programming Languages (POPL'90)*, pages 16–30. ACM Press, Jan. 1990.
11. S. Lippi. Encoding left reduction in the lambda-calculus with interaction nets. *Mathematical Structures in Computer Science*, 12(6), December 2002.
12. S. Lippi. *Théorie et pratique des réseaux d'interaction.* PhD thesis, Université de la Méditerranée, June 2002.
13. I. Mackie. *The Geometry of Implementation.* PhD thesis, Department of Computing, Imperial College of Science, Technology and Medicine, September 1994.
14. I. Mackie. The geometry of interaction machine. In *Proceedings of the 22nd Symposium on Principles of Programming Languages (POPL'95)*, pages 198–208, San Francisco, CA, USA, 1995. ACM Press.
15. I. Mackie. YALE: Yet another lambda evaluator based on interaction nets. In *Proceedings of the 3rd International Conference on Functional Programming (ICFP'98)*, pages 117–128. ACM Press, 1998.
16. I. Mackie. Efficient λ-evaluation with interaction nets. In V. van Oostrom, editor, *Proceedings of the 15th International Conference on Rewriting Techniques and Applications (RTA'04)*, volume 3091 of *Lecture Notes in Computer Science*, pages 155–169. Springer-Verlag, June 2004.
17. J. S. Pinto. Sequential and concurrent abstract machines for interaction nets. In J. Tiuryn, editor, *Proceedings of Foundations of Software Science and Computation Structures (FOSSACS)*, volume 1784 of *Lecture Notes in Computer Science*, pages 267–282. Springer-Verlag, 2000.
18. G. Plotkin. Call-by-name, call-by-value, and the λ-calculus. *Theoretical Computer Science*, 1:125–159, 1975.
19. V. van Oostrom, K.-J. van de Looij, and M. Zwitserlood. Lambdascope: another optimal implementation of the lambda-calculus. In *Workshop on Algebra and Logic on Programming Systems (ALPS)*, Kyoto, April 2004.

Avoiding Equivariance in Alpha-Prolog

Christian Urban[1] and James Cheney[2]

[1] Ludwig-Maximilians-University Munich
urban@mathematik.uni-muenchen.de
[2] Edinburgh University
jcheney@inf.ed.ac.uk

Abstract. αProlog is a logic programming language which is well-suited for rapid prototyping of type systems and operational semantics of typed λ-calculi and many other languages involving bound names. In αProlog, the nominal unification algorithm of Urban, Pitts and Gabbay is used instead of first-order unification. However, although αProlog can be viewed as Horn-clause logic programming in Pitts' *nominal logic*, proof search using nominal unification is incomplete in nominal logic. Because of nominal logic's *equivariance principle*, complete proof search would require solving NP-hard *equivariant unification* problems. Nevertheless, the αProlog programs we studied run correctly without equivariant unification. In this paper, we give several examples of αProlog programs that do not require equivariant unification, develop a test for identifying such programs, and prove the correctness of this test via a proof-theoretic argument.

1 Introduction

Logic programming is particularly suited for implementing inference rules defining relations over terms. Many interesting examples of such inference rules, however, involve terms with binders and α-equivalence, for which Prolog, for example, provides little assistance. In [3] we presented αProlog, which is designed to simplify programming with binders. For instance, the operation of capture-avoiding substitution for λ-terms can be implemented in αProlog as follows:

```
id(X,X).
subst(var(X),X,T,T).
subst(var(X),Y,T,var(X))        :- not(id(X,Y)).
subst(app(M,N),X,T,app(M',N')):- subst(M,X,T,M'), subst(N,X,T,N').
subst(lam(a.M),X,T,lam(a.M')) :- a#T, a#X, subst(M,X,T,M').
```

where the terms `var(X)`, `app(M,N)` and `lam(a.M)` encode variables, applications and λ-abstractions. The predicate `subst(E,X,T,E')` defined by the clauses holds only if `E'` contains the result of the usual capture-avoiding substitution `E[X:=T]` in the λ-calculus.

Two features of αProlog are immediately visible to the user. First, the term language includes the term-constructor $-.-$ for forming abstractions, which are used to encode binding. Second, αProlog has a freshness-predicate, written as $-\#-$, built into the language; this predicate ensures that a name does not occur freely in a term (by a name

P. Urzyczyn (Ed.): TLCA 2005, LNCS 3461, pp. 401–416, 2005.

we mean lower-case symbols, for instance `a` in the expression `lam(a.M)`). In this `subst`-program, the freshness-predicate is used to make sure that no variable capture occurs inside the term being substituted.

To illustrate how the `subst`-program calculates the result of the capture-avoiding substitution $(\lambda b.a\ b)[a := b]$, we consider the query:

```
subst(lam(b.app(var(a),var(b)),a,var(b),R))          (1)
```

To solve this query, αProlog unifies it with the head of the fourth `subst`-clause

```
subst(lam(a1.M1),X1,T1,lam(a1.M'1)):- a1#T1,a1#X1,subst(M1,X1,T1,M'1).
```

where, as in Prolog, the variables `M`, `X`, `T` and `M'` have been replaced with fresh variables (indicated by the subscript), and also the name `a` has been freshened (we shall return to the difference between variables and names later). The unifier that αProlog calculates is $\texttt{app(var(a),var(a}_1\texttt{))}$ for $\texttt{M}_1$, `a` for $\texttt{X}_1$, `var(b)` for $\texttt{T}_1$ and $\texttt{lam(a}_1\texttt{.M'}_1\texttt{)}$ for `R`. Next, αProlog checks that the freshness-predicates $\texttt{a}_1\texttt{\# var(b)}$ and $\texttt{a}_1\texttt{\# a}$ hold, and continues unifying the new query $\texttt{subst(app(var(a),var(a}_1\texttt{)),a,var(b),M'}_1\texttt{)}$ with the third `subst`-clause. Then it uses the first and second `subst`-clause and after they succeed, αProlog returns $\texttt{lam(a}_1\texttt{.app(var(b),var(a}_1\texttt{)))}$ as the answer for `R`.

Another example, which illustrates how easily inference rules can be implemented in αProlog, is the following program

```
mem(X, [X|T]).
mem(X, [Y|T]) :- mem(X,T).
type(Gamma,var(X),T)    :- mem((X,T),Gamma).
type(Gamma,app(M,N),T):- type(Gamma,M,arr(S,T)), type(Gamma,N,S).
type(Gamma,lam(x.M),arr(S,T)):-x#Gamma, type([(x,S)|Gamma],M,T).
```

implementing the usual inference rules for inferring the types of λ-terms.

$$\frac{x:T\in\Gamma}{\Gamma\rhd x:T}\,var\qquad\frac{\Gamma\rhd M:S\rightarrow T\quad\Gamma\rhd N:S}{\Gamma\rhd MN:T}\,app\qquad\frac{x:S,\Gamma\rhd M:T\quad(x\notin FV(\Gamma))}{\Gamma\rhd\lambda x.M:S\rightarrow T}\,lam$$

Note that, in contrast to for example λProlog, abstractions in αProlog bind a concrete name which is *not* restricted to the scope of the abstractions. Therefore it is possible in αProlog to use a name of a binder in the body of the clause, for instance to append `(x,S)` to the context `Gamma` in the third `type`-clause. The implicit side-condition in the rule lam requiring that Γ has no type-assignment for x is implemented in αProlog by the freshness-predicate `x#Gamma`.

We have implemented a large number of such λ-calculus examples, including type systems and operational semantics for System F, $\lambda\mu$ and linear λ-calculi. Our experience from these examples suggests that the combination of concrete names in abstractions and the freshness-predicate is very useful for programming with binders. One question, however, might arise: what are the advantages of αProlog relative to, for example, λProlog [6], which has both α-equivalence and capture-avoiding substitution built-in and the typing rules can be correctly implemented by the two clauses:

```
(type (app M N) T) :- type M (arr S T), type N S.
(type (lam M) (arr S T)) :- (pi x\(type x S => type (M x) T)).
```

(Notice that in this program the typing-context is implicitly given by the "surrounding" program-context. This program-context can be modified using the universal quantification (i.e. `pi x\ ...`) and implications in goal-formulae. Therefore there is no clause for the variable case.) We find the most important reason in favour of αProlog is that by having concrete names (namely `x` in the `type`-example) and freshness-predicates one can almost directly translate the three typing rules into three clauses and obtain a correct implementation. This should be seen in the context that, despite the elegance of λProlog, some recent textbooks use (standard) Prolog for implementing inference rules over λ-terms. For example one of them presents the following implementation of the typing rules:

```
mem(X, [X|T]).
mem(X, [Y|T]) :- mem(X,T).

type(Gamma,var(X),T)   :- mem((X,T),Gamma).
type(Gamma,app(M,N),T):- type(Gamma,M,arr(S,T)), type(Gamma,N,S).
type(Gamma,lam(X,M),arr(S,T)):-type([(X,S)|Gamma],M,T).
```

which calculates the *wrong* type for λ-terms such as $\lambda x.\lambda x.(x\ x)$. Although this problem can be fixed by judicious use of cut or side-effects, first-order terms of Prolog are unwieldy for implementing relations over syntax with binders correctly. On the other hand, λProlog does not allow concrete names as binders and therefore operations such as adding the type for `x` to the typing-context need to be encoded using universal quantification, implications in goals and beta-reduction.

The αProlog language is based on nominal terms and uses the nominal unification algorithm of Urban, Pitts, and Gabbay [8], which calculates (most general) unifiers modulo α-equivalence. For example, the query `?- id(a.a,b.X)` is solved in αProlog by the capturing substitution [`X` := `b`] since `a.a` and `b.b` are α-equivalent. However, nominal unification is not enough to make the programs given earlier function as intended. For this αProlog generates fresh names during proof-search. As seen above, before a query is unified with the fourth `subst`-clause, αProlog generates a fresh name for `a`. This ensures that substitutions can always be "pushed" under a binder without risk of capture.

While in [3] we have described our implementation of αProlog, its behaviour can be justified in terms of nominal logic [7, 2]. For instance, the generation of a fresh name can be expressed in terms of the И-quantifier of nominal logic, and an αProlog clause `A :- B1,..,Bn` can viewed as the formula $\text{И}a_1..a_n.\forall X_1..X_n.B_1\wedge\cdot\cdot\wedge B_n\supset A$, where the X_i and a_i are the variables, respectively names, in the clause. The problem is that the generation of fresh names is more subtle in αProlog than the usual "freshening" of variables when backchaining a Prolog-clause. The reason is that distinct names are always considered to denote different values. Consider the clause $\forall$`X.p(X)` and the query `p(b)` written as a sequent as follows

$$\forall \texttt{X.p(X)} \vdash \texttt{p(b)} \tag{2}$$

When constructing a proof for (2), Prolog generates a fresh name for the variable `X`, say `X'`, and then unifies `p(X')` and `p(b)` giving the solution `[X':=b]`. A similar αProlog-clause that has a name in place of the variable behaves differently: if we have the sequent

$$\text{И}\texttt{a.p(a)} \vdash \texttt{p(b)} \tag{3}$$

with the clause И`a.p(a)`, then "freshening" `a` to `a'` leads to the unification problem `p(a')`$\approx$?`p(b)`. Since nominal unification treats names as distinct constants, this problem is unsolvable. (Treating names as distinct constants is important, because treating them as substitutable entities would break the most-general unifier property of nominal unification, see [8].) On the other hand, (3) *is* provable in nominal logic. This is because after freshening `a` to `a'` one can in nominal logic apply the equivariance principle—expressed as an inference rule[1]

$$\frac{\pi{\cdot}B, \Gamma \Rightarrow C}{B, \Gamma \Rightarrow C}\ \pi$$

where π is a permutation of names, B, C stand for formulae and Γ for a multiset of formulae. This means if the *full* Horn-fragment of nominal logic were used as the basis of αProlog, then we need equivariant unification for complete proof search. Equivariant unification solves a problem not just by finding a substitution but also by finding a permutation; for example in (3) the identity substitution and the permutation `(a' b)`.

The second author has shown in [1] that equivariant unification and equivariant matching problems are NP-hard. For proof-search in αProlog this means that one needs to guess which permutation π leads to a proof. However, in experimenting with αProlog we found that such guessing is never needed in the programs we considered. In this paper we identify a class of nominal Horn-clause programs for which the π-rule can be eliminated from deductions (this is the place where equivariant unification problems arise), and thus nominal unification is complete for proof-search. In order to show this result, we introduce a *well-formedness* condition which guarantees that nominal unification-based proof search is complete. This condition roughly says that a clause is "insensitive" to the particular choice of names occurring in it.

Some programs do not satisfy this condition. For example, in the following program calculating a list of bound variables of a λ-term, the last clause is *not* well-formed.

```
bv(var(X),[]).
bv(app(E1,E2),L)    :- bv(E1,L1), bv(E2,L2), append(L1,L2,L).
bv(lam(x.E),[x|L]) :- bv(E,L).
```

In the last clause, the result accumulated in the second argument depends on which name is chosen for the binder `x`. In contrast, the names chosen in the `subst` and `type` example do not matter (up to α-equivalence) and therefore will satisfy our well-formedness condition.

The existence of a trivial syntactic criterion for deciding when a clause is "insensitive" to the choice of a name seems unlikely. Consider, for example, allowing names

[1] The corresponding right-rule has been shown to be admissible in nominal logic in [5].

to only occur bound or in binding position—then the `type`-program would be ruled out since `x` occurs free in the body of the clause. Restricting free names to occur only in the body of a clause would permit the clause `r(X):-id(X,a)` which *is* sensitive to the choice of `a` since `id` "propagates" the choice for the name `a` back to the head of the clause (`id` is defined in the `subst`-example). Our well-formedness condition is therefore more subtle; it is a test whether a certain matching problem derived from the clause is solvable. Despite being technically relatively complex, well-formedness can be automatically verified.

The paper is organised as follows: Section 2 describes nominal terms, formulae and the inference rules of αProlog's proof-search procedure. Section 3 introduces a well-formedness condition for clauses and shows that the π-rule can be eliminated from proofs involving only well-formed clauses. Section 4 describes how the well-formedness condition can be automatically verified. Section 5 concludes and describes future work.

2 Terms, Formulae and Proof-Search Rules

The terms used in αProlog are *nominal terms* (see [8] for more details) as defined by the grammar:

$$t ::= a \mid \pi{\cdot}X \mid \langle\rangle \mid \langle t, t\rangle \mid a.t \mid \mathtt{f}(t)$$

where a is a name, X a variable, $\mathtt{f}$ a function symbol and π a permutation expressed as a list of swappings $(a_1\, b_1)\cdots(a_n\, b_n)$. We have the operations $-@-$ and $(-)^{-1}$ for composing (list concatenation) two permutations and inverting (list reversal) a permutation, respectively. Constants are encoded as function symbols with unit arguments $\mathtt{f}(\langle\rangle)$, and n-tuples are encoded by iterated pairs $\langle t_1, \cdots \langle t_{n-1}, t_n\rangle\rangle$. Following [8], we refer to terms of the form $\pi{\cdot}X$ as *suspensions*, because the permutation π is suspended in front of a variable waiting to be applied to a term substituted for X.

Formulae are divided into goal formulae G and definite (or program) clauses D defined as

$$G ::= p(t) \mid G{\wedge}G \mid G{\vee}G \mid \top \qquad B ::= G \supset p(t) \qquad D ::= \text{И}as.\forall Xs.\nabla/B$$

where $p(t)$ stands for an atomic predicate with the argument t (we shall also write A for such formulae whenever the argument is unimportant); $\top, \wedge, \vee, \supset$ are standard connectives; and ∇ is a set of freshness constraints of the form $a_1 \# X_1, \ldots, a_n \# X_n$ (X_i and a_i being variables and names, respectively). The intended meaning of ∇ in D-formulae is that a clause is applicable only if its freshness constraints are satisfied. For freshness constraints and quantifier-free formulae we shall use the notation $Q_{as,Xs}$ ($Q ::= \nabla|G|B$) to indicate that the terms of Q are built up from names as and variables Xs (we have the usual convention that as stands for lists of names and Xs for lists of variables; similarly $\text{И}as$ stands for $\text{И}a_1 \ldots \text{И}a_n$ and $\forall Xs$ for $\forall X_1 \ldots \forall X_n$). We call a D-formula *closed* when it has no free variables and free names, that is the formula must be of the form $\text{И}as.\forall Xs.\nabla_{as,Xs}/B_{as,Xs}$. Fig. 1 shows two examples illustrating how D-formulae relate to the αProlog-clauses given at the beginning.

```
subst(var(X),X,T,T).
```
$\forall X,T.\ \varnothing\,/\,\top \supset s(\mathtt{var}(X),X,T,T)$

```
subst(lam(a.M),X,T,lam(a.M')) :- a#T, a#X, subst(M,X,T,M').
```
$\text{И}a.\forall M,X,T,M'.\ \{a\,\#T, a\,\#X\}\,/\,s(M,X,T,M') \supset s(\mathtt{lam}(a.M),X,T,\mathtt{lam}(a.M'))$

Fig. 1. Two examples showing how αProlog-clauses relate to D-formulae (s is a predicate symbol standing for `subst`). We have the usual convention that clauses stand for closed D-formulae

Terms:

$$[]\cdot_{\mathcal{B}} a \stackrel{\text{def}}{=} a \qquad \pi\cdot_{\mathcal{B}}(\pi'\cdot X) \stackrel{\text{def}}{=} \pi@\pi'\cdot X$$

$$((a_1\,a_2)::\pi)\cdot_{\mathcal{B}} a \stackrel{\text{def}}{=} \begin{cases} a_1 & \text{if } \pi\cdot_{\mathcal{B}} a = a_2 \\ a_2 & \text{if } \pi\cdot_{\mathcal{B}} a = a_1 \\ \pi\cdot_{\mathcal{B}} a & \text{otherwise} \end{cases} \qquad \begin{aligned} \pi\cdot_{\mathcal{B}}(\langle\rangle) &\stackrel{\text{def}}{=} \langle\rangle \\ \pi\cdot_{\mathcal{B}}(\langle t_1,t_2\rangle) &\stackrel{\text{def}}{=} \langle \pi\cdot_{\mathcal{B}} t_1, \pi\cdot_{\mathcal{B}} t_2\rangle \\ \pi\cdot_{\mathcal{B}}(\mathtt{f}(t)) &\stackrel{\text{def}}{=} \mathtt{f}(\pi\cdot_{\mathcal{B}} t) \\ \pi\cdot_{\mathcal{B}}(a.t) &\stackrel{\text{def}}{=} (\pi\cdot_{\mathcal{B}} a).(\pi\cdot_{\mathcal{B}} t) \end{aligned}$$

$$\pi\cdot_{\mathcal{B}} X \stackrel{\text{def}}{=} \begin{cases} X & \text{if } X \in \mathcal{B} \\ \pi\cdot X & \text{otherwise} \end{cases}$$

Formulae:

$$\pi\cdot_{\mathcal{B}}(\top) \stackrel{\text{def}}{=} \top \qquad \pi\cdot_{\mathcal{B}}(G\supset A) \stackrel{\text{def}}{=} (\pi\cdot_{\mathcal{B}} G) \supset (\pi\cdot_{\mathcal{B}} A)$$

$$\pi\cdot_{\mathcal{B}}(p(t)) \stackrel{\text{def}}{=} p(\pi\cdot_{\mathcal{B}} t) \qquad \pi\cdot_{\mathcal{B}}(\nabla/B) \stackrel{\text{def}}{=} \nabla/(\pi\cdot_{\mathcal{B}} B)$$

$$\pi\cdot_{\mathcal{B}}(G_1 \star G_2) \stackrel{\text{def}}{=} (\pi\cdot_{\mathcal{B}} G_1) \star (\pi\cdot_{\mathcal{B}} G_2) \quad \text{for } \star ::= \wedge|\vee \qquad \pi\cdot_{\mathcal{B}}(\text{И}a.D) \stackrel{\text{def}}{=} \text{И}a.\pi\cdot_{\mathcal{B}} D$$

$$\pi\cdot_{\mathcal{B}}(\forall X.D) \stackrel{\text{def}}{=} \forall X.\pi\cdot_{\{X\}\cup\mathcal{B}} D$$

Fig. 2. Definition of the permutation operation $\pi\cdot_{\mathcal{B}}(-)$ for terms and formulae. In the clause for the new-quantifier, it is assumed that a is renamed, so that the permutation π can safely be pushed under the binder without capture

There is a delicate point with respect to binding: while in nominal terms the constructor $a.(-)$ is *not* a binder in the traditional sense (it only *acts* as a binder), in formulae the quantifiers $\text{И}a.(-)$ and $\forall X.(-)$ do bind a and X, respectively. Therefore we have the usual convention that formulae are identified if they only differ in the names of binders (i.e. $\forall X.(-)$ and $\text{И}a.(-)$), and operations on formulae need to respect this convention. As a result the definition of the permutation operation introduced for nominal terms in [8] needs to be extended. We define a generalised permutation operation $\pi\cdot_{\mathcal{B}}(-)$ that depends on a set of variables $\mathcal{B}$. The permutation π only acts upon variables *not* in $\mathcal{B}$. Whenever a permutation is "pushed" under a $\forall X.(-)$-quantifier, then X is added to the set of variables the permutation does not affect. The definition of the permutation operation is given in Fig. 2. We use the shorthand notation $\pi\cdot(-)$ in case $\mathcal{B}$ is the empty set. This is a generalisation of the permutation action given in [8]; however, when a permutation acts on a formula with quantifiers, it acts only on the free names and free variables.

Similar problems arise in the definition of the substitution operation—with respect to the abstractions $a.(-)$ substitution is possibly-capturing, whereas with respect to the И- and $\forall$-quantifier it must be capture-avoiding. For terms we can use the definition given in [8]: a substitution σ is a function from variables to terms with the property that $\sigma(X) = X$ for all but finitely many variables X. If the domain of σ consists of

$$\frac{}{\nabla \vdash \langle\rangle \approx \langle\rangle}(\approx\text{-unit}) \quad \frac{\nabla \vdash t_1 \approx t_1' \quad \nabla \vdash t_2 \approx t_2'}{\nabla \vdash \langle t_1, t_2\rangle \approx \langle t_1', t_2'\rangle}(\approx\text{-pair}) \quad \frac{\nabla \vdash t \approx t'}{\nabla \vdash \mathtt{f}\, t \approx \mathtt{f}\, t'}(\approx\text{-fun. symbol})$$

$$\frac{\nabla \vdash t \approx t'}{\nabla \vdash a.t \approx a.t'}(\approx\text{-abs-1}) \quad \frac{a \neq a' \quad \nabla \vdash t \approx (a\, a')\cdot t' \quad \nabla \vdash a \# t'}{\nabla \vdash a.t \approx a'.t'}(\approx\text{-abs-2})$$

$$\frac{}{\nabla \vdash a \approx a}(\approx\text{-name}) \quad \frac{(a \# X) \in \nabla \text{ for all } a \in ds(\pi, \pi')}{\nabla \vdash \pi\cdot X \approx \pi'\cdot X}(\approx\text{-suspension})$$

$$\frac{}{\nabla \vdash a \# \langle\rangle}(\#\text{-unit}) \quad \frac{\nabla \vdash a \# t_1 \quad \nabla \vdash a \# t_2}{\nabla \vdash a \# \langle t_1, t_2\rangle}(\#\text{-pair}) \quad \frac{\nabla \vdash a \# t}{\nabla \vdash a \# \mathtt{f}\, t}(\#\text{-fun. symbol})$$

$$\frac{}{\nabla \vdash a \# a.t}(\#\text{-abs-1}) \quad \frac{a \neq a' \quad \nabla \vdash a \# t}{\nabla \vdash a \# a'.t}(\#\text{-abs-2})$$

$$\frac{a \neq a'}{\nabla \vdash a \# a'}(\#\text{-name}) \quad \frac{(\pi^{-1}\cdot a \# X) \in \nabla}{\nabla \vdash a \# \pi\cdot X}(\#\text{-suspension})$$

Fig. 3. Inductive definitions for $\approx$ and $\#$. The reader is referred to [8] for more details

distinct variables $X_1, \ldots, X_n$ and $\sigma(X_i) = t_i$ for $i = 1 \ldots n$, we sometimes write σ as $[X_1 := t_1, \ldots, X_n := t_n]$. Moreover, we shall write $\sigma(t)$ for the result of applying a substitution σ to a term t; this is the term obtained from t by replacing each variable X by the term $\sigma(X)$ and each suspension $\pi\cdot X$ in t by the term $\pi\cdot\sigma(X)$ got by letting π act on the term $\sigma(X)$. This definition is extended to formulae as follows:

$$\begin{array}{rlrl}
\sigma(\top) & \stackrel{\text{def}}{=} \top & \sigma(G \supset A) & \stackrel{\text{def}}{=} \sigma(G) \supset \sigma(A) \\
\sigma(p(t)) & \stackrel{\text{def}}{=} p(\sigma(t)) & \sigma(\nabla/B) & \stackrel{\text{def}}{=} \sigma(\nabla)/\sigma(B) \\
\sigma(G_1 \star G_2) & \stackrel{\text{def}}{=} \sigma(G_1) \star \sigma(G_2) & \sigma(\text{И}a.D) & \stackrel{\text{def}}{=} \text{И}a.\sigma(D) \\
& \text{for } \star ::= \wedge | \vee & \sigma(\forall X.D) & \stackrel{\text{def}}{=} \forall X.\sigma(D)
\end{array}$$

with the proviso that the quantified names and variables are suitably renamed so that no capturing is possible. For example, if $\sigma = [X := \langle a, Y\rangle]$ and $t = a.X$, then $\sigma(t) = a.\langle a, Y\rangle$, but if $D = \text{И}a.\forall Y.\varnothing/\top \supset A(a, Y, X)$ then forming $\sigma(D)$ gives the formula $\text{И}a'.\forall Y'.\varnothing/\top \supset A(a', Y', \langle a, Y\rangle)$. We use the notation $\sigma(\nabla)$ to mean that every freshness constraint $a \# X$ in ∇ is replaced by $a \# \sigma(X)$.

It is crucial for programming in αProlog that abstractions $a.(-)$ have concrete names. This allows us to formulate the `type`-clause for lambda-abstractions in the usual fashion whereby the abstracted name `x` and its type is just added to the context `Gamma`. Furthermore, the work reported in [8] provides us with a simple algorithm for unifying nominal terms. This unification algorithm does not calculate unifiers to make nominal terms syntactically equal, but equal modulo an equivalence relation $\approx$. For example when unifying the two terms $a.a \approx ?\ b.X$, the nominal unification algorithm produces the unifier $[X := b]$. While the relation $\approx$ is intended to capture the (traditional) notion of α-equivalence, it is in fact a more general relation. For example, $\approx$ is not just a relation between two nominal terms, but a relation that depends on some freshness constraints ∇. Figure 3 gives a syntax-directed inductive definition for judgements of the form $\nabla \vdash (-) \approx (-)$, which asserts that two terms are $\approx$-equal under the hypotheses ∇; the definition depends on the auxiliary relation $\nabla \vdash (-) \# (-)$, which defines when a name is *fresh* for a term under some hypotheses. This definition depends on the auxiliary notion of a disagreement set, ds, between two permutations (the set of names on which the permutations disagree) given by: $\{a \mid \pi_1{\cdot}a \neq \pi_2{\cdot}a\}$.

We can extend $\approx$ to *quantifier-free* G-formulae as follows:

$$\frac{}{\nabla \vdash \top \approx \top} \qquad \frac{\nabla \vdash t \approx t'}{\nabla \vdash p(t) \approx p(t')} \qquad \frac{\nabla \vdash G_1 \approx G_3 \quad \nabla \vdash G_2 \approx G_4}{\nabla \vdash G_1 \star G_2 \approx G_3 \star G_4} \quad \text{for } \star ::= \wedge | \vee$$

The advantage of setting up the formalism in this way is that the $\approx$-equivalence has a number of good properties, which will play an important rôle in our proof for showing that the π-rule can be eliminated. For example, $\approx$ is preserved under (possibly-capturing) substitutions and behaves well with respect to the permutation operation. This is made precise in the following lemma.

Lemma 1. *The permutation and substitution operations preserve $\approx$ in the sense that*

(i) if $\nabla \vdash t \approx t'$ then $\nabla \vdash \pi{\cdot}t \approx \pi{\cdot}t'$ for all permutations π and

(ii) if $\nabla \vdash t \approx t'$, then $\nabla' \vdash \sigma(t) \approx \sigma(t')$ for all substitutions σ with $\nabla' \vdash \sigma(\nabla)$ (whereby $\nabla' \vdash \sigma(\nabla)$ means that $\nabla' \vdash a \# \sigma(X)$ holds for each $(a \# X) \in \nabla$).

The proof of these two facts are a minor extension of the proofs given for [8]; they hold because permutations are bijections on names, and substitutions act on variables only (not names). The properties stated in Lemma 1 should be compared with the notion of α-equivalence we imposed (on the meta-level) on quantified D-formulae. There, whenever a permutation or substitution is pushed under a binder, we might have to rename its binder in order to avoid possible capture.

Next we introduce the inference rules on which proof-search is based in αProlog (see Figure 4). Sequents are of the form $\nabla; \Gamma \Rightarrow G$ or $\nabla; \Gamma \xrightarrow{D} p(t)$ where the former models *goal-directed proof-search* and the latter models *focused backchaining* (the formula above the sequent arrow is usually called the *stoup*-formula). These inference rules are adapted from a standard focusing approach to first-order logic programming (for example [4]).[2] The main novelty of these rules is the presence of the freshness-constraints ∇. Traditionally axiom rules are formulated as

$$\frac{}{p(t'), \Gamma \Rightarrow p(t)}\,\text{Ax}\;, \quad \text{or in focusing proofs as} \quad \frac{}{\Gamma \xrightarrow{p(t')} p(t)}\,\text{Ax}\;,$$

where the terms t and t' need to be syntactically equal. In αProlog this requirement is relaxed: terms only need to be being equal modulo $\approx$. However, $\approx$ only makes sense in the context of some freshness constraints. Consequently, in αProlog, the axiom-rule takes the form

$$\frac{\nabla \vdash t' \approx t}{\nabla; \Gamma \xrightarrow{p(t')} p(t)}\,\text{Ax}$$

[2] The question of establishing the precise relation between the inference rules given here and nominal logic introduced in [7] is beyond the scope of this paper, but will appear in a full version (some results concerning this question have already been presented in [5]).

$$\frac{}{\nabla;\Gamma \Rightarrow \top}\top_R \qquad \frac{\nabla;\Gamma\Rightarrow G \quad \nabla;\Gamma\Rightarrow G'}{\nabla;\Gamma\Rightarrow G\wedge G'}\wedge_R \qquad \frac{\nabla;\Gamma\Rightarrow G_i}{\nabla;\Gamma\Rightarrow G_1\vee G_2}\vee_{Ri} \qquad \frac{\nabla;D,\Gamma \xrightarrow{D} p(t)}{\nabla;D,\Gamma\Rightarrow p(t)}\text{Sel}$$

$$\frac{\nabla\vdash t'\approx t}{\nabla;\Gamma \xrightarrow{p(t')} p(t)}\text{Ax} \qquad \frac{\nabla\vdash\nabla' \quad \nabla;\Gamma\Rightarrow G \quad \nabla;\Gamma \xrightarrow{p(t')} p(t)}{\nabla;\Gamma \xrightarrow{\nabla'/G\supset p(t')} p(t)}\supset_L$$

$$\frac{\nabla;\Gamma \xrightarrow{D[X:=t']} p(t)}{\nabla;\Gamma \xrightarrow{\forall X.D} p(t)}\forall_L \qquad \frac{b\,\#\,Xs,\nabla;\Gamma \xrightarrow{(a\,b)\cdot D} p(t)}{\nabla;\Gamma \xrightarrow{\text{И}a.D} p(t)}\text{И}_L \qquad \frac{\nabla;\Gamma \xrightarrow{\pi\cdot D} p(t)}{\nabla;\Gamma \xrightarrow{D} p(t)}\pi$$

Fig. 4. Proof-search rules of αProlog. In the new-left rule it is assumed that b is a fresh name not occurring in the conclusion and Xs are all free variables in Γ and $p(t)$

where the context ∇ explicitly records all freshness constraints in a sequent. The only inference rule which adds new freshness-constraints to this context is the И-rule; that is whenever a И-quantifier is analysed, a new name is chosen and some freshness-constraints are added to ∇ in order to enforce the "freshness" of this name.

The $\supset_L$-rule includes the judgement $\nabla \vdash \nabla'$ where ∇' is the set of freshness constraints associated with the D-formula in the stoup. This judgement requires that all constraints in ∇' (being of the form $a \# t$) are satisfied by the ∇, that is for all $a \# t$ the judgement $\nabla \vdash a \# t$ defined in Fig. 3 holds.

Of most interest in this paper is the π-rule. In a "root-first" proof-search, this rule is a source of non-determinism. For example, if we want to prove the sequent $\varnothing; \xrightarrow{p(a)} p(b)$, we need the π-rule in order to make the terms a and b $\approx$-equivalent—in this case, only after applying a permutation such as $(a\,b)$ to a may the axiom-rule be used. Prima facie the π-rule is innocuous, however, the problem of simultaneously unifying nominal terms and finding a π is, as mentioned earlier, an NP-hard decision problem. In the next section we shall show that such problems never need to be solved provided the program clauses are well-formed.

3 Elimination of the π-Rule

We implemented αProlog using the nominal unification algorithm. With this implementation we were able to calculate the expected results for programs such as `subst` and `type`. The reason for this is, roughly speaking, that the name we used for specifying the clauses dealing with λ-abstractions does not matter. When using nominal unification, the following renamed clauses (where `a` and `x` are renamed to `b` and `y`, respectively)

```
subst(lam(b.M),X,T,lam(b.M')):- b#T, b#X, subst(M,X,T,M').
type(Gamma,lam(y.M),arr(S,T)):- y#Gamma, type([(y,S)|Gamma],M,T).
```

behave just the same as the original clauses, in the sense that all queries successfully solved by the original versions are solved by the renamed versions. In contrast, the name `a` in the clauses `p(a)`, `q(a.X,X)` and `r(X) :- id(X,a)` determines which queries can be solved successfully using nominal unification and which cannot: given our inference rules, which choose a fresh name for `a`, there are some queries whose answers can only be found using the π-rule, and this means they cannot be solved using nominal unification. Consider for example the following deduction.

$$\dfrac{\dfrac{\dots \qquad \dfrac{\dfrac{\varnothing \vdash c \approx c}{\varnothing;\xrightarrow{p(c)} p(c)}\,\mathrm{Ax}}{}}{\varnothing; \xrightarrow{\varnothing/\top \supset p(c)} p(c)}\supset_L}{\dfrac{\varnothing; \xrightarrow{\varnothing/\top \supset p(b)} p(c)}{\varnothing; \xrightarrow{\text{И}a.\varnothing/\top \supset p(a)} p(c)}\,\text{И}_L}\,\pi\ (c\,b)$$

In this deduction the π-rule, applying the permutation $(c\,b)$ (annotated to the π-rule), is crucial for the sequent being provable and it will turn out that it is impossible to eliminate it from this deduction. Consequently, a proof-search procedure based on nominal unification will not find this proof.

If we impose the following well-formedness condition on D-formulae, we can ensure that the π-rule can always be eliminated from corresponding deductions and hence the nominal unification algorithm alone is sufficient for solving queries.

Definition 1. *A closed D-formula* $\text{И}as.\forall Xs.\nabla_{as,Xs}/G_{as,Xs} \supset A_{as,Xs}$ *is* well-formed *if there exists a substitution* σ *and a permutation* π *such that*

(i) $bs \# Xs, \nabla_{as,Xs} \vdash \sigma(A_{bs,Xs}) \approx A_{as,Xs}$ *and*
(ii) $bs \# Xs, \nabla_{as,Xs} \vdash \sigma(\pi \cdot G_{bs,Xs}) \approx G_{as,Xs}$

where the bs *are some fresh names (different from* as*).*

Let us illustrate this condition with some examples. Clauses without names clearly satisfy the condition. For example the first `subst`-clause in Fig. 1

$$\varnothing \vdash \sigma(S(\mathtt{var}(X), X, T, T)) \approx S(\mathtt{var}(X), X, T, T) \quad \text{and} \quad \varnothing \vdash \sigma(\pi \cdot \top) \approx \top$$

trivially satisfies the condition by taking for σ the identity substitution and for π the empty permutation. More complicated is the case of the second `subst`-clause in Fig. 1

$$\nabla \vdash \sigma(S(\mathtt{lam}(b.M), X, T, \mathtt{lam}(b.M'))) \approx S(\mathtt{lam}(a.M), X, T, \mathtt{lam}(a.M'))$$
$$\nabla \vdash \sigma(\pi \cdot S(M, X, T, M')) \approx S(M, X, T, M')$$

where ∇ is $\{b \# M, b \# X, b \# T, b \# M', a \# X, a \# T\}$. In this case

$$\sigma = [M := (a\,b) \cdot M, X := (a\,b) \cdot X, T := (a\,b) \cdot T, M' := (a\,b) \cdot M'] \quad \text{and} \quad \pi = (a\,b)$$

verify that the clause is well-formed.

Before we formally show that all π-rules can be eliminated from deductions consisting of well-formed clauses only, we outline our proof-plan with some examples. Consider the following deduction, which has a π-rule on the top right-hand side. The

$$\dfrac{\dfrac{\dfrac{.. \quad \dfrac{\vdots}{\Rightarrow s(\mathtt{v}(z),z,\mathtt{v}(y),\mathtt{v}(y))}\star \quad \dfrac{\dfrac{..\vdash\langle \mathtt{l}(b.\mathtt{v}(y)),y,\mathtt{v}(z),\mathtt{l}(b.\mathtt{v}(z))\rangle\approx\langle \mathtt{l}(x.\mathtt{v}(y)),y,\mathtt{v}(z),\mathtt{l}(x.\mathtt{v}(z))\rangle}{..;\xrightarrow{s(\mathtt{l}(b.\mathtt{v}(y)),y,\mathtt{v}(z),\mathtt{l}(b.\mathtt{v}(z)))} s(\mathtt{l}(x.\mathtt{v}(y)),y,\mathtt{v}(z),\mathtt{l}(x.\mathtt{v}(z)))}\text{Ax}}{..;\xrightarrow{s(\mathtt{l}(b.\mathtt{v}(z)),z,\mathtt{v}(y),\mathtt{l}(b.\mathtt{v}(y)))} s(\mathtt{l}(x.\mathtt{v}(y)),y,\mathtt{v}(z),\mathtt{l}(x.\mathtt{v}(z)))}\pi^{\bullet}}{..;\xrightarrow{\nabla/s(\mathtt{v}(z),z,\mathtt{v}(y),\mathtt{v}(y))\supset s(\mathtt{l}(b.\mathtt{v}(z)),z,\mathtt{v}(y),\mathtt{l}(b.\mathtt{v}(y)))} s(\mathtt{l}(x.\mathtt{v}(y)),y,\mathtt{v}(z),\mathtt{l}(x.\mathtt{v}(z)))}\supset_L}{\dfrac{\vdots \qquad [M:=\mathtt{v}(z),X:=z,T:=\mathtt{v}(y),M':=\mathtt{v}(y)]}{\dfrac{..;\xrightarrow{\forall M,X,T,M'.\nabla/s(M,X,T,M')\supset s(\mathtt{l}(b.M),X,T,\mathtt{l}(b.M'))} s(\mathtt{l}(x.\mathtt{v}(y)),y,\mathtt{v}(z),\mathtt{l}(x.\mathtt{v}(z)))}{..;\xrightarrow{\text{И}a.\forall M,X,T,M'.\nabla/s(M,X,T,M')\supset s(\mathtt{l}(a.M),X,T,\mathtt{l}(a.M'))} s(\mathtt{l}(x.\mathtt{v}(y)),y,\mathtt{v}(z),\mathtt{l}(x.\mathtt{v}(z)))}\text{И}_L}\forall_L}\forall_L$$

Fig. 5. Deduction proving the fact `s(l(x.v(y)),y,v(z),l(x.v(z)))` where `l` and `v` stand for lambda-abstractions and variables, respectively

corresponding permutation $(e\,d)$ transforms $p(b.d)$ into $p(b.e)$ so that the axiom-rule is applicable.

$$\dfrac{\dfrac{\dfrac{\dots \quad \dfrac{\dfrac{\vdash b.e \approx d.e}{\varnothing;\xrightarrow{p(b.e)} p(d.e)}\text{Ax}}{\varnothing;\xrightarrow{p(b.d)} p(d.e)}\pi\ (e\,d)}{\varnothing;\xrightarrow{\varnothing/\top\supset p(b.d)} p(d.e)}\supset_L}{\varnothing;\xrightarrow{\forall X.\varnothing/\top\supset p(b.X)} p(d.e)}\forall_L\ [X:=d]}{\varnothing;\xrightarrow{\text{И}a.\forall X.\varnothing/\top\supset p(a.X)} p(d.e)}\text{И}_L\ (a\,b)$$

Observe that the "choice" of the fresh name (namely b) introduced by the И_L-rule has no effect on whether this sequent is derivable, since this binder will not bind anything inside the abstraction. The annotated substitution $[X := d]$ however is important with respect to the π-rule we are trying to eliminate. If we had instead substituted e for X, then the axiom is applicable *without* the π-rule.

Note, however, that changing the instantiation of $\forall$-quantifiers might have some "non-local" consequences in deductions. Consider for example the deduction in Fig. 5. In this deduction, the π-rule (marked by $\bullet$) swaps the names z and y. If we eliminate this π-rule by applying the swapping to the terms instantiated for the variables M, X, T and M', then the π-rule is not needed, but at the same time the subgoal (marked by $\star$) is changed. The well-formedness condition ensures that the modification of the terms introduced by the $\forall_L$-rules does not affect the provability of the sequent.

To show that π-rules can be eliminated from derivations involving well-formed programs, we first prove some auxiliary facts.

Lemma 2. *For all permutations π, the sequent $\nabla;\Gamma \Rightarrow \pi{\cdot}G$ is derivable only if the sequent $\nabla;\pi^{-1}{\cdot}\Gamma \Rightarrow G$ is derivable (where we use the notation $\pi{\cdot}\Gamma$ to indicate that π is applied to every formula in Γ).*

Proof. By induction on the structure of deductions. It makes use of the property of $\approx$ that $\nabla \vdash t \approx \pi{\cdot}t'$ holds only if $\nabla \vdash \pi^{-1}{\cdot}t \approx t'$ holds. By inspection we can further see that no additional π-rule is necessary to show the provability in both directions. □

The following corollary is a simple consequence of this lemma by the fact that for closed D-formulae $\pi{\cdot}D = D$ holds.

Corollary 1. *For all permutations π and contexts Γ consisting of closed D-formulae only, $\nabla; \Gamma \Rightarrow \pi{\cdot}G$ is derivable only if $\nabla; \Gamma \Rightarrow G$ is derivable.*

Lemma 3. *If the sequent $\nabla; \Gamma \Rightarrow G$ is derivable and $\nabla \vdash G \approx G'$, then the sequent $\nabla; \Gamma \Rightarrow G'$ is derivable.*

Proof. Since $\nabla \vdash G \approx G'$ is inductively defined extending the $\approx$-equality of the terms occurring in G and G', we can prove this lemma by inspection of the inference-rules, noting that in the $(-)_L$-rules the right-hand side of sequents is always of the form $p(t)$ and the lemma for axioms follows from the transitivity of $\approx$.

For showing our main result, it is convenient to restrict attention to some specific instances of the π-rule. The next lemma shows that we only need to consider unmovable instances of the π-rule.

Definition 2. *A π-rule is* movable *provided it is not directly under an axiom, otherwise it is said to be* unmovable.

Lemma 4. *All movable instances of the π-rules can be replaced by unmovable instances.*

Proof. We call a derivation π-normalised if all instances of the π-rule are unmovable. We first show that if $\Gamma \xrightarrow{\pi\cdot D} A$ has a π-normalised derivation, then we can construct a π-normalised derivation of $\Gamma \xrightarrow{D} A$. Using this construction, we can eliminate the movable π-rules from any derivation one at a time.

There is one case for each left-rule. For Ax, we have

$$\frac{}{\nabla;\Gamma \xrightarrow{\pi\cdot A} \pi{\cdot}A}\,Ax \quad\longrightarrow\quad \frac{\dfrac{}{\nabla;\Gamma \xrightarrow{\pi\cdot A} \pi{\cdot}A}\,Ax}{\nabla;\Gamma \xrightarrow{A} \pi{\cdot}A}\,\pi^{-1}$$

since $\pi^{-1}{\cdot}\pi{\cdot}A = A$. A π-normalised derivation ending in a π'-rule must be immediately followed by Ax, we can derive

$$\frac{\dfrac{}{\nabla;\Gamma \xrightarrow{\pi'\cdot\pi\cdot A} \pi'{\cdot}\pi{\cdot}A}\,Ax}{\nabla;\Gamma \xrightarrow{\pi\cdot A} \pi'{\cdot}\pi{\cdot}A}\,\pi' \quad\longrightarrow\quad \frac{\dfrac{}{\nabla;\Gamma \xrightarrow{\pi'@\pi\cdot A} \pi'{\cdot}\pi{\cdot}A}\,Ax}{\nabla;\Gamma \xrightarrow{A} \pi'{\cdot}\pi{\cdot}A}\,\pi'@\pi$$

since $\pi'{\cdot}\pi{\cdot}A = \pi'@\pi{\cdot}A$. For $\forall_L$, since $\pi{\cdot}\forall X.D = \forall X.\pi{\cdot}_{\{X\}}D$ and $(\pi{\cdot}_{\{X\}}D)[X := t] = \pi{\cdot}(D[X := \pi^{-1}{\cdot}t])$, so we have

$$\frac{\nabla;\Gamma \xrightarrow{(\pi\boldsymbol{\cdot}_{\{X\}}D)[X:=t]} A}{\nabla;\Gamma \xrightarrow{\forall X.\pi\boldsymbol{\cdot}_{\{X\}}D} A}\forall_L \longrightarrow \frac{\nabla;\Gamma \xrightarrow{D[X:=\pi^{-1}\boldsymbol{\cdot}t]} A}{\nabla;\Gamma \xrightarrow{\forall X.D} A}\forall_L$$

where by induction $\nabla;\Gamma \xrightarrow{D[X:=\pi^{-1}\boldsymbol{\cdot}t]} A$ has a π-normalised derivation obtained from that of $\nabla;\Gamma \xrightarrow{\pi\boldsymbol{\cdot}D[X:=\pi^{-1}\boldsymbol{\cdot}t]} A$. The cases for $\wedge_L$ and И_L are straightforward since $\pi\boldsymbol{\cdot}_{\mathcal{B}}(-)$ commutes with $\wedge$ and И. For $\supset_L$ we have

$$\frac{\nabla\vdash\nabla \quad \nabla;\Gamma\Rightarrow\pi\boldsymbol{\cdot}G \quad \nabla;\Gamma \xrightarrow{\pi\boldsymbol{\cdot}A} A'}{\nabla;\Gamma \xrightarrow{\nabla/(\pi\boldsymbol{\cdot}G)\supset(\pi\boldsymbol{\cdot}A)} A'}\supset_L \longrightarrow \frac{\nabla\vdash\nabla \quad \nabla;\Gamma\Rightarrow G \quad \nabla;\Gamma \xrightarrow{A} A'}{\nabla;\Gamma \xrightarrow{\nabla/G\supset A} A'}\supset_L$$

using Lemma 3 to derive $\nabla;\Gamma \Rightarrow G$ from $\nabla;\Gamma \Rightarrow \pi\boldsymbol{\cdot}G$ and the induction hypothesis to obtain a π-normalised derivation of $\nabla;\Gamma \xrightarrow{A} A'$ from that of $\nabla;\Gamma \xrightarrow{\pi\boldsymbol{\cdot}A} A'$.

Theorem 1. *If Γ consists of well-formed clauses and the sequent $\nabla;\Gamma \Rightarrow G$ is derivable, then it is derivable without using the π-rule.*

Proof. Since Γ consists of well-formed clauses only, all Γ's in the deduction consist of well-formed clauses (formulae on the left-hand side are analysed only if they are selected to be in the stoup-position). By Lemma 4, we can replace this deduction by one in which all π-rules are unmovable. So we need to consider how unmovable π-rules can be eliminated. Recall that unmovable π-rules occur in segments of the form

$$\frac{\dfrac{\begin{array}{c}\vdots\\ \nabla''_{bs},\nabla'\vdash\nabla_{ts}\end{array} \quad \begin{array}{c}\vdots\\ \nabla''_{bs},\nabla';\Gamma\Rightarrow G_{bs,ts}\end{array} \quad \dfrac{\dfrac{\nabla''_{bs},\nabla'\vdash\pi\boldsymbol{\cdot}s_{bs,ts}\approx t}{\nabla''_{bs},\nabla';\Gamma \xrightarrow{\pi\boldsymbol{\cdot}p(s_{bs,ts})} p(t)}\text{Ax}}{\nabla''_{bs},\nabla';\Gamma \xrightarrow{p(s_{bs,ts})} p(t)}\pi}{\begin{array}{c}\nabla''_{bs},\nabla';\Gamma \xrightarrow{\nabla_{ts}/G_{bs,ts}\supset p(s_{bs,ts})} p(t)\\ \vdots \quad \}\text{И}\forall\end{array}}\supset_L}{\dfrac{\nabla';\Gamma \xrightarrow{\text{И}as.\forall Xs.\nabla_{Xs}/G_{as,Xs}\supset p(s_{as,Xs})} p(t)}{\nabla';\Gamma\Rightarrow p(t)}\text{Sel}} \tag{4}$$

where the И-quantifier introduces the names bs and the $\forall$-quantifiers replace the variables Xs with the terms ts. We indicate this by using the notation $G_{as,Xs}$ and $G_{bs,ts}$. The freshness constraints ∇''_{bs} stand for the constraints introduced by the И-quantifiers, that is $b \# FV(t)$ for each b in bs. Let σ be the substitution of the terms ts for the variables Xs, that is the terms introduced by the $\forall$-quantifiers.

Below we give a deduction without the π-rule where the bs and ts are suitably changed. For this we choose first some fresh names cs with the proviso that $\pi\boldsymbol{\cdot}cs = cs$, which means they are unaffected by the permutation introduced by the π-rule (such fresh names always exist). From the well-formedness of the clause in the stoup-position, we know that there is a substitution σ' and a permutation π' such that

$$\begin{array}{l} cs \# Xs, \nabla_{Xs} \vdash \sigma'(p(s_{cs,Xs})) \approx p(s_{bs,Xs}) \\ cs \# Xs, \nabla_{Xs} \vdash \sigma'(\pi'\boldsymbol{\cdot}G_{cs,Xs}) \approx G_{bs,Xs} \end{array} \tag{5}$$

hold where we use the short-hand notation $cs \# Xs$ to refer the sets of freshness constraints $c_i \# X_1, \ldots, c_i \# X_n$ for all names c_i in cs. By Lemma 1*(ii)*, $\approx$ is preserved under substitutions, so we can infer from (5) that

$$\begin{array}{l} cs \# Xs \vdash \sigma \circ \sigma'(p(s_{cs,Xs})) \approx \sigma(p(s_{bs,Xs})) \\ cs \# Xs \vdash \sigma \circ \sigma'(\pi' \cdot G_{cs,Xs}) \approx \sigma(G_{bs,Xs}) \end{array} \tag{6}$$

hold where the right-hand sides are $p(s_{bs,ts})$ and $G_{bs,ts}$, respectively. Note that the ∇_{Xs} "vanish" because we have that $cs \# Xs \vdash \sigma(\nabla_{Xs})$. From (6) we can further infer that

$$cs \# Xs \vdash \pi \cdot \sigma \circ \sigma'(p(s_{cs,Xs})) \approx \pi \cdot (p(s_{bs,ts})) \tag{7}$$

$$cs \# Xs \vdash \pi \cdot \sigma \circ \sigma'(\pi' \cdot G_{cs,Xs}) \approx \pi \cdot (G_{bs,ts}) \tag{8}$$

hold by Lemma 1*(i)* asserting that $\approx$ is preserved under permutations. Recall that we chosen the cs so that π does not affect them. So if we apply the substitution $\sigma \circ \sigma'$ and the permutation π to the left-hand side of (7) we have $\pi \cdot \sigma \circ \sigma'(p(s_{cs,Xs})) = p(s_{cs,ts'})$ for some terms ts'. Moreover we have $cs \# Xs \vdash s_{cs,ts'} \approx \pi \cdot s_{bs,ts}$ which means we can replace in the deduction (4) $\pi \cdot s_{bs,ts}$ by $s_{cs,ts'}$ and get by transitivity of $\approx$ a correct instance of the axiom. Thus we can form the deduction:

$$\dfrac{\dfrac{\dfrac{\begin{array}{c}\vdots\\ \nabla''_{cs}, \nabla' \vdash \nabla_{ts'}\end{array} \quad \begin{array}{c}\vdots\\ \nabla''_{cs}, \nabla'; \Gamma \Rightarrow G_{cs,ts'}\end{array} \quad \dfrac{\nabla''_{cs}, \nabla' \vdash s_{cs,ts'} \approx t}{\nabla''_{cs}, \nabla'; \Gamma \xrightarrow{p(s_{cs,ts'})} p(t)}\,\text{Ax}}{\nabla''_{cs}, \nabla'; \Gamma \xrightarrow{\nabla_{ts'}/G_{cs,ts'} \supset p(s_{cs,ts'})} p(t)}\,\supset_L}{\begin{array}{c}\vdots \quad \}\,\text{И}\forall \\ \hline \nabla'; \Gamma \xrightarrow{\text{И}as.\forall Xs.\nabla_{Xs}/G_{as,Xs} \supset p(s_{as,Xs})} p(t)\end{array}}}{\nabla'; \Gamma \Rightarrow p(t)}\,\text{Sel}$$

without the π-rule. We still need to ensure that $\nabla''_{cs}, \nabla'; \Gamma \Rightarrow G_{cs,ts'}$ and $\nabla''_{cs}, \nabla' \vdash \nabla_{ts'}$ are derivable. The second sequent is derivable because $cs \# Xs \vdash \sigma(\nabla_{Xs})$. For the first sequent we can infer from the original (sub)deduction $\nabla''_{bs}, \nabla'; \Gamma \Rightarrow G_{bs,ts}$ by Corollary 1 that $\nabla''_{bs}, \nabla'; \Gamma \Rightarrow \pi \cdot G_{bs,ts}$ is derivable (this deduction does not introduce any new π-rules). In (8) we can pull out the permutation π' and we have $\pi \cdot \sigma \circ \sigma'(\pi' \cdot G_{cs,Xs}) = \pi @ \pi' \cdot (\sigma \circ \sigma'(G_{cs,Xs}))$. Therefore applying the substitution to $G_{cs,Xs}$ gives $\pi @ \pi' \cdot (\sigma \circ \sigma'(G_{cs,Xs})) = \pi @ \pi' \cdot G_{cs,ts'}$ (taking the ts' we introduced for $s_{cs,ts'}$ earlier). Thus by Lemma 3 we can show that $\nabla''_{cs}, \nabla'; \Gamma \Rightarrow G_{cs,ts'}$ is derivable.

Each transformation decreases the number of π-rules in a deduction by one and thus by repeated application we will eventually end up with a π-free proof. □

We have shown that when all the formulas in Γ are well-formed, every deduction of $\Gamma \Rightarrow G$ containing π-rules can be replaced by one without π-rules. Consequently, nominal unification is sufficient for executing well-formed αProlog-programs.

4 Verification of Well-Formedness Using Nominal Matching

In this section we consider the question of how to verify the well-formedness condition given in Definition 1. For a clause $\mathsf{И} as.\forall Xs.\nabla_{as,Xs}/G_{as,Xs}\supset A_{as,Xs}$, we need to find a substitution σ and permutation π which make the two judgements

$$bs \# Xs, \nabla_{as,Xs} \vdash \sigma(A_{bs,Xs}) \approx A_{as,Xs} \quad \text{and} \quad bs \# Xs, \nabla_{as,Xs} \vdash \sigma(\pi{\cdot}G_{bs,Xs}) \approx G_{as,Xs}$$

hold. For the first judgement, σ can be found by nominal matching. But for the second judgement, finding both substitution σ and permutation π requires solving (NP-hard) equivariant matching problems. This seemingly negative result should, however, be seen in the context that well-formedness only needs to be verified once per clause, rather than repeatedly during proof-search. Thus, the one-time cost of performing equivariant unification in checking well-formedness is negligible compared to the cost of performing equivariant unification throughout computation. Furthermore, as can be seen from the examples, the number of names in a clause is usually small. Taking the following proposition (whose proof we omit)

Proposition 1. *If $G_{bs,Xs}$ equivariantly matches with $G_{as,Xs}$, then a matching exists in which the permutation π consists of swappings $(a_i\ b_i)$ only.*

into account, we can just enumerate all possible cases (2^n given n names) and solve each of the nominal matching problems. If one problem can be solved, then we have a σ and a π as required by the condition.

5 Conclusion

We have shown that for well-formed αProlog programs, all instances of the π-rule can be removed from deductions. As a result, proof search using only nominal unification is complete for such programs, which coincides with our experimental results gained from our implementation of αProlog. This is a significant result, because the alternative is to use an NP-hard equivariant unification algorithm for proof search.

In order to be well-formed, the `type`-program given in the Introduction needs to be stated as follows

```
type(Gamma,lam(x.M),arr(S,T)) :-
                    x#Gamma, x#S, x#T, type([(x,S)|Gamma],M,T).
```

explicitly giving the freshness constraints `x#S` and `x#T`. These constraints do not affect the meaning of the program because term variables are expected (by programmer convention) not to appear in types. In fact, our implementation of αProlog is strongly typed and therefore can determine automatically from type information that lambda-term variables can never occur in types. Thus, our analysis could be made more precise by taking type information into account.

Let us briefly mention whether our result can be strengthened. The logic programming language λProlog [6] has convincingly demonstrated the usefulness of implications in G-formulae (that is extending logic programming to the setting of Hereditary Harrop formulae). In αProlog we would like to allow implications in G-formulae as well. Whether our result extends to such formulae is still open. It seems that our definition of G-formulae can be extended to include existential and universal formulae. However, our proving technique for showing this would require some subtle modifications—for example we would need to define when two formulae with quantifiers are $\approx$-equal, which is non-trivial. However, we expect that this can be done. What is impossible is to allow И-quantifiers in goal-formulae. Such formulae really need equivariant unification.

Acknowledgements. This research was supported by a fellowship for Urban from the Alexander-von-Humboldt foundation.

References

1. J. Cheney. The complexity of equivariant unification. In *Proc. of International Colloquium on Automata, Languages and Programming*, volume 3142 of *LNCS*, pages 332–344, 2004.
2. J. Cheney. *Nominal Logic Programming*. PhD thesis, Cornell University, Ithaca, NY, 2004.
3. J. Cheney and C. Urban. Alpha-prolog: A logic programming language with names, binding, and α-equivalence. In B. Demoen and V. Lifschitz, editors, *Proc. of International Conference on Logic Programming*, volume 3132 of *LNCS*, pages 269–283, 2004.
4. R. Dyckhoff and L. Pinto. Proof Search in Constructive Logic. In S. Barry Cooper and John K. Truss, editors, *Proc. of the Logic Colloquium 1997*, volume 258 of *London Mathematical Society Lecture Note Series*, pages 53–65. Cambridge University Press, 1997.
5. M. J. Gabbay and J. Cheney. A proof theory for nominal logic. In *Proc. of Annual IEEE Symposium on Logic in Computer Science*, pages 139–148, 2004.
6. G. Nadathur and D. Miller. Higher-order logic programming. In D. M. Gabbay, C. J. Hogger, and J. A. Robinson, editors, *Handbook of Logics for Artificial Intelligence and Logic Programming*, volume 5, pages 499–590. Clarendon Press, 1998.
7. A. M. Pitts. Nominal logic, a first order theory of names and binding. *Information and Computation*, 186:165–193, 2003.
8. C. Urban, A. M. Pitts, and M. J. Gabbay. Nominal unification. *Theoretical Computer Science*, 323(1-2):473–497, 2004.

Higher-Order Abstract Non-interference

Damiano Zanardini

Dipartimento di Informatica, Università di Verona,
Strada Le Grazie 15, I-37134 Verona, Italy
zanardini@sci.univr.it

Abstract. This work proposes a type system for checking Abstract Non-Interference in the setting of simply-typed lambda calculus with basic types and recursion. A lambda-expression satisfies Abstract Non-Interference relatively to a given semantic property if an attacker which can only see program data up to that property cannot infer, by observing a computation, private data from public ones. Attackers are abstract interpretations of program semantics. The type analysis infers, for an expression, a security type which approximates the secret kernel for the expression, i.e. the most powerful harmless attacker for which the expression is secure. The type system is proven to be correct, that is, private information is not revealed to an attacker which is unable to distinguish different values belonging to the inferred type.

1 Introduction

Problem. *Information flow* [12] is one of the relevant properties of programs, regarding the possibility that some pieces of secret information can be maliciously acquired by an attacker observing the execution of the program. Data are splitted into *private* and *public*: the requirement for a program to be secure is that no attacker should be able to guess the value of private data by observing only public data and the execution of the program. A program for which this information leakage is impossible is said to have the *Non-Interference* property [8]: two executions differing only on the value of the private input cannot be distinguished by merely observing the public output.

Non-Interference turns out to be too restrictive: some information flows are actually harmless and should be allowed in order not to reject many useful programs. This led to several efforts to weaken the notion of Non-Interference into a more useful and easy to obtain property; in particular, Giacobazzi and Mastroeni [6] proposed Abstract Non-Interference (ANI), an approximated property defined into the framework of Abstract Interpretation [3, 4]. In ANI an attacker can see public data only to a certain degree of precision, then it is not able to exploit some information flows which would be detected (and result in a rejecting of the program) in standard Non-Interference analysis.

Main Contribution. Abstract Non-Interference was first defined for a simple imperative language with integers as the only data type. This paper defines

P. Urzyczyn (Ed.): TLCA 2005, LNCS 3461, pp. 417–432, 2005.

ANI and the relative analysis for a typed lambda calculus with recursion by developing a type system which infers for a lambda-expression a type describing the class of attackers for which the expression is secure.

Dealing with a functional language involves the definition of ANI on higher-order values: two functions can be distinguished by an observer iff, when applied, they give distinguishable results. Our type system is constructive in the sense that it tries to compute the *secret kernel* [6], i.e. the most powerful attacker for which a given program is secure, rather than checking if a program is secure for a given attacker. The result of the type inference is an upper approximation of the secret kernel: some expressions are rejected for a certain degree of precision even if they satisfy Abstract Non-Interference to that degree.

The type system is in general undecidable (even the basic domain of integers does not need to have finite abstract domains); decidability can only be reached if the abstract domains on values are divided into a finite number of classes and some rules are added *at hand* to help the analysis.

Related Work. The type-based approach for security analyses was proposed by Volpano and Smith [14], then it was translated into Abstract Interpretation in [15]. Programs are given security types (*public* or *private*) which are propagated in the composition of bigger programs; the type of the main expression is public if there is not interference. Standard information flow was defined for functional languages in the SLam calculus [9] and in Flow Caml [13], which is a real implementation of control flow analysis. SLam calculus is proven to be a special case of the Dependency Core Calculus [1], a small extension of Moggi's computational lambda calculus which aims to unify into a single calculus several dependency concepts arising in security, partial evaluation, program slicing and call-tracking. In developing the type analysis we use a notion of *ternary relation* similar to [10]; this allows comparing properties displayed by pairs of computations instead of considering a single evaluation.

2 Preliminary Notions

Information Flow and Non-interference. If a user wants to keep some data confidential, he or she could take as a policy requirement that confidential data cannot affect data which are visible to other (untrusted) users. This policy allows programs to manipulate private data as long as the visible outputs of a computation do not reveal information about the hidden data. The notion of *Non-Interference* was introduced by Goguen and Meseguer in [8]: a program has the property of Non-Interference if any two executions differing only in the *private* input data (and therefore indistinguishable by an untrusted user) cannot be distinguished in their output by observing only *public* data: there must be no *information flow* from private to public data. Information flow security techniques are more powerful than standard *access control* methods [11, 12], since they do not deal only with the ability to read information, but also with the possibility that information is dangerously propagated.

Abstract Interpretation. Abstract Interpretation, introduced by the Cousots in [3], is a framework to systematically derive non-standard approximated semantics. The main notion in defining approximation is that of *abstract domain.*

Abstract domains can be formulated either in terms of Galois connections or closure operators [4]. An *upper closure operator* (uco) on a poset $\langle C, \leq \rangle$ is a function $\rho : C \mapsto C$ monotone, idempotent and extensive ($\forall x.\ x \leq \rho(x)$). The set of all ucos on C is $uco(C)$. A closure operator is uniquely determined by the set of its fixpoints (called *abstract values*); this set is (isomorphic to) the abstract domain A approximating the concrete domain C. A set $X \subseteq C$ is the set of fixpoints of a uco iff X is a *Moore-family*, i.e. $X = \mathcal{M}(X) = \{\wedge S | S \subseteq X\}$.

The notion of approximation formalizes the idea that in the abstract domain there is less complexity (A is a subset of C) together with a loss of precision (some elements of C cannot be used when doing computations on A). A computation F_C on C can be approximated with an abstract computation F_A by providing the abstract versions of constants and functions. The abstraction is *sound* if the abstract result is always a correct approximation of the concrete one: $\forall x.F_C(x) \leq F_A(x)$ (where $\leq$ should be read as *more concrete* or *more precise*).

If C is a complete lattice (with $\perp$ and $\top$ as bottom and top elements), then $uco(C)$ ordered pointwise is also a complete lattice with $\lambda x.x$ and $\lambda x.\top$ as bottom and top elements. The first describes the identity abstraction, with $A = C$ and no loss of information; the second is the trivial abstraction that reduces the concrete domain into a one-element abstract domain. The *reduced product* $\overline{\wedge}$ [4] of a set of abstract domains $\{A_i\}$ is the most abstract among the domains more concrete (i.e. closer to C) than each A_i: $\overline{\wedge}_i A_i = \mathcal{M}(\bigcup_i A_i)$.

Abstract Non-interference. The program property of Non-Interference can be weakened (abstracted) by modelling secrecy relatively to some observable property: a secure program is one that preserves secrecy only as regards of a particular amount of information, the one that the attacker can observe.

The concrete domain is the set of all properties of values (e.g. $\wp(\mathbb{N})$ for integers, where $P \subseteq \mathbb{N}$ is the set of values satisfying the property), representing which values can be possibly distinguished by the attacker (Sec. 4). The ability of an attacker to observe data is described by abstract domains: if an attacker has precision ρ it is unable to distinguish two values v_1 and v_2 such that $\rho(\{v_1\}) = \rho(\{v_2\})$ (i.e. values having the same property ρ). A program P is secure for a pair of domains η and ρ (written $[\eta]P(\rho)$) if no information flows are detected by an attacker which can see public input and output data only up to a level of precision characterized respectively by η and ρ:

$$\eta(l_1) = \eta(l_2) \Rightarrow \rho(\llbracket P \rrbracket(h_1, l_1)) = \rho(\llbracket P \rrbracket(h_2, l_2))$$

where l_i are public data and h_i can be any (private) values; if the input values l_1 and l_2 cannot be distinguished, then it is not possibile to guess the value of h_i by observing the (abstracted) output. For a given η, the *secret kernel* is the most concrete ρ_s such that $[\eta]P(\rho_s)$. ANI allows to describe several kinds of attackers by using the opportune abstract domains; standard Non-Interference is a special case, obtained by using the identity abstract domain for all data.

3 Syntax and Semantics of the Language

Syntax. The language is the eager lambda calculus with arithmetical and boolean operations, conditional and recursion μ. $\mathcal{X}$ is the set of variables (denoted by x, y, $F\dots$). The set $\mathcal{E}$ of expressions is defined by

$$e ::= n \mid b \mid x \mid e+e \mid \lambda x.e \mid e(e) \mid \mu F.e \mid \texttt{if } e \texttt{ then } e \texttt{ else } e$$

where n and b are an integer and a boolean constant.

Semantics. The language semantics (see [2]) is described in Fig. 1 (here constants are not distinguished from their semantic interpretation). Every domain of values has a bottom element $\bot$; for functions the bottom element is $\lambda v.\bot$. The denotational semantics $[\![\_]\!] : \mathcal{E} \mapsto \mathcal{S}$ defines a call-by-value evaluation with run-time type checking (checking for type errors is left implicit).

$n \in \mathbb{N}_\bot \triangleq \mathbb{N} \cup \{\bot\}$	integers	$b \in \mathbb{B}_\bot \triangleq \{\texttt{true}, \texttt{false}, \bot\}$	booleans
$f \in \mathcal{U} \triangleq \mathbb{N}_\bot \cup \mathbb{B}_\bot \cup [\mathcal{U} \mapsto \mathcal{U}]$	values	$\mathcal{W} \triangleq \{\omega\}$	wrong value
$\varepsilon \in \mathcal{S}_{env} \triangleq \mathcal{X} \mapsto \mathcal{U}$	environments	$\phi \in \mathcal{S} \triangleq \mathcal{S}_{env} \mapsto \mathcal{U}$	semantic domain

$$[\![n]\!]_\varepsilon \triangleq n \qquad [\![b]\!]_\varepsilon \triangleq b$$
$$[\![x]\!]_\varepsilon \triangleq \varepsilon(x) \qquad [\![e_1 + e_2]\!]_\varepsilon \triangleq [\![e_1]\!]_\varepsilon + [\![e_2]\!]_\varepsilon$$
$$[\![\lambda x.e]\!]_\varepsilon \triangleq \lambda v.[\![e]\!]_{\varepsilon[x \leftarrow v]} \qquad [\![e(e')]\!]_\varepsilon \triangleq [\![e]\!]_\varepsilon([\![e']\!]_\varepsilon)$$
$$[\![\mu F.e]\!]_\varepsilon \triangleq lfp(\lambda v.[\![e]\!]_{\varepsilon[F \leftarrow v]}) \qquad [\![e' = e'']\!]_\varepsilon \triangleq ([\![e']\!]_\varepsilon = [\![e'']\!]_\varepsilon)$$
$$[\![\texttt{if } e \texttt{ then } e' \texttt{ else } e'']\!] \triangleq \text{if } [\![e]\!]_\varepsilon \text{ then } [\![e']\!]_\varepsilon \text{ else } [\![e'']\!]_\varepsilon$$

Fig. 1. The semantics of simply-typed lambda calculus

4 The Type System

Non-Interference refers to the possibility that two computations can be distinguished by observing some public parts of data. By means of security annotations, this type analysis computes a pair of (abstract) values representing the possible simultaneous outcomes of two evaluations of e with indistinguishable input. e is secure if the attacker cannot distinguish the elements of the pair.

The type system has monomorphic types extended with security annotations. The set $\mathcal{T}$ of types contains the basic types `int` and `bool` and has $\rightarrow$ as the only constructor: $\tau, \tau' \in \mathcal{T} \Rightarrow (\tau \rightarrow \tau') \in \mathcal{T}$. Each type is a description of a set of semantic values: the function $\mathcal{V} : \mathcal{T} \mapsto \wp(\mathcal{U})$ is defined as

$$\mathcal{V}(\texttt{int}) = \mathbb{N}_\bot \qquad \mathcal{V}(\texttt{bool}) = \mathbb{B}_\bot \qquad \mathcal{V}((\tau \rightarrow \tau')) = [\mathcal{V}(\tau) \mapsto \mathcal{V}(\tau')]$$

The Abstract Domains. The power of an attacker in observing a computation is described by abstract domains; in general an attacker can see the n input data (free variables) and the output of the computation, then its observational power can be described by at most $n+1$ abstract domains (on various types).

Let $C_\tau = \langle \wp(\mathcal{V}(\tau)), \subseteq \rangle$ be the concrete domain on the type τ, ordered by inclusion ($\bot \in X$ for each $X \subseteq C_\tau$). C_τ describes all the possible properties of values (a property p is described by the set of values satisfying it).

An abstract domain $\rho \in \mathcal{D}_\tau$ is the set of fixpoints of a closure operator $\rho \in uco(C_\tau)$ (we keep the same name for simplicity). The set of all abstract domains is $\mathcal{D} = \bigcup_\tau \mathcal{D}_\tau$.We write $\rho(v)$ for $\rho(\{v\})$. The ordering $\leq$ is $\subseteq$ (the described property is more precise); $\sqcup$ and $\sqcap$ are defined accordingly.

Two values cannot be distinguished by the domain iff they are mapped into the same (abstract) value: $v_1 \equiv_\rho v_2 \iff \rho(v_1) = \rho(v_2)$.

The Security Types. The type system uses normal types equipped with security annotations: this is described by a security relation which links the values of an expression after two possible computations.

Definition 1 (security relations and types). An expression $e : \tau$ is given a *security type* $\{\tau\}_R$, where $R \in \mathcal{R}$ is a *security relation* defined as follows:

$$\mathcal{R} = \wp(P(\tau) \times P(\tau))$$

where $P(\tau)$ is an abstract domain on τ (to be defined in Def. 8). $\bot$ is used as a shorthand for $\{(\bot, \bot)\}$; usually (s_1, s_2) or $s_1 s_2$ is written instead of $\{(s_1, s_2)\}$.

The predicate ST checks if two values v_1 and v_2 belong to the same type σ, i.e. if it is possible that, in two different computations (with possibly different input values) of an expression of type σ, the two outputs are, respectively, v_1 and v_2.

Definition 2 (same-type predicate). The predicate ST describes a ternary relation [10] between a security type and two values: the predicate is true (the triple is an element of the relation) if the values both belong to the security type.

$$\begin{aligned} &\mathrm{ST}_{\{\tau\}_\bot}(v_1, v_2) \equiv v_1 = v_2 = \bot_\tau \\ &\mathrm{ST}_{\{\tau\}_R}(v_1, v_2) \equiv \exists (s_1, s_2) \in R.\ (v_1 \in s_1 \wedge v_2 \in s_2) \end{aligned}$$

- An expression of type $\{\tau\}_\bot$ must have value $\bot_\tau$ in every execution (then its semantics is the constant $\bot_\tau$-function).
- For $e : \{\tau\}_{(s_1,s_2)}$ any two computations must yield values belonging resp. to the classes s_1 and s_2. By definition of $\bot$, $\mathrm{ST}_{\{\tau\}_R}(\bot_\tau, \bot_\tau)$ for every R.
- For functional values the definition amounts to

$$\begin{aligned} \mathrm{ST}_{\{(\tau \to \tau')\}_R}(f_1, f_2) \equiv &\ \forall (s_1, s_2) \in R.\ \forall v_1, v_2. \\ &\mathrm{ST}_{\{\tau\}_{(t_1,t_2)}}(v_1, v_2) \Rightarrow \mathrm{ST}_{\{\tau'\}_{(s_1(t_1), s_2(t_2))}}(f_1(v_1), f_2(v_2)) \end{aligned}$$

ST induces an ordering on security types: $\{\tau\}_R \leq \{\tau'\}_{R'} \equiv \tau = \tau' \wedge R \leq R'$ and

$$R \leq R' \equiv \forall v_1, v_2.\ \mathrm{ST}_{\{\tau\}_R}(v_1, v_2) \Rightarrow \mathrm{ST}_{\{\tau\}_{R'}}(v_1, v_2)$$

On security relations least upper bound and greatest lower buond are defined:

$$\sqcup = \cup \qquad R' \sqcap R'' = \{(s_1 \sqcap t_1, s_2 \sqcap t_2) \mid (s_1, s_2) \in R' \wedge (t_1, t_2) \in R''\}$$

Remark 3. Given a security relation R with $S \times S \subseteq R$ and $\sqcup S = t$, it can be normalized into an equivalent relation R' with $S \times S$ replaced by (t,t), and viceversa. R' is equivalent to R but is structurally (and computationally) smaller: when applying the typing rules we do not need to consider all the pairs in $S \times S$, but only (t,t) (see also the second part of Section 9).

Lemma 4. *$\forall v_1 \leq v_2.\ ST_\sigma(v_2,u) \Rightarrow ST_\sigma(v_1,u)$ (on both arguments).*

Proof.
- Basic types: $\mathbb{N}_\perp$ and $\mathbb{B}_\perp$ are flat domains with bottom; the partial ordering is $v_1 \leq v_2 \Leftrightarrow v_1 = v_2 \vee v_1 = \perp$; lemma holds by def. of $\perp$ and ST.
- Higher-order types: Ordering on functions is pointwise, then, $v_1 \leq v_2$ implies $v_1(x) \leq v_2(x)$ for all x. Result follows by induction and Def. 2 on functions.

Lemma 5. *Let ST^τ be the restriction of ST on the type τ, i.e. $ST^\tau_\sigma(v_1,v_2)$ is defined if $\sigma = \llparenthesis\tau\rrparenthesis_R$ and $v_1, v_2 \in \mathcal{V}(\tau)$. Then ST^τ is continuous on its arguments, i.e. for directed sets S, X and Y*

$$ST^\tau_{\sqcup S}(\sqcup X, \sqcup Y) = \sqcup_{\sigma\in S} \sqcap_{x\in X} \sqcap_{y\in Y} ST^\tau_\sigma(x,y)$$

Proof. ST^τ is a function mapping $\mathcal{T}^\tau_{sec} \times \mathcal{V}(\tau) \times \mathcal{V}(\tau)$ to $\mathbb{B}$ (with $\mathtt{false} < \mathtt{true}$, $\sqcup \equiv \vee$ and $\sqcap \equiv \wedge$). For basic types $v \sqcup v = v$, $v \sqcup \perp = \perp \sqcup v = v$ and $\nexists (v \sqcup u)$ if $\perp \neq v \neq u \neq \perp$; for functional types $(f \sqcup g)(x) = f(x) \sqcup g(x)$. The continuity of ST^τ can be proven separately on the three arguments:

- Continuity on the first argument: $\mathrm{ST}^\tau_{\sqcup S}(x,y) = \sqcup_{\sigma\in S}\mathrm{ST}^\tau_\sigma(x,y)$ for every directed set S. This is easily proven by seeing that on booleans $\sqcup \equiv \vee$ and $\mathrm{ST}^\tau_{\sqcup S}(x,y) = \bigvee_{\sigma\in S} \mathrm{ST}^\tau_\sigma(x,y)$.
- Continuity on the second argument (third is similar): for every directed set X, $\mathrm{ST}^\tau_\sigma(\sqcup X, y) = \sqcap_{x\in X}\mathrm{ST}^\tau_\sigma(x,y)$.
  - Basic types: a directed set on integers or booleans must be either $\{\perp\}$, $\{v\}$ or $\{\perp, v\}$ for a certain v. In the first two cases the result is trivial, in the third it follows from Lemma 4.
  - Functional types: for higher order types X is directed iff for each v the set $X_v = \{f(v) \mid f \in X\}$ is directed. Then (by def. of app, see Fig. 2):

$$\begin{array}{r}
\mathrm{ST}^\tau_{\llparenthesis(\tau'\to\tau'')\rrparenthesis_R}(\sqcup X, g) \equiv \\
\forall v_1, v_2.\ \mathrm{ST}^\tau_{\llparenthesis\tau'\rrparenthesis_{R'}}(v_1,v_2) \Rightarrow \mathrm{ST}^\tau_{\llparenthesis\tau''\rrparenthesis_{\mathrm{app}(R,R')}}((\sqcup X)(v_1), g(v_2)) \equiv [hyp.] \\
\forall v_1, v_2.\ \mathrm{ST}^\tau_{\llparenthesis\tau'\rrparenthesis_{R'}}(v_1,v_2) \Rightarrow \sqcap_{f\in X}\mathrm{ST}^\tau_{\llparenthesis\tau''\rrparenthesis_{\mathrm{app}(R,R')}}(f(v_1), g(v_2)) \equiv \\
\forall v_1, v_2.\ \sqcap_{f\in X}\ (\mathrm{ST}^\tau_{\llparenthesis\tau'\rrparenthesis_{R'}}(v_1,v_2) \Rightarrow \mathrm{ST}^\tau_{\llparenthesis\tau''\rrparenthesis_{\mathrm{app}(R,R')}}(f(v_1), g(v_2))) \equiv \\
\sqcap_{f\in X}\forall v_1, v_2.\ (\mathrm{ST}^\tau_{\llparenthesis\tau'\rrparenthesis_{R'}}(v_1,v_2) \Rightarrow \mathrm{ST}^\tau_{\llparenthesis\tau''\rrparenthesis_{\mathrm{app}(R,R')}}(f(v_1), g(v_2))) \equiv \\
\sqcap_{f\in X}\mathrm{ST}^\tau_{\llparenthesis(\tau'\to\tau'')\rrparenthesis_R}(f, g)
\end{array}$$

In Non-Interference data are splitted into a public and a private part: an attacker can read information from the public but not from the private. In our language input data are the free variables of an expression, and the security type of a variable characterizes it as public or private.

Definition 6 (public and private variables). $E(x)$ is the security type of x in the type environment $E \in \mathcal{T}_{env} = [\mathcal{X} \mapsto \mathcal{T}_{sec}]$.

$$\forall_1(\rho) \triangleq \{(\rho(x), \rho(x)) \mid x \in \mathcal{V}(\tau)\} \qquad \forall_2(\rho) \triangleq \{(\rho(x), \rho(y)) \mid x, y \in \mathcal{V}(\tau)\}$$
$$public(x : \tau) \Rightarrow E(x) = (\tau)_{\forall_1(P(\tau))} \qquad private(x : \tau) \Rightarrow E(x) = (\tau)_{\forall_2(P(\tau))}$$

where $P(\tau)$ is an abstract domain on τ, to be defined in def. 8.

It is now possible, with ST, to understand the meaning of public and private:

(i) In two different computations the values of a public variable must belong to the same element of the domain; if s describes a singleton, then $v_1 = v_2$ as in the definition of standard Non-Interference. In Abstract Non-Interference we allow public data to be different as long as they cannot be distinguished by an observer. It should be noted that no restrictions are posed on the value of a public variable in itself: the constraints apply to values in pairs of computations. For example, in the parity abstract domain $\{\bot, even, odd, \top\}$ a public variable would have $\{(even, even), (odd, odd)\}$ as its security relation.

(ii) Nothing can be said about the values of a private variable: every two values of type τ are possible values in two different computations.

Typing Rules. The type analysis assigns a security type to basic expressions (constants, variables) and infers the types for composed expressions following a set of typing rules. It is an approximate (abstract) analysis because abstract values (sets of values) rather than concrete are taken into account in computing properties: the abstract values are elements of abstract domains.

The observational power of an attacker can be described by the $n+1$-tuple IO of the abstract domains describing the ability to see input and output values (i.e. the n domains ρ_x on the n input variables and ρ_{out} on the result of the computation). When assigning a type to a (public or private) variable the natural choice is to use, in Def. 6, the domain ρ_x as $P(\tau)$. This has some limitations, as shown in the example:

Example 7. Let $e \equiv x$ and IO $= \{\rho_x, \rho_{out}\}$ where $\rho_x = \{\bot, pos, neg, \top\}$ is the domain on x (public) and $\rho_{out} = \{\bot, even, odd, \top\}$ is the one on the output. Then an attacker can observe only the sign of the input and the parity of the output. If x is given a security type based on ρ_x (i.e. $(\mathtt{int})_{\{(pos,pos),(neg,neg)\}}$), then, since two numbers with the same sign can have different parities, the expression is classified as insecure because the attacker can distinguish two computations with the same input sign by watching the output parity.

In the above example ρ_x is a too abstract domain to capture information about parity. Then, in general, we need to choose the right domains to assign types to basic expressions, in order to avoid some unexpected losses of information and to deal with constants. The idea is to build two sets $Z_{\mathtt{int}}$ and $Z_{\mathtt{bool}}$ as follows: while IO $\neq \emptyset$ pick a ρ from IO:

- If $\rho \in \mathcal{D}_{\mathtt{int}}$, then ρ is inserted into $Z_{\mathtt{int}}$.
- If $\rho \in \mathcal{D}_{\mathtt{bool}}$, then ρ is inserted into $Z_{\mathtt{bool}}$.
- If $\rho \in \mathcal{D}_{(\tau' \to \tau'')}$, then there exist ρ' and ρ'' such that the elements of ρ map elements of ρ' to elements of ρ''; ρ' and ρ'' are inserted into IO.

When IO is empty the two sets $Z_{\texttt{int}}$ and $Z_{\texttt{bool}}$ cointain all the relevant information about basic types; collecting the information into a single domain is done by computing the reduced product (Sec. 2) of all the elements of the sets, thus obtaining ρ_i and ρ_b: they are the most abstract domains capturing the relevant properties of the analysis: $\rho_i = \overline{\wedge} Z_{\texttt{int}}$ and $\rho_b = \overline{\wedge} Z_{\texttt{bool}}$. It is easy to see that, in Example 7, using $\rho_i = \overline{\wedge}\{\rho_x, \rho_{out}\}$ instead of ρ_x avoids the loss of information on the variable value: the expression is now considered as secure.

Definition 8 (abstract domains on a given type). The function $P : \mathcal{T} \mapsto \mathcal{D}$ extends the construction of ρ_i and ρ_b to function types:

$$P(\texttt{int}) = \rho_i \qquad P(\texttt{bool}) = \rho_b \qquad P((\tau \to \tau')) = P(\tau')^{P(\tau)}$$

where $\rho^{\rho'}$ is the *Reduced Cardinal Power* [4] of two domains, building the domain of the monotone functions from ρ' to ρ [5].

The syntax of the typing rules is standard: the basic judgement is $E \vdash e : \sigma$ and holds if an expression e is given a security type σ when the computation is performed in a type environment $E \in \mathcal{T}_{env}$ (input variables x have type $E(x)$).

The typing rules are described in Figure 2 and explained below (the function $\mathcal{F}$ is a rewriting of the typing rules: $\mathcal{F}(e, E) = \sigma \iff E \vdash e : \sigma$):

- `Iconst`, `Bconst`: The type for constants expresses the condition that, in any two computations, the value is indistinguishable by the abstract domain.
- `eq`: $\mathrm{eq}(R', R'')$ specifies when it is possible to have equal values for e' and e''. The (dis)equalities in the formula are treated as boolean values.
- `add`: The security type of the sum is such to contain all the values that can be obtained by adding two values of the addendi. Rules `sub`, `mul` and `div` for integers are similar, as well as rules `and`, `or`, `not` for boolean connectives.
- `lam`, `app`: The type of a function is inferred by collecting the types obtained, for all possible types of the abstraction variable, by evaluating the function body in the updated environment. Application rule is dual.
- `rec`: To compute the security type of a recursive function we need to find the fixpoint of a functional $\mathbf{G}_{E,e} = \lambda\sigma.\mathcal{F}(e, E[F \leftarrow \sigma])$. Since $\mathbf{G}$ is continuous, this can be done by starting from $\{\tau\}_\perp$ and iterating the application of $\mathbf{G}$, thus obtaining the least fixed point.
- `if`: In defining if' we have in mind these requirements:
  (1) If $x = y$ we have $\mathrm{ST}_{\{\tau\}_{\mathrm{if'}(\mathtt{tt}, R', R'')}}(v_1, v_2) \Leftrightarrow \mathrm{ST}_{\{\tau\}_{R'}}(v_1, v_2)$. That is, if in two computations the boolean guard is true (false), then the values of the expression are the same as the first (second) branch; therefore they belong to its security type.
  (2) If $x \neq y$, then $\mathrm{ST}_{\{\tau\}_{\mathrm{if'}(\mathtt{tf}, R', R'')}}(v_1, v_2) \Leftrightarrow \mathrm{ST}_{\{\tau\}_{R'}}(v_1, u_2) \wedge \mathrm{ST}_{\{\tau\}_{R''}}(u_1, v_2)$ for each u_1, u_2. That is, if in the two computations the boolean guards evaluate respectively to `true` and `false` (`false` and `true`), then the expression evaluates, in the first one, to the value of the *then* (*else*) branch, and in the second one to the value of the *else* (*then*) branch.

$$\frac{}{E \vdash n : (\!|\mathtt{int}|\!)_{(\rho_i(n),\rho_i(n))}}\,\texttt{[Iconst]} \qquad \frac{}{E \vdash b : (\!|\mathtt{bool}|\!)_{(\rho_b(b),\rho_b(b))}}\,\texttt{[Bconst]}$$

$$\frac{}{E \vdash x : E(x)}\,\texttt{[var]} \qquad \frac{E \vdash e' : (\!|\mathtt{int}|\!)_{R'} \quad E \vdash e'' : (\!|\mathtt{int}|\!)_{R''}}{E \vdash e' = e'' : (\!|\mathtt{bool}|\!)_{\mathrm{eq}(R',R'')}}\,\texttt{[eq]}$$

$$\frac{E \vdash e' : (\!|\mathtt{int}|\!)_{R'} \qquad E \vdash e'' : (\!|\mathtt{int}|\!)_{R''}}{E \vdash e' + e'' : (\!|\mathtt{int}|\!)_{\mathrm{add}(R',R'')}}\,\texttt{[add]}$$

$$\frac{\forall s_1, s_2 \in P(\tau).\ E[x \leftarrow (\!|\tau|\!)_{(s_1,s_2)}] \vdash e : (\!|\tau'|\!)_{R_{s_1,s_2}}}{E \vdash \lambda x : \tau.\ e : (\!|(\tau \to \tau')|\!)_{\mathrm{lam}(P(\tau),\lambda x,y.R_{x,y})}}\,\texttt{[lam]}$$

$$\frac{E \vdash e : (\!|(\tau' \to \tau)|\!)_R \qquad E \vdash e' : (\!|\tau'|\!)_{R'}}{E \vdash e(e') : (\!|\tau|\!)_{\mathrm{app}(R,R')}}\,\texttt{[app]} \qquad \frac{E[F \leftarrow \sigma] \vdash e : \sigma \quad \sigma \text{ minimal}}{E \vdash \mu F.e : \sigma}\,\texttt{[rec]}$$

$$\frac{E \vdash b : (\!|\mathtt{bool}|\!)_{R_b} \qquad E \vdash e' : (\!|\tau|\!)_{R'} \qquad E \vdash e'' : (\!|\tau|\!)_{R''}}{E \vdash \mathtt{if}\ b\ \mathtt{then}\ e'\ \mathtt{else}\ e'' : (\!|\tau|\!)_{\mathrm{if}(R_b,R',R'')}}\,\texttt{[if]}$$

$$\frac{E \vdash e : (\!|\tau|\!)_R \qquad R \leq R'}{E \vdash e : (\!|\tau|\!)_{R'}}\,\texttt{[subt]}$$

$$\begin{aligned}
\mathrm{eq}(R', R'') &= \bigcup \{\{\rho_b(s_1 \sqcap t_1 \neq \bot), \rho_b(s_1 = t_1 = \{v\})\} \times \\
&\qquad \{\rho_b(s_2 \sqcap t_2 \neq \bot), \rho_b(s_2 = t_2 = \{u\})\} | (s_1, s_2) \in R', (t_1, t_2) \in R''\} \\
s + t &= \rho_i(\{v + u \mid v \in s \wedge u \in t\}) \\
\mathrm{add}(R', R'') &= \{(s_1 + t_1, s_2 + t_2) \mid (s_1, s_2) \in R', (t_1, t_2) \in R''\} \\
\mathrm{lam}(X, F) &= \{(t_1, t_2) \mid \forall s_1, s_2 \in X.(t_1(s_1), t_2(s_2)) \in F(s_1, s_2)\} \\
\mathrm{app}(R', R'') &= \{(t_1(s_1), t_2(s_2)) \mid (t_1, t_2) \in R' \wedge (s_1, s_2) \in R''\} \\
\mathrm{if}(R_b, R', R'') &= \bigcup \{\mathrm{if'}(xy, R', R'') \mid (X, Y) \in R_b \wedge x \in X \wedge y \in Y\} \\
\mathrm{if'}(\mathrm{t\,t}, R', R'') &= R' \qquad\qquad (\mathrm{t} \equiv \mathtt{true}, \mathrm{f} \equiv \mathtt{false}) \\
\mathrm{if'}(\mathrm{f\,f}, R', R'') &= R'' \\
\mathrm{if'}(\mathrm{t\,f}, R', R'') &= \{(s', t'') \mid (s', t') \in R' \wedge (s'', t'') \in R''\} \\
\mathrm{if'}(\mathrm{f\,t}, R', R'') &= \{(s'', t') \mid (s', t') \in R' \wedge (s'', t'') \in R''\}
\end{aligned}$$

Fig. 2. The typing rules

The derivation of $\mathrm{if'}(\mathrm{t\,f}, v_1, v_2)$ is illustrated in the following equalities:

$$\begin{aligned}
&\exists u_1, u_2.\ \mathrm{ST}_{(\!|\tau|\!)_{R'}}(v_1, u_2) \wedge \mathrm{ST}_{(\!|\tau|\!)_{R''}}(u_1, v_2) \Leftrightarrow \\
&\exists u_1, u_2, (s_1', s_2') \in R', (s_1'', s_2'') \in R''.v_1 \in s_1' \wedge v_2 \in s_2'' \wedge u_1 \in s_1'' \wedge u_2 \in s_2' \Leftrightarrow \\
&\mathrm{ST}_{(\!|\tau|\!)_{\mathrm{if'}(\mathrm{t\,f},R',R'')}}(v_1, v_2)
\end{aligned}$$

5 Correctness of Type Inference

We are interested in a soundness result for the type inference algorithm: the inferred type is correct if it is not possible to have computations with values not belonging to the type. The function $\mathrm{ENV}_E(\varepsilon_1, \varepsilon_2) = \forall x.\ \mathrm{ST}_{E(x)}(\varepsilon_1(x), \varepsilon_2(x))$ extends the ST predicate to environments.

The correctness theorem is proven by induction on the structure of a derivation: this is the same as induction on expressions (every typing rule *builds* an expression out of zero, one or more subexpressions), except for subtyping (in this rule the expression is not composed). Subtyping rule can be applied virtually everywhere and many times without affecting the validity of the proof. In reasoning about the application of rules, we can infer (backwards) the type of the subexpressions by observing the main type: for example, if add rule is applied, then from the type $\{\mathtt{int}\}_R$ of an expression $e' + e''$ it is possible to say that e_1 and e_2 have types $\{\mathtt{int}\}_{R'}$ and $\{\mathtt{int}\}_{R''}$ with $R = \mathrm{add}(R', R'')$ (otherwise the rule would not have been applicable).

Theorem 9 (Correctness). $E \vdash e : \sigma \ \wedge\ ENV_E(\varepsilon_1, \varepsilon_2) \Rightarrow ST_\sigma([\![e]\!]_{\varepsilon_1}, [\![e]\!]_{\varepsilon_2})$

Proof. Induction on the last rule applied in the derivation (some cases omitted).

- $e \equiv n$: We have $[\![e]\!]_{\varepsilon_1} = [\![e]\!]_{\varepsilon_2} = n$ and $E \vdash n : \{\mathtt{int}\}_{(\rho_i(n), \rho_i(n))}$; then $\mathrm{ST}_{\{\mathtt{int}\}_{(\rho_i(n),\rho_i(n))}}(n, n)$ since, by definition of closure operators, $n \in \rho_i(n)$.
- $e \equiv x : E \vdash x : E(x)$ and $[\![x]\!]_{\varepsilon_i} = \varepsilon_i(x)$ imply (def. ENV) $\mathrm{ST}_{E(x)}(\varepsilon_1(x), \varepsilon_2(x))$.
- $e \equiv e' + e''$:

$$\begin{array}{r}
E \vdash e' + e'' : \{\mathtt{int}\}_{\mathrm{add}(R',R'')} \Longrightarrow \\
E \vdash e' : \{\mathtt{int}\}_{R'} \ \wedge\ E \vdash e'' : \{\mathtt{int}\}_{R''} \Longrightarrow [hyp.] \\
\mathrm{ST}_{\{\mathtt{int}\}_{R'}}([\![e']\!]_{\varepsilon_1}, [\![e']\!]_{\varepsilon_2}) \ \wedge\ \mathrm{ST}_{\{\mathtt{int}\}_{R''}}([\![e'']\!]_{\varepsilon_1}, [\![e'']\!]_{\varepsilon_2}) \Longrightarrow [def.\ \mathrm{add}] \\
\mathrm{ST}_{\{\mathtt{int}\}_{\mathrm{add}(R',R'')}}([\![e' + e'']\!]_{\varepsilon_1}, [\![e' + e'']\!]_{\varepsilon_2})
\end{array}$$

- $e \equiv \lambda x : \tau.\ e_0$: let us suppose to have, for every pair $(s_1, s_2) \in P(\tau) \times P(\tau)$, two values $v_1^{s_1,s_2}$ and $v_2^{s_1,s_2}$ such that $\mathrm{ST}_{\{\tau\}_{(s_1,s_2)}}(v_1^{s_1,s_2}, v_2^{s_1,s_2})$.
Then, by def. of ENV, $\mathrm{ENV}_{E[x \leftarrow \{\tau\}_{(s_1,s_2)}]}(\varepsilon_1[x \leftarrow v_1^{s_1,s_2}], \varepsilon_2[x \leftarrow v_2^{s_1,s_2}])$.
Let $\mathrm{lam}(P(\tau), \lambda x, y.R_{x,y})$ be defined as in the rule for abstraction. Then

$$\begin{array}{r}
E \vdash \lambda x : \tau.\ e_0 : \{(\tau \to \tau')\}_{\mathrm{lam}(P(\tau),\lambda x,y.R_{x,y})} \Longrightarrow \\
\forall s_1, s_2 \in P(\tau).\ E[x \leftarrow \{\tau\}_{(s_1,s_2)}] \vdash e_0 : \{\tau'\}_{R_{s_1,s_2}} \Longrightarrow [hyp.] \\
\forall s_1, s_2 \in P(\tau).\ \mathrm{ST}_{\{\tau'\}_{R_{s_1,s_2}}}([\![e_0]\!]_{\varepsilon_1[x \leftarrow v_1^{s_1,s_2}]}, [\![e_0]\!]_{\varepsilon_2[x \leftarrow v_2^{s_1,s_2}]}) \Longrightarrow \\
\mathrm{ST}_{\mathrm{lam}(P(\tau),\lambda x,y.R_{x,y})}([\![e]\!]_{\varepsilon_1}, [\![e]\!]_{\varepsilon_2})
\end{array}$$

The last step follows from the definition of $[\![\bullet]\!]$, ST and lam.
- $e \equiv e'(e'')$:

$$\begin{array}{r}
E \vdash e'(e'') : \{\tau\}_{\mathrm{app}(R',R'')} \Longrightarrow \\
E \vdash e' : \{(\tau'' \to \tau)\}_{R'} \ \wedge\ E \vdash e'' : \{\tau''\}_{R''} \Longrightarrow [hyp.] \\
\mathrm{ST}_{\{(\tau'' \to \tau)\}_{R'}}([\![e']\!]_{\varepsilon_1}, [\![e']\!]_{\varepsilon_2}) \ \wedge\ \mathrm{ST}_{\{\tau''\}_{R''}}([\![e'']\!]_{\varepsilon_1}, [\![e'']\!]_{\varepsilon_2}) \Longrightarrow [def.\ \mathrm{app}] \\
\mathrm{ST}_{\{\tau\}_{\mathrm{app}(R',R'')}}([\![e'(e'')]\!]_{\varepsilon_1}, [\![e'(e'')]\!]_{\varepsilon_2})
\end{array}$$

- $e \equiv \mu F.e_0$: We take $\sigma = \{\tau\}_R$; the non-security part τ is the type inferred for e by a standard type inference algorithm (we have no problems with non-termination since the type system is monomorphic). Then $lfp(\mathbf{G}_{E,e_0}) = \{\tau\}_R$ where $\mathbf{G}$ is defined above (`rec` rule).
The following result (for each f_1, f_2, σ_0) is true by inductive hypothesis ($\mathbf{H}_{\varepsilon,e} = \lambda v.\ [\![e]\!]_{\varepsilon[F \leftarrow v]}$ is the semantic function for recursion):

$$\mathrm{ST}_{\sigma_0}(f_1, f_2) \Rightarrow \mathrm{ST}_{\mathbf{G}_{E,e_0}(\sigma_0)}(\mathbf{H}_{\varepsilon_1,e_0}(f_1), \mathbf{H}_{\varepsilon_2,e_0}(f_2))$$

So we have the chain of implications

$$\begin{gathered}\mathtt{true} = \mathrm{ST}_{(\tau)_\perp}(\perp,\perp) \Rightarrow \\ \mathrm{ST}_{\mathbf{G}_{E,e_0}((\tau)_\perp)}(\mathbf{H}_{\varepsilon_1,e_0}(\perp),\mathbf{H}_{\varepsilon_2,e_0}(\perp)) \Rightarrow \ldots \Rightarrow \\ \mathrm{ST}_{\mathbf{G}^n_{E,e_0}((\tau)_\top)}(\mathbf{H}^n_{\varepsilon_1,e_0}(\perp),\mathbf{H}^n_{\varepsilon_2,e_0}(\perp))\end{gathered}$$

Let $G_n = \mathbf{G}^n_{E,e_0}((\tau)_\perp)$, $S = \{G_n\}$, $H^1_n = \mathbf{H}^n_{\varepsilon_1,e_0}(\perp)$, $X = \{H^1_n\}$, $H^2_n = \mathbf{H}^n_{\varepsilon_2,e_0}(\perp)$ and $Y = \{H^2_n\}$. Then, by Lemma 5,

$$\mathrm{ST}_{(\tau)_R}([\![e]\!]_{\varepsilon_1},[\![e]\!]_{\varepsilon_2}) \equiv \mathrm{ST}_{\sqcup S}(\sqcup X,\sqcup Y) \equiv \sqcup_{\sigma\in S}\sqcap_{x\in X}\sqcap_{y\in Y}\mathrm{ST}_\sigma(x,y)$$

and, for every $H^1_n \in X$, $H^2_m \in Y$, we can take $p = max(m,n)$ to have $\mathrm{ST}_\sigma(H^1_p,H^2_p) \Rightarrow \mathrm{ST}_\sigma(H^1_n,H^2_m)$ (by Lemma 4) and $\mathrm{ST}_{G_p}(H^1_p,H^2_p)$ (by the chain of implications above).
Therefore it is always possible to find $\sigma \in S$ such that $\mathrm{ST}_\sigma(x,y)$ is true; consequently $\mathrm{ST}_{(\tau)_R}([\![e]\!]_{\varepsilon_1},[\![e]\!]_{\varepsilon_2})$ is also true.

6 Computations and Attackers

As shown above, there is a close correspondence between abstract domains and security types: types identify properties which domains cannot distinguish. This relation between $\mathcal{T}_{sec}$ and $\mathcal{D}$ can be formalized as $\rho \rightsquigarrow \sigma = \forall v_1, v_2.\ \mathrm{ST}_\sigma(v_1,v_2) \Rightarrow v_1 \equiv_\rho v_2$, meaning that ρ cannot distinguish σ-related values. In this case we say that ρ is *corresponding* to σ.

For a given σ there always exists such a ρ (the top abstract domain, characterizing a blind observer, is corresponding to every type). The functions $\alpha : \mathcal{T}^\tau_{sec} \mapsto \mathcal{D}_\tau = \lambda\sigma.\,\bar{\wedge}\,\{\rho \mid \rho\rightsquigarrow\sigma\}$ and $\gamma : \mathcal{D}_\tau \mapsto \mathcal{T}^\tau_{sec} = \lambda\rho.(\tau)_{\{(s_1,s_2)\mid\forall v_1\in s_1,v_2\in s_2.v_1\equiv_\rho v_2\}}$ clearly identify a Galois connection [3] between $\mathcal{T}^\tau_{sec}$ and $\mathcal{D}_\tau$.

We say that a type environment E defines a policy consistent with IO (Sec. 4) if, for every variable x, $E(x)$ is defined (Defs. 6 and 8) using the domains ρ_i and ρ_b induced by IO and the information about public and private data. The meaning of this notion is that the policy, together with the classification of the variables into private and public, is calibrated on the data we want to protect and on the attacker we want to be protected from.

The Abstract Non-Interference condition for an expression e, an attacker IO and a consistent policy described by E can be written as:

$$\mathrm{ANI}_E(e,\mathrm{IO}) \triangleq \mathrm{ENV}_E(\varepsilon_1,\varepsilon_2) \Rightarrow [\![e]\!]_{\varepsilon_1} \equiv_{\rho_{out}} [\![e]\!]_{\varepsilon_2}$$

Thus, if an attacker cannot distinguish inputs, neither can he distinguish outputs. It is easy to see that this is a translation of the original definition of ANI into our functional framework.

A direct corollary of Theorem 9 is (for E consistent with IO and $\rho_{out} \in \mathrm{IO}$):

Theorem 10. $\rho_{out}\rightsquigarrow\sigma \wedge E \vdash e : \sigma \Rightarrow \mathit{ANI}_E(e, \mathit{IO})$

The inferred type is an upper approximation of the secret kernel (Sec. 2): some non-interfering expressions are rejected since the abstraction induced by the abstract domains leads to a loss of information. For example, let ρ_i be the parity domain; then $e \equiv x + x$, where x is a private input variable, would be typed with $(\mathtt{int})_{\top\top}$, even if it clearly is always even. In terms of abstract interpretation, this is an incompleteness situation [7]: viewing the type of an object as an abstraction of its meaning, it turns out that abstracting (typing) the final value of the concrete computation (yielding, in this case, $(even, even)$) is not equal to performing the abstract computation (the type inference process) starting from the abstract values (types) of the input. To avoid this kind of problems there should be a set of axioms and rules (in this case a rule stating that $x+x = 2*x$ is needed) giving informations about special cases; however, in general it is not possible to have a complete rule system to handle such situations.

7 An Example

In this example it is possible to see how an expression showing (standard) dangerous information flows can be accepted by this type system if an attacker cannot see anything but the parity of integer numbers.

The evaluation of the expression yields a function from integers to integers, then the observational power of the attacker on the output must be an abstract domain on $(\mathtt{int} \to \mathtt{int})$. The only input datum is the secret free variable y; since y is referred in the body of the function an algorithm for standard Non-Interference would find a forbidden information flow from y to the result of the computation (in facts, the result of the function applied to a value v depends on both v and y). However, our type system is able to accept the expression as secure since no information about the secret data can be revealed by observing the parity of numbers (for every value of y, $[\![e]\!](v)$ is an even value).

The expression to analyze is

$$e \equiv \mu F.\ \lambda x.\ \mathtt{if}\ x = 0\ \mathtt{then}\ 2\ \mathtt{else}\ 2 * y * F(x-1)$$

and the observational power of a generic attacker is

$$\rho_i = \{\bot, e, o, \top\} \qquad \rho_b = \mathbb{B}_\bot \times \mathbb{B}_\bot$$
$$\rho_{out} = \{\langle e \mapsto e; o \mapsto e\rangle, \langle e \mapsto e; o \mapsto o\rangle, \langle e \mapsto o; o \mapsto e\rangle, \langle e \mapsto o; o \mapsto o\rangle\}$$

- the only visible information on integers is parity (e is even, o is odd);
- no abstraction on boolean values (the attacker can see the truth value of boolean data). In this case we are not following the definition of ρ_b ($Z_{\mathtt{bool}} = \emptyset$ should imply $\rho_b = \overline{\wedge}(\emptyset) = \top$): the analysis will be more precise.
- functions from integers to integers are divided by the abstract domain into five classes (the notation should be clear): functions (i) mapping all numbers to even numbers; (ii) keeping the parity value; (iii) inverting the parity value; (iv) mapping all numbers to odd numbers; (v) all the other functions (these functions are mapped to $\top$). ρ_{out} is an abstraction of $P((\mathtt{int} \to \mathtt{int}))$.

We evaluate e in the type environment E (with $\mathrm{ENV}_E(\varepsilon_1, \varepsilon_2)$); the fact that y is private is written as $E(y) = (\top, \top) = \{ee, eo, oe, oo\}$ (ab stands for (a, b)).

The evaluation begins with the first iteration of the fixpoint construction; let E' be $E[F \leftarrow ((\mathtt{int} \rightarrow \mathtt{int}))_{\perp\perp}]$, and E'_{ab} be $E'[x \leftarrow ab]$.

(0) $E'_{ee} \vdash 0 : (\mathtt{int})_{ee}$	[Iconst]	(1) $E'_{ee} \vdash 1 : (\mathtt{int})_{oo}$	[Iconst]
(2) $E'_{ee} \vdash 2 : (\mathtt{int})_{ee}$	[Iconst]	(3) $E'_{ee} \vdash y : (\mathtt{int})_{ee,eo,oe,oo}$	[var]
(4) $E'_{ee} \vdash x : (\mathtt{int})_{ee}$	[var]	(5) $E'_{ee} \vdash x - 1 : (\mathtt{int})_{oo}$	[(1, 4), min]

(6) $E'_{ee} \vdash F : ((\mathtt{int} \rightarrow \mathtt{int}))_{\perp\perp}$ [var]
(7) $E'_{ee} \vdash F(x-1) : (\mathtt{int})_{\perp\perp}$ [(5, 6), app]
(8) $E'_{ee} \vdash y * F(x-1) : (\mathtt{int})_{\perp\perp}$ [(3, 7), mul]
(9) $E'_{ee} \vdash 2 * y * F(x-1) : (\mathtt{int})_{\perp\perp}$ [(2, 8), mul]
(10) $E'_{ee} \vdash x = 0 : \{\mathrm{tt}, \mathrm{tf}, \mathrm{ft}, \mathrm{ff}\}$ [(0, 4), eq]
(11) $E'_{ee} \vdash \mathbf{if}\ x = 0\ \mathbf{then}\ 2\ \mathbf{else}\ 2 * y * F(x-1) : (\mathtt{int})_{R_{e\perp}}$ [(2, 9, 10), if]
$R_{e\perp} = \{ee, \perp\perp, e\perp, \perp e\} = ee$

To get the value of the lambda-expression the evaluation must be done also in the other E'_{ab}, where $a, b \in \{\perp, e, o, \top\}$; the final security relation is

$$R_0 = \{(f, g) \mid f(e) \in \{e, \perp\} \wedge f(o) = \perp \wedge g(e) \in \{e, \perp\} \wedge g(o) = \perp\}$$

giving the typing judgement $E' \vdash e : ((\mathtt{int} \rightarrow \mathtt{int}))_{R_0}$.

So far the first step of the fixpoint computation; the second step is performed in the type environment $E'' = E[F \leftarrow ((\mathtt{int} \rightarrow \mathtt{int}))_{R_0}]$.

The rest of the computation is omitted; at the second step the fixpoint is reached, giving a functional security type σ_{fix} for which the result of the application is $(\mathtt{int})_{ee}$ for every parity value of the input:

$$\sigma_{fix} = ((\mathtt{int} \rightarrow \mathtt{int}))_{\{(\lambda s.e, \lambda s.e)\}}$$

It is then easy to see that $\rho_{out} \rightsquigarrow \sigma_{fix}$, i.e. if two functions f_1 and f_2 satisfy $\mathrm{ST}_{\sigma_{fix}}(f_1, f_2)$, then they both belong to the first equivalence class described by the abstract domain ρ_{out}: the expression e is secure.

8 Making It More Practical

Type Approximation. Remark 3 shows how a security relation R can be transformed into an equivalent yet simpler one R' by replacing some elements of an abstract domain with their least upper bound; namely, given a set S of elements, the set of pairs $S \times S \subseteq R$ can be replaced by $\{(\sqcup S, \sqcup S)\}$.

This can be done even if some elements of $S \times S$ are missing in R, thus introducing an upper approximation R'' of R: if $X \subseteq S \times S$ and $X \subseteq R$, R'' is obtained by replacing X with $\{(\sqcup S, \sqcup S)\}$, and would be equivalent to $R \cup (S \times S)$.

This approximation could be performed via subtyping after the application of each typing rule. However, it is not clear when such an operation can be applied without losing too much precision; in particular, we have to choose the right S and decide whether X contains *enough* elements of $S \times S$.

A possible approach is to consider S and X good candidates if X contains all the elements of $\{(s, s) | s \in S\}$ plus some pair (s, t) with $s \neq t$, thus leading to the following modified subtyping rule:

$$\frac{E \vdash e : (\tau)_R \quad X \subseteq R \quad X \subseteq S \times S \quad X \supset \{(s,s) | s \in S\}}{E \vdash e : (\tau)_{(R \setminus X) \cup \{(\sqcup S, \sqcup S)\}}} \texttt{[subt2]}$$

The bigger S is, the more the loss of information; then, in order not to lose too much precision, this rule should be applied to a small enough set S. This approximation acts on non-public types (containing at least one pair (s_1, s_2)) and transforms them into approximated (less precise) types with less elements, thus improving complexity results.

Lazy Lambda Abstraction. In the rule `lam` some computations are necessary for every pair in $P(\tau) \times P(\tau)$; however, in many cases most of them are not used in the rest of type inference (e.g. when the function is applied to a constant value). In order to avoid useless computations, the type of a function shall be computed only as long as it is used in the following derivations; for example, if F is applied to a constant with type $(\texttt{int})_{ee}$ it is useless to infer its type for *oo* or $\perp e$. Such a strategy can reduce considerably the complexity of type inference.

Abstract Operators. The application of arithmethic rules, such as `add`, involves performing integer operations on possibly infinite sets (such as even numbers). This is clearly impractical unless some computation rules are provided; for example, rules like *even plus odd equals odd* would solve the problem of adding infinite sets in the parity abstract domain. Such a set of rules cannot, in general, be complete nor automatically generated.

9 Conclusions

This type system is an attempt to compute the secret kernel for a given expression; the inferred security type is an upper approximation of the secret kernel (Section 6), i.e. some harmless attackers are erroneously considered as dangerous.

Computability. This type system is, in general, undecidable: it is not surprising, since there are infinite semantic domains (e.g. integers and functions).

When a concrete domain is infinite, either the abstract domain is infinite or some elements of the abstract domain represent an infinite set of concrete values. In the first case some rules, like `lam`, can diverge, because of the universal quantification on the infinite set $P(\tau)$. In the second some operators on security types must deal with infinite sets (e.g. the sum of the sets of evens and odds).

Then, to have decidability the abstract domains must be finite and some set of rules must be provided to help computations (see third part of Section 8).

Complexity. Provided decidability conditions are met, some complexity results can be obtained. Let N be the (finite) cardinality of ρ_i and p be the highest number of arrow constructors occurring in the type of subexpressions. The cardinality of a domain on functions is, in the worst case, superexponential on N (bounded by $\lambda n.2^n$ applied p times to N); since, in `lam` rule, every pair of elements of the domain must be checked, the complexity of the algorithm is exponential on N.

Section 8 (first part) shows how a security relation can be transformed into a simpler one by introducing some loss of information. This can have significant benefits on complexity, since it decreases the numbers of elements to check in a security relation. Some rule better than `subt2` could be possibly found to improve the ratio *complexity benefits / precision loss*.

Again, Section 8 (second part) outlines lazy type inference as a method to avoid useless computations in lambda abstractions. This is particularly useful in presence of big domains and many applications to constant values.

Future Work. Some features can be added to the language, such as product types or polymorphism. A real-world language could be considered, as in [13].

The complexity of the algorythm could be improved by finding simpler ways to manipulate security types; in particular, the set of operation rules (Sec. 8, third part) should be designed in order to be efficient and partially mechanizable (i.e. automatically generated given an abstract domain).

The approximation of security relations can significantly improve the complexity; however, a proper rule to do abstractions should be found in order to reach the best tradeoff between complexity and precision.

One of the main features of the type system is that it builds the secret kernel rather than checking Non-Interference for a given attacker; this constructive method could be applied to other classes of languages, such as imperative and object-oriented.

References

1. M. Abadi, A. Banerjee, N. Heintze, and J. Riecke. A core calculus of dependency. In *Proc. ACM Symp. on Principles of Programming Languages*, pages 147–160. ACM Press, Jan. 1999.
2. P. Cousot. Types as abstract interpretations, invited paper. In *Proc. ACM Symp. on Principles of Programming Languages*, pages 316–331. ACM Press, Jan. 1997.
3. P. Cousot and R. Cousot. Abstract interpretation: a unified lattice model for static analysis of programs by construction or approximation of fixpoints. In *Proc. ACM Symp. on Principles of Programming Languages*, pages 238–252. ACM Press, 1977.
4. P. Cousot and R. Cousot. Systematic design of program analysis frameworks. In *Proc. ACM Symp. on Principles of Programming Languages*, pages 269–282. ACM Press, 1979.
5. P. Cousot and R. Cousot. Higher-order abstract interpretation (and application to comportment analysis generalizing strictness, termination, projection and PER analysis of functional languages), invited paper. In *Proc. International Conf. on Computer Languages*, pages 95–112. IEEE Computer Society Press, May 1994.
6. R. Giacobazzi and I. Mastroeni. Abstract non-interference: Parameterizing non-interference by abstract interpretation. In *Proc. ACM Symp. on Principles of Programming Languages*, pages 186–197. ACM Press, Jan. 2004.
7. R. Giacobazzi and F. Ranzato. Completeness in abstract interpretation: A domain perspective. In *Proc. International Conf. on Algebraic Methodology and Software Technology*, volume 1349 of *LNCS*, pages 231–245. Springer-Verlag, 1997.
8. J. Goguen and J. Meseguer. Security policies and security models. In *Proc. IEEE Symp. on Security and Privacy*, pages 11–20. IEEE Computer Society Press, 1982.

9. N. Heintze and J. Riecke. The SLam calculus: Programming with secrecy and integrity. In *Proc. ACM Symp. on Principles of Programming Languages*. ACM Press, Jan. 1998.
10. S. Hunt. *Abstract Interpretation of Functional Languages: From Theory to Practice*. PhD thesis, Dept. of Computing, Imperial College of Science Technology and Medicine, 1991.
11. B. Lampson. Protection. In *Proc. Princeton Symp. on Information Sciences and Systems*, pages 437–443, Princeton University, Mar. 1971. Reprinted in *Operating Systems Review*, vol. 8, no. 1, pp. 18–24, Jan. 1974.
12. A. Myers and A. Sabelfeld. Language-based information-flow security. *IEEE Journal on Selected Areas in Communications*, 21(1):5–19, Jan. 2003.
13. F. Pottier and V. Simonet. Information flow inference for ML. *ACM TOPLAS*, 25(1):117–158, Jan. 2003.
14. D. Volpano and G. Smith. A type-based approach to program security. In *Proc. TAPSOFT'97*, volume 1214 of *LNCS*, pages 607–621. Springer-Verlag, Apr. 1997.
15. M. Zanotti. Security typings by abstract interpretation. In *Proc. Symp. on Static Analysis*, volume 2477 of *LNCS*, pages 360–375. Springer-Verlag, Sept. 2002.

Author Index

Lecture Notes in Computer Science

For information about Vols. 1–3358

please contact your bookseller or Springer

Vol. 3467: J. Giesl (Ed.), Term Rewriting and Applications. XIII, 517 pages. 2005.

Vol. 3461: P. Urzyczyn (Ed.), Typed Lambda Calculi and Applications. XI, 433 pages. 2005.

Vol. 3459: R. Kimmel, N. Sochen, J. Weickert (Eds.), Scale Space and PDE Methods in Computer Vision. XI, 634 pages. 2005.

Vol. 3456: H. Rust, Operational Semantics for Timed Systems. XII, 223 pages. 2005.

Vol. 3455: H. Treharne, S. King, M. Henson, S. Schneider (Eds.), ZB 2005: Formal Specification and Development in Z and B. XV, 493 pages. 2005.

Vol. 3454: J.-M. Jacquet, G.P. Picco (Eds.), Coordination Models and Languages. X, 299 pages. 2005.

Vol. 3453: L. Zhou, B.C. Ooi, X. Meng (Eds.), Database Systems for Advanced Applications. XXVII, 929 pages. 2005.

Vol. 3452: F. Baader, A. Voronkov (Eds.), Logic for Programming, Artificial Intelligence, and Reasoning. XI, 562 pages. 2005. (Subseries LNAI).

Vol. 3450: D. Hutter, M. Ullmann (Eds.), Security in Pervasive Computing. XI, 239 pages. 2005.

Vol. 3449: F. Rothlauf, J. Branke, S. Cagnoni, D.W. Corne, R. Drechsler, Y. Jin, P. Machado, E. Marchiori, J. Romero, G.D. Smith, G. Squillero (Eds.), Applications on Evolutionary Computing. XX, 631 pages. 2005.

Vol. 3448: G.R. Raidl, J. Gottlieb (Eds.), Evolutionary Computation in Combinatorial Optimization. XI, 271 pages. 2005.

Vol. 3447: M. Keijzer, A. Tettamanzi, P. Collet, J.v. Hemert, M. Tomassini (Eds.), Genetic Programming. XIII, 382 pages. 2005.

Vol. 3444: M. Sagiv (Ed.), Programming Languages and Systems. XIII, 439 pages. 2005.

Vol. 3443: R. Bodik (Ed.), Compiler Construction. XI, 305 pages. 2005.

Vol. 3442: M. Cerioli (Ed.), Fundamental Approaches to Software Engineering. XIII, 373 pages. 2005.

Vol. 3441: V. Sassone (Ed.), Foundations of Software Science and Computational Structures. XVIII, 521 pages. 2005.

Vol. 3440: N. Halbwachs, L.D. Zuck (Eds.), Tools and Algorithms for the Construction and Analysis of Systems. XVII, 588 pages. 2005.

Vol. 3439: R.H. Deng, F. Bao, H. Pang, J. Zhou (Eds.), Information Security Practice and Experience. XII, 424 pages. 2005.

Vol. 3436: B. Bouyssounouse, J. Sifakis (Eds.), Embedded Systems Design. XV, 492 pages. 2005.

Vol. 3434: L. Brun, M. Vento (Eds.), Graph-Based Representations in Pattern Recognition. XII, 384 pages. 2005.

Vol. 3433: S. Bhalla (Ed.), Databases in Networked Information Systems. VII, 319 pages. 2005.

Vol. 3432: M. Beigl, P. Lukowicz (Eds.), Systems Aspects in Organic and Pervasive Computing - ARCS 2005. X, 265 pages. 2005.

Vol. 3431: C. Dovrolis (Ed.), Passive and Active Network Measurement. XII, 374 pages. 2005.

Vol. 3429: E. Andres, G. Damiand, P. Lienhardt (Eds.), Discrete Geometry for Computer Imagery. X, 428 pages. 2005.

Vol. 3427: G. Kotsis, O. Spaniol, Wireless Systems and Mobility in Next Generation Internet. VIII, 249 pages. 2005.

Vol. 3423: J.L. Fiadeiro, P.D. Mosses, F. Orejas (Eds.), Recent Trends in Algebraic Development Techniques. VIII, 271 pages. 2005.

Vol. 3422: R.T. Mittermeir (Ed.), From Computer Literacy to Informatics Fundamentals. X, 203 pages. 2005.

Vol. 3421: P. Lorenz, P. Dini (Eds.), Networking - ICN 2005, Part II. XXXV, 1153 pages. 2005.

Vol. 3420: P. Lorenz, P. Dini (Eds.), Networking - ICN 2005, Part I. XXXV, 933 pages. 2005.

Vol. 3419: B. Faltings, A. Petcu, F. Fages, F. Rossi (Eds.), Constraint Satisfaction and Constraint Logic Programming. X, 217 pages. 2005. (Subseries LNAI).

Vol. 3418: U. Brandes, T. Erlebach (Eds.), Network Analysis. XII, 471 pages. 2005.

Vol. 3416: M. Böhlen, J. Gamper, W. Polasek, M.A. Wimmer (Eds.), E-Government: Towards Electronic Democracy. XIII, 311 pages. 2005. (Subseries LNAI).

Vol. 3415: P. Davidsson, B. Logan, K. Takadama (Eds.), Multi-Agent and Multi-Agent-Based Simulation. X, 265 pages. 2005. (Subseries LNAI).

Vol. 3414: M. Morari, L. Thiele (Eds.), Hybrid Systems: Computation and Control. XII, 684 pages. 2005.

Vol. 3412: X. Franch, D. Port (Eds.), COTS-Based Software Systems. XVI, 312 pages. 2005.

Vol. 3411: S.H. Myaeng, M. Zhou, K.-F. Wong, H.-J. Zhang (Eds.), Information Retrieval Technology. XIII, 337 pages. 2005.

Vol. 3410: C.A. Coello Coello, A. Hernández Aguirre, E. Zitzler (Eds.), Evolutionary Multi-Criterion Optimization. XVI, 912 pages. 2005.

Vol. 3409: N. Guelfi, G. Reggio, A. Romanovsky (Eds.), Scientific Engineering of Distributed Java Applications. X, 127 pages. 2005.

Vol. 3408: D.E. Losada, J.M. Fernández-Luna (Eds.), Advances in Information Retrieval. XVII, 572 pages. 2005.

Vol. 3407: Z. Liu, K. Araki (Eds.), Theoretical Aspects of Computing - ICTAC 2004. XIV, 562 pages. 2005.

Vol. 3406: A. Gelbukh (Ed.), Computational Linguistics and Intelligent Text Processing. XVII, 829 pages. 2005.

Vol. 3404: V. Diekert, B. Durand (Eds.), STACS 2005. XVI, 706 pages. 2005.

Vol. 3403: B. Ganter, R. Godin (Eds.), Formal Concept Analysis. XI, 419 pages. 2005. (Subseries LNAI).

Vol. 3401: Z. Li, L.G. Vulkov, J. Waśniewski (Eds.), Numerical Analysis and Its Applications. XIII, 630 pages. 2005.

Vol. 3399: Y. Zhang, K. Tanaka, J.X. Yu, S. Wang, M. Li (Eds.), Web Technologies Research and Development - APWeb 2005. XXII, 1082 pages. 2005.

Vol. 3398: D.-K. Baik (Ed.), Systems Modeling and Simulation: Theory and Applications. XIV, 733 pages. 2005. (Subseries LNAI).

Vol. 3397: T.G. Kim (Ed.), Artificial Intelligence and Simulation. XV, 711 pages. 2005. (Subseries LNAI).

Vol. 3396: R.M. van Eijk, M.-P. Huget, F. Dignum (Eds.), Agent Communication. X, 261 pages. 2005. (Subseries LNAI).

Vol. 3395: J. Grabowski, B. Nielsen (Eds.), Formal Approaches to Software Testing. X, 225 pages. 2005.

Vol. 3394: D. Kudenko, D. Kazakov, E. Alonso (Eds.), Adaptive Agents and Multi-Agent Systems III. VIII, 313 pages. 2005. (Subseries LNAI).

Vol. 3393: H.-J. Kreowski, U. Montanari, F. Orejas, G. Rozenberg, G. Taentzer (Eds.), Formal Methods in Software and Systems Modeling. XXVII, 413 pages. 2005.

Vol. 3392: D. Seipel, M. Hanus, U. Geske, O. Bartenstein (Eds.), Applications of Declarative Programming and Knowledge Management. X, 309 pages. 2005. (Subseries LNAI).

Vol. 3391: C. Kim (Ed.), Information Networking. XVII, 936 pages. 2005.

Vol. 3390: R. Choren, A. Garcia, C. Lucena, A. Romanovsky (Eds.), Software Engineering for Multi-Agent Systems III. XII, 291 pages. 2005.

Vol. 3389: P. Van Roy (Ed.), Multiparadigm Programming in Mozart/OZ. XV, 329 pages. 2005.

Vol. 3388: J. Lagergren (Ed.), Comparative Genomics. VII, 133 pages. 2005. (Subseries LNBI).

Vol. 3387: J. Cardoso, A. Sheth (Eds.), Semantic Web Services and Web Process Composition. VIII, 147 pages. 2005.

Vol. 3386: S. Vaudenay (Ed.), Public Key Cryptography - PKC 2005. IX, 436 pages. 2005.

Vol. 3385: R. Cousot (Ed.), Verification, Model Checking, and Abstract Interpretation. XII, 483 pages. 2005.

Vol. 3383: J. Pach (Ed.), Graph Drawing. XII, 536 pages. 2005.

Vol. 3382: J. Odell, P. Giorgini, J.P. Müller (Eds.), Agent-Oriented Software Engineering V. X, 239 pages. 2005.

Vol. 3381: P. Vojtáš, M. Bieliková, B. Charron-Bost, O. Sýkora (Eds.), SOFSEM 2005: Theory and Practice of Computer Science. XV, 448 pages. 2005.

Vol. 3380: C. Priami, Transactions on Computational Systems Biology I. IX, 111 pages. 2005. (Subseries LNBI).

Vol. 3379: M. Hemmje, C. Niederee, T. Risse (Eds.), From Integrated Publication and Information Systems to Information and Knowledge Environments. XXIV, 321 pages. 2005.

Vol. 3378: J. Kilian (Ed.), Theory of Cryptography. XII, 621 pages. 2005.

Vol. 3377: B. Goethals, A. Siebes (Eds.), Knowledge Discovery in Inductive Databases. VII, 190 pages. 2005.

Vol. 3376: A. Menezes (Ed.), Topics in Cryptology – CT-RSA 2005. X, 385 pages. 2005.

Vol. 3375: M.A. Marsan, G. Bianchi, M. Listanti, M. Meo (Eds.), Quality of Service in Multiservice IP Networks. XIII, 656 pages. 2005.

Vol. 3374: D. Weyns, H.V.D. Parunak, F. Michel (Eds.), Environments for Multi-Agent Systems. X, 279 pages. 2005. (Subseries LNAI).

Vol. 3372: C. Bussler, V. Tannen, I. Fundulaki (Eds.), Semantic Web and Databases. X, 227 pages. 2005.

Vol. 3371: M.W. Barley, N. Kasabov (Eds.), Intelligent Agents and Multi-Agent Systems. X, 329 pages. 2005. (Subseries LNAI).

Vol. 3370: A. Konagaya, K. Satou (Eds.), Grid Computing in Life Science. X, 188 pages. 2005. (Subseries LNBI).

Vol. 3369: V.R. Benjamins, P. Casanovas, J. Breuker, A. Gangemi (Eds.), Law and the Semantic Web. XII, 249 pages. 2005. (Subseries LNAI).

Vol. 3368: L. Paletta, J.K. Tsotsos, E. Rome, G.W. Humphreys (Eds.), Attention and Performance in Computational Vision. VIII, 231 pages. 2005.

Vol. 3367: W.S. Ng, B.C. Ooi, A. Ouksel, C. Sartori (Eds.), Databases, Information Systems, and Peer-to-Peer Computing. X, 231 pages. 2005.

Vol. 3366: I. Rahwan, P. Moraitis, C. Reed (Eds.), Argumentation in Multi-Agent Systems. XII, 263 pages. 2005. (Subseries LNAI).

Vol. 3365: G. Mauri, G. Păun, M.J. Pérez-Jiménez, G. Rozenberg, A. Salomaa (Eds.), Membrane Computing. IX, 415 pages. 2005.

Vol. 3363: T. Eiter, L. Libkin (Eds.), Database Theory - ICDT 2005. XI, 413 pages. 2004.

Vol. 3362: G. Barthe, L. Burdy, M. Huisman, J.-L. Lanet, T. Muntean (Eds.), Construction and Analysis of Safe, Secure, and Interoperable Smart Devices. IX, 257 pages. 2005.

Vol. 3361: S. Bengio, H. Bourlard (Eds.), Machine Learning for Multimodal Interaction. XII, 362 pages. 2005.

Vol. 3360: S. Spaccapietra, E. Bertino, S. Jajodia, R. King, D. McLeod, M.E. Orlowska, L. Strous (Eds.), Journal on Data Semantics II. XI, 223 pages. 2005.

Vol. 3359: G. Grieser, Y. Tanaka (Eds.), Intuitive Human Interfaces for Organizing and Accessing Intellectual Assets. XIV, 257 pages. 2005. (Subseries LNAI).